W9-CEA-260

PUBLIC ADMINISTRATION IN CANADA SECOND EDITION

PUBLIC ADMINISTRATION IN CANADA SECOND EDITION

Paul Barker
Brescia University College, Western University

Tim A. Mau
University of Guelph

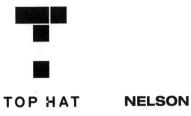

TOP HAT   NELSON

TOP HAT

Public Administration in Canada, Second Edition

by Paul Barker and Tim A. Mau

VP, Product and Partnership Solutions: Anne Williams

Publisher, Digital and Print Content: Alexis Hood

Marketing Manager: Ann Byford

Content Development Manager: Liisa Kelly

Photo and Permissions Researcher: Sandra Mark

Production Project Manager: Hedy Sellers

Production Service: Cenveo Publisher Services

Copy Editor: Elspeth McFadden

Proofreader: N.Manikandan

Indexer: Diana Witt

Design Director: Ken Phipps

Higher Education Design PM: Pamela Johnston

Interior Design: Cenveo Publisher Services

Cover Design: Trinh Truong

Cover Image: IanChrisGraham/Getty Images

Compositor: Cenveo Publisher Services

COPYRIGHT © 2017, 2008 by Tophatmonocle Corp.

Printed and bound in Canada
2 3 4 5   23 22 21 20

For more information contact Tophatmonocle Corp., 151 Bloor Street West, Suite 200, Toronto, Ontario, M5S 1S4. Or you can visit tophat.com

ALL RIGHTS RESERVED. No part of this work covered by the copyright herein may be reproduced, transcribed, or used in any form or by any means—graphic, electronic, or mechanical, including photocopying, recording, taping, Web distribution, or information storage and retrieval systems—without the written permission of the publisher.

For permission to use material from this text or product, submit all requests by email to permissions@tophat.com.

Every effort has been made to trace ownership of all copyrighted material and to secure permission from copyright holders. In the event of any question arising as to the use of any material, we will be pleased to make the necessary corrections in future printings.

Library and Archives Canada Cataloguing in Publication

Barker, Paul, 1953–, author
    Public administration in Canada / Paul Barker, Tim A. Mau. — Second edition.

Includes bibliographical references and index. Issued in print and electronic formats.
ISBN 978-0-17-650239-3 (paperback).—ISBN 978-0-17-676768-6 (pdf)

    1. Public administration—Canada. 2. Canada—Politics and government. 3. Public administration—Canada—Textbooks. 4. Canada—Politics and government—Textbooks. I. Mau, Tim A., 1969–, author II. Title.

JL108.B37 2016   351.71
C2016-906744-0
C2016-906745-9

ISBN-13: 978-0-17-650239-3
ISBN-10: 0-17-650239-4

Contents

The intellectual foundations of this book date back three decades to a time when two leading scholars of Canadian public administration, the late Kenneth Kernaghan and his colleague, David Siegel, endeavoured to produce a comprehensive text that would help to explain the theory and practice of public administration in this country. Over the span of twelve years (1987–1999), Kernaghan and Siegel published four editions of their textbook, which became the academic standard for training a generation of scholars and practitioners of public administration.

By the time that Paul Barker was tasked with providing a brief and updated version of the Kernaghan and Siegel classic in 2008, the academic market for public administration textbooks had expanded considerably. Those teaching public administration had many quality textbooks from which to choose.

Barker, therefore, faced a difficult challenge. On the one hand, a new generation of public administration scholars had firmly established themselves with their own accounts of the evolution of Canadian public administration. But *Public Administration in Canada: Brief Edition*, published in 2008, found a receptive audience. A bigger concern was the fear of tinkering too much with the rich content and analysis contained in the original textbook. Therefore, large parts of the Kernaghan and Siegel book remained untouched, serving as an homage to their groundbreaking work to document the contours of Canadian public administration.

To some extent, this revised edition continues in a similar vein. We remain indebted to the legacy of Kernaghan and Siegel. This is particularly true with respect to how the book is structured and organized, and those familiar with their work will notice that some of their words are still reproduced on the pages of this book. However, with the inclusion of a co-author and the passage of time, bringing with it many new developments in the theory and practice of Canadian public administration to evaluate, this book is increasingly a reflection of our interpretation and understanding of the subject matter.

A familiar refrain that we hear from political science colleagues is that public administration is relatively unsophisticated, while students often bemoan that the subject matter is uninteresting. We hope that this book will correct those impressions. Understanding how the state organizes to govern is a complex undertaking, in part because the institutions of government are constantly evolving. There is plentiful variation within organizational forms, and new organizational entities and service-delivery mechanisms are routinely emerging. Moreover, it seems that governments are undergoing a never-ending series of administrative reforms in their quest to bring greater efficiency and effectiveness to public sector service delivery.

Coming to grips with this diversity is part of what makes public administration so fascinating. Why, for example, does the government establish a regulatory agency to control the telecommunications industry but allow many professional bodies, like those governing our medical and legal professions, to self-regulate? When is it important to reduce ministerial control and allow for greater autonomy and flexibility than the traditional government department would allow? Why control the sale and distribution of alcohol through a provincial Crown corporation instead of letting the (regulated) private sector sell beer, wine, and spirits?

But public administration is also fundamentally concerned with a number of timeless issues that are critical for good governance, such as determining how best to hold our government to account for the policy decisions that it makes. This has become an even more complex and daunting challenge as new forms of service delivery see nongovernmental actors in the private and nonprofit sectors taking on significant roles in that regard through various collaborative partnerships with the state.

Our intention with the second edition of *Public Administration in Canada* is to bring the world of public administration to life for students, demonstrating the intersection of theory with the practice of government program and service delivery. We have provided as many real-life examples of the concepts and ideas contained in the book as space would allow. Our challenge to instructors using this textbook is to identify other concrete illustrations to help reinforce the importance and salience of public administration in the day-to-day lives of those they are teaching. As we often tell our students, one of the most rewarding aspects of teaching public administration is that virtually every day we can open up the newspaper and find practical examples of the issues that we are dealing with in class. In writing this book, we also seek to give the reader a sense of the complexity inherent in the administration of government programs and services. We hope to convey that, despite its challenges and limitations, the public service is a noble and rewarding career choice. Those of us teaching public administration share with government a desire to see the best and brightest Canadians choosing a career of service to the public, be it at the municipal, provincial, or federal level.

The structure of the book is the same as that of the previous edition, save for a couple of important changes, the first of which was to merge Chapters 9 and 10 into one chapter and place the consolidated chapter in a newly constituted Part One of the book, which offers an introduction to the study of public administration in Canada. As in the previous edition, the first chapter investigates the meaning of public administration, draws distinctions between administration and management in the public and private sectors, examines the key environmental influences that impact public administration, and concludes with a discussion of the size of government. Chapter 2 considers public sector values and ethics, with a particular emphasis on the concept of accountability. Placing this chapter in the first part of the book reflects the central place that values and ethics have in public administration.

Part Two of the book examines a number of the key organizational and public administration theories or schools of thought that have shaped the structure and operation of public sector organizations and how they relate specifically to the practice of public administration in Canada. Chapter 3 deals with the early theories of bureaucracy, which include the theories of Weber, Taylor, Fayol, and Gulick and Urwick. We also consider some of the key theorists in the neo-classical school—people like Simon, Merton, Bernard, and Selznick—who began to challenge the structuralists of the classical school and gave rise to the humanist theories, which are addressed in Chapter 4. Chapter 5 reviews the significant influence that new public management (NPM) has had, and continues to have, on the organization and operation of public administration globally; but this chapter has been revised to consider many of the important efforts to move beyond NPM that have emerged since the last edition.

In Part Three, we move from the theories of organizations to the actual structures of government that are used to deliver programs and services and regulate various economic and social processes in Canada. Chapter 6 focuses on the most traditional and commonly used organizational form, namely the government department, as well as the central agency, which is a special type of department that has responsibility for ensuring coordination across government. Chapter 7 is dedicated to an examination of Crown agencies. This includes both Crown corporations, which are similar in nature and function to private sector corporations, and a host of statutory and other agencies that provide a variety of administrative, research, regulatory, and quasi-judicial functions.

These topics were covered as separate chapters in the previous edition of this book. The final chapter in this section of the book, Chapter 8, examines the rise of new organizational mechanisms in government, which are categorized as alternative service delivery.

Part Four addresses the many interactions between public servants employed in the different organizational forms and other actors in the Canadian political process. Chapter 9 examines the relations of the bureaucracy with senior political actors in cabinet, while Chapter 10 shifts the focus to interactions within and between departments and other agencies. Chapters 11 and 12 consider interactions between public servants and the legislature and courts, respectively. Chapter 13 offers an understanding of intergovernmental administrative relations, while the final chapter in this section delves into a review of relations that sometimes receive little attention, namely those between appointed officials and non-governmental actors (pressure groups, the media, the interested public, and social movements).

The book concludes with an examination in Part Five of the two major tasks associated with the management of organizational resources in the public sector, human resources and finance. In other words, this last section of the book gives the reader a view of public servants in action. Chapters 15 and 16 deal with the management of human resources, with Chapter 15 discussing the emergence of the merit principle and the structure of the human resources management system, and Chapter 16 assessing efforts at the federal level to provide for a more representative bureaucracy. The final two chapters address the challenge of managing the country's financial resources. Chapter 17 discusses the various aspects of budgeting in government, which can be considered the first step in the financial management process. Chapter 18 examines the remaining steps in the attempt to ensure that public finances are managed soundly.

A number of new features have been incorporated into this version of the textbook. First, we have included a number of visual images and political cartoons to break up the text. Second, we know that students can sometimes feel overwhelmed by the level of detail contained in introductory textbooks, so with that in mind we added a list of learning objectives at the start of each chapter as well as a concluding section, entitled "Points to Know," both of which highlight the key details that should be gleaned from reading the chapter. Each chapter also includes a number of review questions that students should think about and be able to answer when reviewing the material for an examination. As in the first edition, there is a glossary of terms comprising the bold-faced terms in the text. These are the key terms and concepts in public administration, so students can use the glossary as a study aid to ensure comprehension of the material. Finally, many of the chapters include boxes labelled "What to Do?" These boxes present brief scenarios or issues to the reader to stimulate thinking about difficult public administration issues.

We gratefully acknowledge the critical comments and feedback of our reviewers, which greatly assisted us in revising the book. While many of their suggestions are reflected in this latest edition, it simply was not feasible, without writing a much longer treatment of the subject matter, to incorporate all of their valuable recommendations.

Brendon Boyd	University of Victoria
Charles Conteh	Brock University
Thomas R. Klassen	York University
Rachel LaForest	Queen's University
Andrea Rounce	University of Manitoba

Finally, we would like to express our gratitude to the team at Nelson, firstly, for your belief in and support of this project, and secondly, for your patience and understanding as we required more time than initially anticipated to revise the manuscript.

Paul Barker and Tim A. Mau

Instructor Resources

The following instructor resources have been created for *Public Administration in Canada*, Second Edition. Access these ultimate tools for customizing lectures and presentations at retail.tophat.com.

PowerPoint

Microsoft® PowerPoint® lecture slides for every chapter have been created by Nanita Mohan of the University of Guelph. The slides feature key figures, tables, and photographs from *Public Administration in Canada* and include teaching notes designed to guide your presentation of the material. Principles of clear design and engaging content have been incorporated throughout, making it simple for instructors to customize the deck for their courses.

Test Bank

This resource was also written by Nanita Mohan of the University of Guelph and includes a collection of multiple choice, short answer, and essay questions that you may use with your students for testing, assignments, and practice exercises.

Image Library

This resource consists of digital copies of figures, short tables, and images used in the book that instructors may use to customize the PowerPoint, or to create their own PowerPoint presentations. An Image Library Key is also provided that provides a description and file name for each item.

What Is Public Administration?

Learning Objectives

Reading this chapter allows you to do the following:

- Understand the importance of public administration to the daily lives of Canadians
- Appreciate that public servants and their responsibilities represent the key element in public administration
- Analyze the key differences between public and private administration and explain how these differences contribute to an awareness of the challenges of working in the public sector
- Evaluate the impact of globalization, political culture, the fiscal imperative, and attitudes towards government on the operation of public administration in Canada
- Identify the challenges facing public administration and possible ways these challenges may be addressed

Public administration in Canada is about both continuity and change. This is best seen by looking at **public servants**, who are the appointed officials of government and form the heart of public administration. These officials continue to do basically what they have always done, which is to advise senior politicians and administer government programs and services. Public officials also work in organizational structures whose contours might be recognized by counterparts of a hundred years ago, and they engage in familiar interactions and processes with others both inside and outside of government. But alongside the continuity can be found the signs of change. Public servants once monopolized the provision of advice, but now relatively new players perform a prominent role in shaping the public policies and services offered by government. The new entities include the media, interest groups, social movements, volunteer organizations, and a host of others who wish to participate actively in the decision making of government and whose ambition is effectively to replace government with networks of representatives of the public, private, and nonprofit sectors. Forces of change have as well made government, including its public servants, more visible and more vulnerable to critical scrutiny. The preferences of senior politicians, most especially the prime minister and premiers, have also acted to make things different. Feeling that perhaps their nonpolitical advisors have sometimes had too much influence, these elected officials have sought to centralize power and influence within their offices. The courts and the people's representatives in legislatures, too, have assumed a larger place in public administration. With its interpretation of the *Canadian Charter of Rights and Freedoms*, the judiciary has forever changed the ways public servants go about administering policies and programs, while the House of Commons and equivalents in the provinces have equipped themselves to gain greater control over bureaucratic power. Even within the domain of public

public servant Also referred to as civil servants or bureaucrats, these are the appointed officials who are employed by government. They provide advice, manage resources, and provide services to citizens.

servants—the public service—there have been adjustments in the form of new organizational arrangements and more complex relationships between appointed officials.

There is little doubt that to understand public administration in Canada is to appreciate both the relevant continuities and the changes, to examine where public administration in Canada has been, where it is now, and where it might go. To do so is not to stop at every point in order to recognize continuity or change, but rather to discuss the basic values, structures, and processes that constitute public administration and in so doing see evidence of the old and the new. It is also important to understand that the process of change is gradual and subtle and often becomes entwined with existing practice. With this first chapter, we commence the discussion by becoming clear about the importance and meaning of public administration as well as the external environment in which public administration takes place.

Importance and Meaning of Public Administration

In the past fifty years, there has been an impressive expansion in the activities of Canadian governments. The growth of responsibilities in all spheres of Canadian government—federal, provincial, and municipal—has a great impact on the daily lives and future prospects of Canadian citizens. The degree of happiness and prosperity or misery and poverty experienced by Canadians is affected by the countless decisions made each day by our governments. The range of governmental activities includes the traditional functions of the administration of justice, conduct of external relations, and defence of the country, as well as newer responsibilities such as health care, environmental protection, and scientific research. Federal public servants control and inspect air traffic; protect coastal waterways against pollution and overfishing; guard prisoners in penitentiaries and rehabilitate offenders; protect our health and safety by inspecting food, water, air, and medicine; issue millions of cheques annually to seniors and needy Canadians; help unemployed Canadians find jobs; and support science, technology, and the delivery of foreign aid. The range of activities is wider still when we consider the responsibilities of provincial and municipal governments too, responsibilities which include providing electricity, water, and waste-water treatment, recreational services, public transit, maintenance of local and provincial parks, and so on.

The two major areas of government activities are the provision of services and the enforcement of regulations. The service functions include the delivery of social services, the administration of grants and loans, and the maintenance of roads and highways. Among the regulatory functions are the prevention of unsafe workplaces, the support of Canadian culture, the enforcement of fair housing and employment regulations, and the appropriate use of the Internet. In order to carry out these and other responsibilities as effectively as possible, governments are actively engaged in supporting research on matters ranging from the functioning of struggling families to scientific and medical concerns.

Few Canadians are aware of the importance and the magnitude of their governments' operations. Canadians, like citizens of other countries, tend to be conscious of only those government activities that affect them directly and significantly. Many important functions of government, such as the preservation of internal law and order or the administration of justice, are taken for granted unless the services are discontinued or disrupted for some reason. Once government in Canada was about the provision of security and basic public services; now it does much more. Today, even though many political leaders aspire to limit the size of the public sector, governments involve themselves in all facets of the lives of Canadians.

These extensive and pervasive activities of Canadian governments have a great deal to do with public administration. Public servants play a large role in formulating and implementing policies to fulfill their government's service and regulatory responsibilities.

These responsibilities are performed through what is known as the **public bureaucracy** (also called the public service or civil service), which is an organizational system for achieving government objectives.[1] Elected representatives, especially political executives, participate actively in the making of public policies. However, we will see in later chapters that public servants (also called civil servants, government employees, appointed officials, or bureaucrats) have considerable influence on the content of these policies and make most of the decisions required to implement them. Thus, while a recurring theme in this book is the importance of political actors, the role of the bureaucracy in relation to its responsibilities and interactions with other relevant participants in government is the major focus.

public bureaucracy Also called the public service, it is the system of authority, people, offices, and methods government uses to achieve its objectives; the means by which the practice of public administration is carried out.

Meaning of Public Administration

"Public administration" is a term more easily explained than defined. In the past, this fact did not discourage scholars from trying to capture its meaning in a single sentence. Typical one-sentence definitions of public administration have included "the study and practice of the tasks associated with the conduct of the administrative state" and "the coordination of individual group efforts to carry out public policy."[2] Even today one-sentence definitions can be found—for example, public administration is "the study and oversight of all structures, institutions, policies, and programs of the state."[3] But increasingly the preference is not to define but rather to explain public administration.[4] One such attempt discusses the primary role of appointed officials in the implementation and administration of programs, notes that they assist elected officials in drafting laws and making public policies, reminds the reader that appointed officials sometimes literally make the law through regulations, and observes that "[p]ublic administrators comprise the bulk of government employment and activity." This same attempt at explanation adds that the public service often engages the citizenry directly in various forms and that the job of many senior public-sector employees is now more managerial in nature than administrative or advisory.[5] Understanding public administration through explanation thus appears workable, but it might be best simply to pose questions and promise answers in a subsequent analysis. For example, what are the tasks associated with the conduct of the administrative state? What are the relationships between public servants and such institutions as legislatures, executives, and courts? What is distinctive about organization and management in public administration as opposed to private administration? Has public decision making changed in government and, if so, how has it changed? More fundamentally, does public administration still exist or has it morphed into something else? This text seeks to provide answers to these and many other questions about public administration (see Box 1.1).

Public Administration and Public Policy

BOX
1.1

Our discussion of public administration has referred to "public policies," a term employed to describe the decisions made by government to handle important issues. The term also represents a particular approach that emphasizes the idea of government as a process consisting up to five stages, starting with agenda setting and ending with policy evaluation. Some textbooks on public administration insert the public policy approach into their presentation, which is perfectly acceptable. But other textbooks on public administration, such as *Public Administration in Canada*, leave out the public policy approach. Our decision to forego a chapter dedicated to the policy-making process is not to suggest that it is irrelevant or unimportant. The reason for this omission lies with the fact that an approach already underpins the study of public administration, one that focuses more on institutions than public policies. As a result, the inclusion of the public policy approach may have the effect of combining two different approaches, which can lead to confusion and overlapping discussions.

At this point, where we have a fairly good idea of the meaning of public administration, it seems appropriate to clarify a few matters. The terms "public administration" and "public bureaucracy" are often used interchangeably, but they do not mean the same thing. Public administration refers to a field of practice (or occupation) and to a field of study (or discipline). Public bureaucracy, as mentioned earlier, is the system of authority, people, offices, and methods that government uses to achieve its objectives. It is the means by which the practice of public administration is largely carried on; it is also the main focus of the study of public administration. We use the term public administration to refer to its practice unless we indicate otherwise by specific reference to its study. Accordingly, this text is devoted to studying the practice of public administration as that practice is conducted through the system known as public bureaucracy.

A further matter to make clearer is the relationship between the terms "administration" and "management." The two terms are also often used in a manner that suggests they have the same basic meaning. In a sense they are synonymous because public servants have always engaged in some kind of management. But it is best to see the two as describing separate kinds of activities, the discussion of which forms an important part of this text. For now, it is sufficient to recognize that they are not the same.

Public Administration versus Private Administration

Any discussion of the meaning and operations of public administration can be helped by comparing it with private (or business) administration. There is, in fact, much that is similar in the two sectors. Administration in all organizations involves cooperative group action. Moreover, all large organizations, whether they are government departments, hospitals, universities, labour unions, factories, or commercial enterprises, must provide for the performance of such functions of general management as planning, organizing, staffing, and budgeting. A common observation explaining the differences between public and private administration is that the private sector is more willing to accept risk than the public sector because the latter "operates in a highly charged political environment in which sins are not easily tolerated."[6] Yet, it has been shown that the two types of organizations appear to differ little when it comes to risk.[7] There are, however, distinguishing factors in the administration of public sector organizations, and these differences have important implications for the study and practice of public administration. At the very least, these differences suggest the need for caution in transferring practices and technologies from private sector organizations to public sector organizations (see Box 1.2).

The first and most frequently cited difference is that the overall mission of public administration is service to the public or **public interest**, whereas the primary raison d'être of private administration is profit, or what is often described as "the bottom line." To admit to this difference is not to say that public organizations (and nonprofit organizations) are without concern for financial performance; they, too, need money to survive. The difference emerges when it is understood that public administration is also required to adopt a service orientation to help politicians respond to public demands and requirements for government services. Private administration is profit-oriented because the survival of private sector organizations ultimately depends on making a profit; public administration requires financial well-being, but also has to attend to "producing social value defined in terms of an important mission that they could achieve."[8]

It is normally argued that a second difference, following directly from the service-versus-profit distinction, is that public administration operates less efficiently than private administration. Governments are not oriented toward a single goal such as profit maximization; rather, they typically must satisfy several goals simultaneously, some of which may conflict with one another, and some of which cannot even be stated openly. In this complex environment, it is not surprising that governments sometimes do things that

public interest The common good or welfare of the general public, which guides the actions of government.

Nonprofit Organizations

BOX
1.2

A third type of organization, the nonprofit organization (NPO), is gaining greater attention in both the study and practice of public administration. As the name suggests, NPOs are private organizations whose aim is not to make a profit for distribution to owners or shareholders; rather, the aim of an NPO is to serve a particular social view or purpose. Examples of well-known NPOs in Canada include Mothers Against Drunk Driving, Canadian Association of Elizabeth Fry Societies, the Fraser Institute, Global Vision, and Habitat for Humanity. A way to distinguish more closely differences between NPOs and the two main types of organizations, private and public, is to look at the source of revenue and the ultimate value or mission of the organization. For private and public organizations, the source of revenue is either sales and investment revenues or taxation of one kind or another; for NPOs, it is donations along with government grants, contracts, and earned income. As for the underlying value, again for private and public organization, the value is either profit or electoral mandates; for the NPOs, it is meeting the specified social purpose and expectations of donors.

Source: Mark Moore, "Managing for Value: Organizational Strategy in For-Profit, Nonprofit, and Governmental Organizations," *Nonprofit and Voluntary Sector Quarterly*, 29(1) (2000): 183–208.

would not stand the test of businesslike principles. Inefficiency may also arise from the fact that public sector employees seek through their work to "make a contribution to society," an attitude found less frequently among private sector employees.[9] A public servant may, for instance, interpret rules governing eligibility for payments quite broadly to ensure that struggling families are able to receive additional support from government. Such an action may benefit families and speak to concerns about poverty, but it may not be the most efficient way to spend government revenues. Another consideration is that politicians are concerned, first and foremost, with winning public support. The public judges politicians by their public personae and policy initiatives, not by how well they manage their departments. So even if public managers are inclined to be efficient, they "must serve goals or purposes that are not always the preferences of the agency's senior administrators."[10] Politicians want public servants who provide good policy advice and who keep them out of trouble.

A third difference between public and private administration is the greater emphasis in the public sector on accountability. This emerges in part from the fact that all of us are forced to contribute financially to government and thus we expect some say over its operation or at least an indication that matters are being handled properly. The typical monopoly of government over the provision of services also leads to greater demands for accountability because recipients of the services have nowhere else to go. Parents with children at private schools can always turn to an alternative, for example, but those in the public school system usually have little or no choice. For the latter group of parents, there is an incentive to take a greater interest in the operation of the public function.[11] More generally, in the private sector accountability is mostly confined to pleasing shareholders, whereas in the public sector theoretically the entire population has a stake (see What to Do?).

A fourth difference between public and private administration is that the human resources management system is much more complicated and rigid in government than in private sector

WHAT TO DO?

The mention of government monopolies suggests that it might be wise to consider more competition with regard to the provision of public services. Take, for example, the case of primary and secondary schooling. Providing choice might relieve parents of the burden of constantly checking up on the quality of their children's schooling because students could always leave to attend another school if necessary. It could also lead to higher quality education as the presence of competition may cause schools to take actions that make them more academically attractive. But, interestingly, Canada's secondary school students, who are offered only limited choice, score better on international tests than comparable students from a country known for offering choice in schools, the United States. What are we to do, if anything, with government programs that face little competition?

Source: PISA, What Students Know and Can Do: Student Performance in Mathematics, Reading and Science, http://www.oecd.org/pisa/keyfindings/PISA-2012-results-snapshot-Volume-I-ENG.pdf

organizations. In general, it is harder both to hire and to fire government employees. In the public sector, the merit system of hiring and promoting employees includes several criteria that go well beyond the idea of technical proficiency. To promote sensitivity and responsiveness to the needs of a certain minority group, for example, the government may hire a person from that group who is not as well qualified as other candidates in terms of education and experience. The complexity and inflexibility of human resources management systems also result from the general emphasis on accountability and the need to demonstrate that the required procedures have been properly established and followed.

Fifth, and finally, the public nature of public administration requires that much of it be conducted in a fishbowl of publicity. Many government deliberations are conducted behind closed doors but, compared to the private sector, many more government decisions are subjected to public scrutiny. Members of the media, for example, pay a great deal more attention to the trials and tribulations of ministers and their officials than they do to the goings-on in business life. Front-page headlines are more likely to reveal some inefficiency in government than to cover comparable developments in the private sector. As mentioned earlier, this particular difference does not necessarily mean that public servants are more risk-averse than their counterparts in the private sector. But it does mean, among other things, that nothing in government is too small or unimportant to be considered for public consumption and attention. As Savoie writes, "Any decision [of government] can become the subject of public debate, a question in Parliament, or a ten-second clip on the television news."[12]

Two major characteristics of government account in large part for the differences between public and private administration: (1) the vast scope and complexity of government activities; and (2) the political environment within which these activities are conducted. Given these considerations, the issue of whether public or private administration is more efficient is not the most relevant concern. The critical question is whether public administration is conducted as efficiently as can reasonably be expected; however, we will see at various points in this book that governments are actively engaged in reforms to increase their efficiency, effectiveness, and responsiveness by such means as improved service to the public and the reduction of rules and regulations.

The Study of Public Administration

The systematic study of public administration in North America is a relatively recent development. In the United States, the study of the field is generally acknowledged to date from 1887 with the publication of Woodrow Wilson's essay, "The Study of Administration."[13] Although no single date or publication marks the beginning of the study of public administration in Canada, there are several noteworthy developments in the evolution of the formal study of Canadian public administration.

Several of the 23 volumes of *Canada and Its Provinces*, written by A. Shortt and A.G. Doherty and published in 1914, covered aspects of public administration and public bureaucracy in Canada. In 1918, the first work focusing on a particular problem in Canadian public administration was written by two scholars from the United States.[14] The earliest general work in the field was R. MacGregor Dawson's *The Principle of Official Independence*; that work, published in 1922, was initially written as his doctoral dissertation at the London School of Economics and Political Science. The next significant contribution was his *The Civil Service of Canada*, published in 1929.[15] In 1936, Luther Richter and R.A. Mackay established the first degree program in Canadian public administration at Dalhousie University. Carleton College (now Carleton University) graduated students with a Bachelor of Public Administration degree in 1946, and the University's School of Public Administration was established in 1952. However, it was not until the early 1950s that a group of academic scholars emerged and a more broad-based literature in public administration started to develop. *Canadian Public Administration*, the scholarly journal devoted to the study of the subject, commenced publication in 1958.

The academic study of public administration began to flourish in the late 1960s. This increased attention to research and teaching in public administration is largely due to the growth in the operations, expenditures, and size of the federal, provincial, and municipal bureaucracies. It also coincided with the expansion of Canadian universities and colleges, which were thereby able to devote more resources to teaching and research in public administration. This flourishing could also be seen in the emergence of different models or paradigms that sought to make sense of public administration and how a handful of these paradigms have come to prevail in the study of Canadian public administration.[16] Of course, the road to success can become bumpy at times, and public administration is no exception to this rule. In the 1990s, various developments led to "downsizing" of the size and roles of public services in Canada, and one effect of this action was to reduce the attractiveness of university programs and studies in public administration—a career in government now seemed less likely.[17] But the challenges of the new century and the need for public services to find their place in addressing these challenges have elicited new excitement about studies in public administration. New graduate programs in public administration have emerged, enrolment in these programs has risen, and young scholars are acting to bring new ideas and perspectives into the field[18] (see Box 1.3).

Educational Route to Careers in Public Administration

BOX
1.3

A variety of arrangements exists for the master's-level education of aspiring public servants. Programs leading to a Master of Public Administration (MPA) degree, or to a degree in political science or public sector management, are available in departments of political science or in schools or faculties of administrative studies. However, the most common route to an MPA is through one of the several specialized schools of public administration that have grown rapidly during the past 35 years in Canada. These schools offer an interdisciplinary approach with a professional emphasis. Programs are designed to accommodate students proceeding directly from their bachelor's degree as well as mid-career public servants. The schools require a similar group of core courses (e.g., government structure and organization, policy formulation, quantitative methods, applied economics, the management process in government, evaluation of programs, and public sector financial management and accounting) and a range of elective courses in specialized areas such as local government administration and intergovernmental relations.

In the study of public administration, there is some debate as to whether public administration is a sub-discipline of political science or stands alone. But the reality is that a number of disciplines are relevant to Canadian public administration, including political science, the law, management, economics, sociology, and history. Each of these disciplines has a different focus or object of study; for example, political scientists are concerned with institutions, the role of the state, power relations, and the bureaucracy, while management theorists focus their attention on decision making, the optimal use of resources, and innovation. But all of them together contribute to our understanding of the institutions, programs, and governance processes that are central to public administration.[19] Another defining feature of the study of public administration is its emphasis on practical matters. Public administration, as Henry describes it, "is a broad ranging and amorphous combination of theory and practice."[20] The work of public administration scholars generally has applicability to the day-to-day work of public servants and they, in turn, have much to learn from the wealth of knowledge possessed by the practitioners.[21] The Institute of Public Administration of Canada, a nonprofit organization, has been instrumental in facilitating this coming together of scholar and practitioner in Canada.

Environment and Size of Public Administration

Public administration is greatly influenced by the broad environment within which it is conducted. For example, a public servant may wish to advise a senior politician to move forward with a national child care plan for Canada but decide against it because Canadians traditionally see the family as mainly responsible for the well-being of children. Aside from the political and legal setting of public administration, discussed in detail elsewhere in this book, some of the more important environmental influences of today are globalization, political culture, the fiscal imperative, and public perceptions of government and public servants.

Globalization

globalization A process of integration and interaction between peoples, private sector corporations, and governments around the world that has been propelled by international trade and investment.

Globalization refers to the increasing tendency of people and institutions in various parts of the world to interact with one another without great concern for national identity and borders. As Pal says, globalization reflects "the sense that the entire planet is a single social space, that people carry on conversations and movements within that space irrespective of territoriality...."[22] To give an example of this sense, major movie studios used to focus on generating product mainly for the American market, but now almost everyone wants to go the movies; Thor is a superhero in United States, but also in China. For many, globalization is identified with its economic dimension, which is the movement from a world of distinct economies to a global economy characterized by worldwide markets for investment, production, distribution, and consumption. This in fact is a key element of globalization, and it forces national governments and their bureaucratic agents to be creative in order to remain competitive in the new global marketplace and to guard industries and individuals against the sometimes harsh effects of globalization.[23] Economic globalization also puts a premium on governments' ability to act quickly, so there is pressure to make decision making in the public sector more flexible and open to new ways of organizing itself.

Globalization also has a cultural dimension that puts at risk national cultures as it acts to establish common beliefs and values on a worldwide basis.[24] For governments eager to preserve the cultural uniqueness of their countries, this cultural aspect of globalization represents a tremendous challenge. In Canada, regulatory agencies try to provide for Canadian content in our various cultural products, but the Internet, smartphones, satellite radio, and social media weaken the impact of these efforts. Threats of climate change and signs of widespread damage to the ecosystem demonstrate that globalization also has an environmental dimension, and this too requires governments to act differently. In this instance, the challenge is for the world's governments to coordinate their efforts to ensure that we do not seriously hurt or even destroy the planet.

The same forces of globalization that lead towards convergence and uniformity in the economy and society are similarly felt in the realm of politics and public administration. While governments often embrace distinctive administrative reforms to pursue greater efficiency and effectiveness, we have also witnessed the emergence of a global public management reform initiative in new public management (NPM).[25] (NPM will be discussed in detail in Chapter 5.) However, while there was an assumption with NPM that it could be used almost anywhere to improve public management, there were in fact many different approaches to adopting the NPM prescription for reform. As Painter and Peters noted, "Although there is some reason to think that national public bureaucracies are similar, there are equal or better reasons to think that they are distinctive, and that their distinctiveness is likely to persist even in the face of pressure for convergence."[26] It appears, then, that globalization has some limits.

Political Culture

A second force is the changing **political culture** in Canada (and other developed countries). Political culture refers to the values, beliefs, and attitudes we hold about political life. Surveys show that the political culture in Canada has changed in recent years in a way that makes Canadians less confident in government and not as willing to defer to authority in general. These same surveys also reveal a shift away from traditional ways of participating in politics (voting, for example) and towards a "greater tendency to challenge authority through non-electoral forms of participation."[27] Also interesting, the way Canadians think about politics now includes greater support for social diversity in Canadian politics and the groups that represent this diversity; expressed differently, Canadians want an increased emphasis on the notion of Canada as a mosaic and not a US-style melting pot. For public administration, a major implication of this change is that governments have to consult more widely and in a more varied fashion with the interested public, for people are clearly unhappy with both the level and the type of traditional interactions with government.

> **political culture** The values, beliefs, and attitudes we hold about political life.

All of these shifts in political culture do not necessarily lead to less government; rather, they suggest that governments should consider governing differently—perhaps through the adoption of new management structures in the public sector and inclusion of more non-governmental actors in public decision making. Surveys can also be interpreted to mean that respondents actually wish that government would extend or enlarge itself by going beyond traditional policy concerns for security and the economy and address relatively new matters like the environment and social inequality. However, caution should be exercised in relation to the point just made because, as will be shown, the external environment also includes attitudes that provide support for restrained government.

The Fiscal Imperative

Beginning in the early 1970s, much of the Western world was confronting an economic crisis. The oil shocks of 1973, whereby the price of crude skyrocketed, combined with an economic recession that for the first time was characterized by both high unemployment and high inflation, put an end to the post-World War II economic boom. Governments were also contending with rising levels of government debt and persistent annual budget deficits arising from public expenditures exceeding available revenue. An emerging consensus dictated that governments needed to get their fiscal houses in order. What followed in many countries was a series of cuts in public programs, the privatization of government agencies, and reductions in the number of public servants.

Canada similarly followed a program of austerity measures that ultimately culminated in the federal government's first fiscal surplus in nearly 30 years in the late 1990s. This was the beginning of the "post-deficit era" in Canadian politics;[28] but the balanced budgets did not last long. With the global recession of 2008–2009, Canada, like most developed nations around the world, committed itself to fiscal stimulus spending; as a result, deficits once again became the norm with the debt reduction from the previous decade being completely eliminated. Prime Minister Harper made strong fiscal stewardship, including a return to balanced budgets, the central plank of his re-election strategy in 2014, but the Trudeau Liberals returned to power rejecting that approach in favour of increased government spending. As can be seen from these events in Canada, governing in a climate of scarcity and fiscal prudence constitutes an important part of the environment of Canadian public administration.

Views of Government and Administration

A further force, following in some respects from the three already considered, is changed views about the range and nature of government and the administration of public services.[29] This final force in the external environment has generated a kind of indictment against the public service consisting of three complaints: (1) the bureaucracy has too much influence; (2) it uses delegated power to make decisions that threaten freedoms of the citizenry; and (3) it is a large part of a governing system that badly underperforms and squanders public revenues.[30] The first complaint of excessive bureaucratic influence focuses on the large role of public servants in the making of public policy and the belief that they—and not elected officials—decide on major policy initiatives. People also believe that appointed officials stymie the efforts of political leaders to introduce program initiatives. The second concern arises from the increasing practice of passing broadly-worded laws and allowing public servants to provide the necessary details when carrying out new programs. The fear is that this arrangement results in bureaucrats making decisions that limit individual rights and freedoms. The third and final complaint is that the actions of public servants help explain the failure of public programs to provide the expected benefits. Bureaucrats also allegedly misuse scarce public funds in the pursuit of their own narrow interests. Accompanying these charges is a similarly negative view of government as a whole and its inability to address major societal concerns. Feelings of "hostility, skepticism, frustration, and disappointment" have come to be associated with government and politics in Canada.[31]

Size of the Public Service

The last matter to consider in this chapter is the size of the public service or bureaucracy in Canada. Some of the key issues and controversies relating to public administration and management can be related to the public service and its size.

There are various ways to gain an idea of the size of the public service and government as a whole. One accepted way is to measure total government outlays or expenditures as a percentage of the gross domestic product (GDP), which represents the total value of goods and services in Canada. This approach actually measures government spending and not the public service in particular, but expenditures can be seen as a proxy for the public service. Between the period 1970 to 2014, total federal, provincial, territorial, and local government spending in Canada, expressed as a percentage of GDP, have risen from 35.9% to 39.4%, a relatively small increase that hides rather high percentages in some years during the 25-year period. For example, in the mid-1990s, a period of difficult economic times, the percentages rose to as high as 52.6%. However, since the turn of the century percentages have remained in the high 30s and low 40s, even with the severe economic downturn at the end of the first decade of the twenty-first century. For the United States, a country that actively seeks small government, the percentage increased from 34.2% in 1970 to 38.3% in 2014.[32] If we look solely at the experience of the federal government—a target of critics of government spending—total expenditures as a percentage of GDP declined during the period 1970–71 to 2015–16 from 18.2% to 14.2%.[33] As noted earlier, Canadians are concerned about wasteful spending in the public sector, but the numbers suggest that government in terms of spending is not out of control.

A second way of measuring the size of the public service is to look at the actual number of employees. Chapter 15 discusses the number of public sector employees in Canada within the context of human resources activities and policies in the federal government. At this point, it will be simply noted that growth in public services over the years appears to have been fairly reasonable. Figure 1.1 shows four lines or curves of indexed growth over time for the Canadian economy and population, program spending by the federal government, and the size of the federal public service. The figure shows the economy growing the fastest, then program spending, followed by the population,

Part One / Introduction to Public Administration

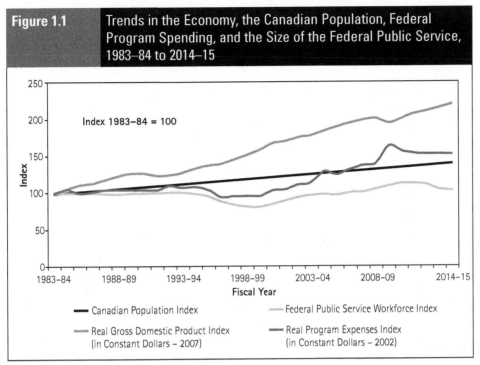

Figure 1.1 Trends in the Economy, the Canadian Population, Federal Program Spending, and the Size of the Federal Public Service, 1983–84 to 2014–15

Index 1983–84 = 100

— Canadian Population Index
----- Federal Public Service Workforce Index
— Real Gross Domestic Product Index (in Constant Dollars – 2007)
— Real Program Expenses Index (in Constant Dollars – 2002)

Source: *Demographic Snapshot of the Federal Public Service, 2015.* https://www.tbs-sct.gc.ca/psm-fpfm/modernizing-modernisation/stats/demo15-eng.asp, Treasury Board of Canada Secretariat, 2015.

and finally the public service. The number 100 represents the size of the public service in 1983–84 (and for the size or amount of the other three indicators) and the movement of the curve for the public service represents annual percentage increases or decreases in overall employment over time. The relatively flat curve for the public service indicates that the size of the service has remained fairly stable for the past thirty years.[34]

The finding that the size of the federal public service over the past three decades has been stable suggests little attention would be paid to this central element of government. However, as we have already shown, this is not the case. The chapters to follow reveal that the public service can represent the continuities inherent in public administration, but they also demonstrate that the public service is hardly immune to the forces of change.

Points to Know

- Public administration is better explained than defined, and an explanation revolves around detailing the duties of appointed officials and their relations with other actors in the political process.

- Public administration is undergoing many changes relating to the formulation and implementation of government programs. These changes include more actors in the decision-making process, the greater transparency or openness in government, and the way public servants administer and manage government programs.

- When compared with their counterparts in the private sector, public servants are expected to adhere to more objectives and act in ways that result in a lesser degree of efficiency. Public servants also face more mechanisms

designed to ensure accountability and face a much more rule-based system of human relations. Finally, the private sector is much less exposed to the public than the public sector.

- Four important forces that constitute the setting or environment for public administration are globalization, political culture, the fiscal imperative, and attitudes about government and bureaucracy. Each has significant effects on appointed officials and others involved in public administration.

- Two ways of measuring the size of the public service overall in Canada and at the federal level in particular suggest that government bureaucracy has experienced only modest growth.

Review Questions

1. Assess the claim that the term "public administration" is difficult to define.

2. How does the comparison of public and private administration help us to better understand public administration?

3. Discuss the impact of globalization and political culture on public administration.

4. Propose a third way of possibly measuring the size of government and the public service.

5. Some argue that public administration is less efficient than private administration. Discuss the validity of this claim.

Notes

1. Strictly speaking, "public bureaucracy" refers to the operation of bureaucracy in government, while "bureaucracy" refers to its operation in any sector (private, public, or nonprofit). But often the two are both used to refer to bureaucracy in the public sector, which will be the practice in this text.

2. Ivan L. Richardson and Sidney Baldwin, *Public Administration: Government in Action* (Columbus, Ohio: Charles E. Merrill, 1976), 3; John M. Pfiffner and Robert Presthus, *Public Administration*, 5th ed. (New York: Ronald Press, 1967), 7.

3. David Johnson, *Thinking Government: Public Administration and Politics in Canada*, 3rd ed. (Toronto: University of Toronto Press, 2011), 19.

4. Kenneth Kernaghan, "Public Administration," *The Canadian Encyclopedia*, accessed July 10, 2016, http://www.thecanadianencyclopedia.ca/en/article/public-administration/.

5. B. Guy Peters and Jon Pierre, "Introduction: The Role of Public Administration in Governing," in *The Sage Handbook of Public Administration*, Concise Second Edition, eds. B. Guy Peters and Jon Pierre (London: Sage Publications, 2014), 2.

6. Donald J. Savoie, *Whatever Happened to the Music Teacher?: How Government Decides and Why* (Montreal & Kingston: McGill-Queen's University Press, 2013), 131.

7. Paul Nutt, "Comparing Public and Private Sector Decision-Making Practices," *Journal of Public Administration Research and Theory* 16(1) (2005): 312; Kristina Jaskyte, "Work Values of Public, Nonprofit, and Business Employees: A Cross-Cultural Evidence," *International Journal of Public Administration*, 39(3) (2016): 190.

8. Mark Moore, "Managing for Value: Organizational Strategy in For-Profit, Nonprofit, and Governmental Organizations," *Nonprofit and Voluntary Sector Quarterly*, 29(1) (2000): 195.

9. Sean T. Lyons, Linda E. Duxbury, and Christopher A. Higgins, "A Comparison of the Values and Commitment of Private Sector, Public Sector, and Parapublic Employees," *Public Administration Review* 66(4) (2006): 613.

10. Savoie, *Whatever Happened to the Music Teacher?* 131.

11. James Q. Wilson, *Bureaucracy: What Government Agencies Do and Why They Do It* (New York: Basic Books, 1989), 348.

12. Savoie, *Whatever Happened to the Music Teacher?* 135.

13. Reprinted in Peter Woll, ed., *Public Administration and Policy* (New York: Harper & Row, 1966), 15–41.

14. H.S. Villard and W.W. Willoughby, *The Canadian Budgetary System* (New York: Appleton, 1918).

15. R. MacGregor Dawson, *The Civil Service of Canada* (Oxford: Oxford University Press, 1929). For a discussion of Dawson's views on the role of the public service, see Ken Rasmussen, "The Administrative Liberalism of R. MacGregor Dawson," *Canadian Public Administration* 33(1) (Spring 1990): 37–51.

16. Iain Gow, "Evolution of Disciplinary Approaches and Paradigms in the Study of Public Administration in Canada," in *The Evolving Physiology of Government: Canadian Public Administration in Transition*, eds. O.P. Dwivedi, Tim A. Mau, and Byron Sheldrick (Ottawa: University of Ottawa Press, 2009), 2–39.

17. Jonathan Malloy, "The Next Generation? Recruitment and Renewal in the Federal Public Service," in *How Ottawa Spends 2004-2005: Mandate Change in the Paul Martin Era*, ed, G. Bruce Doern (Montreal & Kingston: McGill-Queen's University Press, 2004), 287.

18. Barbara Wake Carroll, "Making It Happen: An Introduction to Public Administration in Canada," in *Approaching Public Administration: Core Debates and Emerging Issues*, eds. Roberto P. Leone and Frank L.K. Ohemeng (Toronto: Emond Montgomery Publications, 2011), 5.

19. Gow, "Evolution of Disciplinary Approaches," 5–6.

20. Nicholas Henry, *Public Administration and Public Affairs*, 11th ed. (Toronto: Pearson, 2010), 3.

21. Kenneth Kernaghan, "Speaking Truth to Academics: The Wisdom of Practitioners" *Canadian Public Administration* 52(4) (December 2009): 503–523.

22. Leslie A. Pal, *Beyond Policy Analysis: Public Issue Management in Turbulent Times*, 5th ed. (Toronto: Nelson Education, 2014), 46.

23. Kenneth Kernaghan, Brian Marson, and Sandford Borins, *The New Public Organization* (Toronto: The Institute of Public Administration of Canada, 2000), 5.

24. Pal, *Beyond Policy Analysis*, 55.

25. Donald Kettl, *The Global Public Management Revolution*, 2nd ed. (Washington, D.C.: The Brookings Institution, 2005).

26. Martin Painter and B. Guy Peters, "The Analysis of Administrative Traditions" in *Tradition and Public Administration*, eds. Martin Painter and B. Guy Peters (Basingstoke: Palgrave Macmillan, 2010), 3.

27. Allison Harell and Lyne Deschatelets, "Political Culture(s) in Canada: Orientations to Politics in a Pluralist, Multicultural Federation," in *Canadian Politics*, 6th ed., eds. James Bickerton and Alain-G. Gagnon (Toronto: University of Toronto Press, 2014), 237.

28. Michael Prince, "New Mandate, New Money, New Politics: Federal Budgeting in the Post-Deficit Era" in *How Ottawa Spends, 1998-1999: Balancing Act—The Post-Deficit Mandate*, ed. Leslie Pal (Toronto: Oxford University Press, 1998), 32.

29. Pal, *Beyond Policy Analysis*, 68.

30. Paul Thomas, "Two Cheers for Bureaucracy: Canada's Public Service," in *Canadian Politics*, 6th ed., eds. Bickerton and Gagnon, 182–184.

31. Ibid., 182.

32. Government of Canada, Department of Finance, *Fiscal Reference Tables* September 2015, Table 52, accessed July 9, 2016, https://www.fin.gc.ca/frt-trf/2015/frt-trf15-eng.pdf.

33. Ibid., Table 8.

34. It should be noted that three different federal agencies provide three different counts for the number of federal public service employees. Figure 1 uses the number provided by the Treasury Board Secretariat. The different counts stems from the fact that each agency defines the public service differently. For more on this topic, see Thomas, "Two Cheers for Bureaucracy," 180.

Values and Ethics in Public Administration

Learning Objectives

Reading this chapter allows you to do the following:

- Define and explain the importance of administrative values
- Understand both the old and new values that are found in values and ethics codes for public services
- Identify the elements of political neutrality and their significance for the actions of public servants
- Outline the elements of accountability and apply these elements to determine the success of accountability arrangements
- Develop an understanding of how to resolve ethical dilemmas facing public servants

In the first chapter we saw that the responsibilities and relationships of public servants are central to public administration. This insight clearly indicates that it is necessary for us to discover what shapes and guides the behaviour of appointed officials. There are a number of factors that might be considered here. One is the group of administrative values that are to be found in public services. When faced with the challenge of providing options to deal with a societal problem, chances are that civil servants will look for the more efficient way to address this issue. They will do so because efficiency is an important administrative value. Similarly, appointed officials will strive to treat citizens seeking government services without favouritism because this, too, reflects a value, namely fairness. Some disciplines treat government and its officials as self-seeking individuals wishing to maximize gain, while others see public servants as strict followers of rules and procedure. The study of public administration acknowledges these perspectives but prefers to emphasize the use of a framework of administrative values to explain the decisions and activities of public servants.

This chapter considers the place of values in public administration and the way values provide a framework for better understanding the discussion of public administration and public servants in the chapters to follow. It first defines individual values and how together they form different systems of values; it then establishes that administrative values are the most relevant values for public administration. The chapter proceeds to consider both old and new administrative values and it shows that these values provide the foundation for the present values and ethics code at the federal level of government in Canada. The bulk of the chapter is taken up with an examination of three key administrative values. One is political neutrality, the second is accountability, and the third is integrity and ethics. These values are given prominence because of their significance in shaping what appointed officials do. Absent an appreciation of these values, an understanding of the subject matter of public administration—and of the material in this book—can only be partial.

Public Service Values

values Enduring beliefs that influence the choices made by individuals, groups, or organizations from among available means or ends.

Values are enduring beliefs that influence the choices made by individuals, groups, or organizations from available means or ends. Individual values in turn are organized into value systems that deal with various avenues of life. Accordingly, each public servant has a value system or framework for social, political, administrative, and personal values. The focus in this text is on administrative or public service values. These administrative values can be organized into three categories: ethical, democratic, and professional.[1] Ethical values include such values as fairness and accountability; democratic values address concerns for democracy and responsiveness; and professional values stress beliefs relating to efficiency and excellence. In looking at these categories of values, it is important to appreciate that there is a great deal of overlap. For example, this chapter shows how most or even all values, whatever their types, can be considered ethical values in the sense that they provide direction on appropriate or ethical behaviour for public servants. When values become widely shared within the public service, there are many desirable effects. Shared values generate a sense of community dedicated to beliefs that go beyond self-interest. They also act to limit the need for rules because of their ability to give direction on appropriate behaviour. Research shows as well that organizations produce better work when backed by a set of shared values.[2] For students of administration, the real significance of values lies, however, not in how values are categorized or even in their potential for producing important benefits for society. Rather their importance arises from providing a clue to understanding the behaviour of bureaucrats and their relations with other actors in the political process.[3]

A review of Canadian administrative history shows that among the most important public service values are neutrality, accountability, efficiency, responsiveness, and integrity. These are often described as "traditional" values.

Neutrality

political neutrality A constitutional doctrine or convention according to which public servants should not engage in activities that are likely to impair or appear to impair their impartiality or the impartiality of the public service.

It is essential to distinguish between political neutrality and value-neutrality. Most public servants preserve their neutrality in terms of partisan politics; they carry out their responsibilities without regard to the political party in power. The value of neutrality in this respect is thus the recognition of the non-partisan quality of the duties of appointed officials. Public servants cannot, however, reasonably be expected to be value-neutral in the sense of their own personal values. In making and recommending decisions, the value system of individual public servants is crucial to an analysis of bureaucratic behaviour and bureaucratic power. But the traditional public service value in relation to neutrality is **political neutrality** or non-partisanship.

Accountability

administrative accountability The obligation of public servants to answer for fulfilling responsibilities that flow from the authority given them. Similar in meaning to the concept of objective responsibility.

Administrative accountability involves concern for the legal, institutional, and procedural means by which public servants can be obliged to answer for their actions. The questions commonly asked about the accountability of public servants are: Who is accountable? To whom is accountability owed? For what is accountability owed? By what means can accountability be achieved? Accountability is a pervasive theme in the study of public administration because it has been one of the major values in the evolution of Canadian public administration.

Efficiency

efficiency A measure of performance that may be expressed as a ratio between input and output. The use of administrative methods and resources that will achieve the greatest results for a specific objective at the least cost.

The dominant value in Canadian public administration over the past century has been efficiency. **Efficiency** is a measure of performance that may be expressed as a ratio between input and output, and it can be used as a general indicator of the ability of any individual, organization, or government to expend scarce resources in the most profitable or sensible manner. If a program is operating well but evidence suggests that even more gains could be achieved with certain changes, then efficiency demands that this action be taken. Sometimes efficiency is identified largely with the aim of limiting cost, but an emphasis on cost minimization gives only a partial understanding of the concept.

Responsiveness

Responsiveness refers to the inclination and the capacity of public servants to respond to the needs and demands of both political institutions and the public. Thus, public servants are expected to be responsive to two major groups of participants in the political system. The first includes political executives and legislators; the second includes the general public as well as various public groups and individuals affected by the decisions and recommendations of public servants.

Responsiveness Service both to the public and to political authorities.

Fairness and Equity

For most practical purposes, the terms **fairness** and **equity** can be used interchangeably. Equity is one of the major values to be balanced in determining the merit of persons seeking appointment to the public service, and the courts and governments are now putting greater emphasis on procedural fairness. Considerations of procedural fairness have gradually expanded beyond the boundaries of administrative law to the administrative processes of the public service. Public servants are increasingly expected to consider whether their decisions and recommendations are fair both in substance and in procedure. This heightened emphasis on fairness and equity is based largely on the recognition of the significant power that public servants exercise over the rights and livelihood of individual citizens.

fairness The quality of deciding without discriminatory intent.

equity The act of treating people equally and without bias.

Integrity

Integrity refers here to ethics in public administration. The integrity of public servants is extremely important to the preservation of public trust and confidence in government. Recent experience in Canada and elsewhere indicates that increased vigilance is required to ensure that public servants adhere to high ethical standards.

Integrity A disposition to distinguish right from wrong and to do the right thing.

New Values

As a result of the extensive public service reforms and other developments, new public service values have emerged over the years. The *Values and Ethics Code for the Public Sector* captures the key values for appointed officials at the federal level, and it includes new values (see Box 2.1).[4] One such value is "excellence," which commits public servants to a high level of performance "in the design and delivery of public sector policy, programs, and services". Another is "stewardship." This value states that "Federal public servants are entrusted to use and care for public resources responsibility". Both reflect reforms such as New Public Management, which emphasizes the measurement of performance and the provision of flexibility necessary to achieve greater innovation. Some of the other values in the code employ new formulations, but represent sentiments that have always been implicit in the values of public servants. "Respect for democracy" and "respect for people" fall in this category. As can be seen, the code also includes "integrity," a value that is recognized as a traditional or standard public service value.

BOX
2.1

Values and Ethics Code for the Public Sector

Values and Ethics Code for the Public Sector is a statement of values that guide public servants at the federal level in the carrying out of their duties. The Code comprises the following five values:

Respect for Democracy

The system of Canadian parliamentary democracy and its institutions are fundamental to serving the public interest. Public servants recognize that elected officials are accountable to Parliament, and ultimately to the Canadian people, and that a non-partisan public sector is essential to our democratic system.

Respect for People

Treating all people with respect, dignity and fairness is fundamental to our relationship with the Canadian public and contributes to a safe and healthy work environment that promotes engagement, openness and transparency. The diversity of our people and the ideas they generate are the source of our innovation.

Integrity

Integrity is the cornerstone of good governance and democracy. By upholding the highest ethical standards, public servants conserve and enhance public confidence in the honesty, fairness and impartiality of the federal public sector.

Stewardship

Federal public servants are entrusted to use and care for public resources responsibly, for both the short term and long term.

Excellence

Excellence in the design and delivery of public sector policy, programs and services is beneficial to every aspect of Canadian public life. Engagement, collaboration, effective teamwork and professional development are all essential to a high-performing organization.

Source: *Values and Ethics Code for the Public Sector.* https://www.tbs-sct-gc.ca/pol/doc-eng.aspx?id=25049&section=html, Treasury Board of Canada Secretariat, 2016.

Political Neutrality

As can be seen, a number of values make up the administrative value system of a professional public servant. The remainder of the chapter focuses on three particular values because of their importance in understanding public servants and the carrying out of their duties within the political system. The three values are political neutrality, accountability, and integrity.

Political neutrality is a value that is grounded in a constitutional convention according to which public servants should avoid activities that are likely to impair or seem to impair their political impartiality of the public service. There are six interrelated ideas that are traditionally associated with the concept of political neutrality and that provide a useful model for examining the nature of interactions between public servants and others in the political system. As will be seen, in the Canadian context some of these requirements remain substantially unchanged; but some have never truly been met, and others have been altered.

1. The Politics–Administration Dichotomy

politics–administration dichotomy The idea that a clear distinction can be made between the responsibilities of elected executives, who make policy decisions, and the responsibilities of public servants, who execute these decisions.

The political neutrality of public servants has traditionally rested on the possibility of the separation of politics and administration, and on a related distinction between policy and administration. According to the **politics–administration dichotomy**, political executives and legislators are concerned with the formation of policy, and public servants are concerned with its implementation. Policy decisions are political; administrative decisions are nonpolitical. However, scholars and practitioners in Canada and elsewhere

Part One / Introduction to Public Administration

have over the years become aware that the line between politics and administration has become increasingly indistinct as both politicians and public servants participated actively in policy development. Senior public servants, for instance, made (and continue to make) significant discretionary decisions as to the policy options to be set before their political masters. In the development and presentation of these policy options, public servants are expected to be attuned to the political, as well as the administrative, financial, and technical, implications of their recommendations. In the sphere of the administration or implementation of government initiatives, public servants also exercise substantial power. In the course of interpreting, clarifying, and applying policy, public servants significantly influence the success of policy decisions made by ministers and legislators.

In recent years, the politics–administration dichotomy has made a comeback—but with a twist. Thinking associated with the theory of New Public Management has emphasized the importance of separating policy and administration in order that public servants can direct most of their attention to finding innovative ways of managing public programs. But as the preceding sentence suggests, this thinking has emphasized that the task of public servants is not to administer or follow rules and regulations; rather, it is to manage and discover creative measures by which to deliver services. What has thus emerged is a new dichotomy, namely the "politics–*management* dichotomy."[5] Political developments have also worked in the same direction. Political leaders have emerged who believe that appointed officials wield too much power and that the participation of the bureaucracy in the formulation of policy should be severely limited. Interestingly, some scholars believe that new forces have emerged to politicize the public service and push aside the notion of political neutrality. This perspective, called "New Political Governance," sees disturbing developments: public servants publicly supporting government policies to an unprecedented degree, senior appointments made less on the grounds of merit and more on political acceptability, and deputy ministers and other senior officials working closely with the prime minister and a small group of political advisors to find the most politically satisfactory policies with little concern for effectiveness.[6]

By examining the history of the politics–administration dichotomy, it can be seen that politics and policy cannot be easily separated from administration. Nonetheless, the distinctions commonly made between politics and administration, policy and administration, and policy formation and implementation serve an analytical and practical purpose. They enable political theorists to distinguish—not in an absolute sense but as a matter of degree—between the constitutional and legal functions of political executives and public servants. While the policy role of public servants makes them appear as almost dominant, they remain, in fact and in democratic theory, subject to the overriding authority of elected representatives.

2. Appointments

A second component of the ideal model of political neutrality is the practice whereby public servants are appointed and promoted on the basis of merit rather than of party affiliation or contributions. Political patronage involves the appointment of people to government service on the grounds of contributions, financial or otherwise, to the governing party; it is a blatant violation of the doctrine of political neutrality. Indeed, the appointment is made on the basis that the appointee is, politically, not neutral but partisan. Such appointments clash with the merit principle, according to which Canadians have a reasonable opportunity to be taken into account for any position in the public service. The merit principle also stipulates that selections reflect ability to carry out the requirements of the job. Political affiliation is not a consideration.[7]

In past years, various legislative efforts have been made to put in a staffing system that reflects the tenets of the merit principle, and for the most part these efforts have been successful. But patronage appointments have certainly not disappeared. A review

Chapter 2 / Values and Ethics in Public Administration

of debates in the House of Commons over the years reveals numerous allegations and denials regarding the use of patronage in staffing the public service. Many of the alleged patronage appointments have been to lower-level or part-time positions in which the appointees are so far removed from policy development that their appointment has a negligible effect on the status of political neutrality. Opposition parties, the news media, and the general public have shown greater interest in senior positions that are filled by patronage appointments rather than on a competitive basis by persons from within or outside the public service. The prime minister and the cabinet have the authority to appoint deputy ministers; heads and members of agencies, boards, and commissions; ambassadors; high commissioners; consuls general and certain other diplomatic representatives; and federal judges. Moreover, officials in the Prime Minister's Office are selected by the prime minister, and cabinet ministers' assistants are also chosen in an overtly partisan manner. All these appointments are exempt from the appointing power of the **Public Service Commission**, the agency responsible for overseeing appointments to the federal public service.

Public Service Commission An independent agency that serves Parliament as the guardian of the merit principle in human resources management. It is responsible for recruitment, staffing, and promotion in the public service.

3. Political Partisanship

The ideal model of political neutrality requires that public servants not engage in partisan political activities.[8] However, the relevant history shows that this has not always been observed. During the first fifty years of Canada's political history, the issues of political partisanship and political patronage were intimately linked. Patronage appointments were rewards for service to the governing party. In an effort to eliminate this practice, legislators provided in the 1918 *Civil Service Act* that no public servant could "engage in partisan work in connection with any... election, or contribute, receive or in any way deal with any money for any party funds."[9] Violations were punishable by dismissal. The penalty was so severe and so clearly stated that, with the exception of the right to vote, the impact of the act was the political sterilization of Canada's federal public servants. The rigid restraints imposed in 1918 remained virtually unchanged until 1967. The *Public Service Employment Act* of 1967 liberalized the longstanding restrictions on political activity. Section 33 of the Act provided that public servants (save for deputy ministers) could stand for election to public office if the Public Service Commission believed that their usefulness would not be impaired by their candidacy. Employees were not permitted to work for or against a candidate for election to a federal or provincial office, or for or against a political party; they were permitted, however, to attend political meetings and to make contributions to the funds of a political candidate or party. In 1991, the Supreme Court of Canada in *Osborne v. Canada* struck down Section 33 with the result that, except for deputy ministers, there are virtually no statutory restrictions on the political rights of federal public servants.

The fact that most public servants may now stand for election and engage in a broader spectrum of political activities has heightened the general level of partisan activity and consciousness in Canada's public services, especially among younger employees. However, officials in senior and sensitive posts are usually required to refrain from partisan activity; thus, those officials most actively involved in policy formation and in the discretionary application of policy retain their impartiality. Also, officials with many years of government experience have difficulty overcoming their ingrained avoidance of political activity. Some public servants may justifiably perceive overt partisanship as an obstacle to promotion to the senior ranks of what is, substantially, a politically neutral public service.

4. Public Comment

The admonition that public servants not express publicly their personal views on government policies or administration is an integral component of the ideal model of political neutrality. The prime reason given by contemporary governments for restrictions on public comment is the need to preserve the confidence of the public and of political superiors in the impartiality of public servants.

Strict interpretation of this rule of official reticence requires that public servants not express personal opinions on government policies, whether they are attacking or supporting those policies. This convention has been supplemented by statutory provisions, decisions of administrative tribunals, and written guidelines. But formal written guidelines on public comment are so sparse that considerable uncertainty exists as to the rights of public servants in this area. It is well established in the public service legislation of modern democratic states that the role of public servants in policy development and implementation requires that they enjoy fewer political rights than other citizens. In the area of public comment, the difficulty is to strike an appropriate balance between freedom of expression and political neutrality (see Box 2.2).

The Singing Public Servant

BOX 2.2

In June 2015, a few months before the federal election in October, a scientist employed with Environment Canada performed a song of his on YouTube. The song commented critically on a number of the Harper government's policies and included the line "Harperman, it's time for you to go." The scientist's union found nothing wrong with its member's behaviour, saying that he had not "infracted any laws or policies" and had "the right to express himself through a folk song as a private citizen." For his action, the scientist was placed on leave with pay pending an investigation into whether the he had violated the federal *Values and Ethics Code for the Public Sector.* The scientist, who was planning to retire soon, resigned from the public service before the investigation could be completed.

Source: Madeline Smith, "Public Servant Put on Leave Over Anti-Harper Song," *Globe and Mail*, August 29, 2015, A5; "Federal Government Scientist Suspended Over Anti-Harper Song Retires," *National Post*, October 3, 2015, A7.

Public servants are now involved in forms of public comment not explicitly covered by the conventional rule; the nature of this involvement constitutes a significant departure from a position of political neutrality. It appears that public servants will increasingly be required to attend public meetings to provide information about government policies and programs, and more and more they are asked to arrange and operate the many consultative processes with the interested public. As a result, the public will become more aware of the influence that public servants bring to deliberations on public policy matters. More troubling for some scholars, this change may be evolving further into a requirement that the public service "be publicly supportive, even enthusiastic, about [the government] agenda and … promote it in their consultations…."[10] This is an element of the New Political Governance perspective mentioned earlier.

5. Anonymity and Ministerial Responsibility

As noted early in this chapter, the ideal model of political neutrality requires that public servants provide forthright and objective advice to their political superiors in private and in confidence; political executives protect the anonymity of public servants by publicly accepting responsibility for departmental decisions. The anonymity of public servants depends, in large measure, on the vitality of the doctrine of individual ministerial responsibility, according to which ministers are personally responsible to the legislature both for their own actions and for those of their administrative subordinates. Thus, public servants are not directly answerable to the legislature, and their minister protects

Chapter 2 / Values and Ethics in Public Administration

their anonymity. But over the years events have revealed that ministers will not invariably protect the anonymity of their officials by refusing to name or blame them publicly.

Public service anonymity also depends significantly on factors other than the operation of ministerial responsibility. Departures from political neutrality in the areas of patronage and political activity also diminish official anonymity, but the greatest threat is probably the expansion of public comment described earlier. The increased interaction of public servants with both individual citizens and specific "publics," or clientele groups, reveals the nature of official involvement in policy development. The cumulative impact of the growing information and conciliation functions performed by public servants is a gradual, but significant, decline in official anonymity.

6. Permanence in Office

The preservation of political neutrality requires that public servants carry out policy decisions loyally regardless of the position of the party in power. As a result, public servants have security of tenure during good behaviour and satisfactory performance. Thus, in the event of a change of government, official neutrality helps to ensure continuity of administration by competent and experienced public servants, as well as the provision of impartial advice on policy options and the loyal implementation of policy decisions. Security of tenure enables a career public servant not only to establish and wield influence in the policy process but also to continue to exercise such influence even if there is a change in the governing party. Long tenure allows public servants to acquire knowledge and experience, both in specific policy fields and in the political–administrative system within which policy decisions are made. Permanence in office for public servants increases their power vis-à-vis politicians. Ministers cannot match the expertise of their senior officials, and the frequent rotation of ministers among departments prevents them from accumulating much experience in particular policy areas.

As public servants, especially at the senior levels, become more influential and perhaps more political, the argument for political appointments to senior posts is put forward. There is some support in Canada for a system of political appointments similar to that in the United States. Supporters of a politicized public service usually cite the various benefits from political appointments to senior public service posts. These include a strong commitment to implementing the policies of the new government, an injection of new ideas and approaches toward government policies and processes, advice on policy issues that is more sensitive to their partisan political implications, and greater trust by ministers in their policy advisors. Under this system, the incumbents of the most senior public service positions would be replaced whenever a change in government occurred. Some senior appointments would thus be held on a temporary rather than a permanent basis. The power of career public servants would be reduced, because they would not normally be appointed to the highest administrative positions. However, assuming regular changes in the governing party, the tenure of senior political appointees would be too brief to enable them to exercise as much power based on experience and expertise as do career public servants. At present, a shift to a system of political appointments either in the federal government or in most provincial governments is unlikely.

Accountability

accountability The obligation to answer for fulfilling responsibilities.

For the past half century, public concern about **accountability** in government has been stimulated in Western democratic states, including Canada, by events involving illegal, unethical, or questionable activities by both politicians and public servants. Few public-service values have had the significance and notoriety of accountability. Discussion of incidents of conflicts of interest, disclosures of confidential information, and alleged wasteful spending have also revealed that the this concern for accountability is matched

Part One / Introduction to Public Administration

by disagreement among the general public and students of government over what constitutes irresponsible conduct, who should assume blame in particular cases, and what the penalty should be. The scope and complexity of government activities have become so great that it is often difficult to determine the actual—as opposed to the legal or constitutional—locus of responsibility for specific decisions. Political officials in the executive branch are held responsible for personal wrongdoing. They are not, however, expected to be accountable by way of resignation or demotion for the acts of administrative subordinates about which they could not reasonably be expected to have knowledge. Yet it is frequently impossible to assign individual responsibility to public servants for administrative transgressions either, because so many public servants have contributed to the decision-making process or because public servants place the blame back on the elected officials.

Malcolm Mayes/Artizans.com

While the involvement of political executives in unlawful or questionable activities has drawn much public attention to the issue of political accountability, the status of **administrative accountability** has also become a matter of increasing anxiety. Elected officials make the final decisions on major public policy issues, but public servants have significant influence on these decisions and have authority to make decisions on their own that affect the individual and collective rights of the citizenry. Concern about the preservation of administrative accountability is shared in varying degrees by all major actors in the political system—whether they be political executives, legislators, judges, interest group and mass media representatives, members of the general public, or public servants. As a result of efforts by these various actors to promote responsible administrative conduct, the decisions of public servants are subject to an almost bewildering assortment of controls and influences.

administrative accountability The obligation of public servants to answer for fulfilling responsibilities that flow from the authority given them. Similar in meaning to the concept of objective responsibility.

Chapter 2 / Values and Ethics in Public Administration

Responsibility and Accountability

The current emphasis on accountability is a result of both the need to strengthen accountability in government generally and the very broad interpretations that the word accountability has gradually acquired. These two related causes for concern over accountability point to the need for a clearer and more precise conception of accountability and its application in the case of this text to administrative actors.

The way forward in meeting this need can begin with a consideration of the related concept of responsibility in relation to appointed officials of government. During the period 1935–1941, a celebrated debate over the meaning of administrative responsibility took place between Carl Friedrich and Herman Finer.[11] Both correctly identified the source of burgeoning bureaucratic power as the rapid expansion of government's service and regulatory functions. However, they disagreed vehemently on the most effective means of guarding against abuse of administrative discretion so as to maintain and promote responsible administrative conduct. To achieve administrative responsibility, Finer put his primary faith in controls and sanctions exercised over public servants by the legislature, the judiciary, and the administrative hierarchy. Friedrich relied more heavily on the propensity of public servants to be self-directing and self-regulating, the measure of which was their responsiveness to the dual standards of technical knowledge and popular sentiment.

Two decades later, Frederick Mosher sought to provide a broader, more inclusive classification than the Friedrich–Finer categories by making a distinction between objective responsibility and subjective responsibility. According to his widely accepted definition, **objective responsibility** "connotes the responsibility of a person or an organization to someone else, outside of self, for some thing or some kind of performance." "If one fails to carry out legitimate directives," Mosher continued, "he is judged irresponsible, and may be subjected to penalties."[12] **Subjective responsibility**, by way of contrast, focuses "not upon to whom and for what one is responsible (according to law and the organization chart) but to whom and for what one *feels* responsible and *behaves* responsibly." As Mosher says, this notion of responsibility "is more nearly synonymous with identification, loyalty, and conscience than it is with accountability and answerability."[13]

Mosher thus viewed administrative responsibility as a broad concept that included two major components, which build on the two notions arising from the Finer–Friedrich debate. The one component, following Friedrich, sees responsibility as a psychological phenomenon that creates a kind of "personal responsibility."[14] The public servant believes he or she is personally responsible for carrying out assigned duties and believes that he or she is the person most responsible for any action. The other component, following Finer, is without any psychological orientation and instead emphasizes the presence of an external authority to specify the duties, expectations, monitoring, and application of rewards or penalties for performance. It is this second conception that mostly provides the foundation for building an appreciation and definition of administrative accountability.

Administrative Accountability

Mosher's concept of objective responsibility brings us closer to the essence of administrative accountability. It is, however, necessary to be more precise about the meaning and character of accountability when applied to the public service. One attempt to do this is made by Paul Thomas, who argues that accountability in general is a relationship consisting of these four components:

1. the assignment of responsibilities, ideally based upon agreed-upon goals or purposes;
2. an obligation to answer for the discharge of those responsibilities;

---

objective responsibility The responsibility of a person or an organization to someone else, outside of self, for some thing or some kind of performance. Similar in meaning to accountability or answerability.

subjective responsibility The responsibility a person feels toward others. Often described as personal or psychological responsibility. Similar in meaning to identification, loyalty, and conscience.

3. surveillance of performance to ensure compliance with directions given; and
4. possible sanctions for non-performance and rewards for successful performance.[15]

The four components encompass the qualities identified with much thinking about accountability. There is the presence of external authority whose role begins with the detailing of the duties and responsibilities of those who are at the centre of the accountability exercise. Also included is the notion that the individual or group assigned the responsibilities is answerable for their implementation. The idea of an obligation, which borrows to some extent from subjective responsibility, is also present in discussions of accountability. Mosher's concept of objective responsibility emphasizes the importance of performance in the sense that the person carrying out the responsibilities will be evaluated by the external authority. Finally, accountability in theory includes the view that there will be consequences of one kind or another for performance. Usually, this aspect of accountability revolves around the consideration of the type of penalties that would apply to poor performance, but accountability also makes provision for rewards or recognition for good performance.

These components can be used to give us an understanding of administrative accountability. Public servants in various contexts are assigned explicit responsibilities or are identified with certain expectations. They also develop an obligation to answerability in the carrying out of these responsibilities, which relate to activities concerning formulation and implementation of public policies. An external authority monitors the success of public servants in performing their duties—a minister, a legislative body, or the larger public. Lastly, appointed officials understand that any consideration of performance may have consequences, though the exact nature of the consequences may not be clear and they may differ depending on the context. This mention of context also shows that the application of the components causes us to realize that the accountability of public servants takes place within different settings. In some settings, the components are articulated in only a very general sense; for example, the accountability of public servants to the general public. In other settings, matters are more precise. Within a government department or agency, the superior–subordinate relationships can be quite exacting. And in still others, the accountability arrangements are only broadly outlined, leaving room for flexibility in the implementation of the arrangements. The accountability mechanism involving the legislature, ministers, and public servants is of this type. All of these arrangements in administrative accountability will appear in later chapters, revealing the significance of accountability as a public service value (see What to Do?).

A New Accountability

Some scholars believe that discussion of administrative accountability needs to expand to include consideration of a different conception of accountability. This new conception emerges from the increasing presence of networks of government officials and actors outside government working together to address public-policy objectives. It is argued that these networks require a form of accountability that is "best seen as a series of relational and procedural mechanisms, formal and informal, by which actors sharing authority and responsibility for a given policy or program are obliged to render accounts to another."[16] The traditional understanding of accountability assumes a more top-down arrangement where superiors assign responsibility and subordinates respond with actions and reports on success. But networks are more horizontal and fit uneasily into the top-down approach. A more suitable arrangement, it is claimed, is

WHAT TO DO?

At first glance, the application of the four components of accountability to administration seems to be quite easily done. But the truth is otherwise. One of the more difficult challenges facing attempts to ensure administrative accountability is measuring performance. The private sector has a ready-made performance measure, namely profits. But the public sector is not so fortunate. If you doubt this, try developing performance measures for a government program like student loans or child-care services. It is hard to do and usually we end up measuring things that are measurable but not very important. What to do with this situation? Some suggest that we go back to the old way of gauging performance, which is to see how well the department or agency followed procedures and policies. But this tells us nothing about what has actually been accomplished. So we are back where we started, which is trying to measure the outcomes of actions.

one in which the network participants achieve accountability by being responsible to each other, which amounts to a horizontal type of accountability (see Box 2.3). Proponents of this concept of accountability admit that it might be necessary to keep some aspects of the established way of looking at accountability, but only in the background.

BOX 2.3

Horizontal Accountability in Practice

The federal government and the government of Manitoba have over the years entered into agreements that attempt to foster economic development in Manitoba. Federal–provincial arrangements of this type have typically relied on a vertical style of accountability whereby Ottawa tracks the use of its investment in the economic projects and ensures that the province satisfies the requirements of contracts underlying the agreements. But in Manitoba the direction of the projects and the addressing of any unforeseen difficulties were handled by a group of federal, provincial, and local officials working collectively (and non-government actors also participated). More important, the responsibility for the success of the efforts effectively shifted away from the federal government to the network of government and non-government officials because of the flexibility and consequent achievements of the more horizontal approach to accountability. These agreements were recently discontinued, but this decision was unrelated to this new form of accountability. Horizontal accountability appeared to have some potential.

Source: Charles Conteh, "Rethinking Accountability in Complex and Horizontal Network Delivery Systems," *Canadian Public Administration* 59(2) (2016): 224–244.

Integrity and Administrative Ethics

administrative or public service ethics Principles and standards of right conduct in public organizations. Normally used interchangeably with the term administrative morality.

Integrity is a central public service value. It can be interpreted to cover a broad range of bureaucratic behaviour, but it is used here in a limited sense to refer to **administrative or public service ethics**. Ethics refers to principles and standards of conduct that can serve to guide people towards a moral life and help address ethical dilemmas that may emerge. Accordingly, administrative ethics captures those principles that relate to public servants in the carrying out of their duties.

For some, these principles are those that are applicable to people in all walks of life. One such principle is the utilitarian belief that actions should try to produce the greatest good for all; another is the belief that certain actions causing serious harm to others must be avoided. But scholars in public administration believe that some of the moral principles that guide the behaviour of public servants are indeed unique. For one scholar, these unique principles include the "primacy of rule of law, impartiality in administering public services, and public service as a public trust."[17]

The approach of the federal government (and other governments) has been to pin-point key administrative values that serve to create a "vision" for the public service[18], but also to make clear that these same values act to provide a code of ethical conduct and give direction on resolving ethical dilemmas. Not only is integrity thus a single ethical value relating to honesty, fairness, and other traditional moral principles, but it also can be seen as a kind of recognition of the moral nature of all core values of the civil service. This emphasis on ethics is important because there are opportunities for public servants to become involved in unethical conduct. Such opportunities arise from the power and influence public officials exercise in the development and administration of public policy. Senior public servants with discretionary authority and confidential information have the greatest occasions to benefit from unethical conduct. But temptations to engage in unethical behaviour exist at all levels of the administrative hierarchy and at all levels of government (e.g., a senior official with contracting authority in a federal department or an administrative assistant in a municipal government with access to confidential development plans).

There are many forms of unethical behaviour that can be related to public servants. Some are egregious in nature because they so clearly show a wrong committed for personal gain. But other forms or types emerge from difficult ethical dilemmas where the individual is trying to accomplish beneficial ends through the use of questionable means. One type of behaviour that is clearly unethical is corruption. A civil servant may accept money in exchange for beneficial treatment—the official is given a bribe to favour a particular participant in a tendering process. Few questions arise here about whether the action is right or wrong. A conflict-of-interest situation where the interests of the individual civil servant interfere in the performance of public duties, also is clearly wrong and unethical. For example, an official is required to make a decision to provide financial assistance to a company in which he or she has investments. More difficult situations involve the receipt of gifts of some extravagance. The maxim here "is that civil servants shall not accept or solicit any gifts that could compromise their impartiality or create obligations to the giver."[19] But it is sometimes difficult to determine the effect of receiving a gift.

These are all hypothetical situations but there have been real-life cases of lapses in ethical behaviour committed by public servants in the past decade. An assistant deputy minister with Health Canada received gifts amounting to $200,000 in exchange for helping a private foundation get $70 million in grants from the federal government. A similar case involved a federal official inappropriately assisting a treatment centre to gain access to federal funding. A National Defence official, for his part, was caught "submitting false invoices for information technologies and related services and was later charged with fraud and money laundering."[20] Five immigration officers were found guilty of receiving bribe money to help applicants receive permanent status, and a passport official conceded that he had falsified documents so that non-Canadians could get Canadian passports. The most prominent case has been the Sponsorship Scandal, where a number of unethical and even criminal activities were undertaken, including a senior official with the Department of Public Works and Government Services arranging for the transfer of large amounts of money to advertising agencies for work that was either expensively priced or never completed.[21]

These examples are of the kinds of unethical behaviour that are relatively easy to judge and require little thinking about how to respond to them, and they remind us of behaviour that is unacceptable. But there are other examples where ethical dilemmas become evident. As will be discussed in Chapter 17, the federal Department of Finance and its officials have been accused of purposely underestimating forecasted revenue budgets to increase the chances of promised balanced budgets (or even surpluses).[22] Few believe that this is done through outright falsification of numbers, but rather indirectly through unnecessarily gloomy assumptions about the economy that tend to produce disappointing revenue predictions. At first glance, this alleged misrepresentation might be seen unethical because it amounts to a form of lying. But a closer look might lead to a reconsideration of this initial assessment and focus on the relatively steady fiscal performance of the federal government. In other words, questionable behaviour might be considered more acceptable in light of the positive impact of such behaviour.

The focus on the value of administrative ethics and the attention paid to instances of unethical behaviour follow from a belief that there are important benefits to a public service which clearly places right over wrong. The most obvious benefit is that the effective management of issues of ethics is essential to public trust and confidence in the public service and government in general. As Dimock and her colleagues write, "The public more easily accepts the power of government when that power can be shown

Chapter 2 / Values and Ethics in Public Administration

to be directed at ethically proper ends."[23] A second benefit is the contribution ethical practices make to efficient administration and implementation of programs and policies. The performance of a public service will falter if plagued with corruption, bribes, the provision of misleading information, and other unethical practices. The same holds with respect to the role public servants play in providing advice to elected officials in the formulation of public policies. A final benefit to consider is that ethical practices signify "the value of public service as a career."[24] A public service with a high level of performance is dependent on attracting skilled and gifted men and women. This will not take place in a public service with little concern for moral practices.

Code of Ethics

The importance of ethical behaviour for the public services suggests a need to find ways to articulate the relevant ethical principles and to promote them. Establishing an ethics code or framework is the usual suggestion for the articulation and promotion of ethics. The federal *Values and Ethics Code for the Public Sector* is one example of such a code.[25] The code, shown in Box 2.1, lists five values and expands upon each with three or four statements of expected behaviour linked to the value. As mentioned earlier in the chapter, the values and accompanying definitions act almost as individual vision statements that give direction and inspiration to public servants. But the values also amount to demonstrations of ethical conduct or principles and whose violation warrants attention. A guide to the federal code spells this out in more detail by using hypothetical cases to show how ethical dilemmas may arise and be resolved in the instance of each value.[26] For example, with regard to the value of "respect for democracy," the guide depicts an off-duty public servant publically urging a community group to carry on with its opposition to one of his department's projects. The media gets the comment on tape, broadcasts it, the public servant's superior sees it, and the next day the public servant is told to stop this type of activity. The public servant objects, saying that he has a right as a citizen to voice his options. The guide then suggests a resolution of the issue, using the principle that public servants must appear impartial and non-partisan (which is explicitly stated in the value "respect for democracy").

The federal code might be considered somewhat different from more traditional codes of ethical conduct. An earlier federal code, for example, spent much more time on the common unethical practices that might emerge as public servants carry out their responsibilities.[27] In Ontario, the code for public servants takes the form of a regulation that spells out in detail the different kinds of "prohibited conduct" (for example, use of position to achieve monetary gains, acceptance of gifts under certain conditions, divulgence of confidential information, preferential treatment).[28] Some prefer this more traditional type of ethics code and argue against the present approach of the federal government, which they say is premised on the shaky argument that "fostering core values and building an ethical culture is key for establishing a public service that acts ethically"[29] (see Box 2.4).

Arguably a more important issue than the content and approach of codes is whether even the best-designed codes can actually be helpful. On consideration, there do seem to be benefits to codes of ethics in the public service. They can reduce uncertainty among public servants about what constitutes ethical and unethical behaviour, limit unethical practices by discouraging and penalizing them, and provide a means by which political leaders and senior managers can hold public servants accountable. They also build up the all-important trust in government felt by the citizenry. But there also appear to be problems: the codes can sometimes be difficult to apply and enforce, they can be hard to employ fairly in governments with large numbers of departments, and false accusations related to the codes have the potential to adversely affect the individual rights and private lives of public servants whose ethical behaviour is beyond reproach.

BOX
2.4

Debating Ethics Codes

John Langford, a professor of public administration, dislikes the "values approach" to codes of ethics (caught in the federal *Values and Ethics Code for the Public Sector*). His indictment of the approach is detailed, but the basic message is that the use of values to guide public servants on matters of ethics is poorly conceptualized and too indirect to have the desired effect. The "rules approach," the traditional way of doing things, makes more sense. This approach specifies types of unethical acts and methods of resolving ethical dilemmas—direct and to the point.

Ralph Heintzman, someone with lots of experience working in the federal public service, thinks Langford has it all wrong. There is no replacement of one approach to ethical codes with another. The values are added to give appointed officials a sense or "feeling" of what the public service is trying to accomplish. One effect of this is to give strength to rules of ethical behaviour.

Sources: John W. Langford, "Acting on Values: An Ethical Dead End for Public Servants," *Canadian Public Administration* 47(4) (2004): 429–450; Ralph Heintzman, "Public-Service Values and Ethics: Dead End or Strong Foundation," *Canadian Public Administration* 50(4) (2007): 573–602.

The limitations of the codes of ethics lead to a search for other ways to encourage ethical behaviour. An increasingly important means of promoting such conduct is to sensitize public servants to the ethical and value dimensions of public service through in-service training. At the federal level, a human-relations office in the Treasury Board Secretariat and the Canada School of Public Service work together to provide material for training in ethics. The influence of administrative superiors is also an extremely important means of promoting ethical conduct. The *Values and Ethics Code*, for instance, states that deputy heads of departments are obligated "to model the values found in the Public Sector Code in their daily decision-making, leadership and management styles."[30] Departmental managers must do the same and also be ready to advise subordinates on expectations relating to ethical conduct. Finally, special offices are set up to ensure that the topic of ethical behaviour gets the attention it deserves. The Office of the Public Sector Integrity Commissioner of Canada is an agency to which appointed officials can report instances of wrongdoing in the public service, and the Public Service Commission of Canada is responsible for looking into allegations of wrongdoing relating to staffing. As with codes, these ways of promoting ethical conduct individually have their limits, but together they represent a concerted effort to address and foster moral behaviour.

Points to Know

- Administrative values serve to inspire public servants in their work and to act as ethical standards. In so doing, values represent an important way to understand the behaviour of appointed officials.

- Political neutrality is an important administrative value that comprises six elements seeking to ensure the non-partisan quality of the public service.

- Administrative accountability requires the assignment of responsibilities to public servants, an obligation to answer for these responsibilities, surveillance of performance to provide an incentive for compliance, and an understanding that there are consequences for both satisfactory and unsatisfactory performance.

- Integrity is a value that refers to acting in accordance with the principles and standards of ethical conduct for public servants. The principles and standards also assist appointed officials to address ethical dilemmas that may arise in the carrying out of their responsibilities.

- Political neutrality, accountability, and integrity are three values that form the foundation of values and ethics codes for the public service of Canada.

Review Questions

1. How are values and ethics related in the federal *Values and Ethics Code for the Public Sector*?

2. Discuss three threats to the non-partisanship of public servants.

3. Use the four components of accountability to demonstrate how difficult it might be to ensure accountable government.

4. Demonstrate how values in the federal *Values and Ethics Code for the Public Sector* might conflict with each other. What would you do to resolve the conflict?

5. What could be done to strengthen the politics–administration dichotomy?

Notes

1. Kenneth Kernaghan, Brian Marson, and Sandford Borins, *The New Public Organization* (Toronto: Institute of Public Administration of Canada, 2000), 45. See also Task Force on Public Service Values and Ethics, *A Strong Foundation: Report of the Task Force on Public Service Values and Ethics* (Ottawa: Canadian Centre for Management Development, 1996), ch. 7.
2. Kernaghan, Marson, and Borins, *The New Public Organization*, 48.
3. Research suggests that the actions of public servants are indeed influenced by values. See Paul G. Thomas, "Two Cheers for Bureaucracy: Canada's Public Service," in *Canadian Politics*, 6th ed., eds. James Bickerton and Alain-G. Gagnon (Toronto: University of Toronto Press, 2014), 184.
4. Government of Canada, *Values and Ethics Code for the Public Sector* (Ottawa: Her Majesty the Queen in Right of Canada, 2011).
5. Donald J. Savoie, *Thatcher, Reagan, Mulroney: In Search of a New Bureaucracy* (Toronto: University of Toronto, 1994), 282.
6. See Peter Aucoin, "New Political Governance in Westminster Systems: Impartial Public Administration and Management Performance at Risk," *Governance* 25 (2) (2012): 177–199. In an earlier work, Aucoin referred to this as "new public governance." See Peter Aucoin, "New Public Management and New Public Governance: Finding the Balance," in *Professionalism and Public Service: Essays in Honour of Kenneth Kernaghan*, eds. David Siegel and Ken Rasmussen (Toronto: University of Toronto Press, 2008).
7. R.H. Dowdell, "Public Personnel Administration," in *Public Administration in Canada*, 4th ed., ed. Kenneth Kernaghan, (Toronto: Methuen, 1982), 196.
8. For a definition of political activity and an account of the arguments usually raised for and against the political activity of government employees, see Kenneth Kernaghan, "Political Rights and Political Neutrality: Finding the Balance Point," *Canadian Public Administration* 29(4) (Winter 1986): 639–652.
9. *Canada Statutes*, 8–9 Geo. v, c. 12.
10. Aucoin, "New Political Governance in Westminster Systems," 189.
11. Carl J. Friedrich, "Responsible Government Service Under the American Constitution," in Carl J. Friedrich, William Carl Beyer, Sterling Denhard Spero, John Francis Miller, and George A. Graham, *Problems of the American Public Service* (New York: McGraw-Hill, 1935), 3–74, and "Public Policy and the Nature of Administrative Responsibility," in *Public Policy*, eds. Carl J. Friedrich and Edward S. Mason (Cambridge: Harvard University Press, 1940), 3–24; Herman Finer, "Better Government Personnel," *Political Science Quarterly* 51(4) (December 1936): 569–599, and "Administrative Responsibility in Democratic Government," *Public Administration Review* 1(4) (1941): 335–350. The most comprehensive statements of the opposing positions are found in the 1940–1941 exchange of articles.
12. Frederick C. Mosher, *Democracy and the Public Service* (New York: Oxford University Press, 1968), 7–10.
13. Ibid., 7 (emphasis added).
14. Ibid., 7.
15. Paul G. Thomas, "The Changing Nature of Accountability," in *Taking Stock: Assessing Public Sector Reforms*, eds. B. Guy Peters and Donald J. Savoie (Montreal & Kingston: McGill-Queen's University Press, 1998), 352. Thomas has modified slightly his components of accountability in a more recent publication. See Mark D. Jarvis and Paul G. Thomas, "The Limits of Accountability: What Can and Cannot Be Accomplished in the Dialectics of Accountability?" in *From New Public Management to New Political Governance: Essays in Honour of Peter C. Aucoin*, eds. Herman Bakvis and Mark D. Jarvis (Montreal & Kingston: McGill-Queen's University Press, 2012), 281–282.
16. Charles Conteh, "Rethinking Accountability in Complex and Horizontal Network Delivery Systems," *Canadian Public Administration* 59(2)(2016): 228.
17. Alan Tupper and Lori Turnbull, "The Ethics of Public Service and the Challenge of Public Service Ethics," in *From New Public Management to New Political Governance*, eds. Bakvis and Jarvis, 48–49.
18. Ralph Heintzman, "Public-Service Values and Ethics: Dead End or Strong Foundation?" *Canadian Public Administration* 50(4) (2007): 594.
19. Susan Dimock et al., *Ethics and the Public Service: Trust, Integrity, and Democracy* (Toronto: Nelson Education, 2013), 131.
20. Donald J. Savoie, *Whatever Happened to the Music Teacher: How Government Decides and Why* (Montreal & Kingston: McGill-Queen's University Press, 2013), 209.
21. Ibid., 209–211.
22. Tim O'Neill, *Review of Canadian Federal Forecasting: Processes and Systems*, June 2005; CBC, "Budget Watchdog Questions Flaherty's Deficit Accounting," November 29, 2012, accessed July 19, 2016, http://www.cbc.ca/news/politics/budget-watchdog-questions-flaherty-s-deficit-accounting-1.1173709.
23. Dimock et al., *Ethics and the Public Service*, 83.
24. Ibid., 110.
25. Government of Canada, *Values and Ethics Code for the Public Sector* (Ottawa: Her Majesty the Queen in Right of Canada, 2011).
26. Government of Canada, *Values Alive: A Discussion Guide to the "Values and Ethics Code for the Public Sector,"* accessed June 25, 2016, http://www.tbs-sct.gc.ca/psm-fpfm/ve/code/va-vaq-eng.asp.
27. Government of Canada, *Values and Ethics Code for the Public Service: Democratic, Professional, Ethical and People Values*, accessed July 19, 2016, https://www.tbs-sct.gc.ca/pubs_pol/hrpubs/tb_851/vec-cve-eng.pdf.
28. Government, of Ontario, Reg. 381/07: Conflict of Interest Rules for Public Servants (Ministry) and Former Public Servants (Ministry), accessed June 27, 2016, https://www.ontario.ca/laws/regulation/070381.
29. John W. Langford, "Acting on Values: An Ethical Dead End for Public Servants," *Canadian Public Administration* 47(4) (2004): 430.
30. Government of Canada, *Values Alive*, 18.

Public Administration and Organization Theory: The Structural Foundation

3

Learning Objectives

Reading this chapter allows you to do the following:

- Explain how various organization theories contribute to our understanding of how organizations and the people within them work
- Identify the various characteristics of Weber's ideal-type bureaucracy and relate them to the evolution of the Canadian public bureaucracy
- List the key tenets of classical organization theory
- Assess the contributions of various classical organization theorists to the emergence of the scientific principles of administration
- Criticize the limitations of classical organization theory and explain how it gave rise to the neo-classical school

The study of public administration revolves around the careful consideration of government **bureaucracy**. This means that we investigate the basic structures that constitute the bureaucratic organizations in government and their interactions with other bodies in the political process. It also means taking a close look at some of the essential duties of public bureaucracies. But an important first step in pursuing an appreciation of public administration is the examination of theories of organizations, which is the concern of the various chapters in Part Two of the book. These theories grapple with the challenge of offering clear and accurate descriptions of organizational forms—be they public, private, or non-profit. They also put forward suggestions for enhancing the performance of organizations and ensuring that services are provided more fairly and efficiently. Above all, theories of organization offer us the framework for better explaining the behaviour or operation of various structures that may arise in public administration.

Organization theory is rather diverse and has embraced a wide range of methodological approaches, conceptual frameworks, and levels of analysis. While it is unlikely that we can ever develop a single comprehensive theory of organizations (or public organization), we can, nonetheless, glean important insights about how organizations and the people within them will behave given different structures, cultures, and contexts. Many of the organization theories that have been developed build upon earlier works and, as such, can be grouped together into "schools," "perspectives," or "eras" of organization theory. While the use of such classification schemes can facilitate our understanding of organizations, they can also be problematic since there are disagreements regarding how some of the organization theorists are classified. For example, while the contributions of Chester Barnard on informal organization and the need for cooperation to ensure organizational success are often "taken as a precursor of the rational model of administration ... his work also has interesting humanistic overtones."[1] Therefore,

bureaucracy Literally meaning "rule by desks or offices," it is a method of administratively organizing numerous people who need to work together in large or complex public or private organizations.

whether Barnard is categorized as a classical or neo-classical theorist or part of the human relations school is a matter of personal judgment.

In the influential book on organization theory, *Classics of Organization Theory*, nine distinctive schools of thought are identified: 1) classical organization theory, 2) neo-classical organization theory, 3) human resource theory or the organizational behaviour perspective, 4) "modern" structural organization theory, 5) organizational economics theory, 6) power and politics organization theory, 7) organizational culture and change, 8) theories of organizations and environments, and 9) theories of organization and society.[2] Clearly, the intellectual contributions to these various schools of organization theory over the past century are voluminous; but, notably, there was a time when many of the leading figures in organization studies—people like Max Weber, Frederick Taylor, and Herbert Simon—produced their influential work by examining public organizations. However, since the 1970s there has been a clear divergence between organization studies and public administration to the point where they have been characterized as two ships passing in the night.[3]

Therefore, while Canadian public administration scholars recently have been admonished for failing to adequately keep up with and utilize more recent developments in the organization theory literature,[4] this appears to be a much larger problem that the global public administration community needs to address. Moreover, while we believe that this criticism has merit, it is simply beyond the scope of this introductory textbook on public administration—a field of study with its own distinctive theoretical underpinnings—to provide a comprehensive summary and analysis of the organization theory literature.[5] Our focus, therefore, will be on what can be deemed to be the core contributions of organization theory to public administration.

In this chapter, we begin by discussing the concept of bureaucracy and whether it is relevant in the twenty-first century. We then study the first modern efforts to provide theories and models about the processes and structures of bureaucracy. The chapter examines the pioneering work of Max Weber on the features of traditional bureaucratic organizations as well as his thoughts about the place of bureaucracy in society and government. Frederick Taylor was another early student of organizations, and his endeavour to discover the one best way to organize the workplace is discussed. The chapter also considers the influential thinking of Luther Gulick and Lyndall Urwick on organizations. All together, the theories addressed in this chapter represent the main contributions to classical organization theory.

Classical organization theory is the foundation upon which the other schools of organization theory have been built; it was dominant until the 1930s, although it continues to have influence to this day. Essentially the classical organization theorists were concerned with the structure of formal organizations and developed their ideas on a number of basic tenets that derived from the industrial revolution of the 1700s as well as the professions of engineering and economics. They are as follows:

- Organizations exist to accomplish production-related and economic goals.
- There is one best way to organize for production, and that way can be found through systematic, scientific inquiry.
- Production is maximized through specialization and division of labour.
- People and organizations act in accordance with rational economic principles.[6]

Although classical organization theory expanded and matured over time, these tenets and assumptions have endured.

"Bureaucracy Is Dead—Long Live Bureaucracy?"

While many aspects of the bureaucratic form of organization can be traced back to the ancient Egyptian and Chinese civilizations, the term "bureaucracy" is thought to have been coined by French political economist Vincent de Gournay in 1745. Even from its first conception, the term was used pejoratively to indicate government by officials and excessive official power. Over time, however, efforts were made to cleanse bureaucracy of those negative connotations. "As a result, the properties attributed to bureaucracy (i.e., the qualities of being 'bureaucratic') came to be seen as both efficient and inefficient, both powerful and powerless, both administrative instrumentalism and usurpation of power."[7] In a classic work on bureaucracy, Martin Albrow conducted a thorough examination of the historical evolution of the term and identified a number of "modern concepts of bureaucracy": bureaucracy as rational organization, organizational inefficiency, rule by officials, public administration, administration by officials, the organization, and as modern society.[8] Like many concepts in the social sciences, therefore, "bureaucracy" is a slippery word that has multiple meanings.

But to the average citizen, there is a high degree of uniformity in terms of how bureaucracy is understood. Reflect for a moment on the concept of bureaucracy. What connotations does it evoke for you? Some of you might identify positive elements associated with bureaucracy, such as standardization or fairness, but the reality is that most people tend to have largely negative perceptions of bureaucracy—wastefulness, excessive rules and regulations, inefficiency, "red tape," unresponsiveness, inflexibility, hierarchy, arbitrary and impersonal treatment. It is difficult not to hold such views when the intellectual elite, politicians, and the media are constantly criticizing the public bureaucracy for any number of perceived shortcomings or failures. The chorus of voices denigrating bureaucracy was particularly loud in the 1980s and 1990s, with calls to "break through bureaucracy," "banish bureaucracy," move towards a "post-bureaucratic" model, and, most famously of all, to "reinvent" our bureaucratic governments so as to make them effective.[9] The emerging consensus was that bureaucracy had outlived whatever usefulness it might have had in an earlier era and that it either had been or should be relegated to the dustbin of history.

Against this backdrop of criticism, it is not surprising that Charles Goodsell wrote, "how, then, can any self-respecting professor write a book in *defense* of bureaucracy?"[10] But that is exactly what Goodsell did. As he argued,

> My brief for bureaucracy … is that governmental administration in America may be regarded as generally competent and effective if we look at it in a balanced way and in relation to what is possible. Whereas public bureaucracy in the United States … inevitably involves individual instances of breakdown, it does, *on the whole and in comparison to most countries*, perform surprisingly well.[11]

Similarly, Johan Olsen argued that bureaucratic organization remained relevant and that the time had come to "reconsider and rediscover bureaucracy as an administrative form, an analytical concept, and a set of ideas and observations about public administration and formally organized institutions."[12]

Although Goodsell was writing about government administration in the US, his words would be equally applicable in the Canadian context. As in the US, public perceptions of bureaucracy in Canada have been shaped by media accounts of allegedly egregious bureaucratic blunders and incompetence. Two of the most prominent examples would include the "billion dollar boondoggle" of 2000 and the Quebec Sponsorship Scandal by the Department of Public Works and Government Services Canada in the late 1990s and early 2000s. In the first instance, the media and opposition parties took the results of an internal audit of paper files for a number of programs at the former Human Resources and Social Development Canada to perpetuate a nine-month media storyline that the government had squandered a billion dollars of public money. With respect to the Sponsorship Scandal, which led to the arrest and conviction of advertising executives and public servants for fraud and breach of trust, the issue was the misuse of

The Problem with Bureaucracy

Karsten Schley/CartoonStock.com

public funds that were ostensibly earmarked for sponsorship and advertising activities in Quebec in the aftermath of the failed 1995 referendum. More recently, in 2015, a number of troubling newspaper headlines emerged questioning whether Health Canada had been properly regulating the safe manufacture of pharmaceuticals by Apotex, the country's biggest drug company, at one of its overseas facilities in Bangalore. In this instance, Health Canada was being criticized for allowing Apotex to continue importing and using Indian-made drug ingredients when the US Food and Drug Administration had banned the import of those products over safety concerns.[13] In many instances, these negative portrayals of bureaucracy are further reinforced by the frustrating and problematic experiences that individual citizens have had in their own interactions with civil servants.

When problems arise in the bureaucracy, the public should be concerned and corrective action must be taken. But it is important not to lose sight of the fact that the bureaucracy is not a single amorphous institution; rather, it comprises hundreds of distinct organizations—departments, agencies, bureaus, commissions, Crown corporations, and so on—that process countless transactions on a daily basis. (Chapters 5 to 7 will discuss these organizations.) The vast majority of those transactions are completed quietly and successfully; in many cases, service delivery in the public sector is even quite innovative, but this is not normally deemed to be very newsworthy. There is no denying that bureaucracy can be reformed so as to improve the efficiency and effectiveness of public service delivery, but it should not be viewed as an "organizational dinosaur" that has been vanquished.[14] It has been suggested that rather than creating post-bureaucratic organizations, public sector reforms and the proposed new governance models have merely resulted in new or extended forms of bureaucracy.[15] As Raadschelders and Vigoda-Gadot recently concluded, "Bureaucracy is here to stay; Weber was right about that."[16] Even those who advocated for a shift towards the new public organization that is "post-bureaucratic" in orientation still "note the staying power of the bureaucratic model" and argue that we must "avoid blaming this model for what is really poor design and bad management."[17]

Max Weber and Classical Bureaucratic Theory

It would be difficult to locate the first bureaucratic organization, but the first person who systematically studied the emerging phenomenon of bureaucracy was Max Weber, who was born in 1864. Weber was a brilliant German scholar who sought to examine bureaucracy in the context of authority in any society. For Weber, there were three sources of authority, each distinguished on the basis of its claim to legitimacy. Under traditional authority, the right to rule or exercise authority is legitimated by such factors as heredity, religious beliefs, or divine right. Charismatic authority is based on the outstanding personal characteristics of an individual—for example, Jesus, John F. Kennedy, or Hitler. Finally, legal or rational authority is legitimated by rules and regulations obeyed by both the rulers and ruled. In this last system, "obedience is owed not to a person—whether a traditional chief or charismatic leader—but to a set of impersonal principles."[18] Each type of authority is associated with a different administrative arrangement, and the usual organizational system under legal authority is bureaucracy.

The Characteristics of Weberian Bureaucracy

Weber's empirical study of the German bureaucracy suggested to him that the modern bureaucratic form consisted of a number of related characteristics. When these characteristics were combined in the same organization, the result was what he called the pure or **"ideal-type" bureaucracy**.[19] The main components of bureaucracy, which Weber believed generated a high level of efficiency, were as follows:

Hierarchical Structure

As Figure 3.1 shows, a bureaucratic organization is arranged in a series of superior–subordinate relationships, at the pinnacle of which is one—and only one—superior. This can also be described as **unity of command**, which means that for each position in the hierarchy, there is only one supervisor. The clear line of authority produced by unity of command was one reason Weber felt that bureaucracy was more efficient than previous forms of organization, but there were also other reasons for his belief.

Max Weber

Hulton Archives/Getty Images

"ideal-type" bureaucracy According to Max Weber, complex organizations would be more efficient when they reflected certain key characteristics, including hierarchy, specialization of labour, employment and promotion based on merit, full-time employment, the use of written files, and decisions based on impersonal rules.

unity of command The bureaucratic principle that holds that all employees must report to one, and only one, supervisor in order to minimize confusion and misdirection.

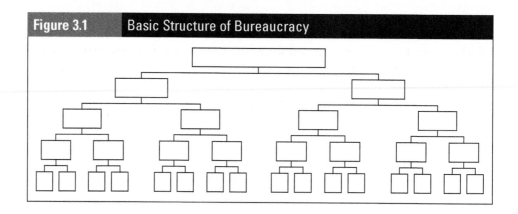

Figure 3.1   Basic Structure of Bureaucracy

Specialization of Labour

The purpose of the hierarchical structure was to allocate responsibilities to subordinates in a clear and unambiguous fashion. This division of responsibilities was significant because a person could become very efficient when able to concentrate on a specific job. Specialization of labour, however, is not enough if the employees are not qualified to learn to perform the work.

Employment and Promotion Based on Merit

In earlier times, people often obtained organizational positions through either heredity or outright purchase. Obviously, this method of staffing provided no guarantee that the person in a particular position was the best person for the job or even a competent one. Without some assurance of competence, no organization could operate efficiently. In the German bureaucracy that Weber studied, employment and promotion based on an objective test of merit provided this assurance and thus increased the efficiency of operation.

Full-Time Employment

An important principle related to employment based on merit was that employment in the bureaucracy was the full-time activity and major source of income of the official. This ensured that the official would develop allegiance to the bureaucracy and that the bureaucrat's hierarchical superior could exercise real control over the day-to-day activities of the official. The superior needed effective control to force the subordinate to abide by organizational regulations in carrying out duties.

Decisions Based on Impersonal Rules

Bureaucrats are bound by certain rules in dealing with the public. These rules are impersonal in the sense that they apply equally to all clients in similar situations. Bureaucrats cannot substitute their own set of rules for those legitimately proclaimed by superiors. If a particular benefit is to be provided without regard to race or religion, then a member of the bureaucracy would risk severe penalties if he or she allowed personal prejudice to affect the decision made. This reliance on impersonal rules increases confidence in the bureaucracy by establishing a regime of certainty in dealings.

Importance of Written Files

The significance of these rules makes written files very important. If the bureaucrat must prove that he or she has abided by the rules in making decisions, then written records must be maintained, first, of the rules themselves, and second, of all decisions made and the rationale for those decisions. It is worth noting here that the bureaucrat's allegiance to the rules takes precedence over allegiance to her or his superior. A superior can exercise judgment in an area that is unclear under the rules, but he or she cannot order a subordinate to violate those rules.

Bureaucratic Employment Separate from the Individual Bureaucrat's Private Life

This is an acknowledgment of both the autonomous nature of the bureaucracy as an organization and the fact that the bureaucrat does not own his or her position and the rights that go with it. Bureaucrats possess a great deal of authority. In the case of members of a government bureaucracy, this could be highly coercive authority. However, it is always clear that the power is attached to the position rather than to the individual. An obvious result of this division is that the bureaucrat is not permitted to obtain any personal gain, other than a fixed salary, from his or her position.

Weber's Views on Bureaucracy

Weber seems to have had a rather difficult love–hate relationship with this new organizational form called bureaucracy. As a serious scholar, he documented the characteristics of the German bureaucracy as he saw them without favourable or critical comment. Beyond that, though, he appears to have been of two minds about bureaucracy. On the one hand, he argued that bureaucracy was the most efficient method of organization:

> The fully developed bureaucratic apparatus compares with other organizations exactly as does the machine with the non-mechanical modes of production. Precision, speed, unambiguity, knowledge of the files, continuity, discretion, unity, strict subordination, reduction of friction and of material and personal costs—these are raised to the optimum point in the strictly bureaucratic administration ... .[20]

On the other hand, Weber foresaw many of the problems familiar to anyone who interacts with bureaucratic organizations. Weber understood that the technical superiority of bureaucratic officials might put them in a position to overwhelm the elected officials leading the organizations. More ominously, he feared that the bureaucratic values of order and security might prevail over those that we cherish and see as essential to an open, thriving community. For Weber, a central challenge for any society was to propose practices that can oppose the "machinery" of bureaucracy and "keep a portion of humanity free from this pigeon-holing of the spirit, from this total domination of the bureaucratic ideal."[21]

In his views on bureaucracy, Weber touched upon the crucial aspects of bureaucracy that still confound us today. It does seem to be the most efficient way of arranging a large number of offices and accomplishing complex, repetitive tasks. It appears that no company, government, or organization of any kind can afford to be without a bureaucratic form. But we also condemn the impersonal, mind-numbing aspects of its operation. Since the advent of bureaucracy in modern times, attempts have been made to find viable alternatives.

Criticisms of Weber

There have been many criticisms of Weber and his work on bureaucracy. A major line of criticism is that Weber dwelt too much on the structural aspects of bureaucracy and not enough on the human side of the organization. It is suggested that because Weber viewed bureaucrats as mere cogs in the mechanism, he overstated the impact of the organization on the worker and overlooked the effect of the worker on the organization. Employees, for instance, may pursue goals that are inconsistent with the professed aims of the organization but that satisfy their particular needs. More generally, informal systems of authority may emerge and effectively displace the formal systems—subordinates become the bosses and the bosses the subordinates. A related criticism is the claim that rational bureaucratic structures may produce irrational or inefficient outcomes. For instance, the emphasis on rules, which are designed as means, may become the ends of the organization. Bureaucrats seek strict compliance with the rules even though such action might be detrimental to servicing customers or recipients of a government service. The well-known term "red tape" arises from this excessive obedience to requirements and regulations.

Others criticized Weber because of perceived internal inconsistencies in his model of bureaucracy. The model relies on professional or expert decision making to ensure efficiency, but it is possible that superiors may lack the knowledge to make the best decision. The dilemma for the subordinate becomes whether to report to the ill-informed boss or seek out someone with the requisite knowledge—a clear violation of hierarchy and the principle of unity of command. Still others contended that bureaucracy was simply outmoded as a form of organization. It was argued that modern trends such as rapid change and the increasing professionalization of the workforce make bureaucracy obsolete. To be productive, organizations require fewer rules, less hierarchy, and employees free to innovate and meet the challenges of an increasingly complex and competitive world.[22]

Surprisingly, even a cursory look at Weber's model points out some obvious problems. A hierarchical organization can soon produce so many levels that it becomes difficult to operate within the firm or government or to comprehend its overall structure. The emphasis on a strict division of labour increases the chances that workers will become bored with doing the same activity every day. It is also easy to require that people be hired and promoted on merit, but measuring merit can be difficult—especially in organizations that wish to build a workplace broadly representative of the society it serves. Full-time employment also appears to ignore the cost advantages of part-time or casual workers, and a government agency can effectively choke on the presence of too many files.

As will be seen later in the text, contemporary theories of organization aim to avoid the pitfalls of Weber's bureaucratic structures. But as suggested earlier, bureaucracy provides insights into the workings of organizations and constitutes part of the repertoire of administrative forms available for structuring organizations. Moreover, some contend that bureaucracy and its qualities of hierarchy, specialization, and standardization represent a necessary condition for achieving sound management in government.[23]

Frederick W. Taylor and Scientific Management

Max Weber was a philosopher who could stand at arm's length from organizations and describe in broad terms their general characteristics. By contrast, Frederick Winslow Taylor, born in 1856, was a mechanical engineer who began his career working as a technician on the factory floor and spent much of his later life in either a supervisory or an advisory capacity dealing with problems of production management. His major concern was the proper arrangement of the human and mechanical resources of the factory so as to minimize waste, particularly the time of workers.

Taylor's experience in the factory showed him that a great deal of slacking off or "soldiering" was taking place. He posited two reasons for this behaviour. One was what he regarded as the natural tendency of employees to do as little work as possible. The second was that work was sometimes arranged in such an awkward manner that no reasonable human being, regardless of how ambitious or honest, could physically perform what their superiors expected. Since soldiering constituted the squandering of a resource, it was important for management to end it. Taylor argued that the resulting increased productivity would benefit both employers and employees.

Fostering Efficiency: The Scientific Approach to Management

Photo Quest/Getty Images

The employee's natural tendency toward soldiering might be eliminated if the employer used scientific principles rather than informal calculations to determine an employee's appropriate workload. Some soldiering was caused by the employee's rational reaction to the method of piecework payment that was prevalent in Taylor's time. Employees knew that in the short run they could earn more by working hard and producing above standard, but they realized that in the long run this was counterproductive, because employers simply raised the standard. It was therefore better to work at a steady pace and receive adequate pay than to be a "rate-buster." The problem was that employers had no idea what an employee could do in an average shift. Thus, most employers used unscientific rules to establish standards and so did not have the confidence of their employees. The obvious solution to the problem was to establish scientific standards based on the proven physical capacities of workers and then refrain from adjusting those standards arbitrarily.

Taylor's usual approach to establishing these scientific standards was to select employees who performed a particular task exceptionally well (e.g., moving the most pig iron, shovelling the most coal). A trained management employee would then carefully scrutinize the actions of these employees, watching and timing their every movement. This was the beginning of the time-and-motion study that has stirred so much controversy on factory floors. The purpose of these studies was to learn the ideal method of performing a particular task from the most efficient employees. This is the "one best way" employed by Frank and Lillian Gilbreth and popularized with humorous effect by their children in the book and movie *Cheaper by the Dozen*.[24] When the best set of physical motions was determined, it was the responsibility of managers to teach this technique to all employees.

The second cause of soldiering was the inability of workers to maintain the pace expected of them because of how the work was organized. Taylor pointed out that workers could be more productive if management took greater care in organizing the work. He put particular emphasis on such factors as determining the optimal working rhythm necessary to maximize output. The next time you are working in the garden or shovelling snow it might be useful to know that, according to Taylor, the greatest tonnage per day can be shovelled when the worker moves twenty-one pounds on each shovel-load.[25]

Taylor felt that it was important to have a clear division of duties between management and labour. It was the job of management to select employees for specific jobs in a scientific manner so that the physical and mental characteristics of the individual fit the job. It was then the role of management to teach labourers the optimum way to perform their duties, while the labourers supplied strong backs.

Taylor emphasized the importance of financial factors as a motivating force. However, he rejected the crude principle of piecework, because he knew that workers could easily manipulate the standard. Instead, he singled out the best workers for the privilege of working in a higher-paid group. By examining their actions as described above, he was able to determine in a scientific manner how much work should be accomplished. In one experiment, workers who had met the standard in their previous day's work were given white slips at the beginning of their next shift, while those who had not were given yellow slips. Those receiving yellow slips obviously did not understand fully how their job should be done, so it was the responsibility of management to provide additional training. The consistent receipt of yellow slips would cause one's return to the lower-paid gang.[26] This was Taylor's method of using financial incentives without the drawbacks identified with piecework.

Some writers suggest that Taylor showed a lack of concern for the workers. It is clear that he viewed management as very enlightened and workers in a rather condescending manner. However, Taylor did strive for harmony between management and workers and was sensitive to the need not to alienate unions. He always argued that cooperation was the best way to maximize productivity—but he gave the impression that it would be cooperation on management's terms. Furthermore, he strongly opposed overworking employees in sweatshop conditions. Although this might well have been more for reasons of productivity than humanity, it was still a fairly radical idea for his time.

Taylor's main contribution to organization theory was his emphasis on the scientific approach to work management—the "one best way"—and his emphasis on the important role of management in organizing the work. But there were certain problems with how Taylor's ideas were implemented. In some cases, management used time-and-motion studies to attempt to extract the maximum possible production from workers. This led to worker resistance to the entire concept. The idea of the narrow subdivision of work into its smallest components created monotony, which led to further worker unrest.

The ideas of Weber and Taylor are significant because they had a great influence on management thinking at one time, and because their influence can still be detected in some mechanistic aspects of organization theory. However, their approaches have been challenged by newer forms of organization. Their ideas made more sense when applied to large factories where workers assembled products manually but make less sense in knowledge-based organizations. However, before these problems became evident, their ideas were tried in a number of places, including the Canadian federal government.

The Canadian Experience—From Patronage to Merit

The Canadian federal government gradually began adopting some of Taylor's ideas to speed up the move from a patronage-based public service to a merit-based one, thus simultaneously moving toward the Weberian concept of bureaucracy. For example, the

Civil Service Commission (CSC) was established in 1908 to act as guardian of the merit principle. The CSC was the outgrowth of a number of reports indicating that the prevalence of **patronage** appointments in the Canadian civil service was having a detrimental impact on its efficiency. The CSC began the process of entrenching the merit principle by administering competitive examinations to applicants for government positions. But the CSC soon discovered that a serious problem existed because the duties of specific positions were not usually well defined. Without a clear description of duties, creating a meaningful competitive examination was problematic.

Gradually the powers and responsibilities of the CSC evolved, until in 1918 it was given the power to make appointments to positions and to reorganize departments, whether this was sought by the department or not. This legislation seemed to be influenced by officials of the CSC, who were in turn influenced by the principles of scientific management that were so prevalent at the time.[27]

The commissioners and the executive secretary of the CSC hired the American consulting firm of Arthur Young & Co. to introduce the principles of scientific management into the Canadian federal government. The exercise began with the systematic description and classification of 50,000 positions. The positions had to be described in great detail because this was the starting point for the mechanistic process of matching the person possessing the proper qualifications with the appropriate position. The next step was to be a sweeping reorganization of the entire governmental bureaucratic apparatus, streamlining and reducing the number of departments and agencies. Obviously, the idea of government reform is not as new and radical as some think.[28]

Arthur Young & Co.'s involvement became bogged down in a series of problems and, as a result, the reorganization did not occur. The sole, but significant, result of the exercise was an extensive and systematic classification of all government positions. The **scientific management** approach to job classification made it possible to match, in a mechanical fashion, the skills required in a particular job with the skills possessed by a given person. When the match was complete, presumably the process would be like pushing a plug into a wall socket—an automatic perfect connection that would last until it was unplugged.

But not everyone was impressed by the neatness of this arrangement. It worked well with positions that required specialized knowledge. A chemist or engineer could easily be placed in the appropriate position. More difficult would be finding the best person for administrative or managerial jobs in which the necessary skills and aptitudes were not so easily discovered.[29]

The impact of scientific management and the Weberian bureaucratic model are evident in Canadian public administration to the present day. As you will discover in Chapter 5, the federal government is still organized around a number of main government departments that are hierarchically structured from the deputy minister, as the administrative head, down to the various street-level bureaucrats who are engaged in direct service delivery to Canadian citizens. Moreover, despite an increasing reliance in recent years on a contingent workforce of part-time and contract employees, the federal government largely comprises a professional, career public service made up of full-time employees who are hired and promoted on the basis of merit (much of which is discussed in Chapter 17). Job classifications, outlining the responsibilities associated with the position, the skills and background required to perform those duties, and pay scales, are still very much a part of the human resource management regime governing the public service. Finally, record keeping remains critical for ensuring accountability,[30] while rules and regulations—even in the face of criticism that there are too many of them—continue to guide the behaviour of public servants as they fulfill their responsibilities.

patronage The appointment of persons to government service or their advancement within the service on the grounds of contributions, financial or otherwise, to the governing party rather than based on merit.

scientific management A management style that emphasizes tailoring the physical nature of work to the physical abilities of workers. Characterized by time-and-motion studies and precise work standards. Usually associated with Frederick W. Taylor.

Fayol's General Principles of Management

Henri Fayol (1841–1925), a French executive engineer, has been credited with being the first person to formulate a comprehensive theory of management. His major work was published in 1916, but his ideas would not become influential in North America for another three decades when his work was translated into English. Fayol outlined six principles of management: technical (production of goods), commercial (buying and selling), financial (generating and using capital), security (protection of property and people), accounting, and managerial. In this final category, he proposed that all managers, irrespective of the organization, engaged in five managerial functions: planning, organizing, coordinating, controlling, and commanding. Fayol devoted most of his attention to these management activities.

As part of the principles of management, he addressed a number of critical components related to the workplace, including the following:

- the division of work (i.e., he advocated for specialization),
- authority and responsibility (which went hand in hand),
- the need for discipline,
- unity of command (employees should receive orders from one superior only),
- **unity of direction** (one head, one plan),
- the remuneration of personnel (which should be fair and reward effort),
- centralization (finding the appropriate balance between centralization and decentralization),
- **scalar chain** (where there is a clear line of authority from the top of the organization to the bottom),
- **esprit de corps** (the spirit or morale of the group),
- the need for order and equity, and
- the stability of tenure for personnel.

Fayol did not envision a limit on the number of principles of management as long as experience proved them to be worthy of inclusion. Therefore, this was not an exhaustive list, but rather an articulation of the ones that were most commonly applied.[31]

Gulick and Urwick and the Scientific Theory of Organization

In the United States in the 1930s, the President's Committee on Administrative Management spurred a great deal of interest by trying to develop a scientific theory of organization. Taylor's work dealt with how to organize work on the factory floor, but Luther Gulick and Lyndall Urwick were concerned with developing broader theories about the ideal structure for any organization. Their concerns were span of control and the proper alignment of related functions.

Span of Control

Span of control refers to the number of subordinates who report to one supervisor. There has long been controversy about what the ideal number should be. As Figure 3.2 shows, the smaller or narrower span provides for better control of employees. However, a span of control that is too narrow can lead to too many supervisors and too much overhead. As Figure 3.2 also demonstrates, a wider span of control avoids these problems and makes communication both up and down the organization considerably easier.

unity of direction The bureaucratic principle that holds that there should be only one leader and one plan for organizing activities to accomplish an objective.

scalar chain The formal line of authority in an organization moving in a straight line from the top to the bottom of the organizational hierarchy.

esprit de corps The morale and sense of unity of a group based on its shared interests and responsibilities.

span of control The number of subordinates reporting to a particular supervisor.

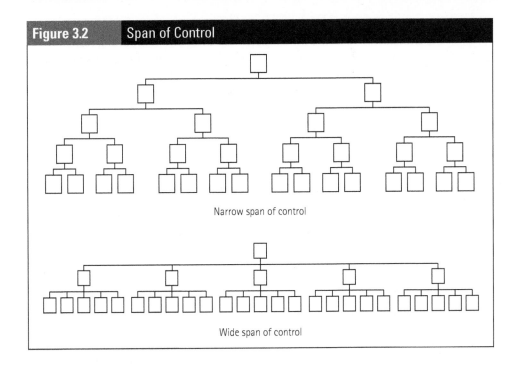

Figure 3.2   Span of Control

Narrow span of control

Wide span of control

But the cost of widening the span of control is the loss of close supervision. Managers now have more subordinates to look after. A dilemma thus presents itself:

> Small spans of control may appear to tighten control for the superior–subordinate relationship, but they loosen the overall control of the organization by extending the number of levels and thereby making the top that much more removed from the bottom. To cut down on the number of levels will reduce the distance between top and bottom, but the resulting increase in the span of control at each level will lessen the control that each level can maintain.[32]

The question of the appropriate span of control is still answered much as it was in Gulick and Urwick's time. It depends on the interaction of several things:

- the nature of the work supervised (routine procedures allow for a broader span of control, but supervision of several heterogeneous activities requires a narrower span of control),
- the level of training of the subordinates,
- the extent of the geographical decentralization of the work, and
- the overall stability of the organization.[33]

Empirical research supports the belief that these four factors largely determine the span of control. However, research also suggests that the weight or importance of these factors differs depending on the level in the hierarchy of the organization. Instability, for instance, may matter more in shaping the span of the control at the lower levels of the organization than it does at the upper levels. Finally, there is evidence that the span of control does indeed have an effect on the productivity or performance of an organization.[34]

The continuing significance of span of control can be seen in such catch phrases as "flattening the hierarchy" and "removing layers of management," which reflected common organizational practice in the 1980s and 1990s. Indeed, this is exactly what the federal government did at that time; as a part of the Public Service 2000 initiative of 1989, a commitment was made to reduce the number of layers of senior management so that for most departments there would be no more than three senior reporting relationships below the deputy minister.[35] A flatter hierarchy will lead to increased spans of control. This can be seen as a cost-saving move, because fewer managers are required. But it can also be justified on several other grounds. Reducing the number of levels between the top and the bottom of the organization decreases the isolation of those at the top and ensures that they will be more in touch with the organization's environment. It also reflects the fact that contemporary workers are much better trained than previous generations and workplaces are more mechanized. Both of these factors reduce the level of detailed supervision needed. However, recent research on flattening or "delaying" organizations has revealed that it may not result in pushing decision making downward, ultimately leading to greater accountability and enhanced market responsiveness. Such firms often exhibit more control and decision making at the top of the organization. "Flattening at the top is a complex phenomenon that in the end looks more like centralization."[36]

Organization of Duties

Aside from span of control, Gulick and Urwick were concerned with the problem of the ideal arrangement of duties within the organization. They argued that the process of organizational design should work simultaneously from the top down and from the bottom up.[37] When working from the top down, the primary criterion was to limit the span of control. Gulick reflected the conventional wisdom of the time that the senior executive should not have more than three direct subordinates. Working from the bottom up, the important factor was to combine homogeneous activities to facilitate coordination and supervision. The analyst then simply built in both directions until the two were joined.

When working from the bottom up, it was important to have an appropriate definition of homogeneity. The definition suggests that people doing similar work ought to be grouped together, but on further analysis this idea is difficult to apply. Gulick suggested that each worker could be characterized in four different ways:

1. the major *purpose* he or she serves, such as controlling crime or conducting education;
2. the *process* he or she uses, such as engineering, medicine, statistics, or accounting;
3. the *persons* or things he or she deals with or serves (immigrants, veterans, Aboriginal peoples, forests, or farmers);
4. the *place* where he or she renders the service (Toronto, Vancouver, or Quebec City).[38]

In designing an organization, employees who had all four things in common would be grouped together in the same organizational unit. If an employee was different in one category—for example, if he or she worked in a slightly different location—that would suggest he or she ought to be in another unit; however, Gulick emphasized the importance of applying pragmatism and judgment to individual cases. Where employees had only one or two things in common, they would likely be in separate units. The question remains as to which of the four should be the dominant organizing principle.[39]

This problem occurs in a very practical way when deciding how to arrange the legal services function in a large, multi-function organization. Figure 3.3 illustrates two ways in which legal services may be organized. The upper half of the figure depicts an organization with one legal department containing all lawyers, who would then provide service to other departments. This is an example of an organization based on process. If, instead, the lawyers are divided and assigned to the units that handle the programs, as in the lower half of Figure 3.3, organization by purpose is being used. At first glance, one arrangement seems to have as many advantages and disadvantages as the other. Gulick admitted that the lack of empirical evidence made serious discussion difficult, but he did suggest some of the pros and cons of each method.[40]

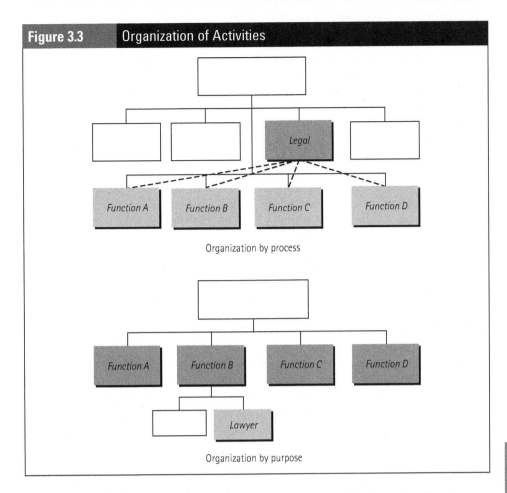

Figure 3.3 Organization of Activities

Legal

Function A   Function B   Function C   Function D

Organization by process

Function A   Function B   Function C   Function D

Lawyer

Organization by purpose

It is difficult to resolve this question of the best method of organization. In general it can be said that governments are most often organized by purpose. There are departments for health, education, labour, and other purposes. But some governments also have departments with a special mandate to look after the unique problems of a particular area. In some cases, these "place" departments actually deliver services provided by the "purpose" departments in designated areas; in others, they act as coordinating bodies.

Staff and Line Functions

Gulick also dealt with the activities of the executive. He argued that words like "administration" and "management" had lost their specific meaning. Building on the managerial functions identified by Fayol, he felt that the job of the executive could be summed up by the acronym **POSDCORB**, which stood for planning, organizing, staffing, directing, coordinating, reporting, and budgeting. Carrying out all these functions as part of managing a complex organization became very difficult, particularly as each of these functions was becoming more complex in itself. Urwick noted that one way many organizations were dealing with this problem was by the use of separate line and staff functions.[41] A **line function** is directly involved in producing and distributing the goods or services provided by the organization. A classic example would be the manufacturing section of an industrial organization. Some typical examples in government would be public health nurses, social workers, or officers dealing directly with social assistance claimants. A **staff function** is a function that aids, advises, and supports the employees providing the line function, usually without dealing directly with the clients or output of the organization. The obvious examples are human resources management, accounting, and legal services.

POSDCORB Building on the work of Henri Fayol, this acronym was developed by Luther Gulick and Lyndal Urwick as a means of highlighting the key steps in the administrative process: planning, organizing, staffing, directing, coordinating, reporting, and budgeting.

line function Any kind of daily operation that is directly involved in provision of goods or services by an organization. In government, those involved in a line function provide services directly to citizens.

staff function Those employed in this capacity, such as those in the accounting, human resources or legal departments, provide advice and support to those who are engaged in a line function.

When organizations are structured in this typical line–staff manner, the organization chart resembles Figure 3.4. Ideally, the two functions work together closely to further the objectives of the organization. The staff units can provide specialized advice to the line units about handling unusual situations. This means that line officers can concentrate on their standard repetitive tasks and do not have to be trained to cope with every eventuality. Another function frequently provided by staff employees is specialized record keeping. Again, this relieves the line officers of the responsibility for a specialized task and allows them to concentrate on their major function. Thus, one would expect a smooth, complementary relationship between these two functions, and this is the case in many organizations.

When problems do crop up in the line–staff relationship, they usually concern the question: Is the staff function a *service* or a *control* function? If the answer to the question is ambiguous, there can be serious problems. In some cases the staff department will render advice that the line department would rather not hear or act upon. Line officials might argue that to carry out their duties appropriately, they cannot be constrained by the whims of some group that does not fully understand the operation of the organization. The line manager may also point out the amount of profit or units of production that her or his unit has contributed to the organization and ask rhetorically how much the staff units have contributed. But the staff official might respond that his or her advice is essential to avoiding legal problems or to hiring the best possible people.

Organizations usually try to resolve possible difficulties between line and staff officials by establishing clear lines of authority and procedures to be followed in particular cases. These procedures seldom anticipate every circumstance. Obviously, both line and staff functions are important in an organization. How well they work together is frequently what separates good organizations from those that limp along from one crisis to the next.

Gulick and Urwick contributed to the theory of organizational behaviour by synthesizing and disseminating other people's ideas. Nevertheless, these two men made a valuable contribution both by forcing people to think about management in a systematic manner and by beginning to set out certain principles—many of which are still seen as beneficial guides to action today.

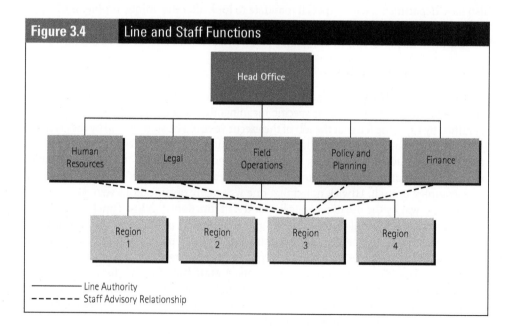

Figure 3.4   Line and Staff Functions

Decentralization and Deconcentration

Gulick and Urwick's discussion of methods of organization opened the way for a serious discussion of decentralization of government services, a very important issue in a country as large and heterogeneous as Canada. The size and diversity of most provinces and even some of our larger cities make decentralization an issue for provincial and municipal governments as well.

An important distinction must be made between decentralization and deconcentration. The difference between the two lies in the amount of real decision-making authority vested in the outlying unit. **Decentralization** suggests a placing of real discretionary authority in the outlying unit. In some cases, this might mean that the unit will also be physically removed from the centre to facilitate an understanding of local conditions, but physical dispersal is not a prerequisite for decentralization. **Deconcentration**, on the other hand, suggests a physical dispersal of members of the organization with only very limited delegation of decision-making authority.

Obviously, the line between the two is sometimes unclear. Even in deconcentration, there is virtually always some limited amount of discretion given to field officials, just as in decentralization there are always some kinds of decisions that can only be made after consultation with head office. Sometimes authority to deal with matters of an operational nature will be decentralized, while matters of a policy or program nature will be retained within the control of head office.

The large size and diversity of Canada causes Canadians to think of decentralization in terms of the physical dispersal of operating units. This is an appropriate use of the term, but it has a more general meaning as well. Geographic decentralization is decentralization by place, but decentralization can also be based on any of Gulick and Urwick's other classical methods of organization—process, purpose, or people.[42] Even an organization with all of its divisions located in the same building can be decentralized if real decision-making authority is vested in each of the separate units.

The large majority of federal government employees in regular government departments work outside the national capital region of Ottawa and Hull. These employees are located across the vast expanse of Canada in field units that vary greatly in purpose, size, and organization. For example, some 65 percent of those who work for Employment and Social Development Canada, which is the fourth largest federal government department, are based outside of the national capital region. This deconcentration of the federal government's operations is essential to the successful development and implementation of its policies and programs. The present balance in each department or agency between the number and level of employees at headquarters and in the field is a culmination of more than a century of political, administrative, economic, and geographical factors. In the earliest days of the Canadian federation, it was necessary to establish outposts for such government services as the post office and customs. The subsequent geographical dispersal of the public service is a government response to the challenge of providing a broad range of services to a population that is spread across a large country. Virtually all government departments now have field units, although the size of these units varies enormously.

Whether this dispersal represents decentralization or deconcentration, the problem remains the same. There must be a balance between accountability to rules specified by head office and responsiveness to regional needs. Officials in the field always feel pulled between the two. On the one hand, the rules and procedures set out by head office must be followed. On the other hand, field workers are sufficiently close to clientele in their everyday work to perceive situations in which an injustice is being done when the general rule is applied without sensitivity. The pressures to bend the rule are sometimes irresistible.

decentralization A system of organization that involves placing actual decision-making power in the hands of units outside the centre of power, either geographically or organizationally.

deconcentration The physical dispersal of operating units with only limited delegation of decision-making authority.

From the standpoint of head office, the problem is to maintain mechanisms to ensure that officials in the field are complying with head office rules and procedures without unnecessarily restricting the freedom of field officials to be responsive to local conditions. After all, it is these officials who are closest to the situation and are most knowledgeable about what should be done. However, they cannot be given carte blanche to do whatever they like without regard to the overall objectives of the department.

Specific approaches to departmental decentralization in Canada will be discussed later in the text, but at this point it is important to consider the general form that decentralization or deconcentration can take. In any organization serving a large geographic area, there must be some form of decentralization. Oversimplifying somewhat, this decentralization can take one of two forms. Figure 3.5 illustrates the two possibilities for an organization carrying out two different functions across the country.[43] The upper half illustrates decentralization by place. This style of decentralization is more likely to be true decentralization rather than deconcentration. In this case there is one main office in each region and that office is subdivided on the basis of the two functions. This kind of structure will tend to improve coordination between the two functions within each region. Because of this ease of coordination and because of the orientation toward place, the regional office of this kind of organization is likely to be highly responsive to the needs of its geographic area. The advantages of this form of organization include good coordination within each region and responsiveness to regional needs; on the other hand, the disadvantages include possible departures from national objectives and a complex form of organization.

The lower half of Figure 3.5 illustrates decentralization based on purpose, although this same form could also apply to decentralization based on process or people. This form is more likely to result in deconcentration than decentralization. In this case, the

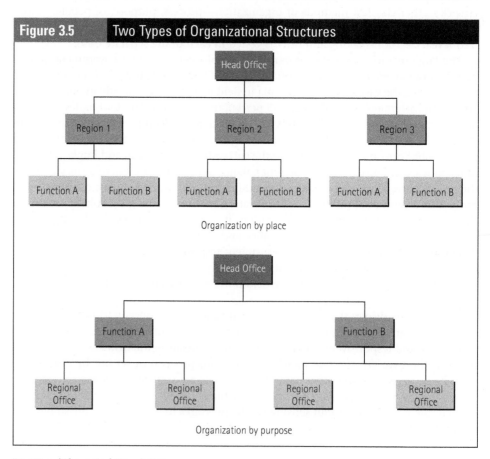

Figure 3.5   Two Types of Organizational Structures

Organization by place

Organization by purpose

primary division is by purpose, with the senior managers responsible for each function remaining in head office. Within each branch there is a subdivision by region, although the geographic areas covered by the regions are not necessarily the same for each branch. This reflects the fact that some programs might be more important in certain areas of the country than in others. Because each branch and each regional office specializes in providing only one function, it is relatively easy to ensure uniformity of administration across the entire country without the awkward organizational structure required in the case of decentralization by place.

The advantages of this style of organization are the simpler form of organization and the uniformity of program administration across the country. Its disadvantages are a lack of coordination of the programs at the regional level and a weaker responsiveness to regional needs.

The best style of organization depends on the nature of the programs to be delivered and the need for regional responsiveness. If good coordination between programs at the regional level and a greater sensitivity to regional needs is important, then the preferable style is decentralization by place. An example of this kind of program would be one aimed at regional economic development. Uniform administration across the country is less important than responsiveness to local conditions. In some cases, the uniform administration of a program across the country is more important than regional sensitivity. When this occurs, deconcentration by program would be preferable. The word "deconcentration" is used here because if there is uniformity of administration across the country, then by definition there will be little scope for decision making within each region. An example of this kind of organization would be a tax collection organization where fairness and equity demand that the same rules apply to everyone in the country.

The Neo-Classical School: Challenging the Structuralists

The neo-classical school, which peaked in terms of its influence from the post-war period to the 1950s, never fully developed to the point where it replaced classical organization theory. Nevertheless, those writers who are typically identified as neo-classical theorists—Herbert Simon, Robert K. Merton, Chester Barnard, and Philip Selznick—are extremely important to the historical evolution of organization theory. This was the case for two principal reasons: (1) they provided a direct challenge to some of the basic tenets of classical organization theory, initiating a movement away from the simplistic mechanistic view that Weber, Taylor, and others had about the role of the worker in the organization; and (2) they raised issues and provided the foundation for many of the subsequent theoretical perspectives that emerged, especially human relations, but also the power and politics, "modern" structural, systems, and organizational culture schools of thought.[44]

Herbert Simon and the Proverbs of Administration

Herbert Simon is a prolific writer on many topics of administration. One of his most widely quoted passages deals with the scientific principles of administration:

> It is a fatal defect of the current principles of administration that, like proverbs, they occur in pairs. For almost every principle one can find an equally plausible and acceptable contradictory principle. Although the two principles of the pair will lead to exactly opposite organizational recommendations, there is nothing in the theory to indicate which is the proper one to apply.[45]

One example of this kind of problematic pair of proverbs is "Look before you leap" and "He who hesitates is lost." If the so-called scientific principles of management could be seen to have similar flaws, their validity would be in doubt.

Simon gives the juxtaposition of these two principles as an example:

Administrative efficiency is supposed to be enhanced by limiting the number of subordinates who report directly to any one administrator to a small number—say six … .

Administrative efficiency is enhanced by keeping at a minimum the number of organizational levels through which a matter must pass before it is acted upon.[46]

Obviously, an organization cannot have it both ways. Earlier in this chapter, Figure 3.2 illustrated how a narrow span of control always results in a large number of layers in the organization. A truly scientific principle of management would not allow this dilemma. If one must exercise judgment and discretion in achieving a blend of the two rules, the rules are not very scientific.

Simon saves most of his attack for the idea of organizing by purpose, process, people, or place. He points out that not only is the overall idea contradictory in that one of the four must take precedence, but that the concepts themselves are fuzzy and that some of them shade into one another. The rebuttal might be made here that Simon is being too fussy. The principles are simply guides to action; they are considerations to be taken into account before acting, to be used to shape our judgment and guide our discretion. This defence might be valid, but the crucial point remains evident: if judgment and discretion are so important in applying these principles, can they really be called "scientific"?

Chester Barnard and the Importance of Cooperation

Chester Barnard was a career business executive, born in 1886, who rose to become president of the New Jersey Bell Telephone Company. In 1938, after his retirement, he wrote his landmark work *The Functions of the Executive*.[47] His crucial idea was that an organization is a cooperative system held together by a good communication system and by the continuing desire of individual members to see the organization thrive.

Members of the organization make *contributions* to it, but only when they receive adequate *inducements* to encourage them to continue to do so. It is important to balance contributions and inducements. If inducements exceed contributions, business failure will result because the organization is too free with its resources. However, if inducements are inadequate, workers will cease making contributions and business failure will result. The essence of good management is maintaining a balance between these two. The inducements offered to workers could be in the form of monetary rewards, but Barnard felt that other forms of inducement such as loyalty, good working conditions, and pride in both the work and the organization were probably more effective.

Barnard tried to be sensitive to the needs of workers, but his basic attitude to workers was somewhat patronizing. The title of his book—*The Functions of the Executive*—probably says it all. He felt that workers were rather docile, uninspired creatures who depended on leadership to accomplish anything. It was the responsibility of the executive to establish good communication systems that would in turn instill the appropriate company spirit in employees.

He recognized that there was an informal organization that could thwart the desires of management; however, he argued that it was the responsibility of management to use the idea of cooperation to harness that informal system for the benefit of the organization. This idea is still found in the argument that job interviews are an important part of the hiring process, not because they disclose specific job skills, but because they can indicate whether the prospective employee's personality fits with the organization's culture.[48]

Robert K. Merton and Bureaucratic Dysfunction

Robert K. Merton (1910-2003) was an American sociologist and is considered to be one of the founders of modern-day sociology. While much of his work concerned the sociology of science, he also wrote on a number of other topics including criminal behaviour and the development of scientific theories. What makes him of interest for public administration is his work on the structure of bureaucracy. Merton recognized that bureaucracy was in many respects the ideal type of formal, rational organization, but he cautioned that bureaucracies could become dysfunctional. He introduced the concept of **trained incapacity** to highlight a flaw associated with the bureaucratic structure. This is a situation whereby "actions based upon training and skills which have been successfully applied in the past may result in inappropriate responses *under changed conditions*."[49] Ultimately, therefore, rigid adherence to the rules becomes an end in itself and the purpose of the organization is lost along the way.

Philip Selznick and the Importance of Non-Rational Aspects of Organizations

Philip Selznick (1919-2010) was another American sociologist, whose major contribution to neo-classical organization theory was a 1948 article published in the *American Sociological Review*.[50] Whereas the structuralists were narrowly concerned with the formal, rational aspects of an organization, Selznick recognized that there were many non-rational and **informal dimensions of organizational behaviour** that had to be understood and accounted for. Individuals within organizations could not simply be controlled and manipulated with respect to their formal roles; they had to be viewed as "wholes." In other words, all individuals within an organization bring with them a series of habits that affect their behaviour as well as personal interests and goals, which may not coincide with the interests and goals of the organization.

Large organizations are prone to experience deviations from the formal system, which results in the emergence of "unwritten laws" and informal associations or cliques. These will often have negative consequences with respect to the formal goals of the organization. Selznick tasked organizational managers and leaders, therefore, with earning the consent and support of their employees. Given the indivisibility of control and consent, Selznick believed that formal organizations had to be viewed as cooperative systems, which are "constituted of individuals interacting as wholes in relation to a formal system of coordination."[51]

Selznick was also interested in understanding how organizations dealt with transformations, be they with respect to their goals, leadership, doctrine, or efficiency. He described a process of organizational adjustment called "co-optation," whereby the organization would bring new elements into its leadership or policy-making process so as to prevent threats to its stability and existence. Clearly, this process is indicative of an adaptive social structure, but the significance of co-optation is not the broadening of leadership but rather that "this change is consequential for the character and role of the organization."[52]

trained incapacity
A concept that refers to the fact that actions continue to be based on skills and training that worked successfully in the past but produce inappropriate responses when circumstances change.

informal organizational behaviour The formal structural aspects of an organization do not fully explain patterns of behaviour and interaction. Organizations contain many informal elements, such as personal interests and goals that may diverge from formally stipulated organizational goals, and informal associations or cliques, which dictate how people actually work together.

Points to Know

- Organization theory, which can be divided into a number of distinctive schools or perspectives, facilitates our understanding of the behaviour of organizations (private, public, and non-profit) and the individuals who work within them.

- The foundation of organization theory is the so-called classical organization theorists (Weber, Taylor, Fayol, Gulick, and Urwick), who were concerned with the structure of formal organizations. They believed that

people and organizations were rational and that it was possible to identify, through scientific inquiry, one best way to organize for production.

- Max Weber was the first person to study bureaucracy systematically and, in doing so, he identified a number of characteristics of the ideal-type bureaucracy. He believed that bureaucracy was the most rational form for all large, complex organizations.

- Although the term "bureaucracy" has been heavily criticized by public administration scholars and it tends to evoke negative perceptions amongst the citizenry, it remains a virtuous and relevant form of organization in the twenty-first century.

- Many of the insights derived from the work of the classical organization theorists were reflected in the design of the Canadian federal public bureaucracy and remain relevant to this day.

- The neo-classical organization theorists—notably Herbert Simon, Robert K. Merton, Chester Barnard, and Philip Selznick—challenged the simplistic and overly-mechanistic view that the classical school had of individuals in organizations.

Review Questions

1. How does classical organization theory as a whole contribute to our understanding of public administration?

2. What are the key elements of Max Weber's ideal-type bureaucracy? How, if at all, do they relate to the structure of the public bureaucracy in Canada?

3. What are some of the criticisms or weaknesses associated with Max Weber's work on bureaucracy and Frederick Taylor's contributions to scientific management?

4. What are the "proverbs of administration" and why were they important?

5. What contributions did the neo-classical theorists make to the evolution of organization theory?

Notes

1. Robert B. Denhardt and Thomas J. Catlaw, *Theories of Public Organization*, 7th ed. (Stamford, CT: Cengage Learning, 2015), 107.
2. Jay M. Shafritz, J. Steven Ott, and Yong Suk Jang, eds., *Classics of Organization Theory*, 8th ed. (Toronto: Harcourt College Publishers, 2015), 7.
3. Jeffrey Pfeffer, "Like Ships Passing in the Night: The Separate Literatures of Organization Theory and Public Management," *International Public Management Journal* 9(4) (2006): 457–465. On the basis of a recent survey examining the extent to which the leading management journals make reference to public management research and vice versa, it has been suggested that it is "not exactly still one of ships passing in the night; rather, there appears to be a dimly lit, one-way street emerging." This reflects the fact that while management and organization studies continue to ignore the influence of public administration, there has been an increasing recognition of the relevance of the scholarship published in generic management journals by public administration scholars. See Rhys Andrews and Marc Esteve, "Still Like Ships that Pass in the Night? The Relationship Between Public Administration and Management Studies," *International Public Management Journal* 18(1) (2015): 48.
4. Evert Lindquist, "Public Administration Research and Organization Theory: Recovering Alternative Perspectives on Public Service Institutions," in *The Physiology of Government: Canadian Public Administration in Transition*, eds. O.P. Dwivedi, Tim A. Mau, and Byron Sheldrick (Ottawa: University of Ottawa Press, 2009), 40–71.
5. See, for example, Denhardt and Catlaw, *Theories of Public Organization*, for a more comprehensive treatment of this subject matter; and Jonathan R. Tompkins, *Organization Theory and Public Management* (Belmont, CA: Thomson Wadsworth, 2005).
6. Shafritz, Ott, and Jang, *Classics of Organization Theory*, 33.
7. Fred W. Riggs, "Introduction: Shifting Meanings of the Term 'Bureaucracy,'" *International Social Science Journal* XXXI(4) (1979): 564.
8. Martin Albrow, *Bureaucracy* (London: Macmillan, 1970), 17–18. Building on the work of Albrow, Riggs identified 11 distinctive meanings for the term "bureaucracy." See ibid., 578–580.
9. Michael Barzelay, *Breaking Through Bureaucracy: A New Vision for Managing Government* (Berkeley and Los Angeles, CA: University of California Press, 1992); David Osborne and Peter Plastrik, *Banishing Bureaucracy: The Five Strategies for Reinventing Government* (Reading, MA: Addison-Wesley Publishing Company Inc., 1997); Kenneth Kernaghan, Brian Marson, and Sandford Borins, *The New Public Organization* (Toronto: Institute of Public Administration of Canada, 2000); David Osborne and Ted Gaebler, *Reinventing Government: How the Entrepreneurial Spirit Is Transforming the Public Sector* (Reading, MA: Addison-Wesley Publishing Company Inc., 1992).
10. Charles Goodsell, *The Case for Bureaucracy: A Public Administration Polemic*, 3rd ed. (Chatham, NJ: Chatham House Publishers, 1994), 1. Emphasis in original.
11. Ibid., 3. Emphasis in original.
12. Johan P. Olsen, "Maybe It Is Time to Rediscover Bureaucracy," *Journal of Public Administration Research and Theory* 16(1) (January 2006): 2.
13. See, for example, David Good, *The Politics of Public Management: The HRDC Audit of Grants and Contributions* (Toronto: University of Toronto Press, 2003); Commission of Inquiry into the Sponsorship Program and Advertising Activities, *Who Is Responsible? Summary* (Ottawa: Public Works and Government Services Canada, 2005); and Jesse McLean and David Bruser, "Inside Ottawa's Fight with a Drug Giant," *Toronto Star*, June 1, 2015, A1, A8. Health Canada lifted the ban against products produced at two Apotex facilities in India on September 1, 2015.
14. Olsen, "Maybe It Is Time," 1.
15. Leslie Budd, "Post-Bureaucracy and Reanimating Public Governance: A Discourse and Practice of Continuity?" *International Journal of Public Sector Management* 20(6) (2007): 531–547.
16. Jos Raadschelders and Eran Vigoda-Gadot, *Global Dimensions of Public Administration and Governance: A Comparative Voyage* (Hobokin, NJ: John Wiley & Sons, 2015), 156.
17. Kernaghan, Marson and Borins, *The New Public Organization*, 1.
18. Peter Blau and Richard W. Scott, *Formal Organizations* (San Francisco: Chandler, 1962), 32.
19. The phrase "ideal-type" has a particular meaning in this context. It is not "ideal" in the sense of "perfect" or "cannot be improved upon": rather, it suggests that Weber's characterization is a polar or extreme description that probably does not exist exactly in the real world. For a good explanation of this, see Michael M. Harmon and Richard T. Mayer, *Organization Theory for Public Administration* (Boston: Little, Brown, 1986), 71–74, 83.
20. Max Weber, *Economy and Society: An Outline of Interpretive Sociology*, eds. Guenther Roth and Claus Wittich (Berkeley: University of California Press, 1978), 2:973.
21. Weber quoted in David Beetham, *Bureaucracy*, 2nd ed. (Minneapolis: University of Minnesota Press, 1996), 55.
22. A discussion of the criticisms of Weber can be found in Albrow, *Bureaucracy*, 54–61.
23. Peter Aucoin, "The Design of Public Organizations for the 21st Century: Why Bureaucracy Will Survive in Public Management," *Canadian Public Administration* 40(2) (Summer 1997): 290–306.
24. Frank B. Gilbreth, Jr. and Ernestine Gilbreth Carey, *Cheaper by the Dozen* (New York: Thomas Y. Crowell, 1948).
25. Frederick Winslow Taylor, *The Principles of Scientific Management* (New York: W.W. Norton, 1967), 65.
26. Ibid., 67–68.
27. J.E. Hodgetts, William McCloskey, Reginald Whitaker, and V. Seymour Wilson, *The Biography of an Institution: The Civil Service Commission of Canada, 1908–1967* (Montreal and Kingston: McGill-Queen's University Press, 1972), ch. 4.

28. For a good historical overview of the evolution of the various federal government departments, see the two volumes by Gordon F. Osbaldeston, *Organizing to Govern* (Toronto: McGraw-Hill Ryerson, 1992).

29. R. MacGregor Dawson, "The Canadian Civil Service," *Canadian Journal of Economics and Political Science* 2(3) (August 1936): 293.

30. See Good, *The Politics of Public Management*, for an account of what can happen when accountability for process (i.e., proper record keeping) becomes secondary to accountability for results, a shift in emphasis that occurred under new public management.

31. Henri Fayol, *General and Industrial Management*, trans. Constance Storrs (London: Pitman, 1971).

32. Robert I. McLaren, *Organizational Dilemmas* (Chichester, U.K.: John Wiley & Sons, 1982), 45–46.

33. Luther Gulick, "Notes on the Theory of Organization," in eds. Luther Gulick and L. Urwick, *Papers on the Science of Administration* (New York: Augustus M. Kelley, 1969), 7–9.

34. See Kenneth J. Meier and John Bohte, "Span of Control and Public Organizations: Implementing Luther Gulick's Research Design," *Public Administration Review* 63(1) (January/February 2003): 61–70.

35. Canada, *Public Service 2000: The Renewal of the Public Service of Canada (Synopsis)* (Ottawa: Minister of Supply and Services, 1990), 15.

36. Julie Wulf, "The Flattened Firm: Not as Advertised," *California Management Review* 55(1) (Fall 2012), 18.

37. Gulick, "Notes on the Theory of Organization," 11–12.

38. Ibid., 15. Emphasis in original.

39. Ibid., 31–32.

40. Ibid., 21–30.

41. Lyndall Urwick, "Organization as a Technical Problem," in ibid., 47–88.

42. McLaren points out that decentralization can occur in several dimensions. *Organizational Dilemmas*, ch. 2.

43. McLaren's enlightening treatment takes a slightly different approach, but deals with the same issues. *Organizational Dilemmas*, 12–17.

44. Shaftritz, Ott, and Jang, *Classics of Organization Theory*, 93–96.

45. Herbert Simon, *Administrative Behavior* (New York: The Free Press, 1957), 20.

46. Ibid., 26.

47. Chester Barnard, *The Functions of the Executive* (Cambridge, Mass.: Harvard University Press, 1962).

48. Glenn Bassett, "From Job Fit to Cultural Compatibility: Evaluating Worker Skills and Temperament in the '90s," *Optimum* 25(1) (Summer 1994): 11–17.

49. Robert K. Merton, "Bureaucratic Structure and Personality," *Social Forces* 18(4) (1940): 562. Emphasis in original.

50. Philip Selznick, "Foundations of the Theory of Organization," *American Sociological Review* 13(1) (1948): 25–35.

51. Ibid., 28.

52. Ibid., 35. Emphasis in original.

Public Administration and Organization Theory: The Humanistic Response and Beyond

4

Learning Objectives

Reading this chapter allows you to do the following:

- List the key tenets of the human relations school of organization theory
- Assess the contributions of the main human relations theorists—Follett, Roethlisberger and Mayo, Maslow, McGregor—whose theories were designed to address the shortcomings of the formal, structuralist perspective of the classical school
- Explain the key criticisms of the human relations theories and how new theoretical developments,

such as participatory management and organizational development, emerged to address those limitations
- Apply systems theory to the study of government as a whole or a particular government department or agency
- Demonstrate how power and politics are inherent in public administration

As noted in the previous chapter, the early theories of organization represented an important first step in the scientific understanding of organizations. They offered a model of bureaucracy and put forward ways of making people more productive. However, the work of Weber, Taylor, Fayol, and Gulick and Urwick also provided the stimulus for a new theoretical perspective on organizations. Initially, there were the criticisms and new perspectives offered by the neo-classical theorists (Simon, Merton, and Selznick), who began to move beyond the formal structures and the significance of rules that preoccupied the classical organization theorists by focusing on informal structures and the need for greater flexibility and autonomy in the workplace. This eventually gave rise to human resource theory or what is otherwise known as the organizational behaviour perspective.

While researchers have been interested in the behaviour of individuals within organizations for quite some time, the humanist perspective, with a different set of assumptions about the relationship between people and organizations, did not emerge until the late 1950s and peaked in terms of its influence in the 1960s and early 1970s. While the early theorists saw the worker at times as little more than a cog in a machine, easily replaceable and controllable through various devices, the humanists believed that employees were as important as the organization itself and the relationship they had with the organization was reconceptualized as one of co-dependence rather than dependence. A fundamentally different set of assumptions guided the thinking of those associated with this new perspective:

- Organizations exist to serve human needs (rather than the reverse).
- Organizations and people need each other (organizations need ideas, energy, and talent; people need careers, salaries, and work opportunities).

- When the fit between the individual and the organization is poor, one or both will suffer.
- A good fit between individual and organization benefits both.[1]

This chapter traces the emergence of the humanist perspective with an examination of the first group of theories to challenge the more mechanist view of organizations and their inhabitants, including the work of Mary Parker Follett, Fritz Roethlisberger, Abraham Maslow, Douglas McGregor, Chris Argyris, and Frederick Herzberg. The chapter also considers more recent work on humanism—called participatory management—that seeks to build upon the earliest attempts to challenge the model of bureaucracy. These theories, which encompass the efforts of Peter Drucker, W. Edwards Deming, and others, tried to correct the failings of organizational humanism and in so doing establish a more sound understanding of organizations and a better basis for effecting greater productivity in the workplace. We then address other contributions to organization theory, including contingency theory (a "modern" structural theory) and concluding with an examination of two additional schools of organization theory that have been particularly relevant to the study of public administration, namely systems theory (part of the theories of organizations and environments) and power and politics organization theory. Each of the perspectives addressed in this chapter has generated insights regarding the ways in which our public institutions are designed and function; they also guide the thoughts and actions of public sector leaders and managers in terms of their interactions with their subordinates as they collectively strive to build high-performing organizations.

Organizational Humanism

organizational humanism (human relations school) An approach to management and motivation that emphasizes the dignity and needs of workers in the workplace. Usually associated with social psychologists such as Roethlisberger and Mayo.

Just as scientific management bore the imprint of production engineers such as Frederick Taylor, **organizational humanism**, or the **human relations school**, bore the imprint of social psychologists. Taylor focused on what *should* happen in the factory to maximize production. The organizational humanists focused instead on what *actually* happened on the factory floor. Their findings seem rather unspectacular now, but they totally upset scientific management theorists. They found that in addition to the formal system of authority through which management controlled workers, there was an informal system of worker control that was in some cases more powerful than the formal system. The informal system was characterized by the network of friendships, workplace banter, and informal sanctions that occur in every work setting. The devastating impact that this finding had on the scientific management theory was obvious. Taylor and his disciples might continue to set their standards, but workers would simply not comply with them if it meant enduring the ostracism frequently accorded the "rate-buster." This meant that Taylor's emphasis on scientific principles to set the work pace and on financial incentives to improve productivity was somewhat misplaced. While these factors had some value, it was becoming clear that another route to increased productivity lay with the informal system.

Mary Parker Follett

One of the first people to understand the importance of the informal system was not a conventional researcher but a very perceptive student of human nature. Mary Parker Follett, born in 1868, did not study organizations systematically in the ordinary sense, but she did use every opportunity to discuss organizational questions with everyone from senior executives to factory workers. From these discussions, she developed a number of important ideas.

Her basic philosophy stemmed from the fact that she rejected the conventional use of raw power in organizations. She felt that its use was either futile or, in some cases, totally counterproductive. Instead, she focused on two related concepts: circular response and integration.

Follett rejected the biological concept of unidirectional stimulus–response relationships as inapplicable in the human setting. Instead, she emphasized shared interaction.[2] Her notion of *circular response* suggested that no one unilaterally acts on someone else; rather, people interact with one another in ways that influence both parties. It was this view that caused her to reject the idea of power as a one-way street. Follett used the term *integration* to refer to the need to combine diverse elements into a useful whole. In some ways, this could be seen as simply a restatement of the old idea of division of labour, but Follett realized that integration was a dynamic concept and not simply the static arrangement of slots on an organizational chart. She understood that conflict would inevitably develop in any organization because of the existence of circular response and the informal organization.

It was, however, the particular genius of Follett's contribution that she recognized and held fast to the notion that the process of change that generates conflict also provides the opportunity for the further changes necessary to resolve that conflict. Each solution contains the seeds of new differences, but these differences also contain the seeds of new solutions. What they need is freedom to grow within a milieu of intelligent and sympathetic cultivation.[3] This latter point was a very important one for Follett. She frequently emphasized the significance of executives exercising leadership rather than wielding power. She felt that the way to motivate employees was through a rational appeal to a person's higher instincts rather than a reliance on fear or threats.

Roethlisberger and Dickson and the Hawthorne Experiments

The beginnings of the human relations school are usually traced to an experiment conducted with workers at the Hawthorne Works (near Chicago) of Western Electric in 1924. The idea was to test the impact of different levels of lighting on employee productivity. The experiments were organized and conducted by an industrial psychologist from Harvard, F.J. Roethlisberger, and a Western Electric management employee, William J. Dickson. They were later joined by another Harvard professor, Elton Mayo.[4]

The experimenters assumed that improving physical working conditions by increasing levels of lighting would increase productivity. The research was poorly designed and the results inconclusive. One problem the researchers encountered was that production tended to move erratically up or down without much regard to changes in the level of lighting. The experimenters had to discard their original hypothesis, because the ambiguity of the results indicated that the physical conditions surrounding work did not have the paramount influence assumed.

The Hawthorne experiment was followed by a series of experiments that tested the impact of many other changes in physical conditions in the workplace. Again, the results were ambiguous, so experimenters began to think about a characteristic of the experiments that they had not considered previously. In every case, the tests were conducted using a group of people who were selected from the workroom, moved to a special place, and singled out for a great deal of consideration from researchers. This led experimenters to focus on the *Hawthorne* or *sympathetic observer effect*—the idea that workers given special attention will experience an increase in morale, which will lead to greater productivity.

This finding has been criticized widely over the years.[5] Some critics have pointed to the poor design of the research, while others have argued that the research findings do not support the conclusions usually drawn from them. Nevertheless, the ideas flowing from the Hawthorne studies "are still widely regarded as the most extensive, systematic and exhaustive study of employees in an industrial setting ever conducted."[6]

Significantly, many of the variables introduced in these studies—employee morale, job satisfaction, informal group behaviour, employee participation and supervisory style—continue to be the focus of a great deal of contemporary organizational research. In the context of public administration, employee morale and job satisfaction in particular have been obvious areas of concern for the federal civil service, with surveys gauging employees' opinions on a range of issues from engagement to leadership to the workplace having been implemented every three years since 1999.[7]

Abraham Maslow's Hierarchy of Needs

Scientific management focused on the idea of monetary rewards as an incentive for good work performance. Maslow argued that this was too simplistic. He said that people are motivated by a hierarchy of five categories of needs ranging from physiological requirements to self-actualization. He believed that a person will first be motivated by a desire to satisfy the most basic physiological needs, but as these are satisfied, the person will strive to meet the next level of needs, and so on up the hierarchy. As an employee attains each succeeding level in the hierarchy, he or she will no longer be motivated by rewards directed at the more basic needs. As shown in Figure 4.1, the five levels in the **hierarchy of needs** are as follows:

1. Physiological needs—food, shelter, clothing, sex and sleep;
2. Safety—security, stability, freedom from fear;
3. Belongingness and love—friendship, love, membership in some community;
4. Esteem—achievement, competence, independence, prestige, status;
5. Self-actualization—self-fulfillment, attaining ultimate goals in life.[8]

Maslow's contention was that there is no "one best way" to motivate employees. Instead, management must be sensitive to the fact that workers have a variety of needs beyond the simple need for money. Thinking about employee needs such as self-esteem and self-actualization posed serious problems for managers who were accustomed to thinking in simple piecework terms.

A discussion of Maslow's complex theory of motivation appears in almost every management textbook, and it is the basis for most participative management philosophy. It also seems to strike a more responsive chord than the simpler, one-dimensional approach of the scientific management school. It agrees with the usual observation that different people, and even the same person, are motivated by different factors at different times.

Despite the widespread repetition of Maslow's ideas, contemporary scholars have taken issue with it. Some of the concepts (especially self-actualization) are poorly

hierarchy of needs
A concept developed by Abraham Maslow that suggests workers can be motivated by the satisfaction of a number of different needs ranging from basic shelter and food to self-actualization. As workers' lower-level needs are satisfied, they are motivated by desires to satisfy higher-level needs.

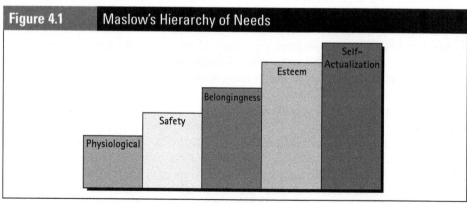

Figure 4.1   Maslow's Hierarchy of Needs

Source: Abraham H. Maslow, *Eupsychian Management* (Homewood, Ill.: Dorsey Press, 1965), 55–56.

Part Two / Theoretical Foundations

defined, and operationalizing the theory for the purpose of scientific testing has been challenging. Even Maslow himself had some reservations about these ideas, but they have been repeated so often that they have taken on a life of their own.[9]

Douglas McGregor's Theory X and Theory Y

Regardless of the caveats to Maslow's theory, McGregor built on his ideas and related them to the attitudes of individual managers.[10] He noted that some managers simply do not trust or respect their employees. He felt that this reflected a group of assumptions about human nature, which he called **Theory X**. This theory depicts people as seeking to do as little work as possible; they must be threatened and closely supervised to ensure that they will do the necessary work. Other managers, however, hold a more optimistic view of their subordinates, which can be captured in **Theory Y**. This theory claims that work is a natural activity—not something to be avoided—and that employees will be quite productive if given the opportunity to reach their potential. There is no need for controls and close supervision. Table 4.1 lists the assumptions underlying these two perspectives on human nature.

Theory X/Theory Y
Developed by Douglas McGregor to describe different managers' views of workers. Theory X holds that workers are basically lazy and need to be closely watched. Theory Y holds that workers are highly motivated and will voluntarily work hard.

McGregor's basic message was that employees react differently depending on how they are treated. If managers convey the impression that they believe their employees are Theory X types of workers, the workers will likely meet those expectations. Conversely, managers who treat employees in a Theory Y manner will likely be more successful. On the basis of their perception of workers, these managers will delegate responsibility, enlarge the duties of their employees, and nurture a more consultative style within the organization.

There are a number of similarities between Maslow's and McGregor's thinking. The most obvious is that they both have a very positive view of human nature. They argue that workers can be positively motivated without recourse to threats, but that this type of leadership requires a certain amount of understanding and sensitivity on the part of managers. Another major similarity is that both theories seem intuitively correct but are difficult to test empirically. In fact, neither has been widely tested, although they are widely discussed in the management literature.

Other Theories of Motivation: Argyris and Herzberg

Earlier ideas of motivation were rather simplistic. Bosses simply told workers what to do and they did it—or were fired. Traditional forms of motivation based on punishment have fallen into disuse for a number of reasons. The strength of unions and recent changes in labour laws to protect workers have reduced the unilateral power that employers once had to discipline employees. However, evidence indicates that motivation by fear of punishment is not very efficient anyway. Negative forms of motivation

TABLE 4.1	Theory X and Theory Y Assumptions
THEORY X	**THEORY Y**
Employees dislike work and will make every attempt to avoid it.	Employees see work as being as natural as rest or play.
Employees must be cajoled or threatened to get them to work.	Employees willingly perform work if committed to the objectives.
Employees will shirk responsibilities and must be told what to do.	Employees can learn to take on and even seek responsibility.
Most workers seek security above all and display little ambition.	The capacity to solve organizational problems is widely dispersed.

might well motivate employees to do just enough to avoid being disciplined. The result might be a continual game of employees trying to find out how much they can "get away with" before they are disciplined. This behaviour might then lead to management continually imposing new controls and restrictions as employees find ways of circumventing them. Positive methods of motivating people are probably much more effective.

Chris Argyris's maturity–immaturity theory represents one development in the attempt to better understand the significance of motivation in organizations. He points out that all social organizations are composed of individuals and a formal structure but that tensions inevitably develop because there is a basic incongruence between the behaviour pattern of mature individuals and the needs of the formal organization. He suggests that the characteristics of a mature individual are, among others, self-determination, increased independence, self-awareness, a longer-time perspective, and a deepening interest in stimulating challenges. He goes on to point out that formal organizations are based on such principles as task or work specialization, chain of command, unity of direction, and span of control.[11] Most of these principles require not mature but immature behaviour on the part of the individual employee. For example, mature individuals capable of complex behaviour and interested in challenges are placed in jobs that require boring, repetitive actions. In such scenarios, "organizations are willing to pay high wages and provide adequate seniority if mature adults will, for eight hours a day, behave in a less than mature manner!"[12]

It is quite rational for employees to react negatively when confronted with this situation. They might simply leave the organization. Or they might stay and become apathetic and/or establish an informal work group that has a detrimental effect on production. Or they might resolve to work their way up the organizational ladder because the incongruity between personality and organizational demands is less pronounced at the higher levels.

In a later work, Argyris presents some tentative suggestions for resolving this basic incongruity.[13] He suggests that organizations of the future will emphasize the pyramidal organizational structure less and recognize that there are other, less formal structures in place that are also important. He strongly supports a form of job enlargement that would ensure that employees develop a greater understanding of, and concern for, the activities of the entire organization, rather than only their narrow portion of it. This should be supplemented by employees meeting in small groups to discuss problems and possibilities for improvement. He argued that autocratic leadership styles should be replaced by situational approaches to leadership—different types of employees and situations call for different leadership styles. Control mechanisms should be oriented less toward detecting transgressions and more toward helping individuals achieve greater self-responsibility and psychological success."[14]

Frederick Herzberg is another scholar who has examined closely the importance and complexity of motivation in the workplace. Herzberg sought to test the conventional wisdom that the factors that cause satisfaction in the work environment are simply the reverse of those that cause dissatisfaction. Herzberg tested this assumption by asking a number of employees to describe work occurrences that led to satisfaction and dissatisfaction. In many cases, the factors causing satisfaction were very different from those causing dissatisfaction.[15] For example, a feeling of achievement tended to satisfy workers, but its absence did not make them dissatisfied; it simply reduced their satisfaction. Conversely, company policy and administration were a frequent source of dissatisfaction, but correcting problems in this area merely lessened dissatisfaction; it did not increase satisfaction.

Herzberg referred to the factors that led to dissatisfaction as "hygiene" factors, because "they act in a manner analogous to the principles of medical hygiene. Hygiene operates to remove health hazards from the environment of man. It is not curative; it is, rather, a preventive."[16] Herzberg labelled the factors that led to satisfaction "motivators," because they had a highly positive effect on people's feelings about their job. Figure 4.2 lists motivators and hygiene factors; it also shows how Herzberg's views differed from traditional ones on satisfaction and dissatisfaction.

Herzberg noted a very interesting difference between the hygiene and motivating factors. The hygiene factors all relate to the general work environment, while the motivating factors are all intrinsic to the nature of the job itself. The implications of Herzberg's theory for management are clear: The general work environment should be pleasant enough to avoid dissatisfaction, but any major improvements in motivation can be made only through changes in the nature of the job itself.

The theories of both Argyris and Herzberg focused on the ability to improve motivation through careful job design. However, two experts in job design, Richard Hackman and Greg Oldham, remind us that sometimes the problem is not with the nature of the job itself. They emphasize the need for proper selection and training techniques to ensure that there is a good fit between the person and the job.[17] As they noted, "When people are well matched with their jobs, it rarely is necessary to force, coerce, bribe, or trick them into working hard and trying to perform the job well. Instead, they try to do well because it is rewarding and satisfying to do so."[18]

However, the job itself must be reasonably attractive. A number of different approaches to improving job designs have been tried. "Job rotation" involves keeping the job descriptions for all positions the same, but shifting the people who fill the position. This could be done for only a half-day at a time or for a few weeks. It adds some variety to an employee's workday and may increase an employee's sense of accomplishment and responsibility if he or she knows how to do several jobs instead of just one. "Job enlargement" tries to relieve the boredom in a job by expanding the size of the job. Instead of spending all day simply examining and filing forms, an employee might also be responsible for working at a counter and helping members of the public fill out forms. Having broader responsibilities and being able to see more of the total process should increase an employee's sense of belonging and accomplishment. "Job enrichment," or "vertical job loading," is a variant of job enlargement proposed by

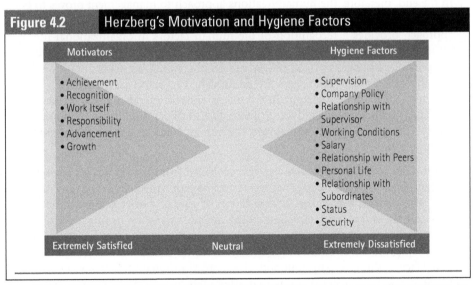

Figure 4.2   **Herzberg's Motivation and Hygiene Factors**

Motivators	Hygiene Factors
• Achievement	• Supervision
• Recognition	• Company Policy
• Work Itself	• Relationship with Supervisor
• Responsibility	• Working Conditions
• Advancement	• Salary
• Growth	• Relationship with Peers
	• Personal Life
	• Relationship with Subordinates
	• Status
	• Security
Extremely Satisfied	Neutral	Extremely Dissatisfied

Source: ROBBINS, STEPHEN P.; COULTER, MARY A., MANAGEMENT, 13th Ed., ©2016. Reprinted by permission of Pearson Education, Inc., New York, New York.

Hackman and Oldham, Argyris, and Herzberg, among many others. Herzberg, in particular, emphasized the importance of expanding jobs not just by arbitrarily adding more duties but by considering the needs of the mature employee. He pointed out the difference between "horizontal job loading," which means simply loading a person with more work, and vertical job loading, which means expanding the job through such means as eliminating controls, introducing more precise and demanding tasks, and setting out a specified area of work in which an employee is assigned new responsibilities.[19]

Criticisms of Organizational Humanism

There have been many criticisms of the philosophy of the human relations school. The most significant are based on the idea that the presumed community of interest between workers and management does not exist. Thus, the entire human relations concept is a method to manipulate employees to behave in the interests of management.

It is obviously in management's interest to extract as much work as possible from employees. This is the profit motive. However, it is in the employees' interest to restrict their output to what they can do in physical comfort. Employees are also aware that the amount of work to be done is usually finite and that their reward for working hard might be a layoff slip when the work is completed. When one views the workplace in this way, the cooperation treasured by the organizational humanists is somewhat elusive.

Critics charge that this is precisely the point where the theories developed by the organizational humanists become important. How does management convince workers to behave in the best interests of management rather than in their own best interests? The human relations response is to establish a feeling of caring and unity in the workplace that can then be used to manipulate employees. Critics like to point to one aspect of the work done at Hawthorne that involved hiring 300 employees to wander the factory floor and listen to complaints of other employees. Management never did anything about the complaints and never intended to do anything; the sole purpose of this action was to create the impression that management actually cared about workers and to maintain control of employees. As Denhardt noted:

> In the end, therefore, the human relations approach to management proves to be simply another technique for managerial control. Although the human relations approach provides a recognition of the human factors in organizational life, it ultimately treats these as just another set of inducements to be manipulated in the pursuit of managerial control. Where conflicts arise between the individual and the organization, managers are admonished to resort to their hierarchical authority. Ultimately, this approach remains simplistic and unfulfilling and, in any case, hardly leads toward a true alternative to the rational model of administration. Though appearing humanistic, the human relations approach may simply be more subtle.[20]

The human relations approach was also criticized from the opposite perspective by production-conscious managers. They were concerned that this school was too employee-centred. Their criticism was that in its rejection of scientific management, it tipped the balance too far in the other direction. Some derisively referred to human relations as "country club" management. Others suggested that for human relations, the "one best way" was employee satisfaction rather than concern for production.

In the face of this criticism from both sides, organizational humanism had to evolve. The next step was a cluster of ideas that attempted to meet both kinds of criticisms. These varying concepts can be loosely grouped under the heading of participatory management.

Participatory Management

Gradually it became accepted that there was an innate tension and conflict in the workplace. This tension could revolve around general issues such as rates of pay and speed of the production processes, or specific issues such as the attitude of a particular supervisor or the quality of food served in the lunchroom. Organizational humanism tried to cover over this tension by in effect bribing employees to accept management views. Participatory theories, on the other hand, held that the tension could be controlled and directed, but probably not totally eliminated, by allowing workers a real decision-making role in the workplace.

There are many approaches to **participatory management**. Peter Drucker is one of the early proponents of participatory management. His view of organizations stood Weber's views of bureaucracy on their head.[21] Drucker argued that the very characteristics that Weber saw as such powerful engines of efficiency—bureaucracy, hierarchical structures, and specialization—were in fact powerful forces for what he termed misdirection. Drucker felt that in large organizations managers and employees became too involved in their own specialty and had a tendency to emphasize this at the expense of the overall good of the organization. For example, if the purchasing department emphasizes buying at low prices rather than the high quality of the product or security of supply, the production department can suffer precisely because the purchasing department is doing its job well—at least, in the view of people in that department. Thus, it frequently happens that inefficiency and misdirection occur because of hierarchy and specialization of labour. The problem is the inability to focus on the overall organizational goal; the solution is a more participatory form of management that would allow managers to have a broader view of the organization and a clearer understanding of its overall goals. Two recent and important approaches to participatory management are discussed here—organization development and total quality management.

participatory management A style of management emphasizing the desirability of workers actually being involved in decision making.

Organization Development

Organization development (OD) is based on the idea that all organizations tend to become rigid or "frozen." While the organization remains rigid, the environment around the organization changes, and this has serious consequences. Usually, conditions gradually deteriorate until a serious crisis occurs, which causes either radical restructuring or even the collapse of the organization. The purpose of OD is to locate the barriers to change and to show the organization how to engage in planned, goal-directed change and not directionless evolution or radical revolution.

Organization development recognizes that all organizations have a history that creates an organizational culture.[22] In some cases this can be a good thing, but in many it is not. This history, or culture, develops as a result of the organization's past successes and failures. For example, when someone responds to a new proposal by saying, "We can't do that because we tried something like it ten years ago and it didn't work," history is at work. The fact that something similar was unsuccessful ten years earlier might or might not be relevant now, but in many cases this kind of argument will carry the day. When the culture or history of an organization has this kind of negative influence, it is referred to as "drag."

organization development (OD) A participative approach to management that emphasizes team development and allows members of the organization to work together to identify and correct problems.

Practitioners of OD warn that the patterns and procedures that create drag are merely symptoms of a more serious underlying problem in the organization's culture. It is pointless to change these patterns and procedures—merely the manifestations of the basic problems—without also changing the underlying culture. Such changes would meet strong resistance, and inappropriate new patterns could possibly be imposed on an unfriendly environment.

There are many practitioners of OD, and each has a slightly different approach. However, they share a belief in a general three-phase approach—unfreezing, moving or changing, and refreezing.[23] The unfreezing stage involves identifying current

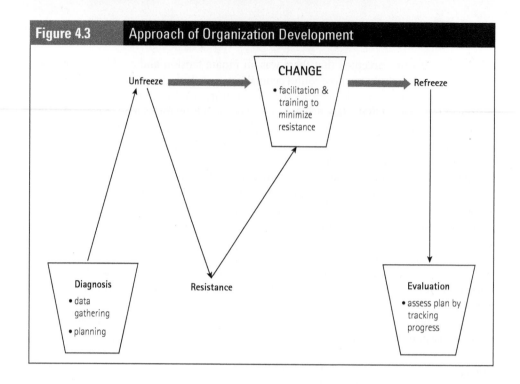

Figure 4.3   Approach of Organization Development

dysfunctional behaviour and helping the organization to "unlearn" that behaviour. In the second phase, the improvements needed are identified and implemented. The third stage involves refreezing the organization with its new behaviour in place so that the organization does not unconsciously revert to the old behaviour. Figure 4.3 offers a visual representation of the three stages.

Total Quality Management

Total quality management (TQM) was the next approach to participatory management. It was popularized in North America in the 1980s and early 1990s as a response to the Japanese system of management, and the focus was on the manufacturing sector. However, it is important to note that there was also a **service quality** stream to TQM that emerged out of the service sector in Europe and North America. Similarly, an emphasis on service excellence was a fundamental aspect of the new public management movement, a topic that will be explored more fully in the next chapter.

We begin by examining the ideas of the leading proponent of TQM—W. Edwards Deming.[24] Deming's work began before World War II in the United States with the development of statistical process control (SPC) to improve production quality. This involved using various statistical techniques to identify and correct deviations from the ideal quality production standard. After the war, he became disillusioned with the way American companies were using his philosophy, because they tended to view the statistical techniques as an end in themselves and did not incorporate thinking about quality into their overall management and organizational culture. When he was given the opportunity to teach his technique to Japanese business leaders after the war, he did not repeat this mistake. He emphasized to them that they must make quality the overall focus of their organizational culture.[25] The Japanese learned this lesson very well.

The basic difference between the American and the Japanese approach to quality can be illustrated by an example from the auto industry. The somewhat exaggerated stereotype suggests that the American auto industry focused on production rather than

total quality management (TQM) A style of participative management popularized in the 1980s and early 1990s. It requires changing an organization's culture to focus on establishing and maintaining high standards of quality, especially with respect to meeting customer expectations.

service quality This is a variation of TQM, which was adopted in the public sector beginning in the late 1980s. While TQM emerged from a manufacturing setting and focused on improving production systems, service quality is concerned with enhancing service and customer satisfaction.

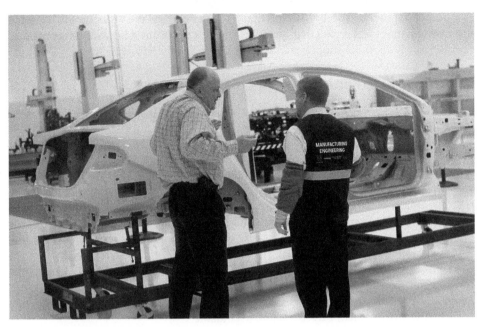

Total Quality Management

Scott Olson/Getty Images

quality. This meant producing the maximum number of cars and then employing a separate quality control group to detect and repair problems after the cars were built. The Japanese approach was to put less emphasis on the raw speed of construction and make every employee responsible for quality control of her or his aspect of the work. Thus, the cars took longer and cost more to build in the first place, but there was greater assurance that the job was done properly the first time and less expense involved in the later correction of errors. The guiding principle of TQM is "get it right the first time."[26]

The basic tenet of TQM is eliminating quality control as a separate function, instead making every employee responsible for quality and giving each a role in designing production processes to ensure maximum quality.[27] TQM has been defined this way:

> a broad-scale approach to changing an organization's entire culture to focus on establishing and maintaining high standards of quality, especially with respect to meeting "customer" expectations. The key of TQM is to serve the "customer," whether the "customer" is internal to the organization or someone outside.[28]

The important point of this definition is that TQM involves the creation of an entire organizational culture based on concern for both quality and production. Garvin and March explain it this way: "Contrary to conventional wisdom in the United States, quality and productivity were not to be traded off against each other. Rather, productivity was a by-product of quality and of doing the job right the first time."[29]

As with most new management processes, there are a number of different ways this technique can be implemented. One method of establishing TQM in the public sector focuses on three basic components:

1. working with suppliers to ensure that the supplies utilized in the work processes are designed for your use,
2. continuous employee analysis of work processes to improve their functioning and reduce process variation, and
3. close communication with customers to identify and understand what they want and how they define quality.[30]

Another important aspect of TQM is that it focuses on how the organization relates to its environment. It recognizes that quality is largely a function of how well the organization works with both its suppliers and customers in the larger environment.

Criticisms of the Participative Approach

One of the criticisms frequently levelled at the participative approaches is that they require a huge commitment of resources on the part of the organization. Another criticism is that these approaches are so disruptive that they can lead to rather lengthy periods of turmoil. The basic principle of the approach is that virtually all employees of the organization must become involved and, in some cases, for fairly lengthy periods. This level of participation imposes a heavy internal cost on the organization. Moreover, there is usually a psychological cost to the organization from undergoing this kind of radical surgery. Even though the actual organizational changes themselves can be planned in an incremental and minimally disruptive manner, the rumour mill that always works full time in these situations can hurt morale.

The obvious response to this criticism is that the end result is worth the short-term trauma, and this has often proven correct. However, given the cost and turmoil engendered in the short run, management's frequent reluctance to become fully involved in a participative management exercise is understandable.

Many of the criticisms of the concept of participative management echo those directed against the organizational humanists. There seems to be a lingering concern that the process is not really participative but is guided—or even manipulated—by management. "Frederick Taylor was satisfied if he could control the physical movements of the workers; OD wants their hearts, souls, and minds."[31] In a true hierarchical setting, those at the pinnacle of the hierarchy have authority over those at lower levels. Given this fact, is real participation possible?

Participative Management in the Public Sector

There is a particular set of problems with the use of participative management in the public sector. The most serious concern is whether a bottom-up participative approach to decision making is consistent with the principle of instilling final responsibility for activities of a department with the minister. A second concern arises when it is suggested that participation should extend beyond employees and allow clients who are affected by the agency to be involved in the decision-making process. Few would argue with the right of clients to have a voice in the consultation process. However, this must be limited because clients of a particular service constitute a special interest group whose perspective on an issue might be at odds with the broader public interest.

In practice, the concern for top-down accountability has often won out over bottom-up participation. At the risk of generalizing, it seems that few government agencies give more than lip service to participatory management. However, this does not preclude certain kinds of OD or TQM approaches that are geared more to operation of the agency than basic public policy decision making. Robert T. Golembiewski, a recognized expert on OD in the public sector, has argued that there are particular problems with the use of OD in the public sector, and that these problems result in a "lower batting average" in the success of OD in the public sector. Nonetheless, he arrives at the conclusion that "the 'lower batting average' is still pretty high."[32]

More Theoretical Developments

As noted in the previous chapter, there are a number of additional schools of organization theory that can be identified. While it is impractical to provide a comprehensive assessment of the various contributions that have been made by scholars writing from each of these frameworks, in the remainder of the chapter we will touch on a few of key thinkers from the "modern" structural (specifically contingency theory), organization and environment (specifically systems theory), and power and politics schools of organization theory.

Many of these new approaches represented significant improvements in organization theory, and they often constituted a continuation of the attack against mechanist thinking in organizational behaviour. But that was not always the case. Structuralist approaches to the study of organizations did not completely fall out of favour. The "modern" structuralist theorists, who wrote in the latter part of the twentieth century, held similar tenets about organizations to those that underpinned the classical school, but they were also heavily influenced by the neo-classical, human relations, and systems theorists of organizations. Elliott Jaques, for example, wrote a seminal article in the *Harvard Business Review* in 1990 where he praised organizational hierarchy. He believed that hierarchies were the only way for organizations to employ large numbers of people and to hold them accountable for their work. In his view, if properly structured, "hierarchy can release energy and creativity, rationalize productivity and actually improve morale."[33] Moreover, contingency theory, considered in more detail below, recognized that various contingencies, such as size, technology, and environmental stability, were relevant in determining how to structure an organization.

Systems theory, part of the organization and environment school, began to dominate organizational theory in mid-to-late 1960s. Some sociologists and social psychologists such as Robert Merton, Talcott Parsons, Daniel Katz, and Robert L. Kahn became disenchanted with the earlier organizational theories because they put too much emphasis on activities of individuals within organizations and on the activities of the organization as a monolithic body, without consideration of the environment within which the organization operated. They criticized this kind of thinking as the "closed system" approach, because, in their eyes, it considered the organization only as a closed system and not as a part of its environment. For example, both Weber and Taylor, in their work, assumed incorrectly that the organization's environment was "regulated and stabilized in such a way that one [could], analytically, ignore the environment when describing, dissecting, and manipulating the system."[34] For systems theorists, organizations had to be viewed as adaptive systems, constantly responding to and affecting their environments.

Another new school of thought was the power school. The power school of theorists also views organizations not necessarily as rational institutions but as complex systems, wherein individuals and coalitions, all with their own interests, values, preferences, and perspectives, are in constant competition for scarce organizational resources. This inevitably leads to conflict. Individuals and groups, therefore, will endeavour to achieve their organizational objectives by deploying various sources of power—personal, positional and relational—in order to influence others. To understand organizations, "one needs to understand organizational politics, just as to understand government, one needs to understand governmental politics."[35]

Katz and Kahn's Open Systems Approach

Followers of **open systems theory** were influenced by biological models that dealt with both the internal organization of organisms and how they interacted with their environment.[36] Natural scientists adopted this approach by thinking in terms of inputs–throughputs–outputs–feedback. To continue to exist, any organism must receive certain inputs from its environment. It then converts these to outputs that, through feedback, help it to attain more inputs. In the case of simple, one-cell organisms, this means capturing some nourishment and converting it to energy, which it uses to move about to

open systems theory An approach to the study of organizations that emphasizes that organizations are a part of, and must interact with, their environment.

capture more nourishment. Human beings operate on the same principle, only with a more complex interaction system. They need nourishment, shelter, and psychic encouragement, which they convert to work effort that can be sold for cash or traded to satisfy such needs as food, shelter, and psychic encouragement.

The open systems theorists felt that organizations could be approached in the same manner (see Figure 4.4). Organizations need inputs in the form of labour power, raw materials, and so forth. These are then converted to finished products or outputs, which are sold for cash so that more inputs can be purchased. Not-for-profit organizations do not follow exactly the same cycle in that their products are usually not sold, but they still must produce an acceptable level of output so that some organization, such as a government, will provide inputs to them. Katz and Kahn argued that successful organizations arrange the input–throughput–output process so as to reverse the normal entropy to which living organisms are subject. Entropy is the process through which organisms are subject to deterioration. In complex physical systems, as the system becomes larger, the individual parts of the system become more disorganized until they are no longer able to sustain the organization as a whole. At this point, the system perishes.

A successful organization overcomes this process by developing negative entropy, which is the process of importing and storing more energy than it expends. This allows the organization to expand and to survive in difficult times by drawing on the stored reserve.[37] This stored reserve could take several forms. An obvious one is cash and other hard assets, but some other forms of stored energy could be the trust and goodwill of important people or a high-quality management team.

The crucial lesson for managers in open systems theory is that all organizations are a part of their environments. Earlier thinkers such as Frederick Taylor and, to a lesser extent, the organizational humanists attempted to see the organization as a closed system unaffected by its environment. The open system concept reminds managers that, in addition to managing the internal aspects of their organization, they must also be sensitive to the rapidly changing environment that affects such things as the acceptance of their product, their relationship with their clientele, the regulatory framework imposed by government (for private firms), and the attitudes of their employees.

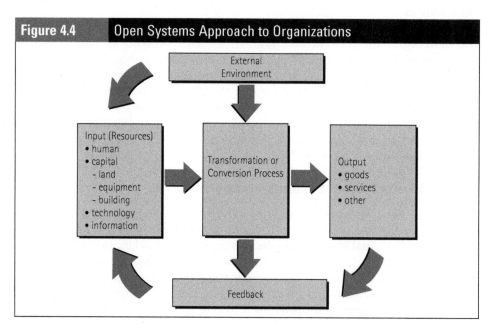

Figure 4.4 Open Systems Approach to Organizations

Contingency Theory

Contingency theory, an example of the "modern" structural organization theories, was first developed in a systematic fashion in the 1960s. Its basic premise is "there is no one best way to organize," but "any way of organizing is not equally effective."[38] Instead, contingency theory suggests that the best way to structure an organization is contingent on a number of factors affecting the organization. The most commonly cited factors are "the task environment of the organization, the technology used within the organization, and the organization's size."[39] The task environment of an organization consists of its clients or customers, competitors, suppliers, regulatory agencies, and, in the case of public organizations, the legislature that established them and provides their funding. Some organizations face a task environment that is uncertain and rapidly changing. These organizations must be very flexible and able to change as rapidly as their environment. Other task environments are considerably more stable and organizations operating in them can become a little complacent.

Technology refers to *the process by which an organization converts inputs into outputs.*[40] In a manufacturing environment, this is the assembly line or other mechanism used to produce the finished product. However, service organizations and even organizations producing such ephemeral products as "policy advice" also have production processes. Where a technology is very routine and repetitive, such as an assembly line, the organization can have a very broad span of control because problems are not likely to occur, and when they do, there is usually a prearranged solution. Where the production process is less highly specified, such as in a policy advice unit, the span of control must be considerably smaller, because each new task is different from previous tasks and superiors and subordinates must work closely together.

The size of the organization also has an impact on its organizational structure. In very small organizations, the chief executive is in daily contact with all her or his subordinates and everyone understands by tradition what is to be done. As organizations become larger, layers of hierarchy are established, and written job descriptions and standard operating procedures are required to delineate responsibilities.

One of the strengths of contingency theory is that, unlike many of the other theories that have been discussed, it is a dynamic approach to organization. Managers must be aware that there is no "one best way" to organize their operation. The structure that was highly successful last year might be a dismal failure with the changed conditions. The need to adjust to the rapidly changing environment is a challenge to all modern organizations.

French and Raven and the Major Types of Power

If politics is essentially the authoritative allocation of values or scarce resources or a mechanism for determining who gets what, when and how,[41] then it should not be difficult to recognize that politics is fundamentally about power. Therefore, just as organization theorists have recognized that power, politics, and influence are integral to understanding organizational life, so too has political science and public administration been preoccupied with the concept of power and its application.[42]

John French and Bertram Raven were American social psychologists, whose 1959 publication outlined what would become the standard classification of the various sources of power.[43] Their work identified five bases or sources of social power available to individuals in order to exert social influence on another person. The first type was **reward power**. Those who possess reward power have the ability to mediate rewards for others, either by administering positive outcomes (such as increasing rates of pay, providing time off in lieu of pay, or providing a bonus) or by removing or decreasing negative perceptions associated with the job (for example, removing boring or repetitive

reward power Individuals who possess this type of power are able to provide some type of tangible or intangible reward (such as better pay, time off, or bonuses) to influence the behaviour of others.

coercive power Individuals who possess this type of power are able to influence the behaviour of others either through punishment or the threat of punishment for non-compliance.

legitimate power Also known as positional power, individuals with this form of power are able to influence the behaviour of others based on their formal position within the organization's hierarchy of authority.

referent power Individuals who possess referent power are able to influence the behaviour of others because those followers admire and respect the power wielder. Followers aspire to be like this person and have a need to gain his or her approval.

expert power Individuals who have specialized knowledge or expertise can exert expert power over those who do not.

tasks from the person's job). **Coercive power** is similar to reward power, but rather than the expectation of rewards for accepting the influence attempt, individuals are motivated by the threat of punishment for non-compliance. This might involve being assigned less desirable shifts or duties when working or being demoted, while the ultimate punishment would be termination of employment. When **legitimate power** is deployed, individuals acquiesce to the demands of another because they believe that this person has a legitimate right to do so. This is typically associated with the position that a person occupies in the organizational hierarchy or when the individual has been delegated authority by a legitimating authority (as would be the case with power that has been granted by a CEO to a department head in a certain area). **Referent power** is based on an individual's identification with and fondness for the other person, which is reinforced by his or her desire to be like that person. It is perhaps most easily recognized in charismatic individuals, who possesses effective interpersonal skills and are likable; these characteristics generate loyalty, commitment, and excitement among staff members who are eager to win the charismatic person's approval. Finally, **expert power** derives from the perception that the individual in question has some specialized knowledge or expertise. This power might originate with formal educational qualifications and training (for example, a lawyer who has completed a law degree and has been admitted to the bar or someone with a graduate degree in a particular area) or a proven track record of success. In this latter instance, an individual who is perennially the top sales person at the company would be afforded expert power and would have the ability to influence his or her colleagues on issues related to the sale of its products.

Not all sources of power, however, are equally effective. While coercive power can be useful and necessary in certain situations, it typically leads to decreased attraction and increased resistance by those being coerced. Legitimate power can be fleeting; people are influenced by the position, not the person, so if that position or title is lost then the legitimate power can instantly disappear. Reward power is often limited by virtue of the fact that the manager is not able to confer pay raises, promotions, or other desirable perquisites to the targets of his or her influence. The most effective leaders are those who rely primarily on referent and expert power. Employee performance will be maximized when they believe that their organizational leaders have expertise and they are drawn to them because of their charisma or other attractive personal characteristics.

Rosabeth Moss Kanter on Power Failure

Harvard Business School professor, Rosabeth Moss Kanter, began her classic essay on power by noting it was a dirty word—that people generally find it easier to talk about money and sex than about power.[44] She argued that power can be both productive and oppressive. In other words, power can help leaders mobilize resources, both human and material, towards the achievement of organizational goals. But it can also be oppressive when those who have formal positional power but are lacking in the other more important forms of power deliberately hold others back and punish by whatever means possible.

Those who possess power have open channels to supplies, information, and support, while those who are powerless are not able to leverage these resources. She identified three groups of employees where powerlessness often prevails: first-line supervisors, who are largely in dead-end positions forced to administer programs and explain policies that they have had no role in creating; staff professionals, who are marginalized both by the peripheral role that they play in terms of the day-to-day functioning of the organization and their lack of career mobility because of their job specialization; and somewhat surprisingly, top executives, who can frequently exhibit powerlessness due to environmental forces beyond their control and because they often get mired in solving routine problems. The challenge for these senior leaders is to insulate themselves from routine operations without compromising their access to information.

Kanter argued that powerlessness in those positions was dangerous for organizations: "Powerlessness...tends to breed bossiness rather than leadership. In large organizations...it is powerlessness that often creates ineffective, desultory management and petty, dictatorial, rules-minded managerial styles."[45] Her prescription was to expand organizational power, which could be achieved by sharing it with others. Moreover, when organizations were being restructured or new programs and policies were being implemented, managers were advised to do so in a way that either prevented or eliminated groups of employees who were powerless. The concern was that those who had been disempowered would provide resistance to the desired change.

Application of Organization Theory to the Public Sector: The Canadian Experience

In the previous chapter, the status of scientific management in the federal government was considered. In this chapter, many other styles of management have been discussed, but there has been very little comment on their impact on Canadian governments. The reason is quite simple: they seem to have had little impact, at least when these theories rose to prominence in the late 1960s.[46] But it would be unfair to say that absolutely nothing of the organizational humanist school filtered into the Canadian public sector. Since the human relations school is, in large part, a prescription for changes in the actions of individual managers, it is likely that certain managers followed the advice of the organizational humanists without any system-wide documentation of the practice. But it is correct to conclude that overall its influence was minimal. Throughout the time of the organizational humanists, Canadian governments continued to exhibit rigid hierarchies, inflexible job classification structures, and the other trappings of scientific management.

When the participatory style of management came into full flower, it found easier acceptance. Many government organizations in Canada have espoused the Total Quality Management (TQM) concept or similar participatory approaches under a variety of different names.[47] TQM thinking, particularly with respect to the service quality stream of the movement, underlay much of the federal government's PS2000 program in the late 1980s and similar initiatives in several provinces.[48] Although the influence of TQM has been waning in management circles since the 1990s, its influence on the federal public sector has been unmistakable.[49] Since the 1990s, government departments have been establishing and reporting on specific service standards for things like the time it takes to respond to electronic and/or written communication from citizens, how long it should take to answer the phone, the amount of time that citizens should wait in line before being served by a frontline public servant, or the speed with which a passport should be delivered to a citizen who applied either through the mail or at a regional Passport Office. Public servants have received customer service training, and many government departments have implemented customer-friendly policies and procedures to simplify forms and make it easier for citizens to access government services. Furthermore, governments have embraced the use of technology to enhance service delivery. This includes the initial move for government departments to have an online presence where citizens can passively access information about more recent initiatives, which allow them to complete transactions online to pay fines, change contact information, or file a tax return.

One of the most recent and important government innovations pertaining to service quality was the establishment of Service Canada, part of the Employment and Social Development Canada portfolio, in September 2005.[50] It was part of a broader government-wide transformation initiative designed to simplify service delivery by providing Canadian citizens—whether in person (with more than 600 locations across the country and an additional 200 points of service through scheduled and mobile outreach services), by phone, or online—with a single point of access for a range of government services, programs, and benefits. This model of government service delivery has proven to be very popular with similar approaches being adopted at the provincial (for example, Service Ontario or Service New Brunswick) and local (Service Guelph) levels.

But the other organization theories covered in this chapter have also had an impact on the federal government. For instance, the language of "systems" is very much a part of the lexicon of political science and public administration. On one level we can refer to our three branches of government—the executive, legislative and judicial—and how they interact as part of the Canadian political system, which comprises various political institutions, political conventions, and traditions. Moreover, it is possible to think about our political system as consisting of a variety of subsystems. Adopting that approach, it is possible to examine specific government departments to ascertain their inputs, conversion process (throughputs), outputs, and feedback and to determine how those particular organizations change and adapt to their environment.

It is also possible to use a systems approach when examining crosscutting elements of the government. Two obvious examples come to mind. First, over the past half century, the government has implemented an expenditure management system; and second, government policies have been the product of a policy-making system. In the case of the former, the Canadian expenditure management system has evolved over time in response to the recommendations of both the 1962 Royal Commission on Government Organization (Glassco Commission) and the 1979 Royal Commission on Financial Management and Accountability (Lambert Commission), while additional changes were introduced to suit the specific needs of different prime ministers (such as the Program, Planning Budgeting System (PPBS), the Policy Expenditure Management System (PEMS), and the Expenditure Management System (EMS), variations of which have been adopted by the Chrétien, Martin, and Harper governments. In the case of the latter, a systems framework can be applied to the formulation of public policies. That is to say, the public policy-making system relies on a number of inputs (e.g., demands from the public or interest groups, and resources) and converts those inputs in the policy formulation, decision-making, and policy implementation stages into various outputs (i.e., public goods and services). Those public goods and services (outputs) can then be evaluated and are subject to feedback from their recipients (and other members of the interested public) so that a decision can be made to either continue, amend, or terminate the policy.

Finally, with respect to power and politics organization theory, a common way of conceiving the relationship between elected officials and public servants is as one of a struggle over power and influence in the policy-making process.[51] Therefore, it is not simply a question of public servants loyally implementing the policy preferences of their political masters; rather, public servants often have their own ideas and preferences (a so-called agency ideology) about the kinds of policies that the government should be pursuing. These ideas may diverge from those of the politicians, resulting in tension between the two groups of actors. But both politicians and public servants have a number of resources as well as ploys and strategies that can be utilized to gain an advantage—and, thus, effective political power—over the other. For the public servants, access to information and technical expertise are their key resources. However, the bureaucracy also has the ability to make decisions more quickly in many instances than the legislature does and it certainly enjoys more permanence and stability, so public servants can often delay decision making in the hope that either their minister or the government changes. The greatest advantage that the politicians have is legitimacy; these individuals were elected by the citizenry to govern on their behalf. In addition, they determine the level of autonomy granted to public agencies and possess the power of the purse; they control the financial resources upon which those public agencies depend for their survival and growth. As will be discussed in the next chapter, one of the core elements of the new public management reform initiative was to enable politicians to reassert their power over the bureaucracy by limiting the role of public servants in the policy-making process.

Points to Know

- The human relations theorists had a very different conception of individuals and organizations than did the earlier structuralists (examined in the previous chapter). For the humanists, employees were as important as the organization; they were perceived as co-dependent and, as such, needed each other.

- While the Hawthorne experiments were designed to advance the scientific management approach of enhancing worker productivity by altering the physical work environment, the results revealed instead that when workers are given special attention their morale increases, as does their productivity. This came to be known as the Hawthorne effect.

- Maslow recognized that a range of factors, not just financial reward, motivate human behaviour from our most basic needs for sex, food, and shelter to self-actualization.

- Human relations theorists were critiqued for both focusing too much on the needs of employees and for simply providing new ways to managers to manipulate their employees to pursue organizational objectives.

- Open systems theory, which moved away from seeing organizations as closed entities by examining the impact of the external environment, has provided a useful framework for understanding organizations and the policy-making process.

- It is impossible to divorce the study of organizations from the concepts of power and politics. The accomplishment of organizational goals requires leaders who are adept at utilizing power and influence.

- Although it may have been challenging to ascertain how the human relations school of organization theory initially had an impact on Canadian public administration, many recent administrative reforms have been inspired by the insights derived from this body of literature.

Review Questions

1. What are the various key tenets or assumptions of the human relations organization theorists? How do they differ from those of the structuralist school that we examined in the previous chapter?

2. The Hawthorne experiments were initially conceived as a way of providing further support to the scientific management approach of analyzing organizations. However, the results of those experiments were unexpected and turned organization theory on its head. How was that the case?

3. Describe how Maslow's hierarchy of needs led to a new understanding of employee motivation in the workplace.

4. McGregor argued that the way in which a manager regarded and treated his or her employees would impact their performance. Outline his theory of management.

5. Despite having a very positive image of the employee in the workplace, the human relations school of organization theory has faced a barrage of criticism. What is the substance of those critiques?

6. What impact did organizational humanism have on the Canadian federal government and public administration?

Notes

1. Jay M. Shafritz and J. Steven Ott, eds., *Classics of Organization Theory*, 5th ed. (Toronto: Harcourt College Publishers, 2001), 146.
2. Mary Parker Follett, *Creative Experience* (New York: Peter Smith, 1951), ch. 3; Mary Parker Follett, *The New State* (Gloucester, Mass.: Peter Smith, 1965), 25–26.
3. Mary Parker Follett, *Dynamic Administration: The Collected Papers of Mary Parker Follett*, eds. Elliot M. Fox and L. Urwick (London: Pitman, 1973), xxv.
4. Their work is described in great detail in Roethlisberger and Dickson's book, *Management and the Worker* (Cambridge, Mass.: Harvard University Press, 1964).
5. Two of the more trenchant critics are Charles Perrow, *Complex Organizations: A Critical Essay* (Glenview, Ill.: Scott, Foresman, 1972), 97–106; and Amitai Etzioni, *Modern Organizations* (Englewood Cliffs, N.J.: Prentice-Hall, 1964), 39–49. A good overview of many of the critical articles can be found in Michael M. Harmon and Richard T. Mayer, *Organization Theory for Public Administration* (Boston: Little, Brown, 1986), 96–102.
6. Jonathan R. Tompkins, *Organization Theory and Public Management* (Belmont, CA: Thomson Wadsworth, 2005), 173.
7. The latest survey of public service employees was conducted in 2014. See Office of the Chief Human Resources Officer, *2014 Public Service Employee Survey: Summary Report* (Ottawa: Her Majesty the Queen in Right of Canada, February 2015), accessed August 6, 2016, www.tbs-sct.gc.ca/psm-fpfm/modernizing-modernisation/pses-saff/dr-rd-eng.pdf.
8. Abraham H. Maslow, *Motivation and Personality* (New York: Harper & Row, 1970), ch. 4.
9. Abraham H. Maslow, *Eupsychian Management* (Homewood, Ill.: Dorsey Press, 1965), 55–56.
10. Douglas McGregor, *The Human Side of Enterprise* (New York: McGraw-Hill, 1960), chs. 3 and 4 and passim.
11. Chris Argyris, *Personality and Organization: The Conflict Between System and the Individual* (New York: Harper & Row, 1957), 50–51 and ch. 3.
12. Ibid., 66.
13. Chris Argyris, *Integrating the Individual and the Organization* (New York: John Wiley & Sons, 1964).

14. Ibid., 275.

15. The results of this research were reported in detail in Frederick Herzberg, Bernard Mausner, and Barbara Bloch Snyderman, *The Motivation to Work* (New York: John Wiley & Sons, 1959). A more elaborate discussion and further verification of the theory are contained in Frederick Herzberg, *Work and the Nature of Man* (Cleveland: The World Publishing Company, 1966).

16. Herzberg et al., *The Motivation to Work*, 113.

17. J. Richard Hackman and Greg R. Oldham, *Work Redesign* (Reading, Mass.: Addison-Wesley, 1980), ch. 2.

18. Ibid., 71.

19. Frederick Herzberg, "One More Time: How Do You Motivate Employees?" *Harvard Business Review* 46 (January/February 1968): 59–62.

20. Robert B. Denhardt, *Theories of Public Organization* (Pacific Grove, CA.: Brooks/Cole, 1984), 97.

21. Peter F. Drucker, *The Practice of Management* (New York: Harper & Row, 1954).

22. A good, complete discussion of the concept of organizational culture is found in Florence Heffron, *Organization Theory and Public Organizations* (Englewood Cliffs, N.J.: Prentice-Hall, 1989), ch. 7.

23. This terminology was first used by one of the founders of organization development, Kurt Lewin, in "Frontiers in Group Dynamics," *Human Relations* 1(1) (1947): 34.

24. Deming's simultaneously insightful and folksy approach to management improvement is well illustrated in his major work, *Quality, Productivity, and Competitive Position* (Cambridge, Mass.: Massachusetts Institute of Technology, Center for Advanced Engineering Study, 1982).

25. Marshall Sashkin and Kenneth J. Kiser, *Putting Total Quality Management to Work* (San Francisco: Berrett-Koehler Publishers, 1993), ch. 1.

26. Joseph R. Jablonski, *Implementing Total Quality Management: An Overview* (San Diego: Pfeiffer & Company, 1991), 7.

27. Armand V. Feigenbaum, "Linking Quality Processes to International Leadership," in *Making Total Quality Happen*, ed. Frank Caropreso (New York: The Conference Board, 1990), 4.

28. Denhardt, *Public Administration: An Action Orientation* (Pacific Groves, CA.: Brooks/Cole Publishing Company, 1991), 316.

29. David A. Garvin and Artemis March, "A Note on Quality: The Views of Deming, Juran, and Crosby," in *Unconditional Quality* (Boston, Mass.: Harvard Business School Press, 1991), 18. For a more complete discussion of this issue, see Deming, *Quality, Productivity, and Competitive Position*, ch. 1.

30. Steven Cohen and Ronald Brand, *Total Quality Management in Government* (San Francisco: Jossey-Bass Publishers, 1993), 18.

31. Heffron, *Organization Theory and Public Organizations*, 161.

32. Robert T. Golembiewski, *Humanizing Public Organizations* (Mt. Airy, Md.: Lomond Press, 1985), 61.

33. Elliott Jaques, "In Praise of Hierarchy," *Harvard Business Review* 68(1) (January–February 1990): 127.

34. Michael M. Harmon and Richard T. Mayer, *Organization Theory for Public Administration* (Boston, Mass.: Little, Brown, 1986), 162.

35. Jeffrey Pfeffer, *Managing with Power: Politics and Influence in Organizations* (Boston, Mass.: Harvard Business School Press, 1994), 8, 36.

36. One of the best discussions of the open systems is Saeed Rahnema, *Organization Structure: A Systemic Approach* (Toronto: McGraw-Hill Ryerson, 1992).

37. Daniel Katz and Robert L. Kahn, *The Social Psychology of Organizations* (New York: John Wiley & Sons, 1966), ch. 2.

38. Jay Galbraith, *Designing Complex Organizations* (Reading, Mass.: Addison-Wesley, 1973), 2.

39. Daniel Robey, *Designing Organizations*, 3rd ed. (Homewood, Ill.: Richard D. Irwin, 1990), 26. See also Rahnema, *Organization Structure: A Systemic Approach*.

40. Robey, *Designing Organizations*, 28. Emphasis in original.

41. We are referring to the classic definitions of politics provided by David Easton, *A Framework for Political Analysis* (Englewood Cliffs, NJ: Prentice-Hall, 1965) and Harold Lasswell, *Politics: Who Gets What, When and How* (New York: McGraw-Hill, 1936).

42. See, for example, Donald Savoie, *Power: Where Is It?* (Montreal and Kingston: McGill-Queen's University Press, 2010).

43. John French and Bertram Raven, "The Bases of Social Power," in *Studies in Social Power*, ed. Dorwin Cartwright (Ann Arbor, MI: The University of Michigan, 1959), 150–167.

44. Rosabeth Moss Kanter, "Power Failure in Management Circuits," *Harvard Business Review* 57(4) (July–August 1979): 65.

45. Ibid.

46. V. Seymour Wilson, "The Influence of Organization Theory in Canadian Public Administration," *Canadian Public Administration* 25 (Winter 1982): 553–554.

47. Denis Martin, "Culture and Client Service at the Department of Fisheries and Oceans," *Optimum* 24 (Winter 1993): 99–104; Tom Rankin and Archie Gardner, "New Forms of Work Organization in the Federal Public Service: The Case of CFB Shearwater/UNDE Local 80409," *Optimum* 24 (Spring 1994): 25–36.

48. Brian Marson, "Building Customer-Focused Organizations in British Columbia," *Public Administration Quarterly* 17(1) (Spring 1993): 30–41.

49. See, for example, Kenneth Kernaghan, Brian Marson, and Sandford Borins, *The New Public Organization* (Toronto: IPAC, 2000), ch. 6, for a detailed discussion of how service quality has been embraced in the federal government.

50. Maryantonett Flumian, Amanda Coe, and Kenneth Kernaghan, "Transforming Service to Canadians: The Service Canada Model," *International Review of Administrative Sciences* 73(4) (December 2007): 557–568.

51. See B. Guy Peters, *The Politics of Bureaucracy: An Introduction to Comparative Public Administration*, 6th ed. (New York: Routledge, 2010), ch. 6.

Public Administration and Organization Theory: The New Public Management, Governance, and Beyond

5

Learning Objectives

Reading this chapter allows you to do the following:

- Identify the reasons why NPM became the prevailing administrative paradigm in the 1980s
- Outline the key elements of the NPM paradigm and how this represented a shift from traditional public administration
- Describe the Canadian approach to NPM and assess how it differed from other Western industrialized democracies
- Differentiate other reform initiatives—governance, new public service, new public governance, and digital era governance—from the NPM
- Assess the continuing relevance of NPM

In the 1970s governments in many of the Western democracies appeared to be living beyond their means as public spending began to outstrip available public revenues. At the same time, the confidence of the public in the effectiveness and value of public services was declining; it seemed that many citizens believed that government policies and programs failed in their many purposes and fell short of the level of quality expected of public agencies. The advent of a globalizing world also translated into a belief that national governments had to be that much more effective in order to compete with other nations in a world that was becoming smaller and smaller. There was as well an uneasy feeling among those close to government that public servants exercised too much influence in making policy. Elected officials, not appointed ones, were supposed to take the lead in formulating government initiatives.

All of these forces created a greater sense of urgency for new thinking about government and its organizations and eventually helped give birth to a new theoretical perspective on organizations called the **new public management (NPM)**. As with the theories of bureaucracy, scientific management and humanism, this new theory sought to provide a sound description and explanation of the behaviour of organizational forms. It also delved into the normative issue of how organizations should be structured for the purpose of achieving effectiveness. But it differed from the preceding theories because it focused mostly on organizations in government. Excessive government spending, declining faith in public programs, the spectre of globalization, and concerns of excessive bureaucratic power supplied fertile ground for a theoretical view centred on the public sector and its shortcomings. The theoretical thrust of NPM was that public bureaucracies had to become less rule-bound and more inclined toward participating in a competitive environment in which government employees would be given a great deal

new public management (NPM) A style of management that borrows heavily from private sector principles and focuses on values like customer service, flexibility in delivery, entrepreneurship, and empowerment.

more autonomy and flexibility. NPM also looked to a more strict division of responsibilities, whereby elected officials looked after policy and appointed officials tended to the implementation and management of public policies. With this orientation, NPM amounted to an attack on the structural or mechanist foundations of organization theory in public administration. NPM was more kind to its immediate theoretical predecessor; it borrowed quite liberally from the ideas of the humanistic perspective. If fact, in some respects NPM was just another aspect or element of the school of participatory management. However, it went beyond humanism in its attempt to locate a more theoretically sound perspective on organizations and their operation in the public sector.

Despite the pervasive influence and widespread endorsement of NPM, which eventually became a truly global reform movement embraced by developed and developing states alike,[1] critical voices began to emerge in the mid-to-late 1990s questioning everything from its applicability beyond a narrow set of countries to a lack of quantifiable outcomes to the emergence of a series of unintended consequences, the latter of which posed a number of serious new challenges for public administration. However, there is disagreement as to whether NPM has been supplanted by a new public administration paradigm and, if so, what exactly has emerged in its stead. For some, the post-NPM reform era is characterized by the shift to the term **governance** (or sometimes the term "networked governance" is used), which is the notion that governments can no longer act alone to provide public services but rather depend on networks and partnerships with other state (i.e., other levels of government—local, provincial, and supra-national) and non-state (i.e., private sector and nonprofit organizations) actors. However, making sense of the post-NPM reform era is further muddied by virtue of the fact that several narrower administrative reform paradigms have been proposed.

In this chapter, we examine the theoretical tenets of the NPM and some of the key contributions to the development of this theory. The chapter also summarizes the elements of NPM in an attempt to bring together the common threads in the relevant writings, and looks at the criticisms directed at this theory of government organization and behaviour. We then consider some of the significant post-NPM administrative reform paradigms that have been articulated. Finally, the chapter reviews the application of NPM and governance in Canada and speculates on the future of organization theory in public administration.

governance A broad category of public administration theories dealing with the distribution and exercise of authority, decision making, and accountability. More specifically, it recognizes that the state is no longer solely responsible for these processes, but rather they are shared with a variety of state and non-state actors.

Theoretical Foundations of New Public Management

In practice, the NPM movement can be traced back to the late 1970s and early 1980s, beginning with a series of administrative reforms that were initiated by Prime Minister Margaret Thatcher of the United Kingdom. This prescription for changing the way that government operated was quickly followed by governments in the US (initially at the local level), New Zealand, and Australia, spreading to most OECD (Organization for Economic Co-operation and Development) countries and other states shortly thereafter. However, it would be about a decade after these reforms were first implemented that they were grouped under the label "new public management."[2]

Intellectually, there is general consensus that NPM has its origins in two separate traditions: **public choice theory** and **managerialism**.[3] In their application, however, these theoretical underpinnings of NPM do not always receive equal attention. In some countries, public choice theory has been emphasized and the result has been reforms consistent with this theoretical perspective. In other countries, such as Canada, managerialism has mostly been the inspiration for efforts at reforming the public sector. But what exactly do these theoretical developments in the behavioural-administrative sciences mean for public administration?

public choice theory The use of economic principles to analyze political activity. It suggests that people take political action to further their self-interest.

managerialism A theoretical perspective on organization that emphasizes setting clear organizational goals and giving employees the flexibility and autonomy to pursue these goals.

In the case of public choice theory, one of the propositions about the nature and operation of organizations is the claim that "career public servants are not primarily motivated by the public interest in good government but by the promotion of their own individual or collective self-interests."[4] More subtle versions of the proposition contend that appointed officials still focus on the public interest but seek to provide their own interpretations of it. However, in all instances the government bureaucrat can be likened to the rational or self-seeking consumer depicted in economic theory, eager to satisfy his or her preferences in the most economical way. Some companion claims to this basic belief include the assertion that the self-interests of appointed officials or their perceptions of the public interest may clash with those of elected officials. For instance, the latter may want to cut spending in response to the wishes of the electorate, but the interest of bureaucrats in maximizing the size of departmental budgets may frustrate movement in this direction. Public choice theory also asserts that public servants often get their way with politicians and their constituents.[5] The kinds of recommendations for organizational reform following from this perspective include more competitive relations within the public sector to counter the will of public servants and the transfer of administrative duties to entities existing outside of government.

The second theoretical proposition is identified with the school of thinking typically called managerialism.[6] Leaning on humanist thinking, managerialism contends that the essence of any large organizational form is not the Weberian ideal-type of bureaucracy. Rather, it is an entity that posits a few basic organizational objectives while providing employees with the autonomy and motivation to achieve these objectives. Managerialism is rooted in practices found in the private sector, but it is assumed that it can be applied to the public sector on the grounds that both sectors amount to large, complex organizations. Thus, managerialism envisions an uprooting of the traditional practice of public administration with its many levels of hierarchy and close attention to established procedures and practices. In some eyes this transformation is symbolized by the substitution of the term "management" for "administration." The latter term "conjures up images of rules, regulations and lethargic decision-making processes"; the former term "implies a decisiveness, a dynamic mindset and a bias for action."[7]

Ultimately, NPM was influenced by a number of organization theory scholars who were trying to foster well-performing organizations—be they in the private or public sector. One of the intellectual foundations was the book *In Search of Excellence*, written in 1982 by Thomas Peters and Robert Waterman. Although the book examined the private sector, focusing on a number of well-run American companies in order to determine the qualities that make for success, many believed their findings had implications for the public sector as well, including an emphasis on the customer and providing high-quality services and products as well as the need to provide employees with sufficient autonomy to be innovative and entrepreneurial.[8]

Another important contribution to the evolution of NPM was the work of Michael Barzelay, who identified the need for **post-bureaucratic organizations** and a corresponding paradigm to deal with the deficiencies of the bureaucratic paradigm. In his book, *Breaking Through Bureaucracy*, Barzelay recommended that government become a "customer-driven service organization." In his view, the "phrase 'the public interest' should be confined to books on the history of American politics and administration." Instead, the focus should be on "results citizens value."[9] The implications of this recommendation mirrored many of those associated with what eventually came to be understood as the NPM: visualizing the citizen as customer, focusing on results or outcomes, creating a competitive environment, providing choice, and empowering frontline public servants to exercise their judgment and authority.

But one work stands out above all others in terms of influencing the way in which public administration scholars and practitioners across the globe thought about public

post-bureaucratic organization A type of organization that eschews the qualities of traditional bureaucracies and stresses flexibility, decentralization, and citizen-centred delivery of services.

management: David Osborne and Ted Gaebler's book, *Reinventing Government,*[10] originally published in 1992. As the title suggests, the book ambitiously aimed to change the way government worked. Though directed at the behaviour of the public sector in the United States, the book spoke to those in other countries wishing to reform their own public services. The two authors felt that the bureaucratic form in most instances had outlived its usefulness and that a new form—a kind of **entrepreneurial government**—was imperative if government were to meet the challenges of the day. The public sector had to contract out services, offer more choice to citizens, develop less controlling budget systems, and eliminate many of its rules and procedures. In short, government had to reinvent itself.

In their book, Osborne and Gaebler made their argument about the need for change through a series of case studies illustrating the wisdom of their approach. One case study examined an aspect of reinventing government that related to the provision of a more competitive environment in the public sector. For example, in the 1980s, the City of Phoenix believed it could save money by requiring its garbage collection department to compete with private collectors over the right to pick up the city's refuse. In the first couple of years, the department lost out to the private interests, who were able to put forward more attractive bids. However, eventually the department regained its responsibility for garbage collection through the introduction of new and more efficient practices and equipment. The result of the competitive process was that the City of Phoenix was able to provide better garbage collection services at a lower cost. For the authors of *Reinventing Government,* this was just one instance of how entrepreneurial government overcame the lethargy of traditional bureaucratic practices.[11]

Osborne and Gaebler reduced their thinking about entrepreneurial government to a set of ten principles or prescriptions:

1. *Catalytic Government.* Conceive government as largely responsible for providing overall direction (what they called "steering") and rely on innovative partnerships with the private and nonprofit sectors to carry out public programs and services (the "rowing" or service-delivery function).
2. *Community-Owned Government.* Empower citizens through participatory democracy to take responsibility for solving their own problems.
3. *Competitive Government.* Encourage competition among government agencies and between public and private suppliers of services in order to take advantage of the benefits available in any competitive situation (lower cost and higher quality).
4. *Results-Oriented Government.* Measure the performance of government agencies and concentrate on the outcomes of government action rather than the actions or inputs of government.
5. *Customer-Driven Government.* See recipients of government services as customers and focus on the provision of quality services through the availability of choice.
6. *Decentralized Government.* When feasible, decentralize agency operations and embrace a participatory form of management.
7. *Enterprising Government.* Rather than simply spending money, earn revenues wherever possible.
8. *Mission-Driven Government.* Pay less attention to rules and rigid budgets; focus instead on the fundamental purpose or mission of the organization to direct and drive the organization.
9. *Anticipatory Government.* Do not simply provide services in response to problems, but rather invest to prevent problems from arising in the first place.
10. *Market-Oriented Government.* Use leverage to structure the marketplace, such as setting the rules of the marketplace, providing information to consumers, creating or increasing demand for services, or changing public investment policy.

At first glance, reinventing government appeared to mean nothing more than government adopting the practices of business. But Osborne and Gaebler knew that

entrepreneurial government A prescription for administrative reform outlined by David Osborne and Ted Gaebler comprising ten key principles that would enable governments to reinvent themselves by becoming more flexible, adaptable, and innovative. Closely associated with the shift towards NPM, particularly in the North American context.

important differences separated the public and private sectors; government could not be "run like a business." However, it was possible for government to be more entrepreneurial without becoming a business. The problem, for the two authors, was not government, but the fact that we had the *wrong kind of government.*[12] The principles of *Reinventing Government* would serve to fix this problem. Notwithstanding this distinction between the reinvented public sector and the private sector, the two authors still emphasized the use of competition and market-based thinking in structuring organizational arrangements for government. As with other proponents of the NPM, they touted the advantages of managerialism and wanted to make sure that it was appreciated that we could learn from the private sector.

Elements of New Public Management

Understanding the concept of NPM is challenging because it has no precise definition and no government went about implementing any administrative reform explicitly identified as such. NPM, it has been argued, "is not a general theory but an eclectic approach," one that was essentially built upon two key ideas—first, that policy should be kept separate from administration, which itself necessitated a stronger focus on management; and second, that the operation of government should rely more heavily on business principles and practices.[13] What emerged in practice, therefore, was a wide range of public sector reforms that were neither consistent nor uniform from one country to the next, but overall were reflective of these fundamental principles. For that reason, there has been variation in terms of what different scholars have classified as being part of NPM, leading some to argue that NPM is similar to an "empty canvas" on which we can paint anything we wish.[14] Nonetheless, it is possible to identify some of the core attributes of NPM that have appeared in the literature.[15]

- *Autonomy and managerial flexibility.* A key element of NPM is the belief that the modern public organization requires fewer rules and more autonomy and flexibility. The public servant of today is highly educated and capable of innovative actions. Rules thus serve only to limit appointed officials unnecessarily and deny society important gains in productivity.
- *Emphasis on results.* Another important quality of NPM is to ensure that results are being achieved, both with respect to programs (requiring evaluation to determine whether programs objectives and outcomes are achieved) and people (through performance measurement). NPM shifts attention away from processes (determining that public servants fulfilled their duties and responsibilities) toward the actual impact of bureaucratic behaviour on society (i.e., outcomes). With this shift in focus, it is believed that a better indication of productivity and effectiveness can be determined. Public servants are motivated to perform through the introduction of private sector techniques like merit pay and the use of mission and vision statements.
- *Client-centred delivery of services.* NPM places special emphasis on ensuring high quality public services that the electorate actually wants. As such, citizens have a key role to play in the determination of the most appropriate services and they are typically referred to as "clients" or "customers" in the belief that the term "citizen" insufficiently conveys the commitment of NPM to providing high-quality programs and policies.
- *Openness to competition.* NPM contends that public agencies should be receptive to competitive arrangements both within government and between the public, private, and nonprofit sectors. This may involve contracting out service delivery to the private and/or nonprofit sector or in some instances transferring responsibility for some public services to the private sector (for example, the privatization of Crown corporations, which is discussed in Chapter 6).

- *Shared values.* The effect of many aspects of NPM is to decentralize operations and to provide public servants with a great deal of discretion. The focus on shared values—which include some traditional values like accountability and a host of new values, such as innovation, leadership, service, quality, and teamwork—tries to balance this effect and provide overall direction for employees of a public agency. The shared values, if properly formulated, also motivate employees and instill in them a sense of the organization's mission.
- *Focus on managing.* Implicit in many discussions of NPM (and explicit in some) is the belief that public servants should concentrate on managing and leave policy making to elected officials. The desired arrangement under NPM is a clear division between politics and administration. Such an arrangement pushes public servants to the area in which they hold considerable expertise and also ensures that elected officials provide the leadership to determine the priorities of government.
- *Cutting costs.* NPM has fundamentally been about "doing more with less," with reductions in both budgetary allocations to public sector organizations and the number of employees working for government.

These various elements are captured effectively in Table 5.1. In addition, this table elaborates on the transformation that has taken place as a result of the shift from the traditional bureaucratic organization to NPM, and subsequently to new public governance. Bureaucracy, for example, is a risk-averse entity, unwilling to take chances and fearful of mistakes, while public sector organizations under NPM recognize that beneficial change and innovation requires taking chances. NPM strives to move away from government appropriations and relies instead on cost recovery for financing programs. It also utilizes a much broader array of mechanisms beyond the traditional government department and Crown agency for delivering programs.

Criticisms of New Public Management

While practitioners and academics were initially largely enticed by the promise of greater efficiency and effectiveness as a result of NPM, over time the chorus of detractors, who believed that many of the aforementioned elements of NPM were unable to survive critical scrutiny, grew louder. Christopher Pollitt was one early critic. He noted that many of the grandiose claims of savings and greater efficiencies for government were really impressions that could not actually be carefully assessed and quantified: "On the one hand it is pretty clear that NPM approaches have worked quite well for some services in some jurisdictions at some times. On the other, it seems equally clear that NPM *isn't* an irresistible wave…and that often its claimed benefits are hard to discern in practice."[16]

Some who have studied NPM claim that greater managerial autonomy and flexibility increases the chances of a loss of accountability. Ministers, who are ultimately responsible for the actions of government, might now find it difficult to oversee the actions of their appointed subordinates. Private sector leaders may be able to suffer a decline in accountability, but such is not the case for senior political officials. Political officials are also reluctant to leave administration solely to the appointed officials, because ministers simply like to be in direct contact with voters; they also wish to be seen to be at the forefront of some important accomplishments.[17] Eventually, the combination of a sense of loss of accountability and a desire to be involved in administration may lead political leaders to develop new rules and requirements. NPM thus succeeds only in returning us to the typical bureaucratic form.

One of the most criticized aspects of NPM is the claim that performance measurement (and the companion concept of **performance management**) is and should be central to the operation of the modern public organization. Such a stance may misinterpret the nature of most public services and the implications of this fact for the measurement

performance management A method for improving the performance and productivity of employees, teams, and organizations. It involves setting performance objectives and expected behaviours, then measuring the results against these measures and providing feedback.

	TRADITIONAL PUBLIC ADMINISTRATION	NEW PUBLIC MANAGEMENT	NEW PUBLIC GOVERNANCE
TABLE 5.1	Traditional Public Administration, New Public Management, and New Public Governance Compared		
Theoretical Foundation	Political science, public policy, and organization theory	Public choice theory and managerialism	Democratic, institutional, and network theory
Focus			
• Recipients of services	Citizens	Clients or customers	Engaged citizens
• Objectives	Public interest	Results (outputs and, more importantly, outcomes)	Public value
	Efficiency	Quality and value	Participation and real influence
• Orientation	Hierarchy (public sector monopolies)	Market (competition)	Networks (collaboration)
Means	Administration (analysts)	Management (entrepreneurs)	Management/Leadership (stewards)
	Departments	Alternative service delivery mechanisms	Mixture of departments, alternative service delivery mechanisms, and non-state actors
	Independent action	Co-ordination, collaboration, partnerships, and networked governance	Dialogue, networks, partnerships, and collaboration
Characteristics	Rules and procedures	Autonomy and discretion	Constitutionally-grounded discretion
	Accountability based on process	Accountability for results	Multifaceted accountability
	Centralized	Decentralized	Co-production
	Status quo	Change-oriented	Change-oriented (transformational)
	Budget-driven	Mission- and revenue-driven (cost recovery)	Problem-solving driven
Values	Ministerial responsibility, neutrality, fairness and equity, responsiveness, efficiency and effectiveness	Innovation, risk taking, leadership, quality, teamwork, service, empowerment	Innovation, empowerment, efficiency, accountability, equity, mutual respect, shared learning, trust

of performance. As Thomas states, "PMMA [performance measurement, management and accountability] appears to be a rational, objective approach, but in practice it is an inherently subjective and interactive process involving 'politics' on a number of levels." This process cannot provide "unequivocal evidence to solve problems"; rather, it must be viewed as a "'political' process involving interaction, communication and consensus-building about what should be measured, how and with what consequences."[18] Also,

Chapter 5 / Public Administration and Organization Theory

BOX
5.1

Savoie versus Borins

The best debate on NPM has involved two prominent Canadian scholars, Donald Savoie and Sandford Borins. The two combatants pulled few punches. Savoie claimed that NPM constituted a "flawed concept" in its attempt to apply business principles and practices to government. For Savoie, the private and public sectors were similar only in insignificant ways. Borins countered that Savoie misunderstood NPM and referred to an earlier work of Savoie's that revealed a more sympathetic appreciation of this perspective. Undeterred, Savoie responded that Borins supplied no real arguments for his position and was no better than a preacher trying to sell some "old time religion." Having the last word in that debate, Borins pointed to all those already engaged in the managerial revolution inspired by NPM.

Sources: Donald Savoie, "What Is Wrong with the New Public Management?"; Sandford Borins, "The New Public Management Is Here to Stay"; Donald Savoie, "Just Another Voice from the Pulpit"; and Sandford Borins, "A Last Word." All from *Canadian Public Administration* 38(1) (Spring 1995): 112–138.

the purposes of a government program or service are often multifaceted, so it is sometimes difficult to interpret the meaning or importance of some performance scores. A school program may do well on standardized tests, but parents may be more interested in safety or accessibility.[19]

Performance measurement, critics say, also pays insufficient attention to the nature of the government environment. Due to political considerations, only a small amount of useful information may be made available, and that information may be ignored by those seeking to establish greater accountability and efficiency. Good explains the dynamics of this problem in the Canadian context:

> It seems that when it comes to program performance information for the purposes of accountability, public servants don't publish for fear of embarrassing their ministers, and Parliamentary Committees don't use what is published because it cannot embarrass ministers. Little wonder progress has been slow and reliable information limited. All this suggests some important limits to new public management.[20]

The focus on citizen input, another key element of NPM, threatens to reduce members of the population to self-interested seekers of government services. Traditionally, the citizenry in a democracy has responsibilities that contribute to the community as a whole. Unlike the consumer in the marketplace, the democratic citizen must think of things other than the satisfaction of personal preferences. The citizen accepts that some sacrifices may have to be made to ensure equitable access to necessary public services and that some effort has to be made to participate in the political process. Some worried that NPM made citizens less willing to make these sacrifices and in the end will turn government into a "supermarket state."[21] The plea for greater competitiveness within government and a greater openness to privatizing public services has also produced concerns. For instance, the belief that many public services ought to be shifted to the private sector may give rise to morale problems in the public service, because it suggests that "public service has no intrinsic value."[22] People decide to work in government not to clean up after the market, but rather to make a contribution to the welfare of the nation.

Although this was not as much of a problem in the Canadian adoption of NPM, which witnessed as much departmental consolidation as it did fragmentation, many critics pointed to the problems associated with disaggregation (i.e., breaking up large public sector organizations into smaller units) and agencification (i.e., the creation of new agencies or the enhanced autonomy of existing ones) that was notable in countries like the UK and New Zealand. Many of the post-NPM reforms that were implemented, therefore, were designed to bring greater coordination and horizontal integration back to government. The desire was to reassert the central capacity and control that had been compromised under NPM.

Reforming New Public Management

Given the limitations of NPM outlined in the previous section, public policy and administration scholars began to articulate new perspectives for understanding the process of administrative reform. As was the case with the neo-classical organization theorists, who began to challenge the ideas of the structuralists (ultimately giving rise to the human relations school), so too can we identify scholars who did not fully embrace NPM and offered different ways of thinking about how the public sector should operate. Some of the early efforts attempted to put a softer face on NPM and shift the focus from markets and efficiency to serving the public interest and the importance of an active, engaged citizenry. Subsequent attempts to alter the discourse were much less subtle with pronouncements that NPM "has essentially died in the water" and the emergence of a number of potential new administrative reform paradigms.[23] The reality is that, similar to NPM, "post-NPM—often labelled governance reforms"—lacks a consistent theoretical framework and, as such, is best understood as offering "a kind of 'shopping basket' of different elements."[24]

Robert Denhardt would be an example of a scholar who began to question NPM without completely rejecting it. In his book, *The Pursuit of Significance*, he identified the need to move away from the bureaucratic form and toward a new way of managing, which led to a number of qualities that were similar or even identical to those in comparable lists seeking to capture the essence of the NPM. Empowerment and shared leadership, and serving the public were two such qualities. But on the basis of his research on organizational change in Canada, Great Britain, Australia, and the United States, Denhardt claimed that public servants were engaged in a "pursuit of significance" in which they strive to have an impact in their work.[25] The primacy of private interest (e.g., competition), which can be found in some of the other works on NPM, was replaced by the pre-eminence of meaning and significance. Thus, Denhardt emphasized in his work the importance of "a commitment to values," which meant that the mission statement and the beliefs contained in the statement became vital to the organization. Similarly, Denhardt included in his list "a dedication to public service." This quality revealed a public servant who goes beyond competition and innovation and toward a commitment to the special place and importance of the public service in a democratic society.[26]

In Denhardt's later work, written with Janet Denhardt, Denhardt expanded upon his earlier ideas, putting forward the model of the "New Public Service." The Denhardts rejected the core elements of NPM in their book, stating at the outset that "government shouldn't be run like a business; it should be run like a democracy," and provided a new perspective on public organizations.[27] This model attempted to provide an equilibrium between the old or traditional public administration at one end of the spectrum and NPM at the other extreme by emphasizing the need to serve and empower citizens. At the centre of their prescription for reform are the public service, democratic governance, and civic engagement. Public servants are not to be entrepreneurs as suggested by NPM; rather, they have a critical role to play in terms of fostering an active citizenry that participates fully in the democratic process. The Denhardts' model never really gained traction as an alternative to NPM, but some of these elements are integral components of efforts to develop a new public administration paradigm, as will be seen later in the chapter.

Another noteworthy contribution to this reform tradition was provided by Canadian academics Kenneth Kernaghan, Brian Marson, and Sandford Borins. Although they acknowledged the failings and limitations of the traditional public administration and were largely amenable to the resultant shift to post-bureaucratic organizations, they nonetheless understood that no "magic pill" exists for addressing the complexities and problems of the public sector.[28] As such, they proposed a structural model for government called the "New Public Organization," which offered a tempered endorsement of the key tenets of NPM. While they believed that there were incontrovertible benefits to the post-bureaucratic model for achieving high-performance organizations, their contribution was to recognize that it had limited applicability. Therefore, each public sector entity would move "along the continua between the bureaucratic and the post-bureaucratic models to the extent that is appropriate to the *type* of organization it is and the *functions* it performs."[29] Therefore, bodies that rely on rules, control and accountability for process to ensure good performance—immigration or environment departments, for instance—may be well advised to stay with the traditional bureaucratic form. This might also be the case for public sector organizations that have a risk-averse and process-oriented culture, like air-traffic controllers. Other entities, for example the Canadian Passport Office, were much better positioned to adopt the principles of the post-bureaucratic organization.

Whither New Public Management?

Is NPM dead and largely irrelevant in the twenty-first century, supplanted by a new paradigm, or does it continue to remain an important means for structuring the public sector in Canada and elsewhere? As is often the case, there is disagreement on this question. One perspective would be that NPM remains the dominant paradigm for understanding administrative reform, immune to efforts to have it replaced by something else. This opinion is included here for the sake of completeness, but we are not making the case that an unmodified NPM paradigm continues to prevail. The contrary view, argued by many scholars, is that a governance-related paradigm has been substituted for NPM.

A third view is that various governance components have bridged the divide between NPM and the post-NPM movement since several aspects of governance, such as public–private partnerships, networks, and increased market orientation, have also been part of NPM. In essence, according to this interpretation, what we have witnessed is the convergence of different reform eras and, because the process of change is gradual, it is difficult to determine exactly when one reform movement ended (NPM) and a new one began (post-NPM). Even in this conception, different interpretations can be identified: on the one hand, it is possible to view both NPM and post-NPM as being important, either independently depending on the policy area or perhaps combined in various ways with respect to different reforms; on the other hand, NPM may be regarded as the dominant reform wave, which has been subject to only minor modifications arising from these governance-related developments.[30]

Christensen and Lægreid support the first approach. They reject the notion that a new paradigm has emerged, but they regard post-NPM reforms as important as the wave of reform ushered in by NPM. They wrote, "we would tend to subscribe to the argument that reform movements are characterized by combination, complexity, layering and hybridization, rather than by dominance, substitution and pendulum swings."[31] Christopher Pollitt, writing in the early 2000s, at a time when some critics had already pronounced NPM a spent force, falls into the latter camp of the convergence perspective. He suggested that "the NPM is by no means 'over.' It may be beginning to seem like 'old hat' in some of the pioneer countries such as New Zealand and the UK, but elsewhere it is still regarded as a central plank in modernization." But even in the Anglo-Saxon countries where NPM first originated, his view was that NPM was not being replaced; rather, new administrative reforms were "being added on to the NPM inheritance."[32]

Therefore, he recognized the pre-eminence of NPM, even though it was evolving in response to new initiatives.

In a more recent study examining whether there has been a shift from NPM to post-NPM in New Zealand, Martin Lodge and Derek Gill reached a similar conclusion:

> NPM was never as purely implemented as the literature has led us to believe, and post-NPM's day is yet (if ever) to come. Indeed, the New Zealand case suggests considerable continuity mixed with ad hoc politically motivated changes that have generated diversification rather than a new era or paradigm.[33]

So they, too, continued to regard NPM as a salient force, while conceding that it has not been without refinement. The change in New Zealand, they argue, "has been one of degree ["layering"], not one of shifting paradigms ["pendulum swings"]."[34]

Post-NPM: Governance and Beyond

The fact that a number of administrative reforms that have emerged over the past two decades have been grouped together under the label "post-NPM reforms" indicates that we are still waiting for an intellectual successor to NPM. For some scholars, however, the concept of governance has come to replace NPM and is at the heart of the latest reforms. Governance essentially emerged in response to dissatisfaction with and efforts to move beyond the NPM model in the centre-left countries of Europe that were trying to deal with increasingly complex public policy problems at the same time as these states were ceding authority to a number of supranational institutions, especially the European Union.[35]

Like NPM, governance is an imprecise concept in that it is a label given to a series of interrelated reforms that are neither clearly defined nor coherent. Therefore, for some commentators, governance can only be considered a weak paradigm at best; it is more properly understood as merely a new "buzz word"[36] or "magic concept"[37] given the various meanings that have been attributed to the term.[38] Nonetheless, advocates of governance posit that we have moved from a focus on hierarchy (under bureaucracy) to markets (NPM) to both partnerships and networks of state and non-state actors sharing power and administrative responsibility. It was understood that governments could no longer act in isolation when making public policy and delivering public services, but instead they increasingly relied on the active participation of a variety of civil society actors. Rhodes noted that "the literature on governance explores how the informal authority of networks supplements and supplants the formal authority of government."[39]

However, even proponents of the concept of governance recognize that there are many similarities between governance and the NPM philosophy.[40] Recall that one of the key principles of Osborne and Gaebler's entrepreneurial government was that the state should focus on "steering" and let the private and nonprofit sector fulfill the "rowing" (i.e., service delivery) function. A number of alternative service delivery mechanisms emerged in that context, including the use of public–private partnerships, which clearly is an example of networked governance since such arrangements involve the state relinquishing a degree of control to the collaborator(s) in question. It also unmistakably leads to a blurring of the boundaries between the public, private, and nonprofit sectors. Another common element would be with respect to user participation: both NPM and governance focus on the role of citizens, but in the case of NPM it was a narrow, consumerist conception whereby citizens were to be consulted as users of public services; the governance framework sees citizens as members of communities who are involved in the planning, design, and management of those services.

Elliassen and Sitter admit that NPM blurs into governance, but as NPM evolves into the six governance themes that they have identified, "the overall result is a system that

Chapter 5 / Public Administration and Organization Theory

differs considerably from the NPM model."[41] They suggest that governance is characterized by the following:

- *Relies on a broader set of policy instruments.* Goals are achieved not solely through the use of formal powers, but rely on persuasion, communication, and monitoring to promote best practice.
- *Boundary between the public, private, and nonprofit sectors blurred.* This is exemplified best through the use of public–private partnerships.
- *Multiple levels of government and mutual power dependence.* It tends to involve cooperation and coordination between several levels of government.
- *A more holistic approach to governing.* This is essentially the concept of "joined-up government," whereby the focus is on enhancing coordination across government departments. It is also reflected in the concept of "horizontal management" and what is known as the "whole-of-government" approach.[42]
- *A reliance on autonomous networks as much as hierarchical organizations.* While the relationship between actors in NPM was defined by contracts, in governance the actors rely on their expertise, skills, resources, and participation in a network for their power.
- *A more flexible regulatory system.* NPM ironically resulted in a great deal of new regulation. The intent of governance is to have more flexible regulatory regimes; at the same time governance maintains and enhances both transparency and accountability.

Digital Era Governance

digital era governance (DEG) One of the governance theories that emphasizes the transformative impact of information technologies and changes to information systems on the practice of public administration.

A number of variations on the governance theme are discernable in the literature. One admittedly ambitious proposition is the concept of **digital era governance (DEG)**. Dunleavy and his colleagues put forth the contention that "the unifying and distinguishing features of the current development of public sector organizational and managerial change mainly revolve around information technology changes and alterations in information systems." While they did note that IT innovations had been producing changes in public administration for decades, their view was that they did not have a transformational impact until the late 1990s. From that point onward, the growth of the Internet and email and the expansion of IT systems began "conditioning in important ways the whole terms of relations between government agencies and civil society."[43]

While IT advancements—in particular Web 2.0 technologies, such as social media, web applications, and blogs—continue to shape the way in which public servants do their work internally and interact with citizens and other external actors in dramatic ways, the relative impact of these technological innovations is perhaps overstated. In many minds, IT advancements were central to NPM in the early-to-mid 1990s, because many of its core elements relied on the Internet, email, and other types of technology (e.g., electronic kiosks) for producing a more citizen-centred delivery of services.[44] To imply that these developments were any less transformational is to forget just how difficult it was for citizens to acquire information about government operations and spending prior to their various organizations having an online presence, which began in 1994 when the first Canadian government websites emerged. Moreover, in the Canadian case at least, the federal government continues to struggle with online service delivery. An internal Treasury Board document recently warned the government that it is lagging behind both the private sector and the expectations of Canadians with respect to online service delivery, revealing that some 77 percent of federal government services still cannot be completed over the Internet.[45]

New Public Governance

new public governance (NPG) First articulated by Stephen Osborne, this is another variant of the governance theories, which is centred on the promotion of the common good and emphasizes collaboration between multiple stakeholders.

Perhaps the most widely cited alternative to NPM is what Stephen Osborne first identified as **new public governance (NPG)**.[46] He made the argument that NPM was merely a transitory stage in the evolution from traditional public administration to NPG, which should be understood as a distinctive regime and not merely an element of either the traditional public administration or NPM. As seen in Table 5.1, while the traditional public administration has political science and public policy as its theoretical foundation and NPM is grounded in public choice theory and management, the roots of NPG are institutional and network theory. This suggests that NPG is fundamentally about collaboration between multiple stakeholders. Osborne writes that NPG "posits both a *plural state*, where multiple interdependent actors contribute to the delivery of public services, and a *pluralist state*, where multiple processes inform the policy-making system."[47] It is also infused with systems theory insofar as NPG is concerned not only with the institutional determinants and constraints of public policy implementation and service delivery, but also with how the external environment similarly impacts these processes.

Other scholars have attempted to elucidate the key characteristics of the NPG. According to Morgan and Shinn, NPG has "three trust- and legitimacy-building characteristics," which NPM does not either address or value appropriately. First, NPG is centred on values; as such, the purpose of government is to promote the common good. Second, it focuses on creating processes that produce agreements between many competing stakeholders. Third, the achievement of the public good is attained jointly involving the public, private, and nonprofit sectors. A key difference here between NPM and NPG is that the former utilized partnerships with the private and nonprofit sectors to deliver services more efficiently and cost-effectively, whereas the aim of NPG is to enhance the capacity of local organizations and build civic infrastructure.[48]

Insofar as common elements of NPG can be identified, then, they would be a process and outcome focus; multi-actor collaboration; empowered participation, both on the part of citizens and other stakeholders in the policy-making process; and multiple forms of accountability.[49] This focus on an active, engaged citizenry harks back to the work of Robert and Janet Denhardt on the New Public Service, which we examined earlier in the chapter. Both the New Public Service and NPG make an assumption that if given opportunities to do so, citizens and other stakeholders will actively participate in the policy-making and service-delivery functions of government. But it would certainly not be unreasonable to challenge that assumption; citizens and stakeholder groups may lack the interest and/or ability to participate and collaborate in these processes. Furthermore, even if these individuals and groups are eager to contribute, there is the thorny issue of unequal participation in the governance process. The fear is that such opportunities to participate will be captured by powerful elites.[50]

Other Post-NPM Reform Developments

If students of public administration were sometimes frustrated by the lack of coherence of the NPM paradigm, then they have been equally disappointed by the nebulousness of the concept of NPG. The fact that various new strands of NPG have been materializing in the literature only serves to produce greater confusion. One such development is **public value governance**.[51] In this particular take on networked governance, the focus of the various participants in the policy-making and service-delivery functions of government is to build public value; in doing so, there is special emphasis placed on public sector values, especially democratic values that go beyond efficiency and effectiveness, which were given such high priority under NPM. Yet another contribution to public management theory under the umbrella of NPG is the "public service dominant" approach, which seeks to reorient the product-dominant bias of public management to better reflect the fact that the public sector largely produces and delivers services, not products.[52]

It should be evident by now that administrative reform is an ongoing process. Governments are continually embracing new reform initiatives in the hope that they can

public value governance One of the most recent governance theories, whereby the purpose of collaboration between various state and non-state actors is to create public value. The focus is on public sector values, particularly democratic values, in place of concerns about efficiency and effectiveness.

bring about greater efficiency and effectiveness to the public sector and new theories are proposed in an effort to understand the transformations that are occurring. A relevant question posed by Christensen and Lægreid at the conclusion of their survey of governance and administrative reforms is whether the governance-related post-NPM reforms will have any staying power or simply be supplemented by new reform measures.[53] As for the fate of NPM? We would agree with the assessment of the late Peter Aucoin, a Canadian public administration scholar of international repute, who wrote in 2008:

> NPM is not going to disappear any time soon, even if this term for public management reform becomes less frequently used or even disappears from the lexicon. Indeed, some critical aspects of NPM no longer exist as a reform movement; it has become the status quo. Everywhere it is now recognized that improved public management requires a necessary degree of management capacity … .[54]

Managerial Reform in Canada

In this final section of the chapter, we will reflect on how both NPM and the post-NPM reform waves have impacted Canadian public administration. As noted at the outset, NPM has affected thinking on public service reform around the world in developed and developing countries alike, but the vanguard countries were the Anglo-American democracies. However, the degree of acceptance of the tenets of NPM and overall enthusiasm for this approach have differed across these countries. Canada has typically been identified as a country that only moderately engaged in NPM reform; in other words, its evolution in this country has been "slow and cautious."[55]

While pragmatic in our approach, the federal government has nonetheless put forward over the years various initiatives that were clearly inspired by one aspect or another of NPM. In the 1980s, it introduced a managerial initiative known as Increased Ministerial Authority and Accountability (IMAA), which made available increased autonomy for individual departments in return for agreeing to explicit performance measures and reviews. A few years later it undertook an effort (Public Service 2000) directed at improving services by fostering a consultative, client-oriented culture in the public service and reducing the reach of agencies whose job entailed coordinating and controlling line departments. The federal government also privatized some major Crown corporations—CN and Petro-Canada, for example—and created special bodies (special operating agencies) that would be granted a greater amount of flexibility in order to meet newly-agreed-upon performance targets. It also experimented with new administrative forms that came to be known as "alternative service delivery mechanisms" (discussed more fully in Chapter 8).

In the 1990s, the federal government launched two major initiatives (Program Review and La Relève) that were conducive to NPM. Program Review mostly amounted to an attempt to increase efficiency through expenditure reductions, but it also entailed a reconsideration of the proper role of the federal government. As a result of that process, there was both a significant reduction in expenditures and a contraction in the number of federal public servants, which mirrored the personnel reductions of the Mulroney era. In the case of La Relève, the intent was to deal with a growing malaise in the federal public service. A critical component of that exercise was to foster leadership capacity in the public service, which was one of the new values resulting from NPM.

A number of additional NPM-inspired administrative reforms were introduced both federally and provincially. In 1995, the federal government launched the Quality Service Initiative. This was designed to improve client satisfaction with government services in part through the use of service standards (e.g., appropriate times for waiting in line to receive services, how quickly phone calls and correspondence would be answered, and so on). But other aspects of NPM were discernable, including the introduction of vision, mission, and value statements for public sector organizations and the introduction of both performance pay for senior executives and departmental business plans. At the provincial level, the new public management received basically the same reception as it had at the federal level of government. Among other developments, there were cutbacks in program expenditures, reductions in the number of civil servants, and the privatization of Crown corporations, although some provinces (Ontario and Alberta) proved to be more aggressive in pushing public service reform.

To be sure, the intensity and reach of these efforts paled in comparison with that of other countries involved in such reform. Some countries, for example, required their agencies to engage in competitions for contracts to offer services. In Canada, contracting-out took place, but not to the same extent as in these other places. Similarly, unlike New Zealand and the UK with its executive agencies, Canada did not engage in a full restructuring of the public sector that resulted in a complete separation of the policy and operation functions of government organizations. In those other nations the majority of public sector entities found themselves in a new organizational arrangement that emphasized autonomy and performance measurement; Canada applied this practice in only a moderate manner.

A selective and experimental approach to public sector reform is really what set this country apart from other early and eager adopters of NPM. In 1998, Jocelyne Bourgon, the head of the federal public service, made this clear, listing the aspects of the Canadian model for reform:

- Unlike some other models of the new public management, the Canadian model rejected NPM's implicit belief that good government was less government. Government and its institutions played an important role in the provision of services and were "essential to a well-performing society."
- The Canadian model agreed to the need for government to enter into alliances with other actors in society—in other words, to embrace new roles—and to think more closely about the role of government in the future.
- The Canadian model affirmed that an effective public service needed both an effective policy capacity and a modernized way of delivering services. The latter part of this affirmation acknowledged the claim of NPM that new organizational forms had to be tried.
- The Canadian model acknowledged the significance of a "well-performing, professional non-partisan public service." With this, the federal government wanted to make obvious the centrality of the public service in any reform efforts and in the delivery of services to Canadians. This was part of the pre-NPM environment and would remain part of any new environment.
- The Canadian model counted on "leadership from both politicians and bureaucrats." Elected officials were essential to finding the appropriate role for government in a changing world, and appointed officials were "relied upon to put bold and creative ideas before ministers." NPM was sometimes interpreted to mean that managers would be limited to managing, but the Canadian model indicated that the public service would be expected to provide some leadership with respect to policy and as well to work closely with ministers.[56]

The Canadian approach to public service reform, therefore, indicated a need to change and to adopt aspects of NPM, but it also represented an approach that wanted to maintain qualities and practices that had served Canada well in the past. So while Canada may have been an obvious outlier relative to the UK, Australia, and New Zealand, all of which were zealous advocates of NPM, ironically, with the "rise of a more hybrid form of public management" it has been proffered that Canada is probably "closer to the mainstream of Anglophone countries," which, over time, saw the more radical features of NPM fade.[57]

But to what extent has Canada moved beyond NPM with its more recent administrative reforms? Like the Canadian approach to NPM, our experience with the emerging governance reforms would have to be characterized as moderate. As has been the situation elsewhere, Canada has experienced a layering of NPM-type reforms with a number of initiatives that could be characterized as post-NPM in orientation. Given that Canada slipped back into deficits as a result of the fiscal stimulus response to the global recession, the Harper government was keenly interested in reducing expenditures. Prime Minister Harper continued with the trend of his predecessors to engage in reviews of government programs and spending, the first of which were his "strategic reviews," implemented in 2006 as a means of finding ongoing and permanent cuts to the budgets of departments and agencies. Those savings were to be redirected to key government priorities. In 2011, "operational reviews" were introduced in order to find substantial one-time cuts to services. Then in the 2012 budget, the government announced plans to eliminate over 19,000 civil service jobs.[58]

The NPM rationale is obvious in these reforms. However, there are also tangible indicators that post-NPM reforms are a part of Canadian public administration. While Canada has a well-documented, long history of centralized control, Prime Minister Harper "has taken complete command of the government by governing from the centre."[59] He has employed strict party discipline on his caucus and there was an expectation that the federal public service would enthusiastically embrace and promote the agenda of his government. This may well have been a result of the prime minister's personal leadership style more so than a reaction to fragmentation under NPM, but it is definitely reflective of a post-NPM practice and is indeed integral to the way in which Peter Aucoin has defined NPG.

A couple of other trends and reform initiatives are indicative of a shift that has occurred. One would be the proliferation of horizontal management initiatives since the mid-1990s. Working collaboratively with other levels of government and civil society actors has been a common approach for dealing with major public policy issues in Canada.[60] More recently, a whole-of-government framework was adopted by the federal government as a complement to its 2005 Policy on Management, Resources and Results Structures, which was introduced to establish a standardized approach across government regarding the "collection, management and reporting of financial and non-financial information on program objectives, performance and results."[61] That policy has elements of both NPM (focus on performance and results) and post-NPM (centralization and co-ordination of information). As part of the whole-of-government framework, which guides how progress is reported to Parliament and could be classified as a post-NPM reform, both the financial and non-financial contributions of government organizations receiving appropriations are mapped against sixteen high-level outcome areas within four areas of expenditure—Economic Affairs, Social Affairs, International Affairs, and Government Affairs.

open government A global movement across all levels of government, the aim of which is to promote greater transparency and accountability, to provide citizens with greater access to information and data, and to foster citizen engagement.

As a final example, consider the widespread movement across all levels of government in Canada to promote **open government**. At the federal level, the government launched its Open Government strategy in March 2011 and became a signatory to the global Open Government Partnership (OGP) in April 2012. Open Government has a number of objectives, including fostering greater transparency and accountability, providing citizens with greater access to data and information, and enhancing citizen engagement across all activities of government and the democratic process more broadly.[62] To fulfill its obligations under the OGP, the federal government had to develop an action plan; it contains twelve commitments as depicted in Figure 5.1.

Open government, with its emphasis on citizen engagement, is exactly the kind of reform initiative that would be characteristic of the NPG reform wave. While there are critics of the Harper government who would question how committed it was to fostering open government, greater openness and transparency has certainly been an important theme for the new Trudeau government. Elements of NPG, therefore, may be more easily discernible in this regard in the coming years.

Part Two / Theoretical Foundations

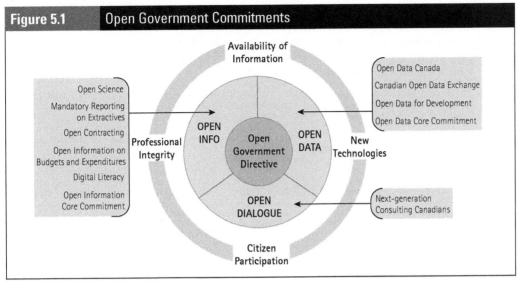

Figure 5.1   Open Government Commitments

Availability of Information

Open Science
Mandatory Reporting on Extractives
Open Contracting
Open Information on Budgets and Expenditures
Digital Literacy
Open Information Core Commitment

Professional Integrity

OPEN INFO

Open Government Directive

OPEN DATA

New Technologies

Open Data Canada
Canadian Open Data Exchange
Open Data for Development
Open Data Core Commitment

OPEN DIALOGUE

Next-generation Consulting Canadians

Citizen Participation

Source: *Canada's Action Plan on Open Government 2014–16.* www.open.canada.ca/encontent/canadas-action-plan-open-government-2014-16, Treasury Board of Canada Secretariat, 2016.

Points to Know

- Beginning in the late 1970s and 1980s, new public management (NPM) became the dominant paradigm across the globe for reforming public administration. The term refers to a broad set of administrative reforms that were designed to bring private sector management principles to government.

- Osborne and Gaebler proposed the concept of entrepreneurial government, built upon ten key principles, many of which reflected the core ideas of NPM. This became the foundation of NPM in North America.

- The core attributes of NPM include greater autonomy and managerial flexibility, an emphasis on results, client-centred service delivery, competition in the provision of public services, a focus on management rather than administration, and a desire to reduce the size and scope of the state.

- Criticisms levelled against NPM ultimately gave rise to a new reform wave, which centred on governance, networks, and partnerships. This has been labelled post-NPM, but includes a number of identifiable strands: digital era governance (DEG), new public governance (NPG), and public value governance among others.

- Canada, with its distinct model of public sector reform, adopted a selective and experimental approach to both NPM and NPG.

- NPM is not a spent force as some critics have suggested. Contemporary public administration reforms are a hybrid of the traditional public administration, NPM, and the governance-related post-NPM initiatives that focus on multi-actor collaboration, empowered participation and enhanced accountability.

Review Questions

1. What was the impetus behind the evolution of NPM?

2. Identify the key elements of NPM and how they were implemented in the Canadian context.

3. Given its emphasis on private sector business principles, was NPM a flawed approach for public sector reform?

4. Is there a distinctive Canadian model of administrative reform? If so, what are the key elements and what makes them unique?

5. Does NPM remain a relevant paradigm of administrative reform? Why or why not? If not, what has emerged to replace it?

6. A central theme in the post-NPM reforms is an emphasis on enhanced participation, particularly by an active, engaged citizenry, in both the policy-making and service-delivery functions of government. Is that a realistic proposition or does that particular focus simply undermine the utility of these proposed public management theories?

Notes

1. See Donald Kettl, *The Global Public Management Revolution* (Washington, D.C.: Brookings Institution Press, 2005).
2. Christopher Hood, a British academic, is generally credited with having coined the term. See Christopher Hood, "A Public Management for All Seasons?" *Public Administration* 69(1) (Spring 1991): 3–19.
3. Gernod Gruening, "Origin and Theoretical Basis of New Public Management," *International Public Management Journal* 4 (2001): 1–25.
4. Peter Aucoin, *The New Public Management: Canada in Comparative Perspective* (Montreal: IRPP, 1995), 31.
5. Agency theory or principal–agent theory is another perspective that captures the basic thrust of public choice theory. See Janet V. Denhardt and Robert B. Denhardt, *The New Public Service: Serving, Not Steering* (Armonk, N.Y.: M.E. Sharpe, 2003), 20–21.
6. Aucoin, *The New Public Management*, 8.
7. Donald Savoie, "What Is Wrong with the New Public Management?" *Canadian Public Administration* 38(1) (Spring 1995): 113.
8. Thomas J. Peters and Robert H. Waterman, Jr., *In Search of Excellence: Lessons from America's Best-Run Companies* (New York: Harper & Row Publishers, 1982).
9. Michael Barzelay, with the collaboration of Babak J. Armajani, *Breaking Through Bureaucracy: A New Vision for Managing in Government* (Berkeley: University of California Press, 1992), 8, 119.
10. David Osborne and Ted Gaebler, *Reinventing Government: How the Entrepreneurial Spirit Is Transforming the Public Sector* (Reading, MA: Addison-Wesley, 1992).
11. Ibid., ch. 3.
12. Ibid., 20, 23. (Emphasis in original.)
13. Iain Gow, "Evolution of Disciplinary Approaches and Paradigms in the Study of Public Administration in Canada" in *The Evolving Physiology of Government: Canadian Public Administration in Transition*, eds. O.P. Dwivedi, Tim A. Mau, and Byron Sheldrick (Ottawa: University of Ottawa Press, 2009), 17.
14. Andrew Stark, "What Is the New Public Management?" *Journal of Public Administration Research and Theory* 12(1) (January 2002): 1.
15. There have been many attempts to list the elements of NPM. See, for example, Hood, "A Public Management for All Seasons?" and O.P. Dwivedi and James Iain Gow, *From Bureaucracy to New Public Management: The Administrative Culture of the Government of Canada* (Peterborough: Broadview Press, 1999), 128–129 (Table 5.1). Dwivedi and Gow summarize the components of NPM as identified by different scholars and government reports and programs.
16. Christopher Pollitt, *The Essential Public Manager* (Maidenhead: Open University Press, 2003), 50.
17. David A. Good, *The Politics of Public Management: The HRDC Audit of Grants and Contributions* (Toronto: Institute of Public Administration of Canada and the University of Toronto Press, 2003), 198.
18. Paul G. Thomas, "Why Is Performance-Based Accountability So Popular in Theory and So Difficult in Practice?" in *Holy Grail or Achievable Quest? International Perspectives on Public Sector Performance Management*, ed. John Herhalt (Brussels: KPMG International, 2008), 185.
19. Christopher Pollitt, "How Do We Know How Good Public Services Are?" in *Governance in the Twenty-First Century: Revitalizing the Public Service*, eds. B. Guy Peters and Donald J. Savoie (Montreal & Kingston: McGill-Queen's University Press, 2000), 119–152.
20. Good, *The Politics of Public Management*, 175.
21. Joel D. Aberbach and Tom Christensen, "Citizens and Consumers: An NPM Dilemma," *Public Management Review* 7(2) (2005): 238.
22. Savoie, "What Is Wrong with the New Public Management?" 118.
23. Patrick Dunleavy, Helen Margetts, Simon Bastow, and Jane Tinkler, "New Public Management Is Dead—Long Live Digital-Era Governance," *Journal of Public Administration Research and Theory* 16(3) (July 2006): 468.
24. Tom Christensen and Per Lægreid, "Governance and Administrative Reforms" in *The Oxford Handbook of Governance*, ed. David Levi-Faur (Oxford: Oxford University Press, 2012), 256.
25. Robert B. Denhardt, *The Pursuit of Significance: Strategies for Managerial Success in Public Organizations* (Belmont, Calif.: Wadsworth Publishing Company, 1993).
26. Ibid., ch. 1.
27. Denhardt and Denhardt, *The New Public Service*, 3.
28. Kenneth Kernaghan, Brian Marson, and Sandford Borins, *The New Public Organization* (Toronto: Institute of Public Administration of Canada, 2000), 4.
29. Ibid., 2.
30. Christensen and Lægreid, "Governance and Administrative Reforms," 261–262.
31. Ibid., 263.
32. Pollitt, *The Essential Public Manager*, 49, 50.
33. Martin Lodge and Derek Gill, "Toward a New Era of Administrative Reform? The Myth of Post-NPM in New Zealand," *Governance* 24(1) (January 2011): 142.
34. Ibid., 160.
35. Kjell Eliassen and Nick Sitter, *Understanding Public Management* (London: Sage Publications, 2008), 104–111.
36. Gow, "Evolution of Disciplinary Approaches and Paradigms," 20.
37. Christopher Pollitt and Peter Hupe, "Talking About Government: The Role of Magic Concepts," *Public Management Review* 13(5) (2011): 641–658.
38. In his classic article on governance, R.A.W. Rhodes, "The New Governance: Governing Without Government" *Political Studies* 44(4) (1996): 652–667, identified at least six different meanings for the term.
39. R.A.W. Rhodes, "Understanding Governance: Ten Years On," *Organization Studies* 28(8) (2007): 1247. See also, Stephen Goldsmith and William Eggers, *Governing by Network: The New Shape of the Public Sector* (Washington, DC: The Brookings Institute, 2004).
40. B. Guy Peters and John Pierre, "Governance Without Government? Rethinking Public Administration," *Journal of Public Administration Research and Theory* 8(2) (April 1998): 227; Christensen and Lægreid, "Governance and Administrative Reforms," 256.
41. Eliassen and Sitter, *Understanding Public Management*, 110.
42. Tom Christensen and Per Lægreid, "The Whole-of-Government Approach to Public Sector Reform," *Public Administration Review* 67(6) (Nov/Dec 2007): 1059–1066.
43. Dunleavy, Margetts, Bastow, and Tinkler, "New Public Management Is Dead," 478.
44. Kernaghan, Marson, and Borins, *The New Public Organization*, ch. 10. See also, David Brown, "Information, Technology and Canadian Public Administration" in *The Handbook of Canadian Public Administration* 2nd ed., ed. Christopher Dunn (Toronto: Oxford University Press, 2010), 521–537.
45. Alex Boutilier, "Ottawa in Internet Dark Ages," *Toronto Star*. March 15, 2016, A2. Interestingly, in a move to better use IT to improve service delivery for Ontarians, Premier Wynne appointed a minister responsible for digital government in 2016; that individual will be hiring the government's first chief digital officer. See Robert Benzie, "Queen's Park to Hire Guru for Online Services," *Toronto Star*, June 15, 2016, A8.
46. Stephen Osborne, "The New Public Governance?" *Public Management Review* 8(3) (2006): 377–387.
47. Stephen Osborne, "The (New) Public Governance: A Suitable Case for Treatment?" in *The New Public Governance: Emerging Perspectives on the Theory and Practice of Public Governance*, ed. Stephen Osborne (New York: Routledge, 2010), 9.
48. Douglas Morgan and Craig Shinn, "The Foundations of New Public Governance" in *New Public Governance: A Regime-Centred Perspective*, eds. Douglas Morgan and Brian Cook (New York: M.E. Sharpe Inc., 2014), 5.
49. Jacob Torfing and Peter Triantafillou, "What's in a Name? Grasping New Public Governance as a Political-Administrative System," *International Review of Public Administration* 18(2) (2013): 16.
50. Ibid., 17–18.
51. See, for example, Gerry Stoker, "Public Value Management: A New Narrative for Networked Governance?" *American Review of Public Administration* 36(1) (March 2006): 41–57; Guoxian Bao, Xuejun Wang, Gary Larsen, and Douglas Morgan, "Beyond New Public Governance: A Value-Based Global Framework for Performance Management, Governance and Leadership," *Administration & Society* 45(4) (2012): 443–467; John Bryson, Barbara Crosby, and Laura Bloomberg, eds. *Public Value and Public Administration* (Washington, DC: Georgetown University Press, 2015).
52. Stephen Osborne, Zoe Radnor, and Greta Nasi, "A New Theory for Public Service Management? Toward a (Public) Service-Dominant Approach," *American Review of Public Administration* 43(2) (2012): 135–158.
53. Christensen and Lægreid, "Governance and Administrative Reforms," 264–265.
54. Peter Aucoin, "New Public Management and New Public Governance: Finding the Balance," in *Professionalism and Public Service: Essays in Honour of Kenneth Kernaghan*, eds. David Siegel and Ken Rasmussen (Toronto: University of Toronto Press, 2008), 29.
55. Ibid., 23.
56. Clerk of the Privy Council, *Fifth Annual Report to the Prime Minister on the Public Service of Canada* (Ottawa: Privy Council Office, 1998), accessed June 24, 2016, www.clerk.gc.ca/eng/feature.asp?pageId=150.
57. John Halligan, "A Comparative Perspective on Canadian Public Administration Within an Anglophone Tradition," in *The Evolving Physiology*

of Government: Canadian Administration in Transition, eds. Dwivedi, Mau, and Sheldrick (Ottawa: University of Ottawa Press, 2009), 302.

58. G. Bruce Doern and Christopher Stoney, "The Harper Majority, Budget Cuts and the New Opposition" in How Ottawa Spends, 2012–2013: The Harper Majority, Budget Cuts and the New Opposition, eds. G. Bruce Doern and Christopher Stoney (Montreal and Kingston: McGill-Queen's University Press, 2012), 10–12.

59. Aucoin, "New Public Management and New Public Governance," 29.

60. See Herman Bakvis and Luc Juillet, The Horizontal Challenge: Line Departments, Central Agencies and Leadership (Ottawa: Canada School of Public Service, 2004). A list of dozens of horizontal initiatives can be found on the federal government's Horizontal Initiatives Database (www.tbs-sct.gc.ca/hidb-bdih/home-accueil-eng.aspx).

61. Treasury Board of Canada Secretariat, "Whole of Government Framework," accessed June 24, 2016, www.tbs-sct.gc.ca/ppg-cpr/frame-cadre-eng.aspx.

62. Treasury Board of Canada Secretariat, Canada's Action Plan on Open Government, 2014–2016 (Ottawa: Her Majesty the Queen in Right of Canada, 2014), accessed June 24, 2016, www.open.canada.ca/en/content/canadas-action-plan-open-government-2014-16.

Government Departments and Central Agencies

6

Learning Objectives

Reading this chapter allows you to do the following:

- Understand the traditional form of government organization for delivering programs and services to Canadians

- Differentiate between the political and administrative head of a government department

- Describe how organizational change in government occurs and assess the costs and benefits associated with it

- Identify the various central agencies and distinguish the critical role they fulfill in public management relative to the line departments

- Explain the difference between the Privy Council Office and the Prime Minister's Office

Agriculture and Agri-Food Canada, the Privy Council Office, Transport Canada, Public Safety Canada, and the Social Sciences and Humanities Research Council of Canada represent a handful of the many administrative bodies at the federal level in Canada. The reality is that government organizations come in a bewildering array of different names and organizational structures. A former senior public servant identified 42 different labels for organizations in the federal government—including department, board, commission, tribunal, agency, advisory committee, and foundation—and argued that part of the confusion in terms of trying to understand the structures of government was the lack of consistency in utilizing these organizational designations. This problem was further compounded by virtue of the fact that often two organizations with the same label (commission, for example) would be structured very differently.[1] Some of the bodies are directly controlled by a minister, others are deliberately kept at arm's length so that there is limited ministerial control, and still others seem almost beyond any kind of control. This huge variety of organizations follows from the diverse functions and duties of government. The problems and challenges facing a society require governments to spend money, regulate behaviour, acquire ownership of companies, and exhort people to act in a particular manner. All of these functions and more require differing kinds of government instruments to achieve the most effective delivery of programs and services.

Historically, government services have been delivered through departments, Crown corporations, and independent agencies, all of which come in many different shapes and forms. But in the last two decades there has been an explosion in the number of different delivery mechanisms that governments employ. This innovation in service-delivery mechanisms has been a response to both financial constraints and citizen demands for improved service delivery. In some cases, the innovation has resulted in governments adopting new structures that are variations of the traditional delivery forms. In other cases, governments have employed new means of service delivery, such as partnerships with non-governmental organizations to share the cost and responsibility for delivering services.

The purpose of Part Three of the book is to consider the organizational mechanisms that governments use to deliver public services, and this chapter considers the most traditional instrument for delivering services, the department. It begins with a discussion of the legal foundations of departments, a discussion which requires an examination of interactions between departments, the legislature, and the political executive or cabinet. The chapter then addresses various aspects of the functioning of departments and finishes with a consideration of the most powerful departmental forms—the central agencies. The next chapter will examine Crown corporations and agencies.

The Legislature, the Executive, and Departments

It is customary to speak of three branches of government—legislative, executive, and judicial. The judicial branch, which consists of the law courts and related institutions, is not discussed in this chapter but will be considered in detail later. In Canada, the legislative branch of the federal government consists of the Queen and two houses or chambers—the House of Commons and the Senate. The executive branch is technically headed by the Queen, represented in Canada by the **governor general** and the **lieutenant governors** of the provinces. In practice, neither the Queen nor any of her vice-regal representatives ever acts except on the advice of the government of the day as embodied in the prime minister (or premier in the case of the provinces) and the cabinet. This means that the responsibilities of the executive branch are carried out collectively by cabinet or what is commonly called "the government." All public servants act under the direction and control of the cabinet and are included, therefore, as part of the executive branch. Thus, in this book, the practical working definition of the executive is the cabinet and the public service.

One sometimes hears that something is done by the **governor-in-council** or the **lieutenant-governor-in-council**. This means that the governor general or the lieutenant governor has taken some legal action after consultation with the cabinet. It actually means that the cabinet has taken some action; the governor general's or lieutenant governor's signature is a formality.

The congressional system of government in the United States is characterized by a balance of powers between the three branches so that no one branch has authority over any other. In parliamentary systems, such as Canada's, it is an important principle that the executive branch is accountable to the legislative branch (i.e., the branch most directly responsible to the general public). Figure 6.1 shows that the two branches are in fact joined, because cabinet ministers are almost invariably members of the legislative branch. This institutional arrangement helps the legislature to hold the executive accountable for its actions. However, it also offers an opportunity for the executive to control the legislature through the use of party discipline, a situation which lessens of influence of the legislative branch.

Definition of a Department

It is difficult to establish a precise working definition of an **operating department**. Legal definitions can be found in pieces of government legislation, but these legislative definitions differ somewhat and they fail to capture the essence of a department, because the purpose of the legislative definition is to determine which organizations will be subject to a particular regime of financial or personnel administration. The definition of an operating department used in this book is that of J.E. Hodgetts, who states that a "department is an administrative unit comprising one or more organizational components over which a minister has direct ministerial management and control."[2]

governor general The representative of the Queen in Canada; functions as the head of state when the Queen is not in Canada.

lieutenant governor The representatives of the Queen in the provinces.

governor-in-council The governor general acting on the formal advice of the cabinet.

lieutenant-governor-in-council The lieutenant governor acting on the formal advice of a provincial cabinet.

operating department An administrative unit comprising one or more organizational components over which a minister has direct ministerial management control.

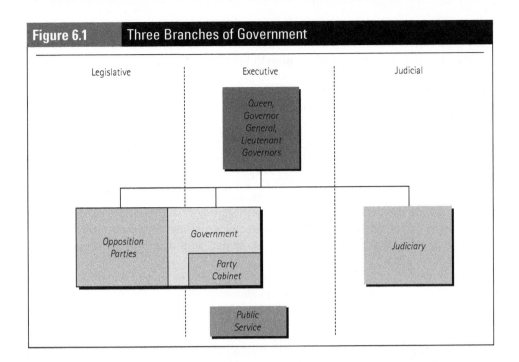

Figure 6.1   Three Branches of Government

Legislative   Executive   Judicial

Queen, Governor General, Lieutenant Governors

Opposition Parties

Government

Party Cabinet

Judiciary

Public Service

This definition emphasizes that traditional government organizations are mainly in the business of administering services and, as Figure 6.2 shows, they are structured hierarchically as per the Weberian bureaucratic model outlined in Chapter 3 with a number of branches or units that serve to carry out their responsibilities. The definition also highlights a characteristic that distinguishes departments from other delivery forms or mechanisms in government, namely that the minister directly controls and manages operations. The positioning of the minister at the top of the organization chart in

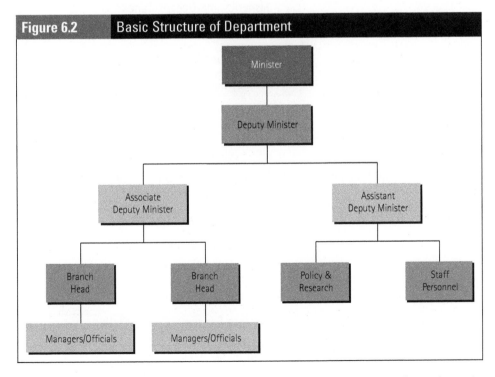

Figure 6.2   Basic Structure of Department

Minister

Deputy Minister

Associate Deputy Minister

Assistant Deputy Minister

Branch Head

Branch Head

Policy & Research

Staff Personnel

Managers/Officials

Managers/Officials

Figure 6.2 and the straight line connecting the minister to the department signify this quality of departments. It is a constitutional convention that the minister should very closely supervise, but resist the temptation to micro-manage, the actions of an operating department.

Classification Systems for Departments

There are so many departments with so many special responsibilities that a number of writers have tried to facilitate understanding of their roles by grouping them in some way. One classification system is based on the general policy fields addressed, or functions carried out by the department, such as "public works, communications, and transportation" and "conservation, development, and promotion of physical resources."[3] Another system adopts a more parsimonious approach and identifies three types of departments by considering the relative power of departments as determined by their function: horizontal policy coordinative, horizontal administrative coordinative, and vertical constituency.[4]

An application of the classification scheme to the present array of departments of the federal government results in the groupings shown in Table 6.1. Of the three types, the

TABLE 6.1 Classification of Federal Government Departments	
HORIZONTAL POLICY COORDINATIVE	**VERTICAL CONSTITUENCY**
Finance Canada	Agriculture and Agri-Food Canada
Justice Canada	Canadian Heritage
Privy Council Office	Immigration, Refugees and Citizenship Canada
Treasury Board Secretariat	Environment and Climate Change Canada
	Fisheries and Oceans Canada
	Global Affairs Canada
	Health Canada
	Employment and Social Development Canada
	Indigenous and Northern Affairs Canada
HORIZONTAL ADMINISTRATIVE COORDINATIVE	Innovation, Science and Economic Development Canada
Public Services and Procurement Canada	National Defence and the Canadian Armed Forces
	Natural Resources Canada
	Public Safety Canada
	Transport Canada
	Veterans Affairs Canada
	Western Economic Diversification

Source: Based on and updated from G. Bruce Doern, "Horizontal and Vertical Portfolios in Government" in *Issues in Canadian Public Policy*, eds. G. Bruce Doern and V. Seymour Wilson (Toronto: MacMillan, 1974), 315–316.

Part Three / Delivering Government Services

horizontal policy coordinative departments tend to be the most influential. Doern explains:

> They have inherent high policy influence because of the formal authority they possess and because they afford their occupants the highest number of strategic opportunities to intervene in almost any policy issue if the occupant wishes. They each deal respectively with the traditionally most basic horizontal or crosscutting dimensions of government policy, namely overall political leadership and strategy, foreign policy and the foreign implications of domestic policy fields, aggregate economic and fiscal policy, the basic legal and judicial concepts and values of the state, and the overall management of government spending programmes.[5]

These departments tend to be small in terms of number of employees and size of budget, but very strong in terms of responsibility for coordination and knowledge or research capability. As a result of this responsibility for coordination across the activities of other departments, some of them are also called central agencies, as will be discussed later in this chapter.

The **horizontal administrative coordinative departments** are usually felt to be the least influential, in that they are assumed to be the "nuts and bolts" departments that provide the wherewithal for other departments to operate. Public Services and Procurement Canada (formerly Public Works and Government Services Canada [PWGSC]), for instance, acts to purchase goods and services for other government agencies at the federal level and ensures that public servants have accommodations necessary to carry out their work. However, even these departments have significance. For example, it was announced in February 2014 that the then PWGSC would assume responsibility for the leadership and implementation of the new Defence Procurement Strategy.[6] This was a direct response to the growing perception that the Department of National Defence was ill equipped to handle procurement; the net result is that Public Services and Procurement Canada is now responsible for billions of dollars of spending associated with defence and major Coast Guard procurements that will be tied to job creation, growth, and economic prosperity.

The **vertical constituency departments** are involved in providing services directly to the public. These are high-profile departments with large budgets and constituencies that they serve. In general, they lack the power to intervene in the affairs of other departments, a power which only comes with the responsibility to coordinate; but their large budgets and vocal constituencies give these departments significant power. It is difficult for the horizontal coordinative portfolios to intervene too much in the affairs of these departments without raising the ire of the large number of constituents who are dependent on the departments for service.

While it is possible to group departments according to characteristics, it is considerably more difficult to rank these portfolios, or the ministers who hold them, in order of importance. Having said that, it is generally understood that there are a number of prestigious ministerial portfolios in the federal government, including Finance, the Treasury Board, Foreign Affairs (now Global Affairs), Industry (now Innovation, Science and Economic Development Canada), and Justice.[7] At the end of the day, however, a minister's relative position in cabinet is determined by her or his portfolio, but also in large part by such other factors as regional power base, personal diplomatic and judgment skills, and, perhaps most significantly, the relationship that the minister has with the prime minister. The importance of the relationship between individual ministers and the prime minister cannot be overstated. This would help to explain why former ministers Jason Kenney (Minister of Employment and Social Development as well as Minister of Multiculturalism) and Diane Finley (Minister of Government Works and Public Services), who headed departments that few would consider top tier, were ranked fourth and fifteenth respectively by the *Hill Times* in the top 100 most powerful and influential people in Ottawa in 2015.[8]

---

horizontal policy coordinative department These are the government departments (also known as central agencies) that have the responsibility for coordinating the overall policy agenda of the government.

horizontal administrative coordinative department Usually considered to be the least influential departments, these entities provide other departments with the various supports (i.e., goods and services) that they require to fulfill their mandates.

vertical constituency department Also referred to as line departments, these are the organizations that have primary responsibility for delivery of programs and services to citizens.

In the final analysis, no portfolio can be deemed unimportant. All portfolios have significant roles, and they can all lead to substantial embarrassment for the government if the occupant of a portfolio is careless or incompetent. This proved to be the case when Rona Ambrose, widely criticized for her poor performance defending the government's opposition to the Kyoto Protocol and its new environmental policy, was replaced as minister in 2007 less than one year into the position. More recently, in an equally embarrassing situation, the Harper government was left reeling after Chris Alexander, Minister of Citizenship and Immigration, mishandled the government's response to the Syrian refugee crisis in the midst of the 2015 general election campaign.

Organizing Departments

The organization structure of the government is the personal prerogative of the prime minister. While most changes must ultimately be approved by Parliament, the *Public Service Rearrangement and Transfer of Duties Act*, which dates to 1918, gives the prime minister a great deal of power to transfer duties among departments and even create new departments. Paul Martin, on becoming prime minister in 2003, and in the wake of increasing concerns about international security and the threat of terrorism, established the new Department of Public Safety and Emergency Preparedness. He also divided the old Department of Human Resources Development into two new entities—Human Resources *and* Skills Development and Social Development—for the purpose of providing a sharper focus for responsibilities in each of the respective departments. As one of his first duties, Prime Minister Stephen Harper, in 2006, also made changes affecting departmental structures. He focused mostly on combining departments in order to produce a more integrated and synchronized approach to the delivery of programs. For example, he brought together the departments of Foreign Affairs and International Trade "to ensure a coherent approach to foreign affairs and international commerce and to better coordinate the provision of services to Canadians both at home and abroad."[9] Then, as part of the 2013 federal budget, the government amalgamated the Department of Foreign Affairs and International Trade (DFAIT) with the Canadian International Development Agency (CIDA), creating a new entity known as the Department of Foreign Affairs, Trade and Development (DFATD). It was suggested that by aligning its foreign, development, trade, and commercial policies and programs, the government would "have greater policy coherence on priority issues [which would] result in greater overall impact of our efforts."[10]

Other prime ministers have also found reason to make adjustments to the departmental structure of government. During her brief stint as prime minister in 1993, Kim Campbell substantially reduced the number of departments because of the difficulty of coordinating the activities of a large array of administrative units. The desire to have a smaller cabinet also played a role. These changes to the machinery of government were largely kept intact when Jean Chrétien became prime minister after the Liberal Party won its landslide victory in the 1993 general election.

Most recently, in November 2015, Prime Minister Trudeau implemented a number of machinery of government changes to better reflect the new government's priorities, including the renaming of DFATD to Global Affairs Canada; Environment Canada to Environment and Climate Change Canada; PWGSC to Public Services and Procurement Canada; Aboriginal Affairs and Northern Development to Indigenous and Northern Affairs Canada; Industry Canada to Innovation, Science and Economic Development Canada; and Citizenship and Immigration Canada to Immigration, Refugees and Citizenship Canada.

It is tempting for each new prime minister to reorganize ministries to suit her or his style of governing, and virtually every prime minister has made certain changes. However, these shifts must be made with care, because major organizational shifts may impose significant tangible and intangible costs on government. The tangible costs arise from the time spent on finding new accommodation, drawing up new organizational structures, preparing new job descriptions, and so forth.[11] Less tangible are the personal costs people feel when their long service in an organization with a particular kind of culture is interrupted by having to integrate into a new department with a vastly different culture:

> Organizing is not a free lunch. Adding new organizations or ministerial portfolios adds complexity, and reorganizing existing ones causes disruption. Neither of these costs should be taken lightly. At a minimum, it can take three years to implement a major organizational change—in many cases five years. Where major adjustments in organizational culture are necessary, even more time may be required. During the time these adjustments are taking place, the time and energy of politicians and officials is occupied with organizational issues, at the expense of the policy and program issues that the organization was meant to address.[12]

There has been a remarkable degree of stability in Canadian government departments. Once created, departments are rarely completely abolished, but that has not translated into the excessive growth of government organizations. However, name changes and the reorganization of responsibilities of federal government departments have been fairly common since Confederation. In an attempt to classify departmental survival in Canada, one study characterized each departmental name change as the death of one organization and the creation of a new one. On that basis, it was noted that 117 federal departments were created and 85 were terminated between 1867 and 2010, leaving a net of 32 departments.[13] This represents an increase of 16 departments in the federal government since 1867, which is hardly evidence of a public sector bloated by the existence of too many public agencies.

One real cost of organizational change is that the resulting departments may be too much for the minister responsible. To address this problem, prime ministers have appointed ministers of state and, less frequently, secretaries of state in addition to the cabinet ministers who head departments. Both the ministers of state and the secretaries of state were assigned specific responsibilities to assist a minister. However, while the ministers of state were junior members of cabinet, the secretaries of state were an intermediate position, in that they were members of the ministry and therefore bound by collective responsibility, but they were not considered to be cabinet ministers. The secretaries of state were created by Prime Minister Chrétien in 1993 and used for a decade before Paul Martin terminated them. Prime Minister Harper briefly resurrected them in 2007, but reverted to using ministers of state in his 2008 cabinet. These positions have been used to indicate the government's concern about certain issues. For example, Prime Minister Paul Martin created a minister of state for public health to reveal his government's commitment to deal with any future epidemics. However, some prime ministers may elect to dispense with ministers of state and rely on a core group of ministers to oversee and direct government departments. Prime Minister Harper, for instance, did not include any ministers of state in his first cabinet in 2006, but there were 12 such positions in a 39-member cabinet when Parliament dissolved for the 2015 general election.[14] For his part, Prime Minister Justin Trudeau chose to eschew the use of both secretaries of state and ministers of state as part of his inaugural cabinet.

The Legislature and Government Departments

Departments are the most closely controlled of all government agencies. Other entities such as regulatory agencies and Crown corporations are deliberately insulated, to some extent, from direct control by the legislature and the executive, but departments have no such autonomy. This control begins at the time of the creation of a new department, because new departments can only be created by an Act of Parliament. This enabling legislation sets out the responsibilities of the department and the limits of its authority. The statute establishing the federal Department of Veteran Affairs is typical, being just six pages long and couched in very general terms imposing only broad conditions on the department's operation. The statute provides in part that

2. (1) There is hereby established a department of the Government of Canada called the Department of Veteran Affairs over which the Minister of Veteran Affairs appointed by commission under the Great Seal shall preside.

(2) The Minister holds office during pleasure and has the management and direction of the Department ... .

4. The powers, duties and functions of the Minister extend and apply to

(a) the administration of such Acts of Parliament, and of such orders of the Governor in Council, as are not by law assigned to any other department of the Government of Canada or any Minister thereof, relating to

(i) the care, treatment or re-establishment in civil life of any person who served in the Canadian Forces or merchant navy or in the naval, army or air forces or merchant navies of Her Majesty, of any person who has otherwise engaged in pursuits relating to war, and of any other person designated by the Governor in Council, and

(ii) the care of the dependants or survivors of any person referred to in subparagraph (i); and

(b) all such other matters and such boards and other bodies, subjects, services and properties of the Crown as may be designated, or assigned to the Minister, by the Governor in Council.[15]

For other departments, the conditions and stipulations are more detailed. The federal Department of Health (or Health Canada) is directed to achieve nine goals.[16] However, even here the minister and the department are allowed a great deal of leeway in the pursuit of these departmental aims.

In addition to the enabling legislation, Parliament sometimes passes other legislation affecting departments. This includes both specific legislation, such as setting up a new program and assigning it to a department, and general pieces of legislation that bind all departments in certain matters. Thus, Parliament can specify a department's mandate as loosely or as tightly as it wants, although the usual practice is to provide a broad mandate that allows maximum flexibility to the executive.

Another important element of Parliament's relationship to the executive is the annual budget. Every year the executive must seek parliamentary approval to spend funds in the upcoming year. At a minimum, the members of parliament, particularly opposition members, use this opportunity to question ministers and public servants about the operation of their departments and programs. In extreme cases, Parliament might decide to reduce, or even entirely eliminate, an expenditure request or appropriation for a department.

While these methods by which the legislature can affect departmental operations are, legally speaking, correct, reality requires some modification in practice. When the government party holds a majority of seats in the legislature, the government has fairly effective control over the legislation passed. Members of the opposition can introduce amendments to proposed legislation, including reductions of appropriations, but these are unlikely to be passed. In the case of a minority government, the situation is more complex, but the government usually finds some method of exercising a certain amount of control over activities in the legislature. If it cannot exert sufficient control, it will not govern long—as Prime Minister Paul Martin discovered in late 2005. This should not be taken to mean that the government can totally dominate the legislature. Opposition members have certain tools at their disposal to thwart arbitrary government actions. The legislature is a highly public forum, and the government is sensitive to the embarrassment it can suffer when the opposition rallies public opinion against some unpopular government action. The government, particularly in a majority situation, has a strong position, but not an absolutely commanding one. Opposition parties still have means of holding a government accountable.

This is where the doctrine of individual ministerial responsibility becomes important. This principle, discussed more fully later in this book, holds that a minister is responsible for all actions carried out by her or his department. This means that, even if the minister did not approve an action in advance or had no knowledge of it, he or she must still accept responsibility for the action. This principle is an important element in a system of responsible government, because the minister is the only link between the legislature and the operating department. If the minister could avoid responsibility for the actions of her or his department, the legislature would have no effective way of holding the executive accountable for its actions. Since the minister is accountable for the actions of her or his department, it is important that there be adequate methods available for the minister to control the department.

The Executive and Government Departments

The minister is the political head of the department, and so has line authority over all public servants in the department. Within the provisions of relevant legislation, he or she has full authority to assign duties to departmental employees and supervise their activities. In the preceding chapters, there was some discussion of the difficulties of administrative superiors holding subordinates truly accountable for their actions. The large size and geographical decentralization of most departments, and the incredible demands made on ministers' time in the legislature and in constituency work, make the enforcement of real accountability problematic. However, ministers have a number of tools to assist them.

All ministers have a small personal staff reporting directly to them. The staff members are selected personally by the minister and are not considered to be public servants, but rather the minister's political assistants. They are selected partly for their administrative competence, but unlike public servants they are also selected for their partisan affiliation. Their roles are difficult to define, since every minister uses them differently; however, one role they have in common is assisting the minister to exercise political control over the bureaucracy. Ministers also have more formal, legal means of controlling their departments. The legislation establishing departments and programs seldom specifies in precise detail how all activities are to be carried out, in large part because the legislature is unable to foresee every future possibility. There is usually a clause in this kind of legislation that allows either the minister or the governor-in-council (i.e., the cabinet) to make certain regulations as long as they are consistent with the terms of the enabling legislation. In some cases, this is done in strict legal form through an **order-in-council**. This is a formal regulation approved by the governor-in-council and, in the case of the federal government, published in the *Canada Gazette,* a bi-weekly listing of official announcements prepared by the government. Provincial governments have similar official publications.

order-in-council An official proclamation made by the governor-in-council; usually a government regulation.

Orders-in-council frequently establish the ground rules governing relationships between public servants and members of the public affected by their actions and decisions. For example, there are lengthy orders-in-council specifying the rules about access to information and privacy. They describe the sorts of information not available to the public, but they also restrict public servants by specifying those items that must be released. In this sense, regulations are an important means of controlling the actions of public servants.

In a less formal manner, ministers frequently issue internal departmental regulations. These are binding on all departmental officials, provided that the regulations are within the terms of the enabling legislation. It is these regulations—covering such matters as which form is to be completed in a given case and how a certain situation is to be treated—that are the lifeblood of most large organizations. Over the years, these regulations can accumulate to several volumes.

Organization of a Typical Operating Department

minister An elected politician who serves as the political head of a government department.

Figure 6.3 shows an organization chart of the federal Department of Transport. At the apex is the **minister**, who sets the priorities and assumes responsibility for all actions taken within the organization. As explained earlier, the minister may also have personal staff members appointed on a political basis to work directly and personally for him or her, and who are replaced when he or she leaves or the government changes. Their role is to provide the minister with overtly political advice. Most ministers also have a variety of additional public sector organizations, often Crown corporations and regulatory agencies, reporting to them in addition to their department. As Figure 6.4 shows, the Minister of Transport has an expansive portfolio with responsibility for an

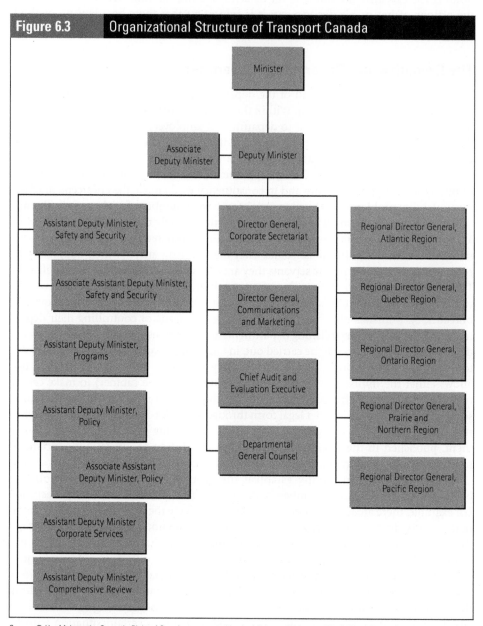

Figure 6.3 — Organizational Structure of Transport Canada

Source: © Her Majesty the Queen in Right of Canada, represented by the Minister of Transport (2016). This information has been reproduced with the permission of Transport Canada.

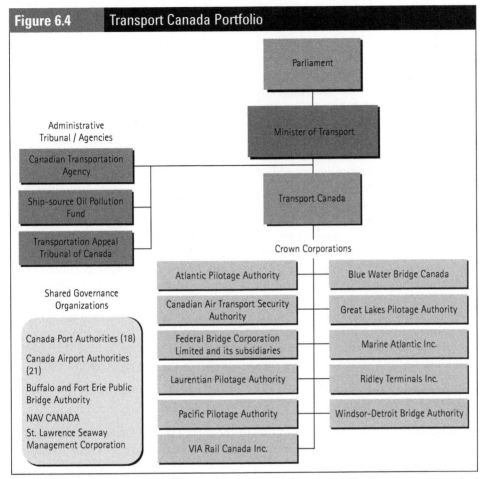

Figure 6.4 Transport Canada Portfolio

Source: © Her Majesty the Queen in Right of Canada, represented by the Minister of Transport (2016). This information has been reproduced with the permission of Transport Canada.

agency, tribunal and fund, 11 Crown corporations and 42 shared governance organizations, including 18 port and 21 airport authorities, in addition to the department itself, which has a staff complement of 5,072 full-time equivalents and planned expenditures of nearly $1.3 billion for the 2016–2017 fiscal year.[17]

The next link in the chain of accountability is the **deputy minister (DM)**. DMs are the administrative (as distinct from political) heads of departments. They are permanent heads of departments in that they do not usually leave when governments change. Unlike ministers, who are politicians, DMs typically work their way up through the ranks of the public service, although in some cases they are brought in directly from other governments or the private sector. In some senses, DMs have the most difficult position in the entire system: they must act as a connection between the political desires of the minister and the administrative concerns of the public servants in the department. Ministers are not totally insensitive to administrative concerns, any more than public servants are totally insensitive to political ones, but each side brings a different dimension to the issue at hand. Ministers, particularly if they represent a new government, often feel under pressure from colleagues to make changes in programs and activities. It would not be appropriate for public servants to oppose these changes, but public servants are frequently more attuned to the administrative problems posed by change than to its political benefits.

A word of caution about terminology is necessary. The term "deputy minister" is not used consistently across departments. There are a number of other individuals working

deputy minister (DM) The administrative head of a government department. Appointed by the prime minister or premier. Also referred to as the deputy head.

in public sector organizations who have the rank of deputy minister, but are known by other titles. This would include the president of an agency or Crown corporation, secretary or commissioner. For example, in the Treasury Board where the minister is called the "president," the senior public servant is called the "secretary." In most government publications, the term "deputy head or equivalent levels" is used to cover all of these senior people. In normal discussion around government offices, one frequently hears reference to "the deputy."

Beneath the level of deputy minister, the nomenclature can become even more confusing. Usually, there will be several "assistant deputy ministers" reporting to the deputy minister. Sometimes the superior status of one of these positions will be established by designating it as "associate deputy minister" or "senior assistant deputy minister." This is usually a sign that the position carries a heavier weight of duties or responsibilities than the other assistant deputy minister positions. Also, in the Department of Transport, there is a regional director general (RDG) (see Figure 6.3) for each of the regions reporting directly to the deputy minister. These positions have almost the same status as the assistant deputy minister in that they report directly to the deputy, but their title indicates that their ranking is slightly lower, usually because they have less weighty responsibilities.

At this point, it is useful to relate this organization chart to some of the material about organizational behaviour covered in earlier chapters. In terms of the line–staff distinction, the line units are the regional directors general, while the staff functions are the assistant deputy ministers in charge of policy and corporate services and the general counsel, who is responsible for legal services. A more complete organization chart would also illustrate the functional lines of authority between the line and staff functions.

Central Agencies

The discussion of span of control in one of the earlier chapters drew attention to the fact that as the number of units reporting to the same person increases, that person has more difficulty maintaining control of the units and coordinating their activities. The organization of the government of Canada demonstrates a very broad span of control with numerous departments, agencies, and so forth coming under the direct control of cabinet. This broad organizational structure requires some method of coordinating the activities of the separate departments to prevent overlap and working at cross purposes. One of the methods employed in Canada is the central agency.

There are other ways of dealing with this problem. In Britain, there are many departments headed by ministers who are not members of cabinet. Ministers heading related departments are then grouped under a senior minister who is a member of cabinet. This creates a situation in which the span of control is reasonable both for cabinet, with a relatively small number of senior ministers, and for the senior ministers, each of whom has a reasonable number of non-cabinet ministers reporting to her or him. It provides for both reasonable spans of control and a relatively small cabinet.

It is this latter characteristic that precludes the use of this system in Canada. In this country, the concept of the representative cabinet is very important. This principle means that many diverse interests must be represented in the federal cabinet. It requires the selection of cabinet members to provide an appropriate balance of geographic, religious, ethnic, linguistic, gender, and other criteria. As a result, the cabinet must be fairly large, to ensure all groups are represented adequately.

central agency An agency that has a substantial amount of continuing legitimate authority to intervene in and direct the activity of departments.

Definition of a Central Agency

A **central agency** (previously also called a horizontal policy coordinative department) is any organization that has a substantial amount of continuing, legitimate authority to direct and intervene in the activities of departments. The application of any definition, particularly one that contains words such as "substantial" and "continuing," is somewhat arbitrary, but it is widely acknowledged that there are four full-fledged central agencies in the government of Canada—the Prime Minister's Office (PMO), the Privy Council Office (PCO), the Treasury Board Secretariat (TBS), and the Department of Finance.[18]

Central agencies obtain their power either from legislative authority to operate in a particular area or from proximity to someone with legitimate authority, such as the prime minister. They usually do not have a large number of employees, although most of the staff employed are relatively high-level, professional people. Indeed, people working in central agencies have been called "superbureaucrats" in recognition of their skills and influence.[19] Table 6.2 shows the number of people employed in these four agencies, and some of the largest and smallest departments. Even the smallest departments typically have more employees than the central agencies, and the largest departments completely dwarf them.

All four agencies discussed in this section have either been created, or have undergone significant change, as a result of the style of government brought to office by Prime Minister Trudeau in 1968.[20] Trudeau's predecessor, Prime Minister Pearson, never had a majority government, and so had to be concerned with conciliation and firefighting. However, with a majority government in his first term, Trudeau had the luxury of focusing on specific goals he wanted to accomplish and using such newly fashionable rational tools as cost-effectiveness and systems analysis to attain those goals. His limited experience in working in large organizations could have made him uncomfortable in a bureaucratic environment. As a result, Trudeau wanted competing sources of information so that he did not have to rely solely on the traditional information sources of the operating departments. This was not evidence of distrust of the traditional organizational structures; rather, it was the understandable desire to obtain more than one point of view on an issue before acting. Thus, another major role for central agencies developed in addition to the coordinating role discussed above. Trudeau began to use these agencies as competing sources of information.

TABLE 6.2	Number of Full-Time Equivalent Employees in Central Agencies and Selected Departments, 2016–2017
CENTRAL AGENCY OR DEPARTMENT	**NUMBER OF EMPLOYEES**
Finance	739
Prime Minister's Office[21]	94
Privy Council Office	954
Treasury Board Secretariat	1,802
National Defence (civilian and military combined)	92,407
Employment and Social Development Canada	20,881
Public Services and Procurement Canada	11,709.07
Justice	4,310
Public Safety Canada	1,081
Global Affairs Canada	11,101
Health Canada	8,913

Source: Figures derived from selected departments' *2016–2017 Report on Plans and Priorities* (Ottawa: Her Majesty the Queen in Right of Canada, 2016).

It is important to understand that, although every prime minister has left her or his own personal stamp on the government bureaucracy, there has been enough consistency that it is still possible to generalize about the duties of the central agencies. They have two related roles: (1) they are responsible for coordinating both the political and the administrative activities of line departments; (2) they are involved in advising the prime minister and cabinet on policy initiatives and shepherding them through the decision-making and implementation processes. These roles and responsibilities can be illustrated best by a discussion of the activities of each of these four agencies.

The Prime Minister's Office

Prime Minister's Office (PMO) The *central agency* providing partisan policy advice to the prime minister. It is most concerned with relations between the prime minister and the media and the party.

The **PMO** works directly for the prime minister and has an overtly partisan political role. For political staff members, securing a post in the PMO is the ultimate end game. As one former PMO insider recently wrote, "If you are a political staffer, the PMO is where you want to be. Politically, it is the centre of your universe and a goal that most want to achieve while on the Hill."* But given its role, status and small size—typically comprising around 100 employees—such appointments typically only emerge after many years of hard work and progressive responsibility. Moreover, being invited to work there should also signify "that you have the political smarts to do the job."[22]

The major responsibilities of those individuals who work in the PMO are to serve the prime minister by providing advice on how policy initiatives will be viewed politically in the country, and to assist in other ways that will cast the prime minister in the best political light. Specifically, these responsibilities include planning and coordinating major new policy initiatives, providing liaison with ministers and the party machinery across the country, maintaining good relations with the media, writing speeches, advising on appointments and nominations, and briefing the prime minister concerning issues that might come up during daily question period and debate (see Figure 6.5 for an approximation of the structure of the PMO as it existed in 2016). Given that the stakes are high when mistakes are made, working in the PMO is filled with pressure and stress.

Most of the personnel in the PMO are junior staff, known for their hyper-partisanship, but the prime minister must also ensure that he or she is surrounded by seasoned senior political staff: "You have to have a few 'grey hairs' with the experience to know when and how to act, i.e., some adult supervision for the boys and girls in short-pants."[23] This was a phrase coined to describe the phenomenon of young staff members in the PMO who routinely bossed around MPs with significant parliamentary experience, telling them how to do politics. Concerns have been expressed, however, that under Prime Minister Harper the PMO was dominated by these young people, who essentially had no real life experience and were unwilling to disagree with the prime minister, which left Harper increasingly isolated and without the sage advice needed to govern effectively.[24]

One thing that the junior and senior staff members have in common is the propensity to work extremely long hours. It is quite common for PMO staff members to be scanning online news as early as 5 a.m., with the first meeting of the day occurring by 7:30 a.m. The work day typically does not end until after the 10 p.m. news, assuming that no urgent matters had arisen that required their immediate attention. The hours in between are filled with an unending stream of emails and dozens of policy files that require review and response. This frenetic pace is also largely maintained over the weekend since news stories potentially damaging to the prime minister and government are not confined to the standard work week.[25]

Since these functions are all overtly political in nature, the people working in the PMO are partisan appointees. Prime Minister Martin's chief of staff—the top official in the PMO—had lifelong ties to the Liberal Party in both an appointed and an elected

---

* Keith Beardsley, "What It's Really Like to Work in the PMO," *Power & Influence* 4(1) (Winter 2015), 4.

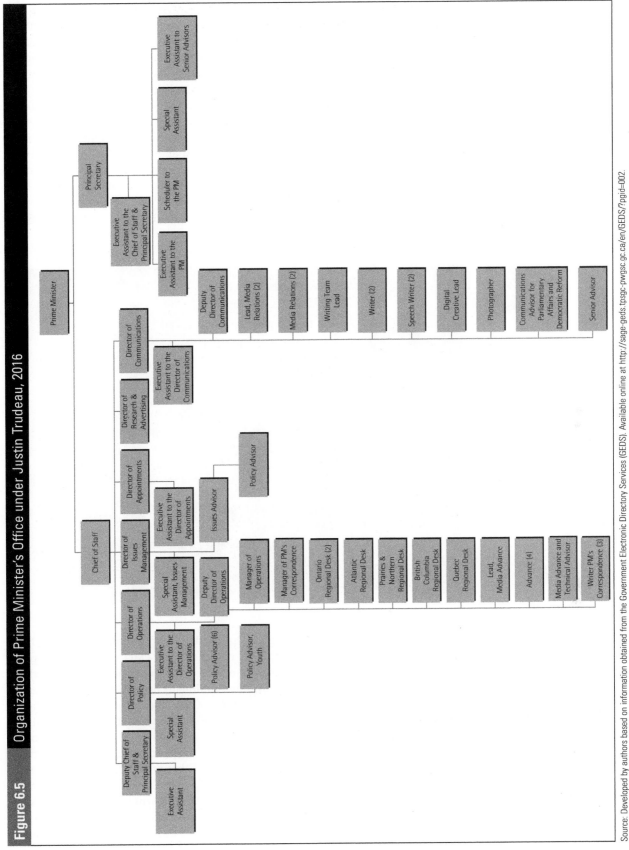

Source: Developed by authors based on information obtained from the Government Electronic Directory Services (GEDS). Available online at http://sage-geds:tpsgc-pwgsc.gc.ca/en/GEDS/?pgid=002.

capacity; Prime Minister Harper's last chief of staff, Ray Novak, has a longstanding relationship with Stephen Harper and the Conservative Party,[26] while Katie Telford, Prime Minister Trudeau's inaugural chief of staff, held a number of positions in both the Liberal Party of Canada and the provincial wing of the party in Ontario prior to assuming this position (see Box 6.1). The partisan nature of appointments to the PMO means that they are there to serve unabashedly the prime minister's political needs and that they hold their positions at the pleasure of the prime minister and always resign when there is a change of government. Sometimes a stay in the PMO can be very short indeed. A few weeks after assuming office, Prime Minister Harper and his newly appointed communications director in the PMO disagreed on the most appropriate manner of handling a delicate situation involving a newly installed cabinet member. The communications officer was relieved of his duties.[27] The incumbents of the chief of staff position have also been known for the brevity of their careers at the PMO—at least while Stephen Harper was prime minister—with four people assuming that role between 2006 and 2015.[28]

BOX 6.1

Profile of a Prime Minister's Chief of Staff

© Jake Wright

Chief of Staff Katie Telford

Date of appointment: November 4, 2015

Age at time of appointment: 37

Education: B.A. (Hon.) in political science from the University of Ottawa

Employment history: Telford, only the second woman ever to be appointed as chief of staff at the PMO, has longstanding connections with the Liberal Party, initially through her involvement with the Ontario Liberal government of Dalton McGuinty, where she served—at the age of 26—as the chief of staff to Gerard Kennedy, Minister of Education. She went on to manage Kennedy's unsuccessful bid for the leadership of the federal Liberal Party in 2006. Telford would then join the staff of Stéphane Dion, the victor of that leadership contest, eventually becoming his deputy chief of staff. She left Ottawa in early 2009 to work briefly for StrategyCorp, a Toronto-based lobbying firm, but was lured back to politics in 2012 to serve as the national campaign director for Justin Trudeau's leadership campaign.

Source: Mark Kennedy, "Katie Telford: 'Hard-Working, Tough, Honest and Wicked Smart'" *Ottawa Citizen*, February 13, 2015, www.ottawacitizen.com/news/politics/katie-telford-hard-working-tough-honest-and-wicked-smart.

A former head of the PMO has argued that the PMO's role should be to establish a "strategic prime ministership."[29] By this, he means that the PMO must assist the prime minister in keeping new policy initiatives on track and avoid being sidetracked. He describes how the prime minister and PMO are continually being confronted with urgent crises. It is imperative, but very difficult, to prevent the urgent from overwhelming the important. He feels that the role of the PMO is to assist the prime minister in identifying the five or six major initiatives he or she wants to accomplish during a term of office, and then making sure the prime minister's energies are expended in this direction rather than on small matters. As seen in Figure 6.5, the PMO has other important activities of a "housekeeping" nature, such as making travel arrangements, which is the largest branch of the PMO,[30] and responding to the huge volume of mail sent to the prime minister.

It is difficult to generalize about the relationship between the PMO and operating departments. The PMO has no statutory authority of its own; the office derives its power from the fact that it is headed by the prime minister, through whom it must act in taking initiatives with departments. Its contact with departments is largely limited to consulting about new policy initiatives or dealing with political problems. There is some evidence that the PMO is becoming more involved in policy matters, a development that worries some because of the political orientation of the PMO. The most notable, and notorious, instance of this concern relates to the earlier-mentioned Sponsorship Program, which operated in the Department of Public Works and Government Services from the mid-1990s to the early part of the new century. The PMO took responsibility for this program, with the chief of staff acting as a *de facto* minister, and failed to provide the necessary direction to officials given the task of administering the program and also "bypassed the normal methods of administration of government programs,"[31] which contributed to the misuse and mismanagement of government funds.

The Privy Council Office

The **PCO** is a relatively small organization that provides policy advice and administrative support to the prime minister, cabinet, and cabinet committees. The title of the office comes from the fact that the formal name for cabinet is the Queen's Privy Council. The status of the PCO is illustrated by the fact that the senior public servant in the agency, who is called the clerk (ordinarily pronounced "clark" in the British tradition) of the Privy Council and the secretary to the cabinet, is officially recognized as the head of the public service.

Unlike the PMO, the PCO is staffed by career public servants rather than political appointees. However, the kind of advice provided by the PCO, while not overtly political in the partisan sense, is certainly sensitive to the political pulse of the nation. A former clerk of the Privy Council described the roles of the PMO and the PCO in this manner: "The Prime Minister's Office is partisan, politically oriented, yet operationally sensitive. The Privy Council Office is nonpartisan, operationally oriented yet politically sensitive."[32]

The Privy Council Office has a number of different roles, including some assigned to it by the prime minister temporarily. However, the major, continuing activities of the PCO fall into the three categories of direct support to the prime minister, assistance to the cabinet and its committees, and advice on machinery of government and operation of the public service. Figure 6.6 provides a depiction of the organization chart for the Privy Council Office and helps to reveal the three roles of the PCO.

In its first activity, the PCO serves as the prime minister's department, providing advice and assistance on a wide range of matters. The PCO keeps the prime minister abreast of developments in key policy areas and pays particular interest to any issues concerning the constitution. The PCO also briefs the prime minister on relations with the provinces and territories and in this role maintains an active liaison with departments to ensure relationships are operating well and that the position of the federal government is not compromised. A further task is to assist the prime minister in the process of making many appointments to important positions within government, and it also prepares the head of government for meetings with counterparts from other countries. If we look at Figure 6.6 we can pinpoint some of the units responsible for carrying out these activities. Certainly, the clerk of the PCO (pictured at the very top) is actively involved and so are parts of the PCO charged with looking after intergovernmental affairs and senior appointments.

The PCO also provides several different kinds of support for cabinet committees. Organizationally, the office is divided so that there is a small secretariat attached to each cabinet committee, except the Treasury Board, which has its own secretarial arm. As the figure shows, there are secretariats for cabinet committees directed at social development, economic and regional development; foreign affairs and security and intelligence;

Privy Council Office (PCO) The central agency, comprising career public servants, providing policy advice and administrative support to cabinet and its committees.

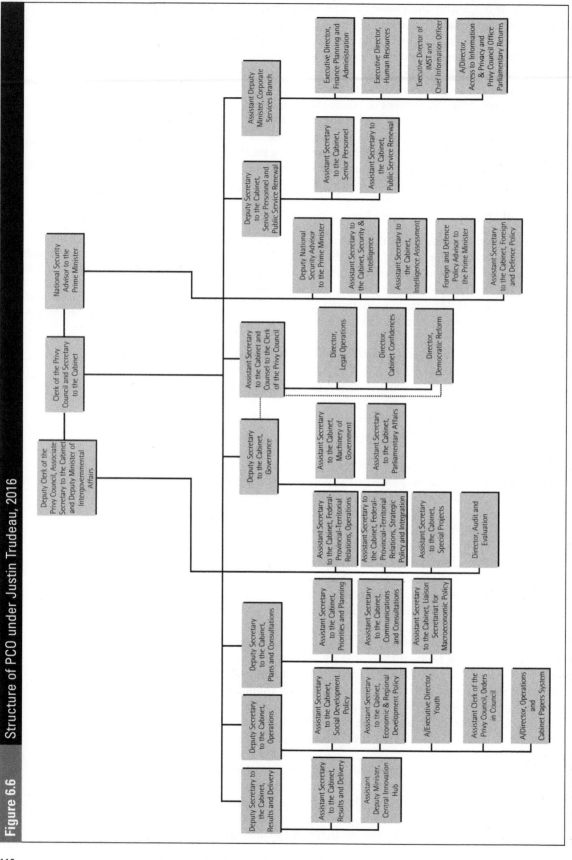

Figure 6.6 Structure of PCO under Justin Trudeau, 2016

Source: Privy Council Office organization chart. Available online at www.pco-bcp.gc.ca//index.asp?lang=eng&page=Org Permission granted by the Privy Council Office (2016). © Her Majesty the Queen in Right of Canada (2016).

and priorities and planning. Each secretariat monitors the general policy environment in the area for which its committee is responsible. The secretariat advises on new policy initiatives or responses to ongoing problems and ensures that all proposals that go before a cabinet committee are in good order. Among other things, this means that the interdepartmental aspects have been discussed and any problems resolved. This aspect of the PCO has prompted some to refer to it as a "gatekeeper." The PCO also assists in the preparation of the agenda of cabinet committee meetings, and in briefing the chairperson of the committee. At the housekeeping level, the PCO arranges for meeting space and maintains the minutes of the meetings.

The last function is in relation to the public service and its operations. In this capacity, the PCO plays a leading role in supporting the government's agenda concerning reform of the public service, and advises the prime minister on the reorganization of departments and agencies. It also advises the prime minister and cabinet about senior appointments within the federal bureaucracy, a reflection of the concern with moving highly competent public servants through senior postings so that they are always employed in a capacity where their talents can be best used and can gain experience for their next position.

The PCO provides a good example of central agency activities and the general position of central agencies in the organizational structure. The duties of the PCO give it the legitimate right to get involved in the activities of every other department of government. It does not have line authority over those departments, but its position as gatekeeper and its proximity to cabinet mean that operating departments always consider advice offered by the PCO very carefully. This helps to explain the complex love–hate relationship operating departments usually have with central agencies.

Notably, there are ongoing concerns that the PCO "has been or is being politicized."[33] The PCO, according to the Gomery commission, is supposed to be a largely nonpartisan agency responsible for tending to the operational and advisory needs of the cabinet decision-making process; but now it appears that the "political and administrative seem to be merging more and more into each other."[34] As one scholar has noted, there has been a blurring of the political and administration at the level of the clerk of the Privy Council and other senior PCO officials, with the latter often being rewarded for being a part of the prime minister's "court" with deputy ministerial appointments.[35]

The Treasury Board and the Treasury Board Secretariat

The **Treasury Board (TB)** is a cabinet committee consisting of the president of the Treasury Board, the minister of finance, and four other ministers appointed by the prime minister. As the general management board of government, the TB has three main roles, which are to foster improved management performance, examine and improve government expenditure plans, and handle labour relations and compensation for the core public service.[36] Unlike the other cabinet committees, the TB is enshrined in legislation—the *Financial Administration Act*—and it is the only cabinet committee that has a large bureaucracy reporting to it—the **Treasury Board Secretariat (TBS)**.

In its support to the Treasury Board, the TBS carries out a number of duties relating to the financial, personnel, and management responsibilities of government. The TBS prepares the expenditure budget that the government proposes in the House of Commons each year. It also assesses the performance of government departments, agencies, and Crown corporations and proposes reallocations of expenditures in light of these evaluations. More generally, it seeks to ensure that the TB functions as a kind of general manager of the entire federal government.

As revealed in Table 6.2, with 1,802 employees, the TBS is considerably larger than the other three central agencies. This is reflective of the breadth of the programs undertaken by the Secretariat in the fulfillment of its strategic outcome, namely "good governance

Treasury Board (TB)
A cabinet committee consisting of the president of the Treasury Board, the minister of finance, and four other cabinet ministers. Responsible for preparation of the expenditure budget and for administrative management in departments.

Treasury Board Secretariat (TBS) The central agency that assists the Treasury Board in carrying out its responsibilities.

and sound stewardship to enable efficient and effective service to Canadians."[37] The TBS is organized into 15 distinct branches and sectors to carry out its responsibilities. This includes, among others, Priorities and Planning, the Expenditure Management Sector and Strategic Communications and Ministerial Affairs as well as a number of critically important organizational units that have a high profile of their own in government: the Office of the Chief Human Resources Officer, which supports the TB in its role as the employer for the public service (explored more fully in chapter 17); the Chief Information Officer Branch, which strives for excellence in information management across the government; and the Office of the Comptroller General of Canada, which takes the lead for providing assurance government-wide for financial management. The Regulatory Affairs Sector, transferred to the TBS from the PCO in 2006, oversees the government's regulatory function.

From the standpoint of operating departments, the TBS is easily the most active—some might say, intrusive—of the central agencies, simply because there are so many points of contact and so many specific activities for which TBS clearance must be obtained. Treasury Board officials are aware that excessive oversight (and accompanying rules and regulations) can stifle department initiatives.

The Department of Finance

Department of Finance
A central agency responsible for advising cabinet on economic matters. The Department also formulates fiscal and tax policies.

The **Department of Finance** is responsible for advising cabinet on matters of economic policy. Thus, the department has an exceedingly broad mandate. It advises on questions of fiscal policy, international trade policy (including tariffs), domestic industrial policy, federal–provincial fiscal relations, taxation policy, and the preparation of the revenue and expenditure budgets. Moreover, much of this advice is in relation to policy and programs developed by the department itself and not in relation to the positions and recommendations of individual departments. For instance, the Department of Finance generates proposals for tax reform (such as the GST or HST) and develops suggestions for adjustments to the major arrangements for transferring financial assistance to the provinces. The Department of Finance is just as much a policy maker as it is a policy advisor, and in this respect might be seen as both a traditional department and a central agency.

With its mandate, the Department of Finance might potentially intervene in the activities of any department involved in policies that touch upon any of the above areas. Moreover, given the breadth of those areas, it is difficult to think of a department that does not. The role of the department does not bring it into the same kind of obtrusive, day-to-day contact with operating departments as that of the TBS, but its concern with economic policy allows it to intervene at strategic points in the policy development process. Its role in the preparation of the expenditure budget helps determine whether the upcoming year will be a lean or a fat one for government agencies. Finance also has a role as the budgetary gatekeeper. Indeed, it has traditionally provided the strongest opposition to new spending programs. This brings the Department of Finance into fairly frequent conflict with operating departments.

Central Agencies in the Provinces

It is obvious that the functions performed by central agencies in the federal government will also be necessary in provincial governments. However, the smaller size of the provincial governments usually means that organizational structures are less complex and differentiated. In some provinces, the functions of the PMO, the PCO, and sometimes the TBS are all carried out in the premier's office.[38] However, there is a general movement toward the establishment of what is commonly described as an institutionalized cabinet, which is an executive system with a formal committee structure and supporting agencies. Moreover, it was a province—Saskatchewan—that first introduced central agencies as an integral part of the cabinet decision-making process.

Points to Know

- Government departments are one of the basic organizational structures for delivering programs and services to Canadians. They have the most stringent degree of oversight and accountability flowing from the minister, who serves as the political head of the department, to the deputy minister (the administrative head) and down through the organizational ranks.

- Sometimes ministers will have one or more additional politicians, designated as either a minister of state or secretary of state, to assist him or her with the task of fulfilling the departmental mandate.

- Departments can be classified as one of three types: 1) horizontal policy coordinative; 2) horizontal administrative coordinative; and 3) vertical constituency.

- The power to establish and reorganize public sector organizations rests with the prime minister through the *Public Service Rearrangement and Transfer of Duties Act.*

- Horizontal policy coordinative departments, also known as central agencies, are a special kind of government organization that have responsibility for coordinating the government's broad policy agenda.

- While the PMO and the PCO both provide advice and support to the prime minister and cabinet, the former central agency comprises partisan appointees while the latter is staffed with career public servants.

- The TBS is charged with providing support to the TB in the areas of finance, personnel and management.

- The Department of Finance serves as a budgetary gatekeeper and is responsible for advising cabinet on matters of economic policy.

Review Questions

1. Describe how accountability is maintained within the traditional government department. Are there any challenges or limitations to ensuring that the department is accountable for the decisions that are made by public servants and the money that it spends on program and service delivery?

2. Identify the central agencies and outline the ways in which they differ from traditional (vertical constituency) departments.

3. What is one of the most common ways for the prime minister to identify his or her priorities and demonstrate a particular leadership style?

4. How are the roles and responsibilities of the PCO and the PMO similar and in what ways do they differ?

Notes

1. Gordon Osbaldeston, *Organizing to Govern* (Toronto: McGraw-Hill Ryerson, 1992), 1:11.
2. J.E. Hodgetts, *The Canadian Public Service: A Physiology of Government* (Toronto: University of Toronto Press, 1973), 89.
3. Ibid., ch. 5. Hodgetts' other categories included "public security and external relations," "coordination and services for the public organization" and "protection and development of human resources."
4. There is a fourth type, but it is no longer in use.
5. G. Bruce Doern, "Horizontal and Vertical Portfolios in Government," in *Issues in Canadian Public Policy*, eds. G. Bruce Doern and V. Seymour Wilson (Toronto: Macmillan, 1974), 310–329. This same idea is also developed in G. Bruce Doern and Richard W. Phidd, *Canadian Public Policy: Ideas, Structure and Process*, 2nd ed. (Scarborough: Nelson Canada, 1992), 316–317.
6. Diane Finley, "Defence Procurement Strategy," Speaking Notes for the Honourable Diane Finley, Minister of Public Works and Government Services, Announcing the Defence Procurement Strategy. Economic Club of Canada, Ottawa, February 5, 2014, accessed February 15, 2015, http://www.tpsgc-pwgsc.gc.ca/medias-media/dm-ms/2014-02-04-eng.html.
7. There has not been much research completed on ranking the prestige of various ministerial portfolios and there are a number of problems associated with such measures. When such references have been made, it has typically been in the context of studies that examine the marginalization of women in less important cabinet positions that revolve around "women's concerns," such as education, culture, social services, health and consumer affairs. See Donley T. Studlar and Gary F. Moncrief, "Women's Work? The Distribution and Prestige of Portfolios in the Canadian Provinces," *Governance* 12(4) (October 1999):

379–395. Manon Tremblay and Daniel Stockemer, "Women's Ministerial Concerns in Cabinet, 1921–2010: A Look at Socio-Demographic Traits and Career Experiences," *Canadian Public Administration* 56(4) (December 2013): 537, refer to a predilection for women's ministerial careers to be concentrated in "pink portfolios," but they conclude that this "does not diminish their importance nor does it imply that women's ministerial careers are of lesser value than those of their male counterparts."
8. See "The Top 100 Most Powerful and Influential People in Government and Politics, 2015" *Power & Influence* 4(1) (Winter 2015): 23. In February 2015, Kenney was appointed as Minister of National Defence in addition to his post as Minister of Multiculturalism.
9. Office of the Prime Minister, "Prime Minister Harper Announces New Ministry and Reaffirms Government Priorities," News Release, February 6, 2006, accessed October 14, 2015, http://pm.gc.ca/eng/news/2006/02/06/prime-minister-harper-announces-new-ministry-and-reaffirms-government-priorities.
10. Canada. Department of Finance, *Jobs, Growth and Long-Term Prosperity: Economic Action Plan 2013* (Ottawa: Her Majesty the Queen in Right of Canada, 2013), 241.
11. Osbaldeston, *Organizing to Govern*, ch. 7.
12. Ibid., 144.
13. Eleanor D. Glor, "Patterns of Canadian Departmental Survival," *Canadian Public Administration* 54(4) (December 2011): 551–566.
14. The Harper cabinet also included an Associate Minister of National Defence, a position that has been used sporadically since 1940 as a means of delegating certain files within the Department of National Defence.

15. *Department of Veterans Affairs Act*, R.S., 1985, c. V-1, accessed September 17, 2015, http://laws-lois.justice.gc.ca/eng/acts/V-1/index.html.

16. *Department of Health Act*, S.C., 1996, c.6, accessed September 17, 2015, http://laws-lois.justice.gc.ca/eng/acts/H-3.2/page-1.html.

17. Canada. Department of Transport, *2015-2016 Report on Plans and Priorities* (Ottawa: Her Majesty the Queen in Right of Canada, 2015), 16.

18. Some argue for the inclusion of additional bodies into the group of central agencies—for example, the Department of Justice. See James B. Kelly, *Governing with the Charter: Legislative and Judicial Activism and Framers' Intent* (Vancouver: UBC Press, 2005), ch. 7.

19. Colin Campbell and George J. Szablowski, *The Superbureaucrats* (Toronto: Macmillan, 1979).

20. Peter Aucoin, "Organizational Change in the Machinery of Canadian Government: From Rational Management to Brokerage Politics," *Canadian Journal of Political Science* 19(1) (March 1986): 3–27.

21. Current employment data for the PMO is not available. This figure, accurate as of February 1, 2012, is based on a response given to a question posed in the House of Commons about the size of the PMO and number of employees working in that organization who made under $50,000 and over $100,000. See Jason Fekete, "Harper's Office Spared Worst of Cuts as Quarter of PM's 100-Strong Staff Paid $100K or More," *The National Post*, April 12, 2002, accessed September 20, 2015, http://news.nationalpost.com/news/canada/almost-quarter-of-pmo-staff-paid-100k-or-more.

22. Keith Beardsley, "What It's Really Like to Work in the PMO," *Power & Influence* 4(1) (Winter 2015): 4, 3.

23. Ibid., 4.

24. Leslie MacKinnon, "How Stephen Harper's Inner Circle Has Changed," *CBC News*, May 24, 2014, accessed September 22, 2015, www.cbc.ca/news/politics/how-stephen-harpers-inner-circle-has-changed-1.2652571.

25. Beardsley, "What It's Really Like," 5.

26. Graham Fraser, "The Man Who Really Saved the Government," *Toronto Star*, May 22, 2005, A4; Daniel Leblanc, "New Chief of Staff Ray Novak has Long Ties to Harper," *Globe and Mail*, May 19, 2013, accessed September 22, 2015, www.theglobeandmail.com/news/politics/new-chief-of-staff-ray-novak-has-long-ties-to-harper/article12023016.

27. Don Martin, "PM Can't Keep Blaming Messenger," *National Post*, February 22, 2006, A8.

28. The four chiefs of staff were Ian Brodie, Guy Giorno, Nigel Wright, and Ray Novak.

29. Thomas S. Axworthy, "Of Secretaries to Princes," *Canadian Public Administration* 31(2) (Summer 1988): 247–264.

30. Ian Brodie, "In Defence of Political Staff," *Canadian Parliamentary Review* 35(3) (Autumn 2012): 33.

31. Commission of Inquiry into the Sponsorship Program and Advertising Activities, *Who Is Responsible? Fact Finding Report*, 99; Commission of Inquiry into the Sponsorship Program & Advertising Activities, *Who Is Responsible? Summary* (Ottawa: Her Majesty the Queen in Right of Canada, 2005), 74.

32. Gordon Robertson, "The Changing Role of the Privy Council Office," *Canadian Public Administration* 14(4) (Winter 1971): 506.

33. Commission of Inquiry into the Sponsorship Program and Advertising Activities, *Restoring Accountability: Recommendations* (Ottawa: Her Majesty in Right of Canada, 2006), 151.

34. Ibid., 143.

35. Donald Savoie, *Whatever Happened to the Music Teacher?* (Montreal and Kingston: McGill-Queen's University Press, 2013), 89.

36. Treasury Board of Canada Secretariat, *Report on Plans and Priorities 2015-16* (Ottawa: Her Majesty the Queen in Right of Canada, 2015), 4.

37. Ibid., 5.

38. Luc Bernier, Keith Brownsey, and Michael Howlett, *Executive Styles in Canada: Cabinet Structures and Leadership Practices in Canadian Government* (Toronto: University of Toronto Press, 2005). See also, Michael M. Atkinson, Daniel Béland, Gregory P. Marchildon et. al., *Governance and Public Policy in Canada: A View from the Provinces* (Toronto: University of Toronto Press, 2013), ch.2.

Crown Agencies

Learning Objectives

Reading this chapter allows you to do the following:

- Identify the structure of Crown corporations and independent agencies, and describe their status as Crown agencies

- Explain the use of Crown agencies instead of departments

- Differentiate between the oversight and accountability mechanisms associated with

Crown corporations and independent agencies as compared to government departments

- Understand the shift towards privatization and deregulation

- Assess the policy of privatizing public enterprise and deregulating market activities

---

In the previous chapter, we examined the first and most common organizational structure that governments have used historically as a means of providing programs and services to Canadians—a department. While there are different types of government departments, all of them are subject to the direct control and oversight of a cabinet minister. This strict ministerial oversight was generally perceived to be advantageous because it was an important mechanism for ensuring that the government remained accountable to Parliament and the citizenry. For certain types of activities, however, the government wanted greater autonomy and flexibility in terms of the structure and operation of an organizational entity than the traditional departmental form would provide. In those instances, the government would rely on the use of **Crown agencies** when organizing to govern, of which there are two broad types: 1) **Crown corporations or public enterprise**; and 2) various **statutory and other agencies**, which are sometimes referred to as agencies, boards, and commissions (ABCs). Both of these traditional organizational forms will be explored in this chapter.

In the first instance, governments would choose to establish a Crown corporation if they were engaging in a commercial or business-like activity. Therefore, despite the ostensible paradigm shift that occurred in the 1980s in Canada as a result of the arrival of new public management (NPM), with its focus on adopting private sector business principles into the operation of government, federal and provincial governments in this country have a long history of engaging directly in the market with organizations that have assumed a corporate form. This practice dates to the early twentieth century with the creation of the Canadian National Railway Company (CNR) in 1922. Since then, the federal government has operated an airline (Air Canada), provided rail service (Via Rail), and filled up cars with gasoline (Petro Canada). The federal and provincial governments have also been directly involved in the broadcasting industry (through the CBC and

Crown agencies A term that applies to two types of public sector organizations: 1) Crown corporations; and 2) statutory and other agencies. Along with government departments, they represent a traditional organizational form.

Crown corporation
A corporation in the ordinary sense of the term, whose mandate relates to industrial, commercial, or financial activities, but that also belongs to the state. Also known as **public enterprise**.

statutory and other agencies A particular type of Crown agency, also known as agencies, boards, and commissions (ABCs), they perform a wide range of functions (administrative, quasi-judicial, advisory, and regulatory) in government. One of the traditional organizational forms.

TVO respectively, for example), competing with a number of private sector broadcasters. The prevailing sentiment was that if government were going to run a business, it had to be structured more like a business and be free of any direct political control and excessive rules and procedures.

A similar rationale is evident with respect to the roughly 50 statutory and other agencies that currently exist. These federal agencies have a wide range of functions; they can be administrative, quasi-judicial, advisory, or regulatory in nature. As one scholar noted, "All these agencies provide services that are either unique or politically or legally sensitive enough to require quasi-independence from the government."[1] For example, while government departments are themselves frequently the source of a variety of rules and regulations that affect the behaviour of individuals and organizations, in certain situations the government would prefer to establish autonomous, arm's-length organizations to make and enforce the various rules and regulations that affect the operation of the public and private sectors. By doing so, the government can ensure that the important policies can be pursued without undue political influence.

Both Crown corporations and the various independent agencies that are a part of the federal government have served important purposes in Canada. Public enterprises have provided services that in many cases the private sector historically was unwilling or unable to provide but which Canadians consider essential; regulatory agencies, although they remain largely enigmatic for most citizens, make and enforce rules and regulations that impact our daily lives in countless ways—from determining which radio and television stations can broadcast on the airwaves, to determining the price that cable companies can charge for their services, to ensuring the safety of our food supply and consumer products, to preventing misleading advertising, and much more. Other ABCs are charged with providing a range of activities from protecting human rights, to providing grants, to undertaking research, to maintaining our security. However, both types of organizations present a number of challenges for public administration, especially with respect to accountability and the public interest.

This chapter first offers a definition of Crown corporations and these various independent agencies and offers a glimpse of the basic structure of these organizational forms. It then discusses the rationale for the use of these particular kinds of government agencies. The means of providing control and oversight of this broad array of Crown agencies are also considered. The chapter concludes by examining a number of issues and trends related to these entities.

Definition of Crown Corporations and Agencies

The focus of this chapter is the non-departmental forms that J.E. Hodgetts referred to as "structural heretics." He argued that the use of these additional organizational forms emerged in the early post-Confederation period for two principal reasons: first, the workload of the conventional government departments had become too great to manage; and second, government started engaging in functions that were considerably different from those of traditional departments. The department as an organizational form was, therefore, no longer totally appropriate. What emerged in conjunction with government departments, then, was "another, numerically much larger, group of administrative entities whose functions and structures are so varied that they virtually defy classification."[2] These are what we identified in the introduction to the chapter as Crown agencies, of which there are two types: corporations and statutory agencies.

The terminology that is used to refer to organizations that are, in effect, government-run businesses is inconsistent and confusing; this is one of the reasons that it is difficult to get a handle on the true scope of public enterprise in this country.[3] At the federal level in Canada, these entities are typically referred to as Crown corporations. That is how the Treasury Board Secretariat (TBS) classifies this particular institutional form. However,

Statistics Canada refers instead to government business enterprise across all levels of government in its statistical tables. At the provincial level, a variety of terms are used, including "operational enterprise agencies," "Crown agencies," and "government enterprise." The picture becomes even more convoluted when trying to account for what is likely to be hundreds of Crown corporations at the local level across thousands of municipalities.

Separating the corporation form from other forms of government organization is relatively easy. Crown corporations are established either through their own legislation or through incorporation under the *Canada Business Corporations Act* (or the analogous provincial legislation) in exactly the same way as any private sector corporation. Determining what constitutes a corporate form, as distinct from other organizational forms, is not difficult; the difficult part is determining what constitutes a Crown corporation (see "What to Do").

The TBS defines Crown corporations as "government organizations that operate following a private sector model, but usually have a mixture of commercial and public policy objectives."[4] This definition highlights the fact that the government will sometimes choose to apply the corporate form to a particular service even though it does not have a commercial or businesslike purpose (e.g., the International Development Research Centre, which provides resources, advice and training to foster the economic and social advancement of developing regions of the world). Most of the federal Crown corporations are listed in Schedule III of the *Financial Administration Act*. These are what the government refers to as **parent corporations**, which are directly and wholly owned by the Government of Canada. In other words, 100 percent of the shares of these entities are held on behalf of or in trust for the government.

Part II of Schedule III of the *Financial Administration Act* identifies those corporations that operate in a competitive environment, do not normally require a government appropriation, ordinarily earn a return on equity, and are expected to pay dividends. Only three parent Crown corporations satisfy those criteria—the Canada Development Investment Corporation, Canada Post, and the Royal Canadian Mint. Figure 7.1 identifies the 44 parent Crown corporations that existed in 2016, according to which department (and specific minister) they are accountable. For instance, Canada Post is accountable to the minister of public services and procurement, while the Canada Mortgage and Housing Corporation (CMHC) reports to Parliament through the minister of families, children and social development, who is one of three ministers associated with the Employment and Social Development Canada portfolio.

In addition to these parent Crown corporations, however, the federal government comprises numerous other corporate interests (see Table 7.1). Although the *Financial Administration Act* does not identify them, there were another 159 **wholly-owned subsidiaries** in 2016. These are corporate entities whereby one or more of the parent Crown corporations owned 100 percent of their shares. In addition, there were 27 corporations that were listed as **other subsidiaries and associates**. The parent Crown corporation(s) owned less than 50 percent of the shares in these companies. While the parent Crown corporations report to Parliament through their relevant minister, these subsidiaries are managed by their parent Crown corporation, reporting to them and their other shareholders rather than directly to the government.

There are four other types of corporations in which the government either has a financial interest or participates in their oversight. **Mixed enterprises** are corporations whose shares are owned partly by the Government of Canada and partly by one or more private sector parties. With the full privatization of Petro-Canada in 2004, there are now no mixed enterprises at the federal level. **Joint enterprises** are similar to mixed

---

WHAT TO DO?

Crown corporations can be classified either by type or degree of ownership. Generally, neither wholly-owned subsidiaries, of which there were 159 across the federal ministry in 2015, nor other subsidiary corporate interests (27 of them), where the government owns less than 50 percent of the shares of these companies, are used to calculate the size of the state-owned enterprise/Crown corporation sector. For example, the CBC owns 20.4 percent of the shares in Sirius XM Canada. Should we be accounting for corporate interests such as these when trying to determine the extent of the SOE sector in Canada? Not to do so seriously underestimates the involvement of the government in the economy.

---

parent corporation
A type of Crown corporation whose shares are directly and wholly owned by the Government of Canada.

wholly-owned subsidiaries These are corporate entities whereby 100 percent of their shares are owned by one or more parent Crown corporations.

other subsidiaries and associates These are corporate entities whereby less than 50 percent of their shares are owned by one or more parent Crown corporations.

mixed enterprise A type of Crown corporation whereby the shares are held jointly by the Government of Canada and one or more private interests.

joint enterprise A type of Crown corporation whereby the shares are held jointly by the Government of Canada and another level of government.

Figure 7.1	Parent Crown Corporations by Ministerial Portfolio (2016)

Agriculture & Agri-Food	Fisheries & Oceans	Natural Resources
• Canadian Dairy Commission • Farm Credit Canada	• Freshwater Fish Marketing Corporation	• Atomic Energy of Canada Limited

Canadian Heritage	Global Affairs Canada	Public Services & Procurement Canada
• Canada Council for the Arts • Canadian Broadcasting Corporation • Canadian Museum for Human Rights • Canadian Museum of History • Canadian Museum of Immigration at Pier 21 • Canadian Museum of Nature • Canadian Race Relations Foundation • National Arts Centre Corporation • National Capital Commission • National Gallery of Canada • National Museum of Science & Technology • Telefilm Canada	• Canadian Commercial Corporation (Min. of International Trade) • Export Development Canada (Min. of International Trade) • International Development Research Centre (Min. of International Development & La Francophonie)	• Canada Lands Company Limited • Canada Post Corporation • Defence Construction (1951) Limited

Employment and Social Development Canada	Innovation, Science, and Economic Development Canada	Transport
• Canada Mortgage and Housing Corporation (Min. of Families, Children, and Social Development)	• Business Development Bank of Canada • Destination Canada (formerly Canadian Tourism Commission) (Min. of Innovation, Science, and Economic Development and Min. of Small Business and Tourism) • Standards Council of Canada	• Atlantic Pilotage Authority • Canadian Air Transport Security Authority • Federal Bridge Corporation Limited • Great Lakes Pilotage Authority • Laurentian Pilotage Authority • Marine Atlantic Inc. • Pacific Pilotage Authority • Ridley Terminals Inc. • VIA Rail Canada Inc.

Finance	Infrastructure & Communities	Treasury Board
• Bank of Canada • Canada Deposit Insurance Corporation • Canada Development Investment Corporation • Canada Pension Plan Investment Board • PPP Canada Inc.* • Royal Canadian Mint	• The Jacques Cartier and Champlain Bridges Inc. (Pres. of the Queen's Privy Council for Canada) • Windsor–Detroit Bridge Authority	• Public Sector Pension Investment Board

*PPP Canada Inc. is a wholly-owned subsidiary of the Canada Development Investment Corporation, but it has been directed by order-in-council to report as if it were a parent Crown corporation.

Sources: Government of Canada http://www.tbs-sct.gc.ca/hgw-cgf/finances/rgs-erdg/cc-se/corporate-societe/ccp-pse-eng.asp; Privy Council Office, "Machinery of Government Changes," November 4, 2015. http://www.pco-bcp.gc.ca/index.asp?lang=eng&page=docs&doc=mog-ag-eng.htm

enterprises, except that the other shareholder is another level of government. Currently, there are only two such entities—Lower Churchill Development Corporation Limited and the North Portage Development Corporation. **Shared-governance corporations** are corporations in which the federal government has no financial interest but can participate in the appointment or nomination of individuals to their governing structures. As of September 30, 2015, there were 83 shared-governance entities at the federal level, including the Canada Games Council, Wildlife Habitat Canada, Waterfront Toronto, and the Canadian Foundation for Innovation. Most of these shared-governance corporations (42 of them) are the port and airport authorities across the country (e.g., the Halifax Port Authority and the Calgary Airport Authority) and report to the minister of transport.

shared-governance corporation A type of Crown corporation in which the federal government retains no financial interest but has the ability to appoint members to its governing structures.

TABLE 7.1	Federal Crown Corporations by Method of Ownership			
	1984	**1994**	**2005**	**2015**
Parent Crown corporations	67	48	43	44
Wholly-owned subsidiaries	128	64	25	159
Other subsidiaries and associates	94	64	25	27
Mixed enterprises	18	5	0	0
Joint enterprises	—	3	3	2
International organizations	—	15	18	15
Shared governance	29	51	141	83

Source: Treasury Board of Canada Secretariat, "Crown Corporations and Other Corporate Interests of Canada," 1984, 1994, 2005; "Organizations by Portfolio and Institutional Form," 2015. www.tbs-sct.gc.ca/hgw.cgf/finances/rgs-erdg/cc-se/institution/organizations-organisations-eng.asp. (Ottawa: Her Majesty the Queen in Right of Canada).

The final category is **international organizations**, which are "corporate entities created pursuant to international agreements under which Canada either holds shares or has a right to appoint or elect some number of members to a governing body."[5] Examples of the 15 international organizations involving the federal government are the International Monetary Fund, the World Anti-Doping Agency, and the African Development Bank.

It is equally, if not more, challenging to define what constitutes those entities identified as "statutory and other agencies." According to the TBS, they are "entities with more narrowly defined mandates than ministerial departments … Their specific functions vary widely but tend to be operational in nature, and they usually operate at a distance from government with varying degrees of autonomy."[6] In a government guidebook, these entities are referred to broadly as "agencies, boards, and commissions," indicating that they are "statutory bodies responsible for administering, determining, establishing, controlling or regulating an economic or business activity, or adjudicating cases that affect individual rights and benefits."[7] As is the case with Crown corporations, these organizations are frequently directed to act in the "public interest."

This category includes an array of federal government organizations, many of which are listed in Schedule I.1 of the *Financial Administration Act*. Statistics Canada, for example, collects and analyzes statistical information about the country's "social and economic structure to develop and evaluate public policies and programs and to improve public and private decision-making for the benefit of all Canadians,"[8] while the RCMP and Canadian Security Intelligence Service (CSIS) provide policing and security services to the nation. These have been variously called "special" and "one-of-a-kind" agencies.[9] Also included in this category are regulatory agencies, like the Canadian Radio-television and Telecommunication Commission (CRTC) and the National Energy Board; administrative tribunals, such as the Canadian Human Rights Commission; quasi-judicial bodies, including the Immigration and Refugee Board and the Parole Board of Canada; and advisory bodies, such as the Public Health Agency of Canada. But even this classification is somewhat misleading in that these entities often carry out multiple roles. For example, the Canadian Transportation Agency both engages in economic regulation and serves as an independent, quasi-judicial tribunal, while the National Energy Board has "statutory duties that are adjudicatory, advisory and regulatory in nature."[10]

international organization A type of Crown corporation established through international agreements whereby Canada either owns shares or has the ability to appoint or elect members to its governing body.

economic regulation
Sometimes referred to as "old" or "direct" regulation, these are the restrictions placed by government on such things as pricing, competition, or the methods of production for particular industries or markets.

social regulation Also known as "new" regulation, these are the restrictions placed by government to control the behaviour of individuals or organizations in order to protect the welfare of society.

Regulatory agencies are the most prominent of the statutory and other agencies. Parliament has delegated these bodies the authority to make regulations, which are, in effect, a type of law and are often referred to as delegated or subordinate legislation.[11] More specifically, regulation can be defined as "government imposition of rules and controls designed to direct, restrict or change the economic behaviour of individuals and business, and these rules and controls are supported by sanctions and penalties for non-compliance."[12] A further distinction is often drawn between **economic regulation** (sometimes referred to as "direct" or "old" regulation) and **social (or "new") regulation**. In the first instance, regulations are typically directed at specific industries or markets and deal with such things as pricing, competition, product content, and methods of production, whereas social regulations tend to focus on controlling behaviour so as to ensure the welfare of society. This would pertain to workplace health and safety provisions, for example, or to the promotion of Canadian content in broadcasting and the protection of human rights or the environment.[13]

At times, the line between these two types of regulation can seem arbitrary. An agency responsible for the regulation of firms—economic regulation, in other words—might take actions to further some social goal. For instance, it may set rates or prices in order to assist disadvantaged groups. Also, it is sometimes believed that the two types of regulation are insufficient to capture the nuances of regulatory activity and that the types of regulation should be expanded to include environmental and moral regulation.[14] Nevertheless, the twofold distinction supplies a helpful reminder that regulatory agencies are about more than fixing the market.

Operation and Structure of Crown Agencies

These various Crown agencies are structured in a number of ways and are tasked with a wide range of duties as outlined in their enabling legislation or other instruments, so it is difficult to generalize about them. Each entity would need to be examined individually to truly understand how they are organized and operate. One similarity is that very few parent Crown corporations are actually operating in competitive markets and earn a profit—or are even financially self-sufficient for that matter. Most of them are dependent on some form of government appropriation to fund their operations and in some instances the level of public funding is substantial. The CBC, for example, with 6,659 permanent full-time equivalent employees, had a government appropriation of $1.04 billion in the 2014–2015 fiscal year, which represented 63 percent of its operating revenue.[15]

But the differences among the other types of statutory and other agencies are extreme. Some of those agencies have a quasi-legislative function in that they have "the ability to make general rules or regulations, in the form of delegated legislation, that have the force of law."[16] The CRTC, for example, has put in place Canadian content regulations as a requirement of being granted a broadcast license. Many of these agencies have staff members who conduct research in the policy area that they are regulating, so as to keep abreast of the most recent trends in the industry or sector. They will often use that research as the basis for providing the minister and the department with advice. Some agencies have direct administrative responsibility for operating programs. For instance, the Canadian Food Inspection Agency (CFIA) undertakes inspections and other similar services to ensure food safety, animal health, and plant protection. A number of these agencies also have an adjudicative function. They act much like a court of law in that they hear evidence and arguments in considering a case (thus, they are quasi-judicial), but they make their decisions on the basis of policy considerations to act in things like "the public interest" or the "protection of society" rather than findings of fact in relation to a relatively precise piece of legislation, as the courts are required to make decisions. In this category would fall such things as CRTC hearings to determine long-distance telephone rates or how much cable companies, like Rogers, can charge for their services;

it would also include the decisions of the Parole Board of Canada in terms of the release of prisoners and immigration cases determined by the Immigration and Refugee Board.

Nonetheless, despite their differences in structure and function, these agencies are united by the fact that they operate at arm's length from the government in terms of their day-to-day operations. In other words, they are insulated from direct political intervention, a situation which is important when the organization either has a predominantly commercial objective and political concerns might interfere with that mandate or when the regulatory agency is making a decision in a specific case. As the government notes:

> Maintaining an arm's length relationship to Ministers is particularly important for those organizations whose mandate is to make decisions that determine or regulate the privileges, rights or benefits of Canadians. Governments delegate decision-making powers to these bodies, in part, to preserve public confidence in the fairness of the decision-making process.[17]

This is not to say that government has no control over these entities; in fact, it is important that organizations that carry out government policy ultimately be subject to the control of the political executive (which will be discussed further later in the chapter).

Another reason why greater autonomy is granted to these Crown agencies is so the government can more easily attract the requisite personnel to work for them. Successful business people frequently have much to offer to government organizations, but they are often uncomfortable coming into an unfamiliar management structure such as an operating department with a political head, central agency controls, and the other trappings of government. They feel more comfortable in the more familiar setting of the corporate form. Similarly, it is thought that the chances of recruiting experts for regulatory agencies increases with the prospect of less political intervention and the relative absence of bureaucratic red tape associated with the greater independence of regulatory agencies. Another advantage is that these agencies are free from the government's central hiring and compensation policies, which allows them to recruit the necessary personnel more quickly at a salary that reflects their skills and expertise.

As illustrated in Figure 7.2, Crown agencies are structured similar to their private sector counterparts. While the administrative head of government departments is the deputy minister, it is typically the president and chief executive officer (CEO) who provides the day-to-day management and oversight of a Crown agency. Furthermore, there is no direct relationship between the president and CEO and the minister of the department to which the agency reports as there would be between a minister and his or her deputy in a government department. This is what provides the agency with autonomy from the political executive. Instead, in these agencies, the president and CEO reports and is accountable to a board of directors; it is this group of individuals that has responsibility for providing overall direction for the organization. The autonomy of these boards is also maintained by virtue of the fact that members are usually appointed by governor-in-council for terms of five to ten years and hold office "during good behaviour." Often the board will have a number of committees responsible for overseeing various aspects of the company's operation; this structure allows the board to break up into smaller groups to examine significant issues in more detail and then to convey the results of their deliberations back to the board for decision. It is the board of directors that ultimately remains accountable to Parliament through the minister responsible for the agency. This is analogous to the corporate governance model in the private sector where the CEO of a company would take direction from and be accountable to his or her board of directors, which, in turn, is held to account by the shareholders of the corporation.

In the case of Crown agencies that have an adjudicative function, in addition to setting policy and overseeing the operations of the organization, the members of the board of directors will serve as panelists, hearing cases and rendering decisions. However, it is unusual for all members to be present at any one hearing. The agency's legislation will

Chapter 7 / Crown Agencies

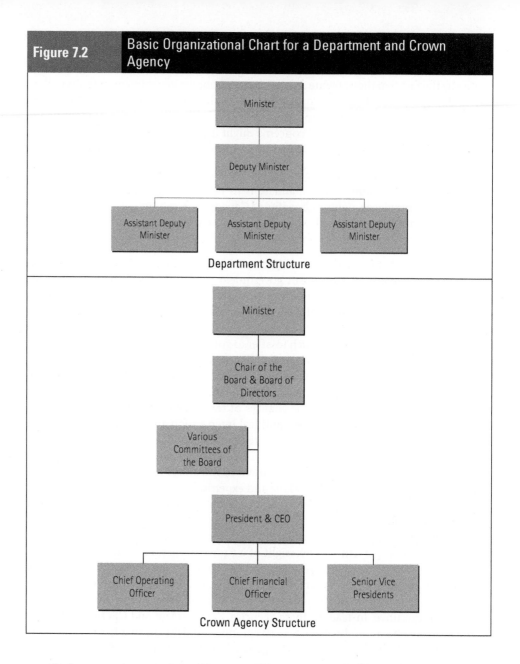

Figure 7.2 Basic Organizational Chart for a Department and Crown Agency

Minister

Deputy Minister

Assistant Deputy Minister | Assistant Deputy Minister | Assistant Deputy Minister

Department Structure

Minister

Chair of the Board & Board of Directors

Various Committees of the Board

President & CEO

Chief Operating Officer | Chief Financial Officer | Senior Vice Presidents

Crown Agency Structure

specify the minimum number of members necessary to conduct a hearing. This can be as few as one member and, notably, the panel may include temporary appointees. In the case of the National Energy Board, "temporary members are typically appointed to add capacity and specific expertise to the Board, on an 'as required' basis."[18] With respect to the Canadian Human Rights Tribunal, which also includes temporary members, it is either one or, in certain circumstances, three of the fifteen members of the Tribunal who are assigned to hear a case. Thus, several hearings can be held at the same time, and the work of the agency can be accelerated. Members can be assigned to cases by the chairperson on a random basis, or there can be a committee system that allows members to specialize.

Crown agencies have a range of staff members who are experts in law, economics, accounting, engineering, or whatever other specialties are required. The main functions of employees are supporting the work of the members in arranging hearings, conducting both general research and specific investigations concerning individual applications,

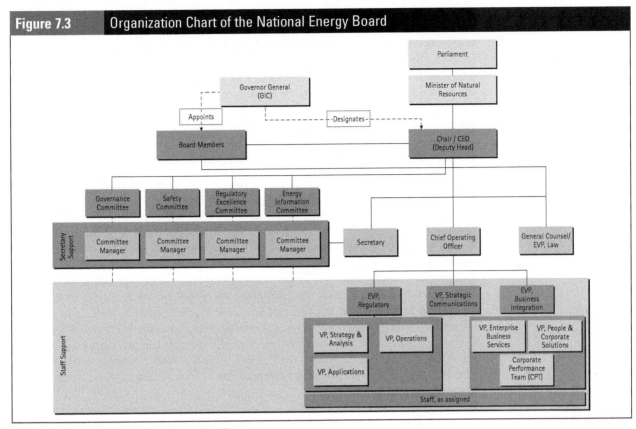

Figure 7.3 — Organization Chart of the National Energy Board

Source: Reproduced with the permission of the National Energy Board.

and advising members on legal and/or technical aspects of their work. With some agencies, the number of staff is rather large, but for many the size of the organization is quite small. In 2016, the CFIA had a staff of just under 6,000 full-time equivalent employees, whereas the Financial Consumer Agency of Canada was anticipating a full-time equivalent staff complement of 89 employees from 2016 to 2019.[19]

A more detailed depiction of the structure of a Crown agency and the relationships between the executive, the board of directors, and the professional staff is provided in Figure 7.3. This chart represents the National Energy Board. As you can see, this agency is ultimately accountable to Parliament through the minister of natural resources. Its administrative head, like its board members, is a governor-in-council appointee and also serves as the chair of the board. The work of the board is carried out through four committees (Governance; Safety; Regulatory Excellence; and Energy Information), all of which receive secretarial support from the professional staff working for the agency. Only the senior leadership team is illustrated in this organization chart, but the National Energy Board had a complement of 460 full-time equivalent employees in 2016.

Rationale for Crown Agencies

There are many reasons why governments have chosen to rely on either Crown corporations or other independent agencies instead of the traditional government department. As noted earlier, to some extent they were born out of necessity since government had grown too large and began to undertake functions for which the departmental structure was no longer suitable. Another important reason for these Crown agencies identified at the outset of the chapter was to escape the tight ministerial control found in departments. But these Crown entities have also been utilized historically as a means for addressing problems with the operation of various dimensions of the private marketplace. Society relies on the market to allocate its scarce resources in the most appropriate way and also to ensure that distribution of these same resources is fair or equitable. But sometimes the market falls short of expectations because of the presence of what are called "market failures." This is the economic rationale for government intervention in the economy, but there can also be ethical or political justifications for doing so.[20]

Nation Building, Community Development, and Externalities

Arguably, the most common rationale for the creation of public enterprises in Canada has been the need to make investments necessary for nation building and community development. Such investments, which have included the establishment of Crown corporations in the areas of telephone services and air and rail travel, amount to an attempt to deal with what are called externalities. Externalities, both positive and negative, are essentially "spillover effects that affect third parties."[21] In the case of positive externalities, producers and consumers in the marketplace fail to take into sufficient consideration that their exchange may have beneficial effects on people outside the transaction. The reason for this is that the two parties accrue no direct benefit from these spillover effects even though the larger society gains from their provision. The result is a shortfall in the supply of some good or service. In Canada's history, the private market has been unwilling, for example, to supply rail or air travel in amounts necessary for the building of this country. The response of government has been to create Crown corporations to make up for this deficiency.

Externalities can also be negative in their effect. The two parties engaged in a market transaction may cause harm to others, but the transaction continues nevertheless because the market provides no way to force the two parties to pay for this cost. The classic example here would be with respect to environmental pollution arising from production or consumption or some other form of economic development activity. The government may choose to establish an independent regulatory agency, like the Canadian Environmental Assessment Agency, to reduce or eliminate a project's potential environmental effects. However, public authorities may also elect to create a public enterprise in order to deal more directly with the matter. Many provinces, for instance, have set up public corporations responsible for the sale of liquor. As Trebilcock and Pritchard say, "To the extent that the excessive consumption of alcohol is seen to generate externalities in terms of health impairment, public rowdiness, moral degeneration and like effects, a case is made for regulating its distribution."[22] Governments might have chosen to apply rules to private retailers of alcohol, but many for one reason or another decided instead to combat the negative externality through the creation of a Crown corporation.

National Goals and Public Goods

Governments have a role to play in ensuring that certain essential "public goods" are provided in a society. These are goods and services that "may be consumed simultaneously by people who cannot be excluded from enjoying such consumption."[23] This tends to lead to a "free rider" problem, where individuals seek to maximize their use of the good or service without having to pay for it. This would include things like the armed forces, police and fire services, and public infrastructure (e.g., roads, street lighting) and parks. That being the case, no private business is willing to provide the good in question. To ensure their provision, governments may elect to create a Crown agency. The creation of the RCMP, our national police force, can be explained in this way. Another example would be the CBC, which was established in part to instill in Canadians a sense of their culture and to help resist the cultural dominance of the United States. Since it is difficult to charge for something as ethereal as "Canadian nationalism," markets in Canada have been reluctant to supply it, making government action necessary.

Natural Monopolies

Societies typically frown upon monopolies in the marketplace because they inevitably lead to such undesirable effects as high prices and low-quality products. The preference is usually to have a competitive situation in which many companies vie for the attention of customers since that competition typically results in better products at cheaper prices. However, in some sectors of economic activity it is not reasonable or efficient to have more than one supplier; this is a situation we call a "natural monopoly." In Canada, the areas of telephone service, power generation, municipal water supply, and some insurance services have traditionally been seen as natural monopolies. Imagine the problems associated with setting up multiple poles and power lines to provide electricity to a community or having companies compete to provide hydroelectric power through the building of huge dams. In these situations, there is no sense in trying to break up the monopoly, but the necessity of some kind of government involvement is apparent, because natural monopolies may seek to take actions that produce unwanted consequences, such as low quality products and price gouging.

As with negative externalities, government may opt for an arrangement in which it oversees a private monopoly by establishing a regulatory agency (such as the CRTC regulating prices that can be charged by telephone companies), but it may conclude that it should assume responsibility for the supply of the service in question. The many provincial power corporations are the results of government deciding that the best way to deal with natural monopolies is to take control of the monopoly itself; a similar situation emerged with respect to the sale and distribution of alcohol at the provincial level.[24]

Incomplete Information

For markets to allocate resources efficiently, they need consumers to have sufficient information to make good, rational decisions about the goods and services available for purchase. Most of the time we have the knowledge required to make sensible decisions in the marketplace, but on some occasions that simply is not possible and the consumer can be misled or exploited by the seller. Pharmaceutical products provide a case in point. The individual consumer would have little way of knowing whether such products are safe and effective and, as such, there would be an incentive for the companies producing those products to sacrifice quality as a means of reducing cost. This may result in the purchase of products that are either ineffective or—worse—physically harmful. Another example would be consumers who are interested in good eating habits, but who may not know the ingredients of a particular product in the grocery store. Government can fix this market failure with the regulation of private sector actors; for example, testing and labelling requirements give us a better idea of the quality of such goods as prescription drugs and household foods.

But government can also seek to acquire the required information—to provide a "window" on the private sector—through the setting up of Crown corporations. In the early 1970s, the federal government found itself without the right information to make sound policy for the increasingly important area of oil. Thus, it created a Crown corporation called Petro-Canada in part "to obtain information and advice ... about market conditions and industry performance [in the petroleum industry] without having to rely on private firms to disclose this information."[25]

Chapter 7 / Crown Agencies

Security of Supply

Over the years, there has been a tendency toward the use of regulatory agencies for "supply management." The best examples are the marketing boards for such farm products as eggs, milk, and chicken. These agencies work by setting quotas on the overall quantity of the product that can be produced and allocating this quota among specific producers. The effect is to ensure that an excess of supply does not reduce prices paid to producers. Marketing boards have been criticized on the grounds that they increase the price consumers pay. However, they also ensure reasonable security of supply by preventing injurious competition that would force some suppliers from the market. This is an area of government involvement that has been heavily criticized by other countries as Canada has been negotiating entry into the Trans-Pacific Partnership, a new regional free trade arrangement.

Fairness or Equity

This constitutes one of the ethical rationales for government intervention into the market. On balance, the private sector works well and provides Canadians with a standard of living that is the envy of many. The market at times fails to work as well as it might, but government can intervene to end the failures. However, sometimes we are still dissatisfied even after these failures in efficiency are eliminated, because an unequal distribution of wealth persists. Wolf explains: "the distributional results of even well-functioning markets may not accord with socially acceptable standards of equity, or with society's preferences for reducing excessive disparities in the distribution of income and wealth."[26]

There are several ways that governments can respond in such situations. One option would be to use both income transfers and the tax system in an attempt to redistribute income. For instance, the federal government has a program called the Canada Child Benefit that provides additional money to families with low and moderate incomes. Another approach would be to rely on regulatory activities to achieve greater equity. Minimum wage laws may be instituted to guarantee that people have access to jobs that pay a decent wage, or rates for basic services may be controlled to increase the chances that all have access to gas, water, and hydro.[27] Finally, public enterprises and Crown agencies can also be established for promoting employment and economic development in particular areas of the country. Numerous examples can be identified, including the Atlantic Canada Opportunities Agency and the Canadian Northern Economic Development Agency, dedicated to economic growth in Atlantic Canada and the three territories respectively. Another such agency is the Northern Portage Development Corporation, a joint enterprise between the federal and Manitoba governments and the City of Winnipeg, whose mission is to act as a catalyst in the revitalization of The Forks and North Portage neighbourhoods of downtown Winnipeg.

Paternalism

Another ethical justification for why governments may want to limit the autonomy of individuals in society is "to reduce potentially self-destructive consequences of their otherwise voluntary choices."[28] Minors and the mentally disabled are two groups of people who are believed to require the protection of the state. But there are other circumstances where the government might want to infringe on individual freedoms in order to protect people, such as regulating the use of tobacco products and narcotics or requiring the use of seatbelts in automobiles and helmets when riding a motorcycle.

Political Considerations

Seeing Crown agencies, especially Crown corporations, as responses to concerns in the marketplace assumes that elected officials focus solely on concerns with efficiency and equity, but politicians also have an interest in remaining in office. Therefore, the final category of reasons why governments rely on Crown agencies is political in nature. In short, this organizational form is often chosen because it enables the government to pursue an important political objective, be it insulating the government from unpopular decisions or contributing to its legitimacy.

As we noted in the previous chapter on government departments, once a government establishes a department it tends not to get eliminated. There is a similar reluctance to change the status quo when considering Crown agencies.[29] Moreover, it is important to remember that these entities fulfill broader public policy objectives and promote the legitimacy of that state:

> They are inherently political entities because they aid governments to resolve important … problems as well as help them to avoid future troubles; in this sense they are critical tools to assist governments to govern effectively … and that … ultimately reinforces a government's overall legitimacy in the eyes of the citizenry.[30]

Crown corporations, for example, will often cross subsidize their operations so that profitable aspects of their business can help pay for those that operate at a loss. In the case of Canada Post, it relies on urban delivery programs to help subsidize the higher costs associated with rural delivery services.

In some instances, Crown corporations may be used to generate revenue for government and hence act as a kind of tax collector with low visibility. When we purchase items at the local liquor store, we rarely think that the profits arising from these transactions are just another form of taxation, but that is what they are. The revenue can be so substantial that governments are reluctant for forego those revenues. In the case of the LCBO, it has been generating in excess of a billion dollars annually to the Ontario provincial treasury for many years.[31]

Political and Judicial Control of Crown Agencies

Crown agencies, despite enjoying a degree of autonomy, are ultimately creatures of the government. As such, a central feature of parliamentary control of Crown agencies is that the legislature, the cabinet, and individual ministers set general policies and guidelines for their activities but are kept at arm's length from their day-to-day operations. This creates a conundrum in that the agency must be accountable to the minister and the legislature, but at the same time it must have autonomy in making individual decisions. The trick, as suggested earlier, is to find the appropriate balance between autonomy and accountability to elected representatives. Weak political control of the agency might allow it to act at cross purposes with other government agencies, or to make decisions that are not in the public interest. However, excessive political control deflates the morale of the agency and might lead to dominance by powerful interest groups. This section will examine how the current system of political control operates.

Establishing Crown Agencies

The establishment of a Crown agency offers elected officials an opportunity to exert control over such entities. Crown agencies can be created in various ways, all of which allow for an opportunity for elected officials to establish some kind of accountability framework. The most effective way involves the passage of separate legislation for each new Crown corporation or agency. The *Canada Post Corporation Act*, for instance, specifies the objects of Canada Post, details the composition and powers of the board, provides for senior officers and administrative staff, authorizes the corporation to make regulations with the approval of cabinet, and sets out arrangements for its financing.[32]

Crown agencies are similar to operating departments and most Crown corporations in that they are formed as a result of enabling legislation, which specifies the structure of the agency, the procedures it must follow in considering cases, the limits of its authority, and the general policies it must apply in making decisions. In some instances, all of these components are specified in one statute; in others, they are divided among several legislative enactments. As an example of the former, the *Royal Canadian Mounted Police Act* specifies that there will be a national police force headed by a commissioner and sets out the organization and operation of the RCMP; it also allows for the creation of the RCMP External Review Committee, the Civilian Review and Complaint Commission for the RCMP, as well as the periodic establishment of boards of inquiry to investigate any aspect of the organization.[33] In the case of the National Energy Board, its mandate, responsibilities, and powers are established under three separate laws: the *National Energy Board Act*, the *Canada Oil and Gas Operations Act*, and the *Canada Petroleum Resources Act*.

Governments can also incorporate companies under the relevant federal or provincial companies' legislation in the same manner as any private citizen. A minister, or a public servant, prepares the necessary documentation and, in due course, the Crown corporation is in business. These companies have share capital that is legally vested in either the minister or the Crown. At one point, this method was relatively common, but now it requires Cabinet approval and so is used very seldom.

Finally, the government can enter into any sort of contract; it may decide to purchase the shares of a company on the open market or through a private arrangement. The shares so obtained are then vested in either the minister or the Crown. This same heading covers those relatively rare situations in which governments have nationalized companies against the will of the previous shareholders. This requires enabling legislation and usually provokes a court challenge.

The *Financial Administration Act*

Financial Administration Act The statute that governs the regime of financial accountability for federal departments and agencies.

With respect to Crown corporations, it is the ***Financial Administration Act*** that establishes a general framework for the allowable activities and their accountability. As outlined in section 88, "Each Crown corporation is ultimately accountable, through the appropriate Minister, to Parliament for the conduct of its affairs."[34] In broad terms, the purpose of the Act is to provide for enhanced accountability and some uniformity in the treatment of Crown corporations, but the provisions of the various acts that created the corporations temper this uniformity.

The specific provisions are discussed at various points in this chapter. The general thrust of the legislation is to stipulate what types of approvals corporations need before they undertake certain activities, and what reports they must file at the beginning (five-year corporate plan) and end of their year (annual report). The *Financial Administration Act* is generally seen as the keystone of formal, legal accountability requirements, but there are a number of other accountability mechanisms based on constitutional conventions.

Ministerial Oversight

Although the responsible minister is expected to avoid intruding into the daily operations of Crown corporations, he or she may employ a range of instruments to achieve some control. The minister may rely on the mandate of the corporation, which is typically broad in expression, to give guidance to a Crown corporation. If the minister believes that the corporation is straying from its mission, the minister can cite the objectives of the corporation to support his or her case. Nearly all Crown agencies are required to present the minister with a corporate plan, which gives the minister some control. Plans are required to outline, among other things, the corporation's objectives for the next five years as well as the annual strategies and expected performance related to those objectives.

A further vehicle for establishing ministerial control over both Crown corporations and other agencies is for the minister to recommend the issuing of "directives," which permit the government "to oblige Crown corporations to deliver on their public policy mandate." What the directive means is that the traditional autonomy of the public enterprise is "set aside" in favour of a government edict requiring the Crown corporation to act in a specific way.[35] In the case of a regulatory agency, while it is inappropriate for a minister to intervene in specific cases before an agency, either the minister, or cabinet collectively, can issue policy statements or directives to inform the regulatory agency of the government's desires in a particular area. These policy statements or directives can be made secretly to the agency, but it is usually considered important that they be made publicly so that all parties appearing before the agency will know what policy statements and directives have been made. Issuing these directives publicly also acts as a constraint on any potential abuse of power by the minister.

For some agencies it is not clear whether these are binding, but for others the legislation makes it clear that they are binding. These must be general policy statements and not directions concerning specific cases. Thus, it would be inappropriate for a minister to tell an agency this: "You must grant this broadcast licence to person A instead of person B." However, it would be quite appropriate for the minister to direct the agency in this way: "The only applicants who should be considered for this broadcast licence are those who will agree to provide X percent of Canadian content."

There are also more informal ways in which the minister may have some say over the activities of a Crown agency. The minister may communicate directly with the chair of the board of directors and rely on his or her departmental officials through various means to convey the concerns and wishes of the government (e.g., attending board meetings or engaging in exchanges with corporations). But these actions typically have less impact than their formal counterparts.

In some instances, the decision of a regulatory agency does not become binding until it is approved either by the responsible minister or by the cabinet collectively. The role of the agency in this situation is to provide an impartial hearing to all concerned and to apply its specialized expertise in arriving at a recommendation for a decision. These recommendations are usually given publicly so that the cabinet must consider very carefully both the recommendations and the supporting documentation. If this advice is ignored, allegations of inappropriate political influence can be made.

In other instances, some legislation dealing with regulation provides the right of appeal to the minister or cabinet. Where this provision exists, the appellant usually has no right to appear personally to argue the case but must state in writing the reasons why the decision should be overturned. The minister or cabinet considers these appeals carefully, but is usually somewhat reluctant to overturn a decision, partly to preserve the morale and integrity of the agency and partly to prevent a flood of similar appeals. This reluctance to overturn decisions probably explains the small number of appeals made to cabinet. Nonetheless, the appeal mechanism can be a valuable safety valve even if no action is taken. The availability of an appeal reminds agencies that their decisions can be reviewed, preventing them from behaving in some entirely inappropriate manner.

Parliamentary Control

Control of Crown agencies by Parliament can take the form of approving appropriations or funding. Only the people's representatives can authorize the allocation of financial resources, so these entities must be somewhat attentive to Parliament. Self-financing Crown corporations like Canada Post have no need for government funding, so they enjoy a high degree of autonomy. But if the corporation and other agencies must return to the public treasury on an annual basis and steer their requests for funding through the surveillance of an operating department, the Treasury Board, a legislative committee, and ultimately the legislature, they have little more autonomy than an operating department. Moreover, members of the legislative branch are recipients of overviews of corporate plans and annual reports of Crown agencies. Each year there is also a consolidated report on Crown corporations. Furthermore, they may also make inquiries of the minister about one aspect or another of their operations.

The committees of Parliament also play a role here. Committee hearings are sometimes instituted as a result of information generated by the auditor general or by public concerns about some controversial actions, and more generally "parliamentary committees have the authority to invite chairs and CEOs [of Crown corporations] to appear before them to explain the activities of their organizations."[36] This is an important element of control, but its usefulness is somewhat limited. Elected members have many responsibilities and little assistance in meeting them; it is, therefore, very difficult for them to use the committee system in an effective manner. This situation is exacerbated in the case of Crown corporations, because they see themselves as somewhat removed from detailed political control anyway. Furthermore, unless a corporation needs additional funding or a change in its legislation, there is no automatic mechanism to bring its affairs before a committee and no incentive for the corporation to be totally forthcoming.

With respect to the various statutory and other agencies, parliamentary committees scrutinize their operation in the same manner as that of operating departments and Crown corporations. Committee members can question the minister responsible for an agency and/or the members of the agency about its implementation of policies or its operating procedures. In addition to that oversight, there can be specialized committees that review all regulations and delegated legislation. This process was first employed in Saskatchewan in the early 1960s and came to the federal government in 1971 in the form of the Senate and House of Commons Standing Joint Committee on Regulations and Other Statutory Instruments, which was renamed the Standing Joint Committee for the Scrutiny of Regulations. All regulations made under delegated legislation by either operating departments or regulatory agencies are referred to this committee. Its mandate includes reviewing whether the regulation is in line with the authorizing legislation, whether it violates the Charter of Rights and Freedoms and whether it intrudes into an area that is the prerogative of Parliament. Beyond these specific areas, it does not generally delve into the merits of the regulation. Therefore, the committee has a somewhat legalistic and limited mandate.[37]

Appointment of Members

Ministers and cabinet also play an important role in the appointment of directors and chairs of corporation boards and agencies as well as the chief executive officer, which provides government with the opportunity to carefully select the most appropriate individuals to run these organizations. In the case of directors, depending on the legislation, either the responsible minister or the cabinet makes the final appointment. Cabinet has the authority to appoint chairs. As for CEOs, the appointment process can vary, but in most instances cabinet has a direct say in who is picked to manage the day-to-day operations of the Crown agency. These governor-in-council appointments normally go to individuals who share the views of cabinet on the policy area in question. Johnson has argued that the power of appointment is the most important of all these powers, because it allows the government to establish the "culture" of the agency, thus fostering accountability.[38] This "cultural" approach is particularly important, since appointees immediately attain a high level of independence after they are appointed.

These appointments are usually held either "for good behaviour" or "during pleasure" of the cabinet for fixed terms—typically of a duration from three to seven years—but appointees may be removed "with cause." This ensures that although it is difficult for the minister or cabinet to interfere with the autonomy of the Crown agency, the minister or cabinet is still effectively remain in control.

Judicial Control of Regulatory Agencies

Courts can also control the actions of independent regulatory agencies. In so doing, a court rarely changes the decision of an agency, a consequence of the traditional deference of judicial bodies to the decisions of regulatory entities. But the courts may consider the process followed by an agency in the making of a decision and use this as grounds for overturning the decision. Accordingly, the process of making a decision—and not the merit of a decision—is the foundation of judicial review of regulatory actions. When a court decides against a regulatory agency, the agency is free to reconsider the matter, follow the proper procedure, and arrive at exactly the same decision as it did prior to the judicial review. The court would then be satisfied. A party interested in challenging the quality or merits of a regulation thus must appeal to political authorities.

Crown Agencies: Trends and Issues

The federal government expanded in size and scope considerably in the post-war period as successive governments, through the creation and evolution of the welfare state, provided a broader range of programs and services to Canadians. This resulted in more public servants working for government across a larger number of traditional government departments and a range of Crown agencies. With the ascendancy of the NPM movement (discussed in Chapter 5) and the desire for a leaner, more efficient state, efforts were undertaken to privatize public enterprises and make government less intrusive in the economy and society through deregulation. In this section we examine the trends pertaining to the use of Crown agencies and some of the emerging issues that pose challenges for this organizational form.

Growth and Evolution of Public Enterprise

Governments at both the federal and provincial level have historically used public enterprises as a means of capitalizing on their vast natural resource wealth as well as to develop industries that the private sector did not determine to be financially viable.[39] The state-owned enterprise (SOE) sector, however, has not been static; there has been a shift over time in terms of the activities in which both federal and provincial Crown corporations have been involved. In the years immediately after Confederation, the federal government was most concerned with nation building, and so focused on transportation undertakings that would unify the diverse parts of the country. During World War II, the major theme of public policy changed from national unity to national defence, with the creation of many new corporations to supply the war effort.[40] Since the end of the war, federal Crown corporations have become more involved in the areas of finance, insurance, and real estate, and the newest corporations address matters of airport security, economic development, and cultural activities.

As Table 7.1 shows, public enterprise remains an important and relevant policy instrument for the federal government (as it does for the provinces). Over the past 30 years, there clearly has been a redistribution in the types of federal SOEs: 23 fewer parent Crown corporations in 2015 than there were in 1984, a complete elimination of mixed enterprise, almost a threefold increase in the number of shared governance corporations, and a modest increase in the number of wholly-owned subsidiaries (from 128 in 1984 to 159 in 2015). There have been a number of factors at play; in some cases high profile privatizations occurred while some inactive corporations were eliminated and others were consolidated. But 26 new Crown corporations were also created between the mid-1980s and the mid-2000s.[41] The most recent federal Crown corporation, PPP Canada Inc., was created by the Harper government in 2009 as a means of promoting the use of innovative public–private partnership models to support public infrastructure projects. This demonstrates that even governments on the right of the political spectrum, which tend to favour markets over state action, have nonetheless utilized the corporate form when it suits their policy goals.

Provincially, one function was dominant in the early twentieth century—power generation—but Crown corporations also emerged in the natural resources (particularly mining and forest products) and agricultural sectors. They initially relied heavily on public enterprises as a policy instrument because they did not control monetary policy and initially had very little taxation capacity to foster economic development. By the end of the 1970s, the provinces had created some 233 public enterprises, more than three-quarters of which were created after 1960 when the trend towards province building was evident.[42] Provincial Crown corporations eventually emerged in a wide cross section of the economy, including economic development, finance, insurance and real estate sectors, gaming and liquor sales, culture, transportation, and research and innovation. As a recent study on public enterprise in Canada revealed, the SOE sector in Canada is much larger than previously thought and the provincial component of it, whether measured by assets, employees, or contribution to Canada's GDP, is much larger than that attributable to the federal government. The study also demonstrated that provincial public enterprises are more financially viable than their federal counterparts, largely due to the sectors that they operate in (notably gaming and liquor, finance, and energy).[43]

Problem of Accountability

Ministers and cabinet have at their behest various instruments for ensuring political control of Crown agencies. However, the actual strength or effectiveness of these instruments raises some concerns. Ministers, for instance, receive corporate plans as part of the accountability process, yet their response to these plans is limited, partly because the ministers' officials may be without the skills to assess such reports. One obvious reform, then, would be to correct the deficiencies and to provide better training and professional development to officials responsible for briefing elected officials on the operations of these entities. Ministers also expect to have some input into determining the direction of Crown corporations and other agencies, but the informal communication channels used to realize this expectation are inadequate and the need for a formal process seems evident.

More worrisome are the indications of confusion about the accountability arrangements between government and Crown corporations. One report found that CEOs and chairs of such corporations believed "that their accountability was to Parliament rather than to their responsible Minister."[44] The participation of a large number of government officials in the review of Crown corporations has also made for some confusion about accountability. The intention is for the board of directors to be accountable to the minister who in turn is accountable and answerable to Parliament. But this seemingly simple arrangement has become muddied. Key here is the need to reinforce the centrality of ministerial responsibility and the fact that Crown corporations are accountable to the responsible minister.

One of the most basic problems facing a Crown corporation is whether it should make a profit or serve a public purpose. There can easily be conflicts between these two objectives. Crown corporations might cease or limit operations in underpopulated areas in order to reduce costs (e.g., Canada Post choosing not to deliver mail to unprofitable rural or remote addresses), but such actions would doubtless clash with their aim of providing services to all Canadians without discrimination.

Determining the amount of control the government should have over the activities of a Crown corporation is not an easy task; it is a delicate balance between accountability and control. This balancing act engenders a number of difficulties. It is sometimes suggested that the managers of Crown corporations engage in activities that are contrary to the desires of politicians and that later cause political embarrassment. This situation is frustrating to politicians, who must bear the criticism even though they feel that in some cases they have very little control over these corporations. The managers of Crown corporations are also placed in a difficult position because they are frequently ridiculed in the media for their inability to make a profit, or to operate more efficiently, when the truth is that profit and efficiency have been sacrificed deliberately to political concerns. Of course, when they sacrifice political sensitivity to the profit motive, they suffer for that as well.

The question of the appropriate role of the minister with respect to Crown agencies seemingly raises a conundrum or puzzle. He or she is responsible for the policy outcomes of the activities of the agency but cannot interfere in the making of individual decisions. The purpose of this apparent contradiction is, in part, to balance the need to ensure that these agencies have sufficient independence to make decisions that are fair, transparent, and non-partisan, with the ministers' need to remain accountable both for the overall policy development of their organizations and the expenditure of the public resources that are used to fund them. In order to serve a constituency interest, a minister with more direct control over agencies might be tempted to intervene in broadcast licensing decisions or in the setting of energy prices. Neither scenario, however, would be in the public interest.

Personnel and Governance System

Boards of directors are central to the successful operation of government's corporate forms. But there have been concerns about the training and capacity of those employed in Crown agencies as well as their governance systems. The federal government itself has recognized that more attention needs to be paid to the appointment process to make it more transparent or public. Moreover, it was recommended that the role of the board of directors be expanded so that they helped to develop the selection criteria for chairs and CEOs as well as competency profiles for directors.[45] Depending on the statutory provisions of the Crown agency, there are several ways in which CEOs are appointed: by governor-in-council, the board of directors on its own or with the approval of cabinet, or by the governor-in-council on the recommendation of the board. Good governance necessitates that one individual should not function as both chair of the board and CEO and that the CEO should be the only member of management to sit on the board. Nonetheless, there are still a number of Crown agencies wherein the CEO also serves as chair of the board.

As is the case with other areas of the federal public service (explored in Chapter 15), regulatory institutions are similarly facing significant staff turnover, which necessitates greater attention to recruitment and retention strategies. Furthermore, the training and development of regulatory professionals is paramount since the type of specialized expertise required by these individuals typically is not addressed by institutions of higher learning. Not only must these professionals have expertise in their given area—for example, animal health, plant protection, drugs, immigration, communication, or environmental protection—but they must also "recognize the impacts and consequences of their regulatory proposals on the operations of the sectors and industries they regulate."[46] Therefore, a strong training and development program is required for these regulatory professionals, and a number of important steps have already been taken in that regard.

Political Interference

Although one of the virtues of the Crown agency form of political organization is its autonomy from direct political control, there have been repeated instances where these entities have not been as free from political interference as should be the case. The most recent troubling examples emerged during the Harper government. In April 2008, for example, the government attacked Elections Canada over its investigation of the so-called "in and out" scheme, whereby the Conservative Party circumvented the campaign spending limits outlined in the *Elections Act* by sending over a million dollars to local candidates, who then returned those same funds to party headquarters to cover advertising costs. Government Leader Peter Van Loan suggested that Elections Canada's investigation was politically motivated, claiming that the agency tipped off the media and the Liberal Party about its warrant and subsequent raid of party headquarters so as to bolster the political damage to the government. This was a direct attack by the government on the credibility of Elections Canada and, as one commentator stated, "No matter how independent, an administrative agency cannot be effective if it is perceived as one party's enemy or another's friend."[47]

Another high profile case emerged when Gary Lunn, Minister of Natural Resources, removed Linda Keen as the head of the Canadian Nuclear Safety Commission (CNSC) in January 2008. This occurred the day before she was to appear before a parliamentary committee to explain the decision to shut down the Chalk River nuclear reactor (operated by Atomic Energy of Canada Limited, a federal Crown corporation) in November 2007. Keen was ostensibly fired over her refusal to adhere to a ministerial directive to revoke that regulatory order. The decision to shut down Chalk River precipitated a national and international health crisis because the reactor was responsible for producing about two-thirds of the world's medical isotopes, which are used for medical procedures and tests.

However, the decision to close Chalk River was not made frivolously or without reason. The CNSC had issued that order over safety concerns that the emergency safety system was not properly connected to cooling pumps. This system was necessary for avoiding a meltdown during disasters such as an earthquake. The crisis was eventually averted when the government used its legitimate authority (by passing an emergency measure in Parliament) to override the decision of the CNSC and restart the reactor. But there was still a problem, as one legal scholar explained with such clarity:

> There is nothing inconsistent with the independence of the CNSC in Parliament trumping one of its regulatory decisions based on an overriding public concern (in this case, the shortage of medical isotopes). Since administrative agencies are created by statute, and can be eliminated by statute, it follows that the authors of a statute can also rewrite any of its decisions. What was a threat to the independence of the CNSC, and to the integrity of independent administrative agencies and quasi-judicial tribunals generally, however, was the decision to remove Keen in the middle of her second five-year term as president. This move was not necessary to ensure a steady supply of medical isotopes. This was payback.[48]

While government interference in the operational autonomy of Crown agencies is not new, it is never welcome. Governments must show restraint and rely on the legitimate control mechanisms at their disposal if they are not satisfied with the decision making of these bodies. Otherwise, they undermine the rationale for providing these entities with autonomy in the first place.

Privatization, Deregulation, and the Move to "Smart Regulation"

One of the most common criticisms of Crown agencies has been that there are simply too many of them, whether it is a case of public enterprises engaged in market activities that could be left to the private sector or independent agencies producing too much regulation with their attendant financial costs and administrative burden. As such, there have been movements to both privatize and deregulate; the intention has been to reduce unnecessary government interference in the operation of the market. In the context of public enterprises, privatization refers to the sale—wholly or partially—of companies owned by the government. This particular reform, which became a central plank in the NPM agenda, was a common approach undertaken by governments around the world in the 1980s and beyond. Prime Minister Margaret Thatcher of the United Kingdom was the first to use privatization. Once elected she proceeded to sell off many of the country's SOEs and deregulate many sectors of economic activity, providing a powerful ideological justification and demonstration effect for other countries to follow suit. Although the Canadian state did not pursue the elimination of public enterprise with the same vigour as the UK, we nonetheless witnessed a wave of privatizations provincially and federally, primarily from the mid-1980s to the mid-1990s. Some of the most high profile privatizations included de Havilland Aircraft Canada Ltd. (1986), Canadair Ltd. (1986), Air Canada (1988), Potash Corporation of Saskatchewan (1989), Petro Canada (partially privatized in 1991 with the government's remaining shares sold in 2004), Telestat Canada (1992), Suncor (1992), Alberta Liquor Control Board (1993), and Canadian National Railway (1995).

There have been a number of arguments put forward in favour of privatization. One is that many Crown corporations constitute a questionable use of the corporate form in that they do not reflect the qualities of a corporation and hence more properly should assume another organizational form. A second reason to support privatization is that many Crown corporations are no longer necessary and relevant given changing circumstances; in other words, an argument can be made that the corporation no longer serves a public policy purpose. Take, for example, Air Canada, which was privatized in 1988. While it was at one time an important tool of nation building and economic development, over time the airline industry in Canada matured to the point where the original market failure disappeared, making the response to this failure no longer necessary. It became clear that the country was reasonably well served by a network of airlines, and no one airline served a more central role than any other. A similar logic may be advanced with respect to the CBC, which remains a Crown corporation. This public enterprise originated partly because of the need for a national broadcaster able to reach all Canadians, but now Canada has a number of private television networks that meet this need. The CBC was also founded to counter the American influence and promote Canadian culture, but given advancements in information and communication technologies this rationale also seems suspect.

A third reason for privatization is that it may improve the efficiency of the privatized company or the services offered by the company. A number of provinces have Crown organizations that have a monopoly over the importation, wholesaling, distribution, and retailing of liquor products. However, one province, Alberta, has privatized the retailing of liquor, and research shows that Albertans have both better access to liquor stores and a richer selection than those residing in provinces that have maintained their public sector monopolies. Improved efficiency was ostensibly the reason behind the Ontario government moving forward with the partial privatization of Hydro One in November 2015; in this instance, the shift to a mixed enterprise has been justified on the basis that it will produce a better-run and more valuable company.

At a more practical level, some governments seem to want to sell some of their more profitable Crown corporations, because the inflow of funds will reduce their deficits and outstanding debt as well as generate revenues for new initiatives. Again, Hydro One is relevant. With plans to eventually sell off a 40 percent stake in the company over several public offerings of shares (with the final one slated for 2017), the Wynne government expects to generate some $9 billion in revenues. This will allow the government to pay off Hydro One's $5 billion debt with the remainder going towards its ambitious ten-year plan to invest in infrastructure, particularly transit.[49]

A final justification for privatization is that some governments have an ideological predisposition to favour the private sector, a predisposition which drives them to privatize corporations even when there are no other sound reasons to do so. In these cases, elected officials believe that a society in general would be better off if the public sector reduced its size and gave the private sector more responsibility to serve the needs of the citizenry. This is the least compelling justification. As a number of scholars have pointed out, a more pragmatic approach would be to examine the specific business interests—and not the corporation as a whole—of these public enterprises on a case-by-case basis to determine whether privatization makes sense, "including a post-privatization regulatory and legislative framework."[50]

Not many public enterprises have been privatized over the past two decades, because most of the obvious candidates at the federal level of government, that is to say commercial Crown corporations operating in competitive markets, have already been privatized. Moreover, the government itself appears to have recognized the "need to reassert the role of Crown corporations as instruments of public policy."[51] Equally relevant is the fact that many public enterprises in Canada have gone through a process of modernization, which has resulted in "much more dynamic, efficient and nimble publicly owned firms."[52] Nonetheless, there are a number of Crown corporations whose continued existence continues to be questioned, including the LCBO (see Box 7.1), B.C. Hydro, Manitoba Lotteries Corporation, Canada Post, Farm Credit Canada, the Business Development Bank of Canada, and the Export Development Corporation.[53]

deregulation The elimination of government regulatory control over an industry so that the industry can operate through the dictates of the private enterprise system.

In Canada, the attractiveness of **deregulation** has not been as great as in some other Western democracies. Nonetheless, governments in Canada have been concerned with the uncoordinated proliferation in the number of regulations and agencies to create and enforce them—what is known as "regulatory congestion." This proliferation led to measures to deal with the regulatory inflation of the 1970s and 1980s. The pressure to pare down the existing set of regulations has not abated. An OECD report published in 2002, for example, suggested that Canada still suffered from substantial regulatory costs and pointed to excessive regulation in such areas as telecommunications and trade between provinces.[54] Experience also suggests that deregulation can be a successful policy—the deregulation of the airline industry in Canada, for instance, led to reduced fares and more efficient use of labour.[55]

Given the obvious pitfalls associated with regulation, it is not surprising that deregulation became part of the NPM mantra in the 1990s. Although regulation is often seen as the low-cost option from the standpoint of government, it can impose sizable costs on other parties. The most obvious examples are the direct costs incurred by the regulated industry and by other affected parties. The firms in the regulated industry must maintain extensive records in a format specified by the regulatory agency. All parties affected by regulatory agencies incur substantial information costs to keep themselves abreast of initiatives by the agency and by other groups affected by the agency. Then there are legal and other costs involved in preparing a case and actually appearing before the regulatory agency.

However, these direct costs might be only the tip of the iceberg. The major costs of regulation could come from complying with regulations. In the past, the automobile industry was forced to conform to regulations relating to seatbelts, air bags, improved door strength, head restraints, and increased bumper strength. These changes helped increase the safety of vehicles, but they also added substantially to the cost of a car. Similarly, expensive pollution-reduction devices, such as scrubbers, contributed to the battle against environmental degradation, but they also represented a substantial cost to the companies and government agencies at which the new measures were directed.

To Privatize or Not? The Case of the Liquor Control Board of Ontario

BOX
7.1

The LCBO—three separate Ontario governments (Harris, McGuinty, and Wynne) seriously examined and ultimately rejected the possibility of privatizing this financially lucrative Crown corporation. The evidence on the impacts of the privatization of the LCBO is somewhat contentious, particularly with respect to government revenues and the cost of purchasing alcoholic beverages. There is disagreement regarding whether market competition would drive prices down (the experience with privatization in Alberta since the early 1990s does not appear to support that conclusion, at least not to any appreciable effect) and lead to a decrease in government revenues. One view is that the Ontario government would need to reduce its markups on alcohol so that the private vendors can make a profit, thus reducing the nearly $2 billion per year in profits that the LCBO is producing. Other studies, however, suggest that government revenues would actually increase as a result of higher volumes of sales due to lower prices. But is profit maintained as a result of increased consumption, with the potential for additional healthcare and social costs (i.e., increased rates of alcohol-related violence and crime), a desirable outcome? Generally, the perceived advantages of privatization are greater product selection, more convenience (more stores to acquire alcohol and greater hours of operation), and cheaper prices. Those opposed to the privatization of the LCBO argue that state ownership is required to control consumption and access (i.e., to prevent minors from acquiring the product); it also ensures better wages and benefits for employees and it allows the government to pursue economic development by using shelf space to promote local wine producers.

Although the Ontario government has continued to maintain the LCBO as a Crown corporation, it has nonetheless undertaken efforts to modernize the way in which alcohol is sold in the province. The process began in the 1990s when significant capital was invested to enhance the LCBO's network of stores with new fixtures, new lighting, better layouts, and improved staff training so as to provide attractive, well-designed retail outlets. These enhancements have resulted in high levels of customer satisfaction. More recently, the Wynne government staved off pressure to privatize the LCBO but opened up the market so that wine and beer can now be sold in a select number of grocery stores throughout the province.

Has the Ontario government made the right decision by making the purchase of alcohol more convenient, but not eliminating public ownership of the sale and distribution of wine and spirits? Is there still a compelling public policy purpose to justify this public enterprise, or should the government let private firms in the marketplace, albeit subject to strict government regulation, take control over responsibility for selling alcoholic beverages?

Sources: Malcolm Bird, "Alberta's and Ontario's Liquor Boards: Why Such Divergent Outcomes?" *Canadian Public Administration* 53(4) (December 2010): 509–530; Paul Masson and Anindya Sen, "Uncorking a Strange Brew: The Need for More Competition in Ontario's Alcoholic Beverage Retailing System," *C.D. Howe Institute Commentary No. 414* (Toronto: C.D. Howe Institute, August 2014).

There are also "induced costs" of regulation. Regulations may hinder innovation, because industry research funds and facilities are moved toward meeting regulatory requirements and away from work on "new technology that might improve productivity, reduce costs, and lead to the development of a wider range of new products and services."[56] The length of the regulatory process—for example, in the approval of new pharmaceutical drugs—may also discourage attempts to develop new products that would increase the effectiveness of the health care sector. Productivity gains, too, may be lost as companies expend valuable resources on addressing regulatory concerns, leaving less available for investment in equipment and machinery that may reduce costs and expand capacity. Employment rates, an important indicator of economic health, can also be affected adversely by regulations. Minimum-wage laws can lead to employment loss, because firms are unwilling to pay the stipulated wage for certain jobs. This has been a concern vocalized by the business community every time the province of Ontario has increased the minimum wage, which has more than doubled since 2003.

Many other pitfalls associated with regulation have been identified. One is the regulatory approval process. A more thorough mechanism should be developed for reviewing the utility of existing regulations—one should never assume that regulations will remain forever effective. One expert has argued that "regulation in the innovation age requires reform that goes beyond *periodic* reform exercises and beyond current federal regulatory policy statements."[57] As such, he has called for the establishment of an annual regulatory agenda and institutional reform as a mechanism for improving regulatory governance.

It is also disconcerting that consultation inherent in the approval process has some problems. The fear is that some groups, especially consumer groups with few resources or the interested public, are unable to make their voices heard (see Box 7.2). This concern, originally articulated in the 2002 OECD report referred to above, was reiterated in a more recent report, highlighting in particular the challenges for consumer groups:

> One objective of public consultations on regulatory issues is to ensure that regulatory authorities are aware of a broad spectrum of perspectives and ideas. In this regard, consumer organizations are under-represented in consultative processes and do not have the resources to undertake the research and develop the expertise required to contribute to consultations on regulatory issues.[58]

BOX 7.2

Regulation of Genetically Modified Crops and Foods

As with all countries, Canada is attempting to determine how best to regulate genetically modified (GM) crops and foods. For the most part, it has left this matter up to science experts and representatives from the agri-food industry. Other countries, such as the United Kingdom, have approached this issue differently, providing for more public input and debate concerning the regulation of GM crops and foods. For some scholars, the Canadian approach is unsatisfactory. A more open process is desirable.

Source: Sarah Hartley and Grace Skogstad, "Regulating Genetically Modified Crops and Foods in Canada and the United Kingdom: Democratizing Risk Regulation," *Canadian Public Administration* 48(3) (Fall 2005): 305–327.

Regulatory congestion, resulting from the existence of a number of uncoordinated regulatory agencies in each of the regulated areas of society, has a number of unwanted effects. It increases the cost of complying with regulatory initiatives and may act to constrain attempts at developing new and interesting production methods. The congestion and the resulting maze of regulation might also discourage groups from participating in the regulatory process. From a global perspective, the congestion "contributes to a perception of Canada and Canadian regulation as being overly complex, which acts as a disincentive to investment in Canada."[59] At the most basic level, the crowded world of regulations and regulatory agencies produces much frustration and confusion. To illustrate this complexity, consider the dizzying array of agencies, regulations, and requirements that a forestry company interested in a new investment would need to confront:

- a provincial timber management plan,
- *Species at Risk Act* requirements,
- permits/requirements under the *Navigable Waters Protection Act*,

- *Fisheries Act* requirements,
- *Canadian Environmental Assessment Act* requirements,
- provincial permits (of various kinds under several statutes),
- further *Fisheries Act* and *Canadian Environmental Assessment Act* processes and requirements, and
- additional requirements downstream or at later stages of the project or investment.[60]

As just demonstrated, Canada's regulatory regimes are complex, but they do not simply involve the federal and provincial governments; increasingly they also involve local and international actors. Moreover, in an increasingly globalized world, it is important that a country's efforts at regulating its interactions with international forces be effective. There is a concern that Canada's actions in this area are "ad hoc and uncoordinated."[61] Too often agencies act to regulate the international sphere without a real sense of overall direction and purpose, and without an awareness of what other Canadian regulatory bodies are doing in this area. Canadian government departments and regulatory agencies also seem to act even though existing internationally negotiated rules and regulations are workable. As a recent report on regulation on Canada states, "In many cases, international standards are sufficiently developed that Canada can achieve its policy goals without the addition of Canada-specific requirements."[62] Of course, this does not mean Canada should bow to pressures from certain sectors for less international regulation, or refrain from acting when necessary; it only means we should be aware of the fact that country-specific solutions to international problems will become less and less effective in an increasingly integrated world.

The charge of ineffectiveness in international regulation includes relations with Canada's largest trading partner, the United States. The two countries often have parallel regulatory bodies and processes, a situation that can lead to higher costs for all concerned. For instance, both countries have bodies that participate together in the regulation of pesticides in North America, but this arrangement is sometimes viewed as "burdensome" and causes some companies to seek approval only in the less-regulated American market.[63] The result is that American farmers may get to use new and more useful pesticides while their Canadian counterparts must be content with older and less effective ones. This problem also reveals a related one: that differences in regulations still exist between the two countries, a condition that "can impede trade and investment." As one report says, "the cross border movement of goods and services is still subject to an array of different regulatory requirements."[64] Some of these differences, to be sure, are the outcome of clear policy differences, but many might be eliminated with little or no detrimental effect to Canadian interests.

The final criticism of regulatory agencies that we will address is **captive agency theory**.[65] In many ways it is complementary to the above arguments about the lack of consumer power in the regulatory process. This theory suggests that, over time, the agency is "captured" by the industry that it was set up to regulate, and so becomes supportive of that industry. It is a gradual process, in which the agency develops a concern for the orderly development of the industry; this concern gradually comes to mean the protection of the companies currently in the industry from any disruptive forces, such as excessive competition from new entrants. The CRTC, for example, is frequently criticized for advancing the interests of the broadcasting industry rather than those of the consumer, although some of its more recent decisions have been characterized as having a more consumer-oriented approach.[66]

Despite these deficiencies, both perceived and real, regulation is an important and necessary aspect of governance. Governments, therefore, must be cautious in their efforts to deregulate so that people are not left vulnerable by a regulatory void. Although the popular press liked to suggest that Canada weathered the 2007 US subprime crisis and ensuing global recession better than other countries because of our more stringent

captive agency theory A theory that holds that regulatory agencies eventually become captive of, or controlled by, the interests they were established to regulate.

Chapter 7 / Crown Agencies

regulatory regime, some scholars have challenged that narrative. In particular, they point to the fact that many of the reckless financial practices that were major causes of the American crisis had started to creep into Canada (e.g., in the 2006 budget the Harper government allowed zero down, 40-year mortgages). Canadian banks did avoid the full effects of the financial meltdown to be sure, but the reason they did so likely had more to do with the conservative, risk-averse culture of the Canadian banking sector than the robustness of the regulatory system in place.[67]

The process of modernizing the federal government's regulatory regime began with the 2002 speech from the throne, at which point the "smart regulation" strategy was announced. Notably, the government has resisted the temptation to simply cut away at rules and regulations. Smart regulation—an acronym for "specific," "measurable," "attainable," "realistic," and "timely"—amounts to an attempt to make the federal regulatory system more effective, and to ensure that the system adapts to the changing economic and social environment. This is to be accomplished in a number of ways, but most particularly through "increased regulatory cooperation at the international, federal, provincial and territorial levels and within the federal government itself" and "the adoption of a regulatory process that is more effective, cost-efficient, timely, transparent, accountable, and focused on results," as articulated in the April 2007 Cabinet Directive on Streamlining Regulations, which was updated and replaced in 2012 by the Cabinet Directive on Regulation.[68] One of the requirements is that all departments and agencies involved with regulation must consult with interested and affected parties at all stages of the regulatory process. In general, the policy of smart regulation recognizes that well-crafted regulations can contribute to the social and economic well-being of a nation.

Points to Know

- Aside from departments, governments have historically relied on two types of Crown agencies—Crown corporations and statutory and other agencies—for delivering programs and services.

- These entities were designed to have varying degrees of autonomy from the government; rather than having tight ministerial control through the deputy minister, these entities typically have a president and CEO as their administrative head, who, in turn, is accountable on a day-to-day basis to an independent board of directors. It is the board of directors that is ultimately accountable, through the appropriate minister, to Parliament.

- Despite operating at arm's length from government, there are several ways that political direction and control are maintained—from the appointment of key personnel to government directives to corporate plans and annual reports.

- The variation in the types of Crown agencies makes it difficult to generalize about their structure and function, but they all typically serve the public interest.

- Crown agencies have been created for many reasons, several of which have to do with a number of failures of private marketplace.

- There have been pressures to privatize public enterprise and to reduce government regulation, but governments in Canada have remained committed to Crown agencies.

Review Questions

1. What are the two types of Crown agencies, and how do these organizational forms differ from the traditional government department?

2. How is accountability ensured in Crown agencies? Are such accountability mechanisms sufficient? If not, how is it possible to balance the need for autonomy with the corresponding need for direction and control?

3. What are some of the reasons that governments have relied on Crown agencies?

4. How important is public enterprise in Canada?

5. Is there still a compelling rationale for public enterprise and regulation, or should governments refrain from direct intervention into the market? Under what circumstances would it make sense for the government to privatize and deregulate?

Notes

1. David Johnson, *Thinking Government: Public Administration and Politics in Canada*, 3rd ed. (Toronto: University of Toronto Press, 2011), 153–154.
2. J.E. Hodgetts, *The Canadian Public Service: A Physiology of Government, 1867–1970* (Toronto: University of Toronto Press, 1976), 138.
3. Daria Crisan and Kenneth J. McKenzie, "Government-Owned Enterprises in Canada," *University of Calgary School of Public Policy SPP Research Papers* 6(8) (February 2013): 1–29. Crisan and McKenzie attempt to assess the size of the public enterprise sector in Canada.
4. Treasury Board Secretariat, "Overview of Institutional Forms and Definitions," accessed May 12, 2016, http://www.tbs-sct.gc.ca/hgw-cgf/finances/rgs-erdg/cc-se/institution/forms-formulaires-eng.asp.
5. Ibid.
6. Ibid.
7. Privy Council Office, *A Guide Book for Heads of Agencies: Operations, Structures and Responsibilities in the Federal Government* (Ottawa: Privy Council Office, August 1999), accessed May 15, 2016, www.pco-bcp.gc.ca/index.asp?lang=eng&page=informatioon&sub=publications&doc=guide2/table-eng.htm.
8. Statistics Canada, "Mandate and Objectives," accessed May 15, 2016, www.statcan.gc.ca/eng/about/mandate.
9. Johnson, *Thinking Government*, 153; Rand Dyck and Christopher Cochrane, *Canadian Politics: Critical Approaches*, 7th ed. (Toronto: Nelson, 2014), 569.
10. National Energy Board, *Board Member Operating Model* (February 2016), 2, accessed May 19, 2016, www.neb-one.gc.ca/bts/whwr/gvrnnc/brdmmbrprtngmdl-eng.pdf.
11. See Privy Council Office, *Guide to Making Federal Acts and Regulations*, 2nd ed. (Ottawa: Her Majesty the Queen in Right of Canada, 2001).
12. John Strick, "Regulation and Deregulation" in *The Handbook of Canadian Public Administration*, 1st ed., ed. Christopher Dunn (Toronto: Oxford University Press, 2002), 263–264.
13. John Strick, *The Economics of Government Regulation: Theory and Canadian Practice* (Toronto: Thompson Educational Publishing Inc., 1994), 8.
14. For example, in addition to economic and social regulation, Johnson, *Thinking Government*, also identifies environmental regulation as a separate category.
15. Canadian Broadcasting Corporation, *#Creating Connections: Annual Report, 2014–2015* (Ottawa: CBC/Radio-Canada Corporate Communications, 2015), 6, 28.
16. Economic Council of Canada, *Reforming Regulation* (Ottawa: Minister of Supply and Services, 1981), 56.
17. Privy Council Office, *A Guide Book for Heads of Agencies*.
18. National Energy Board, *Board Member Operating Model*, 10.
19. Canadian Food Inspection Agency, *2016–2017 Report on Plans and Priorities* (Ottawa: Her Majesty the Queen in Right of Canada, 2016), 18; Financial Consumer Agency of Canada, *2016–2017 Business Plan* (Ottawa: Her Majesty the Queen in Right of Canada, 2016), 20.
20. Edward M. Iacobucci and Michael J. Trebilcock, "The Role of Crown Corporations in the Canadian Economy: An Analytical Framework," *University of Calgary School of Public Policy SPP Research Papers* 5(9) (March 2012): 1.
21. Ibid., 2. See also, Strick, *Economics of Government Regulation*.
22. M.J. Trebilcock and J.R.S. Prichard, "Crown Corporations: The Calculus of Instrument Choice," in *Crown Corporations in Canada: The Calculus of Instrument Choice*, ed. J. Robert S. Prichard (Toronto: Butterworths, 1983), 72.
23. Iacobucci and Trebilcock, "The Role of Crown Corporations," 3.
24. See Malcolm G. Bird, "Alberta's and Ontario's Liquor Boards: Why Such Divergent Outcomes?" *Canadian Public Administration* 53(4) (December 2010): 509–530 for a discussion of the different paths that Alberta and Ontario have taken with respect controlling alcohol sales.
25. Trebilcock and Pritchard, "Crown Corporations," 70.
26. Charles Wolf, Jr., *Markets or Governments: Choosing Between Imperfect Alternatives*, 2nd ed. (Cambridge: MIT Press, 1993), 28.
27. Strick, "Regulation and Deregulation," 266.
28. Iacobucci and Trebilcock, "The Role of Crown Corporations," 5.
29. Ibid., 7.
30. Malcolm Bird, "Canadian State-Owned Enterprises: A Framework for Analyzing the Evolving Crowns," *Policy Studies* 36(2) (2015): 137.
31. The dividend transfer to the Government of Ontario was $1.805 billion in 2014–2015. See Liquor Control Board of Ontario, *Let's Get Together:*

32. *Canada Post Corporation Act* (R.S.C. 1985, c. C-10).
33. *Royal Canadian Mounted Police Act* (R.S.C., 1985, c. R-10).
34. *Financial Administration Act* (R.S.C., 1985, c. F-11), s. 88.
35. Treasury Board Secretariat, *Review of the Governance Framework for Canada's Crown Corporations* (Ottawa: Her Majesty the Queen in Right of Canada, 2005), 18.
36. Ibid., 21.
37. See Audrey O'Brien and Marc Bosc, eds., *House of Commons Procedure and Practice*, 2nd ed. (Ottawa: House of Commons, 2009), ch.17.
38. David Johnson, "Regulatory Agencies and Accountability: An Ontario Perspective," *Canadian Public Administration* 34(3) (Autumn 1991): 417–434.
39. Luc Bernier, "The Future of Public Enterprises: Perspectives from the Canadian Experience," *Annals of Public and Cooperative Economics* 82(4) (2011): 404.
40. Sandford F. Borins, "World War Two Crown Corporations: Their Wartime Role and Peacetime Privatization," *Canadian Public Administration* 25(2) (Fall 1982): 380–404.
41. Treasury Board Secretariat, *Review of the Governance Framework for Canada's Crown Corporations*, 10.
42. Bernier, "The Future of Public Enterprises," 405.
43. Crisan and McKenzie, "Government-Owned Enterprises in Canada," 13–18.
44. Treasury Board Secretariat of Canada, *Review of the Governance Framework for Canada's Crown Corporations*, 14.
45. Ibid., 29.
46. Barry Stemshorn and Robert W. Slater, "Potential for a Regulatory Breakthrough? Regulatory Governance and Human Resource Initiatives," in *How Ottawa Spends, 2008–2009: A More Orderly Federalism?* ed. Allan M. Maslove (Montreal and Kingston: McGill-Queen's University Press, 2008), 73.
47. Lorne Sossin, "Does Independence Matter? From Elections Canada to the Nuclear Watchdog, the Harper Government Seems to Disagree," *Literary Review of Canada* (July-August 2008), accessed June 1, 2016, www.reviewcanada.ca/magazine/2008/07/does-independence-matter/.
48. Ibid.
49. Robert Benzie, "Hydro One's New Share Offer Should Raise $1.7B," *The Toronto Star*, April 5, 2016, accessed June 6, 2016, www.thestar.com/news/queenspark/2016/04/05/next-wave-of-hydro-one-shares-for-sale-soon.html.
50. Anthony Boardman and Aidan Vining, "A Review and Assessment of Privatization in Canada," *University of Calgary School of Public Policy SPP Research Papers* 5(4) (January 2012): 23.
51. Treasury Board Secretariat, *Review of the Governance Framework*, 4. Bolding in original removed.
52. Bird, "Canadian-Owned State Enterprises," 147.
53. See for example, Philippe Bergevin and Finn Poschmann, *Reining in the Risks: Rethinking the Role of Crown Financial Corporations in Canada*, C.D. Howe Institute Commentary No. 372 (Toronto: C.D. Howe Institute, February 2013); Boardman and Vining, "A Review and Assessment"; and Iacobucci and Trebilcock, "The Role of Crown Corporations."
54. OECD, *Canada: Maintaining Leadership Through Innovation* (Paris: OECD, 2002), 25, 29, 41.
55. Strick, "Regulation and Deregulation", 271–272.
56. Strick, *The Economics of Government Regulation*, 116.
57. G. Bruce Doern, *Red Tape, Red Flags: Regulation for the Innovation Age* (Ottawa: Conference Board of Canada, 2007), 133. Emphasis in original.
58. External Advisory Committee on Smart Regulation, *Smart Regulation: A Regulatory Strategy for Canada* (September 2004), 56, accessed June 8, 2016, http://publications.gc.ca/collections/Collection/CP22-78-2004E.pdf.
59. Ibid., 30.
60. G. Bruce Doern, "Smart Regulation, Regulatory Congestion and Natural Resources Regulatory Governance," in *How Ottawa Spends 2004–2005: Mandate Change in the Paul Martin Era*, ed. G. Bruce Doern (Montreal & Kingston: McGill-Queen's University Press, 2004), 247.
61. External Advisory Committee on Smart Regulation, *Smart Regulation*, 17.
62. Ibid., 19.

63. Ibid., 20.

64. Ibid., 21.

65. See Daniel Carpenter and David Moss, eds. *Preventing Regulatory Capture: Special Interest Influence and How to Limit It* (New York: Cambridge University Press, 2014).

66. Robert Armstrong, *Broadcasting Policy in Canada*, 2nd ed. (Toronto: University of Toronto Press, 2016), ch.15.

67. Stephen Harris, "The Global Financial Meltdown and Financial Regulation: Shirking and Learning—Canada in an International Context," in *How Ottawa Spends, 2010-2011: Recession, Realignment and the New Deficit Era*, eds. G. Bruce Doern and Christopher Stoney (Montreal and Kingston: McGill-Queen's University Press, 2010), 68–86; Derek Ireland and Kernaghan Webb, "The Canadian Escape from the Subprime Crisis? Comparing the US and Canadian Approaches," in *How Ottawa Spends, 2010-2011*, 87–106.

68. Treasury Board of Canada Secretariat, *Midterm Evaluation of the Implementation of the Cabinet Directive on Streamlining Regulation* (Ottawa: Treasury Board, May 2011), accessed June 8, 2016, www.tbs-sct.gc.ca/report/orp/2011/cdsr-dcrrtb-eng.asp.

Alternative Service Delivery (ASD)

Learning Objectives

Reading this chapter allows you to do the following:

- Understand the origins of ASD
- Identify many of the various mechanisms that arose as part of NPM that governments have been using for service delivery—beyond the traditional government department and Crown agency
- Distinguish between NPM-inspired ASD and the new forms of service delivery that have emerged as part of the post-NPM reform wave
- Critically assess the successes and limitations associated with ASD

The previous two chapters discussed the traditional types of organizations that governments use for service delivery. Until the late 1980s and early 1990s, this was the end of the story about service delivery—virtually all services were delivered either by a government department, a Crown corporation, or some other type of statutory agency. From that time onward, however, governments have employed many additional—and more flexible—mechanisms for providing services; this is what has come to be known as **alternative service delivery (ASD)**.[1]

As Zussman noted, ASD has been particularly attractive because it has enabled the public service to develop "creative solutions to complex challenges." But while ASD may have been a novel approach to service delivery that emerged with the advent of NPM (new public management), there is nothing extraordinary about it any more: ASD "is now an integral part of the administrative structures and practices of governments around the world."[2] As a part of the NPM administrative reforms, ASD was fundamentally designed to improve organizational performance; while that logic remains pertinent, with the shift to new public governance (NPG) a different theoretical rationale (and associated practical implications) for ASD has started to emerge.

This chapter will focus on a variety of service delivery mechanisms that can be grouped under the very broad heading of ASD. The assertion that governments are slow to espouse new ideas might be correct, but when governments seized upon the idea of ASD, they did so with a vengeance. As a result, there are so many examples of ASD that have been and continue to be developed that there can be no comprehensive catalogue. Rather, the purpose of this chapter is to provide a flavour of the concept of ASD and address some of the political and organizational issues it raises. The chapter begins with a definition of ASD, followed by a consideration of some of the reasons why governments have chosen these mechanisms. The next section will provide a classification and selective discussion of some ASD approaches. The chapter ends with an evaluation of some of the potential problems in the use of ASD mechanisms.

alternative service delivery (ASD) The trend in recent years for governments to search for more innovative and efficient ways to deliver services than through traditional departments and agencies.

Definition of ASD

Governments around the world have been pursuing ASD for decades; given the broad variety of activities that have been subsumed under that label, it is not surprising that a number of definitions have emerged. In its April 2002 Policy on Alternative Service Delivery, the Canadian federal government defined it in the following terms: ASD "entails the pursuit of new and appropriate organizational forms and arrangements, including partnerships with other levels of government and other sectors, in order to improve the delivery of programs and services."[3] A similar, but narrower, definition was offered by Ford and Zussman, who referred to ASD as a "creative and dynamic process of public sector restructuring that improves the delivery of services to clients by sharing governance functions with individuals, community groups and other government entities."[4]

Both definitions emphasize that ASD is not a static process and involves restructuring.[5] The historic approach was that government chose a traditional organizational form to deliver a service (through an operating department, or a Crown corporation or agency) when a policy was created and it stayed with that mechanism for the indefinite future; ASD suggests that there is no "one best way" of delivering a service. Therefore, the best approach is to consider service delivery as a "toolbox from which governments can tailor various options" to meet the needs of a particular set of circumstances.[6]

However, whereas the Ford and Zussman definition regards providing individuals and groups some involvement in the governing process as an essential element of ASD, the government's definition accounts for a wider range of organizational forms and practices. As such, the process of restructuring can be significant to the extent that it involves the adoption of new organizational mechanisms for delivering programs and services (such as departmental corporations, special operating agencies [SOAs], and service agencies) or the use of partnerships with state and non-state actors.

ASD can, however, involve less radical change. Governments may simply promote better coordination and cooperation within and across departments to break down silos and eliminate duplication. Alternatively, a service might be devolved to another level of government to clarify roles and responsibilities and similarly reduce overlap and duplication. For example, several provinces allow the Canada Revenue Agency to collect and remit to them their provincial sales taxes as part of the harmonized sales tax. ASD might also involve bringing together different government departments or offices into the same building—what is known as **co-location**. Increasingly, the discussion around ASD centres on whether programs and services should be provided through traditional service channels (e.g., over the phone, by mail, or visiting a government office) or new digital technologies (e.g., electronic kiosks or self-service technologies like the Internet or mobile devices), not a particular organizational form.[7]

co-location This is the practice of bringing together different government departments or offices into the same building to make it more convenient for citizens to access services. It is one aspect of integrated service delivery.

Origins of ASD: From NPM to New (Integrated) Public Governance

The intellectual origins of ASD were multifaceted. It can certainly be argued that public administration has always been concerned about achieving greater efficiency and effectiveness in the delivery of public services; as such, the government has a legacy of fostering greater cooperation and collaboration between departments as a means of reducing unnecessary overlap and duplication. Another factor in the development of ASD was the declining levels of trust and confidence that citizens had in their governments, resulting in expressions of dissatisfaction about the quality of services that they were receiving for their tax dollars.

However, one especially significant driver in the move towards various forms of ASD was the emergence of NPM. In particular, a central tenet of NPM was the belief that there should be a separation of the policy and service delivery capacities of government. Important in this thinking was the distinction between "steering" and "rowing" and the assertion that government should centre its efforts on the former.[8] Government, it was argued, allocated too many of its scarce resources to administration and too little to providing overall policy direction. What government should do was stick mostly to the crucial task of steering the ship of state and leave the carrying out of public programs to a wide assortment of arrangements, which may or may not involve government directly. In making these claims, the proponents of ASD were not saying that government should never "row." There might be situations in which governments are uniquely situated to implement initiatives, but the point was that in the past governments had been too quick to assume that the "steering" and "rowing" functions are always coupled when in fact they might be easily and beneficially separated.

Other aspects of NPM are discernable in the shift to ASD. One of the most frequent arguments heard in favour of ASD was that it would improve the quality of service delivery. The focus was on the needs and demands of the customer or client receiving the government service rather than citizens.[9] In that regard, some examples of ASD involved restructuring within government to provide the service better at lower cost. ASD was also touted as a way to lower government spending, since it involved giving private sector and non-profit sector organizations a greater role in service delivery. This automatically reduced the size of government by hiving off certain responsibilities. It also transferred certain types of risk, especially cost overruns and delays in large capital projects, to the private sector. But the infusion of competition into the delivery of public services also led to innovation and experimentation, which improved both productivity and service levels; in addition, competition had the benefit of strengthening accountability by allowing for benchmarking across the public sector. Government departments could be compared against the private sector on a number of measures, including cost, outcomes, and service quality.[10] Finally, recall that one of the important elements of NPM was to foster more autonomy and flexibility; this, too, found expression in ASD since it promoted flexibility in the delivery of services. The intent was to move away from the rigid emphasis on process control that was characteristic of traditional service delivery toward other types of organizations that would not be hindered by inflexible budgeting systems and staffing rules.

In the post-NPM era, however, where elements of NPG have started to emerge, the logic—if not necessarily the method or practice—of ASD is undergoing a transformation. The emphasis on efficiency and cost-effective service delivery under NPM is being replaced (albeit gradually and subtly) by a concern for the promotion of the common good. Partnerships, for example, were promoted as part of NPM, and they remain an important element of current public sector reform initiatives; however, rather than viewing them solely from a financial perspective, that is to say of reduced cost and greater efficiency, it has been suggested that partnerships are promoted because of their ability to enhance the capacity of local organizations and build civic infrastructure.

A key element of NPG has been to emphasize the need for and importance of citizen and stakeholder involvement in the policy formation and implementation processes. Citizens and groups are not to be passive recipients of government policy, but rather engage in policy "co-construction" (being involved early in the process to conceptualize and design policy) and "co-production" (delivery or implementation of policy).[11] This would suggest a shift away from the narrow, individualistic NPM conception of the citizen as client or customer to one where individuals are again conceived as citizens who have a "complex, multifaceted relationship with the state."[12] As Heintzman and Marson stated, "They are not just consumers of government services: they are usually also taxpayers and citizens, that is, bearers of rights and duties in a framework of democratic community, with civic and public interests that go well beyond their service needs."[13]

Chapter 8 / Alternative Service Delivery (ASD)

In his discussion of the evolution of public service delivery, Kernaghan wrote of the shift towards single-window service, or what he calls **integrated service delivery**, which "involves bringing together and, where desirable and possible, fitting together related government services so citizens can access them in a single seamless experience based on their wants and needs."[14] In his view, this is part of a broader trend toward integrated public governance (what others have labelled NPG, as discussed in Chapter 5), which has been gaining in influence since the mid-1990s. Central to both integrated service delivery and integrated public governance are coordination, cooperation, and collaboration among individuals, groups, and organizations. This involves the use of partnerships as well as "vigorous and creative community engagement" as a means of improving service to citizens.[15] The creation of Service Canada (see Box 8.1), and analogous organizations at the provincial level, such as Service New Brunswick and Service Ontario, would be an example of integrated service delivery.

BOX 8.1

Service Canada: A Model of Integrated Service Delivery

Announced in the context of the 2005 budget to improve service delivery to Canadians, Service Canada began operations in September of that year. It was designed to be a single service-delivery network whereby citizens could choose whichever channel (phone, Internet, mail, or in-person) they wanted to access government services. Service Canada is currently part of Employment and Social Development Canada and has more than 20,000 employees; it provides services to roughly 36 million Canadians through its integrated website (Canada .ca, and serviceCanada.gc.ca, which has 81.5 million visits per year), over the telephone (1-800-O-CANADA, which has 1.9 million calls per year) and in-person (8.1 million visits) through its 581 Service Canada points of service (this includes full- and part-time Service Canada Centres and 257 scheduled outreach sites). Despite the fact that Service Canada has contributed to improved service for Canadians, concern has also been expressed that "what started out as an exciting initiative seems to have reached a plateau in its evolution."

Sources: Employment and Social Development Canada, *2015–2016 Report on Plans and Priorities* (Ottawa: Her Majesty the Queen in Right of Canada, 2015); Zussman, "Alternative Service Delivery in Canada," in *The Handbook of Canadian Public Administration*, 2nd ed., ed. Christopher Dunn (Toronto: Oxford University Press, 2010), 264.

Classification of ASD

ASD forms and structures can be categorized in many different ways. One way is to use a functional classification system that accounts for the objectives of ASD, namely greater efficiency in service delivery, enhanced management flexibility, and increased reliance on collaborative arrangements.[16] A second approach is to classify mechanisms of ASD using the three dimensions of increased management flexibility (degree of control versus independence), the movement toward greater involvement of non-government sectors in the delivery of services (the public-private continuum), and the increasing commercialization of public services. Figure 8.1 depicts these dimensions along with many of the most common traditional and alternative methods of service delivery.

- Along one dimension, services are moving away from relying on the public sector and toward an acceptance that the private and non-profit sectors are capable of offering public services to citizens in partnership with government.
- A second dimension measures the extent to which government controls the delivery mechanism. The aim is to increase the autonomy of officials responsible for the provision of services to the citizenry and to employ new organizational structures that

Figure 8.1　Options for Service Delivery

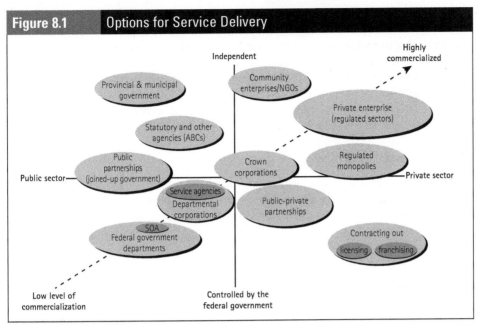

Source: Adapted from David Zussman, "Alternative Service Delivery in Canada" in Christoper Dunn, ed. *The Handbook of Canadian Public Administration*, 2nd ed. (Toronto: Oxford University Press, 2010), p. 253.

exploit new technologies or that involve a relaxation of central rules and controls, including a reduction of direct ministerial oversight.

- A third dimension illustrated in the figure concerns the level of commercialization. This refers to attempts on the part of public agencies to generate revenue and government to transfer responsibility for the delivery of a service to a non-governmental entity.

As can be seen, the combination of the three dimensions produces four quadrants in which we can plot various service delivery mechanisms. The traditional government department can be identified in the lower-left quadrant, signifying a public sector organization with low commercialization and a high degree of government control. The category of "statutory and other agencies" is found in the top-left quadrant, indicating that these public organizations typically have low commercialization but a high degree of autonomy from government. Crown corporations, the third traditional organizational form used by governments, straddle all four quadrants to indicate that these entities bridge the public and private sectors, have operational independence from government, and in many cases are engaged in commercial activities. In addition, the figure situates a number of innovative mechanisms for delivery of public services, including special operating agencies (SOAs), departmental corporations, and service agencies (all of which are firmly in the public sector and are controlled and operated, albeit to varying degrees, by the government), public–public partnerships (or "joined-up government," where multiple public sector entities come together to provide integrated services), and contracting out, which involves a shift to private sector entities for providing service under contract (thus, retaining a fairly high level of government control). Like Crown corporations, public–private partnerships (P3s) are placed at the intersection of the four quadrants because they require a sharing of decision-making authority with their private-sector partners. It is for that reason that P3s have been placed higher on the vertical axis than contracting out; in the case of contracting out, it may be a private sector organization providing the service but government nonetheless retains a relatively high degree of control by virtue of its ability to unilaterally set the terms of the contract.

　　Chapter 8 / Alternative Service Delivery (ASD)

A closer examination of the various new institutional mechanisms that have emerged with ASD will be explored below. These are not watertight categories so their classification according to each of the axes can be disputed. Moreover, while the creation of new organizations and an increasing reliance on private-sector and non-profit organizations has been a critical dimension of ASD, there have been other equally important ways that governments have restructured to improve service delivery to citizens. Many of these enhancements have been attributable to advancements in information and communication technologies (ICTs), which will also be considered.

Management Flexibility

In this grouping of ASD mechanisms, governments have been willing to cede some of the control that was associated with government departments, either by partnering with other public sector entities or, more typically, by establishing new government organizations that had more flexible arrangements for hiring and compensating personnel and freedom from direct ministerial oversight.

Special operating agencies

These are units within departments or agencies that are given a greater degree of flexibility than other units in order to carry out their duties more effectively. In other words, certain bureaucratic controls are eliminated in exchange for a commitment to improved performance. SOAs must still report to the deputy minister and adhere to the performance requirements set out in a framework agreement—negotiated between the minister, deputy minister, and Treasury Board—and an annual business plan; but they are clearly to be "treated specially" within the department.[17] Department units considered for this status are focused on the provision of services, not policy, and offer a service that is discrete within the department and can be easily measured for the purpose of gauging the level of performance.

At present, there are 13 SOAs at the federal level (they have also been extensively used by the provinces), most of which were created in the early 1990s. The novelty of this organizational form has clearly waned, with only three of the existing SOAs having been established since 2000: the Industrial Technologies Office (2007), the Canadian Coast Guard (2005), and Defence Research and Development Canada (2000). The Canadian Conservation Institute, located within Heritage Canada, and the Canadian Intellectual Property Office, which is part of Innovation, Science and Economic Development Canada, are two of the oldest remaining SOAs. The former promotes the preservation of Canada's cultural heritage and advances conservation, while the latter delivers intellectual property products and services in addition to promoting increased knowledge and awareness of intellectual property by Canadians.

Departmental corporations

In contrast with SOAs, **departmental corporations** are "specialized entities, established through legislation, that deliver services, or perform research or regulatory functions."[18] For the most part, these public sector organizations are funded through parliamentary appropriations, although some of them do generate revenue through user fees. They have greater decision-making autonomy than government departments, including more flexibility with respect to financial management and human resources. Accountability structures for departmental corporations are varied; in some instances, the president reports directly to his or her relevant minister (for example, that is the case for both the Canada Border Services Agency [see Box 8.2] and the Canada School of Public Service), whereas in other situations there is either a governing council or some other form of management board. The governance structure of both the Social Sciences

departmental corporation An organizational form, established through legislation, which is responsible for delivering service, conducting research, or performing regulatory functions. It has greater autonomy than a government department, but relies mostly on appropriations (although some do generate user fees too).

and Humanities Research Council and the Natural Sciences and Engineering Research Council of Canada, for example, includes a governing council that has responsibility for setting strategy and high level policy as well as advising the Minister of Innovation, Science and Economic Development Canada. There are currently a total of 14 departmental corporations, all of which are listed in Schedule II (Section 2) of the *Financial Administration Act*.

Profile of a Departmental Corporation

BOX
8.2

Title: Canada Border Services Agency (CBSA)

Appropriate Minister: Minister of Public Safety and Emergency Preparedness

Institutional Head: President of the CBSA

Enabling Legislation: *Canada Border Services Act; Department of Public Safety and Emergency Preparedness Act*

Year of Incorporation: 2003

Financial Information

- 2016–2017 Budget - $1,673,039,553
- 13,565 full-time equivalent employees

Profile

With a work force of roughly 13,500 employees, including over 7,200 uniformed officers, CBSA provides services at approximately 1,200 points in Canada and 39 international locations, including land border crossings, airports, ferry terminals, rail offices, and commercial vessel clearance facilities. Ultimately, the CBSA is responsible for providing "integrated border services that support national security priorities and facilitate the flow of people and goods [including plants and animals] across the border." The CBSA administers more than 90 acts, regulations, and international agreements, including many on behalf of other federal departments and agencies as well as the provincial and territorial governments. Some of its major responsibilities include determining the admissibility of people, goods, plants, and animals in and out of the county; detaining people who pose a threat to Canada; removing those who are inadmissible; protecting food safety and plant and animal health; enforcing trade remedies to protect Canadian business from imported goods that have been dumped or unfairly subsidized; and collecting taxes and duties on imported goods.

Sources: Canada Border Services Agency, *2016–2017 Report on Plans and Priorities* (Ottawa: Her Majesty the Queen in Right of Canada, 2016), 6; Canada Border Services Agency, "What We Do," www.cbsa-asfc.gc.ca/agency-agence/what-quoi-eng.html.

Service agencies

Service agencies are "a specialized form of departmental corporation established through tailored legislation to perform a highly operational function or service for which there is usually no private sector competition."[19] Service agencies, therefore, represent a more ambitious attempt than SOAs to provide for greater managerial flexibility. They have been given separate employer status, which means that they are not bound by central rules and controls related to labour relations and compensation matters. Moreover, those employed in the three service agencies are not included when calculating the number of federal public service employees. These management flexibilities are quite significant, providing these entities with "the greatest degree of autonomy possible as a separate employer short of becoming a Crown corporation."[20]

service agency A special type of departmental corporation that typically provides a service for which there is no private sector competition. As a separate employer, it has greater financial and human resources management flexibility.

In addition to the Canada Customs and Revenue Agency (CCRA), which was created in 1999 and became the Canada Revenue Agency in 2005, there are two other service agencies: Parks Canada and the Canadian Food Inspection Agency (CFIA), which was the first experiment with this ASD approach in 1997. The CFIA was formed by merging parts of four departments into one new agency; it now has responsibility for the delivery of all federal food inspection and quarantine services. With its status, the CFIA is able to engage on its own in a number of activities that are beyond the reach of traditional departments—such as establishing partnerships with the provinces. The agency also nicely captures the spirit of ASD in general in that it concentrates on the delivery of services and leaves policy matters to others.[21] The relationship between the minister and agency head varies, but in each case accountability is maintained through the use of corporate business plans and annual reports, similar to the various Crown agencies.

Public partnerships

Partnerships both within and between governments may also be seen as a way of achieving greater autonomy in order to offer better service. Within a government, separate departments may realize that entering into informal or formal arrangements with each other may contribute to more effective delivery of services. This is another way of expressing the importance of horizontal management and the need for departments to look across departments within a government. Partnerships with other orders of government may also provide for a more flexible and effective approach to the supply of public programs.

Private and Non-Profit Sector Involvement

A number of partnerships between government and either private sector or non-profit organizations can be identified in this second grouping of ASD innovations. These constitute some of the most common, visible, and controversial forms of ASD. The category also includes service provision on a contractual basis with non-governmental entities.

Public–private partnerships

public–private partnership (P3) Arrangement whereby the government partners with one or more private sector entities to deliver a service.

Since the mid-1990s, **public–private partnerships (P3s)** have become one of the most popular forms of ASD employed by governments at all levels, but especially by provincial governments. The Canadian Council for Public–Private Partnerships, a non-profit organization dedicated to the use of P3s as a means of promoting innovation in infrastructure development and service delivery, has a database of 240 Canadian P3 projects since 1991 across all levels of government.[22] This mechanism represents a major way private sector involvement (both private corporations and non-profit organizations), assumes some importance in the provision of public services. The scope of these P3 initiatives is broad, from water and wastewater to information technology to energy and education; but the largest concentration of P3s are in the areas of health (91 partnerships) and transportation (55 partnerships).[23] For the most part, these partnerships are embraced because of the promise of economic gain for all parties, or because governments believe they will result in doing "more or better with less." This is especially thought to be the case with respect to infrastructure projects, given the belief that the private sector has more incentives to provide cheaper, more efficient services than is typically the case under traditional government procurement.[24]

Partnerships may also facilitate the better use of technology or give historically disadvantaged persons a sense of empowerment through participation in decision-making processes affecting their position. This is a particularly attractive notion for voluntary sector organizations, which often make suitable partners for social programs, although for these types of relationships to work effectively they must be truly collaborative. In the face of an unequal distribution of power between organizations, conflicting goals, or a situation of financial dependency of one partner on the other, the arrangement may never become anything more than a pseudo partnership. This proved to be the case when Health Canada ostensibly partnered with various national non-government AIDS organizations from 2000–2004 to pursue the Canadian Strategy on HIV/AIDS.[25]

The partnerships themselves can take a number of different forms: contributory, consultative, operational, and **collaborative partnerships**.[26] This final type is the holy grail of partnerships; it involves both public and private parties bringing their resources together to meet common purposes arrived at together. In addition to sharing financial resources, such arrangements involve mutual dependence, shared risk taking, shared rewards, and shared decision making, all of which means that the public sector partner must be willing to give up some of its power and authority. An example of such a partnership is the agreement between the Ontario Lottery and Gaming Corporation and the Falls Management Company, which operates the Niagara Fallsview Casino and Resort.[27]

What follows are some prominent partnerships between government and the for-profit private sector:

- **BOOT (build-own-operate-transfer)**. This arrangement involves a private sector interest building and operating a service and then turning it over to government after a specified period of time. A good example of this is the Confederation Bridge between New Brunswick and Prince Edward Island. A private sector company built the bridge and was responsible for the full construction cost including any overruns. It was required to complete construction by June 1, 1997, or pay a substantial penalty. The company then operates the bridge for 35 years, collecting the tolls (at a regulated rate) and paying all operating expenses. At the end of the 35 years, ownership is transferred to the federal government. In this arrangement, the government transfers both the cost of the construction and the risk of cost overruns to the private sector. In return, the private sector organization can make a substantial profit if it operates the structure efficiently. Then the government can profit from the operation of the bridge after 35 years.

- **COGO (company-owned-government-operated)**. In this case, a private company builds something for the government, which the government would then operate. For example, Nova Scotia has adopted the P3 program. Under this program, a private company built a large number of school buildings. The company retains ownership of the buildings and the government pays an annual rent to use them. These kinds of arrangements save the government the large initial construction cost, although government ends up paying the same amount eventually (or perhaps more) in annual rents. However, this form of P3 is attractive to elected officials because the cost is deferred over several years, instead of requiring the government to pay a lump sum up front: "Thus, incumbent governments can provide current users and voters with current benefits, thereby garnering political credit, while deferring costs to future politicians, future voters or users."[28]

- **GOCO (government-owned-company-operated)**. This is the inverse of the previous case. In this instance, the government owns a facility and allows a private company to operate it. A good example of this is the situation with regard to several large airports. The government has retained ownership of the building but is allowing the local airport authority to operate it in exchange for a fee. The Greater Toronto Airport Authority, for example, manages and operates Toronto Pearson International Airport under a 60-year ground lease that began in December of 1999. This allows government to withdraw from a commercial-type operation for which it is not suited and transfer its operation to a private sector company, which has greater expertise in this area. It also provides for decentralized, local decision making, rather than having all decisions referred to Ottawa. As of 2016, department officials at

collaborative partnership
This is one of several different types of partnership (the others are contributory, consultative, and operational). It is considered to be the truest form of partnership in that it involves mutual dependency and the sharing of financial resources, decision making, risks, and rewards.

BOOT (build-own-operate-transfer) In this arrangement, the private partner builds and operates a particular service (e.g., bridge, sports facility, etc.) for a specified period of time, after which the facility reverts to the government.

COGO (company-owned-government-operated) In this arrangement, a company owns a facility that it has built for government. The government then pays a fee to the private company to rent the facility.

GOCO (government-owned-company-operated) In this arrangement, the government owns a particular facility and allows a private company to operate it so as to capitalize on the private company's expertise.

Transport Canada are considering the fate of Canadian airports; one option being seriously considered is selling off these assets to private investors and using the money to help pay for the Trudeau government's proposed infrastructure investments.[29] If that decision were to be taken, then this ASD mechanism will shift from a form of partnership to privatization.

Non-governmental organizations/Community enterprises

As government retrenchment was undertaken as part of NPM, there was an expectation that the voluntary or non-profit sector would step into the breach and fill the void that was created by governments abdicating their responsibility for the provision of certain services. This naturally led to concerns in the non-profit sector that it was ill-prepared to assume a larger role. Part of the government's response was to work with the non-profit sector to help build capacity; this led to the launch of the Voluntary Sector Initiative in 2000 and the adoption of the Voluntary Sector Accord in 2001, which had the intent of formalizing the relationship between government and the non-profit sector. As stated in the Accord, "[it] represents a public commitment to more open, transparent, consistent and collaborative ways of working together."[30]

This shift in the relationship between the federal government and the voluntary sector has been characterized as a move away from NPM towards the new governance model, but one that was fraught with challenges due to the accountability regime in place to govern the financial support given to voluntary organizations for project funding and service delivery.[31] Laforest has not been charitable in her assessment. She wrote, "Rather than moving toward a more complex appreciation of the role of civil groups in policy, as one would expect in this context of multilevel governance, the federal government agenda narrowed to the extent that civil society actors are now seen mainly as agents of service delivery."[32] It seems that the full potential of the voluntary sector, at least with respect to the collaboration that is central to post-NPM, remains unrealized.

Contracting-out

contracting-out In this situation the government enters into a contractual arrangement with a private sector company or non-profit organization to provide a publicly-funded service. Also known as **outsourcing**.

Contracting-out or outsourcing involves the government entering into an arrangement with a non-governmental body to provide a publicly-funded service. Instead of supplying the service itself, government elects to buy it from someone else. For some services, such as the building of roads, governments have long engaged in contracting-out practices. However, the practice of contracting-out for services has become more popular across a range of public sector organizations. This would include a government department contracting out its computer services function to a private company or, increasingly, a number of internal services like food service, laundry, and maintenance in prisons and hospitals. Another recent example was the City of Toronto contracting out garbage collection west of Yonge Street to the private company Green for Life.

Employee takeovers

employee takeover This is a type of contracting out arrangement whereby former government employees establish a private company to provide a service that they had previously provided while working for government.

Employee takeovers (ETs) are a specific federal initiative designed to achieve the purposes of contracting-out. It involves former employees of a government agency assuming responsibility for the private delivery of a service they offered while employed in government. ETs are done when governments no longer need to perform a function or if it is believed that the private sector can provide the work better and more cost effectively. For example, six employee takeover corporations emerged out of the National Capital Commission (NCC) in the early 1990s. The Liberal government wanted to reduce expenditures and was looking to privatization as the solution, so former NCC employees formed companies to provide the services they previously provided as public servants. Lafleur de la Capitale, created by former NCC employees Robert Lafleur and Jim Curran, is one such company.[33] Despite this apparent success story, ETs never assumed much prominence as an ASD measure.

Commercialization

This final category of ASD mechanisms refers to attempts on the part of public agencies to generate revenue.

Franchise and licensing arrangements

Given the need for governments to generate revenues, the use of franchising and licensing arrangements has become more common. The Canada Post Corporation is the most obvious example of the former. It has sold franchises to a number of private sector entities to establish postal outlets in their stores. As for a licensing agreement, in the mid-1990s, the RCMP contracted the Walt Disney Company (Canada) to manage and administer the licensing of merchandise using the RCMP logo.

Privatization

The most common form of this type of ASD is the selling of a government entity to profit-oriented concerns. The privatization of some high-profile Crown corporations—Air Canada, CN, and Petro-Canada—falls into this category. But it can also involve non-profit entities as well, an example of which is NavCanada.[34] This non-profit corporation was established when the federal government did not want to continue to provide this civil air navigation service. Although the airlines were not happy with how the government provided the service, they were also worried about turning this service over to a profit-making private monopoly. The compromise reached was a non-profit corporation with a 15-member board of directors consisting of the CEO and 14 individuals selected by those groups with a vested interest: the airlines, employee unions, the Canadian Business Aviation Association, and the federal government. The company receives no government funding; its revenues are generated largely by charging airline companies and other aircraft operators for air traffic control, flight information, and other air navigation services. NavCanada is bound by legislation to set its service charges at a rate that does not exceed the cost of providing civil air navigation services. As discussed more fully in the previous chapter, pressure to privatize state-owned enterprises remains, but there are fewer obvious candidates.

Other Forms of Alternative Service Delivery

Thus far, the examples of ASD that we have been discussing involve either the creation of new types of public sector organizations that have varying degrees of flexibility and autonomy from central rules and control, or a move towards shifting the provision of public services to private sector and non-profit sector organizations. However, some of the most successful innovations that governments have adopted to provide citizen-centred service delivery have not required new institutional design. One example would be the integrated blue pages in the telephone directory using keyword indexes, which simplified the process for finding government services (since citizens often did not know which level of government and/or specific department was responsible for providing particular services). However, it has been both the better use of existing technology and advancements in ICTs that have had a transformational impact on public sector service delivery.

A number of examples where this has been the case can be identified. Many governments have introduced single-window call centres, such as 1-800-O-CANADA at the federal level or Inquiry BC (provincially). Between 1996 and 2012, the Ontario government provided electronic kiosks in more accessible and convenient locations, such as shopping malls, enabling citizens to complete a variety of transactions from updating change of address information to paying fines to renewing licence plate stickers. Despite being extremely popular with citizens they were removed after a security breach raised concerns about the safety of users' personal information. Nova Scotia currently uses electronic kiosks to provide the Bundled Birth Service; this allows parents to apply for a social insurance number, birth certificate, health card, and Canada Child Benefit for their newborn right in the hospital.

Furthermore, website technology facilitates the presentation of information on government services by function rather than by department, a development that pleases citizens eager to acquire services as quickly and easily as possible. Seniors Canada On-Line, for instance, provides information on elderly services available from a variety of federal departments and many provincial governments.[35] The ambition is to employ technology to move right into the homes of citizens. One instance of this already at work is the ability of taxpayers to "e-file" their tax returns from the comfort of their homes.

Government 2.0 Efforts to make government more open, transparent, and engaging by providing open data to citizens and groups and harnessing the power of collaborative technologies.

A number of scholars have written about the apparent transition to **Government 2.0**, or Gov 2.0 as it is also known, whereby technology is harnessed to build government that is by and for the people. It is about making government more open and transparent. In this conception, citizens are no longer seen as passive consumers of government services, but rather are active participants in the policy-making process, who can create value by using government information and their connectedness to build innovative services that unite government to citizens. As an example, citizens might take government crime statistics and use that information to create an application for the Internet or mobile devices. Gov 2.0 is also about promoting real-time public two-way communication between governments and their citizens through text, the web, and social media; governments must engage in conversations with citizens rather than simply having unidirectional interactions whereby governments "talk to" citizens.[36] The move towards open government discussed in Chapter 5 is certainly a move in this direction.

A second important trend with respect to ASD has been the willingness of governments to implement user fees. User fees involve government requiring citizens to pay directly for services that may have been typically available free of charge. These direct payments can be as small as charging for copies of government documents or as large or important as entertaining the idea of asking patients to accept charges at the point of receiving health care. User fees serve the purpose of raising revenue to offset the increasing cost of public services. They also seek to change the behaviour of users or at least make them reconsider their behaviour. For instance, the increasingly common practice of municipalities charging for garbage collection helps the revenue side of the budget and also makes residents more conscious of the cost of garbage and the need to think more seriously about waste management.

Problems with ASD

There is no question but that opening up the issue of service delivery rather than always assuming there is a "one best way" is beneficial. Many of the benefits that are typically identified with ASD were highlighted earlier in the chapter when we examined the NPM roots of this reform initiative. But certain caveats must be raised, because problems may arise with the adoption of ASD.

Steering and Rowing

At the heart of ASD is the belief that a separation of policy and operations results in better performance. Allow the minister to do the steering and develop innovative ways of carrying out the rowing function. But making changes in the service delivery function may produce coordination problems as the public service becomes more complex and increasingly fragmented. As Zussman noted, "The proliferation of semi-autonomous public, private and hybrid entities has become almost dizzying in scale."[37] It may be simply too difficult to move the ship of state in a desired direction with the widespread adoption of ASD. Policy might also suffer, because the separation of policy and service delivery makes it hard for operations people to provide feedback on the workability of policies. More unsettling, the greater use of ASD may produce "policy lock-in," an outcome that emerges when new agencies generate new supporters unwilling to countenance any changes in the operation of ASD. Good and Carin explain:

> Are autonomous agencies undermining policy objectives by creating constituencies that will compel governments to maintain existing policies? Agencies are created but rarely closed or merged. Policy can become what agencies do, not what government proposes.[38]

The separation of steering and rowing duties is meant to make government leaders more able to develop plans and strategies for government. But, ironically, it might do the exact opposite, and the consequence is a weakening of democratic practice. Appointed officials, not elected ones, begin to run government.

Where Is the Public Interest?

Increasing responsiveness to users and more emphasis on the bottom line—two aspects of ASD—sound like two very positive values, but is it possible to be too responsive to users or too profit-driven so that the broader public interest is ignored? The emphasis on the bottom line and being user-friendly is important, but governments are elected to further the public interest. As Stefanick notes with reference to the provision of health care, the system "does not follow the logic of profit-seeking." Contracting out health care service, for example, where the concern of the private service provider will be on profit maximization, may conflict with the government's desire for accessible and affordable medical services.[39]

Loss of Accountability

A major intent of ASD is to offer services at arm's length from government so that they can be delivered in a more flexible manner with greater responsiveness to users. The danger is that accountability linkages may be weakened at the same time. In some cases, other types of accountability mechanisms will supplant the traditional governmental accountability linkages. In the case of NavCanada, the users now have direct representation on the board of directors. But in other instances, the accountability challenge is not so easily surmounted. Let us assume a federal ASD agency has authority to enter into partnerships with either another order of government or an entity in the private sector. Also assume that something goes wrong. Who is accountable? Is it the head of the ASD agency, his or her counterpart at the provincial level, the federal minister formally responsible for the agency, or perhaps the provincial minister to whom the provincial official reports? Some have proposed alternative forms of accountability mentioned earlier in the text to overcome the threats to traditional forms of accountability associated with these types of partnership arrangements, but they too have their limitations. The lesson here is that governments need to choose very carefully the types of services that are given this arm's-length treatment. In some cases, other mechanisms work very well in ensuring accountability, but not always.

Labour Relations

Many forms of ASD involve moving government employees into a different regime within government or even into a private sector organization. On the positive side, this will frequently loosen the constraints of government human resources management systems and allow employees greater flexibility in working conditions, including the opportunity to earn merit pay. However, many employees fear that they will lose the protection that comes with the government human resources management regime. The right to provide merit pay for a job well done is also the right to withhold merit pay for possibly venal reasons. Some employees do not like moving out of the protective situation of the government system. Some make even stronger claims that ASD initiatives are aimed at breaking strong unions or preventing the establishment of a union. Both the government spinning off the service and the organization taking over the service must consider all these issues.

ASD is also changing the nature of the workforce. Long-serving, full-time employees are being replaced by limited-term contract employees. This is beneficial to governments to the extent that it increases their flexibility and reduces labour costs. However, this temporary workforce will have very little loyalty to their employer. It is also very difficult to develop an organizational culture or an organizational memory with so many employees passing through the revolving door.

Savings and Performance

The apparent cost savings and other benefits associated with ASD arrangements involving P3s can go unrealized. Using these arrangements, the government hopes to transfer part of the financial risk to a private partner, but this often fails to happen and the public partner ends up assuming most of the risk. Another expectation is often dashed, namely that the inclusion of the private sector will result in lower costs and greater efficiencies because of economies of scale, greater experience, and better innovation skills. One reason for the unmet expectations is that the price of bargaining, monitoring, and possibly renegotiating partnerships is often high, especially when some of the participants engage in various forms of "opportunism" (threats of bankruptcy).[40] Governments sometimes also believe—mistakenly—that the use of private partners will make hard policy choices more palatable to the public. Then there is the occasional contract failure—a euphemism for a situation in which the arrangement collapses for one reason or another and government is left with the task of cleaning up the mess. That was the case when the partnership between the City of Guelph and Nustadia Developments Inc. (through its subsidiary, Guelph Centre Partners) to build the Guelph Sports and Entertainment Centre (what is now known as the Sleeman Centre) collapsed in 2005 leaving taxpayers with millions of dollars of unanticipated debt. At first, therefore, P3s as a form of ASD appear to offer government substantial benefits, but what limited evidence there is to evaluate them more objectively is mixed: "PPPs are not always 'problem, problem, problem' nor are they the nirvana that many proponents would have one to believe."[41] (See also What To Do? ASD and the Walkerton Tragedy.)

Digital Divide

As discussed in this chapter, public sector services are being delivered by new channels, such as one-stop service centres and the Internet, in addition to the traditional channels of mail, telephone, and office visits to particular government departments. Naturally, governments are particularly interested in promoting the self-help channels—Internet and telephone interactive voice

WHAT TO DO?

In the spring of 2000, the water supply of Walkerton, a town in southwestern Ontario, became contaminated. Seven residents lost their lives, and many more got very sick. Some claim that this was a direct consequence of the provincial government introducing an ASD-like measure. The government had taken away responsibility for water testing from the provincial environment department and given it to private laboratories, and the government only required the labs to report their results to municipal authorities and not to departmental officials. In the case of Walkerton, the labs determined the water was contaminated and sent the results to the Walkerton Public Utilities Commission, but the commission did not act on these results immediately. An inquiry set up to examine the Walkerton crisis observed that the slow response to the results probably caused many more to become sick than would have been the case with a more rigorous reporting system. Was the government misguided in attempting to save money by resorting to ASD— in this case relying on private laboratories for water testing? Or was this tragedy more an unfortunate consequence of poorly conceived reporting protocols combined with the incompetence and neglect of local public utilities officials? How should the provincial government ensure the safety of our water supply?

Source: Judith I. McKenzie, "Walkerton: Requiem for the New Public Management in Ontario?" *International Journal of Environment and Pollution* 21(4) (2004): 309–324.

response—because they are less costly options. However, they must be aware of the existence of a **digital divide** that would result in inequitable access to services by certain segments of the citizenry. The broader literature on this subject suggests that certain groups have less access to the Internet: 1) females, 2) minority groups, 3) those with disabilities, and 4) individuals with lower income.[42] More specifically, in the Canadian context there is some evidence of a digital divide among females and older citizens who are more likely to use the phone to contact the government for information or a service.[43]

With the move towards open government and open data, there have been renewed concerns about this problem. Open government and open data are designed to foster self-empowerment and social participation, but they may produce a "data divide."[44] Much like the problem associated with differential access to online service delivery, noted above, certain segments of the population will undoubtedly find it challenging to access government information that is now being made more readily available to citizens. Furthermore, how many citizens truly want to be anything other than passive recipients of government services? There will be many citizens who have neither the interest nor the ability to be actively engaged in policy development and service delivery, as is the expectation inherent in new public governance. Governments must keep that in mind when attempting to better align strategies for service development and in promoting the concept of open, participatory government.

> **digital divide** This is a situation of inequality in service delivery that arises as a result of the fact that not all citizens have equal access to technology (e.g., the Internet and social media accessed through smart phones).

Limits of Government 2.0

While improvements to public service delivery through Gov 2.0 may one day be profound, the reality is that we have only begun to harness its potential. As noted in a recent book on public service delivery in Canada, we "seem to be having trouble moving to the next level, integrating or aligning more complex interactive services … [We are] 'missing the boat' on key issues such as citizen engagement, performance measurement, cultural change, governance reform and technological adaptation."[45] Moreover, there is little evidence that the federal government is having the kinds of two-way conversations on social media envisioned with Gov 2.0. Writing in 2013, Roy stated:

> the overwhelming usage of social media channels such as Facebook and Twitter is at present broadcast oriented with little in the way of substantive exchange. Indeed, it is telling in this regard that the official Government of Canada website devoted to public consultation exercises is completely devoid of any social media tools and channels.[46]

The federal government is making inroads in that regard, with some of the consultations now including social media tools on them, but most of them continue to be largely informational in nature.

Points to Know

- As part of NPM in the 1990s, governments began to look beyond the three traditional service delivery mechanisms to what has been called ASD.

- There is no longer "one best way" (if there ever was) to deliver government services.

- ASD has been used both in an attempt to improve service delivery to citizens and to save governments money.

- Various ASD mechanisms have continued to be used even as there has seemingly been a transition from NPM to governance, but the emphasis is supposed to be on

- co-construction of public policy and co-production of service delivery rather than simply cost and efficiency concerns.

- It is possible to classify new organizational forms under ASD based on the extent to which these entities have autonomy from government, are engaged in commercial activities, and shift towards the private sector. P3s are some of the more common and popular forms of ASD.

- ASD is not just about creating new organizational forms or entering into partnerships with private and non-profit

Chapter 8 / Alternative Service Delivery (ASD)

sector entities; advances in ICTs have had a profound impact on the way in which services are delivered to citizens.

- Despite the many benefits of ASD, they have not been without their problems, including evidence of a digital divide.

Review Questions

1. Identify the reasons why governments looked beyond government departments and Crown agencies for delivering services to citizens.

2. List some of the most common types of ASD. Are some of these ASD mechanisms more attractive to government than others?

3. How has the nature of ASD changed with the shift from NPM to NPG?

4. What are some of the problems associated with ASD mechanisms?

Notes

1. The government itself has identified Crown corporations as an example of ASD, presumably because a Crown corporation is different from the departmental form. For example, Canada Post was transformed from a government department to a Crown corporation and can be understood in that context as an alternative to the most basic form of service delivery. However, since the government has been using Crown corporations for nearly a century, we have classified them as a traditional method of service delivery (along with departments and other Crown agencies). See, for example, Treasury Board of Canada Secretariat, *People in Transition—Knowing Your Options: Alternative Service Delivery* (Ottawa: Treasury Board of Canada Secretariat, 1996), accessed June 30, 2016, http://www.collectionscanada.gc.ca/eppp-archive/100/201/301/tbs-sct/tb_manual-ef/Pubs_pol/hrpubs/TB_858/ASD_e.html.

2. David Zussman, "Alternative Service Delivery in Canada" in *The Handbook of Canadian Public Administration*, 2nd ed., ed. Christopher Dunn (Toronto: Oxford University Press, 2010), 250.

3. Treasury Board of Canada Secretariat, "Policy on Alternative Service Delivery," April 1, 2002, accessed June 30, 2016, http://www.tbs-sct.gc.ca/pubs_pol/opepubs/TB_B4/asd-dmps01eng.asp#Toc853882. This policy was replaced in April 2007 by the Policy on Reporting of Federal Institutions and Corporate Interests to Treasury Board Secretariat.

4. Robin Ford and David Zussman, "Alternative Service Delivery: Transcending Boundaries," in *Alternative Service Delivery: Sharing Governance in Canada*, eds. Robin Ford and David Zussman (Toronto: KPMG Centre for Government Foundation and Institute of Public Administration of Canada, 1997), 6.

5. See Kenneth Kernaghan, Brian Marson, and Sandford Borins, *The New Public Organization* (Toronto: Institute of Public Administration of Canada, 2000), ch.5.

6. Ford and Zussman, "Alternative Service Delivery: Transcending Boundaries," 7.

7. See, for example, Kenneth Kernaghan, "Serving Seniors: Innovation and Public Sector Service Delivery," *The Innovation Journal: The Public Sector Innovation Journal* 20(2) (2015): 1–18; Christopher Reddick and Michael Turner, "Channel Choice and Public Service Delivery in Canada: Comparing E-Government to Traditional Service Delivery," *Government Information Quarterly* 29(1) (January 2012): 1–11.

8. David Osborne and Ted Gaebler, *Reinventing Government: How the Entrepreneurial Spirit Is Transforming the Public Sector* (Reading, MA: Addison-Wesley, 1992), ch.1.

9. However, it is important to keep in mind that, unlike customers, citizens also have a number of responsibilities and obligations in relation to the state. For a critique of the shift from "citizen" to "customer" or "client," see Joel Aberbach and Tom Christensen, "Citizens and Consumers: A NPM Dilemma," *Public Management Review* 7(2) (June 2005): 225–246. In Canada, the language changed from "client-service culture" as part of the PS 2000 reform initiative and the 1995 Framework for Alternative Program Delivery to "citizen-centred services" in the 2002 Policy on Alternative Service Delivery. This is evidence of the more selective acceptance and endorsement of NPM in the Canadian context.

10. Josh Hjartarson, Alexandra Schwenger, and Liam McGuinty, *Unlocking the Public Service Economy in Ontario: A New Approach to Public-Private Partnership in Services* (Toronto: Ontario Chamber of Commerce, 2014), 10–13.

11. Bryan Evans and Halina Sapeha, "Are Non-Government Policy Actors Being Heard? Assessing the New Public Governance in Three Canadian Provinces," *Canadian Public Administration* 58(2) (June 2015): 250–251. Evans and Sapeha conclude that provincial NGO actors (in Ontario, BC, and Saskatchewan) are involved at various stages of the policy-making process, but that role "is largely focused on implementation and service delivery rather than participation in strategically important design work."

12. Patrick Fafard, François Rocher, and Catherine Coté, "Clients, Citizens and Federalism: A Critical Appraisal of Integrated Service Delivery in Canada," *Canadian Public Administration* 52(4) (December 2009): 565.

13. Ralph Heintzman and Brian Marson, "People, Service and Trust: Is There a Public Sector Service Value Chain?" *International Review of Administrative Sciences* 71(4) (December 2005): 570.

14. Kenneth Kernaghan, "Putting Citizens First: Service Delivery and Integrated Public Governance" in The Evolving Physiology of Government: Canadian Public Administration in Transition, eds. O.P. Dwivedi, Tim A. Mau, and Byron Sheldrick (Ottawa: University of Ottawa Press, 2009): 252.

15. Kenneth Kernaghan, "Moving Towards Integrated Public Governance: Improving Service Delivery Through Community Engagement," *International Review of Administrative Sciences* 75(2) (2009): 240.

16. Zussman, "Alternative Service Delivery in Canada," 253.

17. Treasury Board Secretariat, "Becoming a Special Operating Agency," 1, accessed July 5, 2016, https://www.tbs-sct.gc.ca/pubs_pol/opepubs/TB_B4/bsoa-doss01-eng.asp.

18. Treasury Board of Canada Secretariat, "Overview of Institutional Forms and Definitions," accessed July 5, 2016, http://www.tbs-sct.gc.ca/hgw-cgf/finances/rgs-erdg/cc-se/institution/formsformulaires-eng.asp.

19. Ibid.

20. David Brown, "The Canada Revenue Agency as Separate Employer: Anomaly or Model for the Future?" *Canadian Public Administration* 52(4) (December 2009): 578.

21. Kernaghan, Marson and Borins, *The New Public Organization*, 104.

22. Canadian Council for Public–Private Partnerships, "Canadian PPP Project Database," accessed July 6, 2016, www.projects.pppcouncil.ca/ccppp/src/public/search-project.

23. Ibid.

24. Anthony Boardman, Matti Siemiatycki, and Aidan Vining, "The Theory and Evidence Concerning Public-Private Partnerships in Canada and Elsewhere," *University of Calgary School of Public Policy SPP Research Papers* 9(12) (March 2016), 1–28; Aidan Vining and Anthony Boardman, "Public–Private Partnerships in Canada: Theory and Evidence" *Canadian Public Administration* 51(1) (March 2008): 9–44.

25. Peter Tsasis, "The Politics of Governance: Government–Voluntary Sector Relationships," *Canadian Public Administration* 51(2) (June 2008): 265–290.

26. Kernaghan, Marson, and Borins, *The New Public Organization*, 186–195.

27. It is, however, a collaborative partnership in disguise, since neither the OLGC nor FMC refer to their agreement as such. See Jennifer Berardi, "The Niagara Casinos Partnership: Game of Chance?" in *Professionalism and Public Service: Essays in Honour of Kenneth Kernaghan*, eds. David Siegel and Ken Rasmussen (Toronto: University of Toronto Press, 2008), 207–235.

28. Boardman, Siemiatycki ,and Vining, "The Theory and Evidence," 12.

29. Bruce Campion-Smith, "Major Canadian Airports Could Be Sold Off," *The Toronto Star*, July 4, 2016, A5.

30. Canada. *Voluntary Sector Task Force, An Accord Between the Government of Canada and the Voluntary Sector* (Ottawa: Privy Council Office, 2001), 7.

31. Susan Phillips and Karine Levasseur, "The Snakes and Ladders of Accountability: Contradictions Between Contracting and Collaboration for Canada's Voluntary Sector," *Canadian Public Administration* 47(4) (Winter 2004): 451–474.

32. Rachel Laforest, "Shifting Scales of Governance and Civil Society Participation in Canada and the European Union," *Canadian Public Administration* 56(2) (June 2013): 245–246.

33. Mike Levin, "Company Booms in Wake of Privatization" *Business Edge News Magazine* (May 2005), http://www.businessedge.ca/archives/article.cfm/company-blooms-in-wake-of-privatization-9579. See also Leah Travis, "National Capital Commission Employee Takeover Corporations," in Deputy Minister Task Force on Service Delivery, *Toward Citizen-Centred Service Delivery: Case Studies* (Ottawa: Canadian Centre for Management Development, 1996), 2: 47–62.

34. NavCanada, "Governance." Available online at www.navcanada.ca/EN/about-us/Pages/governance.aspx

35. Kenneth Kernaghan, "Moving Towards the Virtual State: Integrating Services and Service Channels for Citizen-Centred Delivery," *International Review of Administrative Sciences* 71(1) (March 2005), 124–125. The web portal is available at www.seniors.gc.ca.

36. Zachary Tumin and Archong Fung, *From Government 2.0 to Society 2.0: Pathways to Engagement, Collaboration and Transformation* (Cambridge: Harvard Kennedy School of Government, 2010).

37. Zussman, "Alternative Service Delivery in Canada," 262.

38. David A. Good and Barry Carin, draft of "Alternative Service Delivery," August 2003. Prepared by the Canadian Team as part of the CEPRA project on "Sector and Regional Specifics of Reformation of Budgetary Institutions," 23–24.

39. Lorna Stefanick, "Government Outsourcing of Service Provision: Be Careful What You Wish For," in *Approaching Public Administration: Core Debates and Emerging Issues*, eds. Roberto Leone and Frank Ohemeng, (Toronto: Emond Montgomery Publications, 2011), 246.

40. In a review of 74 infrastructure projects either completed or underway in Ontario that utilized Alternative Financing and Procurement, a provincial variant of the P3 model, the auditor general concluded that various tangible costs were $8 billion higher under those arrangements than had the projects been contracted out and managed by the public sector. See Auditor General of Ontario, *Annual Report, 2014* (Toronto: Queen's Printer for Ontario, 2014), ch.3, accessed July 6, 2016, www.auditor.on.ca/en/content/annualreports/arreports/en14/2014AR_en_web.pdf44.

41. Boardman, Siemiatycki, and Vining, "The Theory and Evidence," 17.

42. Reddick and Turner, "Channel Choice and Public Service Delivery in Canada," 4.

43. Ibid., 9.

44. Jeffrey Roy, "Gov. 2.0, Mobility and Inclusion: A Critical Examination of Social Assistance Reform in Ontario, Canada" in *Information and Communication Technologies in Public Administration: Innovations from Developed Countries*, eds. Christopher Reddick and Leonidas Anthopoulos (Boca Raton: CRC Press, 2015), 240.

45. Patrice Dutil, Cosmo Howard, John Langford, and Jeffrey Roy, *The Service State: Reality, Rhetoric and Promise* (Ottawa: University of Ottawa, 2010), 10.

46. Jeffrey Roy, *From Machinery to Mobility: Government and Democracy in a Participative Age* (New York: Springer-Verlag, 2013), 9–10.

The Executive and the Bureaucracy

9

Learning Objectives

Reading this chapter allows you to do the following:

- Understand the principles that shape interactions among elected and appointed officials in the executive branch
- Identify the major executive players and structures

- Outline and evaluate the operation of the cabinet decision-making process
- Analyze claims about the increasing power of the prime minister and the rise of court government

Part Three of the text examined the various administrative bodies at the federal level. Departments, Crown corporations, independent regulatory agencies, and alternative service delivery agencies constitute the administrative or structural dimension of public administration in Canada. The intent in Part Four is to investigate the interactions and relations of appointed officials among themselves and with other actors inside and outside of government. This aim serves to reveal the dynamic quality of public administration, to see that the study of public bureaucracy goes beyond the examination of organizational forms. The chapters in Part Four also show that the lives of public servants can be exciting and tension-filled as they work with powerful public figures and institutions.

There is little disagreement over where the most important interactions of public servants take place. It is in the executive branch. The other two branches of government, the legislature and the courts, are not to be ignored. However, the most significant action occurs elsewhere, in the executive sphere. The significance of the executive lies in its power and responsibilities. Among other duties, it sets the direction for government, formulates policy initiatives, makes the key decisions, and implements the programs and services that Canadians expect. The executive sphere of government includes the Queen's representatives, the governor general at the federal level and his or her provincial counterparts. The key elements in this branch, though, are the political and permanent executives. The political executive refers to the prime minister, cabinet, and individual ministers; the permanent executive refers to public servants, with the most powerful of these being deputy ministers. Each of these two parts of the executive has relations limited to itself; however, the most significant interactions are those which involve both elected and appointed officials working through cabinet, and the most powerful player of them all—the prime minister. These interactions are the concern of this chapter.

In the following pages, the political and permanent executives are fleshed out in some detail to make clearer the interactions. The interactions themselves are also considered, with the greatest attention being given to the interaction that brings all the major players together—the cabinet approval process. The chapter also suggests that a major relationship may be assuming even greater prominence.

Key Interaction Principles

There are principles that shape the dealings involving political executives and public servants. Three of these principles are ministerial responsibility, hierarchy, and influence. The first two principles can also be seen as part of the set of public service values discussed in Chapter 2. The third principle relates to another factor that affects the behaviour of appointed officials, power. Public servants incorporate values, but they also exercise **power**.

power The capacity to secure the dominance of one's goals or interests. There are two forms of power—control and influence.

Ministerial Responsibility

Ministerial responsibility is a general principle, which covers two more specific principles. Collective ministerial responsibility means that ministers as a group—the cabinet— are responsible for the policies and management of the government as a whole. Cabinet must resign if it loses the confidence of the legislature. A loss of confidence is defined as losing the support of the majority of the members of the House of Commons. Individual ministers must publicly support the decisions of cabinet, acting as a collectivity to maintain at least the appearance of solidarity. More specifically, ministers are required to work out a consensus on the content of public policies and on the allocation of resources for developing and implementing these policies. Ministers who are unable to support a cabinet decision are expected to resign from cabinet.

The principle of individual ministerial responsibility, which will be discussed more fully in Chapter 11, refers to the responsibility of the minister, as the ultimate head of a department, to answer to the legislature and, through the legislature, to the public, both for his or her personal acts and for the acts of departmental subordinates.

Coordination and Hierarchy

The principles of collective and individual ministerial responsibility have an important effect on the organizational design of the executive sphere of government. Organization charts of the government typically depict this sphere as a hierarchical arrangement of offices. Aside from the governor general, the prime minister and the cabinet stand at the pinnacle of the hierarchy, and from them the lines of authority flow down to departments headed by cabinet ministers and to Crown or non-departmental agencies reporting to cabinet ministers. Those central agencies that have departmental form and that report to a ministry (e.g., Department of Finance, Treasury Board Secretariat) are normally portrayed as equal in status to the regular operating departments strung horizontally across the chart. Other central agencies (e.g., the Prime Minister's Office and the Privy Council Office) are shown in staff (advisory) relationship to the prime minister and cabinet.

However, the organization chart discloses little about the complex pattern of power relations in the executive realm, especially insofar as these relations involve the exercise of influence rather than authoritative control. It exposes only the bare bones of political–bureaucratic interaction. The organizational skeleton reveals simply the formal lines of authority through which control moves down the governmental pyramid and accountability moves up; the "informal" organization is hidden from view. Similarly, an organization chart of a single department or agency that purports to describe the reality of administrative life as simply a hierarchy of superior–subordinate relationships or as a chain of command is misleading.

The deficiencies or "pathologies" of bureaucracy in general, and of its hierarchical feature in particular, are well-known. Hierarchy does, though, serve important purposes. One of these is particularly relevant to a discussion of ministerial responsibility:

Part Four / The Bureaucracy in the Political Process

hierarchy provides for unity of command and of direction both at the top of government (by the prime minister and cabinet) and at the top of government departments (by ministers). In other words, it promotes accountability. Hierarchy also facilitates coordination. Beginning with the cabinet as the central coordination mechanism of government, hierarchy facilitates the provision of various means of working together to pursue policy and administrative initiatives. This chapter shows that ministers, in fulfilling both their collective responsibility for coordinating government as a whole and their individual responsibility for coordinating their departments, are obliged to rely heavily on senior public servants in central agencies and departments (and the next chapter examines the increasing emphasis in recent years on horizontal relations between government departments).

Influence

Aside from hierarchical control, power in the executive is exercised in the form of influence, and influence in turn stands for the attempts of players in government to secure their interests using various devices of persuasion. Hierarchy remains a force, not in determining the act of decision making but rather as a resource officials can use in bargaining and tussling with others. Fundamentally, the principle of influence means that formal authority, the lines that attach subordinates to their superiors, can on occasion be limited. Even the prime minister, who resides at the very top, may find that others in the executive sphere, those lower in the hierarchy, have through resourceful use of their assets secured a decision contrary to the full wishes of the first minister. These assets can include privileged information, powerful alliances with others either inside or outside government, and personal skills in bargaining and persuasion (see What to Do?).

Influence is thus to be considered in understanding relations with the executive–bureaucratic sphere. It is a useful corrective to those who think interactions in government are basically programmed responses generated by allocations of authority and power; in other words, it disabuses notions of highly predictive behaviour stipulated by organizational charts. At the same time, a sphere of government that allows for influence does not produce a setting of people ruthlessly pursuing their preferences and sometimes succeeding; it also not a super-large depiction of "office politics" that reduces executive decision making to soap-operatic dimensions. What the principle of influence does is introduce a dose of reality into relations that remain to be shaped by hierarchy, authority, and other public service values.

WHAT TO DO?

Assume you are a senior departmental official and one of your subordinates is especially good at getting things done. But this subordinate succeeds in part because she goes around her immediate superiors and has the habit of keeping hidden what she is doing. This subordinate's action has created some turmoil in the department, but her achievements have caught the attention of the minister and his staff. Do you reward or reprimand?

The Prime Minister and Cabinet

The prime minister is the head of the party that controls the House of Commons, and cabinet is a decision-making body whose members include the prime minister and his or her ministers. The latter are typically elected members of the ruling party selected by the prime minister to head government agencies. In the Canadian political system, the prime minister and colleagues in the cabinet possess the foremost power and responsibility for making and implementing public policy. In very large part, they determine the political and policy parameters within which the many participants in the political system interact.

In the executive realm of government, the cabinet, acting in part through committees, provides the general framework of policies for which public servants must devise programs and for which resources must be allocated to the many departments and agencies. Given the individual and collective responsibility of ministers for the performance of the public service, they must strive to control and influence bureaucratic behaviour. They evaluate and coordinate policy and program proposals emanating from departments and bring partisan considerations to bear upon these proposals. Sometimes they initiate policy proposals of their own. In their capacity as cabinet members, federal ministers receive a great deal of political, policy, and administrative support, primarily from the central agencies. This central agency support is generally channelled to ministers in their capacity as members of cabinet and cabinet committees. In their capacity as political heads of government departments, ministers receive the assistance primarily from their deputy ministers and, to a lesser extent, from the political staff in their ministerial offices.

The federal cabinet is located at the centre of a complicated network of political–bureaucratic relations, and the prime minister is the central figure in this network. It is generally acknowledged that the prime minister is much more than "first among equals" in relation to other cabinet members. In fact, it is suggested that the prime minister's power has aggrandized to the point where Canada has "prime ministerial government" rather than cabinet government.[1] Under this alleged governing system, the prime minister makes the final decisions on the most important matters with the assistance of only a few trusted advisors (who include government insiders and outsiders, such as the prime minister's chief of staff, the finance minister, a lobbyist or two, and media experts). The role of cabinet is reduced to dealing with routine matters and acting as a "kind of focus group for the prime minister" when the latter needs to acquire a better understanding of an issue.[2] The notion of the political executive acting collectively disappears and is replaced by one that depicts a high concentration of influence in the hands of one individual. With his impressive set of "levers of power," the prime minister has an "unassailable advantage" over other members of cabinet.[3]

For many, the concentration of power is more than a suggestion. "[N]o one debates whether or not we govern from the centre anymore. It is now a fact," says a senior federal deputy minister.[4] Certainly, the prime minister is a dominant figure by virtue of having responsibility for leading the governing political party, chairing the cabinet, acting as chief spokesperson for the government, and appointing and removing ministers and senior public officials. The first minister can also employ various devices to muzzle (or punish) those in government who dare to take a separate path or pursue a fresh idea of their own. Perhaps the most notorious device is the "mandate letter" ministers receive from the prime minister, detailing the priorities of government in their respective departments and how they are to be addressed (see Box 9.1). But notwithstanding these formidable sources of power, there are constraints on the ability of the prime minister (and provincial premiers) to exercise this power fully. The prime minister's time is so precious

BOX 9.1

Mandate Letters

The Ontario government of Kathleen Wynne, in 2014, released its mandate letters to ministers, so we now know how at least one government writes it mandate letters. The letters are four to five pages long, with the first page being the same for all ministers. This first page welcomes the minister to cabinet and outlines the overall thrust of the government and its key government-wide priorities. The next two or three pages detail the priorities of the department, with each priority supported by a series of bullets. The last part of the letter, which is again the same for all ministers, says that the list of priorities is not necessarily exhaustive and encourages the minister to consider "initiatives not highlighted in this letter." This is a surprising comment given the reputation of mandate letters for limiting ministers.

Source: Ontario government website, Mandate Letters 2014–2015, http://www.ontario.ca/page/mandate-letters-2014-2015.

that he or she can afford to become actively involved only in those few policy areas or issues in which he or she has a personal interest or that command attention on grounds of urgency or partisan politics. As chair of cabinet, the prime minister is the key actor in the central policy-making and coordinating institution of government, but he or she alone cannot direct the activities of the vast number of bureaucratic actors in government; the prime minister must rely on the assistance of cabinet colleagues and central agencies. Also, ministers can through various actions resist the commands of their boss and in so doing reveal the limits of prime ministerial power. Even backbenchers, aligned with cabinet members, can on occasion not only frustrate the will of the prime minister but help precipitate the departure of the most influential person in government. More generally, the demands of governing are just too much for one person (see cartoon).

Cabinet Committees

Taken together, cabinet committees are responsible for helping to coordinate policies and programs, to allocate human and financial resources, and to set priorities and directions for government in various areas of policy. More broadly, cabinet committees expedite careful decision making and assist in ensuring that control and command of events remain in the hands of senior elected government officials. Without committees, the concern is that cabinet alone and with its large size would be unable to collectively consider and decide upon important matters; at most it would be able to rubber-stamp proposals that emerge from individual departments seeking cabinet approval. In a setting that lacked committees, power and influence would move to single departmental ministers and their appointed officials. The ability to coordinate policy, which is the capacity to make sure government initiatives fit together, would also fall away. Basically, the evolution of cabinet decision making has been a shift away from a time when committees were largely absent

© Gary Clement

and cabinet struggled on its own to more recently where committees complement the full cabinet and have an opportunity to situate power in the hands of elected officials working collectively to provide government with overall direction and coordination.

The cabinet committee system at the federal level is now an accepted part of the political executive. Also largely accepted is the type and membership of committees, which comprise a cabinet committee system. The task of the most senior committee, usually called Priorities and Planning, is to advise cabinet on the areas on which government should concentrate; this committee allows government to consider closely what it truly wishes to do and to avoid moving in many different directions all at once. The committee is normally chaired by the prime minister and co-chaired by the finance minister; the two most powerful ministers thus guide the most important committee. Other members, who number from ten to fifteen, include heads of the departments connected with priorities and electoral promises. As Figure 9.1 shows, the Trudeau government, elected in 2015, has given its most senior committee a different name—Agenda, Results, and Communication—but the duties and membership of the committee are comparable to past priorities and planning committees.

Arguably, the second most senior committee is one that provides direction on the day-to-day management of the government's legislative agenda and "thorny issues."[5] The high status of the committee arises from the fact that the legislative accomplishments are central to any government's success as are the resolution of controversial matters. The chair of the committee, which typically goes by the name "Operations," will be someone knowledgeable about parliamentary procedures and comfortable with the often raucous nature of the House of Commons. The Trudeau government has seemingly chosen a different approach with this committee, placing some of the responsibility for operations with the aforementioned committee on agenda setting and getting results. But it has also set up a committee that deals with legislative matters, but it is not clear whether it has the same influence as Operations committees of the past.

The remaining committees in a cabinet system will usually represent the major policy areas in government and will be chaired by ministers closely tied to those areas. This means committees in the areas of social and health services, economic development and prosperity, and foreign affairs and national security; and chairs for these committees will be normally from departments of health, industry, and national defence respectively. The Trudeau government has provided for committees in all of these areas, albeit with names which may be unfamiliar to scholars of Canadian government (and combined economic and social issues into a single committee). Figure 9.1 also shows that the Trudeau cabinet committee system includes committees that address the environment,

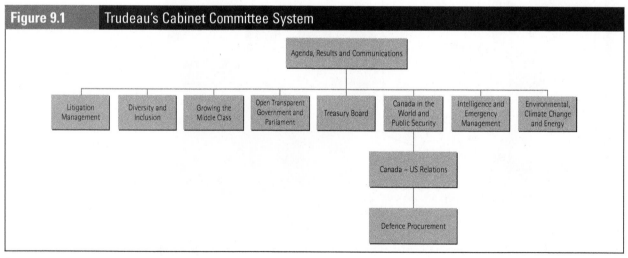

Figure 9.1 Trudeau's Cabinet Committee System

Source: Adapted from http://pm.gc.ca/sites/pm/files/docs/Cab_committee-comite.pdf.

Part Four / The Bureaucracy in the Political Process

diversity, and litigation issues. Initially, the government established a sub-committee on relations with the United States and an ad hoc committee responsible for the purchase of aircraft, ships, and other defence materials; however, both were subsequently made into full committees (see Box 9.2). All committees and their membership are determined by the prime minister save for one—the Treasury Board. In the case of this one exception, The *Financial Administration Act* stipulates that there shall be a cabinet committee for administration as well as the management of financial and human resources in the government of Canada. It should also be mentioned that new committees might be established to reflect new priorities of the government and the prime minister.

Buying Fighter Jets

BOX
9.2

"Ad hoc" refers to something which is arranged or set up for a particular purpose and typically will be discontinued once the aim is achieved. As mentioned, the Trudeau government first set up an ad hoc committee on defence procurement, and its purpose was is to offer options to the entire cabinet on a complex and potentially politically damaging issue: the purchase of fighter jet airplanes (at a cost of $9 billion). The preceding Conservative government had wanted to select a particular type of jet, but during the election campaign of 2015 the Liberals rejected this choice. Now in power the Liberals need to come up with an alternative. The turning of the ad hoc committee on defence procurement into a full committee suggests that the issue demands a body with more than ad hoc status. Using taxpayers' money to buy something costing billions of dollars is no small matter.

Source: Daniel LeBlanc, "Cabinet committee deciding on final options to replace Canada's fighter jets," *Globe and Mail*, June 9, 2016, A1, A11; http://pm.gc.ca/eng/news/2016/08/22/prime-minister-canada-announces-changes-structure-and-mandate-cabinet-committees.

Cabinet committees are an integral part of the political executive, but they are not without their shortcomings. Committee members sometimes feel that the work of the committees is time-consuming and too far removed from their duties as elected officials; in other words, they believe they were elected not to pour over cabinet memoranda and proposals but rather to meet constituents, give speeches at public gatherings, and generally engage in activities that directly increase the popularity of the government. Committees may also be guilty of failing to do their job. Each committee is supposed to collectively consider the value of departmental proposals in their area, a task that may result in rejection of an initiative. Given that the minister of the department that is spearheading a proposal is a member of the committee, other members of the committee may be reluctant to be too critical of a proposal for fear that they may receive the same treatment when one of their proposals comes to the committee. Also, committees feel frustrated at times when the more powerful committees take actions that have the effect of blocking their proposals. Finally, there is a sense in committees that the important work of government is being done elsewhere.

Central Agencies

The major central agencies, save for the Prime Minister Office (PMO), are administrative agencies in the sense that their members are non-partisan public servants. At the same time, they are different from departments, Crown corporations, and other entities associated with administration. The difference begins to become clear when examining roles in the all-important budgetary process. Administrative agencies typically act to press for additional funding; central agencies largely act to guard against expenditure increases.

This difference helps us to better understand central agencies in their capacity as players in the executive branch: they exist to coordinate and control the actions of government. Another quality of central agencies arises from the fact that arguably the most powerful central agency, the PMO, is populated by political appointees. The world of central agencies is highly politicized, where concerns of maintaining the government in power can become paramount.

The role of central agencies in assisting political executives to control and coordinate government policies and programs began to expand in the late 1960s. In serving the prime minister and cabinet, central-agency officials control and influence departmental officials by affecting the allocation of human and financial resources, the organization of governmental and departmental machinery, and the coordination of intergovernmental relations. Central agencies thereby help to promote administrative values such as efficiency, effectiveness, and accountability. Since these same activities help governments to keep their commitments and make them popular as well, central agencies also assist political executives to remain in power.

During the early years of the first government of Pierre Elliott Trudeau, elected in 1968, the PMO and Privy Council Office (PCO) were reorganized and expanded so as to improve their advisory and coordinating functions. The growth in the staff and expenditure of these offices led some commentators to compare them to the White House staff and Executive Office of the President of the United States, and to suggest that the expansion of these offices was part of the prime minister's objective of "presidentializing" the Canadian political system and enhancing prime-minister power.[6] The central agencies, including the Department of Finance and a newly independent Treasury Board Secretariat (TBS) created just before the election of Pierre Trudeau, have continued to play a prominent role in supporting the prime minister and cabinet.

It is notable that the PMO is a central agency unlike the others, being primarily a partisan instrument of the prime minister. The overriding concern of PMO officials is the political fortunes of the prime minister and the governing party. While they owe their first loyalty to the prime minister, the officials also serve the political interests of the cabinet as a whole; they can provide, for instance, guidance on which initiatives to pursue. The same holds for individual members of cabinet, whom PMO officials can work with "hand in hand … to initiate a proposal"; but these same officials can "quickly undercut a proposal when briefing the prime minister." The PMO is not a source of second opinions. It is, as Savoie says, "in the thick of it," an agency to be feared (see Box 9.3).[7]

BOX 9.3

PMO Feared?

The PMO can be intimidating, but it can also look almost inept. In 2013, auditors had determined that a Conservative Senator, Mike Duffy, had made ineligible expense claims. Duffy contested the finding, but the PMO urged him to pay back the expenses to avoid any further damaging publicity to Duffy—and the ruling Conservative Party. The PMO then would reimburse Duffy with funds provided by the federal Conservative Party (CPC). But it was subsequently uncovered that Duffy owed not $32,000, an amount that the CPC would reimburse, but rather $92,000. The party fund balked at paying this amount. Frustrated, the head of the PMO covered the cost with his own money, though efforts were made to make it look as if Duffy had made the payment. But the media soon uncovered what had happened, and the RCMP indicated its intentions to investigate. Almost immediately, Senator Duffy resigned from the Conservative caucus and sat as an independent. Soon after, the PMO head resigned as well. It was not long before there were questions about whether the prime minister had been involved.

Source: Michael Harris, *Party of One: Stephen Harper and Radical Makeover of Canada* (Toronto: Viking, 2014).

In contrast to the PMO, officials in the PCO are generally public servants who are non-partisan; they are, however, highly sensitive to political considerations. Some even go further, saying officials in the PCO are in a position of "near-total submission to the political demands of the Prime Minister's Office."[8] The Department of Finance and TBS are comprised of career public servants. The prime minister and cabinet rely heavily on the central agencies to control and influence the behaviour of departmental public servants.

Departments

Departments represent another key player in the relations within the executive branch, and within these entities the minister and deputy minister stand out. The doctrine of individual ministerial responsibility and legislative enactments give the minister say formal authority over all aspects of departments, but the reality is much different; government actors outside the minister's department carve away at ministerial authority. However, ministers still have some flexibility and independence. All ministers are expected to defend their departments in cabinet at budget time and they understand that reviews of their performance are greatly coloured by their "ability to secure new spending."[9] And truly effective ministers, those able to get things done without controversy, may be invited by the prime minister to attend informal gatherings that can trump the role of cabinet meetings. Ministers thus find themselves immersed in interactions that provide opportunities for securing both departmental interests and individual advancement.

While ministers take the leading part in departments and their relations with others, they share the stage with their deputies. Easily the dominant bureaucratic actors in executive–bureaucratic relations are the deputy ministers of government departments. Deputies concede the spotlight to ministers on policy decisions, but as supporting actors they are found side-by-side with their ministers as they deal with other executive actors. They are, in addition, entangled in the net of bureaucratic politics within their departments, and between their departments and other administrative units (which will be discussed more fully in Chapter 10). Interestingly, in the performance of their roles, deputy ministers appear to be responding increasingly to the prime minister and his or her close set of advisors for advice on priorities and other matters. The belief has been that the deputy is first and foremost a departmental official, but developments suggest that interactions between deputy ministers and central-agency officials—and the prime minister—are gaining greater significance. Some even go so far as to claim that deputies "are now as much a part of the centre of government as they are the administrative heads of their departments."[10]

Cabinet Approval and Cabinet Documents

Figure 9.2 depicts the process that brings together all the major players in the executive branch. This is the set of procedures and rules by which departmental proposals for new public policies and initiatives are approved, amended, or rejected by cabinet committees and by cabinet. Cabinet committees and central agencies clearly play an important role, but proposals for cabinet are formally prepared by government departments and are presented by a minister to the appropriate cabinet committee, usually in the form of a document called a **memorandum to cabinet**. A minister's proposal can be influenced by a variety of sources, including political parties, interest groups, the government caucus, and individual citizens. Central agencies may also intervene to offer direction and in fact they may formulate the proposal and effectively bypass a department if the department is unable for one reason or another to move forward with the proposal. Also, proposals are increasingly a product not of individual departments, but of departments working

memorandum to cabinet The key mechanism by which policy proposals are brought forward by ministers for consideration and approval by their cabinet colleagues. The formal means by which deputy ministers provide confidential policy advice to their ministers.

Figure 9.2   Process of Cabinet Approval

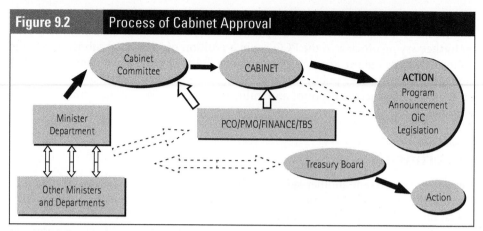

Source: Decision-Making Processes and Central Agencies in Canada: Federal, Provincial and Territorial Practices - Canada. © Privy Council Office, (2015). www.pco-bcp.gc.ca/docs/images/pub_decision_how-iss.gif

together. The dotted arrows in Figure 9.2 between the department and central agencies show that the two entities may meet before submission of the memorandum in order to work out any difficulties in the proposal.

Following its examination of the memo, the cabinet committee makes a recommendation to cabinet in the form of a committee report. Here, too, briefings of central agencies play a part. Approval by cabinet takes the form of a record of decision that is circulated to all ministers for any necessary follow-up; the record of decision also serves as a basis for seeking approval from Treasury Board for any required financial and human resources attached to the policy proposal. Though cabinet is the final decision maker, normally the careful analysis is conducted in the relevant cabinet committee, and cabinet as a result accepts the committee recommendation without much discussion.

The memorandum to cabinet (MC), as already stated, is the mechanism by which policy proposals are brought forward by ministers for consideration and approval by their cabinet colleagues.[11] The MC, which can be only a maximum of ten pages (14 point font), is a product of the PCO and must be structured as follows:

- The memorandum starts with a one-sentence *Issue Statement*, which takes the form of a question to be considered and answered.
- Next is the most important part of the MC, the *Recommendations*. Busy ministers sometimes will limit their reading of the MC to this section. The recommendations outline the course of action to be taken and stipulate the role of the involved ministers in carrying out the decision, the salient policy instruments, and the funding required for the proposal work.
- The *Rationale* section clarifies the reasons for the recommended course of action and how it fits into the strategic direction of the department and the government as a whole. Basically, this part of the MC provides the background necessary to make sense of the departmental proposal.
- The following section—*Proposed Approach and Options*—gives details on the proposed course of action (timeframe, itemizing of costs, supporting evidence, trade-offs, and risks and challenges). Alternatives to the proposed course of actions are offered at this time to give the readers some choice if they find the recommendations unacceptable.
- The *Considerations* part of the MC anticipates concerns cabinet members might have about consulting relevant stakeholders (e.g., provinces, private sector, international interests), offending the Charter of Rights, or heeding various legislative requirements (e.g., environmental, language).

- *Due Diligence* shows that government officials responsible for finances, assets, and human resources have given their approval.
- Appended to the MC are three sets of plans (two pages each) dealing with implementation, communications, and Parliament.

Court Government

In most presentations of government in Canada, the cabinet approval process, along with its MC, represents the most important interaction involving political executives and senior public servants. The federal government's own guide on how government works highlights the cabinet decision-making process.[12] Yet, there is a growing consensus that the cabinet approval process handles only the most mundane and least important of matters. As mentioned earlier, many scholars believe executive decision making has centralized into the hands of the prime minister and his most trusted advisors, who reside both in and outside of government, and who altogether amount to a throwback to pre-democratic times when the King or Queen relied upon secretive advisors lurking in the shadows. Once called prime-ministerial government, the arrangement is now more aptly named **court government**.[13] This transformation can be seen as a defensive manoeuvre designed to stave off the collective pressure of globalization, a 24/7 media, parliamentary oversight bodies, and a less deferential population wanting government to do more with less. But it can also be seen to reflect an aggressive mindset. Governments, and this includes those outside Canada as well, feel that effective power is concentrated power, and that timely, coordinated, and well-received initiatives are not the product of a formalized cabinet approval process but rather the result of a coterie of gifted and trusted people able to act quickly and creatively (see Box 9.4). This sentiment has gained currency among Canadian political leaders for the past three or four decades, but now it seems that the intensity of this feeling is heightening. As stated, it also seems that court government has emerged in other countries.[14]

court government A type of government that places a great deal of power in the hands of the prime minister and a select group of valued counsellors. Employed by some to describe the nature of the Canadian government.

Court Government and the New Prime Minister?

The notion of court government was certainly associated with former prime minister Stephen Harper and his government, but the hope is that Justin Trudeau will reject this approach and opt for a more open and inclusive government. But a media report based on insider interviews states that the Trudeau government is forming a decision-making system which "uses high-level 'delivery units' to push key goals across the entire public service, sometimes bypassing the hierarchy of cabinets, departments, and administrations ...."

Source: Doug Saunders, "How the Liberal Dream Machine Will Work," *Globe and Mail*, October 24, 2015, section F, F1-2.

BOX
9.4

Points to Know

- Three principles that shape interactions between and among elected and appointed officials in the executive branch are ministerial responsibility, hierarchy, and influence.
- The major players interacting with one another are the prime minister and cabinet, central agencies, and departmental ministers and appointed officials.
- Each interaction among key players has particular qualities. For example, the prime minister in his interactions with individual ministers tends to dominate using devices such as mandate letters.
- The cabinet decision-making process is the major interaction because it involves all the primary players in the executive sphere of government.

- There are indications that the cabinet decision-making process is being eclipsed by a new process called court government. It is a process that reflects an even more powerful prime minister working with a select group of advisors.

Review Questions

1. What is the nature of the relationship between cabinet and the prime minister?

2. What is the role of cabinet committees?

3. How does a policy proposal move through the cabinet decision-making process?

4. What do the contents of a memorandum to cabinet tell us about the concerns of cabinet members?

5. What is the best explanation for the emergence of court government?

Notes

1. Stephen Brooks, *Canadian Democracy*, 8th ed. (Toronto: Oxford University Press, 2015), 280.
2. Quoted in Donald J. Savoie, "The Federal Government: Revisiting Court Government in Canada," in *Executive Styles in Canada: Cabinet Structures and Leadership Practices in Canadian Government*, eds. Luc Bernier, Keith Brownsey, and Michael Howlett (Toronto: University of Toronto Press, 2005), 31.
3. Ibid., 33.
4. Quoted in Donald J. Savoie, *Whatever Happened to the Music Teacher? How Government Decides and Why* (Montreal & Kingston: McGill-Queen's University Press, 2013), 85.
5. Bruce Carson, *14 Days: Making the Conservative Movement in Canada* (Montreal & Kingston: McGill-Queen's University Press, 2014), 151.
6. Thomas A. Hockin, ed., *Apex of Power: The Prime Minister and Political Leadership in Canada*, 2nd ed. (Scarborough: Prentice-Hall, 1977); Jeffrey Simpson, *The Friendly Dictatorship* (Toronto: McClelland & Stewart, 2001).
7. Donald J. Savoie, "Power at the Apex: Executive Dominance," in *Canadian Politics*, 6th ed., eds. James Bickerton and Alain-G. Gagnon (Toronto: University of Toronto Press, 2014), 140.
8. Michael Harris, *Party of One: Stephen Harper and Canada's Radical Makeover* (Toronto: Viking, 2014), 6.
9. Savoie, *Whatever Happened to the Music Teacher?* 77.
10. Savoie, "The Federal Government," 41.
11. Privy Council Office, *Memorandum to Cabinet*, July 2014, http://www.pco-bcp.gc.ca/index.asp?lang=eng&page=information&sub=publications&doc=mc/mc-eng.htm (accessed November 8, 2016).
12. Government of Canada, *Open and Accountable Government: A Guide for Ministers and Ministers of State* (Ottawa: Her Majesty the Queen in Right of Canada, 2015), Appendix D.
13. See Savoie, "Power at the Apex."
14. C. Dahlstrom et al., eds., *Steering from the Centre: Strengthening Political Control in Western Democracies* (Toronto: University of Toronto Press, 2011).

Interdepartmental and Intradepartmental Relations

10

Learning Objectives

Reading this chapter allows you to do the following:

- Understand the causes and importance of interdepartmental relations and horizontal management
- Analyze efforts at horizontal management by comparing the causes and possible costs of horizontal management
- Identify the key intradepartmental relationships within a government department
- Appreciate the complex nature of interactions between the minister and deputy minister
- Propose the appropriate relationship between appointed officials and ministerial assistants

Within the executive branch, the most significant interaction takes place as cabinet considers policy and proposals. This interaction, involving key ministers, central-agency guardians, determined deputy ministers, and the prime minister, defines a government. But another set of relations within the executive also deserves attention. These are the interactions that emerge both within a department (**intradepartmental**) and between departments (**interdepartmental**). Within a department, we see the responsible minister, the ministerial assistants, the deputy head, and public servants all acting with each other to create and carry out public programs. Also significant are the relationships that have lately gained greater attention. These are relations that cut across departmental boundaries in pursuit of solutions to problems that resist easy placement within a single department. The realization that arrangements involving two or more departments have secured high priority forces students of public administration to expand their traditional emphasis on the activities of departments acting alone. If asked to choose the most important department out of, say, industry, justice, health, social services, and environment, the best answer may be all of them working together. Intradepartmental relations remain worthy of our consideration, but increasingly the focus is shifting to interdepartmental relations and beyond that to include not only government departments but also actors existing in the larger society.

This chapter first explores interdepartmental relations in recognition of their growing prominence. It suggests that there are various forces pushing government towards arrangements that call for departments to coordinate their efforts. The chapter also proposes qualities that increase the chances that **horizontal management**—another name for interdepartmental relations—will achieve success, and urges us to see that true success often requires including non-governmental entities. The second half of the chapter returns the reader to the more traditional territory of relations within departments. The focus at this point is on the interactions consisting of the primary departmental players—the minister, the deputy minister, senior public servants, and ministerial assistants.

intradepartmental interaction Interactions within one department.

interdepartmental interaction Interactions between different departments.

horizontal management A type of management process that involves two or more departments and, increasingly, non-governmental bodies.

Interdepartmental Relations

Interdepartmental relations represent an increasingly important element in the operations of governments in Canada and elsewhere. An ever-expanding number of issues are now handled through horizontal arrangements in which departments and agencies combine their actions in one way or another; the traditional reliance on vertical relations within a single department no longer suffices. Health departments wishing to consider new initiatives need to check with social service and treasury departments to ensure that the full implications of their action are appreciated. The same holds for the formulation of taxation proposals, where the views of finance, revenue, and justice departments are typically required. The successful implementation of programs, in addition to their formulation, also often depends upon agencies working with one another. Moreover, vigorous attempts are made to involve all the relevant interests, including those outside government, in order to increase the chances that issues are handled effectively and fairly. This last development has become so evident that the equating of horizontal management with interdepartmental relations is increasingly rejected. Other levels of government, citizens groups, and non-governmental organizations at times must also be counted among the participants in horizontal relations.

The reasons for the increased emphasis on interdependent relations start with public issues that require more than the efforts of an individual department. The complexity of problems facing government necessitates departments and agencies coming together to coordinate their actions—to act horizontally. Especially relevant here are "wicked" problems which typically cut across departmental boundaries and whose solutions appear within reach only using the kind of organizational approaches associated with joint departmental exercises (see Box 10.1). Globalization with its stipulation that national governments act in compliance with new global rules and regulations has made it essential for government departments to better coordinate their actions, and this too leads to greater horizontality in government. The competitiveness inherent in globalization also requires that public agencies act as a team in order to succeed. A further reason for the significance of horizontal relations is the heightened expectations of the citizenry who insist that government be able to deliver services and programs that compel the participation of more than one department; citizens resist any attempt to force them to go from one department to another to get what they want from government. These same citizens also "demand equal and fair treatment from their governments," an outcome that also requires public agencies to better harmonize and coordinate their services.[1] Finally, the inefficiencies inherent in overlap and redundancy can be more easily discovered and eliminated through attempts at managing horizontally. Only by going beyond the perspective of individual departments can we see the unnecessary duplication in government.

BOX 10.1

Wicked Problems

Wicked problems are "wicked" not because they are evil but because they are difficult to solve. The difficulty arises from their complexity. Poverty is an example of a wicked problem. Poverty is always with us, whether in a modern city or in a village in an underdeveloped country. One of the proposed ways to address particularly difficult challenges is to engage all the relevant stakeholders. In Canada, federal and provincial governments along with anti-poverty groups combine their efforts to tackle poverty.

Source: H.W.J. Wittel and M.M. Webber, "Dilemmas in the General Theory of Planning," Policy Sciences 4, pp 155–169. Amsterdam: Elsevier Science, 1973.

Horizontal Management

Interdepartmental relations and the more general concept of horizontal management have been defined in various ways. According to the Government of Canada, "a horizontal initiative is defined as an initiative in which partners from two or more federal organizations have established a formal funding agreement (e.g., Memorandum to Cabinet, Treasury Board submission) to work toward achieving shared outcomes."[2] There are others who agree with this definition, but emphasize the need to include other governments and non-government entities in any understanding of horizontal management.

In recent years, the major horizontal initiatives at the federal level have largely been restricted to federal departments and agencies. For example, the Youth Employment Strategy is a horizontal initiative involving eleven federal agencies with the purpose of equipping young people aged 15–30 with job skills and experience. The Federal Tobacco Strategy, headed by Health Canada, is another horizontal initiative with only federal membership, and a host of other initiatives dealing with various concerns (border control, infrastructure, money laundering, firearms) are also basically interdepartmental arrangements.

At the same time, however, some initiatives go beyond federal agencies. The Canadian HIV Vaccine Initiative involves various federal departments and the Bill and Melinda Gates Foundation joining forces to contribute to the discovery of "a safe, effective, affordable globally accessible HIV vaccine"[3] (see Box 10.2).

Case of Horizontal Management

BOX
10.2

The Canadian HIV Vaccine Initiative (CHVI) employs horizontal management to engage the efforts of government departments and a prominent non-profit agency in an effort, as stated, to help discover an HIV vaccine. The initiative also pursues a related goal, which is to support services that prevent the transmission of HIV from mother to child. The federal-government agencies involved include Health Canada, Industry Canada, Foreign Affairs, Trade and Development Canada, Canadian Institutes of Health Research, and the Public Health Agency of Canada (PHAC). All of these federal bodies contribute in one way or another to the initiative. The non-profit agency involved is a foundation supported by the former head of Microsoft, Bill Gates, and his wife. Both the federal government and the Bill and Melinda Gates Foundation offer financial support to the initiative and its activities, with the total amount reaching up to $139 million and possibly beyond this figure. The PHAC serves to coordinate the actions of the federal participants. An advisory body monitors the carrying out of the objectives of the initiative and also provides advice on allocation of available funds to appropriate projects. Progress reports are made available every six months until the termination of the ten-year initiative, in 2017.

As can be seen, the CHVI is an ambitious endeavour, which recognizes that a collective effort is required to address the problem of AIDS. It also recognizes that horizontal management can only work if attention is given to mechanisms for bringing the participants together and keeping them together.

Source: Government of Canada, Memorandum of Understanding Between the Government of Canada and the Bill & Melinda Gates Foundation, Canadian HIV Vaccine Initiative http://www.chvi-icvv.gc.ca/mou-eng.html.

Effectiveness of Horizontal Management

The sheer abundance of horizontal relations in government indicates that we expect such relations to lead to more effective government actions. The causes of horizontality in government suggest that no public authority can be satisfied with departments and agencies acting on their own. Moreover, the relevant evidence points to successes in horizontal relations - the HIV initiative outlined in Box 10.2 is an example of such evidence. However, interdepartmental relations and those that include interests outside government can also have their problems and costs. The cost most identified is the amount of time required to operate in a horizontal manner. Interdepartmental relations translate into more meetings, more planning, more drafting, and generally more talking. Further, the cost in time is sometimes not worth the effort involved in horizontal management. A second problem is the possibility that the best policy response may not be chosen. Instead, a compromise will be put forward in order to resolve differences. As one participant in interdepartmental relations testifies, "your position gets diluted because you have to compromise with the other guys."[4] This also means that skills at decision making start to atrophy and officials "spend much more of their time explaining situations, setting out various options and tradeoffs, and persuading those involved, before proposed solutions become acceptable."[5]

Arguably, the most important concern is the possible loss or blurring of accountability. With single department initiatives, the line of accountability is clear, running from the bottom to the top of the organization; with interdepartmental initiatives, the line is less clear as these initiatives involve officials working across and outside organizations without any specific link back to their formal superiors. If something goes wrong in a horizontal initiative, it is not immediately evident who takes responsibility and who enforces any necessary remedies and sanctions. Some claim that a new kind of accountability emerges in horizontal relations, one that relies on "the mutual accountability of collaborators, partners, or co-producers of policy and services to each other, and the accountability of each to citizens and users."[6] But the notion of "horizontal accountability" does not sound quite right; accountability, it appears, requires hierarchy.

A final concern to consider is that interdepartmental relations and horizontality as a whole erase the boundaries created by a more vertical or department-based view of public management. Departmental boundaries are important because they provide a sense of order, telling people where they are to work, how they are to work, with whom they are to work, and to whom they are accountable. The collapse of these boundaries offers a feeling of freedom and greater possibilities for creativity, but it also generates an uneasiness borne of uncertainty and confusion over where one goes and what one does. One of the qualities of interdepartmental relations involves the building of a new culture that binds together participants; but it can be argued that public servants already have a culture centred within their home departments.

These problems do not mean that interdepartmental relations should be rejected, because such relations are here to stay. The causes of such relations are too powerful to be brushed aside in favour of old ways of doing things. But these concerns do mean that architects of horizontal management need to anticipate and to take into consideration the challenges of getting people in different departments to work together. Horizontal initiatives often require skills that departmental officials may be without, so some officials may be reluctant to participate in endeavours with other agencies. These skills include the ability to negotiate and to engage in consensus building. It is also important to grasp the sheer magnitude of the task facing those who engage in truly ambitious horizontal relations. Figure 10.1 depicts the many federal departments and programs (and other actors) that have sought to address the homeless problem in Toronto, many of which must eventually be coordinated through horizontal relations if this social issue is to be addressed successfully.

Network Governance

Another type of horizontal arrangement called "network governance" has begun to emerge in Canadian public administration.[7] As the name indicates, the arrangement relies on a grouping or network of actors dedicated towards achieving public purposes.

Part Four / The Bureaucracy in the Political Process

Figure 10.1   The Challenge of Horizontal Relations

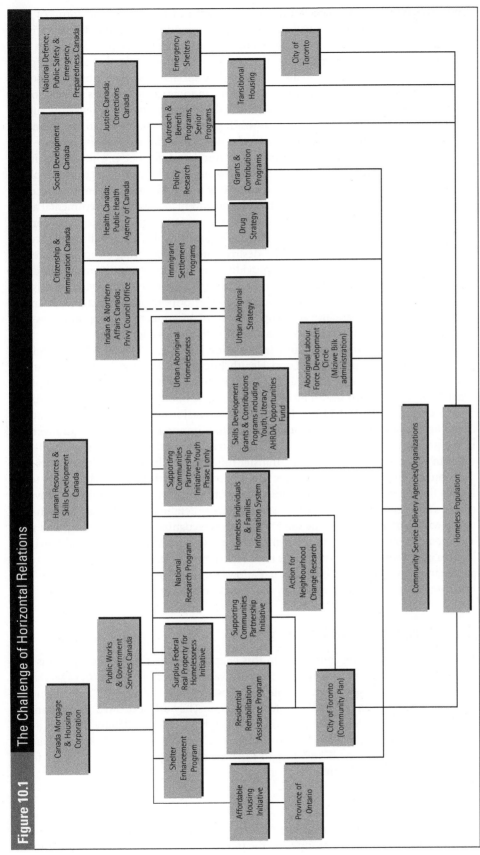

Source: *Report of the Auditor General of Canada* (2005), Office of the Auditor General of Canada. Reproduced with the permission of Her Majesty the Queen in Right of Canada, as represented by the Auditor General of Canada, 2016.

Networks appear to be able to produce a workable balance between autonomy and accountability. The LHINs seemingly have the required amount of autonomy to achieve their purposes, while the provincial government has the control necessary to ensure accountability. In reality, this balance between the LHINs and the health ministry is difficult to achieve, with both parties often feeling that the other side is getting the better of the arrangement. This tension needs to be resolved to achieve effective networking. What is the appropriate balance? For example, should the autonomy of the LHINs be maximized to the point where the central ministry of health simply sends the money and allows the LHINs to do the rest?

This characteristic makes it similar to more traditional forms of horizontal management, but there are differences. One difference is the inclusion of entities outside government playing an important role. Network governance recognizes that the complexities of societal problems and challenges facing any social entity require both public and private actors; this recognition in some cases even goes so far as to suggest government is now unable to govern by itself, hence the suggestion, in the use of the word "governance" as opposed to "government," that the problems of today necessitate the participation of more than just governmental players. Another difference is a somewhat ironic one: the greater inclusiveness of networks leads to a greater emphasis on maintaining accountability in the hands of government. In other words, the attempt to expand governance to non-governmental actors leads to efforts to ensure that government has some degree of control. These efforts include giving government responsibility for steering the network in the desired direction, ensuring acceptable levels of performance, and providing the appropriate resourcing. A third and final difference, in the Canadian context, is the focus on initiatives at the local level. Traditional types of horizontal management appear resistant to network governance at the upper levels of government, but opportunities for a more ambitious type of interaction are available within cities and regions.

An example of network governance in operation is the set of 14 relatively new regional health bodies in Ontario called Local Health Integration Networks (LHINs). The networks are led by a board of community representatives assisted by a small team of public officials, who work with health providers, health-care boards, citizens of the region, and others to fund, manage, and provide many of the major institutional and community-based health care services in the province. Another important actor in this arrangement is the provincial ministry of health, which enters into agreements with each LHIN in order to set performance indicators, transfer funding, and lay out health priorities. The decision to transfer authority for many health services from the provincial ministry to the LHINs flowed from the belief that only a network of citizens and health care providers close to the community could ensure a health care system that provided services sensitive to the wishes of residents. At the same time, it was recognized that the transfer had to be accompanied by an accountability regime that allowed political leaders at the provincial level to play a role as well. The LHINs represent the elements we identified with network governance: an inclusive orientation that allows for many actors, close attention to both horizontal *and* vertical accountability, and a focus on the local (see What to Do?).

Intradepartmental Relations

The other relations to be considered in this chapter are those within departments. The internal structure of government organizations varies from one category of organization to another, but in general departments and those central agencies with a departmental form are organized in a broadly uniform manner. They are structured in a pyramidal fashion, with a minister as the political head (with staff) and a deputy minister as the lead administrative official of a formal organization with layers of interlocking superior–subordinate relationships descending to the base of the pyramid. This structure forms the basis for intradepartmental relations.

The Minister

At the top of all departments sits the minister, who is usually an elected member of the party in power and who is appointed by the prime minister. In this position, the minister is responsible for all actions of the department, a reality confirmed by the convention of individual ministerial responsibility. Individual statutes also seek to specify the duties of the minister in relation to the department. Within this legal framework, ministers undertake certain actions necessary to their position within the department. They will need, first of all, to define departmental priorities in order to give direction to the department. In this exercise, the ministers are aided by the deputy minister, political advisors, and most importantly, the "mandate letters" from the prime minister. In some cases, the minister rests content with serving the interests of his or her departmental clients and staying away from the larger policy issues; indeed, it is expected that ministers come to work with "no view on policy."[8] This means that any major plans or adjustments articulated by the minister are strongly discouraged; it also means that some may emerge from their experience as minister feeling "powerless and outside the system."[9] In all cases the minister realizes that there is a certain "sink or swim" quality to being a minister. The job requires ensuring problem-free administration of department programs and exercising some initiative with the guidance of the prime minister.[10] If the minister doesn't accomplish these things, the department flounders and eventually someone else assumes effective control. Government, like nature, abhors a vacuum.

Facing all ministers is the challenge of ensuring that departmental personnel work diligently to serve the government and the country. Given the significance of this challenge, the temptation on the part of the minister is to manage the department; but to do this is a mistake. A minister actively engaged in department management soon "becomes so swamped with work that he or she cannot spend the time required to set the agenda and define the major policy or management thrusts for the department."[11] Most ministers appreciate this problem; they limit themselves to setting out their broad expectations about the management of the department, and then leave the actual managing to the appointed officials. Ministers also seek to establish good relations with their senior administrative staff and ensure that the latter are able to work with any political appointees in the minister's office. In addition, they make efforts to get to know not only the senior personnel, but also the department as a whole and what is key to its operation. Furthermore, minister ought to represent the department effectively in various political arenas. The minister defends the department in Parliament, pursues its priorities in cabinet, and puts the department's best face forward when dealing with interest groups and the media.

The individual responsibility of ministers as political heads of departments links the cabinet to the bureaucracy, and it establishes the minister as the locus of formal authority in the departmental hierarchy for both policy formulation and policy execution. Not only do ministers make the final decisions on policy questions, but they also bear constitutional, legal, and political responsibility for the proper administration of their departments. In practice, ministers look to their senior departmental officials for assistance, especially to the deputy minister. But the deputy minister and other departmental officials know that ultimately it is the minister who makes the final decision when it comes to the daily operation of the department. Admittedly, relations between the deputy and the minister are complicated by the fact that the prime minister appoints all deputies. This appointment arrangement, among other things, reminds the deputy ministers that they must take into consideration the collective concerns of the entire government as well as the wishes and goals of the first minister. It also means that deputies are expected to answer to both the minister and the prime minister. This is a reality that all ministers need to consider carefully and manage to their benefit and that of the government.

The Deputy Minister

The authority of the deputy minister, who is the senior administrative official in a department, is based on both statutes and conventions. These authorities can be translated into a set of basic roles for the deputy minister (see Figure 10.2). The role most apparent in relation to intradepartmental interactions is the provision of advice and assistance to the minister. This advice, which is to be timely, frank, and "presented fearlessly," includes the offering of the "best possible policy options based on impartial review of the public good and the declared objectives of the Minister and the government."[12] Aside from policy advice, the deputy minister can put forward his or her views to the minister on legal, administrative, or technical issues that concern the department and the minister, and the deputy is also instrumental in ensuring that the parliamentary duties of the minister are carried out. The deputy minister provides counsel on the political dimensions of any issue, but this is not guidance on how the minister and the government can best remain in government but rather views on how program initiatives will fare in light of the existing pressures both in and outside government. The deputy may, for instance, suggest to the minister that a particular proposal will be received poorly because of the opposition of powerful interest groups or because of the strong objections of other departments or influential central agencies. Perhaps above everything else, ministers "expect their deputies to help them get their proposals through the system...", which is to say that the deputy minister is able to navigate the obstacles that inevitably await ministerial initiatives and related actions both in and outside departments.[13] In all cases, the minister has the authority to ignore the advice and proposed actions of the deputy and act against them. Nevertheless, the deputy minister has the duty and responsibility to make known his or her opinions—both policy and political—to the minister.

Deputy ministers are also expected to carry out another role relating to relations within departments, and that is to spend some of their precious time on the internal management of their departments. The average line department has thousands of employees, often located in a maze of regional and local offices and all attempting to respond to a multitude of demands. So the deputy has to pay attention to what goes on in his or her department. Much of this work is delegated to associate and assistant deputy ministers and middle-level managers, but the deputies nevertheless have to concern themselves with such issues as the hiring of senior people, the articulation of preferred management approaches, the formulation of workable policies, the administration of financial resources, and the provision of overall leadership. This last duty, leadership, has become especially important, as deputies are expected to "frame a vision for the department" and "lead by inspiring and galvanizing employees."[14] Many of these departmental responsibilities are prescribed in law. The *Financial Administration Act* makes the deputy minister directly responsible "for the prudent management of allocated resources" and the *Public Service Employment Act* places many duties affecting human resources management in the hands of the deputy. To perform this role of managing departments, the deputy has to have a good understanding of the substance of the department and an appreciation of "how to manage in a government environment."[15]

A final role of the deputy concerns the department but its overall orientation resides outside the department. This role involves the collective or corporate management of government, a role that is becoming more significant; in fact, some argue it has assumed the top spot in the list of deputy-ministerial duties. This particular role refers

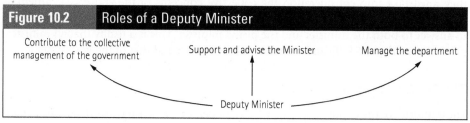

Figure 10.2 Roles of a Deputy Minister

Contribute to the collective management of the government

Support and advise the Minister

Manage the department

Deputy Minister

Source: Gorden Osbaldeston, Job Description for DMs, Policy Options, January 1988. Montreal: Institute for Research on Public Policy, 1988.

to a number of activities. Some of these are centred within the department; for example, the deputy works with the minister to make certain that the contents of the prime minister's mandate letter shape the formulation of departmental priorities. Other instances include guaranteeing that the department respects government-wide practices and standards set by such bodies as the Treasury Board and the Public Service Commission. But many of the activities connected to corporate management cause the deputy minister to go beyond the department. The deputy, for instance, meets with other deputies through numerous committees "to exchange information and discuss approaches to shared files in order to foster improved collaboration,"[16] and deputies together will go on a number of one- or two-day retreats annually. Meetings with senior central agency representatives also form part of the corporate management role. Each week, all deputy ministers will have breakfast with the head of the Privy Council Office to discuss issues of the day for the government, and a select group of deputies will meet on a weekly basis with Treasury Board Secretariat (TBS) officials to consider initiatives suggested by the TBS. Then there are the informal processes where deputies—often only a chosen few—will meet with other very influential players in the political arena. The most important of these processes is the one with the prime minister and other close advisors to consider the most senior priorities of the government and the taking of appropriate action. All of these activities relating to corporate management have become so numerous and prominent that they have fundamentally changed the work of deputy ministers. Deputies traditionally focused on their individual department, but now they concentrate more and more on the collective interests of the government and their varied processes.

The shift in the nature of deputy-minister duties towards an emphasis on corporate management in one sense is unsurprising. As noted earlier, the complexity of public policies is forcing government to develop a more horizontal or cross-departmental perspective toward its operations, and the enlargement of the deputy's corporate role is one manifestation of this adjustment. It also has to be remembered that deputy ministers are appointees of the prime minister and as such are accountable to the first minister and his or her government. Deputies are also accountable to their individual ministers, but one might claim that the deputy's top boss is the prime minister and the larger government of the day.

So the aforementioned shift should not be considered unexpected; but in another sense the development is somewhat surprising and even disturbing. A successful department requires that a deputy "manage down," which means the deputy is oriented toward meeting the needs and requirements of the department and its minister. But the adoption of a more corporate orientation produces a deputy who "manage up" and cares increasingly about the survival of the government and leaves the department to subordinates.[17] The fear here is that the readjustment of deputy minister roles may eventually lead to deputies who worry more about the welfare of the prime minister and less about the public interest. In addition, the tradition of non-partisanship within the public service may be seriously challenged as its most senior members risk becoming politicized. Getting too close to the centre of political power has its dangers.

Ministerial Staff

A consideration of interactions within government departments focuses on the minister, deputies, and other public servants within the organization. But a look at departmental relationships should also include staff attached to the minister's office. These assistants to the minister, who are often referred to as political aides or political staff, are appointed by the minister and are usually described as "exempt staff" because they are not subject to rules governing the recruitment of public servants.

The tenure of ministerial assistants is tied directly to that of the minister and thus the minister's staff is subject to the fluctuations of partisan politics; for instance, they lose their jobs if the minister leaves office because of poor performance or electoral upheaval. In the past, a measure of employment protection was assured by the *Public Service Employment Act*. A person who served at least three years as an executive assistant, a special assistant, or a private secretary to a minister was entitled to a position in the public service for which he or she was qualified at a level at least equivalent to that of private secretary to a deputy minister. However, legislation ended this practice, replacing it with a provision that only permits ministerial staff to enter into internal job competitions within the federal public service for up to one year after leaving their position. The best former ministerial assistants can get now is limited entrance to job competitions restricted to people already employed within the public service. Not surprisingly, the absence of job security means ministerial staff tends to be young people willing to accept the risky tenure of the position in return for employment and work experience in politics (see Box 10.3).

BOX 10.3

Working for the Minister

The youth of ministerial assistants means that recent political science graduates are prime candidates for work in a minister's office. Below are the types of job requirements that have been associated with the exempt staff position of Policy Advisor:

- working together with departmental personnel on policy reviews or consideration of specific policy issues
- briefing the minister on matters relating to policies under the responsibility of the minister
- helping to coordinate government policies and programs through relations with the Prime Minister's Office and other ministerial staff
- ensuring that the policy actions and initiatives of the minister are in keeping with the overall goals and priorities of the government
- meeting with groups outside government who have an interest in the policy developments of the department

Source: Based on: Treasury Board Secretariat, Policies for Ministers' Offices. Available at http://www.tbs-sct.gc.ca/pubs_pol/hrpubs/mg-ldm/2011/pgmo-pldcm12-eng.asp#tocAppA.

Since the early 1960s, the size of the minister's office staff has increased. Recent counts of ministerial staff (outside the Prime Minister's Office) put the number of assistants at 559, an increase of 24% over the 10-year period from 2005–2015.[18] The current number of ministerial staff suggests a commitment to staffing, but in the past the support for ministerial staff has been often inconsistent and sometimes weak or nearly absent. Until the Progressive Conservative government of 1984, ministers were usually authorized under Treasury Board guidelines to hire only an executive assistant, a policy advisor, as many special assistants as funds permitted, one private secretary, and support staff. Some ministers supplemented this staff by seconding departmental public servants and/or using departmental funds to hire employees on a contract basis. Upon its election in 1984, the Progressive Conservative government upgraded the quality of ministerial staff by authorizing each minister to hire a chief of staff at a substantial salary. The chiefs of staff were intended to function, not as senior policy advisors to the minister, but as the minister's chief political advisors and as the managers of the minister's office. They did, however, play a more significant policy role than their predecessors. Following its election in 1993, the Chrétien government abolished the chief of staff role and reduced the resources devoted to ministerial staff. On coming into office in 2004, Prime Minister Paul Martin reinstated the position of chief of staff with a substantial increase in remuneration over the salary paid to senior ministerial assistants in earlier years, and the Harper government continued to appreciate the value of ministerial assistants and, as already shown, increased their numbers. Early reports show that the Trudeau government is working hard to fill positions in the offices of ministers.[19]

The Functions of Ministerial Assistants

An authoritative government document drafted by the Privy Council Office (PCO) states that the overall intent of a minister's office is to "provide Ministers with advisors and assistants who are not departmental public servants, who share their political commitment, and who can complement the professional, expert and non-partisan advice and support of the public service."[20] A former chief of staff of the Prime Minister's Office (PMO) concurs, saying that "the government has long recognized that ministers require something more than the expert, but non-partisan, advice of the public service to meet the demands on them."[21] These statements clearly show that the main function of ministerial assistants is to offer political advice on all matters coming into the minister's office, including proposals emanating from the department and its public servants. In offering this advice, the primary motivation of the assistants is to "protect their Minister and government from any action or issue that might adversely affect their chances of re-election."[22] The major players in the minister's office—the Chief of Staff, the Director of Policy, the Director of Communications, and the Director of Parliamentary Affairs—are all focused on this particular function. A related function concerns liaising with senior departmental officials, the PMO, ministerial chiefs of staff, and any other bodies crucial to the political survival of the minister. A third function is managing the minister's office, which means handling the office budget, correspondence, work flow, and staff. A still further function relates to managing a most important commodity in political life, namely the minister's time. This last duty, the role of time manager, involves juggling the minister's extremely onerous schedule. See Figure 10.3 for the structure of a minister's office.

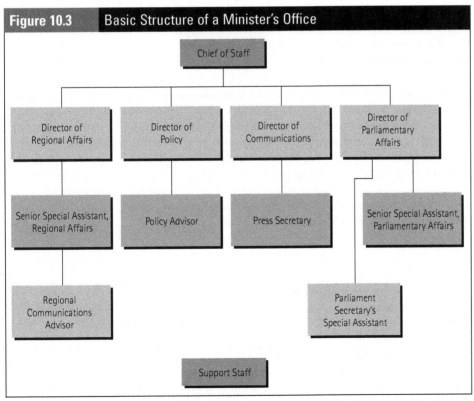

Figure 10.3   Basic Structure of a Minister's Office

Source: Adapted from Treasury Board of Canada Secretariat, *Guidelines for Ministers' Offices* (Ottawa: Her Majesty the Queen in Right of Canada, February 2006).

Ministerial Staff and Departmental Officials

Any government hopes that there will be harmonious and productive relations between ministerial staff and departmental officials, and that this can be achieved through a clear understanding of the respective duties. The PCO document mentioned above emphasizes the complementary relationship between the two, one being non-partisan and the other clearly partisan. It also lays out rules of engagement; for example, exempt staff members are forbidden to "give direction to departmental officials on the discharge of their responsibilities" and "relations between officials and exempt staff should be conducted through the deputy minister's office."[23] Sometimes the hope of harmonious relations is achieved, but other times difficulties arise between the two parties. The precipitating factor usually is the belief of departmental officials that the minister's staff has intruded too much into the process of policy formulation. This type of intrusion is easy to imagine given that some of the listed duties of ministerial assistants—for example, "assisting the Minister in developing policy positions"—seem almost indistinguishable from those of public servants.[24] One former deputy minister conveys the exasperation of some departmental officials:

> The role of the ministerial assistant should centre around the relationship with the caucus, the constituency and the Minister's personal schedule; when they stick to that kind of knitting there is no problem. The difficulties arise when they start to act like Leo the 10th, "God has given us the papacy, now let us enjoy it." They want to be policy hounds and think they know all about it, and usually the intellectual apparatus is an ideological disposition—Christian, free market, union—and on that basis, they try to influence departmental policy.[25]

As the quotation suggests, departmental members feel that ministerial staff are without the technical skills to contribute to the formulation of policy and programs, and instead merely trumpet one belief system or another. Public administration scholars add that the lack of training extends to the near-absence of any appreciation of the constitutional pillars of government as well as the values that animate public servants.[26] Ministerial staff, of course, can also add to the discomfort felt by deputies and scholars by voicing beliefs that the bureaucracy is bereft of innovative policy ideas and lacking in its understanding of the minister's political needs. There are thus reasons for affixing the blame for turbulence in relations between public servants and ministerial assistants to those close to the minister. But it might be said that appointed officials are not totally blameless, that their criticisms of ministerial assistants reveal a wish to remove ministerial assistants from any consideration of policy. Yet, the needs of the minister and the necessity of balancing bureaucratic power and influence require their presence. As noted, relations between the two parties can be good, usually when each side respects the other and especially when departments understand that political staff can make important contributions to the development of politically acceptable policies.

Points to Know

- Interdepartmental relations and horizontal management are becoming increasingly important in government. The major cause of this development is the advent of policy challenges that do not fit neatly within the confines of individual departments and spill over into other departments.

- Problems with interdepartmental relations include time-consuming meetings, seeking compromise instead of the best solution, confusion over accountability, and the loss of the benefits tied to vertical management.

- In their relations within the department, the minister must set priorities, avoid the temptation to manage the department, and establish a partnership with the deputy minister, while at the same time making clear that he or she has the final word.

- The intradepartmental or within-department relations of the deputy minister revolve around the three roles of a deputy. These three roles are to support and advise the minister, to manage the department, and to contribute to the corporate management of the government.

- An important relationship within a department is between appointed officials and ministerial assistants. Ministerial assistants act to complement the policy advice of appointed officials with the provision of political advice to the minister.

Review Questions

1. What are the causes for the increasing importance and prominence of interdepartmental relations?

2. Discuss how a policy initiative might benefit from horizontal management.

3. How might the problems that afflict exercises in horizontal management be addressed and eventually solved?

4. How do intradepartmental relations shape the activities of ministers and deputy ministers?

5. It is sometimes said that relations between senior public servants and ministerial assistants are naturally conflictual. Is this true, or can actions be taken to remedy the tension between these two important actors in public administration?

Notes

1. Task Force on Horizontal Relations, *Managing Horizontal Policy Issues*, December 1996, 4, accessed July 11, 2015, http://publications.gc.ca/collections/Collection/SC93-8-1996-3E.pdf.
2. Treasury Board of Canada Secretariat, *Horizontal Initiatives Database*, 2015, accessed July 11, 2015, http://www.tbs-sct.gc.ca/hidb-bdih/home-accueil-eng.aspx.
3. Ibid.
4. Herman Bakvis and Luc Juillet, *The Horizontal Challenge: Line Departments, Central Agencies, and Leadership* (Ottawa: Canada School of Public Service, 2004), 48, accessed July 11, 2015, http://publications.gc.ca/Collection/SC103-1-2004E.pdf.
5. Quoted in Donald J. Savoie, *Whatever Happened to the Music Teacher? How Government Decides and Why* (Montreal & Kingston: McGill-Queen's University Press, 2013), 111.
6. Cosmo Howard and Susan Phillips, "Moving Away from Hierarchy: Do Horizontality, Partnerships, and Distributed Governance Really Signify the End of Accountability?" in *From New Public Management to New Political Governance: Essays in Honour of Peter C. Aucoin*, eds. Herman Bakvis and Mark D. Jarvis (Montreal & Kingston: McGill-Queen's University Press, 2012), 315–316.
7. Carey Doberstein, "Metagovernance of Urban Governance Networks in Canada: In Pursuit of Legitimacy and Accountability," *Canadian Public Administration* 56(4) (December 2013): 584.
8. Quote from former deputy minister in Donald J. Savoie, *Breaking the Bargain: Public Servants, Ministers and Parliament* (Toronto: University of Toronto Press, 2003), 193.
9. Quoted in Savoie, *Whatever Happened to the Music Teacher?* 77.
10. Gordon Osbaldeston, "Dear Minister," *Policy Options* 9 (June/July 1988): 5.
11. Ibid., 10.
12. Privy Council Office, *Guidance for Deputy Ministers*. accessed August 4, 2016, http://www.pco.gc.ca/index.asp?lang=eng&page=information&sub=publications&doc=gdm-gsm/doc-eng.htm#TOC1_3.
13. Donald Savoie, *Breaking the Bargain*, 138.
14. Jacques Bourgault, "Federal Deputy Ministers: Serial Servers Looking for Influence," in *Deputy Ministers in Canada: Comparative and Jurisdictional Perspectives*, eds. Jacques Bourgault and Christopher Dunn (Toronto: University of Toronto Press, 2014), 387–388.
15. Gordon Osbaldeston, "Job Description for DMs," *Policy Options* 9 (January 1988): 34.
16. Bourgault, "Federal Deputy Ministers," 392.
17. Savoie, *Whatever Happened to the Music Teacher?* 113.
18. David Akin, "Non-Partisan to Partisan: Federal Politicians Pluck their Staff from the Civil Service," *Toronto Sun*, March 15, 2016, accessed June 21, 2016, http://www.torontosun.com/2016/03/15/non-partisan-to-partisan-federal-politicians-pluck-their-staff-from-the-civil-service.
19. Simon Doyle, "Chiefs of Staff: Meet the People Behind All of Trudeau's Ministers," *Toronto Globe and Mail*, accessed June 21, 2016, http://www.theglobeandmail.com/news/politics/globe-politics-insider/chiefs-of-staff/article28148253/.
20. Government of Canada, *Open and Accountable Government: A Guide for Ministers* (Ottawa: Her Majesty the Queen in Right of Canada, 2015), 46.
21. Ian Brodie, "In Defence of Political Staff," *Canadian Parliamentary Review* (Autumn 2012): 33.
22. Liane E. Benoit, "Ministerial Staff: The Life and Times of Parliament's Statutory Orphans," in Commission of Inquiry into the Sponsorship Program & Related Activities, *Restoring Accountability: Research Studies, Volume 1: Parliament, Ministers and Deputy Ministers* (Ottawa: Her Majesty in Right of Canada, 2006), 178.
23. Government of Canada, *Open and Accountable Government*, 47.
24. Ibid., 46.
25. Benoit, "Ministerial Staff," 185.
26. Paul Thomas, "Who Is Getting the Message: Communications at the Centre of Government," in Oliphant Commission, *Public Policy Issues and the Oliphant Commission: Independent Research Studies* (Ottawa: Public Works and Government Services, 2010), 90.

The Legislature and the Bureaucracy

11

Learning Objectives

Reading this chapter allows you to do the following:

- Identify the conventions that shape the unique relationship between the legislature and the bureaucracy
- Assess the conventions of individual ministerial responsibility and political neutrality
- Understand the impact of officers of Parliament and parliamentary committees
- Evaluate reforms for strengthening legislative scrutiny of the public service

Interactions between public servants and the legislative branch are unlike any other relationship involving appointed officials and actors in the political process. When public servants deal with senior politicians in the cabinet decision process or appointed officials in other departments, the relationship is usually a direct one. The public servant helps to draft a memorandum for the minister and cabinet members or engages in exercises of horizontal management with counterparts in other agencies. But a large part of the public servant's relationship with legislative members is conducted *indirectly* through individual ministers. Constitutional conventions require that elected officials in the executive assume responsibility for the actions of government and that appointed officials remain mostly out of sight. The intent of the legislative branch is to exercise a degree of control over the executive branch in order to make the latter accountable, so legislators have an interest in knowing about the efforts of public servants. But if members of the House of Commons wish to better understand policy developments in a department or get to the bottom of an apparent mistake in the administration of a program, they are unable to interact with officials literally responsible for the action. Rather, they must go to the minister in charge of the department.

Members of the legislature are not always satisfied with this arrangement and have worked to assemble other more direct relations with appointed officials. Though always acting on behalf of the minister, public servants may sometimes be called to appear before parliamentary committees. There have also emerged a number of officers of Parliament who report to members of the House of Commons on the administrative operations of government and seek to help individual constituents deal with the frustrations of bureaucratic practices. But even with these relations, the most important way the legislature interacts and attempts to shape the actions of public servants is to do so indirectly through their questioning and investigation of the responsible ministers.

The main concern of this chapter is to examine the doctrine of individual ministerial responsibility. This is the convention that structures the indirect relations between legislators and public servants. The chapter defines the convention and assesses its ability to provide for government that is both answerable and accountable to the people and their representatives. As we shall see, Parliament falls short of achieving full accountability and indeed it is argued by some that the best the legislature can do is to give scrutiny to the activities of the executive. The chapter also looks at how a series of offices assist Parliament in dealing with the public service in relation to such matters as information, privacy, and the finances of the nation. Lastly, the chapter considers reform proposals for making the convention of individual ministerial responsibility work better.

Ministerial Responsibility and Political Neutrality

The conventions of collective and individual ministerial responsibility are separate but interrelated unwritten rules of behaviour in the operation of parliamentary government. **Collective ministerial responsibility**, in its application to the government as a whole, prescribes that the prime minister and the cabinet must resign or ask the governor general for dissolution of Parliament if the House of Commons expresses an absence of confidence in the government. In its application to individual ministers, collective responsibility prescribes that a minister must support government decisions in public or at least suppress any public criticism of them. If ministers find a particular decision unacceptable, they must either stifle their objections or submit their resignation. A few years ago, in 2014, the federal finance minister resigned seemingly because of differences with the prime minister and cabinet over proposed tax policies.

This chapter centres on individual rather than collective responsibility. In the academic literature, several meanings and implications are given to **individual ministerial responsibility**, but it can be said that the doctrine stipulates that the "minister is responsible for everything done in the department."[1] Two components flow from this pithy formulation of this important constitutional convention (see Box 11.1). The first is that the minister is accountable to Parliament for all the administrative errors of his or her departmental subordinates, in the sense that he or she must resign in the event of a serious error by these subordinates. This component of ministerial responsibility is often described as a myth, but it will be shown that this criticism follows from a misunderstanding of the operation of individual ministerial responsibility. The second component of the convention is that the minister is answerable to Parliament in that he or she must explain and defend the actions of his or her department before Parliament. The importance of this component is, unfortunately, sometimes ignored or minimized in considerations of ministerial responsibility in Canada; at the same time there is admittedly cause for some concern about its workability.

collective ministerial responsibility The responsibility of ministers as a group (i.e., as members of the cabinet) for the policies and management of the government as a whole.

individual ministerial responsibility The responsibility of the minister, as the political head of the department, to answer to the legislature and through the legislature to the public both for his or her personal acts and for those of departmental subordinates.

BOX 11.1

What Is a Constitutional Convention?

A constitutional convention is an unwritten rule of a constitution. The intent of these rules is either to fill gaps in the written constitution or to effectively amend the written rules. Unlike the written constitution, the conventions are not enforceable by the courts, but they are typically followed because of their importance to governing. The convention of individual ministerial responsibility is an instance of filling in the gaps.

Though separate from the doctrine of individual ministerial responsibility, the convention of political neutrality deserves attention because it also shapes relations between the legislature and the public service. Political neutrality implies a number of elements, which were discussed in detail in Chapter 2. But it is sufficient to observe that the convention (and public service value) can—as with the doctrine of individual ministerial responsibility—be reduced to two propositions. One is that all activities of public servants are carried out "in the name of the minister" and that appointed officials are for all intents and purposes invisible in the public sphere. Recent reforms in Canada have weakened the impact of this proposition, but it still remains operational. The second proposition is that public servants neither "promote" nor "defend" the policies and decisions of government. Their job begins and ends with the supply of facts and information; public servants "should not act or be seen to act as the 'agents' of Ministers by publicly defending their Minister."[2] Also, public servants ought to refrain from engaging in any overt political activity that may detract from their ability to serve the minister. This second proposition, like the first one, has experienced some weakening in recent years; but it, too, remains effective. This diminishing of both propositions will be explored later in the chapter.

The Resignation of Ministers

The first component of ministerial responsibility requires that a minister resign if a serious administrative error committed by her or his department is exposed. Despite frequent calls by opposition parties for ministerial resignations on the grounds of actual or alleged departmental mismanagement, ministers do not resign because of administrative bungling in their department. It is now almost universally accepted that it is unreasonable to hold ministers personally responsible for the administrative failings of their subordinates. Ministers cannot hope to have personal knowledge of more than a small percentage of the administrative actions taken by their officials. A report of a parliamentary committee makes the point, saying that a minister in the past might have had "intimate knowledge of the daily workings of his or her department" but this "is no longer so under contemporary circumstances."[3] It might even be said that at no time was it realistic, as demonstrated in the fact that not a single federal minister has resigned because of administrative misdeeds. Moreover, it is not clear whether it would ever be in the public interest for ministers of government to become too concerned with departmental operations, for they have more important matters to address. A more sensible and acceptable approach to this first component of individual ministerial responsibility is articulated in a government document written for federal ministers:

> Ministerial accountability to Parliament does not mean that a Minister is presumed to have knowledge of every matter that occurs within his or her department or portfolio, nor that the Minister is necessarily required to accept blame for every matter. It does require that the Minister attend to all matters in Parliament that concern any organizations for which he or she is responsible, including responding to questions. It further requires that the Minister take appropriate corrective action to address any problems that may have arisen, consistent with the Minister's role with respect to the organization in question.[4]*

Authorities on the doctrine of individual ministerial responsibility agree with this type of interpretation, saying that in cases of "administrative shortcomings" the minister "is expected to take corrective action and is personally responsible for that action."[5] The corrective action inevitably involves an internal investigation of the matter and an attempt to make changes that limit the chances of the mistake occurring again. Corrective action may also involve disciplinary action of one kind or another against one or more appointed officials.

This interpretation of the first component of individual ministerial responsibility falls well short of claiming there is no obligation for ministers to resign or to accept personal responsibility under any circumstances. Cases do arise in which personal culpability of

---

* Government of Canada, *Accountable Government: A Guide for Ministers*, 2011, p. 3. Ottawa: Her Majesty in Right of Canada, 2011.

a minister is evident—for example, the personal conduct of the minister violates societal norms—or where the magnitude of the error causes the government considerable embarrassment. A failed policy initiative intimately connected to the minister may also offer grounds for resignation. But even if the minister accepts full responsibility in such situations, the practical effects on his or her career depend largely on personal, partisan, and situational factors. Parliament itself has no authority to unseat the minister; only the head of the government has that power. However, if the minister under attack is an unpopular member of cabinet, if the electorate is unusually enraged, or if the government is in a minority position in Parliament, the prime minister might be tempted to seek or accept the minister's resignation. In the past ten years, a dozen ministers have left the federal cabinet, none of which reflected administrative problems within their department. Four of them resigned because of a genuine wish to leave public life, another two because of disagreements with government policies, and the remaining number because of personal errors or problems. With respect to this last group of resignations, one minister left cabinet after it was revealed that he had left sensitive government documents at his former girlfriend's house, another resignation followed from a minister's questionable expense claims, and still another resigned because of allegations relating to dealings with criminal elements (see Box 11.2). Two other ministers left cabinet because of personal missteps, one for violating campaign spending rules and the other for trying to influence a court; and yet another minister resigned because of an addiction problem.

BOX 11.2	**Resignation of Bev Oda**

What does it take for a government minister to resign? How about travel expenses over a three-day stay that included a hotel room at $665 per night, room-service charges of $1,995, and a car and driver costing $1,000 per day? Remarkably, the room service bill included $16 for a single glass of orange juice. Bev Oda, the Minister of International Cooperation, generated these expenses on a trip to London, England. But this episode only capped a long list of missteps that involved charging excessive travel expenses, misleading the House of Commons, and allegedly engaging in a "reign of terror" within her department. The prime minister defended his minister until the London trip, but the symbolism of the expensive orange juice was too much. Bev Oda had to go.

Source: Meagan Fitzpatrick, "Bev Oda apologizes for swanky hotel stay," CBC News, April 24, 2012 <cbc.ca/news/politics/bev-oda-apologizes-for-swanky-hotel-stay-1.1169374>; Joanna Smith and Allan Woods, "Bev Oda resigns as Conservative MP for Durham," *Toronto Star*, July 3, 2012 <http://www.thestar.com/news/canada/2012/07/03/bev_oda_resigns_as_conservative_mp_for_durham.html>.

These resignations show clearly that ministers do not resign to atone for either serious mismanagement by their officials or personal administrative or policy mistakes. Thus, the demand for ministerial resignations on the grounds of misadministration may appear to be a feeble weapon in the parliamentary arsenal of opposition parties. Yet this component of ministerial responsibility has important consequences for both ministers and public servants. At a minimum, parliamentary and public calls for a minister's resignation attract public attention and put at risk ministerial careers; they may also harm public servants tied to the ministers in question. Moreover, calls for a minister's resignation preserve the commitment to having a single entity formally responsible for the operations of government.

The Answerability of Ministers

The second component of ministerial responsibility has until recently corresponded closely to expectations. Ministers have explained and defended their department's policies and administration before Parliament. Opposition members and, on occasion, government backbenchers have used a variety of other opportunities (e.g., motions, Opposition

Part Four / The Bureaucracy in the Political Process

days) to seek information and explanations from ministers. But an inordinate amount of parliamentary, media, and public attention centres on the daily Question Period. It is notable that ministers have almost always responded to questions in their sphere of responsibility, although they can be obliged neither to answer nor to give reasons for refusing to answer. The strongest impetus to answer to Parliament is that a minister may suffer adverse political consequences for declining to do so. The Speaker of the House of Commons has observed that he "is not in a position to compel an answer—it is public opinion which compels an answer."[6] Certainly, a minister who refuses to answer questions on an important issue, especially if he or she does not provide a reasonable explanation for his or her position, has traditionally received severe criticism from Opposition members and the media. There has, therefore, been both constitutional and political pressure on ministers to justify their department's actions to Parliament.

However, in the past few years a number of developments affecting the House of Commons suggest a decline in ministerial answerability. Question Period has become less civil and more politicized, making it difficult to receive clear answers from the responsible minister. Efforts on the part of government to limit the usefulness of Question Period led to greater use of the mechanism of written questions to the minister, but this practice has been discouraged with the government's publication of the costs for responses to the questions.[7] House of Commons committees have also become less effective in investigating government actions because of excessive politicization, and even government backbenchers now find it difficult to ask serious questions of their own political party. Perhaps most threatening to the answerability of ministers is that some governments in Canada increasingly believe their own authority is derived directly from the people and that listening to parliamentary members is not required.

These developments and others do indeed point towards a possible weakening of an important component of ministerial responsibility. But the evidence also reveals that ministers are still obliged to answer queries about their departments and that there is public pressure to respond appropriately. "[T]he government will pay a political price if it routinely attempts to evade important questions or to obfuscate when asked to defend its actions," admits a former Conservative MP who left his party because of disagreements

Graham Harrop/CartoonStock.com

with the party's practices.[8] Governments still struggle, and in some cases lose electoral support if the legislature is able to uncover administrative wrongdoings.

Political Neutrality

The convention of political neutrality entails an attempt to make certain that public servants remain both anonymous and politically neutral in their actions. This convention consists of six supporting ideas or prescriptions (see "Political Neutrality" in Chapter 2). Some of these prescriptions, such as maintaining a strict separation between policy and administration or prohibiting public servants from engaging in some political activities, are clearly unrealistic, or their violation is not fatal to the operation of responsible government. But any serious challenge to two of the prescriptions—maintaining anonymity and resisting any public comment on the attractiveness of government initiatives—puts at risk the doctrine of individual ministerial responsibility. For some, such a challenge is taking place. In the past few decades, events have chipped away the anonymity of public servants. One has been the refusal of some ministers to accept responsibility for a certain action; instead, the ministers name the public servant responsible or place blame on the departmental bureaucracy as a whole. The other developments, though less sensational, may be even more important because they involve institutional changes and not the wishes of a few ministers to escape responsibility:

- Public servants now routinely appear before legislative committees to provide factual answers to queries of elected representatives. Though every effort is made to ensure that the public servants do not use these appearances to defend or justify the actions of the minister, the fact is that public servants are becoming well known to people within the legislative branch.
- Access to information legislation allows any interested party an opportunity to gain access to documents that may reveal the role of administrative officials. It is possible now to follow the decision-making trail associated with a decision whose controversial nature may concern those outside the department.
- There exist now a number of officers of Parliament whose task is to help elected representatives to examine the actions of public servants. More on this topic is provided in the next pages.
- The media have become much more pervasive and aggressive in their efforts to tell their readers and listeners about the activities of government. As a result, public servants find themselves increasingly a part of the media's stories. Also, the desire of government to consult more with interest groups and the public has brought public servants more into personal contact with a greater and greater number of people.[9]

The declining anonymity of public servants can have serious implications for the doctrine of individual ministerial responsibility. Arguably the most important achievement of ministerial responsibility is that it clearly establishes a locus of responsibility for any wrongdoings within a department. If a problem emerges, members of legislature know where to go for answers. There is no need to go looking for the actual culprit; an MP only has to determine the identity of the responsible minister. But the loss of anonymity blurs this locus of responsibility, and tempts some to pursue civil servants in the hope of locating the individual truly responsible for some disturbing development. With this blurring comes the fear that determining responsibility amounts to trying to find a needle in a haystack.

Another challenge related to political neutrality is the belief that senior public servants are being used "to advance the government's agenda."[10] It has always been understood that public servants provide advice on achieving government goals; but some now say now they are expected "to enthusiastically and aggressively support government policy and actions."[11] With the lessened degree of anonymity, public servants now find themselves more publicly exposed; and in this new setting, their political superiors expect them to champion the initiatives of government. The obvious implication here is the loss of non-partisanship, a quality which supported the public image of a professional and competent public service. There is evidence to support this particular claim, but some scholars are not convinced. They believe that select public servants have always advocated proposals of government without great harm to the doctrine of individual ministerial responsibility; the lack of harm stems from the fact that the phenomenon of partisan public servants has never been and still is not far-reaching.[12]

Legislative Control and Influence

The convention of individual ministerial responsibility is the major means by which elected representatives in the legislative branch hold appointed officials accountable. When an administrative error occurs, the minister in theory accepts responsibility and promises to take remedial actions. But these actions are handled internally, and the public rarely finds out what penalties, if any, are imposed. And if a minister refuses to accept responsibility, the doctrine of political neutrality makes it difficult to affix the blame on the public servant actually responsible. Clearly, there is a need for further mechanisms by which the legislature can control appointed officials and their actions without undermining their neutrality.

Officers of Parliament

A second way of ensuring responsibility in government involves officers of Parliament who report directly or indirectly to Parliament. These agents serve two related purposes. One is "to assist [Parliament] with the task of holding ministers and public servants accountable."[13] It is difficult for Parliament by itself to ensure responsible action in the executive and the bureaucracy, so agencies have been set up "to supplement the principles of ministerial responsibility as a basis for accountability."[14] The second purpose of these agencies is to handle concerns and complaints of citizens about the actions of government. In these two capacities the agencies act as watchdogs, helping members of the legislature to ensure that officials in the executive are acting responsibly and assisting members of the public with their own particular concerns or needs.

At the federal level there exists no authoritative statement on which government bodies qualify as officers of Parliament. However, most agree that any list of such agents would include the following:

- *The Office of the Auditor General (OAG)* is one of the watchdog agencies that report directly to Parliament rather than through a minister. This status symbolizes the importance of the OAG, easily the most prominent and probably the most influential of all the officers of Parliament. The auditor general, the lead official in the office, reports annually to Parliament on whether departments have kept proper financial records and whether public funds have been spent as appropriated by Parliament. The auditor general also carries out audits of select government programs whose regard for economy and efficiency are in question and that have failed to put in place measures to determine their effectiveness. This office, which has seen its influence increase, is discussed more fully in Chapter 18, which is concerned with government financial estimates and the management of spending.
- *The Office of the Information Commissioner (OIC)*, set up in 1983, administers the *Access to Information Act* by investigating complaints about denial of public access to government information. The office has no authority to force government to provide access; instead, it acts as a mediator between the complainant and government. However, the Information Commissioner may ask for a review of a complaint by the Federal Court of Canada if he or she believes that requests for information have been denied. This office, too, has become more prominent.

- *The Office of the Privacy Commissioner*, also established in 1983, implements the *Privacy Act* and looks into complaints from individuals who believe that their privacy rights have not been properly respected. This involves either violation of privacy rights or a failure to recognize a person's right of access to her or his own personal information, which may be under the control of private companies or the federal government. Reporting directly to Parliament, the Privacy Commissioner seeks to resolve complaints through mediation and conciliation but has the authority to force people to give evidence in an attempt to resolve cases.
- *The Office of the Commissioner of Official Languages*, created in 1970, administers the *Official Languages Act* by, among other things, protecting the right of any citizen to deal with and be a recipient of services from the federal government in either French or English and to ensure the right of any person at the federal level to work in either of the two official languages. As part of his or her duty, the Commissioner of Official Languages addresses any complaints in relation to the *Official Languages Act* and may appeal to the Federal Court of Canada for the purpose of seeking an appropriate resolution of a matter.
- *Elections Canada* is an independent body reporting directly to Parliament and whose responsibilities include ensuring compliance with federal electoral legislation, making Canadians aware of elections in Canada, and reviewing the amount of spending by candidates, parties, and others during elections. The Chief Electoral Officer heads the agency.
- *The Office of the Ethics Commissioner*, set up in 2004, has the task of administering the *Conflict of Interest Code* for members of the House of Commons and the *Conflict of Interest and Post-employment Code for Public Office Holders*. The first refers to all members of the House of Commons when they are carrying their parliamentary duties, and the second refers to elected, and some appointed, officials in the executive branch (ministers, ministers of state, parliamentary secretaries, ministerial staff, and others).
- *Office of the Public Sector Integrity Commissioner* receives and looks into complaints made by public servants relating to various forms of mismanagement or wrongdoing in the public service. Mismanagement includes improper use of public funds, violation of the code of conduct, contravention of legislation, and serious mismanagement. This office also deals with claims of reprisals against public servants who have made complaints about mismanagement in the public service.
- *The Office of the Parliamentary Budget Officer (PBO)* reports indirectly to the House of Commons and Senate through the Library of Parliament on matters relating to the financial situation of the country, estimates of government revenues and spending revenues, and costs of government initiatives presented to Parliament for its approval. Creation of the budget office was part of a group of actions taken by the Harper government to strengthen democracy in Canada, the rationale being that the PBO helps to keep the government responsive to the will of the people by showing what government is doing and what it could be doing even better.
- *The Office of the Commissioner of Lobbying* is responsible for the upkeep of the Registry of Lobbyists, which provides the public with information on lobbyists at the federal level. The office also seeks to educate the public on legislation regulating lobbyists and engages in investigations pertaining to compliance with the aforementioned legislation and the *Lobbyists' Code of Conduct*.

All of these agencies provide new sources of information concerning the activities of the executive branch. These officers of Parliament thus act to complement the efforts of Parliament to make government more accountable. But it is also possible to see them in a negative light. They can put at risk the political neutrality of public servants and no country with a British government system spends as much as Canada on officers of Parliament. There are also other concerns, all of which act to support the belief that there is no consensus on the value of officers of Parliament (see Box 11.3).

Do Officers of Parliament Improve Government?

BOX
11.3

Robert Shepherd, a political scientist at Carleton University, believes officers of Parliament do improve government. They offer specialized expertise and carry out impartial evaluations. Most important, says Shepherd, they raise public awareness of significant issues. Christopher Stoney, also a professor at Carleton, disagrees. The agents are too narrowly oriented and fail to see the bigger picture, he believes.

They are also often very critical in their analysis, which serves to weaken public trust in government. And, finally, officers are too intent on raising their own profile and forget that they act through Parliament, not on their own.

Source: Roberto Leone and Frank Ohemeng, eds., *Approaching Public Administration: Core Debates and Emerging Issues* (Toronto: Emond Montgomery Publications, 2010), ch. 7.

House of Commons Committees

House of Commons committees are another means used to exercise parliamentary control over the public service. The functions of these committees may be divided into policy development (primarily involving evaluation of the purpose and content of proposed legislation), review of existing policies, and scrutiny of departmental administration (especially through examination of the estimates). In practice, these functions often overlap, and committee members put varying emphasis on each function.

The House of Commons has three basic types of committees: standing (or permanent) committees, special committees, and legislative committees (and subcommittees may also emerge). Most of the standing committees (e.g., Agriculture and Agri-Food, Canadian Heritage, Environment and Sustainable Development) focus on a substantive sphere of government policy. Each committee covers one or more departments and agencies; in some cases the list of organizations can appear almost overwhelming. For example, the Committee on Agriculture and Agri-Food deals with the Department of Agriculture, the Canadian Grain Commission, the Canadian Food Inspection Agency, the Canadian Dairy Commission, the Farm Credit Corporation, the Farm Products Council, and the Pest Management Regulatory Agency. There are at present 24 standing committees in all, but the number can change from time to time. There are also a few joint standing committees of the Senate and the House of Commons (at present, the Joint Committee on Scrutiny of Regulations and the Joint Committee on the Library of Parliament).

Special committees represent a second type of committee, and they are set up as required to examine such specific issues as acid rain, child care, or same-sex marriage; once the special committee presents its final report, it ceases to exist.

Legislative committees are established to examine specific government bills. One advantage of legislative committees has been that the expertise, experience, and interests of the legislators can be matched to the subject matter of the legislation.

The Public Accounts Committee; the Access to Information, Privacy and Ethics Committee; the Government Operations and Estimates Committee; and the Standing Joint Committee on Scrutiny of Regulations all deserve special attention. They enjoy a greater measure of independence from cabinet control because, unlike other committees, they are chaired by a member of the Opposition. The Public Accounts Committee examines both the public accounts (i.e., the government's year-end financial statements) and the auditor general's report as a basis for making recommendations to the House of Commons. With the assistance of the auditor general, the committee has uncovered, investigated, and reported on several scandals involving the expenditure of public funds, and it has recommended corrective action in many other instances in which public money has been improperly spent. The primary function of the Standing Joint Committee on the Scrutiny of Regulations is to scrutinize the use of delegated legislative authority by cabinet, ministers, and public servants. The committee reviews statutory instruments—that is, the rules, regulations, and orders made by the executive under delegated legislative authority. The other two committees, which are relatively new, deal with issues relating to information and ethics (Access to Information, Privacy and Ethics) and the examination of central agencies and the process of financial management (Government Operations and Estimates).

Figure 11.1 shows the floor plan of a typical committee room. The setup resembles the House of Commons in some respects, with government members on one side of the room and Opposition members on the other (with the chair at the head of the table). Committees often invite individuals (experts, representatives of organizations, public servants) to appear in order to give the committees a better insight into some matter, so provision is made for witnesses. Journalists and members of the general public may attend committee meetings, and staff resources are available for committee members. Usually, committees have ten members, picked from representatives of the major parties sitting in the House of Commons.

At first, it might be concluded from Figure 11.1 that the parliamentary committee system is equipped to monitor the activities of the executive branch and the public service. There are opposition members to challenge the government, witnesses to help with finding the answers, journalists to report on proceedings, and staff to provide the necessary background material. The formal powers of the committees—committees are authorized to undertake inquiries, assess any aspect of a department's functioning, summon reluctant witnesses, and require that documents be made available—also give an impression of substantial influence. The reality, however, is otherwise.

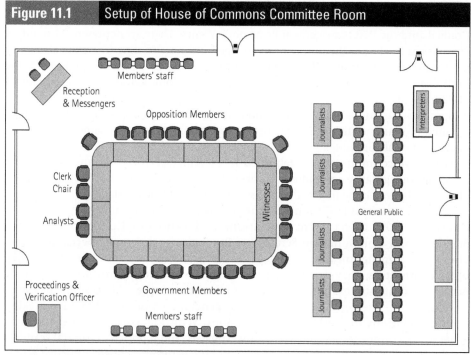

Figure 11.1 Setup of House of Commons Committee Room

© The House of Commons, Canada

In the past, public servants have expressed the belief that parliamentary committees represent only a minor constraint on efforts to develop policy.[15] The presence and power of party discipline in committee increases the chances that the impact of legislative committees on the public service will be only minimal. In recent years, governments have promised to strengthen committees and sometimes the promises have been kept, in whole or in part. One change allowed committee members to vote for committee chairs without any direction from the prime minister and his or her advisors; such a change provided for the possibility that the hold of party discipline on committees would weaken. But the reversal of some of the changes that were intended to strengthen committees and the introduction of new ways to impose the will of senior political leaders has limited the impact of parliamentary committees[16] (see Box 11.4).

Committees of the Senate

BOX
11.4

Reference to parliamentary committees typically means committees of the House of Commons. But the other house of Parliament, the Senate, also has committees. The fact that Senate members are unelected largely explains the lack of attention paid to Senate committees (and scandals over expenses of Senators have brought the wrong kind of attention to the Senate). This slighting is unfortunate because Senate committees are quite effective in scrutinizing government operations and programs—and they are especially effective in undertaking full-scale investigations of policy issues. The fact that Senate members often bring relevant expertise and experience to the Senate is one reason for the effectiveness of Sentate committees. Another is the non-partisan approach to committee responsibilities, and still another reason is the dearth of media attention and consequent absence of members playing to the cameras. Members of the Senate typically get down to business.

Source: Paul Thomas, "Parliament and the Public Service," in *Handbook of Canadian Public Administration*, 2nd ed., ed. Christopher Dunn (Toronto: Oxford University Press, 2010).

Reform

A number of proposals have been put forward over the years to change relations between the legislature and the public service. One set of changes has just been mentioned: adjustments to the operation of legislative committees. But it has been the doctrine of ministerial responsibility and a rethinking of it that has received the most attention. And this rethinking has centred on making senior public servants, specifically the deputy minister, more directly responsible for the administration of public programs and services.

Already, the deputy minister is assigned statutory responsibilities relating to financial management, personnel, and use of the two official languages; but these are seen as exceptions to the doctrine that the minister, and only the minister, is truly responsible and accountable for all department activities. Serious thinking on the role of the deputy minister began over 30 years ago, in 1979, when the Royal Commission on Financial Management and Accountability noted that "deputy heads are not regularly held accountable in a systematic or coherent way for program management and departmental administration." The Commission recommended that deputy ministers "be liable to be held to account directly for their assigned and delegated responsibilities before the parliamentary committee most directly concerned with administrative performance, the Public Accounts Committee."[17] In 1985, a special House of Commons committee looking into parliamentary reform observed that the operation

Chapter 11 / The Legislature and the Bureaucracy

of individual ministerial responsibility "undermines the potential for genuine account-ability on the part of the person that ought to be accountable—the senior officer of the department."[18]

The thinking and recommendations of these two bodies went unheeded, but interest in the issue continued. In 2002, former prime minister Jean Chrétien promised that "new measures [would] be introduced to provide for more explicit accounting by deputies for the affairs of their department" and he also mentioned in this context the British tradition of designating their senior officials (equivalent to deputies) as "accounting officers" responsible for answering directly to Parliament "for the finan-cial administration of departmental funds voted by Parliament."[19] This promise went unfulfilled, but a report of the House of Commons Standing Committee on Public Accounts on a case of serious mismanagement—the infamous Sponsorship Program—carried on with the idea of accounting officers and recommended their adoption. With this change, deputy ministers could be questioned more directly by Parliament, with the understanding that they would be held personally responsible for the "finan-cial accounts of their departments and held to account for the performance of their duties before the Public Accounts Committee."[20] The committee made it clear that such a proposal would be consistent with the convention of ministerial responsibility, because the minister would have the opportunity to overrule a deputy in instances when the two disagreed on a course of action relating to the administration of the department. The commission of inquiry set up to examine the Sponsorship Program came to similar conclusions as the Public Accounts Committee about the operation of the doctrine of ministerial responsibility.

In 2006, the newly elected Conservative government, headed by Stephen Harper, passed legislation incorporating the new position of accounting officer into the responsibilities of the deputy minister. With this act, it appears at first glance that the doctrine of individual ministerial responsibility has now been substan-tially changed. Deputy ministers in their guise as accounting officers are personally responsible and accountable for a series of administrative duties. According to a respected authority on ministerial responsibility, this means that the deputies as accounting officers "appear before parliamentary committees to explain and defend their use of power they hold in their own right" and "do not appear to support the accountability of their ministers."[21] One implication of this alleged change is that appointed officials can be blamed for administrative wrongdoings. Also, public servants and legislative members interact *directly*. But for the government little has changed with the appearance of accounting officers. It says that legislation autho-rizing the new position merely makes clear the traditional practice of senior officials going before parliamentary committees to provide information and explanation in support of ministerial accountability.[22]

Supporters of accounting officials with personal responsibility and accountability are disappointed with the government's interpretation. They feel that an important opportunity for establishing more responsible government has been missed. But there are problems with accounting officers representing a major change in the doctrine of ministerial responsibility. Deputy ministers, like ministers, can hardly be expected to know all the details of administration in their departments. The change also assumes that it is easy to make clear distinctions between administrative and policy matters (the deputy attends to the former, the politician to the latter) yet this kind of separa-tion is difficult to establish. And then there is the concern, already mentioned, that the proposal weakens the major attraction of the convention of ministerial responsibility, which is its ability to place the locus of responsibility clearly with one individual, the minister. With a strong accounting officer, we now have two people who are responsible, an arrangement that opens up the possibility of each shifting responsibility and blame to the other. More generally, it would "weaken the accountability and the authority of ministers, and going forward would create greater confusion as to who is responsible for future errors."[23]

An Independent Public Service

The discussion of relations between appointed officials and the legislature leads to an important and controversial issue: whether the public service should be seen in some instances as an independent branch of government. The prevailing belief is that public servants have only one commitment: they serve the minister and the interests of the government in power as part of the executive branch. But developments in the past decade suggest that public servants may have a commitment that goes beyond the minister. This new commitment arises as a possibility in the acts of deputies as accounting officers, who in this role may serve to challenge government behaviour. The operation of the Sponsorship Program also proves instructive on this point. An official with the Department of Public Works and Government Services, the agency responsible for the Sponsorship Program, felt that the administration of the program amounted to an illegal activity and looked for an opportunity to report this matter to someone outside the department and the executive branch. The same wish to be able to make known a questionable activity to a body external to the executive branch led to the decision to create the Office of the Public Sector Integrity Commissioner, which provides an agency receptive to public servants wishing to report cases of administrative misconduct.

All of these developments point to the conclusion that the bureaucracy has in some circumstances an obligation that competes with its loyalty to the minister and the government in power. When the law is broken or when the actions of government put in peril people's health or safety (including that of public servants), appointed officials are obliged to act in the public interest and divulge these unwelcome events. The fact that such divulgences may harm the government is unimportant. Sossin discusses the important implication of this line of reasoning:

> The conventional view is that the civil service has no constitutional identity apart from the government it is serving at the time. ... I suggest an alternative view, one that sees the constitutional identity of the Crown as constituted by both a political executive and the civil service as *independent* and interdependent components.[24]

The quotation suggests that the interdependent nature of the relationship between the civil service and government remains intact. But added to this relationship is the notion that the bureaucracy is also independent from the political executive. For constitutional support of this claim, it might be argued that inherent in the convention of political neutrality is the contention that appointed officials in some instances must have the authority to deny proposals of governments that threaten the non-partisan quality of the public service. In Sossin's words, "it is not constitutionally permissible for public servants to discharge their loyalty to the government of the day where to do so would require public servants to take part in partisan activities."[25] An arguably more powerful constitutional convention, the rule of law, also gives support to the notion of an independent public service. The rule of law speaks to the notion that no one is above the law, and the duty of the public service is to refuse to follow government directives that break it (see What to Do?).

WHAT TO DO?

Should we take seriously the idea of an independent public service? Sossin certainly thinks so. Two constitutional conventions, political neutrality and the rule of law, provide a solid foundation for independence. But critics of the proposal argue that an independent public service would be accountable to no one. Under the present system, the public servant is accountable to a minister who in turn answers to the people's representatives in the House of Common. But a public service on its own could do what it wanted. At least that it what the critics say.

Points to Know

- The convention of individual ministerial responsibility largely shapes relations between the legislature and public servants. The convention stipulates that ministers ought to resign in the event of serious administrative error and that ministers are to explain the actions of their department.

- The convention of political neutrality complements individual ministerial responsibility by requiring that public servants remain anonymous and politically non-partisan.

- Officers of Parliament have been appointed to help Parliament ensure that ministers and administrators remain accountable to the people's legislative representatives.

- Parliamentary committees represent another means by which the legislature attempts to influence public servants and the executive.

- Reforms have been introduced to increase the capacity of the legislature to influence ministers and public servants. The most prominent change is to make deputy ministers (as accounting officers) more responsible for the administrative actions of government.

Review Questions

1. What are the strengths and weaknesses of the doctrine of individual ministerial responsibility?

2. Why is the political neutrality of public servants key to the success of individual ministerial responsibility?

3. What are the effects of officers of Parliament and parliamentary committees on the activities of the executive branch?

4. There is some disagreement over the role of accounting officers. What is the appropriate role of these officials?

5. Does Parliament succeed in making public servants accountable for their actions?

Notes

1. Donald J. Savoie, *Breaking the Bargain: Public Servants, Ministers and Parliament* (Toronto: University of Toronto Press, 2003), 3.
2. Peter Aucoin, Jennifer Smith, and Geoff Dinsdale, *Responsible Government: Clarifying Essentials, Dispelling Myths and Exploring Change* (Ottawa: Canadian Centre for Management, 2004), 37.
3. Standing Committee on Public Accounts, House of Commons, *Governance in the Public Service of Canada: Ministerial and Deputy Ministerial Accountability*, May 2005, 19, accessed August 18, 2015, http://www.parl.gc.ca/HousePublications/Publication.aspx?DocId=1812721&Language=E&Mode=1&Parl=38&Ses=1.
4. Government of Canada, *Open and Accountable Government 2015* (Ottawa: Her Majesty in Right of Canada, 2015), 3.
5. Aucoin, Smith, and Dinsdale, *Responsible Government*, 32.
6. House of Commons, *Debates*, February 8, 1978, 567.
7. Brooke Jeffrey, *Dismantling Canada: Stephen Harper's New Conservative Agenda* (Montreal & Kingston: McGill-Queen's University Press, 2015), 125–126.
8. Brent Rathgeber, *Irresponsible Government: The Decline of Parliamentary Democracy in Canada* (Toronto: Dundurn, 2014), 69.
9. Ibid., 38–39.
10. Evert Lindquist and Ken Rasmussen, "Deputy Ministers and New Political Governance: From Neutral Competence to Promiscuous Partisans to a New Balance?" in *From New Public Management to New Political Governance: Essays in Honour of Peter C. Aucoin*, eds. Herman Bakvis and Mark D. Jarvis (Montreal & Kingston: McGill-Queen's University Press, 2012), 191.
11. Peter Aucoin, quoted in Ibid., 191.
12. Ibid., 194–195.
13. Paul Thomas, "Parliament and the Public Service," in *The Handbook of Canadian Public Administration*, 2nd ed., ed. Christopher Dunn (Toronto: Oxford University Press, 2010), 119.
14. Paul G. Thomas, "The Past, Present and Future of Officers of Parliament," *Canadian Public Administration* 46 (3) (Fall 2003): 293.
15. Parliamentary Centre, *Backgrounder*, September 2004, accessed August 19, 2015, http://www.parlcent.org/en/wp-content/uploads/2011/04/articles_and_papers/MPs_and_Committees_Backgrounder_EN.pdf.
16. Peter Aucoin, Mark D. Jarvis, and Lori Turnbull, *Democratizing the Constitution: Reforming Responsible Government* (Toronto: Emond Montgomery Publications, 2011), 137–139. See also Jeffrey, *Dismantling Canada*, 126–130.
17. Quoted in Standing Committee on Public Accounts, *Governance in the Public Service of Canada*, 17.
18. Quoted in Ibid., 18.
19. Aucoin, Smith, and Dinsdale, *Responsible Government*, 41–42.
20. Committee on Public Accounts, *Governance in the Public Service of Canada*, 20.
21. Prof. Ned Franks (Professor Emeritus of Political Science, Queen's University, as an individual) at the Public Accounts Committee, March 21, 2007, accessed August 6, 2016, https://openparliament.ca/committees/public-accounts/39-1/44/prof-ned-franks-1/only/.
22. Privy Council Office, *Accounting Officers: Guidance on Roles, Responsibilities and Appearances Before Parliamentary Committees*, 2007, accessed August 19, 2015, http://www.pco-bcp.gc.ca/docs/information/publications/ao-adc/2007/ao-adc-eng.pdf/.
23. Jonathan Malloy and Scott Millar, "Why Ministerial Accountability Can Still Work," in *How Ottawa Spends: The Harper Conservatives - Climate of Change, 2007–8*, ed. G.B. Doern (Montreal and Kingston: McGill-Queen's University Press, 2007), 112.
24. Lorne Sossin, "Speaking Truth to Power? The Search for Bureaucratic Independence in Canada," *University of Toronto Law Journal* 55(1) (Winter 2005): 15–16. Emphasis added.
25. Lorne Sossin, "Bureaucratic Independence," in *Handbook of Canadian Public Administration*, ed. Dunn, 366.

The Judiciary and the Bureaucracy

12

Learning Objectives

Reading this chapter allows you to do the following:

- Identify the structure and operation of the Canadian court system
- Explain administrative law and its pertinence for government tribunals and other related administrative bodies within government
- Apply the various grounds for judicial review to administrative actions and behaviour
- Appraise the significance of the *Canadian Charter of Rights and Freedoms* for the study of public administration
- Assess the impact of the judiciary on the activities of public servants

The interactions of public servants with the political process reach beyond the legislative and executive branches. They also include relations with the third branch of government, the judiciary or court system. These relations between the bureaucracy and the courts revolve around the courts and their judges attempting to ensure that government officials function within the confines of legal rules concerning procedure, jurisdiction, and respect for individual rights and freedoms. When it appears that bureaucrats may be overstepping the line separating the legal from the illegal, the courts may be asked to intervene in order to review an allegation of administrative wrong. A citizen might, for example, appeal to the courts to look at a government action that fails to respect a procedural rule, or a corporation might seek access to the courts because of a belief that public officials acted outside their authority. A multitude of situations dealing with the administration of government programs and policies can precipitate dealings between the courts and the permanent executive. Also important in approaching this aspect of public administration is to appreciate that the courts have assumed in the past couple of decades a much larger role in the professional lives of public servants. It is not only the entities in the executive and legislative branches that catch the attention of those whose job is to administer the business of government. The judiciary, too, deserves to be respected since it now wields much more influence.

The intent of this chapter is to investigate that part of the political process that deals with public servants and the judiciary. The chapter outlines the structure of the Canadian judiciary and discusses how a body of law called administrative law has arisen to shape judicial review of bureaucratic actions. The grounds or reasons for the courts intervening in the work of public servants are also examined. It is here that we most clearly see the larger role of judges in the administration of public programs, with the greatest emphasis given to the *Canadian Charter of Rights and Freedoms*. Appointed officials undertake their duties knowing that the courts may intervene at any time.

The Canadian Judiciary

Unlike the executive and legislative branches of government, which are integrally linked, the judiciary is independent from the other two branches. The independence of judges is considered crucial to the impartial or unbiased administration of justice. Without this separation, the courts would be vulnerable to political pressures emanating from the other branches and would find themselves unable to carry out the unbiased adjudication of disputes about the law. Various measures, including tenure in office for judges, are used to guarantee that judges remain independent.

The structure of the judicial system in Canada is shown in Figure 12.1. This structure is determined by the *Constitution Act of 1867*, which provides for federal and provincial courts, but permits cases to be appealed from provincial to federal courts. Section 101 of the act authorizes the Parliament of Canada to establish a court of appeal for the entire country and for any other courts required for the "better administration of Canadian laws." This is the legal foundation for the federal courts. As for the provincial courts, s. 92 (14) grants the provinces exclusive authority over the administration of justice in the provinces, "including the Constitution, Maintenance, and Operation of Provincial Courts, both of Civil and Criminal Jurisdiction, and including procedure in Civil Matters in those Courts." But s. 91 (27) of the act confers on the federal Parliament exclusive jurisdiction over the making of criminal law, and ss. 96, 99, and 100 give the federal government power over the appointment, salaries, and removal of all judges found in the upper tier of provincial courts. Clearly, the drafters of the Constitution wished the two levels of government to act together in the administration of justice.

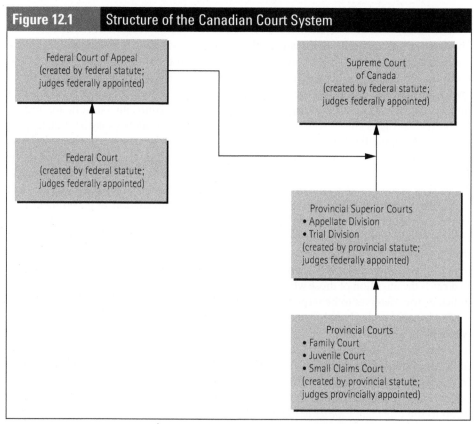

Figure 12.1 Structure of the Canadian Court System

Source: From DICKERSON/FLANAGAN. *An Introduction to Government and Politics*, 7E. © 2006 Nelson Education Ltd. Reproduced by permission. www.cengage.com/permissions

The names of the courts in the provinces vary, but the structure is basically the same for all provinces. In the upper tier of the provincial court system in each province is a superior court that, depending on the province, bears the name of Supreme Court, Superior Court, or High Court. As the figure shows, this court has both trial and appellate divisions, which consider cases arising out of federal, provincial, or constitutional laws. (In some provinces the divisions are two separate courts.) They also hear appeals from the lower provincial courts. The lower tier of the system encompasses courts usually referred to as the "provincial courts." These courts handle such matters as minor criminal acts, juvenile offences, family problems, and legal conflicts concerning small amounts of money. The provinces have the authority to appoint justices to these courts.

The major federal courts are the Federal Court, the Federal Court of Appeal, and the Supreme Court of Canada. The Supreme Court, the highest court in the land, hears appeals from the other federal courts and the superior provincial courts. It also considers questions of law referred to it by the federal cabinet when there is some doubt about the legality of a proposed legislative enactment. This expansive jurisdiction of the Supreme Court makes it a truly national court for it can hear cases arising from all types of laws operating in all regions of the country.[1]

The two other prominent federal courts are central to the study of administration and law, and figure prominently in the study and practice of administrative law. (A less prominent federal court is the Tax Court of Canada, whose jurisdiction largely concerns considering income tax appeals.) The Federal Court has jurisdiction to first hear cases involving claims made against the federal government and decisions of most federal boards, commissions, and other regulatory bodies. In other words, it is set up primarily to adjudicate disputes about how appointed officials at the federal level carry out and implement laws and regulations. The Federal Court of Appeal considers appeals from the decisions of the Federal Court and has exclusive jurisdiction to review the decisions of select federal tribunals. These two courts are unique in the sense that they are established to hear matters relating only to federal law.

Judicial Review of Administrative Action

The role of courts in relation to public administration is to review the actions and decisions of appointed officials. Judicial decisions in this area have led to a body of **administrative law**, which "deals with the legal limitations on the actions of government officials, and with the remedies which are available to anyone affected by a transgression of these limitations."[2] This definition of administrative law tells us that judicial review can lead to concrete actions that can reverse or nullify the behaviour of public officials. A court may quash the decision of a regulatory agency to deny a license to a radio station, for example, or rule against a government body responsible for the administration of pension benefits.

In earlier years, **judicial review** of administrative action and the accompanying body of administrative law have received relatively little attention from students of public administration. But interest in this area has increased substantially in the past four decades. This development was largely due to the recognition of the extensive regulatory and adjudicative powers now exercised by administrative officials. As Gall writes, "[T]here has been a proliferation of legislation at both the federal and provincial levels of government delegating authority to … tribunals composed of persons possessing expertise in particular areas to set policy and render decisions accordingly."[3] These tribunals represented, and continue to represent, the major concerns of courts when it came to administrative law. Interestingly, the Chief Justice of the Supreme Court of Canada, Beverly McLachlin, has written quite eloquently on this matter, saying that the growing prominence of tribunals and the body of administrative law signifies a

administrative law The branch of public law concerned with relations between the government and individual citizens. It deals with the legal limitations on the actions of governmental officials and on the remedies that are available to anyone affected by a transgression of these limits.

judicial review Authority of the courts to assess the legality of an action of the legislative or executive branches of government.

Chapter 12 / The Judiciary and the Bureaucracy

"revolution in governance."[4] A related stimulus for increased interest in administrative law was the creation in 1970 of the Federal Court of Canada and the court's review of administrative behaviour. The establishment of this court meant that there was now a judicial body set up specifically to deal with administrative law. A still further factor was the passage of the *Canadian Charter of Rights and Freedoms* into law in 1982, an action whose implications will be addressed more fully later in this chapter.

Judicial review of administrative action can apply to any government form that is perceived to be in violation of principles of administrative law. Appointed officials located in departments, Crown corporations, independent regulatory agencies, and any other agency are vulnerable to court action. But typically the focus of administrative law is on non-departmental structures that are given a degree of independence unavailable to most departments and that address regulatory matters. In other words, judicial review concentrates on independent regulatory agencies or what administrative law often refers to as "tribunals." The presence of this heightened degree of independence from direct ministerial control makes judicial review especially important with respect to regulatory agencies; the fact that regulatory agencies are often obliged to follow a due process of rules and procedures also makes them worthy of consideration by the courts. Included among these tribunals are those that perform centrally important and politically sensitive regulatory functions, such as the National Energy Board, as well as those that play a specialized adjudicative role bearing on individual rights, such as the Immigration and Refugee Board (see Box 12.1).

BOX 12.1

The Competition Tribunal

The Competition Tribunal is a court-like body that adjudicates disputes over competition in the marketplace. Cases that have come before the tribunal include those relating to misleading advertising, practices which restrict trading, and proposed mergers of companies. A case that has taken up a lot of the tribunal's time involves the attempt of the federal government—representing the public interest—to force the Toronto Real Estate Board to give greater access to privileged house-sales information. At present, access to information on prevailing house prices, broker commissions, and length of time houses have been on the market is limited to licensed real-estate brokers in the Toronto area, and this limitation has the effect of hindering competition among brokers and keeping agent commissions artificially high. It also makes it difficult for house buyers to do their own searching. Case proceedings started in 2011 and, finally, in the spring of 2016, the tribunal made a decision, ruling against the real estate board. But this is not the end: the board has indicated its intention to appeal the decision of the tribunal to the Federal Court.

Sources: CBC, "Competition Bureau Rules Against TREB in Dispute Over Home Sales Data, April 28, 2016, http://www.thecourt.ca/sailing-in-uncharted-waters-the-duty-to-consult-for-administrative-tribunals/.

Discretionary Powers

The importance of judicial review and other means of control over administrative action emerge largely from the exercise of discretionary powers by public officials. Discretionary powers "are those which involve an element of judgment of choice by persons exercising them and comprise all government functions from fact finding to setting standards."[5] Public servants exercise a striking number and variety of discretionary powers under delegated legislative authority. Most of these powers are delegated to cabinet, but they are also conferred on ministers and individual officials and on various departments and tribunals. With the prominence of discretionary powers comes the greater possibility of actions that contravene laws of administration. A regulatory agency might make a decision that violates rules of procedural fairness, or it might act without the necessary legislative authority. Yet there are good reasons for discretion. A minister could hardly find time to decide upon every application for a license or to ensure that environmental standards are being properly observed. The desire to put more decision-making authority in the hands of experts also explains the acceptance of giving officials choice in the administration of government affairs; elected officials understand that the complexities of government require that knowledgeable appointed officials be given the opportunity to grapple with the challenges of governance. The same desire for discretion also reflects the need to shape the actions of government to serve the differing demands of individual citizens.

Classification of Function

A central issue with respect to judicial review of administrative discretion has traditionally been the classification of the function being performed by the tribunal or other type of government organization. The functions are "judicial," "quasi-judicial," and "administrative." The nature of the function being exercised is important in deciding whether and on what grounds the courts will grant relief. Though there is a distinction between judicial and quasi-judicial—the latter involves some discretion and the former none—historically the courts have used the terms interchangeably, because the rules of natural justice apply to both and because each directly affects the rights of a person. The more important distinction is between the administrative and the quasi-judicial or judicial functions. If the function affects individual rights and is based on law, it is considered quasi-judicial or judicial; if the function is without effect on rights and emerges out of a policy decision, it is thought to be administrative in nature.

Until recently, the courts usually reviewed the exercise of a judicial or quasi-judicial function, but not of an administrative function. This practice placed restrictions on the application of administrative law. However, this distinction has become significantly less important. The courts now see themselves as capable of considering all three functions. This development might seem to mean at first glance that the reach of administrative law extends to all actions of government, in light of the fact that all government decision making includes an element of administration. However, this perception exaggerates the implication of applying administrative law to administrative functions. Policy and legislative decisions whose purpose carries right across the country or province and that are without application to individual persons, groups, or corporate entities are usually considered beyond the reach of administrative law and the courts. Thus, administrative law and its grounds for judicial review could not be used against government decision making that led to new federal–provincial fiscal arrangements or international trade agreements. Alternatively, a decision to deny a radio licence or refuse compensation for an alleged workplace injury would be fair game for court action.

Grounds for Review

A key aspect of the role of the courts in public administration is the set of reasons or grounds for pursuing judicial review of the actions of appointed officials. Statutes or written laws may provide citizens with an opportunity to ask courts to consider their concerns. In the absence of such legislation, a person may rely upon **common law** or judge-made grounds for challenging administrative action (see Box 12.2). The advent of the *Canadian Charter of Rights and Freedoms*, which is part of the written *Constitution of Canada*, has supplied a further basis for gaining access to the courts. This basis is the violation of a right or fundamental freedom protected by the Charter. Accordingly, then,

common law Law derived from custom and judicial precedent rather than statutes.

Chapter 12 / The Judiciary and the Bureaucracy

outside of ordinary statutory law, there are four grounds that can be used to review the legality of an administrative action:

1. breach of rules of natural justice;
2. acting outside the jurisdiction conferred by the law by exceeding its powers, abusing its powers, or committing errors of procedure;
3. making errors of law; and
4. violating provisions contained in the *Canadian Charter of Rights and Freedoms*.

BOX 12.2

The Common Law

The term "common law" refers to legal rules developed over the centuries by judges in the area that became England in order to resolve disputes and issues that came to their courts. Judges denied creating these rules and asserted that they were largely applying traditions and customs common to the citizenry. This type of law formed the basis of the law in England and its colonies for a long period of time and it still has effect. However, much of the common law has been translated into statutory or written law, which is the product of elected officials. Also, the introduction of new legal rules is largely reliant on the passage of statutes. The preference in modern times is for written law expressed in statutes and put in place by governments responsible to the citizenry. However, one aspect of the common law remains quite active—judicial interpretation of written laws precipitated by disagreement over the meaning of those laws. This kind of common law is often called "case law."

Source: Richard A. Yates, Ruth Whidden Yates, and Penny Bain, *Introduction to Law in Canada*, 2nd ed. (Scarborough: Prentice Hall, 2000), 22–23.

Natural Justice

The two fundamental principles of natural justice are, as expressed in Latin, *Audi alteram partem* (Hear the other side) and *Nemo judex in sua causa debet esse* (No one should be a judge in his or her own cause). The *audi alteram partem* principle encompasses the notions that a party whose rights might be affected should, among other things, have the following:

- adequate notice of the allegations against him or her and of the tribunal's intention to make a decision, and knowledge of the case to be made against him or her;
- the right to be heard, specifically to present proofs and arguments;
- the right to cross-examine witnesses and sometimes the right to legal representation; and
- the right to an adjournment for a reasonable period of time to allow for preparation of his or her case.

In *Canada v. Mavi*, the governments of Ontario and Canada sought reimbursement for social assistance payments made to recent immigrants who were the responsibility of private sponsors.[6] The sponsors refused to pay partly on the grounds that the two governments had failed to respect various components of procedural fairness in seeking reimbursement (with the most important one being no opportunity to make an argument for a delay in reimbursement). The Supreme Court of Canada ruled that procedural fairness was indeed a pertinent issue but that the relevant components had been sufficiently observed. The case reveals that natural justice and its insistence on *Audi alteram partem* remain important.

A case with a similar issue, *Liquor Control Board of Ontario v. Vin de Garde Wine Club*, involved a government agency—and not a private individual—challenging the actions of an administrative tribunal.[7] The Liquor Control Board of Ontario contested a decision of the Information and Privacy Commissioner of Ontario (IPC) that forbade the LCBO from collecting personal information from a wine club for which it had filled an order (and required the LCBO to destroy any information it had already collected); the Commissioner had ruled that that Crown corporation failed to make a convincing case for securing the private information. The LCBO argued that it had not been given a chance to respond to the complaint of the wine club and that the commissioner had proceeded without giving prior notice. The Superior Court of Justice (Divisional Court) found that there was indeed a violation of procedural fairness, saying in part that such a finding was "supported by case law on what constitutes adequate notice in an adjudicative administrative proceeding".[8] The court ordered that the IPC to consider the case again in light of the court's decision.

According to the *nemo judex in sua causa* principle, all forms of bias should be excluded from the proceedings and decisions of tribunals. The courts may intervene if there is evident "reasonable apprehension" of bias; this may arise as kinship, friendship, or business relations with a party to the proceedings, from hearing appeals from one's own decisions, or from manifestations of undue hostility toward one of the parties. In the leading case on bias, parties expressed concern that the chair of the National Energy Board, a government tribunal, might be unable to act in a disinterested fashion during hearings that included a consortium with which the chair had been formerly involved.[9] In a split decision, the Supreme Court of Canada found against the National Energy Board; but, interestingly, it was a dissenting judge who articulated the "reasonable apprehension" test that would guide the courts when dealing with bias. The test itself asks what an informed person would decide after having considered thoroughly the claim of bias.

A lively case dealing with bias involved former Prime Minister Jean Chrétien, who sought to have quashed the findings of a one-person commission that blamed Mr. Chrétien (and his former chief of staff) for the failings of the Sponsorship Program. The commissioner had stated, during inquiry proceedings, that the program had been "run in a catastrophically bad way"; he also described evidence relating to the former prime minister as "the juicy stuff."[10] Lawyers representing Mr. Chrétien believed that these comments and others indicated that the commissioner was biased against their client and could not objectively assess the facts. The Federal Court agreed and ordered that sections of the commission's final report on the Sponsorship Program dealing with the prime minister and his chief of staff be stricken from the record.

Ultra Vires

The Latin phrase *ultra vires*, which means "beyond the power," represents a second ground for legal challenges of administrative actions. The courts will generally intervene and grant relief where a tribunal has acted outside the scope of authority bestowed on it by its governing statute. Where there has been an excess of powers, the courts have found all types of decisions ultra vires, whether judicial, quasi-judicial, or administrative. To take a hypothetical and extreme example, the action of a pension tribunal in granting a driver's licence would be declared ultra vires. The determination of whether there has been an excess of powers obliges the courts to examine the enabling statute very carefully to see if Parliament has empowered the tribunal to act in a certain situation. Recently, the Supreme Court of Canada decided a case that involved the federal government denying it had authority to act in a certain area—a kind of a reverse ultra vires case (and one not directly related to administrative law). Ottawa had said its constitutional authority over "Indians" included only status Indians, who are indigenous peoples either registered with the federal government or part of a band that has dealings with Ottawa. Non-status Indians were thus outside the authority of the federal government and hence were ineligible for any federal benefits; the same applied to Metis, who are a product of the union

Chapter 12 / The Judiciary and the Bureaucracy

of an Aboriginal and non-Aboriginal person (typically First Nations women and French or British men). The Supreme Court sided with the Metis people and Aboriginal peoples classified as non-status Indians.[11]

Another aspect of this second ground, that of errors of procedure, requires that the courts look to the enabling statute. Parliament may specify that a tribunal exercise its powers according to specific procedures. We have already seen that on grounds of natural justice the courts may require tribunals performing judicial or quasi-judicial functions to follow certain rules of procedure. Regardless of natural justice principles, the courts will insist that tribunals follow the procedural rules set out in the statute; otherwise, the decision stemming from errors of procedure will be declared ultra vires.

An abuse of power occurs when a tribunal uses its power for a purpose not authorized by Parliament under the enabling statute. Thus, in considering whether there has been an abuse of power, and consequently whether a decision is ultra vires, the courts tend to look beyond the enabling statute to examine Parliament's intent. Abuse of power is usually expressed in terms of discretion exercised by a tribunal for ulterior purposes, in bad faith, or on irrelevant grounds. In the celebrated case *Roncarelli v. Duplessis*, the Supreme Court of Canada found abuse of power when the attorney general (who was also the premier) of Quebec directed a licensing commission to cancel a tavern owner's liquor permit because he had acted as bondsperson for persons accused of distributing allegedly seditious literature. The commission's decision was declared to be beyond its powers, and Justice Rand stated:

> In public regulation of this sort there is no such thing as untrammelled "discretion," that is, that action can be taken on any ground or for any reason that can be suggested to the mind of the administrator; no legislative act can, without express language, be taken to contemplate an unlimited arbitrary power exercisable for any person, however capricious or irrelevant, regardless of the nature or purpose of the statute. … "Discretion" necessarily implies good faith in discharging public duty; there is always a perspective within which a statute is intended to operate; any clear departure from its line or objects is just as objectionable as fraud or corruption.[12]

Errors of Law

The courts may also review the decisions of tribunals for errors of law on the face of the record. The "record" for this purpose includes not only the formal decision but also the reasons for the decision, documents initiating the proceedings, documents on which the decision is based, and documents cited in the reasons for the decision. The words "on the face of the record" indicate that the courts will not review a decision unless the error is apparent.

Forms of Relief

Before turning to a consideration of judicial review in relation to the Charter, we will examine the common-law remedies or forms of relief that the courts may use in determining the appropriate response to a case under review. Here are some of the forms of relief that can be employed:

- The most frequently used writs in Canada are certiorari and prohibition. *Certiorari* is a writ issued by a superior court to quash a decision already taken by an inferior tribunal, whereas *prohibition* is a writ to restrain a tribunal from taking a certain action.
- *Mandamus* is a writ used to compel an inferior tribunal to exercise the authority conferred on it by statute. Unlike certiorari and prohibition, this writ is not restricted to tribunals exercising a judicial or quasi-judicial function. To obtain the writ of

mandamus, an affected party must show that the tribunal is authorized or required to perform a certain duty, that it has been asked to perform that duty, and that it has refused to perform the duty.

- *Habeas corpus* is used to require that a person who has been detained be brought before a court for the purpose of determining whether the detention is legal. This writ is not used much in the sphere of administrative law. It is normally restricted to immigration cases, where it is often used to challenge orders for custody or deportation.
- An *injunction* is a remedy that requires an inferior tribunal to take a particular action or, more commonly, to refrain from taking some specified action beyond its powers. An injunction is generally available only if an equally effective alternative remedy is not available. It can be used against tribunals exercising administrative, as well as judicial or quasi-judicial, functions.
- An *action for declaration* (or *declaratory judgment*) asks the court to declare and define whether some act taken or proposed by a tribunal is beyond its powers. Like an injunction, a declaration is available for administrative as well as judicial or quasi-judicial decisions. Actions for declaration are infrequent. Moreover, they are normally combined with requests for other forms of relief, notably injunctions.
- *Awarding damages* is a remedy that requires that a certain amount of money be paid to compensate for an injury or wrong done to an individual. Tribunals, like ordinary citizens, are liable to an action for damages. Obviously, the remedy of damages is most useful in situations where the tribunal has already taken some action or decision. A remedy like certiorari that simply quashes the original decision would be of little help once the harm has been done. The remedy of damages is available for administrative as well as judicial and quasi-judicial functions. Damages were awarded against the attorney general (and premier) of Quebec in the case of *Roncarelli v. Duplessis* mentioned earlier.

Privative Clauses

The courts clearly have the authority and grounds to review administrative action and to apply the appropriate remedies. But equally clear is the power of the legislative authority through the doctrine of parliamentary sovereignty to restrict the actions of judicial bodies. With a view to allowing administrative tribunals to operate efficiently and quickly, Parliament and the provincial legislatures have used this power to enact **privative clauses** to deprive courts of the power to undertake reviews of administrative action. Sometimes the clauses take the form of straightforward provisions that specifically state that no judicial review shall take place or that the tribunal has "exclusive jurisdiction" over its area of responsibility.[13] At other times the effect is achieved through such a wide grant of power that the grounds for any kind of judicial review fall away. Here is how a privative clause might be worded that seeks to explicitly deny the possibility of judicial review of an administrative action:

privative clause Statutory provision designed to prevent judicial review of the decisions of administrative tribunals.

> No decision, order, direction, declaration, or ruling of the Board [or Tribunal] shall be questioned or reviewed in any court, and no order shall be made or process entered, or proceedings taken in any court, whether by way of injunction, declaratory judgment, certiorari, mandamus, prohibition, quo warranto, or otherwise, to question, review, prohibit, or restrain the Board [or Tribunal] or any of its proceedings.[14]

Until the late 1970s, Canadian courts generally paid little attention to privative clauses because of the belief that the courts should exercise their inherent supervisory jurisdiction over inferior tribunals if these made unreasonable decisions. Since that time, however, the courts have taken greater heed to privative clauses as part of a growing confidence in the role of tribunals:

> Traditionally, the courts often intervened and substituted their opinion for the opinion of the administrative tribunal. In contrast, the more recent trend is for the courts to "defer" or respect the decision of the administrative tribunal especially dealing with matters where the courts recognize that the administrative tribunal has more expertise.[15]

The increasing deference of the courts, however, fails to extend to a total acceptance of privative clauses. Judges assume in their decision making that the authors of the privative clauses never intended to provide protection against instances of tribunals acting outside their jurisdiction or functioning in an unfair or incorrect fashion. It is through the straightforward interpretation of the actions of tribunals and other bodies—and not through claims of acting in accordance of the rule of law—that the judiciary handles the delicate topic of privative clauses. Moreover, a series of court decisions have led some legal scholars to believe that there now exists "a constitutional prohibition on privative clauses that purport to exclude judicial review for jurisdictional error."[16]

Canadian Charter of Rights and Freedoms

The *Canadian Charter of Rights and Freedoms*, which became law in 1982, has had a significant effect on the role of the courts in public administration. Prior to the Charter, judicial review of administrative actions relied on rules limited to issues of procedural fairness, appropriate jurisdiction, and errors of law. Also important, these were rules that legislative authorities could seek to nullify through privative clauses and other statutory enactments. The Charter enlarged the reach of judicial review of public administration to include the rights and freedoms contained within it and gave a constitutional basis to important aspects of administrative law; no longer, for example, could elected officials deny rules of natural justice because they were now entrenched in a constitutional document. Judicial review of administrative action had lived in the shadow of parliamentary supremacy and the authority of the legislature to make or remake any laws it wished. The Charter has ushered in a new era that gives the courts a final say (see What to Do?).

The Charter has already had a considerable effect on the working lives of public servants at all levels of government. Many decisions have greatly affected public servants' day-to-day work, especially in the area of criminal justice. Police officers, for example, must be aware of a person's right to be informed of his or her right to counsel, and they have to be careful about how they conduct their searches and detain individuals suspected of illegal action. The Charter has also forced governments in Canada to engage in "Charter-proofing" exercises in order to protect both existing and proposed legislation from constitutional challenges. The federal Department of Justice, for instance, has examined statutes "to forestall litigation by identifying and removing provisions that might violate the Charter." It has also supported new legal units within departments and agencies that seek to defend new policies and programs against a Charter challenge.[17] The efforts of the justice department have in the past been quite successful in limiting Charter challenges, but in recent years the Supreme Court of Canada and other courts have

WHAT TO DO?

The increasing impact of the courts has caused a greater interest in individuals who make the important legal decisions. Certainly, public servants anxious about the legality of the policies that they propose and implement would like to know more about judges. This interest is especially evident when it comes to members of the top court, the Supreme Court of Canada. Senior judges in the United States are almost household names because Supreme Court nominees have to undergo a public hearing process during which probing questions are asked. Canada has experimented with such hearings without much commitment to this practice. But in 2016 the Trudeau government proposed a new selection process for Supreme Court justices that allows House of Commons and Senate committee members to ask questions of the chosen nominee to the Supreme Court. The issue is whether Canada should follow the American example. Public hearings allow citizens to get to know the top judges in the country; however, judicial hearings in the United States have at times become almost circus-like as questioners seek to discredit nominees.

acted to knock down a number of significant legislative and policy initiatives of the federal government not only in relation to the Charter but also in other areas of the law (see Giving the Minister Advice below). For students of public administration, the most important implication of attempts to forestall legal actions is the greater significance of the courts for public servants.

Many sections of the Charter are pertinent for administrative law, but ss. 7, 8, and 15 have an especially important effect on the conduct of public administration. Section 7, on legal rights, provides in part that "[e]veryone has the right to life, liberty and security of the person and the right not to be deprived thereof except in accordance with the principles of fundamental justice." In the *Charkaoui* case, the Supreme Court held that the process employed to grant a security certificate used to arrest a suspected terrorist living in Canada amounted to a violation of a person's liberty.[18] The offending part of the process was the refusal to allow the suspect or his lawyers to view the evidence employed to gain the certificate, an action inconsistent with rules of natural justice. A further s. 7 case involved the issue of a person's right to be remain silent during a police interrogation.[19] In this instance, the person expressed his wish to remain silent, but the police continued with the interrogation and eventually the accused uttered statements used in court. A slim majority of the Supreme Court of Canada ruled that there was no violation of the right to liberty under s. 7; four of the nine Supreme Court justices decided that a right to silence, inherent in s. 7 and the common law, had indeed been encroached upon.

Section 8 of the Charter provides that "[e]veryone has the right to be secure against unreasonable search and seizure." A recent case involving s. 8 considered the important issue of privacy on the Internet, a concern relevant to both constitutional and administrative law.[20] In this case, the police asked an Internet service provider for the identity of a person who used an IP to download and view child pornography; with this information, the police would be able to secure a search warrant to enter the person's home. The provider supplied the name, a search warrant was granted, and subsequently it was used to gather evidence to charge the named person. The Supreme Court of Canada ruled that the request for information amounted to a search of premises; given that no warrant was obtained for the search, the request for information constituted a violation of s. 8, which requires warrants for a reasonable search to take place. But the Charter allows evidence garnered through procedures in violation of a Charter right to be used if it does not act "to bring the administration of justice into disrepute." The Supreme Court ruled that admission of the evidence would not have this effect.

Section 15 provides that "[e]very individual is equal before the law and has the right to the equal protection of the law without discrimination and, in particular, without discrimination based on race, national or ethnic origin, colour, religion, sex, age, or mental or physical disability." There have been a number of legal cases involving this provision of the Charter and the daily work activities of public servants. In the *Little Sisters* case, the Supreme Court addressed the actions of customs officers charged with the duty of determining whether books entering Canada from the United States were obscene. The court held that the officers violated the equality provision by "targeting" or giving special attention to shipments to a Vancouver bookseller that focused on books for gays and lesbians (an action that also amounted to abuse of power or discretion in administrative law).[21] In *Eldridge*, the Supreme Court ruled that hospitals in employing their discretion refused to provide sign-language interpreters to deaf patients and thereby offended s. 15.[22] In *Halpern v. the Attorney General of Canada et al.*, a City of Toronto clerk declined to issue a civil marriage licence to gay and lesbian couples until she received further direction.[23] This action helped precipitate a challenge of the common-law definition of marriage (union of two people of the opposite sex) and a decision of the Ontario Court of Appeal that found the definition inconsistent with s. 15. This and similar decisions in other provincial courts led to the introduction of a new federal law that defined marriage in a way that provided for same-sex marriages. (see Box 12.3.)

BOX 12.3

Aboriginal Rights

The *Canadian Charter of Rights and Freedoms* constitutes strong support for challenging the legality of administrative action. But another rights-based rationale for judicial review of tribunals and other administrative actors is also assuming significance. Section 35 of the *Constitution Act, 1982*, which immediately follows the provisions of the Charter, recognizes the Aboriginal and treaty rights of Aboriginal peoples of Canada. But a legal case has called into question whether the Aboriginal rights provision has much relevance for administrative tribunals. The courts have interpreted Aboriginal rights to include the stipulation that the Crown has a duty to consult with Aboriginal groups on decisions affecting indigenous peoples. But the Federal Court of Appeal has ruled in *Chippewas v. Enbridge* that this duty does not apply to administrative tribunals. Accordingly, tribunals can make decisions without formally consulting the relevant Aboriginal parties or ensuring some other government agency has done so. This is what happened in *Chippewas v. Enbridge*.

Source: 2015 FCA 222; Lillianne Cadieux-Shaw, "Sailing in Unchartered Waters: The Duty to Consult for Administrative Tribunals," http://www.thecourt.ca/sailing-in-uncharted-waters-the-duty-to-consult-for-administrative-tribunals/.

Giving the Minister Advice

In the summer of 2011, the federal Minister of Citizenship and Immigration requested advice from his officials concerning "rules requiring that when people take the oath, their face must be uncovered." The oath was in reference to the oath of citizenship, which is part of the ceremony for becoming a Canadian citizen. The minister had learned that some had taken the oath with their face covered with the Muslim niqab, and he felt that this was wrong. The officials reacted to the request with caution and reminded the minister that the "federal-level response to recent high-profile incidents ha[d] been to accommodate religious beliefs when no security reasons existed." More directly, they said that existing regulations required that religious beliefs and practices have to be given "the greatest possible freedom." The minister's demand for a mandatory policy forbidding the niqab thus might be challenged in the courts because it conflicted with present regulations which in turn sought to respect the Charter right of freedom of religion. The minister would have none of this thinking and eventually a new policy emerged, saying that "candidates are required to remove their face coverings for the oath-taking portion of the ceremony."[24] Four years later, the policy was challenged in court on the grounds that it violated rights of religious freedom contained in the Charter. The Federal Court sided in favor of the complainant, Zunera Ishaq, but not on Charter grounds. Rather the court ruled that the regulation requiring the greatest possible freedom took precedence over the policy of wearing face-veils. Regulations were laws and policies were only statements, which fell short of the legal status of laws. The federal government appealed the decision to the Federal Court of Appeal but lost again. The federal government has no plans to appeal the decision.[25]

Zunera Ishaq takes the citizenship oath wearing her niqab.

Sylvia Thomson/CBC Licensing

Utility of Judicial Review

Even though the importance of judicial review of administrative action has increased substantially as a result of the Charter, judicial review has several deficiencies as a means of preventing and remedying abuses of bureaucratic power. The courts review only a miniscule number of the millions of decisions made annually by administrative authorities; the success rate of litigants is not high; neither the amount of money nor the issue involved is usually significant enough to justify the high cost of the proceedings; and judicial review tends to focus on certain areas of public administration (labour relations, tax assessment, and licensing) so that many other areas are relatively untouched. However, the evidence also suggests that public servants believe that the courts over the recent past have changed the way they function. A quarter of a century ago, appointed officials "rarely thought about the courts as they went about their work," but now federal officials claim that the "courts are never far from people's minds when planning departmental activities."[26] As with many other players in the political process, the courts have seemingly made life more complicated for appointed officials and their superiors.

Points to Know

- The Canadian court system consists of provincial courts, federal courts, and, at the very top of the judiciary, the Supreme Court of Canada.

- An important role of the judiciary is to review the actions and behaviours of appointed officials for the purpose of determining any transgressions of the law.

- Administrative law is the body of law that has arisen from judicial review of the administration of government programs and policies.

- Four major grounds or reasons for legal review of the behaviour of public servants are breach of natural justice, acting outside the law, making errors of law, and violating the *Canadian Charter of Rights and Freedoms*.

- Judicial review of alleged administrative wrongdoings has become a more pronounced part of public administration in recent years.

Review Questions

1. Discuss the uniqueness of the Federal Court and the Federal Court of Appeal.

2. What are the rules of natural justice and how have they been applied in the courts?

3. What are the reasons for the increased importance of judicial review of administrative actions?

4. How might the courts be seen as having only a limited effect in their review of appointed officials?

5. What are the pros and cons of judicial review of administrative actions?

Notes

1. Peter W. Hogg, *Constitutional Law of Canada* 5th ed. Supplemented, Loose-Leaf (Toronto: Carswell, 2015), 7–3.
2. David P. Jones and Anne de Villars, *Principles of Administrative Law*, 6th ed. (Toronto: Carswell, 2014), 3.
3. Gerald Gall, *The Canadian Legal System*, 5th ed. (Toronto: Thomson Carswell, 2004), 540.
4. Rt. Hon. Beverly McLachlin, Chief Justice of Canada, "Administrative Tribunals and the Courts: An Evolutionary Relationship," May 27, 2013, accessed June 20, 2016, http://www.scc-csc.ca/court-cour/judges-juges/spe-dis/bm-2013-05-27-eng.aspx.
5. Law Reform Commission of Canada, *A Catalogue of Discretionary Powers in the Revised Statutes of Canada* (Ottawa: Information Canada, 1975), 2.
6. *Canada (Attorney General) v. Mavi*, 2011 SCC 30, [2011] 2 S.C.R. 504.
7. *Liquor Control Board of Ontario v. Vin de Garde Wine Club*, 2013 ONSC 5854.
8. Ibid., paragraph 30.
9. *Committee for Justice and Liberty v. Canada (National Energy Board)*, [1978] 1 S.C.R. 369.
10. Campbell Clark and Bill Curry, "Absolving Chrétien, Judge Blasts Gomery," *Globe and Mail*, June 27, 2008, accessed August 7, 2016, http://www.theglobeandmail.com/news/national/absolving-chretien-judge-blasts-gomery/article675611/.
11. CBC, "Unanimous Ruling Says Ottawa Has Jurisdiction Over All Indigenous People," April 14, 2016, accessed August 7, 2016, http://www.cbc.ca/news/aboriginal/metis-indians-supreme-court-ruling-1.3535236; Daniels v. Canada (Indian Affairs and Northern Development), 2016 SCC 12.
12. *Roncarelli v. Duplessis* (1959) S.C.R. 121 at 140.
13. Peter W. Hogg, *Constitutional Law of Canada*, 5th ed. Supplemented, Loose-Leaf (Toronto: Carswell, 2015), 7–53.
14. Ontario, *Labour Relations Act*, 1995, s. 118.
15. Lisa Braverman, *Administrative Tribunals: A Legal Handbook* (Aurora: Canada Law Book Inc., 2001), 92.
16. Hogg, *Constitutional Law of Canada*, 7–53.
17. Heather MacIvor, *Canadian Politics and Government in the Charter Era* (Toronto: Nelson Thomson, 2006), 185. See also James B. Kelly, *Governing with the Charter: Legislative and Judicial Activism and Framers' Intent* (Vancouver: UBC Press, 2005), ch. 7.
18. *Charkaoui v. Canada (Citizenship and Immigration)*, [2007] 1 S.C.R. 350, 2007 SCC 9.
19. *R. v. Singh*, [2007] 3 S.C.R. 405, 2007 SCC 48.
20. *R. v. Spencer*, 2014 SCC 43, [2014] 2 S.C.R. 212
21. *Little Sisters Book and Art Emporium v. Canada (Minister of Justice)*, [2000] 2 S.C.R. 1120.
22. *Eldridge v. British Columbia (Attorney General)*, [1997] 3 S.C.R. 624
23. *Halpern et al. v Attorney General of Canada et al.* (2003), 65 OR (3d) 161.
24. Sean Fine, "Documents Reveal Government's Scramble to Enact Niqab Requirements," *Globe and Mail*, September 23, 2015, accessed August 7, 2016, http://www.theglobeandmail.com/news/national/documents-reveal-governments-scramble-to-enact-niqab-requirements/article26486680/.
25. Sean Fine and Gloria Galloway, "Ruling Makes Niqabs an Election Issue," *Globe and Mail*, September 19, 2015, A16.
26. Donald J. Savoie, *Breaking the Bargain: Public Servants, Ministers, and Parliament* (Toronto: University of Toronto Press, 2003), 249.

Intergovernmental Administrative Relations

13

Learning Objectives

Reading this chapter allows you to do the following:

- Understand the meaning of intergovernmental relations and intergovernmental administrative relations in a federal state
- Identify the implications of the evolution of Canadian federalism for intergovernmental relations at the political and administrative levels
- Analyze the various federal–provincial policy arrangements which have arisen out of relations between governments

- Explain the machinery of intergovernmental relations and the primary role of intergovernmental experts in this machinery
- Evaluate the ability of the federal, provincial, and territorial levels of governments to address together important policy concerns in Canada

Relations and interactions between governments in Canada represent an important aspect of the Canadian political system. An expert on Canadian federalism once said with humorous intent that national security, garbage collection, and the post office appeared to be the only matters that existed outside the boundaries of intergovernmental relations.[1] But the truth is that no public issue truly escapes the attention of those engaged in affairs between governments in Canada. The prime minister meets with provincial and territorial counterparts, either one-on-one or as a group, in order to revolve issues of national importance, and ministers from all kinds of departments at both levels are given responsibility for seemingly everything else. One consequence of this situation is that public servants are necessary to assist elected officials in the management of the Canadian federation. Public administration thus concerns itself with relations not only *within* government, but also *between* governments. Appointed officials are often close by when prime ministers and premiers negotiate the major concerns of the day, and ministers depend on their advisors when seeking to formulate policies that concern both federal and provincial governments. Public servants, particularly those who specialize in intergovernmental relations, are also expected to take the lead in sorting out the administrative details of federal–provincial agreements and to address matters whose significance requires the attention of appointed officials at both levels of government.

In recent years the federal government, under the leadership of Prime Minister Stephen Harper, sought to limit intergovernmental relations. Harper felt that both orders of government should focus on their constitutional responsibilities and leave the other order to their responsibilities. In some respects this effort at disentanglement succeeded. First-minister conferences involving the prime minister and premiers, a staple of federal–provincial relations, were held infrequently, and the prime minister at times appeared determined to resist meeting with premiers on an individual basis. But the federal election of 2015 ushered in a new government that is more than willing to re-engage governments in Canada. Moreover, it was always the case that relations below the first ministers' level continued to take place.

This chapter seeks to provide a comprehensive view of intergovernmental administrative relations. It discusses the meaning and evolution of federalism in Canada and examines key areas of federal–provincial–territorial (FPT) relations. It also provides a close-up view of the machinery that facilitates relations between elected and appointed officials of the different orders of government. An attempt is made as well to reveal the nature of relations between intergovernmental officials and the capacity of these relations for successfully addressing the challenges of Canadian federalism.

Federalism and Intergovernmental Relations

Federalism may be defined as a political system in which the powers of the state are formally divided between central and regional governments by a written constitution but in which these governments are linked in an interdependent political relationship.[2] In the Canadian context, this definition captures the enduring legal and constitutional rudiments of Canadian federalism, the politics that pervade the federal system, and the necessity for intergovernmental interaction. Though federalism entails an element of independence in the sense that each level of government is sovereign in its areas of responsibility, the fact is that in modern federal states the orders of government tend to be highly interdependent and interactive. Uncertainty over the interpretation of areas of responsibility, the tendency of most policy areas to spill from one area of jurisdiction into another, and the sheer competitive nature of the federal relationship ensure that the two orders of government will interact with each other. There have been attempts, as already mentioned, to disentangle the two orders of government, but the reality of "shared rule" nearly always prevails.[3] Broadly interpreted, the term **intergovernmental relations** embraces not only federal–provincial relations but also interprovincial, federal–provincial–territorial, federal–municipal, and provincial–municipal relations. The main emphasis in this chapter is on FPT liaison (and often only federal-provincial relations), but specific reference is made also to the activities of officials involved in interprovincial relations and with the municipalities of Canada.[4]

Evolution of Federalism

Figure 13.1 depicts the various periods in the evolution of federalism in Canada, differentiated by the distribution of power and influence between the two orders of government. An appreciation of this evolution helps us to understand the changing nature of federalism and the settings in which intergovernmental relations take place; it also helps us to better comprehend the actions of elected and appointed officials and their resolve to find the limits of what is possible in any one period (see What to Do?).

The term **quasi-federalism** characterized the first period of the Canadian federation, during which the federal government dominated the provincial governments in part by making frequent use of the federal constitutional powers to disallow and reserve provincial legislation. The degree of subordination of provinces to the federal government has led some to call this period "colonial federalism." The next stage was

federalism A political system in which the powers of the state are formally divided between central and regional governments by a written constitution but in which these governments are linked in a mutually interdependent political relationship.

intergovernmental relations The interactions between and among the federal, provincial, and territorial governments in the Canadian federal system.

quasi-federalism A term used to describe the early decades of the Canadian federation during which the federal government dominated the provincial governments, in part by making frequent use of the federal constitutional powers to disallow and reserve provincial legislation.

WHAT TO DO?

Let us assume the federal government wishes to make additional cash transfers to the provinces and territories for healthcare but to do so with a difference. Normally, Ottawa attaches very broad conditions to health-care transfers. But in our scenario the federal government now wants the provinces and territories to spend the new monies on a health service that it has deemed very important to the future of the Canadian healthcare system, namely home care. Assume that the division of political power between the two orders of government is roughly even. If you were a federal official, what would you recommend to your political bosses? Would you urge them to push for conditions that require spending the additional financial assistance on home care, or would you suggest a less aggressive approach and hope that the provinces will spend the money sensibly?

Part Four / The Bureaucracy in the Political Process

Figure 13.1   Evolution of Canadian Federalism

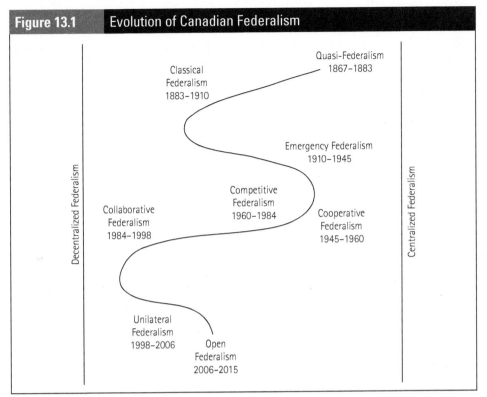

Source: Based on Robert J. Jackson and Doreen Jackson, *Politics in Canada: Culture, Institutions, Behaviour, and Public Policy*, 6th ed. (Pearson Education Canada, Inc., 2006), Pg 194. Reprinted with permission by Robert J. Jackson.

classical federalism, which approached K.C. Wheare's celebrated "federal principle": Wheare held that the powers of government are divided "so that the general and regional governments are each, within a sphere, coordinate and independent."[5] Between the late 1800s and 1930, with the exception of World War I, provincial powers gradually increased as a result of strong political leadership in certain provinces and judicial decisions favouring the provinces in constitutional disputes with the federal government. Both the federal and provincial governments enjoyed exclusive jurisdiction in certain policy fields, and jurisdictional conflicts were resolved by the courts. Increased federal–provincial consultation was formally recognized by the first federal–provincial conference of first ministers (the prime minister of Canada and the provincial premiers), held in 1906, and federal assistance for the financing of provincial responsibilities began in such areas as transportation and agriculture. The growing importance and expense of the provinces' responsibilities for health, education, and welfare required not only federal subsidies but also a provincial search for new revenues through the use of such forms of taxation as personal and corporate income taxes.

The period of World War I was one of **emergency federalism**. The courts supported the federal government's exercise of broad powers, enshrined in the Constitution, over the economy and matters of property and civil rights, which, in peacetime, were clearly within provincial jurisdiction. After the war, including the Depression years, the courts resisted the exercise of this emergency power. During World War II, and for a short time afterward, the federal government again used the emergency power to control many matters that were normally within provincial jurisdiction. "There can be little quarrel with Professor Wilfred Eggleston's observation that 'in 1914–19 and again in 1939–45 … the emergency provisions of the constitution turned Canada for the time being into a unitary state.'"[6]

classical federalism A concept according to which the powers of government are divided so that the general and regional governments are each, within a sphere, coordinate and independent.

emergency federalism A term used to describe federal–provincial relations during the two world wars and the Depression; these relations were characterized by a growth in federal power vis-à-vis the provinces.

cooperative federalism A term used to describe federal–provincial relations when the constitutional division of powers is preserved but federal and provincial ministers and public servants engage in consultation and coordination to reach joint decisions on matters of mutual concern.

executive federalism A term used to describe federal–provincial relations characterized by the concentration of authority at the top of each participating government and the formalized quality of the relations between the two orders of government.

competitive federalism A term used to describe highly conflictual federal–provincial relations during the 1960s, 70s, and 80s, when the provinces challenged the federal government on major issues relating to energy, fiscal arrangements, and the Constitution.

collaborative federalism A term employed to characterize a period in the 1990s when both orders of government realized the importance of cooperation in achieving policy outcomes important to the federal government and the provinces.

unilateral federalism A depiction of a short period at the turn of the century where the federal government imposed its views on arrangements involving both Ottawa and the provinces and enacted programs largely in areas of provincial jurisdiction.

It is difficult to pinpoint the precise date when **cooperative federalism** (or **executive federalism**) emerged, but Donald Smiley noted in the early 1960s that the development of Canadian federalism since 1945 had been "a process of continuous and piecemeal adjustment between the two levels of government," and that these adjustments had overwhelmingly been made through "interaction between federal and provincial executives" rather than through formal constitutional amendment or judicial interpretation.[7] Under cooperative federalism, the constitutional division of powers was preserved, but federal and provincial ministers and public servants engaged in consultation and coordination to reach joint decisions on policies and programs of mutual concern. However, it was clear during this period of cooperation that the federal government was the senior partner and that intergovernmental relations relied on direction from national authorities.

In the 1960s provincial governments gradually acquired the expertise and influence to deal with the federal government from a stronger position. The Quiet Revolution, which "unleashed a progressive nationalism that transformed Quebec,"[8] helped precipitate this movement toward what came fittingly to be known as **competitive federalism**.[9] Regional loyalties, especially in western Canada, contributed as well to the increasing combativeness of federal–provincial relations. For the next three decades or so, the two orders of government wrangled over the likes of fiscal transfers to the provinces, the pricing of oil, and amendment of the Constitution. In the early 1990s, the character of federalism in Canada began to change again, partly because of fiscal difficulties at the federal level and partly because of the recognition that some challenging policy issues required the participation and agreement of both orders of government. **Collaborative federalism** led to important agreements between federal and provincial governments in areas such as trade, the environment, social policy, and income support for families.[10] What underlay this period was a belief that "national goals are achieved … by some or all of the 11 governments and territories acting collectively."[11]

Some believe that in the late 1990s federalism assumed a new form, **unilateral federalism** or "federal unilateralism."[12] With its fiscal problems fixed, the federal government was now better positioned financially to impose new arrangements on the provinces and to even act independently in areas largely provincial. A short period, unilateral federalism soon receded into the background, to be replaced by a preference for allowing the provinces to look after their areas of policy (albeit with help of federal money) and for the federal government to pursue its constitutional duties in the areas of security and the economy. With the election of a Conservative government at the national level, in 2006, federalism entered into a new stage characterized by the "withdrawal of Ottawa from working directly to shape the operation of the federal system."[13] This approach, known as **open federalism**, worked to reduce the importance of the machinery for facilitating intergovernmental relations and reminded some of the classical approach to federalism and its emphasis on the independence of governments in Canada.

At present, forces appear to be pushing for a type of federalism that emphasizes the need for both orders of government once again to act in concert. One of these forces is a new perspective at the federal level, one that sees value in collaboration. "I believe that confronting our collective challenges can only be achieved by sitting down together and engaging in open dialogue," wrote the leader of the Liberal Party in a letter to the premiers during the election campaign of 2015.[14] Now, as prime minister, Justin Trudeau has a chance to act on his belief. A related force is the set of policy issues facing Canada—climate change, healthcare demands, the global economy—whose resolution seemingly demands the contributions of both Ottawa and the provinces as well as other state and non-state actors. It is, in essence, emblematic of the shift to new public governance that was discussed in Chapter 5.

There is one last development to mention in the evolution of intergovernmental affairs, and that is the efforts of new entities to acquire literally and figuratively a seat at meetings involving the two orders of government. Aboriginal peoples constitute one such entity striving to open up the intergovernmental process. For Canada's Indigenous peoples, the long-term goal is recognition as a third order of government with its own exclusive set of powers in a reconstituted Canadian federalism. But in the meantime Aboriginal representatives have worked to gain access to relevant intergovernmental dealings at the political and administrative levels (though often only at the whim of the two orders of government). More important, responsibility for administering many of the public programs directed at Aboriginal communities is now in the hands of Aboriginal organizations. One result of this has been to increase interactions between the two orders of government and Aboriginal representatives to ensure successful policy coordination. Notwithstanding these recent developments, "[t]he relationship between Aboriginal peoples and Canadian federalism remains uncertain and tentative."[15] However, the federal government, under new leadership, has committed itself to "recognize First Nations, Metis, and Inuit communities as full partners in the federation."[16]

Cities represent another entity wishing to break into the intergovernmental process in the sense of being given a greater voice or even expanding relations between the two orders of government to include a new third partner. The challenges facing cities, which include addressing growing populations, ensuring efficient public transit, and exploiting the economic opportunities, all demand a **multilevel governance** approach in which federal, provincial, and urban governments get together to exploit their respective "comparative advantage" to address problems in large metropolitan areas.[17] As with Aboriginal peoples, the federal government has expressed its belief that more has to be done for the cities, starting with an affirmation of the cities' "rightful place at the national decision-making table" (see Box 13.1).[18]

open federalism A term used to describe the period of federal–provincial relations during the early 2000s, where the federal government worked to bring a return to a classical type of federalism in which each order of government tended to its own constitutional responsibilities.

multilevel governance An intergovernmental arrangement whereby city governments enter into working relations with federal or provincial governments (or both together) to address policy challenges that are important to urban areas; arrangement may also include the participation of non-governmental actors.

Multilevel Governance

BOX
13.1

Increasingly, scholars are using the term "multilevel governance" in place of federal–provincial–territorial relations. The increasing prominence of cities and their governments (and non-governmental actors, too) has given intergovernmental relations in Canada a more expansive look. More and more, cities see themselves in arrangements with provincial and federal governments, with either all three acting together or the cities partnering with one of the two constitutionally recognized orders of government. Especially noteworthy is the greater presence of the federal government in city affairs. Municipal government is a constitutional responsibility of the provinces, but Ottawa has over the years begun to establish a greater presence at the local level. For a period of time, the Conservative government of Stephen Harper limited the federal presence in municipal matter, but Ottawa has recently renewed its interest in the cities and their needs.

Climate Change and the First Ministers: A Case Study

On assuming the position of prime minister of Canada in late 2015, Justin Trudeau made clear his intentions to work with the provinces to develop measures to deal with climate change and greenhouse gas emissions. He told his environment minister that he expected her to forge a partnership with the provinces on climate change, set out national carbon emission targets, and ensure that the provinces "have targeted federal funding and the flexibility to design their own policies [to meet the targets]." This represented a near monumental shift in federal–provincial relations and a solid rejection of the Harper government's go-it-alone approach to federalism.[19] At a first ministers' conference on climate change, held one month after the election, the prime minister's positive attitude appeared to have the desired effect. Though no concrete decisions were made, not even on the all-important national targets for carbon emissions, all present agreed on the need for a "national climate strategy." A few premiers introduced a little reality into proceedings; the Saskatchewan leader, for example, reminded all present at the meeting that movement on climate change could not come at the expense of the country, and Ontario's premier said it would be nice if the federal government confirmed that its role was basically to support the provinces in their individual efforts to address climate change.[20] But all in all it seemed that a new era in federal–provincial–territorial relations might be possible. A trip by the prime minister, along with invited premiers, to a UN conference on climate change in Paris a week after the first minister's meeting appeared to cement good relations between Ottawa and the provinces.

In the early part of 2016, divisions and differences began to appear on the appropriate response to the challenge of climate change. Ottawa, naturally, wanted a "pan Canadian" solution to limiting carbon emissions, and provinces had initially seemed willing to accede to this vision. But then the provinces appeared to go off in all directions to address (or not address) climate change. An assortment of policies emerged from some provincial capitals, while in others the policy was either to do nothing until clearer direction was forthcoming from the federal government or to redefine old practices as a way of limiting carbon emissions.[21] The result of these developments was Ottawa pulling back from the promise that a forthcoming first ministers' meeting in March would produce the national plan on climate change. At that meeting, the provinces rejected a federal proposal for a national minimum tax on carbon emissions. Ottawa relented for the moment and allowed for further discussion on carbon emissions and climate change; but the threat of unilateral federal action on the matter in the future was not outside the realm of possibility. As the end of the conference neared, it seemed that the consensus achieved at the first meeting of the first ministers had all but disappeared. However, all parties were able to take a small step forward together, agreeing that there was a need for "carbon pricing mechanisms adapted to each province's and

Federal Minister of Environment and Climate Change Catherine McKenna meets with her provincial counterparts in Ottawa to discuss carbon-cutting strategies.

THE CANADIAN PRESS/Adrian Wyld

territory's specific circumstances."[22] A compromise in intergovernmental relations had thus been achieved: the federal government got to keep carbon policies on the table, and the provinces and territories got a commitment to provincial and territorial flexibility.

This episode in relations between governments shows that change can occur in relations between the two orders of government. The Liberal government of Justin Trudeau brings a different attitude towards federalism than the preceding Conservative government and this has made a difference. But negotiations over climate change also show that some qualities of intergovernmental relations never really change. Ottawa serves the national interest; the premiers serve their provinces and territories.

Intergovernmental Relations

Intergovernmental relations can be broken down into a series of specific relations shaping areas important to the governing of Canada. Three of the most important areas are those that affect fiscal matters, the Constitution, and policies addressing major public concerns.

Federal–Provincial Fiscal Relations

While federal financial assistance to provincial governments dates to Confederation and was especially important during the Depression, federal–provincial fiscal relations (and now territorial) have been an especially prominent theme in Canadian federalism since World War II. At present, the federal–provincial financial relationship consists of four major elements: Tax Collection Agreements, the Canada Health Transfer, the Canada Social Transfer, and Equalization.

The Tax Collection Agreements (TCAs) are an arrangement between the federal government and provinces that allows the federal government to collect both federal and provincial personal income taxes (except for Quebec) and corporate taxes (except for Alberta, Ontario, and Quebec), and to remit the provincial portion of the taxes to the provinces. The purpose of this agreement is twofold. One is to provide an administrative convenience to provincial governments; the other is to limit tax competition between provinces by establishing some uniformity in the method of calculation of federal and provincial taxes on personal income and corporate revenues. However, in the past two decades, many provinces have sought to vary the method of calculation in their respective jurisdictions by introducing new tax measures for personal incomes. The result has been to reduce the degree of uniformity in the taxation of personal incomes but also to give the provinces more opportunity to act in a manner consistent with their individual needs (see Box 13.2).

Accounting or Politics?

BOX 13.2

A description of the workings of the Tax Collection Agreements makes one believe that the agreements are a largely technical document put together by accountants. But the changes to the methods of calculating provincial taxes in some provinces reveal the political nature of the TCAs. These changes are not a response to an accounting problem; rather the changes represent an attempt by the provinces to gain more control over the taxation system. Why would the provinces want this? Because the taxation system produces the fiscal resources that are the lifeblood of any government. The fact that Quebec refuses to participate in the agreements should also make clear the political nature of the agreements.

The other three elements of the federal–provincial financial relationship—the Canada Health Transfer, the Canada Social Transfer, and Equalization—involve transfer payments from the federal government to the provinces and territories. Figure 13.2 shows

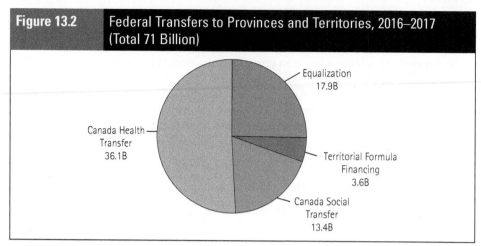

Figure 13.2 Federal Transfers to Provinces and Territories, 2016–2017 (Total 71 Billion)

Equalization
17.9B

Territorial Formula
Financing
3.6B

Canada Social
Transfer
13.4B

Canada Health
Transfer
36.1B

Source: Government of Canada, Finance Canada, www.fin.gc.ca/FEDPROV/ftpte.html. Permission granted under Open Government License - Canada, http://open.canada.ca/en/open-government-licence-canada.

that federal funding made available under these arrangements in 2016–2017 was equal to $71 billion, which amounted to roughly one-quarter of total federal expenditures.

- The Canada Health Transfer (CHT) helps establish the foundation for Canada's healthcare system, called medicare. Under this arrangement, the federal government provides financial assistance to help the provinces and territories pay for their healthcare plans. The assistance takes the form of cash grants. Cash grants, as the name suggests, are simply transfers of money, which are allocated on an equal per capita basis to the provinces and territories. The CHT represents a huge transfer of money—estimated at a little over $36 billion in the 2016–2017 fiscal year—so it is not surprising that the federal government attaches conditions to its health transfers. To be eligible for the transfers, the provincial and territorial health plans must respect the five principles of medicare: each plan must be universally available to all; comprehensive in its coverage of healthcare; administered on a nonprofit basis; reasonably accessible to all Canadians, with no direct patient fees for insured services; and portable, in the sense that citizens remain covered when outside their home province. Failure to observe these principles may result in a withdrawal of federal funding, a possibility that makes the provinces unhappy with the attachment of strings to federal assistance.

- The Canada Social Transfer (CST), which is expected to amount to $13.4 billion in 2016–2017, is directed at postsecondary education and social services and assistance. As with the CHT, the CST comprises cash grants; but unlike the health transfer, very few conditions are attached to this transfer. Indeed, there is only one stipulated condition: that provinces cannot impose residency requirements on persons seeking social assistance or social services. The absence of conditions is explained in part by provincial sensitivity to any federal attempt to influence educational programs in the provinces and the recognition that the administration of social services programs requires much flexibility.

- Equalization is a program through which the federal government makes cash grants to provinces that have a weak tax base and are as a result unable to generate sufficient revenues. For the fiscal year 2016–2017, it was estimated that the Equalization program would transfer $17.9 billion dollars to the "have-not" provinces (the name given to eligible provinces). In the fiscal year 2016–2017, this list of recipients included all provinces save the three most westerly provinces in the Confederation. The purpose of the program is to allow the have-not provinces to provide adequate public services to their citizens without imposing excessively high taxes. A similar transfer called Territorial Formula Funding is provided for the territories. Given that the program aims to assist provinces in building up all their services, there is no need for accompanying conditions targeted at any particular program.

This summary of federal–provincial financial arrangements may imply a fair amount of stability in fiscal relations between the two levels of government, but this could not be further from the truth. At one time, the Tax Collection Agreements involved the provinces agreeing not to levy personal and corporate income tax in return for payment from the federal government; now the provinces are on the brink of changing the agreements so much that there may be little sense in maintaining them. Initially, health arrangements relied on the federal government matching provincial spending on medical and hospital services; then, healthcare was combined with postsecondary education to create a new arrangement; next it was combined with postsecondary education and social services; and at present it is by itself in the Canada Health Transfer. As the experience of healthcare shows, arrangements for postsecondary education and social services have also been quite fluid. And Equalization has similarly experienced changes over time because of shifts in the well-being of various provinces (for example, Ontario at the turn of the decade become for the first time a recipient of Equalization payments).

Federal–Provincial Constitutional Relations

The impact of federal–provincial relations on the evolution of Canada's constitution is a long and intricate story in which many of the constitutional issues have had an important financial aspect as well. There have been, however, a number of constitutional developments with special relevance for contemporary federal–provincial relations and consequently, for the officials involved in these relations. A series of federal–provincial conferences that began in the 1960s sought agreement on various matters relating to constitutional reform. These efforts were given enormous impetus by the election of the separatist Parti Québécois government in Quebec in 1976 and the 1980 referendum campaign on "sovereignty-association," at which time the federal government promised constitutional change. Also, during the 1970s and early 1980s, intergovernmental tensions were severely exacerbated by sharp disagreements over the ownership of natural resources, especially petroleum, and over the allocation of the revenues flowing from the exploitation of these resources. The dispute raged not only between the federal government and the energy-producing provinces but also between these provinces and the energy-consuming provinces (especially Ontario).

For the 1980–1981 constitutional meetings, the first ministers agreed upon an agenda containing many contentious items. However, following the failure of the September 1980 meeting of the first ministers to achieve constitutional reform, and after lengthy debate in the federal Parliament, the provinces were presented in November 1981 with a federal proposal for constitutional change, which all provinces, except Quebec, only grudgingly supported (partly because they had no part in crafting the proposal and because some of the provinces opposed some of the proposed changes).

Agreements were reached on only a few of the agenda items, and these agreements were enshrined in the *Constitution Act of 1982*. This act provided an amending formula ensuring that all changes to the Constitution would henceforth be made in Canada. It also created the *Charter of Rights and Freedoms* along with a commitment to the principle of equalization, confirmation of provincial ownership of natural resources, and affirmation of the existing rights of Aboriginal peoples.

During the late 1980s and the early 1990s, the major focus of attention in intergovernmental relations was on the Meech Lake Accord and the Charlottetown Agreement. The Meech Lake Accord was negotiated by the first ministers, with the assistance of their public service advisors; it was signed in June 1987. The Accord consisted of a number of proposals for constitutional amendment that would serve "to bring Quebec back into the constitutional family" after Quebec's refusal to accept the *Constitution Act of 1982*. The Accord was to come into effect when it was ratified by the legislatures of all eleven governments. Under the terms of the *Constitution Act*, that ratification had to occur within three years, that is, by June 23, 1990; but two provinces (Newfoundland and Manitoba) failed to obtain ratification before the stipulated deadline. Among the major objections to the Accord were its recognition of Quebec as a distinct society, its decentralization of power from the federal government to the provinces, its requirement of unanimous consent for Senate reform, and its lack of recognition of the rights of Aboriginal peoples. Following the death of the Meech Lake Accord, the province of Quebec announced its unwillingness to participate in any constitutional conferences for the foreseeable future and began formal consideration of its future association with the rest of Canada.

Beginning in 1991, a renewed effort to reach agreement on constitutional reform began. Widespread consultations involving participants from all parts of the country and many meetings of the first ministers and senior public servants led to the August 28, 1992, Consensus Report on the Constitution. This report was known generally as the Charlottetown Agreement and was agreed to by first ministers (including the premier of Quebec), territorial leaders, and Aboriginal leaders. The agreement's comprehensive proposals for constitutional change included, among other things, provisions for a social and economic union, the recognition of Quebec as a distinct society, the protection of minority language rights, the reform of the Senate and the Supreme Court, a reduction of overlap and duplication among governments, and the recognition of the inherent right of self-government for Aboriginal peoples. These proposals were submitted for approval in a national referendum held on October 26, 1992. The agreement was rejected by a majority of almost 55 percent of voters.

The period since the rejection of the Charlottetown Agreement has been called a return to "constitutional normalcy."[23] There have been no major constitutional proposals, and the emphasis has been on meeting the challenges of Canadian federalism through non-constitutional means. However, dissatisfaction with various aspects of the functioning of the Senate of Canada has led recently to a call for reform of the Senate, which would require the consent of the federal government and the ten provinces. The period of normalcy may be coming to an end.[24]

Federal–Provincial Policy Relations

Since the movement away from constitutional reform, there have been important policy developments involving the two orders of government. In some instances, these developments have witnessed useful collaboration between the two orders of government; in others, the relations have been less than successful:

- In the past three decades, the federal government and the provinces have combined their efforts to put into place important international trade agreements. Normally, trade agreements are the product of national governments, but the Supreme Court of Canada ruled that responsibility for implementing the provisions of a trade agreement depended on whether the substance of the provision fell within federal or provincial jurisdiction. The federal government could negotiate and ratify an agreement, but it could not necessarily put the agreement into place. Accordingly, Ottawa has invited the provinces to provide input through various consultative mechanisms during the negotiation of trade agreements with other countries. The adoption of this "shared jurisdiction model" facilitated the successful implementation of various trade agreements, including the North American Free Trade Agreement, the Multilateral Agreement on Investment, and the Canada–EU Comprehensive

Economic and Trade Agreement.[25] The recent negotiation of the Trans-Pacific Partnership trade initiative has, however, revealed a possible moving away from the shared jurisdiction model—some provinces have voiced their opposition to provisions in the proposed agreement.

- In response to pressure emanating largely from Quebec, the federal government agreed, in the 1990s, to devolve much of its responsibility for labour market training to the provinces. Some of the provinces fully accepted the offer; others decided to enter into a shared management relationship with the federal government. In 2007, the new Conservative government of Stephen Harper reaffirmed federal support of provincial responsibility for job training, but six years later unilaterally introduced a new *federal* job grant initiative that would reassert Ottawa's role in this area. The provinces and territories strenuously objected to the measure, with the result that the federal government modified the initiative to make it more consistent with provincial and territorial control over labour market training.

- Climate-change policy is a responsibility of both orders of government, a reality that has elicited little progress on this most important area of public policy and its aim "to reduce greenhouse gas (GHG) emissions."[26] At the Kyoto Conference in 1997, the world's first attempt to address climate change, the federal government committed Canada to reduce GHGs by 6 percent below 1990 levels, which went against a consensus previously achieved by a federal–provincial committee to support an approach which relied on voluntary efforts to reduce emissions. The federal action undermined any joint federal–provincial initiative on climate change and forced Ottawa to seek agreements on emissions with individual provinces. With provinces worried that any emission policy may have a negative effect on their economies, the bilateral approach achieved little. The election of a Conservative government at the federal level in 2006 led to a weakened commitment to climate change at the national level, but at the same time some of the provinces acting alone or in tandem with other provinces (and American states) began to seriously address GHG emissions. In 2015, the new Liberal federal government has already shown an interest in climate change by meeting with the provinces to create a consensus on how best to address the problem of global warming. But as the case discussed earlier shows, this new attitude of the federal government is not a guarantee for an accepted approach to climate change.

- Beginning in 2000, the federal government and the provinces (sometimes without Quebec) agreed to a set of arrangements that culminated, in 2005, in a national program for early childhood education and care.[27] It seemed that Canada would join many other nations in ensuring the availability of high-quality care provided by qualified child-care workers located in regulated locales. But the Harper government quashed the agreement, saying that it wanted to give parents choice in selecting their child-care arrangements by providing them with cash payments. This action effectively ended, during the Harper years, relations between the two orders of government when it came to child care. Ottawa would provide eligible families with money, which parents could use to shop for childcare services. As for the provinces, from the federal perspective, they could do what they wanted but without much additional federal help. Interestingly, some provinces have transformed child care for the very young into an educational program by offering full-day kindergarten and the "blending" of child care and kindergarten services. During the 2015 federal election, the New Democratic Party promised, if elected, to construct a national childcare program along the lines of the one rejected by the Conservative government. The NDP failed to win the election, but the Liberals did unseat the Conservatives, providing the possibility for change in the area of early childhood education and care.

- The two orders of government, in the first years of the new century, negotiated a series of healthcare accords through which the provinces received additional federal funding on condition that they move ahead with key healthcare reforms.[28] The reform areas included primary healthcare, home care, prescription drugs, and wait lists for care, actions that suggested a more aggressive role for the federal government in healthcare. These negotiations culminated in a ten-year agreement, in 2004, that seemingly confirmed this new relationship where Ottawa would have an important role in healthcare. But as we have seen in other areas of public policy, Prime Minister Stephen Harper and his government members had ideas different from those who preceded them. The prime minister believed there was little role for Ottawa in healthcare, a position that followed from his "classical" view of federalism. Accordingly, when the 10-year agreement came up for renewal, the federal government eschewed any meetings with the provinces or any stipulation of conditions; instead, it unilaterally announced that funding under the arrangement would remain unchanged for three years into the new agreement; after that point, the annual rate of increase would drop from 6% to the three-year moving average of growth in GNP without falling below 3% (predicted to be about 4%). Ottawa would thus limit itself to helping with the financing of medicare without any intent to specify how the money would be spent. Now a new prime minister has emerged, one who wishes for a stronger federal role without upsetting the provinces. The fear of some is that such a stance will only cause the provinces to bargain hard for more money without consenting to any new federal conditions.

Machinery for Intergovernmental Relations

The expansion of the activities of all governments and the increased interdependence of federal and provincial responsibilities has led to a need to design and operate machinery to manage contacts between governments. The result is a hierarchical network of intergovernmental structures (see Figure 13.3). At the top are found "peak" institutions, which

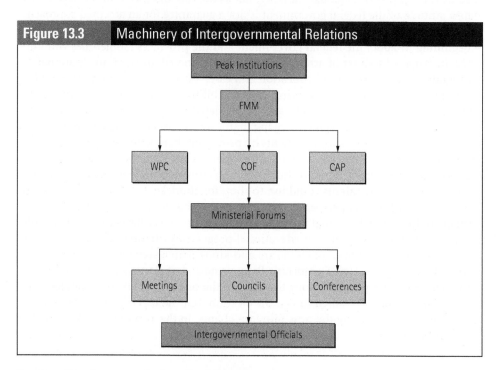

Figure 13.3   Machinery of Intergovernmental Relations

are "central to determining the direction of Canadian federalism in a wide variety of policy areas, including federal–provincial financial relations, trade, health care and social policy."[29] Easily the most important peak institution is the First Ministers Conference (FMC), where Canada's prime minister and premiers, both provincial and territorial, meet to discuss and resolve the most important intergovernmental issues. A couple of decades ago, FMCs were renamed First Ministers Meetings (FMMs). This action signalled the beginning of a decline in the use of this particular body and a greater reliance on bilateral relations between the prime minister and individual premiers. Another peak institution is the Council of the Federation (COF), whose members include the provincial and territorial leaders. The aim of the agency is to "promote interprovincial–territorial cooperation and closer ties between premiers" and to "foster meaningful relations between governments based on respect for the Constitution and recognition of the diversity within the federation." The COF also endeavours to "show leadership on issues important to all Canadians," an intent that reveals the ambition of the provinces and their possible willingness to act without federal participation.[30] Two additional bodies at the top are the Western Premiers' Conference (WPC) and the Council of Atlantic Premiers (CAP), which allow premiers in two of Canada's regions to meet to consider matters specific to their area. The most senior elected officials in government are associated with these peak institutions, but appointed officials located in central agencies, intergovernmental departments, and secretariats also play an important advisory role here.

Immediately below the peak institutions are the councils, conferences, forums, and meetings populated by departmental ministers. The task of these intergovernmental bodies is to act on directives issued by FMMs and other peak organizations, and to address less pressing matters with their counterparts in other governments. For instance, federal, provincial, and territorial ministers responsible for immigration had to coordinate the directive relating to welcoming 25,000 Syrian refugees into Canada by early 2016. During the same period, energy ministers from the two levels of government and the territories held an important conference to discuss energy priorities sensitive to environmental considerations.

The last basic piece of intergovernmental machinery is the variety of intergovernmental institutions and interactions involving appointed officials. As in any area of public administration, administrators and analysts must complement and support the work of the country's elected representatives. Of special importance here are the designated intergovernmental officials, residing largely in central agencies but also in special units within line departments at both the federal and provincial levels. Those located in central agencies and other bodies specializing in relations between the orders of government (and called "intergovernmental generalists") focus on the "coordination of relations with other governments and of intergovernmental activities within their own government," thereby ensuring that the interests and views of the government are properly represented within and outside their home base. Those in line departments are called "intergovernmental specialists" because they address substantive policy issues that arise in relations with other governments.[31] Senior departmental officials such as deputy and associate deputy ministers also serve to represent governments in their dealings with other public authorities.

In many policy areas, formal arrangements have been made to facilitate bureaucratic dealings on intergovernmental matters. In the field of fiscal relations, for example, a permanent committee of the deputy ministers of finance from the federal, provincial, and territorial governments (called the Continuing Committee of Officials) carries out the necessary preparation for meetings of finance ministers and resolves issues not requiring ministerial attention. Informal interactions are also a crucial part of the machinery of intergovernmental relations at this level. Appointed officials emphasize the "importance of being able to connect with their counterparts in other governments on the phone or via email, sometimes on an almost daily basis."[32] The respect and trust among officials developed during formal contacts pave the way for frank and productive discussions outside of, and between, formal meetings. During these discussions, officials exchange a great deal of information about their government's position on matters of continuing concern and negotiation. An essential attribute of intergovernmental officials is their ability to obtain current knowledge of the perceptions and positions of other governments.

Types of Intergovernmental Administrative Interactions

The preceding section shows that interactions involving senior elected representatives and their officials are important to intergovernmental affairs. These interactions are many in number, but they can reduced to three types of relationships. Each type reveals a particular pattern to the way in which officials—whether elected or appointed—relate to one another when addressing intergovernmental issues. Earlier, we looked at federal–provincial relations in terms of particular policies or arrangements; now, the aim is to examine federal–provincial relations in terms of the nature of the interactions between intergovernmental officials.

One of the three types of relationships concerns intergovernmental specialists from each of the two orders of government. The interactions between the specialists at the federal and provincial level tend to be harmonious and quite productive because they share a body of knowledge and skills. The fact that they also possess a common set of professional attitudes and values relating to their particular policy fields also contributes to good relations. Equally important, the focus is on reaching sound decisions about policy initiatives and not on process and guarding jurisdictional responsibilities.[33]

A second type of relationship describes intergovernmental interactions involving primarily ministers and intergovernmental generalists residing in each of the two orders of government. The interactions take the form of a bargaining process in which the ministers and their officials at one level of government present and defend their government's position on specific public policy issues to ministers and their officials at the other level. Intergovernmental conflict is more prevalent, because ministers and the intergovernmental generalists tend not to share values, attitudes, and skills to the same extent as policy specialists; the interests of minister and their intergovernmental generalists lie less in resolving technical program issues and more in achieving broader policy and political goals.

A third set of relationships refers to interactions between intergovernmental generalists and specialists within each order of government; it is *intra*governmental rather than *inter*governmental bargaining that is involved here. As individual governments seek to define their positions on an intergovernmental issue, generalists in the field may advise that process considerations be paramount while the specialists might side in favour of policy substance. For instance, the specialists at the provincial level may recommend accepting federal conditions in return for more federal funding, but the generalists may counter by warning against federal interference in areas of provincial jurisdiction. Differences can also arise in these kinds of relations because of the "implicit hierarchy" which places the generalists above the specialists.[34] At times, say the specialists, the hierarchy means that the central agency officials can move into the departments to take away responsibility for issues that became important. The central agencies, not surprisingly, downplay any talk of hierarchy, saying that their job is essential to ensuring a coordinated approach within the government to intergovernmental matters. Too often, say the central-agency generalists, the specialists in the individual departments are unable to see the intergovernmental connections between the policy initiatives of the various departments. For example, the overall goal of a province might be to achieve consistency in its relations with Ottawa, but one department may allow a fairly prominent role for the federal government while another offers it little or no role.

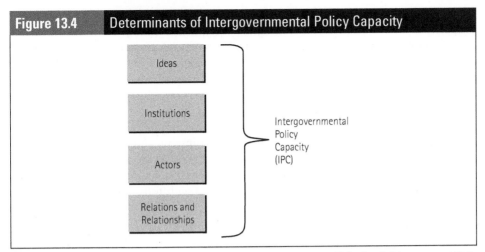

| Figure 13.4 | Determinants of Intergovernmental Policy Capacity |

Ideas

Institutions

Actors

Relations and Relationships

Intergovernmental Policy Capacity (IPC)

Source: Inwood, Gregory, Johns, Carolyn and O'Reilly, Patricia. "Determinants of Intergovernmental Policy Capacity." *Intergovernmental Policy Capacity in Canada*. Montreal: MQUP, 2011. Print.

Intergovernmental Policy Capacity

The processes and interactions of intergovernmental officials are important, but ultimately it is **intergovernmental policy capacity (IPC)** that matters the most. This capacity refers to the "ability of national and sub-national governments in a federal system to work together to address public policy problems."[35] Whether this capacity develops depends on four determinants (see Figure 13.4). One is the ideas that shape thinking about the role of government and the policy challenges facing a federal state. A second factor relates to the workability of the institutions important to the functioning of a federal state. A third determinant concerns the relevant actors in and outside the institutions of federalism. The relationships, both formal and informal, between and among the actors constitute the final factor affecting the quality of IPC.

There is evidence to suggest that all four determinants fall short of reaching their potential for contributing to IPC in Canada.[36] The set of ideas prominent in interactions between governments fail to include vision statements and other proclamations that act to bring policy makers together. For their part, the institutions fail in their inability to use FMMs and other senior bodies to jump-start action in various areas. As for the actors, the appointed officials need to be better skilled at networking, and the presence of leadership qualities appears to be limited among both elected and appointed officials. The final determinant, the intergovernmental relations themselves, also suffer from various ailments, the most important one seemingly being the turf wars at both the political and administrative levels; these wars work to undermine the cooperation necessary for success in intergovernmental relations. Participants in the relations also express the wish for more informal relations so that "trust ties" can be established between people who work together.[37]

The conclusion from the consideration of the four determinants is an obvious one: the policy capacity of intergovernmental relations has to be strengthened. This lack of capacity would matter little if it were the case that federalism works best when governments have

intergovernmental policy capacity (IPC) A measure of the ability of governments in a federal state to combine their efforts to create effective policy outcomes.

WHAT TO DO?

The recent actions of the federal government in the area of postsecondary education have been directed towards providing financial assistance to students. But the federal government has also been concerned that young people may be graduating from university and college without the skills and competencies required to succeed in the job market. The federal government as well feels that the two orders of government need to work together to address this problem. But the provinces are protective of their constitutional responsibility for education and are reluctant to acknowledge officially the existence of the need for any federal involvement in dealing with postsecondary education. However, unofficially, some of the provinces concede that federal assistance might be necessary, especially when it comes to helping to pay for any reforms of colleges and universities. What might be done to bring about a federal–provincial partnership to ensure today's young people are properly equipped to enter the workplace? Part of your consideration of this query should be proposing ways of affecting positively one or more of the determinants of intergovernmental policy capacity in Canada.

Chapter 13 / Intergovernmental Administrative Relations

few dealings with other governments in Canada. But most scholars argue against this proposition. As Inwood and his colleagues say, "In most policy areas it is no longer a question of exclusive jurisdiction of federal, provincial, or territorial governments, but a question of how jurisdiction, responsibility, accountability, policy purposes, and public resources are shared."[38] Interestingly, when asked about IPC, some government officials identify it with their own government's policy capacity and not the capacity of governments to work together. Perhaps this indicates that the importance of IPC is exaggerated and that governments think in terms of other governments as at most sometime-participants in their policy-making process. Another interpretation, however, is that this perception is part of the failure associated with ideas. Within the set of ideas that inform intergovernmental relations in Canada, "[t]here appears to be little political awareness, will or capacity in the federation as a whole to deal with today's realities on anything but an ad-hoc, crisis-led basis...."[39]

Points to Know

- Intergovernmental relations refer to the interactions of federal, provincial, and territorial governments at both the political and administrative levels. Non-governmental actors are also playing an increasing role in these relations.

- Relations between the federal and provincial governments—the most salient part of Canadian federalism—evolve over time in terms of the relative power of each order of government. At times the federal government dominates, at other times the provinces are in the ascendency, and in still other times the two find themselves evenly matched.

- The organizational machinery supporting relations between governments includes peak organizations involving first ministers, forums that allow departmental

ministers to discuss and decide matters, and a web of formal and informal administrative relationships among appointed officials expert in the area of intergovernmental arrangements.

- Intergovernmental relations at the administrative level largely involve officials who are either proficient in coordinating and managing interactions between governments (intergovernmental generalists) or specialists in public policies requiring the participation of both federal and provincial governments (intergovernmental specialists).

- Intergovernmental policy capacity is the ability of any federation to bring governments together to produce sound public initiatives and arrangements.

Review Questions

1. Outline the evolution of Canadian federalism and explain its significance.

2. Discuss trends in intergovernmental relations based on your understanding of recent developments in public policy.

3. Propose a new network of intergovernmental structures that would result in better relations between the orders of government.

4. What are the appropriate roles for the two types of intergovernmental officials?

5. What might strengthen the intergovernmental policy capacity of federalism in Canada?

Notes

1. Richard Simeon, "The Federal–Provincial Decision Making Process," in Ontario Economic Council, *Issues and Alternatives—1977: Intergovernmental Relations* (Toronto: Ontario Economic Council, 1977), 26.

2. Adapted from M.J.C. Vile, *The Structure of American Federalism* (London: Oxford University Press, 1961), 199.

3. Daniel Elezar, quoted in Douglas M. Brown, "Getting Things Done in the Federation: Do We Need New Rules for an Old Game?" *Constructive and Cooperative Federalism?* (Montreal: Institute for Research on Public Policy,

2003), 2, accessed August 11, 2016, www.policy.ca/policy-directory/Detailed/890.html.

4. The territories have now achieved a status almost equal to federal and provincial governments in intergovernmental relations, so increasingly we refer to federal–provincial–territorial relations (FPT relations) when discussing federalism in Canada. However, this chapter will sometimes revert to the traditional practice of using federal–provincial relations, especially when relations literally apply only to the two orders of government (e.g., the Equalization program).

5. K.C. Wheare, *Federal Government*, 4th ed. (London: Oxford University Press, 1963), 10.
6. Quoted in Edwin R. Black, *Divided Loyalties: Canadian Concepts of Federalism* (Montreal: McGill-Queen's University Press, 1975), 43.
7. Donald V. Smiley, "The Rowell-Sirois Report, Provincial Autonomy, and Post-War Canadian Federalism," *Canadian Journal of Economics and Political Science* 28 (February 1962): 54.
8. David Cameron and Richard Simeon, "Intergovernmental Relations in Canada: The Emergence of Collaborative Federalism," *Publius: The Journal of Federalism* 32(2) (Spring 2002): 51.
9. Richard Simeon and Ian Robinson, "The Dynamics of Canadian Federalism," in *Canadian Politics*, 4th ed., eds. James Bickerton and Alain-G. Gagnon (Peterborough: Broadview Press, 2004), 113. This period is often given the name "executive federalism."
10. Ibid., 117–122.
11. Cameron and Simeon, "Intergovernmental Relations in Canada," 54.
12. Gerard Boismenu and Peter Graefe, "The New Federal Tool Belt: Attempt to Build Social Policy Leadership," *Canadian Public Policy* XXX(1) (2004): 71–89.
13. Richard Simeon, Ian Robinson, and Jennifer Wallner, "The Dynamics of Canadian Federalism," in *Canadian Politics*, 6th ed., eds. James Bickerton and Alain-G. Gagnon (University of Toronto, 2014), 83.
14. Letter of Justin P.J.Trudeau to the Hon. Paul Davis, September 2, 2015, 1, accessed August 11, 2016, https://www.liberal.ca/letter-to-the-council-of-the-federation/.
15. Martin Papillon, "Canadian Federalism and the Emerging Mosaic of Aboriginal Multilevel Governance," in *Canadian Federalism: Performance, Effectiveness, and Legitimacy*, 3rd ed., eds. Herman Bakvis and Grace Skogstad (Toronto: University of Toronto Press, 2012), 297.
16. Letter of Justin P.J. Trudeau to the Hon. Paul Davis, September 2, 2015, 2.
17. Neil Bradford, "Canada's Urban Agenda: A New Deal for the Cities?" in *Canadian Politics*, eds. Bickerton and Gagnon, 431, 435.
18. Justin Trudeau's Speech to the Federation of Canadian Municipalities Conference, June 10, 2015, accessed October 11, 2015, https://www.liberal.ca/justin-trudeaus-speech-to-the-federation-of-canadian-municipalities-conference/.
19. Prime Minister Justin Trudeau, Minister of Environment and Climate Change Mandate Letter, 2. http://pm.gc.ca/eng/minister-environment-and-climate-change-mandate-letter accessed August 11, 2016.
20. Shawn McCarthy and Gloria Galloway, "First Ministers Agree to Forge National Climate Strategy," *Globe and Mail*, November 24, 2015, A1, A4.
21. Bill Curry, "Ottawa Lowers Expectations for Climate Deal with Provinces," *Globe and Mail*, February 10, 2016, accessed September 27, 2016, Shawn McCarthy, "Ottawa Seeks to Set National Minimum on Carbon Pricing" *Globe and Mail*, February 17, 2016, accessed September 27, 2016, http://www.theglobeandmail.com/news/politics/ottawa-seeks-to-set-national-minimum-on-carbon-pricing/article28792641/.
22. SCICS, Press Release – Communique of Canada's First Ministers, accessed June 17, 2016, http://www.scics.gc.ca/english/Conferences.asp?a=viewdocument&id=2400.
23. Peter Russell, *Constitutional Odyssey: Can Canadians Become a Sovereign People?* 3rd ed. (Toronto: University of Toronto Press, 2004), 228.
24. See Patrick Boyer, *Our Scandalous Senate* (Toronto: Dundurn Press, 2014).
25. Grace Skogstad, "International Trade Policy and the Evolution of Canadian Federalism," in *Canadian Federalism*, eds. Bakvis and Grace Skogstad, 206.
26. Mark Winfield and Douglas Macdonald, "Federalism and Canadian Climate Change Policy," in *Canadian Federalism*, eds. Bakvis and Skogstad, 241.
27. See Martha Friendly and Linda A. White, "'No-laterialism: Paradoxes in Early Childhood Education and Care Policy in the Canadian Federation," in Ibid., 183–202.
28. See Antonia Maioni, "Health Care," in Ibid., 165–182.
29. J. Peter Meekison, Hamish Telford, and Harvey Lazar, "The Institutions of Executive Federalism: Myths and Realities," in *Canada: The State of the Federation 2002: Reconsidering the Institutions of Canadian Federalism*, eds. J. Peter Meekison, Hamish Telford, and Harvey Lazar (London: McGill-Queen's University Press, 2004), 16.
30. All quotations taken from the Council's website at http://canadaspremiers.ca/en/about, accessed June 17, 2016.
31. Gregory J. Inwood, Carolyn M. Johns, and Patricia L. O'Reilly, *Intergovernmental Policy Capacity in Canada: Inside the Worlds of Finance, Environment, Trade and Health Policy* (Montreal & Kingston: McGill-Queen's University Press, 2011), 80.
32. Gregory J. Inwood, Carolyn Johns, and Patricia L. O'Reilly, "Intergovernmental Officials in Canada," in *Canada: The State of the Federation 2002*, 268.
33. Inwood, Johns, and O'Reilly, *Intergovernmental Policy Capacity in Canada*, 113.
34. Ibid., 112.
35. Ibid., 14.
36. The evidence emerges from interviews conducted with intergovernmental officials a decade ago, but the decision of the Harper government in the past 10 years to downplay relations between the two orders of government suggests that little has changed with respect to intergovernmental policy capacity. See Ibid.
37. Inwood, Johns, and O'Reilly, *Intergovernmental Policy Capacity in Canada*, 449.
38. Ibid., 414.
39. Ibid., 469.

Non-Governmental Actors and the Bureaucracy

14

Learning Objectives

Reading this chapter allows you to do the following:

- Understand that public administration extends beyond the three branches of government to include non-governmental bodies

- Identify the key activities of interest groups and successfully apply them to real-life situations

- Assess the dynamics of relations between the media and appointed officials and design new ways of shaping these relations

- Propose actions that enrich public consultations between government and citizens

- Appreciate the debate over the impact of social media on public administration and government

The most significant relations involving appointed officials are often thought to be those that involve either one of the three branches of government or another level of government. Appointed officials exist in a governmental setting, so it is natural to infer that what happens within and between governments is central to public administration. This line of thinking has an element of truth to it: the interactions of public servants with ministers, cabinet, the legislature, the courts, and other orders of government are important. But the world of public administration also includes entities that exist outside of government. It has to be appreciated that **non-governmental actors** also form part of the world of the public servant. To believe otherwise is to miss an increasingly large part of the study of public administration in Canada.

The key non-governmental actors are interest groups, the media, and the concerned public. These entities all interact with public servants because they contribute to the goal of addressing the needs of Canadians. Interest groups can help the government administer public initiatives, the media are able to assist the government in supplying the citizenry with information about important public programs, and consultations with the public can contribute to the design of better public policy. But these interactions are not always a product of civility and common interests. The media may select a particular program for extensive criticism, interest groups might attempt to force senior elected officials to make a decision inconsistent with the mandate of the government, and members of the public sometimes make proposals that clash with government preferences. This same mix of cooperation and conflict also applies to the newer non-governmental actors, which include social movements, social media, and the Internet.

This chapter seeks to provide an understanding of the relations between the public bureaucracy and the major non-governmental actors. The chapter outlines the nature of

non-governmental actor Citizens and representatives of institutions located outside of government who strive to influence elected and appointed officials and participate in the making and administration of public programs and policies.

each of the non-governmental actors and reveals how they affect the political process. It also discusses the often strategic or game quality of the relationship between non-governmental actors and government. The interaction between the two sometimes at times appears as a contest in which all sorts of tactics are employed to secure preferences and goals.

Interest Groups

interest group Organizations of private persons who join together to further their mutual interests by influencing public policy.

A good place to start an investigation of **interest groups** is with the disagreement over whether the term "interest group" is appropriate. Some scholars like the term "pressure group" because they believe the essence of groups is to place pressure on government to act in a particular way. However, this may be too narrow a view, with its nearly exclusive focus on the adversarial nature of the relationship between groups and government; relations between groups and government can also be cooperative. Other scholars prefer "advocacy group" and its connotation that groups are basically about pursuing ideas and beliefs regardless of their impact on government. The problem with this term is that the adversarial quality almost disappears when all that is necessary is to find a balance between the cooperative and conflictual orientation of groups. Still others favour defining groups in terms of one of two types: one type is the public interest group, which has a wide breadth of membership and acts with little heed of material gain; the other type has a more narrow membership that seeks private gain. But research shows that it is sometimes hard to make such a distinction between groups. Almost by default, the preferred term is "interest group" if we understand "interest" to signify both the narrow, self-regarding definition of the term and the broader, other-regarding meaning. By using "interest group," we avoid the usual temptation to see groups always acting selfishly while at the same time realizing that they are not always proponents of the public interest. With this in mind, a definition of interest group can be offered: interest groups are organizations of private persons who have joined together to further their mutual interests by influencing public policy, with "interests" defined both narrowly and broadly.[1]

Types of Interest Groups

All groups can be covered by the definition just provided, but it is also true that interest groups are not all the same. Interest groups have been classified into a variety of types according to such criteria as objectives, activities, and structure; but a broad distinction can be made between "institutionalized groups" and "issue-oriented groups."[2] Institutionalized groups are characterized by organizational continuity and cohesion. They are highly knowledgeable about the policy-making process and about how to get access to public officials, in part because they usually employ a professional staff. The membership of institutionalized groups is stable. They have concrete and immediate operational objectives, but their ultimate aims are sufficiently broad that they can bargain with government over achieving particular concessions. Last but not least, their long-term credibility with government decision makers is more important than any single issue or objective. Examples of institutionalized groups are the Canadian Medical Association, the Canadian Chamber of Commerce, the Canadian Bankers Association, and the Canadian Labour Congress.

Issue-oriented groups tend to be less organized and to have less knowledge of government and of how to contact public officials. There is a constant turnover in their membership, they usually focus on only one or two issues, and they are not typically concerned about their long-term credibility with the bureaucracy. Examples of issue-oriented groups are those troubled by a particular threat to the environment or those opposed to specific projects of developers. Recently, the policy influence of certain issue-oriented groups has increased substantially, as they have learned to use the Internet and gain better access to the media and outside expertise.

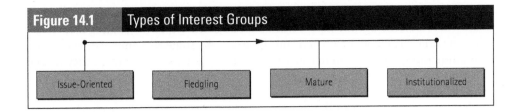

Figure 14.1   Types of Interest Groups

| Issue-Oriented | Fledgling | Mature | Institutionalized |

In reality, virtually all interest groups fall on a continuum between the two extremes of institutionalized and issue-oriented groups, and they can be discussed in terms of the extent to which they possess the characteristics of one type or the other (see Figure 14.1). A few additional types of interest groups—"fledgling" and "mature"—can be placed on the continuum to suggest the character of groups at various points.[3] As well, some issue-oriented groups may gradually move along the continuum, shifting to fledgling status, then to mature, and finally to institutionalized—and some of the more mature groups may at times find it necessary to adopt some of the extreme tactics associated with issue-oriented and fledgling groups.

What Does an Interest Group Do?

The most important and interesting aspect of interest groups is what they do. Any activity of interest groups can be associated with one or more of six basic activities.[4] The best-known activity is **lobbying**, which "typically involves voicing preferences or transmitting demands to government, exclusively on behalf of and for the benefit of members."[5] The voicing can encompass informal meetings between interest group leaders and their counterparts in government, access to cabinet and senior party members at fundraising gatherings, arranged meetings with government officials, and the employment of professional lobbyists to make the case of interest groups to government. As can be seen, lobbying reflects that quality of groups which relates to their capacity to be self-centred.

A second activity, **advocating**, is similar to lobbying save for the important fact that the benefits of successful advocacy efforts go beyond group members. For example, a successful letter campaign by a parent–teacher association wishing to convince the local school board to upgrade computers in the schools confers benefits upon parent members of the association; but it does the same for parents who are non-members. The parents who worked hard for the association get the new computers, but so do those parents who did little to help, and the first group of parents know this to be the case. Accordingly, we have an action that generates gains that go beyond the group itself (Box 14.1).

Sometimes groups feel that any action directed towards government through lobbying or advocacy is fruitless and thus subscribe to a third type of activity that centres on gaining the attention of the media and the larger public. The hope associated with this activity

lobbying A legitimate means by which groups and individuals try to influence government decisions by direct contact with politicians or public servants. Usually associated with the activities of interest groups.

advocating An activity similar to lobbying except that the impact of the activity addresses not only to the interests of group members but also those interests located outside the group.

Free Riders

The concept of "advocating" brings up an issue crucial to the study of interest groups. It has been argued that it is difficult to sustain groups whose efforts produce benefits for those outside the group. Why? Because people will refrain from joining groups if the benefits are available to those who are not part of the group. People will naturally "free ride" because they feel that it makes little sense to incur group costs for something which they can get for nothing. Yet the phenomenon of advocacy suggests otherwise. Are people who join advocacy groups acting irrationally or are the free-rider theorists missing something in their analysis?

BOX 14.1

is that the media, the public, or some other valid target will put pressure on government to act. This would be like the parent-teacher group discussed earlier shifting their attention away from the school board and launching a media strategy to embarrass the school board into acting. If the board refuses to listen to the parents, then perhaps they will be more receptive to media stories that put the school trustees and administrators in a poor light. Using the courts to find government in violation of the law is another example of this type of activity. Scholars call this kind of activity "contesting." "Retreating" is a term applied to groups who experience failure with their lobbying and decide to fall back and wait for a more opportune time to make their case: sometimes to act is not to act.

A fifth action, called "participating," refers to the actions of groups who "cooperate with government, as well as with other actors, in the development of policy for the betterment of their community (or their country)."[6] The activities here include formal presentations to legislative bodies, membership in government-established commissions, and media strategies supportive of the issue at hand. This type of activity shows that interest groups are more than capable of acting in a way that almost exclusively concerns itself with the larger public interest. We often think that groups are only in it for their own material interests, yet there are a number of well-known interest groups famous for their commitment to making things better for everyone. Greenpeace and Amnesty International are two examples of such groups acting on the international stage. In Canada, groups that act this way include the John Howard Society, the Canadian Civil Liberties Union, and the Non-Smokers Rights Association. Perhaps the best-known public interest group is Mothers Against Drunk Driving, which has been more than instrumental in getting tougher laws for drunk driving.

A final type of interest-group activity is "regulation," which involves the solving of public-interest problems with knowledge only available to interest groups. In these situations, which typically entail issues relating to the application of expert knowledge, government is largely unable to participate and the group gains the right to regulate itself. Groups representing doctors, lawyers, accountants, and other professions applying important expertise to their patients or clients are the ones that fall into this category. In accepting this responsibility, interest groups serve the public interest by ensuring that expert knowledge is applied properly. But there is also a suspicion that self-regulation is used to produce benefits solely available to regulated body. Doctors regulate themselves in order to ensure that only properly educated physicians provide medically required care and that these same physicians practise medicine without imposing injury on their patients. This is the public interest side of regulation. However, self-regulation can be seen to allow doctors to shape health care systems to reflect the preferences of doctors. This brings up the possibility of a private interest side of regulation.

In observing these activities of interest groups, it is important to understand that groups are often part of a larger system of decision making for each sector of public policy. The terms **policy community** or **policy network** identify this system of governmental and non-governmental actors. Figure 14.2 shows that each policy community consists of an inner circle or "sub-government" of key governmental and non-governmental actors—cabinet, the lead department or agency, and major interest groups—who make the actual decisions, and an outer circle (or "attentive public") of players, who indirectly influence policy through discussion and debate of the issues of the day. Many of the political activities of interest groups take place in relation to these policy communities.

policy community or **policy network** A cluster of interested groups (government organizations, interest groups, international agencies, interested companies and individuals, and journalists) organized around a particular policy. This group has a strong influence on the making of that policy.

Targeting and Accessing Government

It is critical to the success of interest groups that in their interactions with government they identify and aim at the right targets. With this task of targeting, groups must first decide whether to direct their efforts to the federal, provincial, or local spheres of government (or to all of them). The federal nature of Canada has important effects on the organization and operations of interest groups. Many Canadian groups are

Figure 14.2 The Policy Community

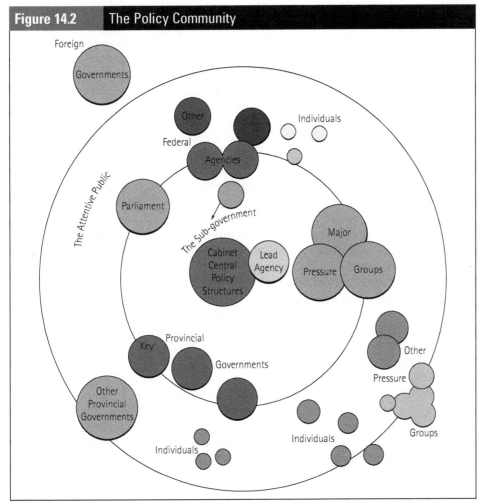

Source: Pross, Paul, *Group Politics and Public Policy* 2e © 1993 Oxford University Press Canada. Reprinted by permission of the publisher.

themselves federations composed of provincial bodies that give their attention to provincial governments and a national organization that focuses its efforts on Ottawa. But some groups are not large enough to have provincial components or affiliates of a national organization and are thus obliged to channel their limited resources to those governments where the resources will do the most good. A further impact of federalism on group activity is that groups may be required to lobby federal, provincial, and local governments simultaneously.

Whether interest groups lobby federal or provincial governments, the usual targets of their activity are cabinet ministers, public servants, and legislators, all of whom play important roles in the public policy process. This process may be divided into pre-legislative, legislative, and post-legislative stages. Public servants are influential in the pre- and post-legislative stages, making them entities to which interest groups will address many of their efforts. In the pre-legislative stage, the temptation for interest groups may be to concentrate their attention on cabinet and the prime minister, who are formally responsible for proposing legislative enactments to Parliament. However, at this stage public servants play a key role because senior elected officials rely on the administrative arm of government to provide the options for action and the drafting of key decision documents. Accordingly, well-informed groups expend much of their energies on dealing with the relevant public servants.[7]

The influence of public servants does not give them the final say on major public policy issues at the legislative stage; that authority belongs to cabinet ministers. Therefore, interest groups are frequently obliged to approach ministers to influence both the decisions of individual departments and those of cabinet committees and cabinet at the legislative stage. Parliament, too, becomes a target at this point, especially when legislative committees hold hearings on bills vying to become laws. But at the last stage, the post-legislative stage, the significance of public servants as targets of groups becomes salient again. Cabinet ministers have enormous power, which allows them to be dominant in all three stages; in theory, they can be the most powerful voice when it comes to the post-legislative stages. In practice, though, ministers have neither the time nor the inclination to participate actively in the post-legislative stage; rather, they tend to leave policy implementation to the public servants. Because of this decision, interest groups will be encouraged to turn most of their attention in this last stage to appointed officials. In this post-legislative stage, interest groups know that public servants have some discretion in the carrying out of government policies and programs. Though some may believe that the policy process ends with the passing of proposed legislation into law, knowledgeable actors in the political process appreciate that the truth is something quite different.

The ability of interest groups to select the right targets requires having the necessary appreciation of the operation of government. As Savoie writes, "It is ... vitally important to know how to access the [political] process, whom to talk to, when, and what arguments should be marshalled to have an impact."[8] This in turn relies on having the available resources for acquiring such knowledge, so it is usually well-funded groups that best understand where the power lies in government.

On completion of targeting, interest groups next have to access those targeted. As with targeting, resources increase the chances of gaining access. A major concern of appointed officials is the availability of the knowledge and expertise necessary to ensure the efficient formulation and administration of public programs. An interest group that has the economic power to meet this particular need will be recognized favourably by appointed officials and their superiors. Once again money is the key to success:

> It is simply the case that the more an interest group has the resources to move beyond communicating demands, to become instead a source of knowledge (and thereby a potential source of effective administration), the more it becomes of interest to civil servants.[9]

Certain groups also gain access and maintain recognition more easily than others because they constitute a large part or even the sole clientele of a specific department (for example, a labour union might be highly influential with the labour department). A department can rely on a clientele group as a source of information and as a channel of communication to the group's members. It can also use the group to gain support for its policies from other departments and, indeed, from the general public, by claiming to speak for the interests of the major group affected by the department's policies.

A further basis of interest group access and recognition is the group's political clout. Ministers, legislators, and public servants are interested in the political impact interest-group activity can have on the next election and on the overall fortunes of the party in power. While public servants are expected to be non-partisan, they are at the same time supposed to be politically sensitive. They should be able to advise the minister as to the likely effects of proposed policies on various segments of society, including those represented by influential interest groups. Thus, public servants will strive to be aware of the possible effects of government decisions on the voting behaviour of an interest group's membership. Similarly, public servants are aware of the capacity of groups to shape public opinion on an issue. Public servants are thus more likely to grant access to groups that have the resources to influence the political fortunes of their minister or of the government as a whole (see Box 14.2).

BOX
14.2

A New Governance?

Many believe that the success of interest groups and other types of non-governmental actors has been shaped by a change in the nature of governance in Canada. This new governance model, outlined in Chapter 5, visualizes a shift away from a top-down approach to governing dominated by government to one that emphasizes collaboration between government and non-governmental actors, and a greater reliance on networks rather than strict hierarchical arrangements. There is evidence to support such a view, but the failures and frustrations of non-governmental groups—some of which are discussed in this chapter—suggests that the alleged new governance model has its limits.

Source: Susan Phillips, "Policy Analysis and the Voluntary Sector: Evolving Policy Styles," in *Policy Analysis in Canada: The State of the Art*, eds. Laurent Dobuzinskis, Michael Howlett, and David Laycock (Toronto: University of Toronto Press, 2007).

Finally, a primary function of interest groups is the provision of legitimacy to government actions. A group can thus gain access to government if it can serve to increase the acceptability of government. This means that public servants and other actors in government seek out those groups that can facilitate legitimating government initiatives.[10] The importance of interest groups in this regard is revealed in the fact that governments actively support the creation of groups who have the potential to support public initiatives.

Interest Group Tactics

The success of pressure groups depends on their ability to target the right entities for attention and for their appreciation of the factors that increase the chances of gaining access to these targets. It has also been shown that interest groups have available six basic types of activities that can be employed in pursuing their goals. But success may also reflect the use of tactics to complement the other factors important to a group's ability to get what it wants. These tactics can be seen as a set of tips for interest groups:

- Groups are advised to attempt to influence policy at the earliest possible stage of its development and to follow the progress of that policy all the way through the policy-making process, including the post-legislative or implementation stage. Groups can perform this task more successfully if their contacts with government officials are sufficiently cordial and continuous so that they are able to anticipate or learn quickly about policy initiatives.
- Both common sense and the present nature of the policy process suggest that interest-group representations to government should, where feasible, be framed in terms of the public interest. The requests of interest groups are more likely to be met if they are attuned to the priorities and plans of the government than if they amount to blatant, self-interested pleading. For example, in a time of high inflation and high unemployment, officials are likely to look favourably on proposals that may reduce these. Similarly, proposals that require the expenditure of substantial public funds during a time of severe economic restraint are unlikely to receive a sympathetic hearing.
- Interest groups typically rely on quiet, behind-the-scenes consultations rather than media campaigns and public demonstrations designed to influence decision makers indirectly. Aside from the fact that public protests and the like may embarrass the government (not a good thing to do), the quiet approach allows groups to convey their concerns more effectively and to offer any possible help to government. Certainly, groups within the inner circle of the policy community rely on the more discrete manner of approaching government. But those in the outer circle may find

that a less discrete approach is the only way to make known their views. Inner-circle groups also sometimes come to the same conclusion if they find that the discrete approach is not working or that aggressive action is more beneficial.

- One effective and frequently used tactic is cooperative lobbying. This requires groups to create formal or informal alliances with other groups who share their views on a particular policy issue. Cooperative lobbying enables several groups to present a united front to government as an indication of widespread concern. At the same time, groups profit from this cooperative arrangement by sharing information and contacts (see the following case study).

Interest Group Politics: A Case Study

In 2013, the Government of Canada issued new regulations to generate greater competition in Canada's wireless technology industry, which was dominated by the Canadian companies Rogers, Bell, and Telus. The regulations, though complex, gave smaller Canadian wireless companies advantages that were unavailable to the three big telecommunication corporations. The regulations also allowed foreign companies to purchase smaller Canadian wireless companies and have access to the advantages offered to them. A huge American wireless firm, Verizon, soon expressed interested in buying Wind Mobile, a small Canadian wireless entity. The development alarmed the big three Canadian companies, who initiated a campaign, which included some of the activities that interest groups which may use to achieve their goals (this joining together revealed that within an industry a handful of individual firms—or even single ones—can act to create an ad hoc interest group).[11] The first move was a combination *lobbying–advocacy* tactic: a letter to the prime minister signed by the heads of Rogers, Bell, and Telus.[12] The letter complained that the new regulations were unfair and put the big three companies at a distinct disadvantage; the regulations also put at risk the benefits now available to all Canadians through the present wireless market (reasonable prices, employment, good wireless access). The letter constituted lobbying with the focus on private interest; advocacy also could be seen with the reference to public benefits.

The big three sensed, rightly, that the letter would not be nearly enough, and that it would be necessary to embrace a *contesting* technique: a media campaign that spoke directly to Canadians. A few weeks after the letter, Bell published in newspapers a full-page "An Open Letter to all Canadians," which repeated the arguments made in the letter to the prime minister.[13] The media campaign then expanded to include radio commercials featuring ordinary Canadians expressing fears about recent developments in the wireless industry. Then the contesting escalated with Telus taking the government to court, saying that it was "seeking clarity from the court" on whether the new regulations were legal.[14] At the same time, the big three reverted to an old-fashioned *lobbying* tactic: a meeting with the responsible minister. The government agreed to a meeting with the heads of Rogers, Bell, and Telus; but the meeting went badly. According to a Bell director, the minister gave the three CEOs little time to make their arguments and seemed to be "just going through the motions."[15]

As the meeting with the minister suggested, the efforts of the three majors had little effect on the federal government. The minister himself said that he respected the fact that the wireless companies had a commitment to their shareholders; but his responsibility was to a "broader public interest." In other words, the companies were pursuing narrow self-interest, and the government was

WHAT TO DO?

Let us assume that Verizon continued to take an interest in buying Wind Mobile, rather than deciding not to come to Canada (see Interest Group Politics: A Case Study). Would the federal government have eventually backed down and agreed to the demands of the big three telecommunication companies? There is pretty strong evidence to indicate that the regulations instituted to create more competition in the wireless industry would have remained in place. Letters to the prime minister and the responsible minister seemed to have little effect. The creation of a government website to defend the regulations and emergence of consumer lobbies point to the same conclusion. So the question becomes as follows: what went wrong with the efforts of Rogers, Bell, and Telus? What would you have suggested if you had been advising the three Canadian companies?

"serving Canadians."[16] And to make their point even clearer, the government set up a website supporting its position and indicated their intentions to enlist consumer groups in the fight against the wireless-industry giants. Rogers, Bell, and Telus, however, had not given up. They continued their lobbying efforts, getting some of their high-profile directors to approach important members of the government; and unions with members employed with the big three entered the fray to support the Canadian companies with public rallies and the like.

After two months of interest group activity and government responses, the whole issue came to an anti-climactic end: Verizon announced that it would not be proceeding with plans to buy Wind Mobile. "Verizon is not going to Canada," said the company's CEO.[17] The reason offered for the action was that Verizon had never seriously contemplated buying into the Canadian wireless market (see What to Do?).

Media

Like interest groups, the media act as intermediaries between the government and the public. The term "media" includes traditional transmitters of mass communication, such as radio, television, newspapers, and magazines. But arguably more important are the new purveyors of information to the public—the Internet, social media, and smart-phone technology. Research shows that increasingly people are moving towards use of the new forms of media, a development which has significant implications for both political and appointed officials in government. One implication is the enhanced immediacy of political events. **Social media** such as Facebook and Twitter allow for instantaneous reporting, which demands quick responses from government if it wishes to stay on top of the issues. The popularity of the new forms has led as well to a coming together of the old and the new as radio, television, and printed news find their way onto the Internet and social media outlets (see Box 14.3).

Interest groups and the media are also similar in the sense that each wields more and more influence in the political process and therefore has increasing relevance for appointed officials. Once the institutions of government were the stars of political life in Canada, and attention was riveted on the activities of the three branches of government. But now power and influence have moved outside of government and allowed such institutions as interest groups and the media to acquire greater distinction. It is important to see, however, that interest groups and the media have their differences

social media A term that refers to electronic communication that conveys information, ideas, videos, proposals, and other items of interest. Relevant for public administration is the use of social media to marshal or organize public sentiment about a particular event or action and to allow for quick and easy availability of government messages and policies.

Facebook—A New Media Empire?

BOX
14.3

In the pre-Internet days, the media tended to be dominated by television networks and a handful of cable companies; for example, NBC, CBS, ABC, Fox, and CNN in the United States and CBC and CTV in Canada. One effect of the Internet and social media outlets has been to end this domination and allow viewers and readers various ways in which to get their news. But it is argued that new media empires are emerging in the form of supposedly harmless social media sites. Facebook, for example, provides a list of "trending topics" in the news, topics which relate to the interest of the viewer as determined by Facebook. People are more than ever using their Facebook topics to give them their news for the day. Unlike the older television networks, Facebook does not generate the actual news; it just sends its users to a newspaper article, magazine story, or television news item reporting on the trending topic. But Facebook does decide which topics are trending and which news sources do the best job on the topic. This gives the social network a great deal of influence on what we consider as news.

Source: Ross Douthat, "Facebook's Subtle Empire," *New York Times*, May 22, 2016, 9.

as well. Interest groups seek directly to influence public policy while the media are more focused on servicing customers and generating economic returns for their owners and shareholders. As well, groups tend to represent well-defined interests to carefully identified officials. On the other hand, the media's audience inside and outside governments tends to be broader and more diffuse.

Operation of the Media

The media perform a number of important public functions. They provide the information necessary for a citizenry to become informed about the operation of its government; in a way, they constitute democracy's oxygen. Without this information, a political system committed to democratic norms would be hard pressed to represent the people and their wishes. The media also offer analyses of political events, and in so doing give greater sense to the large amount of information available on the political process. It is also appreciated that newspapers, television, radio, and social media investigate and uncover serious abuses of power in government (and elsewhere). At times, it seems now with the Internet and social media that nothing can really remain secret. This is a new phenomenon that has its good side in the sense that wrongdoing can be more easily identified.

These are all important duties, but arguably more important for government officials and their interaction with the media is how the latter go about making news concerning government and politics. There are a number of theories about the news-making activities of the media. The theory with the greatest resonance is that "journalists and news organizations are not passive, neutral, and objective reflectors of reality but active agents that change the reflection in various ways."[18] (The same can be said of those outside formal media institutions who provide information through social media.) Moreover, the media use various techniques to mold their stories and to develop an audience for their work. It is these techniques that public servants must always keep in mind when dealing with the media:[19]

- *Simplicity.* In reporting on events, the media look for occurrences that are straightforward and easy to explain and understand. If an important event fails to reflect these qualities, the media will be tempted to simplify it even at the risk of losing some meaning or distorting the truth.
- *Dramatization.* The "story" is central to the journalistic enterprise. The media thus look to provide drama in their reports. Conflict, surprise, and juxtaposition are highlighted to make the story work.
- *Personalization.* Successful media reports rely on personalities. A news event without identifiable individuals is more likely than not to be rejected in favour of one that includes people. These people can be both elected and appointed officials, which makes this technique especially crucial for public servants and their superiors.
- *Preformed storylines.* Journalists usually frame an event in a particular way and interpret any developments in accordance with this interpretation. Facts that conflict with the storyline can be ignored, downplayed, or made to fit the storyline.
- *The unexpected.* News reports thrive on the unexpected, especially if it involves a serious error on the part of government. The unexpected event can form part of the preformed storyline—the surprise development becomes an expected event.

These techniques have become even more prominent with the heightened importance of social media. Facebook, Twitter, YouTube, and other social media "fuel a fast-paced political environment," a development that gives even less time for journalists to tackle the difficult issues.[20] This in turn results in a continued "focus on conflict or personalities rather than on more substantive issues."[21] Social media also respond easily to a public "fascinated with celebrity," an amplification of the wish for stories which emphasizes personalities.[22] Finally, social media have also made the media much more willing and able to challenge ministers and their senior officials—and at times to become part of the story as defenders of the public interest. The old days when ink-stained newspaper reporters dutifully recorded the pronouncements of government are over.

Government and the Media

As with the media, governments also seek to shape reality and to present information in a manner that meets their goals. Most government contacts with the media are handled by appointed officials assigned to the media; these officials strive to use the media to support their political superiors, to publicize their department's activities, to obtain favourable comment on these activities, and to measure public reaction to proposed policies and programs. To achieve these goals, attempts will be made to satisfy the needs of the media. Information will be available to meet tight deadlines, and sources within government will work hard to ensure that journalists have something important to report (and some media outlets with limited resources will welcome these entreaties). This category of interaction between the media and government typically involves an exchange of largely factual information on the content and administration of government programs.

Another category of interaction entails an exchange of views on controversial issues. In this instance, partisan officials in the central agencies and media experts in departments rely on their own set of techniques to please their political superiors. Sometimes the techniques are used to counter those of the media. At other times the government will take the offensive and use the following techniques to shape the story:

- One thing public servants must do is to be prepared for the media, especially in relation to possible crises that can do great damage to the political fortunes of government. Witness the efforts of one department to be ready: "most 140-character tweets issued by the department of Industry are planned weeks in advance; edited by dozens of public servants; reviewed and revised by the minister's staff; and sanitized through a 12-step protocol …."[23]
- How a government is perceived or "framed" will help determine the attitude of the public. As Marland writes, the media and government are "locked in a perpetual struggle of public persuasion, jockeying for power to frame events and control the public agenda."[24] So every attempt to prevail in this struggle must be made.
- Mistakes in government, even small ones, often form an important part of any storyline. Public servants thus must be sensitive to the making of errors and make every effort to limit them. To achieve this end, governments sometimes allow only specialized spokespeople to talk to the media; public servants who are experts on a particular issue are muzzled for fear they may reveal too much. Even if government officials are permitted to talk to the media, extensive vetting must first take place (see Box 14.4).
- Politicians and public servants may provide privileged access to journalists in return for favourable coverage. All media types require sources who can provide scoops on forthcoming government initiatives. Government officials can put this basic truth to good use.

These techniques of government put up against techniques employed by the media suggest an almost Machiavellian interaction between government and the media. The two sides have differing aims and each at times uses morally questionable tactics to prevail over the other. To employ a favourite simile, relations between the two are "like 'a chess game' where each player seeks to exploit their symbiotic relationship and never truly trusts the other's motives or agenda."[25] But each requires the other, and hence they must learn to cooperate as well. The media rely on government for stories that people

BOX
14.4

Message Event Proposal

When in power, the federal Conservative government instituted a procedure to prevent mishaps with the media. Called the Message Event Proposal (MEP), it required that a precise communication strategy accompany any government event or announcement. The MEP had to specify such things as wished-for headlines, the important message being delivered, the lines most likely to dominate media copy, the expected sound bite, and even the photo opportunities and dress of those involved. And the whole package had to be approved by the two most powerful central agencies, the Privy Council Office and the Prime Minister's Office.

Source: Alex Marland, "Political Communication in Canada: Strategies and Tactics," in *Canadian Politics*, 6th ed., eds. James Bickerton and Alain-G. Gagnon (Toronto: University of Toronto Press, 2014).

like to read and listen to; the government relies on the media to get its views and programs out to the public. Relations between media and government, as with political life overall, amount to an interdependent situation in which the temptation to deceive or manipulate is present but where long-term gains are to be had if cooperation is practised.

Public Participation and Consultation

A further type of interaction important to public administration in Canada involves public servants and their consultations with the public. The traditional mechanisms for allowing **public involvement** in the governmental process, which include elections, political parties, interest groups, and the media, also represent accepted aspects of the democratic process. But there is a demand for a more direct relationship between those responsible for designing government initiatives and individual members of the public. Part of this demand arises from a desire on the part of government to enhance the legitimacy or acceptability of public programs. In its effort to achieve efficiency and effectiveness in its offerings, government sometimes fails to appreciate sufficiently that legitimacy "is conferred upon policies when a large public feels it has been consulted and heard."[26] A force complementary to this first one is the wish of the public to be more actively involved in the design of public actions. Canadians appear less willing to defer to experts in government and increasingly express their desire to take a more direct part of the policy-making process.

The demand for public consultation also springs from the belief that it may lead to better public policy. Not only will government initiatives be more readily accepted if they are the product of public consultation, but they will also constitute a more effective response to the problem at hand. Scholars believe that the advent of social media has greatly increased the potential of public involvement affecting and enriching the processes of government. Laforest, for one, claims that "the proliferation of social media tools is now single-handedly reshaping the nature of interaction between governments and citizens."[27] Such a claim requires careful consideration because there are some who urge caution in gauging the effect of social media on public involvement with government (see The Internet and Social Media later in the chapter).

The push for greater public consultation and citizen engagement has special relevance for public servants. The focus of this push is typically on the design of public programs. Most forms of public participation seek a capacity to intervene before governments make a final decision. In the Canadian political process appointed officials play a large role in the formulation or design of public programs. Montpetit writes that "the prime responsibility for drafting policies before their presentation to Cabinet, and possibly Parliament, falls upon civil servants."[28] Accordingly, much of the consultation process entails

public involvement A broad range of direct and indirect forms of participation by members of the public in government decision making.

relations between appointed officials and the public. Politicians are eager to see the public play a greater role in designing policies, but more often than not it is the civil servant who represents government. A related reason for the prevalence of public servants in the consultation process is a more mundane one: only the public service has the capacity to handle the increase in the volume of public consultations.[29]

Mechanisms of Public Involvement

Public involvement can take a number of forms distinguished by the purpose of the consultation and the accompanying degree or level of citizen involvement. One way to conceptualize public consultation is to see it as comprising five levels of interaction with the citizenry (see Figure 14.3).[30] Level 1 involves a "low level of public involvement and influence," because the purpose here is merely to "inform or educate" the public on an issue of importance. The mechanisms used with this level of consultation include fact sheets, backgrounders, press releases, information fairs, open houses, and the use of 1-800 numbers to convey information to the public. Social media now play a large role in this first stage, too, succeeding "in offering citizens greater visibility into government".[31] This has been achieved through the use of Facebook, Twitter, and special social media efforts designed to inform and educate. (For example, the federal government has established a website called Consulting with Canadians which alerts Canadians to opportunities for public input and consultation.[32])

Level 2 represents an attempt on the part of government to "gather information" and a corresponding rise in the intensity of citizen involvement. An important distinction between this level and the preceding one is that at Level 2 government has typically not made a final decision on a matter. To gather information, departments may simply invite citizens to submit electronically their feelings about some matter to be examined, or ministers may instruct their officials to arrange for a public or town hall meeting at which members of the public express their sentiments about a proposed public initiative. Public hearings or seminars constitute another mechanism for gathering information. This mechanism involves selecting a panel of individuals—public servants, experts, and informed members of the public—to conduct an open forum on a specific topic. In the past few years, social media have facilitated all of these consultation types and more. The Consulting with Canadians website lists numerous departmental reviews that include invitations for comment; other government agencies go a little further, offering citizens an opportunity to have on-line workbooks which keep track of their comments and for selected stakeholders to become part of one of many planned cross-country roundtable meetings.

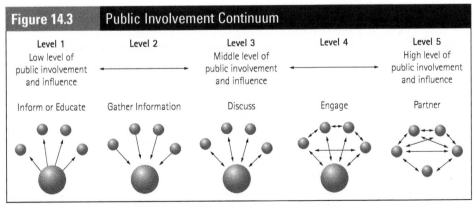

Figure 14.3	Public Involvement Continuum

Level 1	Level 2	Level 3	Level 4	Level 5
Low level of public involvement and influence		Middle level of public involvement and influence		High level of public involvement and influence
Inform or Educate	Gather Information	Discuss	Engage	Partner

Source: © All rights reserved. *Health Canada Policy Toolkit for Public Involvement in Decision Making.* Health Canada, 2000. Adapted and reproduced with permission from the Minister of Health, 2016.

Chapter 14 / Non-Governmental Actors and the Bureaucracy

Level 3 moves beyond the gathering of information and toward the discussion of issues. For this purpose, advisory boards or councils may be employed. These mechanisms of participation typically entail government selecting public representatives to offer input on a matter and to hold conferences that lead to the provision of helpful advice to government. Various forms of computer-assisted participation—televoting, online discussion groups, and electronic conferencing—may also be used to permit the public to comment on public matters. Again, social media has been at work at this level. In Ontario, regional health agencies have used on-line discussion groups to help determine priorities.[33] At the federal level, consultation efforts through social media also include on-line discussion groups.

The first three levels are usually considered to be fairly traditional forms of participation and are linked with the rather passive involvement of the public in government decision making. The next two levels try to involve the public more actively in government affairs, a shift signified by the substitution by some of the term "citizen engagement" for "public participation" or "public consultation."[34] Citizen engagement means that the consultation process—the agenda, the invitees, and the use of generated information—will be less controlled by government. With regard to the role of public servants, they assume a more open stance with respect to public input and effectively change from "substantive policy experts to public consultors."[35] Mechanisms used at Level 4 include joint working groups, retreats, round tables, and citizen dialogues. Each is distinguished by the fact that active deliberation takes place among the participants and that the results of the deliberation will play an important part in the final resolution of the issue at hand.

Level 5 represents the ultimate in participation, because it allows the public to manage the consultation process and to put forward solutions that government will seriously consider. Citizen juries represent one kind of mechanism found at this level. This mechanism involves the selection of community representatives who hear expert evidence on a particular matter and who then make a decision for government to consider seriously. Deliberative polling is another activity that can be used to achieve a relatively high level of citizen participation. The government first polls a sample of the population on an issue, and then selects a small number of individuals in the sample to hear expert opinion on the issue and to discuss the matter among themselves. The process ends with a polling of the selected group in an effort to gauge the opinions of well-informed citizens and to use these opinions in the making of policy. Citizen panels, search conferences, and study groups are other modes of participation that may be used at this level. Each of these modes is different in the way it operates, but similar to the others in the sense that all involve citizens actively deliberating on a matter and recommending a clear course of action for government.

Effectiveness of Public Consultation

There are various concerns about the effectiveness of exercises in public consultation. One is that the participating public is unrepresentative of the general public. For public participation to achieve its various purposes—to produce better policy, engage Canadians from all walks of life, and contribute to civil literacy—it must ensure that more than just select portions of the Canadian population take part in the interaction between government and individual citizens. The attraction of public participation is that ordinary Canadians, those unattached to any formal group or cause, are provided with an opportunity to influence their government. But this attractiveness quickly dissipates if we realize that only the like-minded and well-organized participate;[36] often interest groups and quasi-interest groups dominate because they have the expertise and the time and familiarity with consultation practices. A related concern is that participants are without the necessary information to make informed judgments on what has to be decided; even if the information is provided, experience shows that there is always the possibility that the information will be presented in a way accessible to only the very expert. A third and final concern to consider is that the methods of consultation rarely go beyond the first three levels of consultation. At times, it appears that government has developed a standard operating procedure that discourages citizen engagement. It circulates an information document for discussion, holds a series of stakeholder meetings, sets up a website for citizen responses, makes available a workbook for the interested to complete, and includes many people to protect itself against claims of insufficient consultation. Nowhere in this process is there an opportunity for informed discussion and the making of a recommendation (see What to Do?).

WHAT TO DO?

The possibility of tightly knit policy communities rejecting new players is a further worry for those hoping for differing ideas and interests to emerge in public consultation efforts. But perhaps the exclusion is a good thing. The involvement of the public may disturb carefully crafted policy compromises. More important, the public, as stated, may have neither the expertise nor the experience necessary nor the time to make a contribution. The healthcare field, a crucial area of public policy, is coming to this conclusion after disappointing exercises in community engagement.[37] What are we to do to maximize the effectiveness of public consultation?

The Internet and Social Media

The Internet and accompanying social media have generated large claims about their capacity for changing relations between government and citizens. Roy, for example, writes that information technology "is transforming public administration and democratic governance in profound ways,"[38] and earlier we noted Laforest's belief that social media alone would make major changes to how the people and their government relate to each other. The supportive evidence begins with observations about the breadth and depth of information now available from social media; it seems that insufficient information will no longer inhibit consultation efforts. Then there are the applications of social media to government: departments employ Twitter and Facebook to provide details on their operations, crises are more easily managed because of quick delivery of necessary information, "crowdsourcing" allows ordinary people working together to solve problems with access to newly available government data, and police on the frontlines can "connect with citizens" and avoid the sluggishness of bureaucratic media procedures.[39] We also get directed towards government websites and declarations dedicated to new consultation opportunities dependent on social media.

All of this is impressive. Social media do indeed appear to be playing a large role in government operations; the question is whether citizen consultation is enhanced. To the credit of social media supporters, they find it difficult to answer yes. The enthusiasm for the new information technology is tempered with an appreciation of the advances so far, or lack thereof. Governments use social media to keep in touch with constituents, but advocates of social media concede that the conversation in Canada and elsewhere seems to be largely one-way. Plus, when engagement does takes place, "citizens are seldom told how their ideas and comments have an impact on policy and why decisions were made"[40]; it seems that social media so far have done little about old problems with engagement exercises. Also of concern, the nature of social media—their ability to generate almost instantaneous responses without much contemplation—allows for quick escalation of argument and thus generates debates often long on nastiness and short on reasoned exchange and deliberation. Another quality of social media may also be at work here, which is the ease with which individuals can find like-minded believers who serve to confirm wholeheartedly positions that deserve second thought. It seems that social media may serve to close minds rather than to open them.[41] Finally, social media and the Internet may indeed make possible greater breadth and depth in relation to information: we may know more things and we may know more about each of these things. But does this translate into real knowledge and understanding, useful qualities in any productive relationship between citizens and their governments?[42] At a minimum, the appropriate reply to this query is that information technology is not a panacea and must be combined with more traditional modes of securing public consultation in order to achieve successful interactions between citizens and government.

Social Movements

social movement Informal networks of private citizens with shared beliefs who seek to influence government and the larger society, through protest and other non-traditional modes of influence.

The Internet and social media are not the only new actors in the area of non-governmental actors. **Social movements** have always been part of political life in Canada, but they have achieved a higher profile in recent years, to the point that they are effectively new additions to the study of public administration. Social movements can be seen in the efforts of various groups—university students, indigenous peoples, environmental activists, and a host of others—to seek and sometimes achieve adjustments in government policies and programs. More ambitiously, they may also bypass government and endeavour to change society-wide thinking and values about social issues and institutional arrangements. The significance of social movements for public administration arises mostly from their ability to place pressure on government through actions aimed at the media and the larger society. Leaders of social movements at times give little credence to traditional mechanisms for interacting with elected and appointed officials of government.

Though social movements are clearly evident, their exact nature is hard to pin down. One way to attempt to acquire a good picture of these entities is to show what they are not. Like interest groups, social movements have goals. However, unlike interest groups, their structure often tends to be more informal than formal and they are more than willing to use disruptive tactics in pursuing their ends. A second way to clarify the picture of what a social movement amounts to is to admit differences within social movements. Some movements are consensus-based, meaning that the goals resonate with much of society; but other movements, the better known and more common ones, are conflict-based, find little explicit support in the larger society, and also face organized opposition. A definition which follows from this brief analysis could be as follows: social movements are "informal networks based on shared beliefs and solidarity which mobilize about conflictual issues, through the frequent use of various forms of protest."[43]

Social movements have recently been engaged in some well-known events in Canada. One event is actually a series of actions connected to the indigenous movement "Idle No More." The movement protested against a federal bill that allegedly violated Aboriginal treaty rights, supported native chiefs in their tussles with federal government departments, and even launched a campaign to unseat the head of the Assembly of First Nations (the lead Aboriginal body in Canada). It did all this (and more) using various tactics, including protests on Parliament Hill, social media presentations, and informal lectures at various colleges and universities. A second event has been the closely covered protests of students in Quebec against proposed tuition hikes. For many nights on television, Canadians watched students fill the streets of Quebec cities with raucous protests, an action which eventually led to meetings between student leaders and elected officials. A final event to consider was the G-20 meetings in Toronto, which drew the attention of protesters opposed to the event's agenda. With this event, violence between police and protesters escalated quickly and smoke from burning cars filled the skies of Canada's largest city. (See Box 14.5 for the discussion of another social movement.)

The business of public servants rarely concerns itself directly with burning cars, violent student protests, and the hunger strikes of chiefs. But appointed officials do deal with student tuition, negotiation of native treaties, and global free trade agreements—under conditions conducive to discussion and cordial exchange of information. However, the cozy policy communities may be outdated. The number and nature of non-governmental actors is growing and the responsibilities of both elected and appointed officials will have to grow with them.

Disability Rights Social Movement

BOX
14.5

The Disability Rights Social Movement (DRSM) is a social movement that has sought to use fairly traditional methods of influencing government while pursuing the kind of ambitious society-wide goals associated with more aggressive social movements. Arguably the most ambitious goal, a goal which has largely been met, is to get society as a whole to stop thinking of disabilities as impairments to be treated. The better way to look at people who have a disability is to see them as individuals wishing to live in the community but who are unable to because of the failure of society to make the necessary accommodations; in other words, people with disabilities are victims of discriminatory behaviour.

This shift was achieved in large part through the DRSM using advocacy to influence governments and employ the courts, and especially the Charter, to knock down barriers facing people with disabilities. This two-prong political strategy, complemented with other methods of persuasion, has led to other victories for people with a disability. But the movement has recently failed to secure its wishes to block movement towards legalizing physician-assisted dying, perhaps because some members of the movement support legalization.

Source: Lisa Vanhala, "Meaning Frames, Opportunity Structures, and Rights in the Canadian Disability Rights Movement," in *Group Politics and Social Movements in Canada*, ed. Miriam Smith (Toronto: University of Toronto Press, 2014).

Points to Know

- Non-governmental bodies represent an important part of the study of public administration.

- Interest groups are group of citizens with common interests who seek to influence government in a way that can serve private and public interests. Interest groups affect government through various activities, which include lobbying, advocating, contesting, retreating, participating, and regulating.

- The media perform public functions that act to enrich any democracy, but they also shape the news in a way that increases audiences and at times causes difficulty for governments. Public servants play an important role in the attempt by government to manage the media in order to get their messages across to citizens.

- Public consultations are becoming a more important element of public administration, but these consultations still fall short of expectations of full citizen engagement in public affairs.

- The Internet and social media constitute a new non-governmental entity and are also responsible for change in the behaviour and tactics of traditional non-governmental actors. Social movements represent another new non-governmental actor, and they are gaining prominence.

Review Questions

1. What kind of activities would you associate with institutionalized interest groups eager to persuade government? Give reasons for your answer.

2. Assess the efforts of the three telecommunications giants to influence the federal government.

3. Assume the government wishes to announce a new plan for addressing the growing problem of obesity in Canada. Propose a media strategy for the government that would draw the maximum amount of attention from both old and new media.

4. How might relations between government and the media be made more cooperative and less combative?

5. What level of public involvement would you propose for public servants wishing to draft a plan for consulting with Canadians on the issue of reforming the Canadian health care system? Be sure to explain your answer by considering all viable options.

Notes

1. Éric Montpetit, "Are Interest Groups Useful or Harmful? Take Two," in *Canadian Politics*, 6th ed., eds. James Bickerton and Alain-G. Gagnon (Toronto: University of Toronto Press, 2014).
2. Paul Pross, *Group Politics and Public Policy* (Toronto: Oxford University Press, 1986), ch. 5; Paul Pross, "Pressure Groups: Adaptive Instruments of Political Communication," in *Pressure Group Behaviour in Canadian Politics*, ed. Paul Pross (Toronto: McGraw-Hill Ryerson, 1975), 9–18.
3. Pross, *Group Politics and Public Policy*, 122.
4. All six are discussed in Éric Montpetit, "Are Interest Groups Useful or Harmful? Take Two."
5. Ibid., p. 335.
6. Ibid., p. 335.
7. Éric Montpetit, "Governance and Interest Group Activities," in *Canadian Politics*, 4th ed., eds. Bickerton and Gagnon (Peterborough: Broadview Press, 2004), 316.
8. Donald J. Savoie, *What Is Government Good At? A Canadian Answer* (Montreal & Kingston: McGill-Queen's University Press, 2015), 87.
9. Montpetit, "Governance and Interest Group Activities," 317.
10. Lisa Young and Joanna Everitt, *Advocacy Groups* (Vancouver: UBC Press, 2004), 99.
11. Peter Clancy, "Business Interests and Civil Society in Canada," in *Group Politics and Social Movements in Canada*, 2nd ed., ed. Miriam Smith (Toronto: University of Toronto Press, 2014), 11–13.
12. Letter to Prime Minister Harper from Bell, Rogers, and Telus Regarding Upcoming Spectrum Auction, July 9, 2013, accessed March 10, 2016, https://www.northumberlandview.ca/?module=news&type=user&func=display&sid=23576.
13. "An Open Letter to all Canadians," accessed March 10, 2016, http://www.bell.ca/an-open-letter-to-all-canadians.
14. Christine Dobby, "Telus Takes Battle Over Ottawa's Wireless Spectrum Policy to Federal Court," *Financial Post*, July 29, 2013, accessed May 20, 2015, http://business.financialpost.com/fp-tech-desk/telus-takes-battle-over-ottawas-wireless-spectrum-policy-to-federal-court?__lsa=d42c-e709.
15. Anthony Fell, "Canada's Telecom Arrogance, August 12, 2013, accessed May 20, 2016, http://business.financialpost.com/fp-comment/canadas-telecom-arrogance.
16. Hon. James Moore, PC, MP, Minister of Industry, "A Telecom Policy for All Canadians," accessed May 20, 2016, http://www.jamesmoore.org/august132013/13, 2016.
17. "Verizon Not Entering Canada's Wireless Market After All," accessed August 10, 2016, http://www.cbc.ca/news/business/verizon-not-entering-canada-s-wireless-market-after-all-1.1339361.
18. David A. Good, *The Politics of Public Management* (Toronto: University of Toronto Press, 2003), 61.
19. Ibid., 63.
20. Savoie, *What Is Government Good At?* 40.
21. Ibid., 40.
22. Alex Marland, "Political Communication in Canada: Strategies and Tactics," in *Canadian Politics*, 6th ed., eds. Bickerton and Gagnon, 320.
23. Quoted in Savoie, *"What Is Government Good At?"* 43.
24. Marland, "Political Communication in Canada, 312.
25. Ibid., 318.
26. Éric Montpetit, "Public Consultations in Policy Network Environments: The Case of Assisted Reproductive Technology Policy in Canada," *Canadian Public Policy* XXIX (2003): 97.
27. Rachel Laforest, "Deep and Wide: Citizen Engagement in the Era of Social Media," in *Canadian Public Administration in the 21st century*, eds. Charles Conteh and Ian Roberge (Boca Rotan, FL: CRC Press, 2013), 61.
28. Montpetit, "Public Consultations in Policy Network Environments," 96.
29. Rachel Laforest and Susan Phillips, "Citizen Engagement: Rewiring the Policy Process," in *Critical Policy Studies*, eds. Michael Orsini and Miriam Smith (Toronto: UBC Press, 2007), 76.
30. Health Canada, *Health Canada Policy Toolkit for Public Involvement in Decision Making* (Ottawa: Minister of Public Works and Government Services, 2000), 12.
31. Laforest, "Deep and Wide: Citizen Engagement in the Era of Social Media," 69.
32. Government of Canada, "Consulting with Canadians," accessed August 10, 2016, http://www1.canada.ca/consultingcanadians/.
33. Kristin Shields, Gwen DuBois-Wing, and Ellis Westwood, "Share Your Story, Shape Your Care: Engaging the Diverse and Disperse Population of Northwestern Ontario in Healthcare Priority Setting," *Healthcare Quarterly*, 13(3) (May 2010): 86–90. doi:10.12927/hcq.2010.21821.
34. See, for example, Susan D. Phillips and Michael Orsini, *Mapping the Links: Citizen Involvement in Policy Processes* (Ottawa: Canadian Policy Research Networks, 2002), 3, or Health Canada, *Health Canada Toolkit*, 14–16.
35. Montpetit, "Public Consultations in Policy Network Environments," 97.
36. Health Council of Canada, *Primer on Public Involvement*, 17, accessed August 10, 2016, http://www.cprn.org/documents/45131_en.pdf.
37. Katherine Fierlbeck, *Health Care in Canada: A Citizen's Guide to Policy and Politics* (Toronto: University of Toronto Press, 2011), 76–80.
38. Jeffrey Roy, "The Promise (and Pitfalls) of Digital Transformation," in *Approaching Public Administration: Core Debates and Emerging Issues*, eds. Roberto P. Leone and Frank L.K. Ohemeng (Toronto: Emond Montgomery Publications, 2011), 279.
39. Laforest, "Deep and Wide: Citizen Engagement in the Era of Social Media," 65.
40. Ibid., 71.
41. Frank Bruni, "How Facebook Warps Our Worlds," *New York Times*, May 22, 2016; Eli Pariser, *The Filter Bubble: What the Internet Is Hiding from You* (New York: Penguin Press, 2011), ch. 3.
42. See Michael Patrick Lynch, *The Internet of Us: Knowing More and Understanding Less in the Age of Big Data* (New York: Liveright Publishing Corporation, 2016).
43. Quoted in Michael Orsini, "Of Pots and Pans and Radical Handmaids: Social Movements and Civil Society," in *Canadian Politics* 6th ed., eds. Bickerton and Gagnon, 351.

The Management of Human Resources

15

Learning Objectives

Reading this chapter allows you to do the following:

- Identify some of the critical challenges facing the public sector with respect to human resources management

- Explain why it is difficult to establish the size and scope of the public sector

- Differentiate key eras in the evolution of human resources management

- Distinguish between the HRM roles of individual departments and agencies and other institutional actors

The last part of the book strives to offer a close-up view of how public servants go about managing organizational resources in the public sector. This purpose might encompass the examination of a number of activities—engaging in strategic planning, meeting the information technology requirements of the organization, structuring procedures for collective bargaining—but Part Five focuses on two central challenges facing appointed officials: the management of human resources and the management of financial resources. This chapter and the next consider the first test, and the final two chapters discuss the second.

One of the most important aspects of the management of organizational resources, if not the most important, is addressing the human resources needs of the organization. To carry out this task, it is necessary first of all to determine an underlying principle or philosophy that guides the terms and conditions for employment in the public sector. In Canada, and other countries, the merit principle—the notion that employees must be qualified to do the job—has come to be accepted as the foundation for human resources systems. However, other principles, such as a public bureaucracy that is broadly representative of the society it serves, ought to be considered as well. The management of human resources includes the creation of a process that allows for, among other things, the classification of jobs and the training and evaluation of employees. We must also provide for the organizations necessary to this managerial effort and do so in a way that facilitates respect for the merit principle and other principles while allowing managers to tend to the personnel needs of the organization without facing a web of rules and regulations.

In this chapter, we explore the processes, structures, principles—and frustrations— integral to the management of human resources. The chapter commences by identifying what is meant by human resources management (HRM) in the public sector and some of the key challenges facing government in that regard. It then provides some context for understanding the public service today, including its size and scope, before addressing the critical importance of the merit principle and an historical overview of the evolution of the human resources system. The chapter then examines the legislative and organizational framework for managing federal employees, and follows this with a discussion of the separate steps—job classification, human resources planning, staffing, training, and performance evaluation—that make up the actual management of people in the public service. The following chapter offers a detailed review of a crucial issue in the management of human resources, namely the concern for a public bureaucracy that includes representation of many key target groups in society.

Human Resources Management in the Public Sector

In essence, HRM in the public sector is about "managing people within the employer–employee relationship" and it entails everything from the recruitment, retention, motivation, and reward to development and departure (for other opportunities or retirement) of employees from the public service.[1] While one approach is to provide an array of disparate programs to cover these various human resources elements, such as recruitment plans, customized training and development programs, career planning, compensation and reward systems, and so on, many organizations, including the federal and several of the provincial governments, have adopted a more comprehensive approach to HRM known as talent management. In these instances, this broad range of human resources activities is more fully integrated to ensure that talented individuals are hired at the right time and deployed in the right place for the proper purpose.[2] Such approaches are an explicit recognition of the ongoing "war for talent" in the labour market, whereby both public and private sector organizations are competing to hire the best and brightest employees.

While historically the Canadian federal public service, "regarded as one of the best in the world," may have been the obvious destination for the country's brightest minds, this so-called golden era came to an end by the early 1970s.[3] Over time, the morale of public sector employees plummeted and, according to a 2001 EKOS survey, it was a career that less than half of Canadian adults (45 percent) would want their children to pursue.[4] However, the government eventually recognized the need to address the human resource issues that were beleaguering the public service in order to build a world class institution. For example, as part of the PS 2000 initiative of the late 1980s, the federal government indicated that those who worked in the public service were "not simply resources"; rather, they were regarded as "its most important asset." The initiative recognized that "a professional, career public service, capable of attracting and retaining Canadians of talent, commitment and imagination, is essential to Canada's national well-being." As such, the government introduced a number of administrative reforms that were designed to renew the public service to prepare for the twenty-first century by fostering a new consultative and client-oriented culture.[5]

Although the Mulroney government was much criticized for the obvious disconnect between the rhetoric of PS 2000 and the reality of working in the public service during that time—an era characterized by wage and hiring freezes as well as a significant contraction in the number of people working for the federal government—the focus on the importance of human capital was not misguided. Globalization, with its attendant need for rapid and constant change, has had a profound effect on organizations. To be successful in the new knowledge-based economy all organizations, be they public, private, or non-profit, have been facing a significant challenge, namely to attract and retain highly-skilled and highly-educated employees.

For governments the challenge has been even more pronounced. The public policy issues they confront are increasingly complex, often necessitating a horizontal or networked approach to provide an adequate response, and they are under constant pressure to deliver services to the public more efficiently and effectively. To succeed in this environment, governments must possess a talented pool of committed public servants with wide-ranging knowledge, technical skills, and abilities:

> Ultimately, the ability of government to provide services effectively and efficiently depends upon a competent cadre of civil servants. Good government requires good people. This has always been true, but its importance to the international community has probably never been more critical than it is today.[6]

Over time, the Canadian government, like its counterparts around the world, began to embrace a process of HRM reform for the public sector.[7] The government shifted from a traditional model of personnel administration that was highly centralized and rule-based as per the tenets of the Weberian rational–legal bureaucracy to one that was more in line with the market-based orientation associated with the new public management (NPM) movement. The traditional model was based on notions of a career service whereby public sector employees had security of tenure and lifetime employment; jobs were very specialized and routinized; seniority was the basis for promotion, which largely occurred from within a "closed" public service; and remuneration was based on the job or position rather than performance. A greater degree of flexibility was introduced with the new HRM regime in the public sector. Although great efforts have been made to ensure that a career public service is retained, the concept has evolved to recognize that the federal public service has become a much more porous institution, with employees entering later in life and at higher ranks as well as leaving before retirement to pursue other employment opportunities both within and outside the broader public sector. Moreover, it has been punctuated by periods of significant downsizing—or "rightsizing" as advocates of the NPM agenda would prefer to say—in the 1980s and 1990s and after the Conservative majority government of 2011. Performance pay has been introduced and seniority is no longer the basis for promotion. Greater emphasis has been placed on career planning and skills development, especially in the area of leadership capacity, and the system has been decentralized so that deputy ministers have far greater delegated authority for fulfilling their staffing needs.[8]

The preceding paragraph provides a broad overview of the transformation that has occurred with respect to HRM in the federal public service. A more nuanced assessment of the evolution of HRM will be presented later in the chapter. But first, we identify some of the most pressing human resources challenges confronting the government and provide an overview of the public service today.

Human Resources Challenges

A number of the critical human resources challenges confronting the federal government are linked with the changing nature of the HRM regime outlined in the previous section. First, there are lingering negative perceptions about the public service. Beginning in the 1980s, the attractiveness of working in the public sector was waning, both among public servants themselves and the citizenry. Public servants began to question their career choice because of their deteriorating working conditions, while citizens began to view government as part of the problem rather than the solution because of their declining confidence in the ethical standards of public servants and dissatisfaction over the quality of public services they had been receiving. That Brian Mulroney came into power in 1984 on a promise to issue pink slips and running shoes to federal public servants, whom he viewed as the source of waste and inefficiency in government and as "self-serving, incompetent and certainly unable to earn a living in the real world,"[9] only served to exacerbate matters. While it was primarily as a result of attrition and limitations on recruitment rather than dismissals of public servants by a government that was antagonistic towards the bureaucracy, employment in the federal public service nonetheless decreased by more than 65,000 people between 1977 and 1986.[10] These reductions, along with wage and hiring freezes, naturally had a discernable impact on the collective morale and psyche of public servants who felt neither valued nor respected by their political masters.

The election of an ostensibly more centrist Liberal government in 1993 had little impact in terms of rectifying the situation. In fact, the rightsizing agenda was pursued with equal vigour and success after the Liberals swept to power. Notably, Prime Minister Chrétien launched Program Review in 1994 with clear deficit reduction targets in mind, and ultimately this exercise was intended to fundamentally question the role of the federal government in the Canadian economy and society. The net result was a reduction of some 50,000 more public service positions, including many clerical and operational positions, as well as scientists, policy analysts, and other technical experts needed to cope with the various critical scientific and social issues beleaguering society.[11] At the same time, there were restricted opportunities for executive promotion, transfer, and development. What remained was a public service workforce suffering from high levels of stress and increased workloads with a disproportionate number of older, predominantly knowledge-based employees.[12]

The second challenge relates to this shift to the knowledge economy. With public sector employment comprising fewer clerical and operational positions, there is even more intense competition with the private sector to recruit the best and brightest employees with the requisite technical skills and knowledge to succeed in this new labour market. Significantly, the public sector must do so without the same range of inducements as their competitors to sway new recruits.[13] When focusing on the issue of financial remuneration, private sector employers, with their ability to offer incentives such as signing bonuses, stock options, and access to leading-edge technologies, are thought to have a distinct advantage over the public sector. However, there are studies that suggest public sector employees actually enjoy a wage premium over their private sector counterparts.[14] Moreover, with respect to some of the other factors that are important to students in terms of choosing a career—such as interesting work, work–life balance, long-term job security, and opportunities for promotion[15]—the public sector fares much more favourably. Nonetheless, the government has a formidable challenge to educate prospective employees that it can offer a competitive salary and benefits.

Third, the demographic shift that has been occurring more broadly in Canadian society is particularly acute in the public sector, resulting in an aging workforce and the loss of key personnel through retirement. In Canada, the clarion call for acknowledging and addressing the HRM challenge was made by Jocelyne Bourgon, former clerk of the privy council, who in 1997 wrote of a "quiet crisis" in the public service in her fourth annual report to the prime minister. At the time, she noted that the public sector was going to find it "increasingly difficult to retain, motivate and attract people essential to the work of the Public Service." Moreover, she indicated that more than 30 percent of the executive group would be eligible to retire by 2000, a figure that would increase to 70 percent by 2005. This represented the potential loss of significant experience and expertise. More troubling, however, was the fact that few people recognized the problem or were prepared to do anything about it.[16] Sheila Fraser, the Auditor General, expressed similar concerns in her 2001 annual report. In her view, the problem was exacerbated by the fact that the number of public service employees under the age of 35 was about half the number in the workforce more generally. Therefore, there were not enough younger employees in the public service ready to assume the leadership positions that would be vacated as a result of the impending retirements.[17]

As some commentators observed, however, the so-called quiet crisis did not emerge as predicted, in part because many of those public servants who were eligible to retire chose not to do so.[18] Others, including several senior officials in both the Public Service

Commission (PSC) and Treasury Board Secretariat (TBS), believe that there never was a human resources crisis in the federal public service; in their view, Madame Bourgon manufactured one in order to garner support for "a sweeping set of reform initiatives—La Relève—that would have been difficult to achieve otherwise."[19] La Relève, which is an acronym for leadership, action, renewal, energy, learning, experience, values, and excellence, was a reform initiative designed to reinvigorate the federal public service in the aftermath of the failed PS 2000 exercise, although it too has critics who argued that it was largely irrelevant to the day-to-day lives of public servants.[20] A third perspective has also been posited, namely that Bourgon was correct in diagnosing the HRM crisis but that her timing was off by at least a decade with the problems emerging in the second decade of the twenty-first century.[21] What is incontrovertible, however, is that with the average age of employees being 44.9 years in 2014 (versus 39.3 in 1983) while the corresponding average age of executives is 50.4 years (versus 48.1 in 1983), the public service is an aging workforce (see Box 15.1).[22]

This particular problem is exacerbated by the fact that about 40 percent (4800 to 6000 people) of the 12,000 to 15,000 employees that the federal government has been recruiting every year since 2000 to replenish the ranks of the public service must be bilingual. The vast majority of these positions will also require a post-secondary education. The challenge will be to find a cross-section of Canadians who are bilingual to work in the federal public service at a time when there are fewer bilingual high school graduates than in the past and post-secondary institutions no longer have language competency requirements. Francophone Canadians have a distinct advantage in that regard since they have a much higher rate of bilingualism than Anglophone Canadians. The government, therefore, will need to take action so as to increase the representation of Anglophones across the entire public service, but especially at the most senior levels where a greater percentage of the positions are bilingual.[23]

Fourth, with the downsizing of the public sector and the increased reliance on a variety of alternative service delivery mechanisms that were introduced with NPM, such as contracting out to the private corporations and non-profit agencies or the use of public–private partnerships, there has been a blurring of the public and private sectors; this has meant that those Canadians who are interested in careers dedicated to working in the "public interest" have options outside of the public service for satisfying their aspirations.

Finally, the NPM reforms that were introduced in Canada have resulted in changing notions of what constitutes a "career service." With three significant periods of contraction in the size of the federal bureaucracy, public servants have come to realize that security of tenure means protection from partisan dismissal and not "lifetime employment." The reality is that employees exhibit far less loyalty now that the concept of "employability," which has replaced the notion of permanent employment, has been introduced into the public service. This essentially means that the government no longer has an obligation to provide public servants with a job; instead, it is the government's responsibility to provide employees with the skills that they need to function in their current role and to secure future employment—whether in the public sector or not.[24] The notion of a career service has also been undermined by a heavy reliance on contingent labour as well as the fluidity with which employees have been entering and exiting the public service in recent years. Short-term hiring has definite advantages, but it also may make it more difficult for government to attract and retain the highest quality employees since they can likely find full-time employment elsewhere. But the public service has also been losing permanent employees. Although historically denigrated, the reality is that many public servants are knowledge workers, who are particularly adept at dealing with complexity, forging strategic alliances with various partners and balancing competing objectives to create consensus, all of which are skills in high demand by private sector organizations.

That being the case, retention of public servants is as critical as recruitment, and it is not at all unreasonable to refer to a "brain drain" in the public sector.[25]

BOX 15.1	So You Want to Work for the Federal Public Service? A Demographic Snapshot (as of March 31, 2014)

- Number of employees – 257,138
- Female employees – 54.9%
- Female executives – 45.3%
- Employees in the National Capital Region – 41.7%
- Indeterminate (full-time) employees – 86.6%
- Term employees – 8.3%
- Casual and student employees – 5.1%

- Employees for whom English is their first language – 71.1%
- Average age of employees – 44.9
- Average age of executives – 50.4

Source: *Demographic Snapshot of the Federal Public Service*, 2014, http://www.tbs-sct.gc.ca/psm-fpfm/modernisation/stats/demo14-eng.asp, Office of the Chief Human Resources Officer, Treasury Board of Canada Secretariat, 2014.

The Public Service Today

core public administration The more than 75 federal departments, agencies, and commissions identified in Schedules I and IV of the *Financial Administration Act* for whom the Treasury Board is the employer and that are the main part of the federal public service.

separate agencies Government organizations for which the Treasury Board is not the employer, although the Public Service Commission retains exclusive authority to make appointments. Some, but not all, of the employees working in the separate agencies are counted as members of the federal public service.

How large is the public sector in Canada? This seemingly straightforward question requires a nuanced response. Focusing only on the federal public service, it should be noted that a distinction is made between the **core public administration** and what are known as **separate agencies**. The core public administration includes over 75 federal departments, agencies, and commissions that are listed in schedules 1 and 4 of the *Financial Administration Act*, while the list of separate agencies, of which there are 25, can be found in schedule 5, including the Canada Revenue Agency, the Canadian Food Inspection Agency, Parks Canada, the National Film Board, the National Energy Board, and the Office of the Auditor General. While both the core public administration and separate agencies are typically combined when calculating the total population of the federal public service, it is important to note that the separate agencies are given discretion to conduct their own negotiations with employees and establish their own classification levels. However, the PSC has exclusive authority to make these appointments. In the case of the core public administration, the Treasury Board is identified as the employer for that part of the public service.

As Table 15.1 reveals, after the cuts to the federal public service in the 1990s, there was annual growth in the size of the public service until 2011, reflecting, in part, the continual growth of the Canadian population and an increased demand for services. After that point there have been persistent reductions down to a total federal public service of 257,034 employees as of March 31, 2015. This is consistent with the message delivered by the Conservative government after securing its first majority government in the 2011 general election, where it was intimated that the public service could be reduced by a staggering one third of its size through attrition as a means of balancing the budget.[26] While the cuts to the federal public service have not been as drastic as projected, there were roughly 25,000 fewer people employed by the government in a span of just three years. To put this in perspective, while the Canadian population increased 40 percent from 1983 to 2014 (from 25.3 to 35.4 million people), the number of federal public servants only increased 2.5 percent during that time (from 250,822 to 257,138). Furthermore, the federal public service in 2014 comprised about .73 percent of the Canadian population, whereas the ratio of civil servants to Canadians from the 1980s to the early 1990s was about one in one hundred.[27]

Thus far, we have only considered those individuals who work for the federal government and even these numbers do not give a complete picture of the size of the

TABLE 15.1	Population of the Federal Public Service			
YEAR	POPULATION OF THE FEDERAL PUBLIC SERVICE	POPULATION OF THE CORE PUBLIC ADMINISTRATION	POPULATION OF THE SEPARATE AGENCIES	CANADIAN POPULATION (STATISTICS CANADA) CANSIM SERIES V1 (1ST QUARTER)
2000	211,925	152,070	59,855	30,525,872
2001	223,933	161,505	62,428	30,824,441
2002	237,251	170,779	66,472	31,172,522
2003	242,737	174,581	68,156	31,476,734
2004	244,158	177,136	67,022	31,776,075
2005	243,971	184,083	59,888	32,077,339
2006	249,932	189,280	60,652	32,394,898
2007	254,622	192,683	61,939	32,739,308
2008	263,114	200,575	62,539	33,113,330
2009	274,370	209,523	64,847	33,527,199
2010	282,980	216,596	66,384	33,930,830
2011	282,352	217,224	65,128	34,278,406
2012	278,092	212,028	66,064	34,670,352
2013	262,817	200,516	62,301	35,056,100
2014	257,138	195,330	61,808	35,427,524
2015	257,034	195,565	61,469	35,749,600*

*StatCan Quarterly Demographic Estimate for April 2015.

Source: Treasury Board of Canada Secretariat (http://www.tbs-sct.gc.ca/res/stats/ssen-ane-eng.asp)

public service because excluded from these calculations are members of the RCMP and the Canadian Armed Forces as well as the more than 85,000 individuals (as of 2013) who work for federal Crown corporations. Moreover, if we were to think of the public sector more broadly, by including those who work for the provincial, territorial, and local governments, educational, social services, and health care institutions and various local, provincial, and federal government business enterprises, then roughly one in ten Canadians works for government. Table 15.2 outlines the employment numbers in the Canadian public service for each of these various categories.

A number of interesting observations can be derived from the data in Table 15.2. One is that since the mid-1980s there has been a fairly consistent increase in the number of Canadians (to more than 3.6 million in 2012) working in the public sector, but there has not been consistent growth in all segments of public sector employment. While there was modest growth and contraction in the number of employees working for the provincial and territorial governments over the past 30 years, there are virtually an

TABLE 15.2 Public Sector Employment in Canada

YEAR	PUBLIC SECTOR	FEDERAL GOVERNMENT	PROVINCIAL AND TERRITORIAL GOVERNMENTS	HEALTH AND SOCIAL SERVICES	UNIVERSITIES AND COLLEGES	LOCAL GOVERNMENT	SCHOOL BOARDS	GOVERNMENT BUSINESS ENTERPRISES (ALL LEVELS)
1984–85	2,768,481	397,211	355,354	619,764	222,225	313,444	444,879	415,605
1989–90	2,979,662	402,754	374,807	710,211	266,105	347,227	504,584	373,975
1993–94	3,027,162	402,791	367,825	744,406	280,077	367,933	539,580	324,550
1994–95	2,991,504	389,817	360,099	736,785	275,601	365,548	543,158	320,497
1995–96	2,932,748	364,157	352,068	732,905	274,811	367,029	542,696	299,083
1996–97	2,839,142	352,458	336,943	702,096	271,990	355,678	551,077	268,900
1997–98	2,783,572	335,818	337,080	693,333	270,496	348,206	539,565	259,074
1998–99	2,772,917	328,913	333,515	692,932	269,849	340,803	545,194	261,712
1999–2000	2,777,444	329,319	337,105	689,956	269,494	341,523	541,873	268,174
2000–01	2,839,739	338,525	340,298	694,094	278,032	359,730	557,705	271,356
2001–02	3,060,886	354,608	337,582	715,044	304,500	466,310	610,004	272,837
2002–03	3,101,800	361,835	329,220	733,583	316,924	463,144	621,391	275,703
2003–04	3,178,305	367,087	332,793	750,128	329,112	494,409	624,450	280,326
2004–05	3,201,746	367,260	331,685	742,416	335,760	502,972	634,088	287,564
2005–06	3,261,264	372,370	341,943	754,911	340,248	521,796	643,299	286,696
2006–07	3,324,899	388,006	345,959	767,723	349,113	533,364	651,592	289,144
2007–08	3,413,707	390,385	355,482	787,971	361,310	557,887	663,650	297,022
2008–09	3,513,780	403,476	361,850	805,479	367,426	584,376	677,962	313,212
2009–10	3,577,915	418,456	358,900	829,163	377,710	598,546	679,911	315,229
2010–11	3,615,508	420,548	357,600	848,972	388,393	606,580	678,362	315,054
2011–12	3,633,407	425,909	356,884	862,949	378,976	608,417	680,980	319,293

Notes: Employment data are not in full-time equivalents and do not distinguish between full-time and part-time employees. These figures are year-to-date averages and not raw data. Federal general government data includes reservists and full-time military personnel. Data may not add to the total due to rounding.

Source: Statistics Canada, CANSIM, Table 183-0002.

identical number of people working as public servants for those governments in 2012 as there were in 1984. Employment in government business enterprises across all levels of government, however, has decreased nearly 25 percent over that same time period; this undoubtedly reflects the decisions of governments both provincially and federally in the late 1980s and 1990s to privatize Crown corporations.

At the federal level, the numbers clearly show that the arrival of the Liberal government in 1993 initially resulted in a period of contraction in public sector employment, but that by the turn of the century the federal public service began to increase in size once more. This pattern of growth continued even with the transition to a Conservative government under Stephen Harper in 2006, although, as noted earlier in the chapter, a new period of retrenchment in federal public sector employment was initiated after the 2011 general election. While it is too early to know exactly how the federal public service will fare under the new Liberal government of Justin Trudeau, the party did campaign on an activist agenda, which suggests that there could be another period of expansion. Scott Brison, President of the Treasury Board, has intimated as much by referring to an "opportunity to restore and create another golden age of public service where we actively recruit the best and brightest millennials to the public service."[28]

Finally, all of the remaining categories of public sector employment—health and social services, colleges and universities, local government, and school boards—have all seen significant increases. This is particularly pronounced at the local level of government, where the number of employees has almost doubled since 1984, which is a clear indication of the increasing importance of this level of government as the provinces have downloaded the provision of numerous services to the municipalities.

RCMP Recruitment Campaign

© (2015) HER MAJESTY THE QUEEN IN RIGHT OF CANADA as represented by the Royal Canadian Mounted Police (RCMP). Reproduced with the permission of the RCMP.

The Concept of Merit

Merit is the most pervasive and enduring theme in HRM. Despite the significant changes highlighted earlier, which have transformed the way in which the government deals with and relates to its employees, merit has not been compromised. To understand the concept of merit, one must distinguish between the merit principle and the merit system. The

Chapter 15 / The Management of Human Resources

merit principle A principle according to which (1) all citizens should have a reasonable opportunity to be considered for employment in the public service and (2) selections must be based exclusively on qualification or fitness for the job. To be distinguished from the *merit system*.

merit system The mechanism in use at any time by which the goals of the *merit principle* are achieved. An administrative device that can and should be adapted to changing circumstances.

merit principle has often been explained as requiring that public service appointments be based exclusively on merit, in the sense of fitness to do the job, and that citizens have a reasonable opportunity to be considered for public service employment. Yet this definition allows for considerable interpretation as to what is meant by "reasonable"; moreover, fitness for the job does not necessarily require that the most qualified person be chosen. The merit principle is often interpreted solely in terms of appointing the best-qualified person—that is, the "reasonable opportunity" component is omitted. For their part, the courts in Canada have consistently interpreted merit to mean "best qualified."

In practice, the meaning of the merit principle is worked out through the **merit system**, which is the mechanism, consisting of policies, procedures, and regulations, by which the merit principle is pursued. The merit system is a dynamic concept in that it can be adapted to changing circumstances. The federal PSC, which is responsible for safeguarding the merit principle through implementation of the merit system, is obliged to reconcile the merit principle with several other important principles. These other principles include a public service that is representative of the larger population, and a process of staffing which is fair and transparent and appointees who are competent and able to work in both of the official languages. A further principle is that the merit system itself should be flexible and conducive to the efficient staffing of positions. However, there have been concerns expressed about the operation of the merit system—that its procedures are inflexible and that the rigidity of system actually impedes the satisfaction of the merit principle. The oft-expressed wish of many is a merit system that gives managers a better opportunity to use their own judgment in the selection of personnel while still working within a framework of general policies and procedures. In 2003, the federal government passed legislation that provided a definition of merit that attempts to introduce more flexibility into the merit system, for it allows managers to move away from the idea of locating the best-qualified candidate and instead to hire people on the basis of the requirements of the agency and any qualifications deemed necessary for the performance of the work. The chapter discusses this in more detail later.[29]

There have been few significant events, developments, or reforms in the public service that have not affected HRM in general and merit in particular. Merit has been pursued within the broader context of the traditional public service values, namely neutrality, accountability, efficiency and effectiveness, responsiveness, representativeness, integrity, fairness, and equity. The priority that public servants assign to each of these values at any given time is a reflection of the desires and expectations of the various actors in the political system who control or influence public servants. Among the most important of these actors are political superiors. The uniqueness of HRM in the public sector can be explained in large part by the political environment within which public servants work. Evidence of the importance of the politics of HRM has been provided in earlier discussions of such matters as political appointments, political partisanship, public comment, anonymity, permanence in office, and ministerial responsibility.

Evolution of Human Resources Management

The development of HRM in Canada may be viewed in terms of the effect of the shifting importance of the dominant administrative values on merit. In the federal sphere of government, this evolution may for analytical purposes be divided chronologically into seven periods. In each of these periods, HRM has been affected by a different mix of administrative values as the priority of the various values has risen and declined.

The Patronage Era (Pre-1918)

This period was dominated by efforts to promote political neutrality by eliminating, or at least minimizing, political patronage in the appointment of public servants.[30] Indeed, between 1867 and 1918, as many as five royal commissions and a judicial inquiry on the federal public service devoted considerable attention to the evils of patronage. In relation to the staffing of the public service, patronage took several forms. The most common form was appointments based on party affiliation, which occurred at the level of the local constituency and which involved both the member of parliament and the local party members. Most of these appointments were to lower-level positions in the public service, and many of the positions were of a seasonal nature. A second form was appointments made by the cabinet to senior-level positions, largely on the basis of partisan political considerations. A third form of appointments related to positions to be filled from within the public service; since many deputy ministers were political appointees themselves, it is not surprising that some "bureaucratic" patronage occurred. Lastly, there were a greater number of appointments following a change of government when some appointees of the outgoing governing party were dismissed and replaced by supporters of the incoming party.

The first major step toward the abolition of patronage was the *Civil Service Amendment Act* of 1908, which established the Civil Service Commission. The Act also provided for appointment on the basis of merit and for heavy penalties for partisan political activities by public servants. However, the Act applied only to the "inside service" or public servants working in Ottawa.

From Patronage to Merit (1918–45)

This period began with the passage of the *Civil Service Act* in 1918. The search for political neutrality was supplemented by concern for efficiency. The major objective of the Act was the "promotion of economy and efficiency in the non-political public service." Merit was to be achieved through "selection and appointment without regard to politics, religion or influence," and through "the application of methods of scientific employment to maintain the efficiency of these selected employees after they enter the service." The Act applied to both the "inside" and "outside" services. Severe restrictions in this Act on partisan political activities remained virtually unchanged until 1967.

Continued pursuit of political neutrality and efficiency had important effects on HRM. The emphasis during the 1920s on eradicating patronage rather than on improving efficiency led to a significant decline in patronage appointments and partisan political activities by 1930. In the 1930s, the Civil Service Commission, with its persistent focus on merit in terms of selection of the most qualified candidates, lost ground to the Treasury Board, which emphasized economy and efficiency, not only in the human resources area but throughout government. This emphasis continued during the war years.

The Roots of Reform (1946–66)

This postwar period provided a strikingly different environment for HRM. The rapid expansion of government activities in an increasingly complex and technological society required a much larger number of employees and a greater proportion of employees with professional, technical and managerial skills. By the end of this period, public service unions had won the right to bargain collectively and to strike. Efficiency remained the paramount public service value as the Royal Commission on Government Organization (the Glassco Commission)[31] examined HRM as part of its task to recommend changes to "promote efficiency, economy and improved service in the dispatch of public business." Political neutrality was a continuing, but secondary, concern. Also, representativeness emerged as a primary public service value, specifically in regard to remedying the longstanding discrimination in the public service against French-speaking Canadians.

Public Service Alliance of Canada, Founding Convention (1966).

© Public Service Alliance of Canada

The Fruits of Reform (1967–78)

This period was an especially momentous one in the evolution of HRM. Public service managers in general and human resources managers in particular felt the full effects of reforms generated in the previous period. Among the most important reforms were collective bargaining, language training, new management techniques, and departmental reorganizations.

A larger number of public service values contended for precedence during this period. The former emphasis on economy and efficiency was supplemented by vigorous concern for effectiveness. Disclosures of mismanagement and of inefficient and ineffective use of public funds led to widespread anxiety about the accountability of public servants. Revelations of numerous incidents of unethical conduct involving government officials aroused unprecedented concern about their integrity. The representativeness of the public service also became a major issue as the claims of women, Aboriginal peoples, and the disabled were added to those of French-speaking Canadians. The Trudeau government's promises of participatory democracy gave responsiveness a higher place among the public servants' value priorities. Finally, the importance of political neutrality was renewed with the increased recognition of the changing role of public servants in the political system.

The Failure to Reform (1979–89)

It was evident by the end of the 1970s that the traditional concept of merit would have to be reinterpreted to take account of important public service values. Since that time, the federal government has consistently argued that the principles of the merit system noted earlier in this chapter (e.g., fairness, equity, efficiency) should govern all aspects of HRM. During the 1980s, the values of efficiency and accountability had an especially important impact on HRM.

In 1979, the Special Committee on Personnel Management and the Merit Principle[32] (the D'Avignon Committee) reported that the basic human resources problems were a lack of leadership, excessive and inflexible regulation, managers who were ill equipped for managing, and an absence of accountability for the proper management of human resources. The report rejected "authoritarian, non-participative, uncommunicative and centralized systems" and proposed "a flexible, entrepreneurial, professional and participative style of management."[33] Other studies documented the deficiencies of HRM,[34] including low morale caused in part by staff and expenditure reductions. Since the government's efforts to remedy these problems during the 1980s enjoyed little success, in 1989 the government launched Public Service 2000 (PS 2000), an initiative to revitalize the public service, especially in the sphere of HRM.

The Road to Renewal (1990–2002)

By the time the authors of PS 2000 reported in late 1990,[35] HRM was being affected by the emergence of new values that had arisen from extensive public service reform. Notable among these new values were innovation, service, quality, and teamwork. There was also continuing emphasis on the traditional values of efficiency and accountability. PS 2000, which viewed people as the main asset of the public service, recommended the pursuit of such human resources objectives as the empowerment of employees, enhanced career planning and professional development, and improved union–management relations.

In late 1996, to reinforce the actions taken to achieve these objectives, the government first announced La Relève, the initiative discussed earlier, which was designed to address a kind of malaise in the public service brought on by downsizing, pay freezes, and minimal recruitment, and thereby build a modern and efficient public service able to take on the challenges of the twenty-first century. As Jocelyne Bourgon, Clerk of the Privy Council, who launched La Relève in her 1997 report to the prime minister noted, "[It] is a challenge to build a modern and vibrant institution able to use fully the talents of its people."[36] This ambitious initiative endeavoured to go beyond structural adjustments and to change the very culture of the public service, but assessments of La Relève suggest that its reach may have exceeded its grasp.[37]

Initially that cultural change was intended to establish the public sector as a learning organization. For Bourgon, a learning organization focused on much more than learning and development opportunities for its employees; it was one that would learn from and rectify the mistakes that would inevitably arise in administering government programs and services, generate new ideas and incorporate ones identified elsewhere, and modify behaviour on the basis of new knowledge and insight.[38] Eventually, several clerks of the Privy Council honed in on the importance of fostering leadership throughout the public service.

The recruitment and retention of highly qualified and capable public servants was a recurring theme during this period of HRM. To deal with this challenge of reinvigorating the public service, the government ultimately embraced the idea of positioning itself as an "employer of choice," a goal that could be achieved by focusing on recruitment, workplace well-being and retention, and the promotion of learning and development for all employees.[39]

From Renewal to Modernization (2003–Present)

While the renewal imperative, particularly with respect to "branding" the public sector as an "employer of choice," has continued in the most recent period of HRM reform, there

BOX 15.2	The Merit Principle

In the *Public Service Modernization Act*, the merit principle is defined in law for the first time. The Act states that an appointment has respected the merit principle when "the person to be appointed meets the essential qualifications for the work to be performed, as established by the deputy head". The deputy head also has the authority to consider other qualifications that might be considered an "asset" to the organization now or in the future, and may as well take into account "the current or future operational requirements [and] needs of the organization." The definition has some important implications. One is that there is no longer any need to show that the chosen candidate is the "best" in comparison to others; it only has to be demonstrated that the appointed person has the necessary qualifications. Another is that merit criteria can be quite broad and aware of the needs of the organization.

has been a subtle shift in the rhetoric from renewal to modernization. One aspect of the modernization agenda was to introduce legislation to address precise concerns about the inefficiency of the merit system and the alleged absence of an effective definition of the merit principle. The *Public Service Modernization Act* of 2003, which introduced what has been described as "the most important legislative, institutional and policy reforms of the human resources system of the federal public service in almost four decades,"[40] equates merit with meeting "essential qualifications" necessary for the position in question and any "additional qualifications" or needs of the organization (see Box 15.2). The definition acts to broaden the traditional conception of merit "to allow departments to meet multiple considerations when hiring and promoting staff, such as the ability to work in teams and enhancing diversity."[41] The Act also leaves much of the determination of qualifications and needs of the department to senior department officials and thus "underscores the closer alignment of staffing with the business needs of an organization."[42] In general, the legislation was designed to build a values-based, flexible HRM system in place of the rules-based, prescriptive approach.

Modernizing the way in which the federal public service works was a key theme articulated in the 2011 throne speech and given the perception that numerous aspects of the public service employment model—from performance management to labour relations to classification and total compensation—were considered to be outdated, modernizing the public service employment model was identified by the Prime Minister's Advisory Committee on the Public Service as "the key challenge" to be addressed. At the same time, the Committee acknowledged that having emerged from a period of significant downsizing, renewal of the public service was still central to the government's management agenda.[43]

For Wayne Wouters, who served as clerk of the Privy Council from July 2009 to October 2014, the cultural change needed for the public service took on new meaning. It meant working towards a public service that is performance-oriented, innovative, and collaborative; it meant taking full advantage of technological advancements like Web 2.0 tools, and promoting intelligent risk taking. Many of these aspects were evident in the government's latest human resources reform initiative, Blueprint 2020, which was launched in June 2013.

Blueprint 2020 was designed to be a different type of reform initiative, likely as a response to the shortcomings of both PS 2000 and La Relève, which were criticized for being top-down, elite-driven exercises. This initiative was unique in that this was a transparent, bottom-up transformation project where all public servants were given the opportunity to offer their opinions, ideas, and solutions for helping to ensure that the vision of making the federal public service in Canada a world-class institution is attainable. Four guiding principles underpin this vision for the federal public service:

1) an open and networked environment that engages citizens and other governance partners; 2) a "whole-of-government" approach to service delivery; 3) a workplace that fully capitalizes on the use of new technologies for networking, accessing data, and delivering services; and 4) a high-performing workforce that employs a diversity of talent.[44] More than 110,000 public servants were engaged in this process, and this feedback contributed to the development of five priority areas for action (see Box 15.3).

This latest HRM reform initiative, however, has not been immune to criticism. Former Parliamentary Budget Officer, Kevin Page, has called Blueprint 2020 "an empty vessel" while Donald Savoie, one of the country's leading public administration scholars, is on the record as making this assessment:

> I can't figure out Blueprint 2020. It's like grabbing smoke. I don't understand where it is going. Maybe something fundamental or important is taking shape in the system and if that's the case, good luck, but for someone from the outside looking in, there's nothing there. It seems vapid … and until you deal with the role of ministers, Parliament and their relationship with public servants … the vision is only sentences in a report and will not have any legs.[45]*

Like previous administrative reform initiatives, Blueprint 2020 is not a panacea. Nonetheless, it has contributed to the ongoing dialogue of how the public sector needs to respond and adapt to the various environmental factors—political, economic, technological, legal, and so on—that shape it on an ongoing basis.

Blueprint 2020: Priority Areas for Action

BOX
15.3

Innovative Practices and Networking. Public servants will be encouraged to individually and collaboratively develop innovative solutions to complex problems.

Processes and Empowerment. Rules and processes will be reduced and simplified and employees will be empowered to get things done on time and in the proper way.

Modern Technology. Modern technologies will be more effectively integrated into the workplace to ensure faster, more efficient service delivery.

People Management. HRM practices will be refined to improve the recruitment, development, and retention of talent. All core training will be provided to public servants at no cost.

Fundamentals of Public Service. Efforts will be made to raise awareness of the pride that public servants feel in delivering non-partisan advice to government and high-quality services to Canadians.

Source: Canada, *Destination 2020*, May 2014, http://www.clerk.gc.ca/local_grfx/d2020/Destination2020-eng.pdf.

The Legislative and Organizational Framework

The function of HRM pervades government, but the development and administration of human resources policy in the federal government is determined largely by a few key statutes and organizations. The scope and objectives of human resources activities and their allocation among these organizations are set out in three major statutes. The *Financial Administration Act* states that the Treasury Board is charged, among other things, with broad responsibility for "personnel management in the federal public administration, including the determination of the terms and conditions of employment of persons employed therein." The *Public Service Employment Act* grants the PSC authority to

---

* © Donald Savoie

Chapter 15 / The Management of Human Resources

appoint persons to and within the public service according to merit and to handle matters relating to political partisanship and principles concerning layoffs and priorities for appointments. The *Public Service Labour Relations Act* sets out the responsibilities of the Public Service Labour Relations and Employment Board and provides for the structure and operation of the collective bargaining process and for the resolution of disputes and grievances.[46] (See Box 15.4.)

BOX
15.4

Collective Bargaining

Collective bargaining refers to the process by which parties negotiate the pay, hours of work, and other conditions of employment, and it is an important part of the operation of the public sector. At the federal level there are laws and structures set up to manage the collective bargaining process, and the same can be found at the other levels of government. The process of bargaining requires, among other things, the establishment of bargaining units, the determination of the scope of bargaining, the identification of bargaining agents, and the manner of resolving differences within and between parties in the bargaining process. Given the nature of collective bargaining, it should not be surprising that it represents one of the more controversial issues in HRM. Disputes over such matters as pay, benefits, and the right to strike can lead to acrimony and work stoppages.

Historically, the TBS and the PSC constituted the two major bodies in the area of HRM at the federal level. Acting on behalf of the Treasury Board, the Treasury Board Secretariat's responsibilities in the human resources field traditionally included the following: the development and interpretation of policies, programs, and procedures in regard to the organization of the public service; public service positions; compensation; training and development; official languages; discipline; working conditions; human resources needs and their utilization; classification of employees and employee benefits; and other terms and conditions of employment necessary for effective HRM. In addition, the secretariat represented the government as employer in the collective bargaining process. As for the PSC, it had the responsibility to recruit, select, promote, transfer, demote, and dismiss public servants; to provide staff development and training, including language training, within the framework of Treasury Board policies; to hear and decide appeals relating to appointments or to demotions and dismissals for incompetence or incapacity; to investigate allegations of discrimination in public service employment practices; and to administer regulations on political activities by public servants, including decisions on requests for leave of absence to seek political office.

In addition to these two key bodies, other federal organizations with important roles in HRM include the Deputy Ministers Human Resource Management Advisory Committee (MAC), the External Advisory Committee on Senior Level Retention and Compensation, the Human Resources Council, and the Privy Council Office. Set up to oversee the introduction of the *Public Service Modernization* Act, the MAC now has an expanded mandate that encompasses the review of all major reforms in HRM in the federal government. The External Advisory Committee on Senior Level Retention and Compensation, created in 1997, provides advice to the president of the Treasury Board on the management and compensation of senior executives. The Human Resources Council, which comprises senior human resources personnel in departments and central agencies, "provides advice and leadership in strategic resources management for the Federal Public Service."[47] For its part, the Privy Council Office (PCO) exercises a major influence on human resources policy and appointments for the most senior ranks of the public service. It is the prime minister's prerogative to make a large number of order-in-council appointments, including deputy ministers, heads of Crown agencies, and federal judges. The clerk of the Privy Council, who is also secretary to the cabinet, advises the prime minister on the qualifications of existing and prospective order-in-council appointees. The PCO also assumes a leadership position in advancing the agenda for public service management and the clerk speaks for the public service.

The aforementioned *Public Service Modernization Act* and complementary decisions, however, have caused a realignment of roles and responsibilities in the area of HRM. Many of the historic human resource functions of both the TBS and the PSC were initially allocated to a new body, the Public Service Human Resources Management Agency of Canada (PSHRMAC), which reported to the Treasury Board. Another new body, the Public Service Staffing Tribunal, was tasked with managing complaints concerning such matters as layoffs, cancellation of appointments, and general abuse of authority in the appointment process—once a responsibility of the PSC. Responsibility for professional and language training was allocated to a newly established Canada School of Public Service, an amalgamation of the Canadian Centre for Management Development, Training and Development Canada, and Language Training Canada. While the changes were supposed to modernize people management in the public sector, if anything the new structure only served to foster greater overlap and confusion regarding the allocation of HRM functions. PSHRMAC (2003-07) was ultimately short-lived, having been replaced by another fleeting organization, the Canada Public Service Agency (2007–2009).

In February 2009, Prime Minister Harper announced further reorganization of the governance of HRM in the public sector based on the recommendations of the Prime Minister's Advisory Committee on the Public Service, which had noted that the human resources system was inefficient because it was "overly complex, with multiple players and a resulting burden of duplicative and often unnecessary rules."[48] The new structure is shown in Figure 15.1. The changes introduced in the new structure were designed to "simplify, streamline and improve our management of human resources."[49]

The Office of the Chief Human Resources Officer, which is housed in the TBS, emerged to replace the Canadian Public Service Agency and parts of the TBS that dealt with pensions and benefits, labour relations and compensation. Moreover, it is responsible for formulating broad framework policies, ensuring that departments are meeting performance expectations, providing human resources support across the government and talent management for the senior leadership group. In short, it focuses on those activities that must be provided corporately, while leaving primary responsibility for HRM at the departmental level with the deputy ministers, their management teams, and human resources professionals. This further solidifies changes that were introduced with the new definition of merit contained in the *Public Service Modernization Act*, whereby deputy heads of departments took on more responsibility for determining departmental needs and policies relating to learning, training, development, discipline, and dismissal for unsatisfactory performance.

It is now the Chief Human Resources Officer who represents the government as "employer" and who provides strategic leadership with respect to human resources issues. The Canadian School of Public Service continues to be responsible for learning and leadership development programs, but it has been stripped of its policy role. The PCO similarly retains responsibility for deputy ministerial and governor-in-council appointments as well as the broader renewal of the public service by providing support to both the Prime Minister's Advisory Committee on the Public Service and the Deputy Minister Committee on Public Service Renewal. Finally, the PSC remains the guardian of the merit principle and non-partisanship in the public sector.

As for the Public Service Staffing Tribunal, as of November 1, 2014, it was merged with the Public Service Labour Relations Board (PSLRB), which was a quasi-judicial tribunal that was given responsibility for administering the collective bargaining and grievance adjudication systems for the public service and Parliament, into a new

Figure 15.1   Human Resources Governance Structure

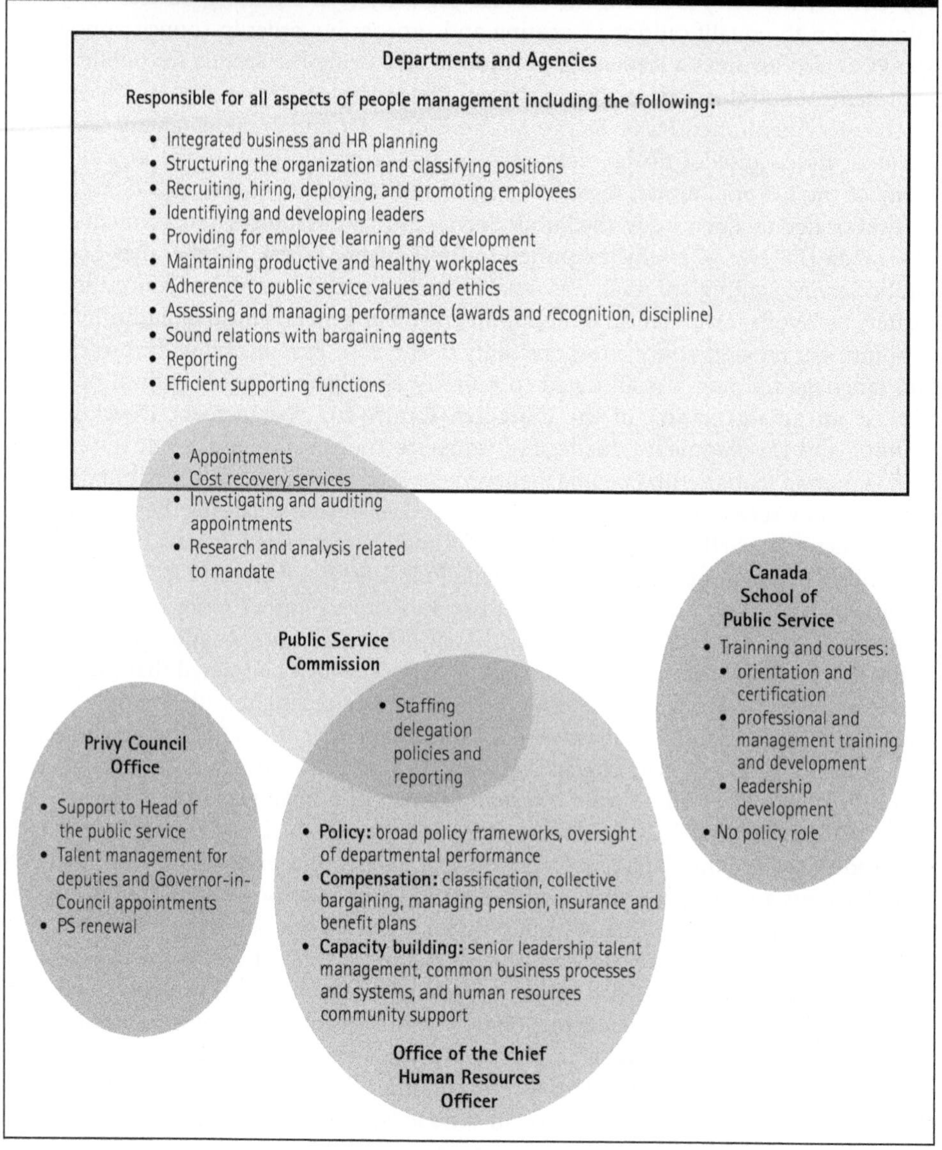

Departments and Agencies

Responsible for all aspects of people management including the following:

- Integrated business and HR planning
- Structuring the organization and classifying positions
- Recruiting, hiring, deploying, and promoting employees
- Identifying and developing leaders
- Providing for employee learning and development
- Maintaining productive and healthy workplaces
- Adherence to public service values and ethics
- Assessing and managing performance (awards and recognition, discipline)
- Sound relations with bargaining agents
- Reporting
- Efficient supporting functions

Public Service Commission

- Appointments
- Cost recovery services
- Investigating and auditing appointments
- Research and analysis related to mandate
- Staffing delegation policies and reporting

Canada School of Public Service

- Training and courses:
  - orientation and certification
  - professional and management training and development
  - leadership development
- No policy role

Privy Council Office

- Support to Head of the public service
- Talent management for deputies and Governor-in-Council appointments
- PS renewal

Office of the Chief Human Resources Officer

- **Policy:** broad policy frameworks, oversight of departmental performance
- **Compensation:** classification, collective bargaining, managing pension, insurance and benefit plans
- **Capacity building:** senior leadership talent management, common business processes and systems, and human resources community support

Source: *Sixteenth Annual Report to the Prime Minister on the Public Service of Canada* – March, 2009. © Permission granted by the Privy Council Office (2016).

organization known as the Public Service Labour Relations and Employment Board. All of the responsibilities of the former Public Service Staffing Tribunal and the PSLRB have been subsumed under this new organizational entity, including the resolution of "pay equity complaints filed by, or on behalf of, groups of employees pursuant to the *Canadian Human Rights Act*," which was a responsibility granted to the PSLRB in 2009.[50]

Major Human Resources Management Processes

In practice, the distribution of responsibilities for HRM among the key organizations discussed above and the many other administrative bodies within government is very complex. A comprehensive examination of the entire field of HRM in Canadian government cannot be provided here, but an explanation of the major human resources processes—employee type and classification, human resources planning, staffing, training and development, and performance evaluation—is provided.

Employee Type and Job Classification

As mentioned previously, when identifying members of the public service, the standard definition would include employees in both the core public administration and the separate agencies. Furthermore, a person appointed to the public service would be classified according to a particular employee type—indeterminate, term, seasonal, casual, and student—and would either be working as a full-time or part-time employee (unless on leave or extended leave, with or without pay). **Indeterminate employees** are those whose tenure in the public service is of an unspecified duration; in other words, they assume the coveted permanent positions, which are relatively few in number when compared with the total annual hires. **Term (determinate) employees** are those individuals whose appointments are for a specified period in accordance with the *Public Service Employment Act*. **Casual employees** can either be full-time or part-time, but their appointments cannot exceed 90 working days in a calendar year in any given government department or organization. To be considered for a position as a student employee under one of the government's student employment programs, the individual in question must be registered as a full-time student at an accredited secondary or post-secondary institution and must be returning to full-time studies in the next academic term. Finally, seasonal employees are those individuals who are hired to work a portion of the year (season) each year.

Job classification is the process by which jobs are assigned to an occupational group or sub-group within an occupational category and to a level within that group. Both logically and chronologically, classification usually precedes the other main human resources processes. It supplies an essential basis for effective HRM in general and appropriate wage and salary administration in particular.

An **occupational category** includes a broad range of occupations of the same type, distinguished by the nature of the duties performed and the education required. The six occupational categories in the federal public service and the number of full-time employees in each category in 2014 were as follows: Executive Group (5,252), Scientific and Professional (31,854), Administrative and Foreign Service (82,710), Technical (12,593), Administrative Support (19,891), and Operational (28,971).[51] An occupational group within a category includes occupations that require similar types of work involving similar skills (e.g., the actuarial science group within the Scientific and Professional category or the firefighters group within the Operational category) and that are often related to the labour market outside the public service.

Human Resources Planning

Human resources planning is the process through which a government strives to ensure that it has—and will continue to have—the appropriate quantity and quality of employees to carry out its responsibilities. This process aims to eliminate the gap between the existing supply of qualified employees and the current and anticipated demand. It involves a number of steps, including determining the overall goals and priorities of the organization with corresponding human resources plans for each department and agency, understanding the demographic makeup of the public service, forecasting future needs, and evaluating to measure for success. There is a close relationship between this planning and virtually all other areas of HRM.

Staffing

The integral link between attracting capable employees and attaining program objectives suggests that staffing may well be the key element of HRM. We have already seen that

indeterminate employee Individuals who are appointed to the public service for an unspecified period of time (i.e., these are permanent positions).

term (determinate) employee Individuals who are appointed to the public service for a specific period of time (e.g., a contract of six months or more).

casual employee Individuals who are appointed to the public service for no more than 90 days in a calendar year in any one government department or agency in either full- or part-time positions.

job classification The process by which jobs are assigned to an occupational group within an occupational category and to a level within that group.

occupational category A broad range of occupations of the same type, distinguished by the nature of the duties performed and the education required. Examples in the federal public service are the Executive Group and the Operational categories.

human resources planning The process through which a government strives to ensure that it has the appropriate quantity and quality of employees to carry out its responsibilities.

determining staffing needs and the means of meeting these needs is a central feature of human resources planning. At the beginning of this chapter, we also saw the importance in the staffing system of balancing the merit principle with other principles. The PSC sets out the following guiding principles to which the entire staffing system should conform:

- *Fairness.* Staffing decisions must be made objectively and be without favouritism and political interference.
- *Access.* Interested persons must have a reasonable opportunity to apply for positions and to be considered for employment.
- *Transparency.* Any information about decisions, policies, or procedures relating to staffing must be communicated to the public openly and in a timely fashion.[52]

Staffing is a complex process, especially in government, where account must be taken of policy and procedural considerations absent in most private sector organizations (e.g., language requirements). However, the staffing process in Canadian governments is normally characterized, and to some extent simplified, by a number of policy and program components (e.g., delegation of staffing authority, open and closed competitions) and of sequential and interrelated steps (e.g., written tests, interviews). Moreover, these policies, programs, and procedures are usually spelled out in a HRM manual.

The central activities in staffing are recruitment, promotion, and deployment. **Recruitment** involves identifying candidates for public service positions from outside the public service by such methods as inviting job applications from within and from outside the public service and using a human resources inventory system. Promotion involves the appointment of an employee from within the public service to a position for which the maximum rate of pay is greater than that of the employee's current position. **Deployment** involves the appointment of an employee to another position at the same level as his or her existing position, or to a higher or lower level, provided that there is no change in the employee's personnel classification. In turn, all of these activities involve **selection**—that is, the screening of candidates through such means as application forms, written examinations, interviews, and a review of the candidate's credentials and past performance. The activities of recruitment and selection are followed by appointment to a specific position or level in the public service.

It is difficult to design and operate a staffing system that will fully satisfy all the parties affected. In a report, the Office of the Auditor General of Canada found that "managers continue to view staffing as unduly complex, inflexible and inefficient, and [that] many employees still are not confident that the system is fair."[53] A major concern expressed in the report related to the slowness of the staffing system, especially when compared with the staffing decisions made in Crown corporations and other government agencies existing outside the core public service. The proposed solution to this problem (and others) was to give individual departments and their managers more leeway in the appointment of officials, a proposal that was acted upon in the *Public Service Modernization Act*. Nonetheless, the efficiency gains that were expected to materialize with the 2003 reforms have been slow to materialize. As the PSC noted, "overall, the average time to staff indeterminate positions through an advertised process has remained virtually unchanged since the coming into force of the Act [*Public Service Employment Act*] … ."[54] In response, the federal government adopted the New Direction in Staffing, which came into effect on April 1, 2016, so as to give individual departments and agencies greater flexibility to customize their approaches to staffing in order to "attract talented people, with modern skills, in a timely fashion."[55]

Training, Development, and Learning

Training, development, and learning are related activities centred on the desire to ensure that employees are properly equipped and disposed to successfully implement present duties and

recruitment The process of attracting suitable candidates for employment in the public service.

deployment The appointment of an employee to another position at the same level as his or her existing position, or to a higher or lower level, provided there is no change in the employee's personnel classification.

selection The process through which candidates for public service positions are screened by such means as application forms, written examinations, and interviews.

any future requirements that might arise from the needs of the organization. For the federal government, training refers to "the transfer of knowledge and know-how that is required for the successful performance in a job, occupation or profession," while development represents "an activity that assists employees [to] further their careers and is aligned with departmental priorities and management objectives of the government." Learning involves the process of acquiring "new knowledge and ideas that change the way an individual perceives, understands or acts."[56] At the national level, the Canada School of Public Service is the lead agency in providing overall direction in training, development, and learning. It offers more than 350 learning products—from courses to programs and seminars, many of which are available online or by webcast—to ensure that employees of the federal public service have the requisite skills and knowledge. This includes providing second language maintenance courses and online tools and courses as well as ensuring the quality of language training services provided by contractors to public service employees. The Canada School of Public Service also provides development programs to ensure that employees at various stages of their career are provided with an opportunity to build upon their skills and knowledge. Such programs include the Management Trainee Program, the Accelerated Executive Development Program, and Living Leadership: The Executive Excellence Program.[57] It is also understood that individual departments will develop training and development programs to suit their specific needs and to complement the School's efforts.

The varied activities of the Canada School of Public Service reveal a trend in HRM away from simply providing courses to supplying a rich menu of services. The underlying aim of this shift is to support a culture of continuous learning and education within organizations so that training and development become a natural part of public agencies. More specifically, for at least the past two decades, the focus of these training and development efforts has been to foster leadership capacity among federal public servants at all levels, but especially in those working in the senior executive service. The importance of fostering leadership within the public service became particularly pronounced with the adoption of the key leadership competency model in 2004, which was revised in 2015. Federal public servants from the supervisory to the deputy ministerial level, are expected to demonstrate six required competencies: they must be able to create vision and strategy, mobilize people, uphold integrity and respect, collaborate with partners and stakeholders, promote innovation and guide change, and achieve results.[58] The acquisition and development of these leadership competencies can be built into the individual learning plans of public servants; furthermore, a number of highly specialized leadership development programs offered through the Canada School of Public Service have been designed to build on this competency profile.

Performance Management

It is important to have quality information about the performance of people over time. Employees must be recruited, selected, trained, and paid; they must also be evaluated in terms of their overall performance. Performance review and appraisal are part of the broader process of **performance management**, which is "a comprehensive approach that includes setting commitments, performance objectives and expected behaviours, assessing results and providing continuous feedback and coaching."[59]* Employees are given informal mid-year reviews to discuss accomplishments in relation to performance commitments; in addition, they receive a formal annual written performance assessment.

The overriding purpose of performance management is to improve the contribution of each employee by ensuring that his or her work is aligned with departmental as well as government-wide strategic and operational goals. It also contributes to employee

performance management
A method for improving the performance and productivity of employees, teams, and organizations. It involves setting performance objectives and expected behaviours, then measuring the results against these measures and providing feedback.

---

* *Directive on Performance Management*, Treasury Board of Canada Secretariat, 2014, www.tbs-sct.gc.ca/pol/doc-eng.aspx?id=27146.

Chapter 15 / The Management of Human Resources

motivation by recognizing strong performance (and dealing with unsatisfactory performance). More specifically, it provides a means of assessing the advisability of pay increases and promotion, the strengths and weaknesses of an employee's present performance, and his or her potential for advancement and need for training and development. Performance management is a component of the federal government's Policy Framework for People Management, which has been designed to foster a culture of excellence in the pursuit of a high performing public service by promoting a number of outcomes, including leadership, empowerment, and employee engagement at all levels of the organization, trust and horizontal collaboration, innovation and creativity, and linguistic duality and diversity.[60]

Points to Know

- It is difficult to identify the size of the public sector since there are many different categories of public sector employment.

- If governments are going to be able to provide a range of services efficiently and effectively to their citizens, then they require competent people to so do. Human resources management deals with all aspects of the employer–employee relationship from recruitment to retention to training and development to motivation and reward to retirement.

- Governments want to attract the best and brightest to the ranks of the public service, but face a number of challenges in achieving that goal.

- Merit has long been a foundational principle for hiring and promotion decisions in the public service. While

merit-based appointments remain the backbone of the federal public service, the concept of merit has evolved over time. Those responsible for hiring no longer have to appoint the "best" candidate; rather, there is greater flexibility for making hiring decisions amongst a pool of candidates who possess the "essential" and "asset" qualifications for the position in question.

- Individual departments and agencies now have responsibility for all aspects of people management, but there are a number of other organizations that also have an important role to play in HRM in the public sector, including the Office of the Chief Human Resources Officer, the Privy Council Office, the Public Service Commission, and the Canada School of Public Service.

Review Questions

1. What is human resources management and how has HRM in the public sector evolved over time in response to various internal and external pressures?

2. Defining the size and scope of the public sector can be problematic. Why is that the case? What are some of the relevant factors that must be considered when making that determination?

3. How does the merit principle influence HRM in the public sector? Is the concept of merit still pertinent in the context of a modern public service?

4. What are the key institutional actors that have a role to play with respect to HRM in the public sector?

Notes

1. Kerry Brown, "Human Resource Management in the Public Sector," *Public Management Review* 6(3) (2004): 304.
2. Ted Glenn, "The State of Talent Management in Canada's Public Sector," *Canadian Public Administration* 55(1) (March 2012): 25–51. The goal of talent management is to maximize the contributions of employees through "ensuring better utilization of their skills and experience; identifying learning and development needs including mentoring and coaching; finding the 'right fit' of skills, experience and career plans; and facilitating succession planning and management" (See Treasury Board of Canada Secretariat, *Talent Management*, accessed May 31, 2015, http://www.tbs-sct.gc.ca/chro-dprh/tal-eng.asp.
3. Donald Savoie, *Breaking the Bargain: Public Servants, Ministers and Parliament* (Toronto: University of Toronto Press, 2003), 63. See also, Savoie, *Court Government and the Collapse of Accountability in Canada and the United Kingdom* (Toronto: University of Toronto Press, 2008), 53.
4. Cited in Public Service Commission of Canada, *The Road Ahead: Recruitment and Retention Challenges for the Public Service* (Ottawa: Public Service Commission of Canada, February 2002), 12. This represented a drop from 52 percent of those surveyed a year earlier. On a more positive note, recent surveys of federal public servants reveal that they have a very high level of engagement with their work and are committed to their organization. See Canada, *2014 Public Service Employee Survey: Summary Report* (Ottawa: Her Majesty the Queen in Right of Canada, February 2015), 6.
5. Canada, *Public Service 2000: The Renewal of the Public Service of Canada - Synopsis* (Ottawa: Minister of Supply and Services, 1990), 16, 13.
6. Robert J. Lavigna and Steven W. Hays, "Recruitment and Selection of Public Workers: An International Compendium of Modern Trends and Practices," *Public Personnel Management* 33(3) (Fall 2004): 237.
7. Despite the common trend of HRM reform, the extent of those reforms and the speed with which they were introduced varied from country to country. See Deok-Shob Shim, "Recent Human Resource Developments in OECD Member Countries," *Public Personnel Management* 30(3) (Fall 2001): 323–347, and Lavigna and Hays, "Recruitment and Selection of Public Workers."

8. Brown, "Human Resource Management in the Public Sector"; Luc Juillet, *The Public Service Commission and the Implementation of the Public Service Employment Act (2003)* (Ottawa: Public Service Commission, March 2011).

9. Cited in Savoie, *Thatcher, Reagan, Mulroney: In Search of a New Bureaucracy* (Toronto: University of Toronto Press, 1994), 94.

10. O.P. Dwivedi and James Iain Gow, *From Bureaucracy to Public Management: The Administrative Culture of the Government of Canada* (Toronto: Broadview Press, 1999), 90.

11. Patricia W. Ingraham, B. Guy Peters and Donald P. Moynihan, "Public Employment and the Future of the Public Service" in *Governance in the 21st Century: Revitalizing the Public Service*, eds. B. Guy Peters and Donald J. Savoie (Montreal & Kingston: McGill-Queen's University Press, 2000), 385–422. More specifically, the public service comprised far fewer secretarial and clerical positions in 2007 than it did in 1983, while it employed three times the number of economists and five times the number of computer specialists. See Clerk of the Privy Council, *Fifteenth Annual Report to the Prime Minister on the Public Service of Canada* (Ottawa: Privy Council Office, 2008), 9.

12. Graham Lowe, *Employer of Choice? Workplace Innovation in Government: A Synthesis Report* (Ottawa: Canadian Policy Research Network, 2001).

13. Public Service Commission, *The Road Ahead*; Lowe, 2001; Office of the Auditor General, *Report of the Auditor General of Canada to the House of Commons—2001* (Ottawa: Supply and Services Canada, 2001), ch. 2.

14. See, for example, Ted Mallett, *A Comparison of Public-Sector and Private-Sector Salaries and Benefits* (Toronto: Canadian Federation of Independent Business, March 2015); Charles Lammam, Milagros Palacios, Feixue Ren, and Jason Clemens, *Comparing Government and Private Sector Compensation in Ontario* (Vancouver: The Fraser Institute, February 2015); Milagros Palacios and Jason Clemens, *Comparing Public and Private Sector Compensation in Canada* (Vancouver: The Fraser Institute, 2013); Richard Mueller, "Public- and Private-Sector Wage Differentials in Canada Revisited" *Industrial Relations* 39(3) (July 2000): 375–400.

15. Public Service Commission, *The Road Ahead*, 17.

16. Clerk of the Privy Council. *Fourth Annual Report to the Prime Minister on the Public Service of Canada*. (Ottawa: Supply and Services Canada, 1996), ch. 6.

17. Office of the Auditor General, *Report—2001*, ch. 2.

18. David Johnson and Andrew Molloy, "The Quiet Crisis and the Emergence of La Relève: A Study of Crisis Perception and Executive Leadership within the Canadian Federal Public Service, 1997-2002" *Canadian Public Administration* 52(2) (June 2009): 210; Jonathan Malloy, "The Next Generation? Recruitment and Renewal in the Federal Public Service," in *How Ottawa Spends 2004-2005: Mandate Change in the Paul Martin Era*, ed. G. Bruce Doern (Montreal & Kingston: McGill-Queen's University Press, 2004), 284.

19. Johnson and Molloy, 209.

20. Evert Lindquist and Gilles Paquet, "Government Restructuring and the Federal Public Service: The Search for a New Cosmology" in *Government Restructuring and Career Public Services*, ed. Evert Lindquist (Toronto: Institute of Public Administration of Canada, 2000), 94.

21. Johnson and Molloy, 216.

22. Treasury Board of Canada Secretariat, *Demographic Snapshot of the Federal Public Service, 2014*, June 1, 2015, www.tbs-sct.ca/res/stats/demo14-eng.asp.

23. Canada. House of Commons. *5,000 Bilingual Positions to Be Filled Every Year: The Role of Post-Secondary Institutions in Promoting Canada's Linguistic Duality. Report of the Standing Committee on Official Languages.* (Ottawa: Communication Canada, 2009), 1.

24. Savoie, *Breaking the Bargain*, has meticulously documented how the traditional bargain between public servants and their political masters has been compromised. It was the report of one of the deputy ministerial task forces launched in the mid-1990s by the clerk of the Privy Council that introduced the concept of employability to the federal public service. See Task Force on Public Service Values and Ethics, *A Strong Foundation: Report of the Task Force on Public Service Values and Ethics* (Ottawa: Canadian Centre for Management Development, 1996).

25. B. Guy Peters, "The Future of Reform" in *Governance in the Twenty-First Century: Revitalizing the Public Service*, eds. B. Guy Peters and Donald Savoie (Montreal and Kingston: McGill-Queen's University Press, 2000), 425–435.

26. Les Whittington, "Flaherty's Message: Victory Opens Way to Spending Clampdown" *The Toronto Star*, May 13, 2011, accessed June 2, 2015, www.thestar.com/business/2011/05/13/flahertys_message_victory_opens_way_to_spending_clampdown.html.

27. Treasury Board of Canada Secretariat, *Demographic Snapshot*.

28. Cited in Kathryn May, "The 'Golden Age' of Public Service is on the Horizon—If Canada Hires More Millennials: Scott Brison" *The National Post*, February 16, 2016, accessed May 2, 2016, www.news.nationalpost.com/news/canada/canadian-politics/the-golden-age-of-public-service-is-on-the-horizon-if-canada-hires-more-millennials-scott-brison.

29. Public Service Commission, *Annual Report 2004–2005* (Ottawa: Her Majesty the Queen in Right of Canada, 2005), 11–12.

30. Valuable information and analysis on the nature and extent of patronage from the pre-Confederation period to the mid-1930s are provided by R. McGregor Dawson in *The Principle of Official Independence* (London: P.S. King and Son, 1922), ch. 3; *The Civil Service of Canada* (Oxford: Oxford University Press, 1929); and "The Canadian Civil Service," *Canadian Journal of Economics and Political Science* 2 (August 1936): 288–300. For a detailed treatment of the evolution of merit in the Canadian federal public service, see Luc Juillet and Ken Rasmussen, *Defending a Contested Ideal: Merit and the Public Service Commission of Canada, 1908–2008* (Ottawa: University of Ottawa Press, 2008).

31. Royal Commission on Government Organization, *Report*, 5 vols. (Ottawa: Queen's Printer, 1962–63).

32. D'Avignon Committee, *Report of the Special Committee on the Review of Personnel Management and the Merit Principle* (Hull: Supply and Services Canada, 1979), 5.

33. Ibid., 46.

34. See, notably, David Zussman and Jak Jabes, *The Vertical Solitude: Managing in the Public Sector* (Halifax: The Institute for Research on Public Policy, 1989).

35. Canada, *Public Service 2000: The Renewal of the Public Service of Canada* (Ottawa: Supply and Services Canada, 1990).

36. Clerk of the Privy Council. *Fourth Annual Report*, ch. 6.

37. Malloy, "The Next Generation?" 279.

38. Clerk of the Privy Council. *Fifth Annual Report to the Prime Minister on the Public Service of Canada*. (Ottawa: Supply and Services Canada, 1997), ch. 3.

39. Clerk of the Privy Council. *Seventh Annual Report to the Prime Minister on the Public Service of Canada*. (Ottawa: Privy Council Office, 2000).

40. Juillet, *The Public Service Commission*, 3.

41. Evert Lindquist, Ian Clark, and James Mitchell, "Reshaping Ottawa's Centre of Government: Martin's Reforms in Historical Perspective," in *How Ottawa Spends 2004–2005*, ed. Doern, 333.

42. Public Service Commission of Canada, *Annual Report 2004–2005*, ch. 2, 12, accessed July 27, 2016, http://www.collectionscanada.gc.ca/webarchives/20071121062637/http://www.psc-cfp.gc.ca/arp-rpa/2005/rpt-eng.pdf#page=12&zoom=auto,-73,702.

43. See Governor General, *Here for All Canadians: Stability, Prosperity, Security. Speech from the Throne to Open the First Session of the Forty-First Parliament of Canada*, June 3, 2011, 15; Prime Minister's Advisory Committee on the Public Service, *Seventh Report to the Prime Minister: Modernizing the Employment Model*, March 2013, 8. Prime Minister Harper established the Prime Minister's Advisory Committee on the Public Service in 2006 as a mechanism for providing counsel to both the prime minister and the clerk on its renewal and future development.

44. Canada, *Blueprint 2020: Getting Started—Getting Your Views. Building Tomorrow's Public Service Together*, June 2013, accessed June 9, 2015, www.clerk.gc.ca/local_grfx/bp2020/bp2020-eng.pdf.

45. Cited in Kathryn May, "Kevin Page Dismisses Privy Council's Blueprint 2020 as 'Empty Vessel'" *Ottawa Citizen*, December 25, 2013, accessed June 10, 2015, www.ottawacitizen.com/news/national/kevin-page-dismisses-privy-councils-blueprint-2020-as-empty-vessel.

46. Some other pieces of legislation might be mentioned, including the *Official Languages Act* and the *Canadian Human Rights Act*.

47. Public Service Human Resources Management Agency of Canada, "Welcome to HR Council Online," *Human Resources Council*, July 12, 2006, www.hrma-agrh.gc.ca/ hr-rh/hrc-crh/index_e.asp.

48. Prime Minister's Advisory Committee on the Public Service, *Second Report of the Prime Minister's Advisory Committee on the Public Service*, 6.

49. Canada, *Sixteenth Annual Report to the Prime Minister on the Public Service of Canada* (Ottawa: Her Majesty the Queen in Right of Canada, 2009), 33.

50. Public Service Labour Relations Board, accessed June 25, 2015, http://pslreb-crtefp.gc.ca/index_e.asp.

51. Treasury Board of Canada Secretariat, *Employment Equity in the Public Service of Canada, 2013-14: Annual Report to Parliament* (Ottawa: Her Majesty the Queen in Right of Canada, 2015), (Table 3), 12.

52. Public Service Commission, *Annual Report 2004–2005*, ch. 2, 12.

53. Auditor General of Canada, *Report of the Auditor General of Canada* (Ottawa: Department of Public Works and Government Services, April 2000), ch. 9, "Streamlining the Human Resource Management Regime," 9–20.

54. Public Service Commission of Canada, *Merit and Non-Partisanship Under the Public Service Employment Act (2003)* (Ottawa: Public Service Commission of Canada, 2011), 9.

55. Public Service Commission, "New Direction in Staffing—Message from the Public Service Commission to All Public Servants," April 1, 2016, accessed June 29, 2016, www.psc-cfp.gc.ca/plcy-pitq/message-eng.htm.

56. Treasury Board of Canada Secretariat, *Policy on Learning, Training and Development* (January 1, 2006), 9–11, accessed July 14, 2016, http://www.tbs-sct.gc.ca/pol/doc-eng.aspx?id=12405.
57. See the website of the Canada School of Public Service at www.csps-efpc.gc.ca/index-eng.aspx.
58. Treasury Board of Canada Secretariat, "The Key Leadership Competency Profile, March 2015," accessed July 14, 2016, www.tbs-sct.gc.ca/psm-fpfm/learning-apprentissage/pdps-ppfp/klc-ccl/klcp-pccl-eng.asp. See also Glenn, "The State of Talent Management"; and Tim A. Mau, "Is Public Sector Leadership Distinct? A Comparative Analysis of Core Competencies in the Senior Executive Service," in *Public Sector Leadership: International Challenges and Prospects*, eds. Jeffrey A. Raffel, Peter Leisink, and Anthony E. Middlebrooks (Cheltenham, UK: Edward Elgar, 2009), 323–326.
59. Treasury Board of Canada Secretariat, *Directive on Performance Management* (April 2014), Appendix, accessed June 20, 2016, www.tbs-sct.gc.ca/pol/doc-eng.aspx?id=27146.
60. See Treasury Board of Canada Secretariat, *Policy Framework for People Management* (July 2010), accessed June 20, 2016, www.tbs-sct.gc.ca/pol/doc-eng.aspx?id=19134.

Representative Bureaucracy and Employment Equity

16

Learning Objectives

Reading this chapter allows you to do the following:

- Distinguish between affirmative action and employment equity
- Identify the four target groups and explain why a representative bureaucracy is considered to be an important policy objective for the federal government
- Assess whether passive representation in the federal public service is sufficient for ensuring responsive public policies

- Explain how merit can be reconciled with employment equity
- Determine the representativeness of the federal public service
- Discuss how pay equity relates to the broader goal of employment equity

When we look at public bureaucracies in Canada or elsewhere, sometimes we can see that the composition of the organization is not representative of the population it serves. This result may arise from a very strict application of the merit principle, or it might be a consequence of discrimination inherent in the system of human resources management (HRM). Whatever the reasons, governments—and their societies—are usually unhappy with this situation, because they understand it is unfair and most likely detrimental to the responsive delivery of services. Accordingly, governments will take action to correct it. In Canada, the actions taken to provide for a more representative bureaucracy constitute an effort typically called employment equity. Another unsettling aspect of the public bureaucracy is evidence that there may be discrimination in the payment of public servants. Even though women may carry out a job comparable to one carried out by men, they may find that they are paid less than men. Pay equity is the program in Canada established to address this problem.

This chapter first examines the philosophical and logical underpinnings of representative bureaucracy. We will see that representative bureaucracy has its supporters, but that it is not without its critics. The chapter also considers employment equity efforts at the federal level and their effects. These efforts are intended to benefit four groups: women, visible minorities, the disabled, and Aboriginals. There is also an effort at ensuring that the distribution of jobs broadly reflects the presence of Francophones in the larger population. The chapter ends with a discussion of pay equity.

Representative Bureaucracy

representative bureaucracy The idea that the social composition of the bureaucracy should reflect that of the population as a whole. Also that larger numbers of persons from certain under-represented groups (e.g., women, minority groups) should be brought into the public service.

Representative bureaucracy is a difficult concept that has been interpreted in a variety of ways. A strict interpretation would require that the public service be a microcosm of the total society in terms of a wide range of variables, including race, religion, language, education, social class, and region of origin. Most governments would probably see this interpretation as too literal and probably impossible to achieve. But these same governments would most likely accept the following sentiment as the foundation for their efforts in this area: that a public service that is representative of the larger society will be responsive to the needs and interests of the public and will thus be more responsible.[1] This belief in turn would be based on several propositions:

- If the values of the public service as a whole are similar to those of the total population, the public service will tend to make the kinds of decisions the public would make if it were involved in the decision-making process.
- The values of public servants are molded by the pattern of socialization—education, social class, and race—that they experience before they enter the public service.
- The values arising from this socialization will not be modified by prolonged exposure to bureaucratic values.
- The values arising from socialization will be reflected in the behaviour of public servants and, therefore, in their recommendations and decisions.

Thus, the various groups in the general population should be represented in the public service in approximate demographic proportion so that public servants will be responsive to the interests of these groups both in policy development and in program delivery.

passive representation A situation whereby the demographic makeup of the bureaucracy reflects that of the general population. An assumption is made that a passively representative bureaucracy will act in the interests of their counterparts in the general population when formulating public policy.

active representation A bureaucracy is only considered representative if the policies emanating from the policy-making process actually reflect the interests of the groups in the general population that are being passively represented.

But in terms of ensuring representativeness, is it sufficient that the public service reflects the broader demographic makeup of society? This is what Frederick Mosher referred to as **passive representation**. Or is it more critical to determine whether the bureaucracy ensures **active representation**? In this latter instance, the bureaucracy is considered representative only if the interests and desires of those who are passively represented are reflected in the formulation of public policies.[2] Many contemporary scholars argue that active representation can only be realized if passive representation is first achieved, but Mosher asserted that the former could occur without the latter. In other words, while senior public servants might not passively represent the population, they could nonetheless actively represent those broad interests because of their education and experience. Much of the scholarship on representativeness, especially outside of the US, has tended to focus only on descriptive representation with race and gender being the two most common characteristics identified as being important.

In addition to the concerns identified above, there are other scholars who believe that the theory of representative bureaucracy and its supporting propositions are vulnerable.[3] The critics of representative bureaucracy contend, for instance, that it is insufficient for the public service as a whole to be broadly representative of the total population; for all interests to be represented in the decision-making process, each major administrative unit must be representative of the total population, especially at its senior levels where the most important recommendations and decisions are made. In other cases, it has been suggested that passive representation should not be determined on the basis of the percentage of public servants within a given department or agency relative to the population at large; rather, representativeness with a given public organization must be compared with the specific population it serves. It is also pointed out that a public servant with certain social and educational origins will not necessarily share the values of those outside the public service with similar origins. The lifelong process of socialization continues after entry to the public service in the form of resocialization to the values of the service as a whole or of particular administrative units. Moreover, representatives of a specific group in the population, particularly if they achieve high office in the public service, are likely to be upwardly mobile and may well share the socioeconomic and other values of those with whom they work, rather than of the group from which they came. It is also possible, as suggested above, that an unrepresentative bureaucracy may successfully represent the various groups in a society, and indeed some claim that this has happened in some civil services. All in all—and somewhat ironically—it is possible to have a representative public service that is not responsive and a responsive public service that is not representative.

Canadian Writings

First, it should be noted that not much has been written about the importance of having a representative bureaucracy in the Canadian context.[4] That being said, the major points of contention in the historical debate on representative bureaucracy in Canada involve the extent to which the values of efficiency, effectiveness, neutrality, and responsiveness conflict with, or complement, that of representativeness.[5] In this debate, Donald Rowat objected to John Porter's sacrifice of representativeness for the sake of efficiency and suggested that both values can be achieved. He argued that representativeness "is essential to the efficiency of the bureaucracy, in the sense of the latter's effectiveness in a democratic, pluralistic society."[6] Porter asserted that people of various social origins will be found in the bureaucracy in roughly the same proportion as in the population as a whole *if* government recruitment and promotion policies do not discriminate against particular groups, *if* educational facilities to qualify persons for public service appointments are equal among these groups, and *if* these groups are equally motivated to join the public service. He contended that "in the theoretically ideal bureaucracy, the candidate for office neither gains nor loses as a result of ethnic, religious or regional origins."[7]

Rowat, who was more concerned with what can be realized in practice than with a search for a theoretically ideal bureaucracy, observed that Porter's conditions of equality did not exist and cannot be easily achieved. He contended that representativeness must be actively sought, even at the expense of technical efficiency and neutrality. Moreover, competent members of under-represented groups could be brought into the public service from outside. Porter opposed the recruitment of outsiders on the grounds that this practice threatened the neutrality of the service and the concept of the bureaucratic career. He stated that "since the basis of power associations are frequently ethnic, regional or religious, the idea that these groups should be represented in the bureaucracy contradicts the notion of the official as the servant of the state."[8] Rowat did not agree that the appointment of "bureaucratic outsiders" would endanger political neutrality, and he argued that a public service that complemented career public servants with outsiders would be more responsive, since a career bureaucracy tends to "lose contact with and lack understanding of the changing feelings, needs and desires of the great variety of people and groups found in our dynamic, pluralistic society."[9]

Porter objected on several grounds to Rowat's plea for representativeness. He first posed the basic question as to which of the many groups in society should be represented in the public service. He then asserted that Rowat's proposals for recruiting members of under-represented groups and providing them with in-service training serve the principle of equal opportunity rather than representativeness. Porter also stated that "in a society of classes, the upwardly mobile are seldom representative of the social interests from which they originated."[10] Finally, he noted the assumption in the theory of representative bureaucracy that political institutions are inadequate to cope with modern demands and questioned the view that "ways can be found for governmental bureaucracy to make up for the deficiencies in our representative political institutions."[11]

The Representativeness of the Canadian Bureaucracy

The federal public service is not a microcosm of Canadian society, but it is not the policy of the federal government to pursue an exact demographic representation of all groups in society; rather, the government's aim is to achieve a more proportionate representation of a limited number of politically significant, but under-represented, groups. In this regard, the government has argued that the under-representation of such groups as Francophones, women, and Aboriginal peoples may diminish the sensitivity of the public service to the needs of certain segments of the population. Thus, a prime motivation underlying efforts to represent these groups more adequately is to make the public service more responsive, in both the provision of policy advice and the delivery of services. As explained above, the assumption that representativeness will promote responsiveness is central to the theory of representative bureaucracy. The government also presumes that members of under-represented groups who join the public service will remain sensitive to the needs and claims of these groups.

In view of the deficiencies of the theory of representative bureaucracy outlined earlier, the benefits of representation in terms of increased responsiveness are likely to be less than anticipated. However, we know little about the extent to which the expanded representation of members of under-represented groups has had a policy impact by advancing the substantive interests of these groups.[12]

Increased representation has effects that are not covered by the theory of representative bureaucracy. Representation has a symbolic impact that helps to promote quiescence and stability in the Canadian political system and explains, in part, its appeal to government officials. The statutes, regulations, and administrative units designed to increase the representation of under-represented groups evoke symbols of equality of opportunity and upward mobility for members of these groups. In the name of equal opportunity, the government has instituted programs to recruit and train members of groups who have not enjoyed equal access to the public service. Also, recruitment to senior posts from outside the service and post-entry training geared to promotion to the higher ranks of the service demonstrate the opportunities for group members to attain senior policy-making posts. Thus, group members who are appointed to, and promoted in, the public service provide role models for other members of their group.

Government actions to increase the representativeness of the public service serve a partisan political purpose in that they help to sustain or increase electoral support for the governing party. Evidence of partisan motivation can be seen in the fact that the groups for whom increased representation has been sought have mobilized for political action and are highly visible and vocal in their demands for greater participation in the political and administrative systems. The government's efforts on behalf of under-represented groups have brought about a more representative public service.

target (designated) group Since it is not feasible to have a bureaucracy that is an exact representation of all key demographic groups in society, the Canadian government has decided to ensure that the federal bureaucracy is representative of four target groups: women, visible minorities, Aboriginals, and persons with disabilities.

Equal Opportunity and Employment Equity

The issues of representative bureaucracy and equal opportunity are closely linked: the attainment of a representative public service depends largely on the extent to which various groups in society have equal access to employment in the public service. The federal, provincial, and municipal governments have adopted a wide range of programs to promote equal opportunity in the public service for segments of the population that have historically been under-represented. As explained above, the federal government is committed to improving the representation of certain **"target" ("designated") groups**, namely women, members of visible minority groups, persons with disabilities, and Aboriginal peoples. In the federal sphere, Francophones are not treated as one of the target groups; rather, they are treated separately as part of the government's efforts to ensure equitable participation in the public service of Canada's two official language communities.

Part Five / The Management of Organizational Resources

Despite the lack of guaranteed representation for Francophones in the federal public service, we have witnessed a shift from the under-representation of Francophones to a situation of over-representation. This has been achieved through the adoption of the principle of individual bilingualism. Since Francophones have a much higher level of bilingualism than English-speaking Canadians, they have had an advantage in the hiring process.[13]

The term "equal opportunity" was largely displaced in the early 1980s by "affirmative action," which was in turn soon displaced by **employment equity**. "Affirmative action" and "employment equity" are often used interchangeably; both can usefully be viewed as means to the end of equal opportunity, although in the former instance—at least as practised in the US—has typically meant the use of racial or gender quotas and mandatory compliance. As such, affirmative action has often been criticized for promoting reverse discrimination. In June 1983, the federal government announced its continued commitment to a bureaucracy that is representative of and responsive to the people it serves,[14] and introduced an affirmative action program to accelerate the participation of the target groups in the public service. Affirmative action was defined as "a comprehensive systems-based approach to the identification and elimination of discrimination in employment. It makes use of detailed analyses to identify and systematically remove employment policies, practices, and procedures that may exclude or place at a disadvantage the three target groups"[15] (which at that time included women, Aboriginal peoples, and disabled persons).

The government stressed that the merit principle would be preserved, and that the numerical goals being set were not quotas but "an estimate of what can be achieved when systemic barriers are eliminated and some temporary special measures are put in place to accelerate training and development experience."[16] The president of the Treasury Board announced that implementation of the affirmative action program would be viewed as a major consideration in the performance of deputy ministers. Thus, while this program did not establish quotas, it moved in that direction by using temporary special measures, numerical goals, and pressure on senior public servants to achieve these goals.

The legal basis for affirmative action programs was laid in 1977 by the *Canadian Human Rights Act*, which also established the Canadian Human Rights Commission. Section 16(1) of the Act provides in effect that measures taken to redress historical imbalances in the participation of certain groups do not amount to reverse discrimination. Since that time, the recommendations of the Royal Commission on Equality in Employment[17] (the Abella Commission) and the coming into force of Section 15—the equality rights section—of the *Canadian Charter of Rights and Freedoms* have supported the federal government's affirmative action programs.

Section 15 guarantees "equal protection and equal benefit of the law without discrimination," and then goes on to say that this guarantee "does not preclude any law, program or activity that has as its object the amelioration of conditions of disadvantaged individuals or groups including those that are disadvantaged because of race, national or ethnic origin, colour, religion, sex, age or mental or physical disability." In other words, preferential treatment for groups that have historically been disadvantaged does not constitute reverse discrimination.

As noted, the term employment equity, which came into frequent use in 1985, is very similar in meaning to affirmative action. However, when Justice Abella produced her royal commission report in 1984, she coined the term "employment equity" with the "aim of avoiding the contentious type of debate that characterized the discourse on affirmative action in the United States."[18] As defined by the Public Service Commission (PSC), an employment equity program includes "positive policies, practices or elements of an employment equity plan designed to address identified disadvantages and under-representation of one or more designated groups."[19] In the Canadian context, employment equity has two elements: first, it is about fair treatment and the removal of barriers; and second, it is designed to address historic imbalances through the adoption of positive actions to foster a representative workforce.[20]

employment equity An approach or program designed to identify and systematically remove employment policies, practices, and procedures that exclude or place at a disadvantage certain groups that have been historically under-represented in the public service.

A positive, albeit incomplete, step towards employment equity occurred in March 1986 when the House of Commons passed the federal *Employment Equity Act*, which required Crown corporations and federally regulated employers with 100 or more employees (primarily in the banking, transportation, and communication industries) to report annually to the government on the extent to which they have achieved results in promoting employment equity programs for designated groups. The problem was that the legislation did not apply to the federal public service. In the same year, however, the Treasury Board issued an employment equity policy for the public service that required departments and agencies, among other things, to identify systemic barriers to equitable participation by designated groups, adopt special measures to remedy imbalances in the public service workforce, and meet numerical objectives for the representation and distribution of the designated groups.[21]

In early 1991, the Treasury Board announced a new approach to setting employment equity targets on the basis of rates of recruitment, promotion and separation, not just on representation. "This reflects the principle that the workplace should be conducive to attracting and retaining designated group members, that they should receive a fair share of recruitment and promotion opportunities, and that their rate of separation from the Public Service should be no higher than that of other employees."[22] In 1995, a new *Employment Equity Act* replaced the 1986 Act. The new Act applied to public servants as well as the previously covered Crown corporations and federally regulated industries; it also authorized the Canadian Human Rights Commission to audit employers to verify their compliance with the Act.

In the federal government, the Treasury Board Secretariat (TBS) and the PSC have played the leading roles in developing, implementing, and monitoring employment equity programs. The two agencies devised programs for Francophones and women in the 1960s, initiatives that were strengthened and supplemented by programs for Aboriginal peoples, visible minorities, and the disabled during the 1970s and 1980s. Table 16.1 shows the distribution of employees by designated group and occupational category as of March 31, 2015. As this data reveals, the federal public service has achieved full representativeness at the aggregate level, with the percentage of employees in each of the four targeted groups exceeding workforce availability. This has now been the case for three consecutive years. However, more representation is still required at the executive level where only one (Aboriginals) of the four target groups exceeds workforce availability.

Employment equity programs can be grouped into three categories: training and development (e.g., special training opportunities for women); new or modified administrative units and practices (e.g., a special office for Aboriginal employment); and vigorous recruitment (e.g., various programs to recruit qualified persons from every target group). Departments and agencies are required to run employment equity programs to promote representativeness and fairness in the public service. But a big part of the challenge has been to overcome attitudinal barriers—notably prejudice against the target groups—that existed in the public service and Canadian society as a whole.

Employment Equity in Practice

Under the *Public Service Employment Act, 2003*, the PSC retains the exclusive authority to make appointments to and within the public service, but much of this authority has been delegated to deputy heads and their sub-delegated managers. These individuals have similarly been delegated responsibility for employment equity and fulfilling the obligations outlined in the *Employment Equity Act*. Ultimately, it is the PSC that is accountable to Parliament for the overall integrity of appointments to the public service. The PSC, in turn, holds deputy heads accountable for their delegated authorities through a variety of means, including the Staffing Management Accountability Framework; a variety of PSC policies, including a number related to achieving employment equity objectives; requiring deputy heads to report on the exercise of their delegated authorities; conducting audits, studies, and investigations; monitoring appointment patterns,

TABLE 16.1

OCCUPATIONAL GROUP	ALL EMPLOYEES (NUMBER)	WOMEN (%)	ABORIGINAL PEOPLES (%)	PERSONS WITH DISABILITIES (%)	MEMBERS OF A VISIBLE MINORITY GROUP (%)
Executives (Workforce Availability)	5,228	46.4 (47.8)	3.4 (5.2)	5.3 (2.3)	8.8 (9.5)
Scientific and Professional	31,974	52.0	3.2	4.4	17.7
Administrative and Foreign Service	82,802	63.0	5.3	6.2	14.7
Technical	12,569	25.5	4.4	4.5	8.1
Administrative Support	19,144	78.7	6.8	7.7	15.2
Operational	28,889	29.4	6.1	4.5	8.9
Undetermined	75	60.0	N/A	8.0	16.0
Total	180,681	54.3	5.1	5.6	13.8
Workforce Availability		52.5	3.4	4.4	13.0

Distribution of Public Service of Canada Employees by Designated Group, Occupational Group, and Workforce Availability as of March 31, 2015

Source: *Employment Equity in the Public Service of Canada 2013–14: Annual Report to Parliament*, http://www.tbs-sct.gc.ca/psm-fpfm/ve/dee/reports-rapports/2013-2014/ee-eng.pdf, Treasury Board of Canada Secretariat 2014.

information gathering, and risk assessment; and providing feedback to delegated organizations so that they can improve their staffing systems.

With respect to employment equity, it is the responsibility of deputy heads to determine whether their departments and agencies are under-represented by conducting surveys and doing workforce analyses. They are also responsible for developing an Employment Equity Plan, either as a stand-alone document or as part of the Human Resources Plan for their organizations. As a part of those Employment Equity Plans, organizations would have their own employment equity programs. These are established by the deputy head and can either be distinct to the organization in question or modeled after the Framework for Employment Equity Programs established by the PSC in 2004. Such programs can be in place for no more than five years at which point they are evaluated and a decision would be made to either extend or modify the program.

There are a number of key decision points in the appointment process, and deputy heads and their sub-delegated managers should take employment equity considerations into account at each of these stages.[23] We examine below four of these decision points, which should clarify how employment equity is integrated into the appointment process:

1. *Human resources planning.* As part of the integrated business and human resources planning, the deputy head would include an employment equity gap analysis along with strategies and plans to reduce those gaps.
2. *Establishing merit criteria.* The deputy heads can establish employment equity objectives as part of the criteria for determining merit for positions, in addition to the essential and asset qualifications, either as a current or future need for the organization or the public service as a whole. This organizational need merit criterion can be applied in any order at any stage of the appointment process. In other words, if employment equity has been identified as an organizational need,

then the hiring manager can either choose to apply this criterion at the start of the assessment process and eliminate all candidates who are not members of the designated group(s), or he or she can assess all of the other merit criteria first and then use the employment equity organizational need criterion at the end of the process as a means of choosing the candidate to appoint.

3. *Choice of appointment process.* Deputy heads have the authority to set the criteria for all non-advertised appointment processes. If a non-advertised process is being used to improve employment equity representation, then the deputy head must establish and communicate the criterion for the appointment of designated group members through such a process. The appointment of members of designated groups should be identified as an organizational need. The use of a non-advertised process can be justified when the department has a skills shortage, when there is a high rate of turnover among certain designated groups or when it has been a challenge for the department to recruit designated group members to a specific field.

4. *Area of selection.* For all advertised external appointment processes, PSC policy dictates that there is a national area of selection. However, in other appointment processes the area of selection may be limited by one of four criteria—1) geographic, which is where a person must reside or be employed to be considered for an appointment; 2) organizational, in which case the potential applicant must be employed by a particular organization; 3) occupational, which may restrict eligibility to a specific occupational stream or a particular occupation; and 4) employment equity, whereby jobs are restricted to one or more of the four designated groups. Deputy heads, therefore, are given the flexibility of establishing an area of selection that is limited to one or more of the designated groups as long as the decision to do so is consistent with the organization's Employment Equity or Human Resources Plan. For example, a job posting might be restricted to persons with disabilities or to members of a visible minority group and Aboriginals (as was the situation in the case study considered below). In some instances, the deputy head may choose to expand an area of selection so as to create a pool of candidates with additional designated group members. For example, a department may identify a need to increase the number of Aboriginal people in an occupational group (through an internal advertised process), but since their number in the region is insufficient the position could be opened up to both employees of the organization in that particular region and individuals who are employees of Aboriginal origin based in other regions.

There have been complaints from public servants and from their unions that equal opportunity programs violate the merit principle and discriminate against candidates outside the designated groups for appointment and promotion.[24] This issue also drew national media attention in 2010 when an Ottawa-area woman publicly complained that she was prohibited from applying for an administrative assistant job in the federal public service because she was white (see Box 16.1). The PSC has responded by explaining that merit is a dynamic principle; its application must be reconciled with such other values as responsiveness, representativeness, fairness, equity, and economy.[25]

Box 16.1

Employment Equity—Progressive Policy or Reverse Discrimination?

The issue of whether employment equity provisions in the public sector constitute reverse discrimination gained national prominence in 2010 when Sara Landriault, a Caucasian woman from Kemptville, Ontario, attempted to apply for an administrative assistant position with Citizenship and Immigration Canada.

Chris Roussakis/Toronto Sun. Material republished with the express permission of: *Toronto Sun*, a division of Postmedia Network Inc.

Landriault felt that she was qualified to apply for this job, but she was ultimately prevented from submitting her resume when she identified herself as white during the online application process since the position in question was restricted to two employment equity groups—Aboriginal people or visible minorities. It was little consolation to the unsuccessful applicant that only about 1 percent of the approximately 20,000 jobs overseen by the PSC were exclusively for Aboriginals or visible minorities. As Landriault stated, "No government should have the right to ask you your race or gender to see if you are qualified for a job. That is discrimination."

Administrative Assistant

Department Name: Department of Citizenship and Immigration Canada
Location: Ottawa
Classification: AS - 01
Salary: $46,321 to $51,807
Closing Date: July 19, 2010 - 23:59, Pacific Time Useful Information
Reference Number: IMC10J-010980-000002
Selection Process Number: 2010-IMC-EA-10297
Vacancies: 1

Website: For further information on the department, please visit Department of Citizenship and Immigration Canada

Who Can Apply:

Useful Information

Applicants must meet at least the first requirement:

- **Open to:** Members of the following Employment Equity groups: Aboriginal persons, visible minorities

---

© Immigration, Refugees and Citizenship Canada

Despite such restrictions being permissible under both the Charter and the provisions of other relevant legislation (*Public Service Employment Act, Employment Equity Act,* and *Canadian Human Rights Act*), the issue gained traction because two government ministers expressed sympathy for her concerns. Jason Kenney, Minister of Citizenship and Immigration, the department at the centre of this controversy, went on the record stating that individuals should be hired on the basis of merit, not ethnicity. Another minister, Stockwell Day, President of the Treasury Board, the minister who ultimately had responsibility as the head of the entity that serves as the general manager and employer for the public service, ordered a review of the government job-application process that allowed for job restrictions to one or more of the designated employment equity groups.

In an apparent rebuke of the government's actions and statements regarding the employment equity laws, Maria Barrados, President of the PSC, issued a letter to the heads of human resources in the federal government to reaffirm the PSC's policies and guidelines with respect to employment equity. The November 2010 letter highlighted the link between merit and representativeness, and it identified the various special measures that could be undertaken to foster employment equity, including identifying employment equity in the merit criteria for a job posting or restricting candidate selection to one or more of the four designated groups if that were consistent with the department's Employment Equity or Human Resources Plan.

What are your views on the matter? Are Landriault and others justified in their criticism of the federal government's practice of reserving some public service positions for candidates belonging to one or more of the four designated employment equity groups? Or is the purpose of the *Employment Equity Act,* namely to achieve workplace equity by correcting the disadvantages experienced by the four designated groups through the use of special measures and the accommodation of difference, still relevant?

Sources: Public Service Commission of Canada, Guidance Series – Integrating Employment Equity in the Appointment Process (Ottawa: Public Service Commission of Canada, December 2005). Available online at www.psc-cfp.gc.ca/plcy-pltq/guides/equity-equite/guid-orie-eng.htm; Joe Friesen, "Tories Take Aim at Employment Equity," *The Globe and Mail.* Thursday, July 22, 2010. Available online at http://www.theglobeandmail.com/news/politics/tories-take-aim-at-employment-equity/article1389384/; Maria Barrados, "Employment Equity Hiring (10-23)," Letters to Heads of Human Resources (Ottawa: Public Service Commission of Canada, November 12, 2010).

To assess the extent to which the federal government's employment equity programs have been successful, it is useful to examine briefly the experience of five major groups that, historically, have been under-represented in the public service: Francophones, women, Aboriginal peoples, members of visible minorities, and disabled persons.

The Representation of Francophones

Barriers to equal opportunity for French-speaking people existed both in the government and in the Francophone community itself for much of this century. During the post-Confederation period before the 1918 *Civil Service Act,* Francophones were numerically well represented in the public service. They were not, however, as well represented as Anglophones at the senior levels. Also, many of the Francophone appointments rested on patronage, whereas the 1918 Act emphasized merit and efficiency. Especially after 1918, the public service was pervaded by an Anglophone linguistic and cultural bias. Merit and efficiency were linked to formal education and technical qualifications. French-language, or bilingual, competence was not considered a component of merit or likely to enhance efficiency. Furthermore, written examinations and interviews for recruitment and promotion reflected Anglophone values and the Anglophone educational system, to the disadvantage of Francophones. Finally, the view was widely held that the Quebec educational system was a significant barrier to Francophone representation, because it emphasized education for such occupations as law, medicine, and the priesthood instead of the technical, scientific, and commercial skills required for appointment to the public service.

All these factors combined to reduce the motivation of Francophones to seek or retain positions in the federal public service. The result was a decline in the proportion of Francophones from 21.58 percent in 1918 to 12.25 percent in 1946, and a decline at the deputy minister level during the same period from 14.28 percent to zero.[26]

During the early 1960s, the so-called Quiet Revolution in Quebec focused national attention on Francophone grievances about their inadequate participation in the public service. The Royal Commission on Government Organization (Glassco Commission) reported in 1963 that Francophones were poorly represented in the service. The commissioners noted that public confidence in the public service will depend on "how representative it is of the public it serves," and that to achieve representativeness, "a career at the centre of government should be as attractive and congenial to French-speaking as to English-speaking Canadians."[27]

Then, in 1966, Prime Minister Pearson promised that the "linguistic and cultural values of the English-speaking and French-speaking Canadians will be reflected through civil service recruitment and training."[28] The Royal Commission on Bilingualism and Biculturalism, which reported in 1967, gave enormous impetus to this objective. Prime Minister Trudeau, in his comments on the commission's report, stated that "the atmosphere of the public service should represent the linguistic and cultural duality of Canadian society, and ... Canadians whose mother tongue is French should be adequately represented in the public service—both in terms of numbers and in levels of responsibility."[29] Then, in keeping with the aim of the *Official Languages Act* passed in 1969,[30] the Treasury Board established the Official Languages Program, with three major objectives—providing services to, and communicating with, the public in both official languages; enabling public servants to work in the official language of their choice; and achieving the full participation in the service of members of both the Anglophone and Francophone communities.

In a concerted effort since the late 1960s to increase Francophone representation in the public service, the major strategies adopted by the government have included more active recruitment of Francophones, the designation of language requirements for public service positions, and the development of an extensive language training system. In 2003, the government launched the *Action Plan for Official Languages*, whose purpose was to supply additional financial assistance to language training services, the recruitment of bilingual personnel, the study of the administration of language training and testing, and innovative programs designed to support official languages. Then in 2008, the government announced the *Roadmap for Canada's Linguistic Duality 2008–2013: Acting for the Future*. This initiative involved a five-year commitment of funds "to enhance and expand action across the Government of Canada to increase the benefits of linguistic duality and extend them to all Canadians."[31]

These strategies have helped to reduce institutional barriers in the government to Francophone representation. As of 2014, Francophones represented 31.9 percent of employees in the core public administration, which comprises people working in government departments (but not Crown corporations and separate agencies). Also, as Table 16.2 shows, their presence in each of the occupational categories in the public service (other than the Operational group at 22.3 percent) either equals or exceeds their representation in the population of Canada (which is 23.2 percent); for example, Francophones constituted 33 percent of those in the management category and 39 percent in the administrative and foreign service category. At the most senior levels of the public service, Francophones are doing better as well. During the period 1987–97, Francophones represented 23 percent of the deputy minister appointments; in the ensuing period 1997–2003, they constituted 40 percent of the appointments.[32] If we look at the entire number of people working in all institutions that are subject to the *Official Languages Act*, including the core public administration of the federal government as well as Crown corporations, separated agencies, and so on, Francophones represent 26.5 percent of the total number, again higher than their representation in the general population.[33]

The Representation of Women

The historic under-representation of women in Canada's public services, especially at the middle and senior levels, resulted from obstacles to equal opportunity, both in the government and in society generally. By 1885, only 23 of 4,280 public servants were women and more than one-third of these were junior clerks in the Post Office Department. The proportion of women in the service rose gradually to 14 percent in 1928 and to 17.7 percent in 1937. It accelerated during the war years, reaching 35 percent in 1943, but declined after the war and remained at about 27 percent during the 1960s.

TABLE 16.2	Participation of Anglophones and Francophones in the Core Public Administration by Occupational Category		
	1984	**2004**	**2014**
Canada:			
Anglophones	72%	68%	68.1%
Francophones	28%	32%	31.9%
Total	227,942	165,679	183,201
Management:			
Anglophones	80%	71%	67%
Francophones	20%	29%	33%
Total	4,023	3,872	5,040
Scientific and professional:			
Anglophones	78%	74%	74.2%
Francophones	22%	26%	25.8%
Total	22,826	23,772	31,801
Administrative and foreign service:			
Anglophones	71%	63%	61%
Francophones	29%	37%	39%
Total	56,513	68,033	82,594
Technical:			
Anglophones	79%	76%	76.4%
Francophones	21%	24%	23.6%
Total	27,824	16,828	12,590
Administrative support:			
Anglophones	67%	67%	68.3%
Francophones	33%	33%	31.7%
Total	72,057	32,888	20,841
Operational:			
Anglophones	75%	76%	77.7%
Francophones	25%	24%	22.3%
Total	44,699	20,286	30,335

Sources: Adapted from Public Service Human Resources Management Agency of Canada, *Annual Report on Official Languages 2003–04* (Ottawa: Her Majesty the Queen in Right of Canada, 2004), 53; Treasury Board of Canada Secretariat, *Annual Report on Official Languages 2013–14* (Ottawa: Her Majesty the Queen in Right of Canada, 2014), 25.

Part Five / The Management of Organizational Resources

Canadian Women Contributing to the War Effort

Capt. Jack H. Smith / Canada. Dept. of National Defence / Library and Archives Canada / PA-162428.

By 1970, women constituted about 30 percent of the total labour force, so they were not badly under-represented in the public service compared to the private sector. However, they faced a "glass ceiling" and were poorly represented at senior levels of the service. In 1971, women held only 14.1 percent of officer positions, whereas women made up 29.3 percent of the service as a whole.[34] Therefore, the introduction of the merit system did not serve to eliminate the problems encountered by the female pioneers in the public service. In fact, as one scholar noted, "merit and women were seen as contradictory," ultimately leading to the establishment of a "modern federal civil service [that] was developed on a highly gendered basis."[35]

Before 1970, the government took little action to promote female representation in the public service. It was not until 1955 that the restriction against hiring married women for government employment was abolished. The Glassco Commission called upon the government in 1963 to show "creative leadership in providing equal opportunities for women."[36] In the 1967 *Public Service Employment Act,* sex was included with race, national origin, colour, and religion as a basis on which it was forbidden to discriminate. Then the Royal Commission on the Status of Women reported in 1970 that women do not enjoy equal opportunity to "enter and advance in Government Service, and that their skills and abilities are not being fully used there. Attitudes and practices seem to be at fault."[37] In effect, women not only confronted a glass ceiling in terms of reaching the upper echelons of the public service, but they also faced a "glass door" by virtue of being concentrated in certain "female" occupations and professions, which typically had lower pay scales. The commissioners made numerous recommendations to ensure equality of opportunity for women in the public service, and the government implemented several of them.

Barriers to equal opportunity for women have been similar in the public and private sectors of society. The under-utilization of women has generally been attributed to

Chapter 16 / Representative Bureaucracy and Employment Equity differences between men and women in formal education and work experience, and to low career expectations, high absenteeism, and high turnover among female employees. Studies on the role of women in the public service conclude that these factors are not sufficient to explain fully the lower salaries and subordinate positions received by women. Additional factors include attitudes that militate against women advancing and developing, corporate cultures that women find stultifying, and the difficulty of balancing work and family duties.

As with Francophones, the government has used a variety of strategies to remove barriers to female representation, including new administrative structures, active recruitment, and training. But other measures have been deemed to be equally important. The Consultation Group on Employment Equity for Women, which advises the Treasury Board and deputy ministers on the recruitment, retention, and advancement of women in the federal public service, noted that "simply increasing the representation of women in all occupations and levels … was not a sufficient goal. It was also necessary to put in place measures to build an environment, infrastructure and culture that encourage and support the employment of women."[38] Therefore, the government has been supportive of progressive HRM policies such as job-sharing, working from home, and a variety of leave options, including parental leave, care and nurturing leave, leave for family-related reasons, and self-funded leave. The impact of these activities leads one to be cautiously optimistic about the efficacy of employment equity. As Table 16.1 shows, women now represent more than half of all employees (54.3 percent) in the core federal public service, and they constitute 46.4 percent of those in the Executive occupational category—which is slightly below their workforce availability (47.8 percent). More significantly, it is double the percentage (23 percent) of women in the executive cadre in the 1996–97 fiscal year and up dramatically from 5.2 percent in 1983.[39] Women have also made impressive gains in other occupational categories (Administration and Foreign Service, and Scientific and Professional) that require higher levels of education.

Not all the signs, however, are positive. Women still represent the vast majority of employees in Administrative Support, the occupational category that encompasses most of the low-paying and low-skilled positions. Also, while 32.2 percent of all federal employees earn less than $60,000 per year, nearly 41 percent women earn a salary figure in this range. At the top end of the public sector salary scale, some 18.7 percent of all employees earn in excess of $95,000, but only 14.8 percent of women are earning salaries at that level.[40] Women also remain under-represented in occupational groups relating to computers and engineering—areas with high hiring potential in an increasingly technological world. Finally, until the appointment of Janice Charette to the position of Clerk of the Privy Council in October 2014, only one of the previous 21 clerks (Jocelyne Bourgon from 1994–99) had been female. As the head of the public service, with responsibility for providing leadership and direction, it is critical that more talented women are identified and appointed to this position.

The Representation of Aboriginal Peoples

The historic under-representation of Aboriginal peoples reflects the lack of effective Aboriginal participation in the Canadian labour force as a whole and results from a formidable array of institutional and attitudinal barriers to representation, both in the government and in the Aboriginal community. Aboriginal peoples have been isolated culturally and geographically from the mainstream of Canadian society. Inadequate educational facilities and opportunities have made it difficult for them to obtain the academic qualifications required for entry into the public service, especially at the senior levels. As a result of their small numbers in the public service and their concentration in the lower ranks, they have not been sufficiently aware of career opportunities in the more senior echelons. There was no visible cadre of Aboriginal public servants whose achievements they were motivated to emulate. Furthermore, the government's recruitment practices tended to emphasize formal academic qualifications rather than practical experience, and stressed competence in the French or English languages rather than in an Aboriginal language. Discriminatory attitudes toward Aboriginal peoples that are widespread in Canadian society have in the past been found also in the public service.[41] In addition, some Aboriginals choose not to work for the Canadian government because they do not recognize this government as their government.

These various governmental and societal factors have combined to discourage Aboriginal peoples from seeking positions in the service and to confine those who do enter primarily to lower-level positions. To overcome these obstacles, the federal government has adopted strategies similar to those used to increase the representation of Francophones and women; new administrative units, such as the creation of the Aboriginal Centre of Excellence in Winnipeg in 2007, have engaged in active recruitment and training of Aboriginal peoples, and these efforts appear to have had a positive effect.

As Table 16.1 reveals, Aboriginal peoples constitute 3.4 percent of the labour force, but as of 2015 they make up 5.1 percent of the public service, more than double their representation (2.4 percent) in 1997.[42] Moreover, Aboriginal representation in the important Executive category has increased significantly in the past two decades, from 1.7 percent in 1997 to 3.4 percent in 2015, although this remains one of three designated groups whose representation in the Executive group still does not exceed its workforce availability (5.2 percent) for executives.[43] This ongoing lack of representativeness needs to be rectified because, as the PSC noted, "the Executive (EX) cadre provides the leadership and role models that are important to effect the necessary changes in corporate culture in departments and agencies."[44]

There are other notable issues with regards to the representation of Aboriginal peoples in the federal government. First, more than 40 percent of the public servants in this employment equity group work in just three organizations: Indigenous and Northern Affairs Canada (formerly known as Aboriginal Affairs and Northern Development Canada), which has a 50 percent Aboriginal hiring policy in place given its unique mandate; Correctional Service Canada; and Employment and Social Development Canada (formerly Human Resources and Skills Development Canada).[45] Second, as with women, Aboriginals are over-represented in the low-paying Administrative Support category.

The Representation of Visible Minorities

Visible minorities make up an increasing percentage of the Canadian population, and thus of the labour force. By 2031, it is projected that the number of visible minorities will more than double the nearly 5.3 million that were identified in the 2006 Census, so that visible minorities will constitute anywhere from 29 to 32 percent of the Canadian population.[46] Given that the working age population in the coming decades will increasingly come from visible minorities and Aboriginal groups (whose population is growing by about 22 percent every five years as compared to the non-Aboriginal population, which is only growing at a rate of about 3.4 percent),[47] it is important that the federal government be able to recruit and retain individuals from these two designated groups, as well as to provide them with equal opportunities for career advancement. The government, however, may face some significant challenges in that regard. A recent survey of nearly 13,000 Canadian college and university students indicated that Aboriginals, persons with disabilities, women, and LGBT people were more likely to indicate a preference for work in the public sector than their majority group counterparts (i.e. non-Aboriginal, non-disabled, men, and heterosexuals), but visible minorities were more interested in a private sector career. This suggests that the motivation to join the public service among different groups in Canadian society is not equal.[48]

visible minority A person (other than an Aboriginal person) who is non-white in colour/race, regardless of place of birth.

Workplace Diversity in the Public Sector

Monkey Business Images/Shutterstock.com

Like the other designated groups, visible minorities have historically been significantly under-represented in the federal public service. In 1997, visible minorities constituted 9.4 percent of the Canadian population and 9 percent of the labour force, but only 4.7 percent of all federal government employees. A decade earlier, that figure was only 2.7 percent. In terms of the public sector leadership group, merely 2.6 percent of the Executive category comprised visible minorities in 1997. On a more positive note, slightly less than 14 percent of new employees in a visible minority group that year entered the Scientific and Professional category, which was twice the proportion of the federal public service as a whole.[49]

There was a steady increase in the representation of visible minorities over the next decade to the point where this group made up 8.8 percent of the federal public sector labour force by 2007 and 9.2 percent a year later, but the workforce availability of visible minorities was 12.4 percent. There were also improvements made with respect to the proportion of visible minorities occupying positions in the Executive category—6.2 percent in 2007 and 6.7 percent in 2008. Quite significantly, between 2000 and 2007, the number of visible minority executives almost trebled from 103 to 290.[50] However, these numbers remained smaller than what would be expected based on workforce availability for this category.

The federal government has made various efforts to address this slow rate of progress. In 1995, it announced that special measures would be taken to increase the presence of visible minorities in the national public service, including allowing members of visible minority groups to self-identify on employment application forms. Several years later, the government embraced benchmarking targets of "one in five" in various staffing areas (e.g., recruitment and entry into executive levels) by a certain time. In the fall of 2011, the federal government adopted a new Employment Equity Governance Model, which aims to ensure that employment equity resonates at the most senior levels of the public service and to help focus on assuming responsibility for issues, advancing solutions, and sharing best practices. There is now also a Champions and Chairs Committee for the Aboriginal, employees with disabilities, and visible minority designated groups.

The government achieved a major milestone in 2013: this was the first time that all four of the designated groups were represented in the public service at a level that exceeded their workforce availability. Some 12.6 percent of the federal public service comprised visible minorities (against a workforce availability of 12.4 percent) as of March 31, 2013;[51] Table 16.1 reveals a further increase to 13.8 percent in 2015. With 8.8 percent of the Executive group comprising visible minorities, this occupational group is slightly under its workforce availability numbers (9.5 percent). Therefore, the government clearly has to make further progress with respect to achieving representativeness among its senior executives. Moreover, the challenge for the government will be to sustain the representativeness of visible minorities in the public service moving forward, especially since they will constitute an increasingly large percentage of the Canadian labour force and they may continue not to perceive the federal public service to be the most attractive place of employment.

The Representation of Disabled Persons

As Table 16.1 shows, the representation of disabled persons in every occupational category and for the public sector as a whole (5.6 percent) equals or surpasses the percentage of disabled persons in the Canadian labour force (at 4.4 percent). The same table in an earlier edition of this text (for the year 1997) showed the exact opposite—that representation of disabled people in the federal public service and its occupational categories fell well short of their participation in the overall labour force of Canada. Significantly, the gains for persons with disabilities also hold true for the all-important Executive group. Individuals in this designated group constituted 5.3 percent of the most senior public servants, which is more than double their workforce availability of 2.3 percent.

Pay Equity

Since the 1980s, **pay equity**—or equal pay for work of equal value—has been an issue of considerable importance in the management of human resources in both the public and private sectors of the economy. It is one component of the broader concept of employment equity already discussed. Although employment equity supports movement into new occupational categories, pay equity accepts differences in representation in occupations and seeks to eliminate pay differences among these occupations.

Pay equity is a shorthand term for equal pay for work of equal value. This concept must be distinguished from that of equal pay for equal work, which requires that men and women be paid the same for doing the same job, or for a job that is very similar. The concept of equal pay for work of equal value permits comparisons of different jobs performed for the same employer. For example, if one job classification, such as public health nurse, is of equal value to another, such as public health inspector, employees in these two categories should receive the same base pay.

A primary purpose of pay equity programs is to ensure that women receive equal pay for doing work that has the same value as that done by men. Historically, women have been segregated into certain low-paying jobs (e.g., clerical, sales, and service jobs); these jobs have received lower rates of pay than those of equivalent value traditionally performed by men. Pay equity programs strive to devise a job evaluation method that removes sex bias from job classifications. If the requirements of a female-dominated job category, such as secretary, were found to be equivalent in terms of skill, effort, responsibility, and working conditions to those of a higher-paid job category in which males predominated, such as machinery repairs, a pay adjustment would be made for the female-dominated category.

One concern about pay equity programs is that "all evaluation techniques are fundamentally arbitrary and can at best only estimate the comparable value between one job

pay equity A system that permits comparisons to be made between different jobs performed for the same employer. A shorthand term for equal pay for work of equal value. To be distinguished from equal pay for equal work, which requires that men and women be paid the same for doing the same job.

and another." Another is that both the pay adjustments and the administration of pay equity programs are very costly.[52] It is also argued that higher wages mean higher prices for the affected jobs, which in turn may lead to less demand for these positions. Despite these and other concerns about pay equity, most governments in Canada are convinced that the benefits outweigh the disadvantages. Beginning with the province of Manitoba in 1986, six out of the ten Canadian provinces have enacted pay equity legislation for their employees based on a "proactive" system-wide approach that requires employers to implement pay equity regardless of whether a complaint has been made or whether there is solid evidence of wage discrimination.[53]

Therefore, in the federal government, and in most provincial governments (only Alberta has no pay equity law or framework, while Saskatchewan, Newfoundland, and British Columbia have policy frameworks for negotiating pay equity, but no specific pay equity legislation), the battle for pay equity legislation has been won albeit after a protracted fight dating back to the adoption of the International Labour Organization Convention 100, the Equal Remuneration Convention of 1951, which Canada ratified in 1972. Then, in 1977, the government implemented the *Canadian Human Rights Act*. According to Section 11(1) of this Act, which applies to federally regulated employers, "it is a discriminatory practice for an employer to establish or maintain differences in wages between male and female employees employed in the same establishment who are performing work of equal value."[54] However, the Canadian Human Rights Commission was only able to investigate and refer cases of wage discrimination to the Canadian Human Rights Tribunal after receiving a complaint from an employee, a group of employees, or their union. More than 400 such complaints were filed with the Commission between 1977 and 2001, most of which were dismissed.[55]

This approach to wage discrimination has been heavily criticized for being reactive (by having to respond to complaints) as well as a slow, cumbersome, costly, and largely ineffective process. It was not unusual for employees to wait an inordinate amount of time (often more than a decade) and endure a costly and divisive court battle before seeing a resolution to their pay equity complaints. A complaint of wage discrimination filed by the Public Service Alliance of Canada (PSAC) in 1984, for example, was only settled in 1999 after two Canadian Human Rights Tribunal decisions. In another case, it took 18 years and multiple legal proceedings to settle a pay equity complaint launched by Bell Canada employees. The longest wage discrimination case on record was a 1983 complaint against Canada Post, which was only referred to the Tribunal after remaining with the Commission for 8 years. The Tribunal only disposed of the complaint in 2005, ruling that the Crown corporation pay $150 million in back pay and interest to the female employees subject to the discrimination in question, at which time Canada Post applied to the Federal Court for judicial review. Both the Federal Court and the Federal Court of Appeal sided with Canada Post, but the decision was finally resolved in November 2011 when, after an appeal by the PSAC, the Supreme Court of Canada restored the 2005 Tribunal decision. Remarkably, it took another 18 months after that decision to reach an implementation agreement.

Given these issues, the government appointed the Pay Equity Task Force in 1999 to conduct a review of section 11 of the *Canadian Human Rights Act*. The Bilson Report, with 113 recommendations in a nearly 600-page document, was released in May 2004 and echoed some of the earlier criticisms that had been levelled against the existing system. Despite acknowledging that the legislation did have some success in placing pay equity on the agenda and assisting those who wanted to challenge wage discrimination, the Task Force concluded "that the regime in place under section 11 has provided an inadequate foundation for significant and systematic progress towards the goal of pay equity across the federal jurisdiction as a whole."[56] Its recommendation was to replace the complaint-based system with a proactive model underpinned by stand-alone pay equity legislation. Such an approach had the advantage of including timelines for the elimination of inequalities and promoting cooperation instead of confrontation, which was characteristic of the existing system; it also placed "positive obligations on employers to review their compensation practices, identify any gender-based inequities, and take steps to eliminate them."[57]

The government was initially dismissive of the Task Force report, with the Ministers of Justice and Labour suggesting that it "did not provide an adequate blueprint for implementation of pay equity in a broad range of federally-regulated workplaces."[58] However, the government eventually responded by introducing the *Public Sector Equitable Compensation Act* in February 2009 as part of the omnibus budget implementation legislation. As noted by the Treasury Board Secretariat, in addition to recognizing that the previous complaints-based system under the *Canadian Human Rights Act* was ineffective and did not serve employees well, the government chose to introduce the new legislation over concerns about the potential drain on taxpayers' money arising from future pay equity complaints. While in many respects this Act reflects the positive features of the laws in place at the provincial level, it is unique in that it holds the employer and the unions jointly responsible for ensuring that gender-based discrimination in compensation is eliminated. Bargaining units, therefore, will be accountable for achieving equitable compensation for their members by demonstrating that they were actively engaged in pursuing that objective in the collective bargaining process.[59]

Whether the new legislation is an improvement upon the previous system remains to be seen. As of July 2015, more than six years after the legislation received royal assent, the *Public Sector Equitable Compensation Act* had still not come into force; this will remain the case until the Governor-in-Council approves all of the various regulations pertaining to the legislation that are in the process of being developed by the TBS. While the government has insinuated that the legislation is not yet in force because of the complex nature of the regulatory process and the need for broad consultation when dealing with such a wide array of stakeholders, the final in-depth round of consultations occurred more than two years earlier (February and March of 2013). It is more than a little curious that the regulations pertaining to this Act have not yet been developed and approved.

From the perspective of the Canadian Labour Congress, the *Public Sector Equitable Compensation Act* is problematic in several respects:

- The new legislation only covers the federal public service and not federally-regulated industries like Canada Post, which were included in the previous legislation.
- In addition to assessing skill, effort, responsibility, and work conditions when determining the value of work, the new Act also introduces the notion that women's work in the public sector should be valued by prevailing market conditions in the private sector, which would presumably have a downward effect on their wages.
- Workers lose the right to challenge gender-based wage discrimination under human rights law and instead their complaints go before the Public Service Labour Relations and Employment Board, which, according to the PSAC, "further entrenched the notion that pay equity was a commodity to lose or win at the bargaining table, rather than a fundamental human right."[60]
- Unions are prohibited from providing any form of assistance to employees launching a complaint under this Act and can be fined $50,000 for doing so.
- While the Act confers joint responsibility on management and labour for identifying and addressing wage inequalities in the federal public sector, it does so without recognizing the power imbalance that exists with unions lacking access to critical pay equity information. The authors of the report concluded, "The new regime promises to be unworkable, contentious, lengthy, and costly. Again, the conclusion we reach, is that the government is not interested in ending the wage gap between men and women, but has other goals in mind."[61]

Points to Know

- The federal government has embraced the importance of having a representative bureaucracy, which is thought to be more responsive to the needs and interest of the public.

- Canada has embraced employment equity rather than a policy of affirmative action (which adopts quotas) and has chosen to focus on the representativeness of four key designated groups: women, Aboriginals, people with disabilities, and visible minorities.

- Francophones are not a designated group in the federal public service, but their historic under-representation has been overcome through the adoption of the principle of individual bilingualism.

- Employment equity programs do not constitute reverse discrimination and are protected by both provisions of the *Canadian Human Rights Act* and the equality rights section of the Charter. Moreover, employment equity objectives can be included as merit criteria in addition to the essential and asset qualifications for a position.

- Although the gains have been slow to materialize, as of 2013 the federal public service in Canada has been fully representative of the four designated groups. However, in the Executive group category, only persons with disabilities are fully represented relative to their workforce availability.

- Concerns remain about gender wage discrimination, which pay equity legislation has been introduced to address, and the fact that some of the designated group members remain "ghettoized" in certain low-paying job categories.

Review Questions

1. Why is it important that the federal government embrace the notion of having a representative bureaucracy?

2. The federal government chose to adopt employment equity rather than affirmative action in order to pursue the goal of a representative bureaucracy. Distinguish between the two concepts and explain how employment equity has evolved in the Canadian context.

3. How representative is the federal bureaucracy today? How has representativeness evolved over time? What specific measures undertaken by the government have helped to foster greater representativeness of the bureaucracy?

4. Does the pursuit of employment equity constitute reverse discrimination?

5. Is it still appropriate for the government to focus on the four designated employment equity groups or are there other groups in Canadian society that should be reflected in the composition of the federal public service?

6. Although governments have long supported the goal of equal pay for work of equal value, eliminating wage discrimination has proven to be extremely challenging. Identify some of the impediments to promoting pay equity and assess whether the *Public Sector Equitable Compensation Act* has addressed the limitations of the previous legislative approach to pay equity.

Notes

1. Brandy Kennedy, "Unraveling Representative Bureaucracy: A Systematic Analysis of the Literature," *Administration & Society* 46(4) (2014): 396.
2. Frederick Mosher, *Democracy and the Public Service* (New York: NY: Oxford University Press, 1968). Active and passive representation are the equivalent of what Hannah Pitkin, in *The Concept of Representation* (Berkeley and Los Angeles, CA: University of California Press, 1967), referred to as "substantive" and "descriptive" representation in her classic book on the subject matter.
3. For a discussion of some of the potential costs of representative bureaucracy, namely that increasing representation for one group may come at the cost of another group, and the limitations of these underlying propositions, see Kennedy, "Unraveling Representative Bureaucracy."
4. Eddy S. Ng and Greg J. Sears, "Toward Representative Bureaucracy: Predicting Public Service Attraction Among Underrepresented Groups in Canada," *Review of Public Personnel Administration* (2014), DOI: 10.1177/0734371X14544546, 2.
5. John Porter, "Higher Public Servants and the Bureaucratic Elite in Canada," *Canadian Journal of Economics and Political Science* 24 (November 1958): 483–501; Donald C. Rowat, "On John Porter's Bureaucratic Elite in Canada," *Canadian Journal of Economics and Political Science* 25 (May 1959): 204–207; and John Porter, "The Bureaucratic Elite: A Reply to Professor Rowat," *Canadian Journal of Economics and Political Science* 25 (May 1959): 207–209.
6. Rowat, "On John Porter's Bureaucratic Elite," 204.
7. Porter, "Higher Public Servants," 490–491.
8. Ibid., 490.
9. Rowat, "On John Porter's Bureaucratic Elite," 207.
10. Porter, "The Bureaucratic Elite," 208.
11. Ibid., 209.
12. Most of the research in this area examines the impact of gender representation in the legislature on policy outcomes. See, for example, Manon Tremblay and Réjean Pelletier, "More Feminists or More Women? Descriptive and Substantive Representation of Women in the 1997 Canadian Federal Election," *International Political Science Review* 21(4) (2000): 381–405. Geneviève Bouchard and Barbara Carroll, "Policy-Making and Administrative Discretion: The Case of Immigration in Canada," *Canadian Public Administration* 45(2) (Summer 2002): 239–257, argue that street-level bureaucrats have a great deal of discretion in making policy decisions and intimate—but do not empirically demonstrate—that enhanced representativeness amongst the ranks of employees at Citizenship and Immigration Canada will have positive impacts with respect to the use of discretion on immigrant communities. Richard Ogmundson, "Does It Matter If Women, Minorities and Gays Govern? New Data Concerning an Old Question," *Canadian Journal of Sociology/Cahiers Canadiens de Sociologie* 30(3) (Summer 2005): 315–324, makes an appeal for further research on the social composition of Canadian elites so as to develop a better understanding of how various social characteristics like gender, race, and sexual orientation impact on the decision-making process of those in positions of authority.

13. Luc Turgeon and Alain-G. Gagnon, "The Representation of Ethnic and Linguistic Groups in the Federal Civil Service of Belgium and Canada," *Canadian Public Administration* 56(4) (December 2013): 578–579.

14. Treasury Board of Canada Secretariat, "Affirmative Action in the Public Service," news release, June 27, 1983.

15. Ibid.

16. Ibid.

17. Royal Commission on Equality in Employment, *Report* (Ottawa: Minister of Supply and Services, 1984).

18. Public Service Commission of Canada, *History of Employment Equity in the Public Service and the Public Service Commission of Canada* (Ottawa: Public Service Commission of Canada, October 2011), 20. Ultimately, it was the use of quotas and preferential hiring that proved to be controversial.

19. Public Service Commission of Canada, *PSC Glossary* (Ottawa: Public Service Commission of Canada, February 2012), 10, accessed June 30, 2105, www.psc-cfp.gc.ca/abt-aps/gls/index-eng.htm#e.

20. Public Service Commission of Canada, *Merit—Achieving Representativeness* (Ottawa: Public Service Commission of Canada, March 2008), 2.

21. Public Service Commission of Canada, *History of Employment Equity*, 16–23.

22. Paul Tellier, Clerk of the Privy Council and Secretary to the Cabinet, *Public Service 2000: A Report on Progress* (Ottawa: Minister of Supply and Services, 1992), 59–60.

23. Public Service Commission of Canada, *Guidance Series – Integrating Employment Equity in the Appointment Process* (Ottawa: Public Service Commission of Canada, December 2005), accessed July 21, 2015, www.psc-cfp.gc.ca/plcy-pltq/guides/equity-equite/guid-orie-eng.htm.

24. A recent study by the PSC suggested that employment equity status does have an impact on perceptions of merit and fairness in the staffing practices of the federal government. See Public Service Commission of Canada, *Members of Employment Equity Groups: Perceptions of Merit and Fairness in Staffing Activities* (Ottawa: Her Majesty the Queen in Right of Canada (March 2014).

25. Public Service Commission of Canada, *History of Employment Equity*, 25.

26. V. Seymour Wilson and Willard A. Mullins, "Representative Bureaucracy: Linguistic/Ethnic Aspects in Canadian Public Policy," *Canadian Public Administration* 21(4) (Winter 1978): 520.

27. Royal Commission on Government Organization, *Report* (Ottawa: Queen's Printer, 1963), 1:27–29.

28. House of Commons, *Debates*, April 6, 1966, 3915.

29. Ibid., June 23, 1970, 8487.

30. A new *Official Languages Act* was proclaimed in September 1988. Among other things, the new act recognizes that the participation rates of Anglophones and Francophones may vary from one department to another, depending on such considerations as the department's mandate, clientele, and location.

31. Treasury Board of Canada Secretariat, *Evaluation of the Official Languages Centre of Excellence* (Ottawa: Her Majesty the Queen in Right of Canada, May 2013), accessed July 23, 2015, www.tbs-sct.gc.ca/report/orp/2013/olce-celo/olce-celopr-eng.asp.

32. Jacques Bourgault, *Profile of Deputy Ministers in the Government of Canada* (Ottawa: School of Public Service, 2004), Table 2.

33. Treasury Board of Canada Secretariat, *Annual Report on Official Languages 2013–14*, 26.

34. Calculations based on Public Service Commission, *Annual Report 1971* (Ottawa: Information Canada, 1972), 44–45.

35. Caroline Andrew, "Women and the Public Sector" in *The Handbook of Canadian Public Administration*, ed. Christopher Dunn (Toronto: Oxford University Press, 2002), 160.

36. Royal Commission on Government Organization, *Report*, 275.

37. Royal Commission on the Status of Women, *Report* (Ottawa: Information Canada, 1970), 138.

38. Treasury Board of Canada Secretariat, *The Public Sector Equitable Compensation Act and the Reform of Pay Equity* (Ottawa: Her Majesty the Queen in Right of Canada, November 2012), 8.

39. Treasury Board of Canada Secretariat, *Employment Equity in the Federal Public Service 1996–97* (Ottawa: Public Works and Government Services Canada, 1997), 35; Treasury Board of Canada Secretariat, *Demographic Snapshot of the Federal Public Service, 2014*, accessed July 11, 2016, http://www.tbs-sct.gc.ca/psm-fpfm/modernizing-modernisation/stats/demo14-eng.asp.

40. Authors' calculation using data from Treasury Board of Canada Secretariat, *Employment Equity in the Public Service of Canada 2014–2015* (Ottawa: Her Majesty the Queen in Right of Canada, 2016), 12–13.

41. See "Native People and Employment in the Public Service of Canada", A Report prepared by Impact Research for the Public Service Commission, October 1976, 40–44.

42. Treasury Board of Canada Secretariat, *Employment Equity in the Federal Public Service 1996–97*, 55.

43. Ibid., 57; Treasury Board of Canada Secretariat, *Employment Equity 2014–15*, 2. For a more critical look at employment equity efforts in relation to Aboriginals, see Pay Equity Task Force, *Pay Equity: A New Approach to a Fundamental Right - Pay Equity Task Force Final Report* (Ottawa: Her Majesty the Queen in Right of Canada, 2004), 41–42. This report also takes a more critical stance on the other designated groups under the employment equity program.

44. Public Service Commission of Canada, *History of Employment Equity*, 40.

45. Ibid., 43.

46. Statistics Canada, *Projections of the Diversity of the Canadian Population 2006 to 2031* (Ottawa: Minister of Industry, 2010), 23, accessed July 21, 2015, www.statcan.gc.ca/pub/91-551-x/91-551-x2010001-eng.pdf.

47. Statistics Canada data as report in Public Service Commission of Canada, *Guidance Series – Integrating Employment Equity in the Appointment Process* (Ottawa: Public Service Commission of Canada, December 2005), accessed July 21, 2015, www.psc-cfp.gc.ca/plcy-pltq/guides/equity-equite/guid-orie-eng.htm.

48. Ng and Sears, "Toward Representative Bureaucracy," 10. These results mirror a summer 2000 survey of student employees and a February 2001 survey of new indeterminate hires in the federal public service, which revealed that visible minority students were among those least attracted to public service jobs and, along with more highly educated employees and younger employees, new hires in the visible minority designated group were more likely to be planning to leave the public service within five years. See Public Service Commission of Canada, *The Road Ahead: Recruitment and Retention Challenges for the Public Service* (Ottawa: Public Service Commission of Canada, February 2002).

49. See Treasury Board of Canada Secretariat, *Employment Equity 1996–97*.

50. See Treasury Board of Canada Secretariat, *Employment Equity in the Public Service of Canada 2006–07 and 2007–08* (Ottawa: Her Majesty the Queen in Right of Canada, 2009), accessed July 24, 2015, www.tbs-sct.gc.ca/rp/0608ee01-eng.asp.

51. Treasury Board of Canada Secretariat, *Employment Equity in the Public Service of Canada 2012–13* (Ottawa: Her Majesty the Queen in Right of Canada, 2013), 12.

52. Patrick Luciani, *Economic Myths: Making Sense of Canadian Policy Issues* (Toronto: Pearson Education Canada Inc., 2004), 11–12.

53. For an overview of the various legislative responses to the pay equity issue, see Pay Equity Task Force, *Pay Equity*, ch. 2.

54. *Canadian Human Rights Act* (R.S.C., 1985, c. H-6). The federal government then adopted the Equal Wages Guidelines in 1978 (revised in 1982 and again in 1986) to provide guidance on the application of the pay equity provisions under this Act. Specifically, the Guidelines elaborate on the various factors used to determine the value of work—skill, effort, responsibility, and working conditions—for the purpose of comparison under section 11.

55. Pay Equity Task Force, *Pay Equity*, 98.

56. Ibid., 108.

57. Ibid., 111.

58. Cited in Treasury Board of Canada Secretariat, *The Public Sector Equitable Compensation Act*, 15.

59. Ibid., 16, 22.

60. Public Service Alliance of Canada, "Economic Leadership and the Prosperity of Canadian Women," A Submission to the House of Commons Standing Committee on the Status of Women, May 14, 2014, accessed July 27, 2015, www.psacunion.ca/economic-leadership-and-prosperity-canadian-women.

61. Theresa Healy and Sue Genge, *Pay Inequity: Canadian Labour Congress Analysis of the "Public Sector Equitable Compensation Act,"* Research Paper #47 (Ottawa: Canadian Labour Congress, February 27, 2009), 10.

The Budgetary Process

17

Learning Objectives

Reading this chapter allows you to do the following:

- Identify functions and processes of government budgeting
- Understand the types of budgets
- Analyze the quality of expenditure budget styles
- Create a workable budgetary process for government
- Demonstrate the game-like nature of budgeting

In government—as elsewhere—"money talks."[1] It talks because it makes possible large public projects like medicare and income-support plans for families. It also makes possible government agencies—departments, Crown corporations, and regulatory agencies—that are able to deliver goods and services, which in turn means that money also provides for public administration. Money, acting almost as a lure, encourages people to enter public life, to become politicians in order to propose new ideas for Canada. Money in government also speaks to baser instincts, the desire to win and to be rewarded, or in some instances to seek private gain at the expense of the public interest. Money does indeed talk, and because of this effect it is necessary for public officials to manage it. This requires generating the necessary public revenues (another name for money) through various forms of taxation and making plans for spending or allocating these monies. Budgeting is the tool used to carry out these two actions. Managing public resources also requires gaining formal approval of budgetary proposals from the people's representatives in the legislature. The approved programs then have to be administered, an activity that entails following procedures for distributing the money and ensuring that the money is used effectively and in accordance with the law.

This chapter concerns the budgeting of money. It considers the primary functions of budgets in government and the types of budgets. Also examined is the basic dynamic of an expenditure budget, the most prominent kind of budget. The specific process of expenditure budgeting at the national level in Canada also receives attention, and the chapter ends with an appreciation of an important fact: budgeting is a political act which sees officials, political and appointed, competing for control over public money.

The Budget

The managers of public money have three basic duties. Two of these duties deal directly with the preparation of the budget—the subject of this chapter. The other relates to the implementation of the budget, which is handled in the next chapter. The first two tasks are sustaining overall fiscal discipline and distributing the public money in a way that respects government priorities. Fiscal discipline refers to maintaining both short- and long-term control of the "totals" in the budget, which are the fiscal numbers detailing revenues, expenditures, deficit, and debt.[2]

In the past, the discipline or control in Canada and other developed countries translated into a commitment to budgets in which expenditures and revenues were roughly even and produced no serious deficit (deficits occur when expenditures exceed revenues). The absence of a deficit in turn controlled the overall debt, which was the sum of all deficits or monies owed to people and institutions that had lent money to government to make up the shortfall in revenues.

In the more recent past, there have been periods in Canada, such as the years between the mid-1970s and the 1990s, when discipline has been lax or pressures have pushed for substantial increases in expenditures. There also have been times when external events or crises, such as the Great Recession of 2008, have required sudden and unexpected spending to stimulate the economy and end the economic downturn. Governments in Canada and elsewhere have learned that deficits may be a normal part of the economic cycle. In the last two decades or so, though, it seems that those charged with fiscal discipline have lost sight of the need for flexibility and seek only budgets without deficits.[3] Government went so far as to pass legislation that requires balanced budgets except in times of recessions or emergency situations (see Box 17.1). But in the budget of 2016, a new Liberal government at the federal level went against the trend and projected a modest deficit of nearly $30 billion with the promise that efforts would be made to reduce and eventually eliminate the deficit.

BOX 17.1

A Political Imperative

In 2015, falling oil prices threatened a promised deficit-free budget for the 2015–16 fiscal year. The Conservative federal government panicked, delayed the budget, and searched for ways to keep the promise (but ultimately failed). Andrew Coyne, one of Canada's most respected political columnists, observed that the small size of the projected deficit would cause little fiscal harm. But this mattered not—absence of deficits, as Coyne wrote, had become "a political imperative, not an economic one."

Source: Andrew Coyne, "Rush to balance budget is a political imperative, not an economic one," *National Post*, January 19, 2015, http://news.nationalpost.com/full-comment/andrew-coyne-rush-to-balance-budget-is-a-political-imperative-not-an-economic-one.

Table 17.1 shows budgetary totals for the federal budget in Canada. The table displays the core totals—budgetary revenues, total expenses, budgetary balance (or deficit), and federal debt—over a period of time (which reveals an important element in fiscal discipline, namely planning). For the present budget year 2016–17, a deficit is projected at $29.4 billion dollars, to be followed by a series of declining deficits over the following budget years. These deficits add to the debt, which can be seen to grow along with the deficits, but at a declining rate.

The second task of budget preparation is spending public money to reflect the priorities of government. This is the task which results in the funding of government services and programs well-known to Canadians—health care, armed forces, support for seniors, social assistance and the like. All of the spending on these programs and others is incorporated under "program expenses," which can be seen in Table 17.1 Importantly, the first task, fiscal discipline, adopts an overall perspective on the budget, but this second task concentrates on only one element, the spending of money. The task suggests an almost pinpoint allocation of funds following the clearly defined priorities of the

TABLE 17.1   Budget Transactions

| | PROJECTION (BILLIONS OF DOLLARS) | | | | | | |
	2014–2015	2015–2016	2016–2017	2017–2018	2018–2019	2019–2020	2020–2021
Budgetary revenues	282.3	291.2	287.7	302.0	315.3	329.3	344.4
Program expenses	253.8	270.9	291.4	304.6	308.7	314.2	323.2
Public debt charges	26.6	25.7	25.7	26.4	29.4	32.8	35.5
Total expenses	280.4	296.6	317.1	331.0	338.0	347.0	358.6
Budgetary balance	1.9	−5.4	−29.4	−29.0	−22.8	−17.7	−14.3
Federal debt	612.3	619.3	648.7	677.7	700.5	718.2	732.5

Source: Reproduced with the permission of the Department of Finance, 2016 (http://www.budget.gc.ca/2016/docs/plan/budget2016-en.pdf)

governing political party. But in reality the allocation is mostly a reflection of traditional spending patterns, which may or may not be linked with the priorities of government. The actual priorities of a government typically represent only a small portion of expenditures. A more important quality of this second function of budgeting is the constant push for additional spending which emerges from all departments and agencies. This second task is an invitation to spenders in government to do what they are naturally disposed to do, which is to spend.

The two tasks tied to budget preparation can complement each other—but they can also be in conflict. Fiscal discipline can lead to funds available for priority spending, a complementary effect. But the aggressive pressure for additional funding can hinder efforts to produce deficit-free budgets. The trick is to produce a balance between the two to allow each to satisfy their respective goals. Those responsible for fiscal discipline need to realize that a zealous type of discipline can ruin expenditure planning and leave priorities unfunded; those responsible for allocating spending have to appreciate that expenditures can careen out of control and ruin the foundations of sound budgeting.

Revenue Budgets

There are two types of budgets, one of which is the revenue budget. At least once each year, the federal minister of finance and all provincial finance ministers prepare their revenue budgets that contain a request to their respective legislatures to impose new taxes or modify existing ones. The revenue budget will accomplish other purposes, such as providing overviews of the economy and announcing changes in expenditures; but the primary intent is to give a picture of the revenue structure and to announce changes in taxes and other means of raising revenue. Table 17.2 outlines the basic revenue structure of the federal government of Canada. It shows that the revenue structure consists of three revenue sources: income taxes, excise taxes or duties, and miscellaneous revenue sources such as premiums for the federal employment insurance program. It also shows that personal income taxes—levies on the salaries and other forms of employment payments to individual Canadians—are by far the most important source of income for the federal government (at $143.9 billion in 2016–17). The revenue budget seeks to ensure that this revenue yields the money necessary to fund expenditures and provide some semblance of control over the fiscal aggregates—and preferably do all this and produce a balanced budget. Any proposed changes in taxes and other revenue

WHAT TO DO?

Reducing taxes is easy, but increasing them is not. To see why, let's assume government needs to raise taxes. What might it do? It could increase taxes on personal incomes, but ordinary Canadians already pay a lot of taxes. Corporation taxes might be bumped up, but companies may leave the country. Perhaps reverse the 2% GST decrease. But this looks bad—give a tax break, then take it back? If you were a senior federal tax official, what tax measure would you recommend?

sources will be reflected in the revenue structure. For example, shortly after winning a minority government in 2006, the Harper government lowered the rate of the Goods and Services Tax (7% to 5%), a decision that decreased the yield of this particular tax and caused a decline in overall revenue ("yield" refers to how much money a tax can generate). More recent changes have had the effect of lowering the yield of the personal income tax (see What to Do?).

The fiscal year of the federal and provincial governments begins on April 1 and ends the following March 31, so the practice is to present the revenue budget shortly before the beginning of the fiscal year, usually in February or March. But there is no set rule for this timing; budgets are sometimes presented at other times of the year

TABLE 17.2	Revenue Outlook						
	PROJECTION (BILLIONS OF DOLLARS)						
	2014–2015	2015–2016	2016–2017	2017–2018	2018–2019	2019–2020	2020–2021
Income taxes							
Personal income tax	135.7	142.7	143.9	153.7	160.9	168.5	177.0
Corporate income tax	39.4	38.8	37.9	39.9	40.4	42.1	44.5
Non-resident income tax	6.2	6.3	6.3	6.3	6.6	6.9	7.2
Total income tax	181.4	187.8	188.0	199.9	208.0	217.5	228.7
Excise taxes/duties							
Goods and Services tax	31.3	33.1	33.5	35.2	36.7	38.3	40.0
Customs import duties	4.6	5.2	5.0	4.5	4.7	4.8	4.9
Other excise taxes/duties	11.3	11.5	11.1	11.2	11.2	11.2	11.2
Total excise taxes/duties	47.2	49.8	49.6	50.9	52.6	54.3	56.2
Total tax revenues	228.6	237.6	237.6	250.8	260.6	271.8	284.9
Employment Insurance premium revenues	22.6	23.0	22.4	21.0	21.8	22.7	23.5
Other revenues							
Crown corporations	13.5	13.1	10.4	11.6	12.7	13.5	13.6
Other programs	16.4	15.5	15.3	16.3	17.7	18.6	19.3
Net foreign exchange	1.4	2.1	1.9	2.2	2.5	2.8	3.1
Total other revenues	31.2	30.6	27.7	30.2	32.9	34.9	36.0
Total budgetary revenues	282.3	291.2	287.7	302.0	315.3	329.3	344.4

Source: Reproduced with the permission of the Department of Finance, 2016 (http://www.budget.gc.ca/2016/docs/plan/budget2016-en.pdf)

Part Five / The Management of Organizational Resources

and more than one budget can be presented in the same year. These deviations stem from either political considerations (for example, the desire to present an attractive budget on which to fight an election), or from volatile economic conditions such as changing international economic situations.

The revenue budget is presented as a part of the finance minister's budget speech (and accompanying budget plan). There is no set format for the speech, but it typically congratulates the government on its accomplishments and outlines a plan of action involving tax and spending initiatives. The 2016 federal budget, for instance, focused on painting a better picture for Canada's struggling middle class through enriched family tax credits, new spending on education, and investments in the infrastructure of the nation. The minister's budget speech is given much more attention than other speeches in the legislature, because it says so much about the government's financial situation and may include proposals that affect the daily lives of Canadians. The date and time of the speech are set several weeks in advance at an hour when stock markets are closed so that the contents of the speech will not affect stock prices precipitously. The media focus on the event, and portions or even all of the speech are broadcast live on radio and television, followed by analyses by learned commentators, representatives of interest groups, and the inevitable interviews with Canadians on the street. Several days of the legislature's time is set aside for debate on the budget speech and plan, but opposition parties often use this time to criticize the finance minister for past mistakes and anticipated future mistakes.

After the debate on the budget speech, there is a vote of confidence concerning the overall budget. If the government survives the initial vote of confidence, the minister of finance will then introduce, over the next few months, a series of motions implementing the specific taxation measures presented in the budget. Votes on these motions can be matters of confidence if the specific measure is central to the budget package, but they are not ordinarily considered matters of confidence. However, a defeat of a major tax measure poses a serious problem for a government, for an alternate source of revenue will have to be found.

Budget Making

Traditionally, it has been difficult to discuss the making of the revenue budget in great detail; it is very much the personal work of the minister of finance or provincial treasurer and her or his senior public servants. The secrecy of the revenue budget has been considered important because taxpayers with advance information about revenue provisions might profit unfairly or evade the intended effects of the provisions. The parliamentary tradition is that a minister of finance must resign if there is any leak of information about the budget. However, in the past decade the secrecy has abated somewhat. The process now typically includes a statement on the economic and fiscal outlook four or five months before the actual budget, which gives the context in which the budget will be prepared. Following this are a series of formal and informal consultations with stakeholders or groups interested in the contents of the budget. At this point, the government may even hint at its intentions, either because of a desire to gauge reaction to some proposals or to move the debate about revenue provisions in the desired direction. The final product is a budget with few surprises.

Unfortunately, new concerns about budget making have arisen to replace old ones. For one, it is felt that budget documents now provide less economic and fiscal information, with the result that it is difficult to assess the forecasts used for determining budget aggregates such as total budgetary revenues or allowable total expenses.[4] It was hoped that the Parliamentary Budget Office (PBO), an agency assigned to review the anticipated cost of government initiatives, would have the information necessary to

Chapter 17 / The Budgetary Process

review the tenability of federal budget forecasts and related issues, especially given that the office, when set up in 2006, was promised full access to budgetary information. But up to now the federal government has either refused requests from the PBO for the desired data or complied with requests only reluctantly (and usually with the provision of little information).[5]

Another arguably more serious new concern about budget making has been the use of omnibus budget bills. Normally, budget bills or legislation providing authority to items proposed in the budget are relatively short and offer not much more detail than available in the budget plan.[6] But omnibus bills covering the budget are much longer (one in 2014 reached almost 400 pages). They are longer because they supply a lot of detail on budget proposals and even address matters not foreshadowed or even addressed in the budget. The government's intention behind the omnibus procedure is to move more quickly—normal procedure might require separate pieces of legislation for various budget proposals—and also to effectively hide or protect controversial measures. The latter aim reflects the belief of the government that no elected member would have the courage to vote against a bill with many desirable measures for Canadians just because of one or two questionable items. The downside to the omnibus bill is that it limits legislative review of budgetary proposals and precludes the people's representatives in Parliament addressing major proposals, which should be assessed and not hidden. The new Trudeau government, elected in 2015, promised to stop the use of omnibus bills, which had become quite prevalent under the preceding government of Stephen Harper. But the proposed legislation to implement the first budget of the Trudeau government, with its nearly 200 pages, drew charges that it constituted an omnibus bill.[7]

© Gary Clement

Part Five / The Management of Organizational Resources

Expenditure Budgets

The preparation of the expenditure budget, the second type of budget, is a much more open process. It usually involves almost everybody within government and actively seeks the views of interested groups and the general public. The remainder of the chapter discusses some of the different styles of preparation of the expenditure budget, but suggests that a basic style underlies many of the purportedly different styles. The chapter also provides a step-by-step illustration of how a budget is prepared, and finishes with a discussion of some of the strategies and tactics employed by organizations to maximize their budgetary allocation.

Styles of the Expenditure Budget

Many different styles of budgeting have been in use and still are in use in various jurisdictions. There is no general agreement among governments about the ideal approach to the expenditure budget; each seems to adopt a slightly different style. Regardless of the approach employed, the ideal budgeting system should serve the two purposes outlined earlier: to provide for fiscal control or discipline, and to allocate resources in a way that recognizes the wishes or plans of the government and takes into account program effectiveness. Another way of expressing these purposes is to say the perfection in budgeting allows for the achievement of control, management, and planning and choice.[8]

Line-Item Budgeting

Line-item budgeting was the first style of budgeting employed in modern public administration and was used in Canada right up to the 1960s. Table 17.3 provides a hypothetical example of a line-item budget. It shows that it involves a line-by-line itemization of *inputs*, which represent the activities of the organization—there is no mention of the *outputs* or effects of the activities. The figure also shows that annual changes in the budget typically amount to across-the-board incremental increases in funds allocated to the respective activities. For the most part, this style of budgeting places much of the budget-making

line-item budgeting
A style of budgeting that emphasizes the object of expenditure (salaries, stationery) rather than the purpose of the expenditure.

TABLE 17.3	Expenditure Line-Item Budget of Hypothetical Government Department	
OBJECT OF EXPENDITURE	**2017 BUDGET ($000s)**	**2016 ACTUAL ($000s)**
Salaries—regular	112,000	110,000
Salaries—overtime	9,100	9,000
Casual labour	8,100	8,000
Employee benefits	11,300	11,000
Equipment	10,200	10,000
Uniforms	5,100	5,000
Building rent	22,000	22,000
Stationery	5,100	5,000
Cleaning supplies	2,100	2,000
Total	185,000	182,000

Chapter 17 / The Budgetary Process

authority in the hands of departmental officials, who are responsible for specifying the inputs and making requests for the marginal adjustments in expenditure allocations.

The line-item style of budgeting serves the goal of fiscal discipline and control, for it is quite easy to prevent overspending or to determine who is responsible if it should occur. But it hardly allows for the funding of government priorities and successfully resists any endeavour at assessing performance or effectiveness. The emphasis on inputs makes consideration of priorities and performance impossible, for the latter require a focus on programs and the results of organizational activities. It also makes it difficult to shift resources from one line of expenditure to another. All in all, merely giving costs of salaries, benefits, uniforms, and the like is not good enough for modern public administration.

Performance Budgeting

performance budgeting A style of budgeting that relates expenditure to specific activities to determine unit costs of providing services.

The next style of budgeting to emerge was performance budgeting. The basic difference between line-item and **performance budgeting** is the output orientation of performance budgeting. Line-item budgeting measure only inputs used; performance budgeting establishes a relationship between inputs employed and outputs attained. The basic building block of performance budgeting is the unit cost of providing a service (inputs) and the number of units of service provided (outputs). So, for example, Table 17.3 might be the budget for a local Service Canada office; it could be adjusted to include information on the cost of providing information and services to a set number of Canadians. With this adjustment, a budgetary allocation would be established by multiplying units of service (people served) by the unit cost of providing each service.

The unit-cost information creates an additional method of evaluating an organization and its employees besides looking for overspending. Managers performing similar duties could be evaluated by comparing the unit costs of their operations. In making budgetary allocations, it is possible to escape from small adjustments in a limited way. Reasonable estimates could usually be made about changes in the demand for the service, although, even here, managers frequently had to use past spending allocations as an aid in calculation. The strong point of performance budgeting is that it adds a management improvement focus to the control focus of line-item budgeting. It provides decision makers with enough information to consider management improvement and cost-minimization techniques. But when used for government budgets, performance budgeting provided neither techniques for planning nor enough information to make tradeoffs between programs.

Program Budgeting

program budgeting A style of budgeting that allocates funds by program and attempts to measure the impact of expenditures on the goals and objectives of programs.

In proceeding chronologically through the adoption of various budgetary styles, we can see a steady ascendancy in the basic building block from the object of expenditure, to the unit of service, to the entire program. Many further changes came with program budgeting that involved more than just the emphasis on programs. In general, **program budgeting** aims to adapt rational decision-making techniques to the budgetary process, in an attempt to find the ideal style of expenditure budgeting. Objectives are set, proposals for meeting these aims are outlined, costs and benefits of each proposed program are determined for a number of years, and the most appropriate choices are finally made.[9] Program budgeting also brings with it a large set of economic tools such as cost–benefit analysis, cost–effectiveness analysis, and systems analysis. These tools can maximize government performance by providing a rational economic comparison of different methods of attaining goals and even comparing the worth of trying to attain different goals.

The strength of program budgeting is that it includes, in theory, all the requirements of an ideal budgeting system. The projection of program costs or spending allows for control of the budget and thus there will be no sudden and surprising increases in spending; the primacy of objectives highlights the importance of priorities; the availability of

Part Five / The Management of Organizational Resources

choices helps to ensure that only the best programs for meeting the priorities will be selected; and the emphasis on yearly evaluations appear to guarantee continuous quality in programming. It was indeed ideal, but impossible to do.

The impossibility stems in part from the cognitive challenges. Take, for example, the challenge of measuring quantitatively the benefits derived from government action. Everyone agrees that it is beneficial for the garbage to be picked up or for property to be saved from fire, but how is this value determined objectively in dollars and cents so that costs and benefits can be compared? Some of the core benefits can be measured, but what about the esthetic, practical, and other benefits? Or take the planning demands of program budgeting. For some managers, the very notion of planning is a contradiction: is it really possible to know the future costs of any program in light of the unknown things that inevitably happen as we move through time?

Probably the most serious failing of program budgeting is its inability to appreciate sufficiently the political nature of the budgeting process. Program budgeting foresees the possibility of major adjustments to the list of government expenditures, yet interested parties that are negatively affected by these proposed changes will oppose them. This third style of expenditure budgeting assumes that budgeting is a rational or technical process in which all participants can agree on the best course of action. The reality is otherwise. Budget allocations represent substantial benefits to various societal groups, and these groups will fight to maintain and enhance these benefits. A program might be shown to be inefficient or unfair, but this may matter little to parts of the electorate who benefit from it and to the public servants who administer the program.

Incremental Budgeting

The failures of program budgeting point to an expenditure style that might be seen as ideal in the sense that it is the best we can do.[10] This style borrows from some of the styles mentioned above but acknowledges the cognitive and political limitations facing any budgeting system. It is also a style that most governments have been using, even if not explicitly acknowledged. The style, called **incremental budgeting**, is supported by five concepts: base, increment, fair share and priorities, equal sacrifice, and shift points.

incremental budgeting A style of budgeting characterized by small annual adjustments in spending accompanied by occasional large increases or decreases in expenditures.

- *Base and Increment:* The incremental style starts with the notions of base budgets and increments. The base budgets take on the guise of "A," "B," and "X" budgets. The A budget is the base of programs and their expenditures, which shall receive little or no attention during any one budget year aside from small increments to account for inflation and increases in workload. The B budget consists of a relatively small number of expenditures dedicated toward government priorities, which may include new initiatives or substantial adjustments in existing services. Lastly, the X budget is made up of expenditure reductions in existing programs, the money from which will be used to finance the B budget. This structuring of the budget allows for fiscal discipline in that little or no additional spending is planned. It provides a small increment of money either distributed evenly to all departments or intended for the funding of priorities; but it avoids the Herculean attempt to deal with the entire budget. Action is focused on either all agencies or only a handful of programs, minimizing the demands on the cognitive and political abilities of budget makers.
- *Fair Share and Priorities:* Fair share comes into play when deciding how to allocate any surplus funds, those found mostly in the B budget. To respond again to cognitive and political limitations, the practice is to share the surplus among most of the departments. With this practice, there is little need to calculate costs and benefits to determine the most deserving departments; there would also be little fear that politics would emerge because all would receive a portion of the surplus. In recent years, priority funding, the practice of targeting money to select departments, has at times

replaced the fair share philosophy. However, the fact that the priorities are "sharply limited" and strongly supported by the prime minister allows the new practice to fit into the budgetary process.[11] Interestingly, in Canada the notion of fairness has re-emerged most recently through the need for spending reductions. These reductions have been achieved through across-the-board cuts, which amount to "equal sacrifice" on the part of departments.

- *Shift Points:* The incremental style allows for the abandonment of incrementalism in favour of major adjustments or shift points in the budget, whether large increases or decreases in funding allocations. Typically, it is an external event—for example, the global economic crisis of 2008—that causes this moving away from incremental budgeting. The advent of actors in the budgetary process who are more attuned to articulating priorities also plays a role here, for they are able to do the translating of the external shock into action. Not surprisingly, the shift points create the political problems borne of non-incremental budgeting; however, experience shows that emphasizing the temporary nature of the shift point helps to limit the dissatisfaction. In cases of shift points requiring expenditure reductions (the more common type of shift point in the most recent years), the attempt to spread the cutbacks evenly can also help to diminish opposition to less spending (see Box 17.2).

BOX 17.2

Incremental Style

As the figure below shows, the incremental budgeting style can be visualized as a line or curve representing real percentage increases in government expenditures (Y axis) over years or time (X axis). The curve has a gentle upward movement, with the small up and down bumps representing the success of incremental budgeting in limiting expenditures to small increases or decreases. The overall upward movement reflects the fact that the marginal adjustments are typically increases in spending. The curve also has three points—shift points—that indicate large expenditure increases in the one year and substantial reductions in the other two.

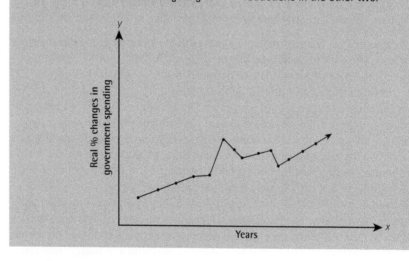

Government Expenditure Budgeting System

The government expenditure system of the federal government involves the expenditures themselves and the process of making and carrying out the expenditure budget. Table 17.4 provides details on program expenditures of the federal government, which

TABLE 17.4	Program Expenses Outlook						
	PROJECTION (BILLIONS OF DOLLARS)						
	2014–2015	2015–2016	2016–2017	2017–2018	2018–2019	2019–2020	2020–2021
Major transfers to persons							
Elderly Benefits	44.1	45.6	48.4	51.1	53.9	56.9	60.1
Employment Insurance Benefits	18.1	19.4	21.1	21.6	21.3	21.5	22.1
Children's Benefits	14.3	18.1	21.9	22.8	22.4	22.1	21.8
Total	76.5	83.1	91.4	95.5	97.7	100.5	104.0
Major transfers to other levels of government							
Canada Health Transfer	32.1	34.0	36.1	37.1	38.5	40.2	41.9
Canada Social Transfer	12.6	13.0	13.3	13.7	14.2	14.6	15.0
Equalization	16.7	17.3	17.9	18.3	19.0	19.9	20.7
Territorial Formula Financing	3.5	3.6	3.6	3.7	3.8	3.8	3.9
Gas Tax Fund	2.0	2.0	2.1	2.1	2.2	2.2	2.2
Other Fiscal Arrangements	−3.7	−4.0	−4.4	−4.7	−5.0	−5.3	−5.6
Total	63.1	65.8	68.6	70.3	72.7	75.4	78.1
Direct Program Expenses							
Transfer Payments	35.1	34.1	41.7	45.3	44.0	44.3	46.0
Capital Amortization	4.8	5.2	5.8	6.1	6.2	6.3	6.5
Operating Expenses	74.4	82.8	83.9	87.4	88.1	87.8	88.7
Total	114.3	122.0	131.3	138.8	138.3	138.3	141.1
Total Program Expenses	253.8	270.9	291.4	304.6	308.7	314.2	323.2

Source: Reproduced with the permission of the Department of Finance, 2016 (http://www.budget.gc.ca/2016/docs/plan/budget2016-en.pdf)

are divided into transfers to persons, major transfers to provinces and territories, and direct program expenses. The first category includes such initiatives as the Old Age Security program for seniors and the Canada Child Benefit for moderate and low-income families with children under 18. The second category represents efforts to assist the provinces and territories in financing health care, post-secondary education, social programs, and other necessary activities. The third category covers operating costs and services of government departments, Crown corporations, and other agencies at the federal level. For a full picture of expenditures, it is necessary to add additional expenses for paying interest on the public debt to Canadians and others who have lent money to the federal government. In 2016–17, interest expenses equalled $25.7 billion dollars. This would mean that total expenditures for 2016–17 would be the program expenses of $291.4 billion plus the public debt expense of $25.7 billion, which would equal $317.1 billion in overall expenditures.

Expenditure Management System (EMS) The federal government's expenditure budget process, which is designed to provide more information to Parliament and other decision makers. Its centre point is each department's business plan, an approach that ensures that the department is focusing on its main area of responsibility.

The process for preparing and adopting the expenditure budget at the federal level is outlined in the **Expenditure Management System (EMS)**.[12] The EMS, introduced in 1995 and amended in 2007,[13] reflects many of the features inherent in incremental budgeting and the other styles of expenditure budgeting discussed earlier. For example, it provides for fiscal discipline and planning and certainly anticipates shift points; indeed, it might be argued that it encourages such points in order to combat the incrementalism found in expenditure budgeting. As well, implicit in EMS are the three types of budgets, A, B, X, and the increments used in times of fiscal abundance and scarcity. Figure 17.1 outlines the cyclical process of EMS; the basic elements of the process are as follows:

- The process begins a little less than one year before the presentation of the budget, with cabinet and its committees meeting in the spring to consider plans and priorities that can be used to shape the allocation of revenues in the forthcoming budget. Around this same time, departments lay out business plans for present operations and develop outlooks on their future operations and priorities within their area. The outlooks effectively involve development of A, B, and X budgets within the individual departments and other agencies.
- In the summer period, the Department of Finance, with other central agencies, meets with departments to bring together the planning done in the first stage in order to come up with proposals and resulting documents or papers that can be employed

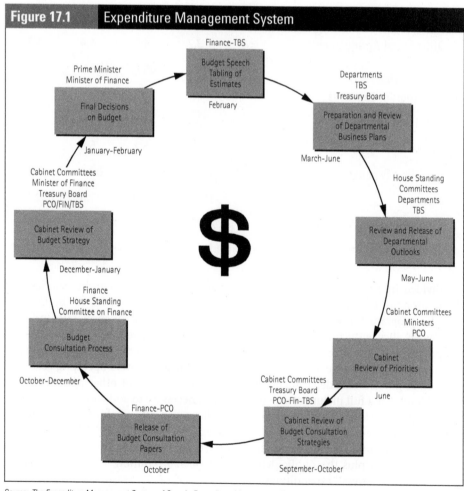

Figure 17.1   Expenditure Management System

Source: *The Expenditure Management System of Canada*, Expenditure Management Sector, Treasury Board of Canada Secretariat, 2015.

Part Five / The Management of Organizational Resources

in the forthcoming public consultation process. The proposals may involve new spending, reallocations, or reductions, depending on the fiscal and economic outlook and the consequent revenue and expenditure targets presented by Finance at this time.

- In the fall and early winter, the minister of finance releases the consultation papers and begins meeting with parliamentary committees, provinces, groups, and the interested public. Within the government, central agencies and departments continue their work on fine-tuning proposals, while cabinet committees propose expenditure priorities to cabinet. This part of the cycle ends with the minister of finance developing a budgetary strategy that takes into account recommendations and decisions flowing from the various actors and processes involved in the budgetary cycle up to this point (e.g., public consultation, central agencies and departments, cabinet committees).

- In the few months preceding the budget, cabinet examines the budgetary strategy, and the prime minister and the finance minister make the final decisions on the contents of the budget. In February, the finance minister concludes the budgetary cycle by the presentation of the budget in the House of Commons. At this time, the Treasury Board Secretariat tables documents called the Estimates, which lay out the allocation of resources to departments for the forthcoming fiscal year and constitute a request of the House of Commons for authority to expend these resources. The Estimates are referred automatically to various parliamentary committees for review, and by the end of May the committees report back on their consideration of the Estimates (more on this in the following chapter).

Budget Gaming

The expenditure budgetary process is a series of processes and institutions working to produce a budget. But it is also a game in the sense of real people interacting and competing with each other to realize their interests. Historically, the game has consisted of two players: spenders and guardians.[14] The spenders, located in departments and agencies, search for more and more budgetary expenditures; at the extreme, they acquire an almost insatiable appetite for new monies. The guardians are the Finance Department and Treasury Board Secretariat, committed to fiscal discipline, balanced budgets, efficient use of monies, and anything else that blocks unreasonable spending. The game is conflictual, and each side employs tactics to achieve its end. Spenders inflate their budget requests to defend themselves against possible cutbacks, they mobilize interest groups to press for more spending, they manufacture crises to stampede guardians into acquiescing to their demands, they propose programs with small demands initially but with the potential to grow large—the "thin edge of the wedge" strategy—and they attempt to end run guardians to get to the top, where the prime minister resides.

Guardians, too, have their manoeuvres. One adage in war is "know thy enemy," so guardians recruit former spenders from departments. They can also tie up spenders with procedural rules or requests for studies supporting the proposed new spending. Most unsettlingly, allegedly fiscal frameworks are constructed to eliminate any available increments for new spending or, worse, demonstrate the need for reductions. The belief that the Department of Finance in the past continually underestimated available revenues at budget time gave life to the possibility of this particular tactic.

Clearly, the spenders and guardians generate conflict but the reduction of the game to two parties simplifies the complexity of budgeting and ensures the performance of two primary functions of budgeting, fiscal discipline and expenditure allocation. Moreover, both sides understand that an element of cooperation permeates the budgeting game; each knows that unrestrained pursuit of self-interest may preclude agreement on a budget, an outcome neither side wants. The budget, with its fiscal framework, workable

Chapter 17 / The Budgetary Process

levels of aggregates, and list of expenditures, is the product of the two players engaging where both aggression and restraint play a role. Sometimes one side wins the game, the odd time the game ends in disarray, and most times neither side gets all it wishes, but neither side is left with nothing (see Box 17.3).

BOX 17.3

Play the Game

The spender–guardian game can be likened to the prisoners' dilemma situation (see below). In this game, the two players each have two choices, cooperate or compete. The first number in each cell represents the spender score and the second number the guardian score. If they both cooperate, the two each get 3 points, a pretty high score for the two players—but the not the highest *individual* score. But if they both are tempted to get the highest score of 5, they end up getting only 1. Or if one wants to cooperate and thinks wrongly that the other player has a similar intent, he or she gets nothing. So what to choose? Select a partner and on the count of three simultaneously select cooperate or compete and see who wins.

		Guardian	
		Cooperate	Compete
Spender	Cooperate	3, 3	0, 5
	Compete	5, 0	1, 1

Recently, a new player, the priority setter, has entered the budgeting game.[15] Historically, the budgeting game took place against a background of revenues available for the fair sharing of expenditures: everyone got a piece of the expenditure pie. But in the last few decades revenues have become less available, necessitating the positing of carefully-sculpted priorities to guide spending directed at only the few or supplying direction to where savings are to be found. And this task has fallen to the priority setters, located in the Privy Council Office (PCO) and the Prime Minister's Office (PMO). This, in turn, has led to more active participation of the person who is served by these two agencies, namely the prime minister. With guardians and spenders only, the game looked mostly to the minister of finance to set any necessary priorities. Now, with the advent of the priority setters, the prime minister along with the PCO and PMO largely set the priorities for the federal budget.

A New Process?

The emergence of the priority setters, which includes the prime minister, is more than simply adding another player to the budgeting game. It also means that the expenditure budgeting process may be changing in a fundamental way. Figure 17.1 shows that the formal budgetary cycle of the Expenditure Management System includes a wide range of people engaged in various duties and strategies for the purpose of preparing a budget.

But as indicated in earlier chapters, scholars claim that decision making in the federal government, which includes decisions on the budget, is "centralized in the hands of the prime minister and a small group of carefully selected courtiers."[16] When it comes to the budget, courtiers include the senior guardians (most especially the minister of finance) and priority setters, with a few spenders added along with advisors outside of government. The effect is to include the roles of guardian, spender, and priority setter in one group, a centralization of influence over the budget that is almost breathtaking in its ambition and audacity. The sheer force of prime-ministerial power overwhelms all else in the budgetary process, placing power over money with a single person. Yet, there are signs of exaggeration when contemplating the new process. Publications of the federal government refer to the Expenditure Management System when discussing financial management, which suggests that cabinet, cabinet committees, and departments still play a role in the budgetary process. Moreover, it would be challenging for the prime minister and a handful of senior ministers and officials to run the budget system. Budgeting appears too complicated and expansive to be in the hands of only a few.[17] Still, the significance of the budgetary process in the world of public administration requires that we be alert to possible changes in the handling of public money.

Points to Know

- The preparation of budgets has two sometimes conflicting duties—to establish fiscal discipline and to generate expenditures based on government priorities.

- Budgets include both revenue and expenditure budgets. Revenue budgets outline the revenue structure and any changes in taxes and other means of raising revenue; the expenditure budget allocates monies to the varied programs and services of government.

- There are various styles of budgeting, each of which seeks to carry out the two duties of any budgetary process. The most workable style is the incremental system of budgeting, which is based on five concepts: base, increment, fair share, priority, and shift points.

- The expenditure budgetary process of the federal government is the Expenditure Management System, which has many qualities of the incremental style of budgeting.

- The process of making budgets can be seen as a strategic game between spenders and guardians. The one participant wishes to spend; the other seeks to protect revenues. A new player, the priority setter, may cause the budgetary process to change entirely.

Review Questions

1. Why is the budgetary process seen as both a fiscal and a political activity?

2. What are the two types of budgets, and how do they relate to each other?

3. What are the concepts that support the incremental style of expenditure budgeting?

4. How can budgeting be seen as a kind of game, and how is this budgeting game changing?

5. Why are budgeting and budgets central to public administration?

Notes

1. David A. Good, *The Politics of Public Money*, 2nd ed. (Toronto: University of Toronto Press, 2014), 3.
2. Allen Schick, "The Changing Role of the Central Budget Office," *OECD Journal on Budgeting* 1 (2001/02): 1.
3. Andrew Coyne, "Rush to Balance Budget Is a Political Imperative, not an Economic One," *National Post*, January 19 (or January 20), 2015, accessed July 18, 2016, http://news.nationalpost.com/2015/01/19/andrew-coyne-rush-to-balance-budget-is-a-political-imperative-not-an-economic-one/.
4. Scott Clark and Peter Devries, "Restoring Integrity to the Budget Process," *Inside Policy*, February–March, 2013.
5. Kevin Page, *Unaccountable: Truth and Lies on Parliament Hill* (Toronto: Viking, 2015).
6. C.E.S. Franks, "Omnibus Bills Subvert Our Legislative Process," *Globe and Mail*, July 14, 2010, accessed January 1, 2015, www.theglobeandmail.com/globe-debate/omnibus-bills-subvert-our-legislative-pro.
7. CBC, "New Liberal Budget Bill Raises Old Concerns about Omnibus Legislation," April 24, 2016, accessed June 8, 2016, http://www.cbc.ca/news/politics/budget-omnibus-wherry-1.3550676.
8. David Gow, *The Process of Budgetary Reform in the Government of Canada* (Ottawa: Information Canada), 1.

9. C.M. Drury, *Planning-Programming Budgeting Guide* (Ottawa: Queen's Printer, 1969), 8.
10. David A. Good, "Still Budgeting by Muddling Through: Why Disjointed Incrementalism Lasts," *Policy and Society* 30:1 (February 2011).
11. Ibid., 47.
12. Treasury Board of Canada Secretariat, *The Expenditure Management System of Canada* (Ottawa: Minister of Supply and Services, 1995).
13. Department of Finance Canada, *Advantage Canada: Building a Strong Economy for Canadians* (Ottawa: Her Majesty the Queen of Right in Canada, 2007), 34–35.
14. Good, *The Politics of Public Money*, 21.
15. Ibid., 30.
16. Donald J. Savoie, "The Federal Government: Revisiting Court Government in Canada," in *Executive Styles in Canada: Cabinet Structures and Leadership Practices in Canadian Government*, eds. Luc Bernier, Keith Brownsey, and Michael Howlett (Toronto: University of Toronto Press, 2005), 17. Savoie sticks to his position in more recent publications. See Donald J. Savoie, *Whatever Happened to the Music Teacher? How Government Decides and Why* (Montreal and Kingston: McGill-Queen's University, 2013).
17. G. Bruce Doern, Allan M. Maslove, and Michael J. Prince. *Canadian Public Budgeting in the Age of Crises: Shifting Budgetary Domains and Temporal Budgeting* (Montreal and Kingston: McGill-Queen's University Press, 2014), 96.

Management of Financial Resources

18

Learning Objectives

Reading this chapter allows you to do the following:

- Identify and understand the process of financial management
- Outline the duties of the players involved in managing public monies
- Analyze the actions taken to achieve efficiency in using expenditures
- Recommend reforms that address the shortcoming of financial management in government
- Understand the place and status of managing public monies in the budgetary process

The budgeting of money in government attempts to achieve three aims or tasks. One is to establish control over the basic aggregates of any budget—the revenues, the expenditures, and the resulting fiscal balance—and a second aim is to allocate budgetary resources to government programs and priorities. These two aims have been examined in the preceding chapter. A third aim, the concern of this chapter, is to secure the efficient delivery or management of government services arising from the application of revenues. This last aim of budgeting involves transforming contents of the budget into law; no spending of public monies can be done without the approval of elected representatives sitting in the legislature. A corollary of this action is ensuring that the law is observed and that public funds are spent in accordance with the will of the legislature. Another activity entails attempts to achieve high levels of performance out of budgeted programs.

This third aim is important, but it fails to receive the kind of public notice accorded to the first two, a reality that leaves this aim often unmet. The separation of the treatment of budgets into two chapters in this text is a reflection of an inability to squeeze a discussion of all three budgetary aims into one chapter. But it also serves to symbolize the relative importance of the budgetary aims and tasks. The first two duties get a lot of attention; the last one does not.

This chapter constitutes the second of two chapters on government budgeting. The presence of two chapters on budgeting confirms the significance of money in government. With this chapter, the management of budgetary resources is considered, by looking at a process that involves the institutions or players trying to satisfy the requirements of managing the finances of government. These players include Parliament as a whole, a senior central agency, government departments, auditors of one type or another, and committees of the House of Commons—with one being especially important.

The players engage each other to achieve the third aim of any government budget: the successful adoption and management of public money.

The Process

There are many approaches to examining the management of money in government. One such approach it is to see it as a yearly process. Figure 18.1 describes the process, showing the players from the executive and legislative branches interacting to achieve the best use of government finances. With its position in the centre, the Treasury Board and its Secretariat perform a central role in managing money. However, the symbolic leader of the process is Parliament, for it is the body that gives life to the process by making budgetary proposals the law of the land. From this point, the budget process moves to government agencies, where auditing officials with the help of the Treasury Board Secretariat act to ensure the appropriate expenditures of funds. The Department of Public Works and Procurement (formerly the Department of Public Works and Government Services) receives special attention among the departments for serving as the central accounting agency of the Canadian government. The process then moves out of the executive and into the legislative branch, where the Office of the Auditor General provides assessments of the programs and services that arise from the spending of public monies. These assessments are given to House of Commons' Public Accounts Committee, which holds hearings on the auditor general's evaluations and makes a report to the House of Commons on the general management of government finances.

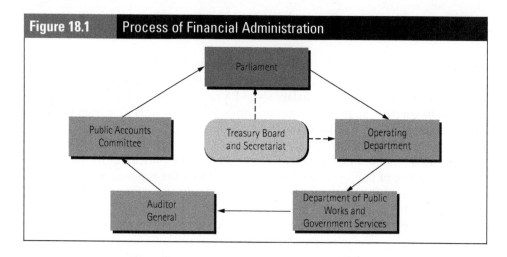

Figure 18.1   Process of Financial Administration

Treasury Board Secretariat

Estimates Documents that lay out the allocation of proposed expenditures to departments for the forthcoming fiscal year and constitute a request of the House of Commons for authority to expend these resources.

The process of financial management begins with Treasury Board and its Secretariat preparing and eventually tabling the **Estimates** in the House of Commons. The Estimates list the budget allocations requested by each government agency for the upcoming fiscal year, including those connected to initiatives and proposals outlined in the budget. The expenditures are organized by program and their intended strategic outcome. Table 18.1 provides expenditure estimates for Environment Canada, which is responsible for a variety of issues relating to the environment. The table shows that one strategic outcome is ensuring that "Canada's natural environment is conserved and restored for present and future generations"; it also shows that a series of programs—biodiversity, water resources, sustainable ecosystems—are directed towards meeting this outcome and that designated expenditures are attached to each of these programs.[1] The table also reveals that Environment Canada is accepting a decline in total expenditures over

Part Five / The Management of Organizational Resources

TABLE 18.1 Expenditure Estimates of Environment Canada

Expenditures by Strategic Outcome and Program

	2014–2015 expenditures	2015–2016 Main Estimates (dollars)	2016–2017 Main Estimates
Budgetary			
Canada's natural environment is conserved and restored for present and future generations.			
Biodiversity – Wildlife and Habitat	140,408,483	122,779,285	137,912,691
Sustainable Ecosystems	72,619,888	91,480,613	88,026,739
Water Resources	92,453,058	95,770,859	80,035,023
Compliance Promotion and Enforcement – Wildlife	17,058,497	16,115,510	16,652,429
Threats to Canadians and their environment from pollution are minimized.			
Climate Change and Clean Air	121,061,134	122,872,074	97,030,449
Substances and Waste Management	86,779,805	85,149,099	74,912,985
Compliance Promotion and Enforcement – Pollution	42,309,866	37,560,222	34,672,528
Canadians are equipped to make informed decisions on changing weather, water and climate conditions.			
Weather and Environmental Services for Canadians	174,493,294	192,103,008	174,382,678
Weather and Environmental Services for Targeted Users	25,886,657	15,792,293	19,267,384
The following program supports all strategic outcomes within this organization.			
Internal Services	203,115,955	181,428,113	179,196,292
Total	976,186,637	961,051,076	902,089,198

Note: Additional details by organization are available on the Treasury Board Secretariat website—http://www.canada.ca/en/treasury-board-secretariat.html.

Source: *Estimates 2015–16*, II-13. Estimates for Environment Canada www.tbs-sct.gc.ca/hgw-cgf/finances/pgs-pdg/gepme-pdgbpd/20162017/me-bpd-eng.pdf. Expenditure Management Sector, Treasury Board of Canada Secretariat, 2015

the previous fiscal year, a somewhat surprising action given the tendency of departments to ask for additional expenditures. The Estimates are accompanied by detailed reports on expected results of expenditures and follow-up reports on whether these results have been achieved. **Supplementary Estimates** always follow the Estimates because of new spending developments; they emerge at a later date. Typically, three sets of Supplementary Estimates are submitted during the fiscal year.

The Estimates and the supporting reports contain a great deal of detail. Even their authors housed in the Treasury Board Secretariat are almost overwhelmed by the details and decisions to be made about final expenditure requests. But the primary intent of the Estimates is straightforward: to lay out the government's annual spending plans for approval by Parliament.

Supplementary Estimates
A request for funds in addition to the original Estimates. Usually requested towards the end of the fiscal year.

Parliament

The tabling of the Estimates in Parliament is the next step in the process of managing the money. Parliament is involved because laws and conventions require that any plans for spending public money must have the consent of the legislature. On receipt of the Estimates, the House of Commons and then the Senate assign them to committees with the mandate to review the proposed expenditures of the government. These committees study the Estimates and hold public hearings at which ministers and public officials explain and defend their budget requests. Representatives of interest groups, appropriate experts, and others may also find themselves testifying before committees. The committees then recommend to Parliament their view on the appropriate response to the request for expenditures. They may say yes or no to the request, or deny certain requests within the Estimates; but they are without the authority to increase the expenditures, to change the way the money is used, or to move it to some other purpose. The full House or Senate can accept the recommendations or take actions that go against committee wishes to reduce or reject an expenditure item.

With committee reports in hand, the House of Commons and then the Senate vote on the entire budget as contained in the Estimates. As with most items in Parliament, the vote is a test of the House's confidence in the government. In other words, a lost vote on the budget would most likely mean the end for the prime minister and his government. Accordingly, the government usually secures approval of the Estimates without any change, but this outcome can be otherwise for governments lacking majority support. When the estimates receive approval and become law, they become known as the *Appropriation Act* for that year.

The review of Estimates is a time-consuming task. This creates the possibility that the Estimates will be without approval by the beginning of the new fiscal year, April 1. This situation leads to the passage of legislation, called **Interim Supply**, which provides government with the funds necessary to operate until approval for **Full Supply** is given. The interim funding equals about one-fourth of the total budget requested and runs from April 1 to June 30. Typically, interim funding is only for established programs and is unavailable for new initiatives.

This description of Parliament's role suggests a useful contribution to the management of money. Expenditures have been carefully reviewed and are now in place for transfer to the departments, which in turn will use the money to pursue budgetary initiatives. But the reality is different: there are problems with the Estimates process. The time to consider the Estimates is limited, Members of Parliament are without the expertise to review expenditures, and important budgetary items are often missing in the Estimates. It may even be the case that even with the time or expertise supplied by additional staff there may be little incentive to examine the Estimates without any promise of political gain. It has to be remembered that legislators are politicians, not accountants. A House of Commons committee recently offered suggestions for getting greater value out of parliamentary review of Estimates. These included ensuring the presence of budget items in the estimates and having greater access to the parliamentary budget officer. It is not clear whether these types of recommendations hit the spot (See What to Do?).

It is clear that parliamentary review of Estimates has serious shortcomings. But it is also true that it is not without positive attributes. The prospect of review forces the government to organize and account for their spending proposals; the Estimates offer useful information to anyone wanting to know what government is doing with the people's money. It is also unrealistic to expect a consideration of all the material presented in the estimates. A wiser tack is to work on the margins, to look at the relatively small handful of new or high priority expenditure items that require serious attention. This is within reach of Parliament; indeed, it is likely that more than a few members engage in this practice already. And the hearings and

Interim Supply A limited appropriation of funds provided by Parliament at the beginning of the fiscal year until the full Estimates have been improved.

Full Supply An appropriation of funds provided by Parliament that covers the difference between the total funds requested in the Estimates and funds initially made available through Interim Supply.

WHAT TO DO?

"If they can play, they will come." David Good, an authority on budgeting in Canada, suggests this reformulation of the well-known cliché "if we build it, they will come" points to a possible way of making the Estimates review process more productive. For politicians, to "play" is to have a real effect. Good says this might be achieved by giving MPs the ability to shift monies in the estimates from one area to another—say, more for job skills, less for income security of individuals and families. Would this cause MPs to become more engaged in assessing the Estimates?

Source: David Good, *The Politics of Public Money*, 2nd ed. Toronto: University of Toronto Press, 2014, p. 259.

Part Five / The Management of Organizational Resources

reports of Parliament also act to draw public attention to issues even if it is conceded that the legislature will have no real effect on these issues.

A Second Appearance: Treasury Board Secretariat

With the passage of the annual *Appropriation Act*, Parliament recedes into the background and Treasury Board and its Secretariat (TBS) emerge as an important player in the process of managing government resources. The role of the TBS at this point is to ensure the "prudent and effective use of public resources" within government agencies, which are now ready to receive the funds authorized by Parliament.[2] To achieve this end, TBS undertakes three basic tasks. One is to formulate, approve, and encourage use of management policies such as appropriate accounting standards for departmental reporting of budgetary expenditures. A second task is the allocation and tracking of monies; past controversies over the use of public funds have made this a very important part of TBS duties. A final task is "overseeing department performance" by working with departmental units responsible for evaluation of their units.[3] This last task addresses directly the third aim of budgeting, which is the provision of a high level of performance in using government expenditures.

The TBS has a little over 1800 employees and all of these people doubtless are important to financial management. But a single person within the Secretariat, the Comptroller General of Canada (CGC), and his small office are the most important when it comes to ensuring the successful implementation of the budget. As with all major players in government, the CGC has a long list of duties and activities. But to understand the CGC it is best to appreciate that the purpose of the CGC office "is to put the focus on financial management in government and also to create a champion for the financial management issues... ."[4] In the budgetary process and in government as a whole, the emphasis is on formulating new ideas and policies; management, on the other hand, receives relatively little consideration and *financial* management even less so. The job of the CGC is to change this situation, and efforts to do so have indeed focused on building a champion of financial management for all of government—the CGC—as well as champions in the individual departments.

Operating Departments

The turning of budgetary allocations into law and the oversight readiness in place in the TBS mean that monies can now be actually allocated to departments and other government agencies. This allocation of funds facilitates the emergence of the champions of financial management at the departmental level, the department's Chief Financial Officers (CFOs). The CFOs have three basic roles. One role is the usual one associated with the third aim of budgeting, which is guaranteeing the efficient use of scarce resources, with efficiency defined as "getting things done for the least cost and best value."[5] A second and related role is to have access to the information necessary to head off any serious disruptions that may result in loss of efficiency and a blow to the department's reputation. Disruptions can be relatively minor, perhaps one that involves a cost overrun for a particular project; but they can also be major if they involve misuse of funds and activities of criminality (see Box 18.1). In this capacity as crisis-avoider, the CFOs are aided by both the departmental internal audit bureau and departmental audit committees; both are bodies set up to support the commitment to sound accounting and use of public monies within departments. The final role of CFOs is one that effectively jump-starts government actions in the new fiscal year: securing the money allocation provided through the budget and ensuring that these funds are always sufficient to support departmental activities.

CFOs face many challenges in carrying out their roles, but one looms as being absolutely central to the basic exercise of governance in the modern world: finding

BOX 18.1

The Sponsorship Scandal

Easily the worst case of abuse of funds and criminal behaviour in recent times is the Sponsorship Scandal, which exploded onto the scene in 2004. A public inquiry discovered that officials in the federal Department of Public Works and Government Services (now called Public Works and Procurement) had misused funds intended to give more presence to the federal government in Quebec. Funds had been awarded to advertising companies close to the governing Liberal Party for doing very little or even nothing, and some of these funds had been effectively rerouted back to the Liberal Party to help finance political activities. Some officials involved in the scandal were forced to resign, and one senior public servant responsible for running the Sponsorship Program was convicted of fraud. The scandal played a large role in the Liberal Party, in 2006, losing power to the Conservative Party and Stephen Harper.

the appropriate amount of control over bureaucratic activity and the use of financial resources. Financial managers like CFOs are naturally inclined to set rules and regulations that specify quite closely how money is to be used. There are rules that give direction on how to access money in the Estimates, there are rules that specify procedures for accounting and tracking the money, and there are rules for making year-end reports on the use of the money. Rules are also enacted to give guidance on the procedures for gauging performance, hiring personnel, outsourcing tasks, and other actions necessary to the provision of programs and services. These are all connected to getting value for money. But one person's rules are another person's red tape. The complexity and demands of modern government require flexible government. Excessive rules tie the hands of public servants who face clients impatient with slow government; excessive rules also prohibit the release of creative activity that government can achieve with private partners and other governments—and by itself. Accordingly, rules can actually work against their primary mission, which is to ensure the most effective use of public monies.

CFOs are sensitive to this challenge and believe they may have found the answer. The answer exists in changing the nature of the rules. Traditional rules tend to focus on process from beginning to end. This guarantees the presence of rules at every stage of delivering services and programs—a recipe for inflexibility. New rules tend to focus on outputs and outcomes, which occur at end of the process. Thus, public officials are relatively free from the restraints of rules throughout the process of meeting the needs of the public. This is the same transition witnessed in the styles of budgeting, the movement away from measuring inputs and towards considering outputs. But as seen with budgeting styles, it is hard to measure outputs in terms of satisfying performance standards. The fear is that the shift leads to excessive flexibility and fails in the hunt for the ideal amount of control over public monies.

Public Works and Procurement Canada

One agency holds a special place in the world of federal departments and agencies seeking to provide sound financial management. This is a department with the rather unwieldy name Public Works and Procurement Canada (formerly Public Works and Government Services Canada). It provides a wide array of services to organizations of the federal government. One of these services is to act as the central accounting centre for the government. It is responsible for the receipt and disbursement of all public monies and for accounting for those funds in the Consolidated Revenue Fund. This fund is one large cash account, which the government maintains for all federal funds not earmarked for some special purpose. This consolidation of funds allows for easy tracking of federal monies and decreases the chances of inappropriate use of funds. The department also handles day-to-day financial transactions, issuing cheques to departments and agencies that have submitted cheque requisitions to the department; it also takes care of all receipts and deposits of public funds. And along with the Treasury Board Secretariat, the department is responsible for the establishment of the government accounting system.

Another notable duty of the department is to prepare the government's year-end financial statements, referred to as the **Public Accounts**. These statements include the government's balance sheet, lists of assets owned and liabilities owed, a statement of revenues and expenditures, and other financial declarations. The Public Accounts are important because they represent a complete and true picture of the government's fiscal situation.

Public Accounts The series of documents containing the government's year-end financial statements.

Public Works and Procurement Canada makes a significant contribution to the management of financial resources in the Canadian government. But, as mentioned earlier, the department was seriously implicated in the Sponsorship Scandal. The accountant for government departments at the federal level had betrayed the trust of the Canadian people. The lesson of this occurrence is that impediments to the successful management of financial resources are not always related to lack of expertise or the absence of sufficient time to review important documents. Sometimes the impediment is the failure to respect the ethical values that are meant to shape and guide the actions of public servants.[6]

Auditor General

The **Office of the Auditor General (OAG)** includes the Auditor General of Canada and almost 600 audit professionals. The agency reports to the Parliament of Canada on the actions of the government of the day, and it has become a prominent part of the financial management system. In fact, its prominence is so great that it has achieved formal status in the budgetary game; it is the watchdog, joining the spenders, guardians, and priority setters as key players in the budgetary game. But it is a player with a difference. The other three reside within the government of the day and have a direct and immediate effect on the budget. The OAG stands outside the government in its role as an officer of Parliament, a situation that makes its effect "indirect, long term, and subtle."[7] Still, the OAG wields considerable influence, so much so that it is held partly responsible for the political executive seeking greater power in order to defend itself against aggressive agencies like the OAG. In recent years, OAG influence has increased to the extent that many think it has a political agenda of its own. Such perceptions in the long run weaken the agency because the reason people listen to the OAG is that it is not a political player.

Office of the Auditor General (OAG) The officer of Parliament who performs an annual audit of the public accounts and prepares reports to Parliament on the government's financial stewardship.

As watchdog, the office carries out two basic roles, one expected of auditors and accountants and the other not so expected. The expected role is simply to conduct audits to ensure that what government agencies say what they have done with the public money is the truth. In the words of the OAG, "auditors test whether financial transactions support the amounts and disclosures in the financial statements."[8] The result is the type of accounting report found at the back of the annual reports of organizations, public or private. An additional intent of these audits is to determine whether the activities and spending of departments respect laws and regulations concerning how and where government finances have been spent. For example, a legislative enactment may state that Health Canada is budgeted to spend a certain amount on assuring food safety, and the task of the audit is to determine if this requirement has been met. Up until the 1970s, these audits, which could be called financial audits, represented the main role of the OAG. If this had remained the case, then the watchdog label would have been undeserved. But political developments, namely concern over the quality of government spending, provided the grounds for a different, more controversial and more powerful role for the OAG. With this role, the watchdog tag becomes appropriate.

Chapter 18 / Management of Financial Resources

This second role of the OAG centres on an audit that goes beyond counting the money. As the name of the audit suggests—the performance audit—it relates to the heart of the third aim of budgeting. It seeks to determine how well the government is using public funds. More precisely, the audit measures government programs and practices using the criteria of economy, efficiency, and environmental impact; it also tries to gauge whether government agencies are themselves capable of measuring program effectiveness. Recent examples of performance audits include assessing the ability of the Department of Finance to manage tax-based expenditures, the extent to which federal health agencies have dealt with the issue of anti-microbial resistance, the actions of Corrections Canada to prepare male offenders for release, and the progress of the Canada Border Agency towards introducing information technology. Typically, there are 25 to 30 performance audits annually, to be found in two or three reports; the audits consume about 60% of the OAG budget. As to the programs or areas to be audited, the agency says it selects "those that cost taxpayers significant amounts of money or that could threaten the health safety of Canadians," or areas that are "of great interest to parliamentarians and Canadians (such as national security)."[9] When completed, the audits are tabled in Parliament and sent to the Public Accounts Committee of the House of Commons, the latter of which asks for public comment on the audits and their recommendations.

With this type of audit, the OAG denies any attempt to "question the merits of government policies."[10] Rather, it is only considering the "government's practices, controls and reporting systems based on its own public administration policies and on best practices." Yet, to assess performance is to assess the suitability of the government in power; it helps to determine whether this government should remain in office. Admittedly, a perusal of OAG performance audits shows some to involve little questioning of the government; it is not clear, for instance, whether information technology investments at border crossings would interest many people in government or the general public. But others audits do question the government, and it can even be argued that audits have helped bring down governments. The very selection of performance audits by OAG, which entails choosing areas with high costs or high-profile issues such as national security, also speaks to an agency that seeks a watchdog role.

The OAG knows that the performance audit is controversial, but at the same time it feels that this type of audit is necessary to successful budgeting. The emphasis in budgeting is on the first two aims, so there is a need to balance this emphasis with an agency that stresses the third aim of managing the allocated resources. "The Office of the Auditor General of Canada (OAG) serves Parliament," says that OAG, "by providing it with objective, fact-based information and expert advice on government programs and activities… ."[11] As the quotation suggests, the agency gives a professional edge to its work and exists independent of the government in power. People turn to the agency because it can be counted on to provide something close to the truth about government; in other words, it has credibility. All of this may be accepted without denying that OAG is an important player in the budgetary process and in so being is a political entity.

Public Accounts Committee

The OAG is an agent of Parliament and serves Parliament and its committees. The committee that receives and acts upon the reports of the OAG is the Standing Committee on Public Accounts (PAC) of the House of Commons. The PAC, whose members are from the three major parties in the House of Commons, has a mandate to review the *Public Accounts of Canada* (the record of government revenues, expenditures, assets, and liabilities) and other matters referred to it by the House of Commons. But its key task is to consider the reports of the Auditor General of Canada and his or her office. The committee selects chapters within the reports that it believes to be the most important and calls for the auditor general and senior public servants from audited agencies to appear before it to discuss the reports. The committee then, if warranted, makes its own report to the House of Commons, usually with recommendations to address the shortcomings in the audited agencies. These reports close the loop set out in Figure 18.1. Parliament now has the recommendations of the PAC before deciding upon expenditures proposed for the next budget.

As with Parliament in the review of Estimates, it looks at first as if the PAC has real influence. It can use the analytical and sometimes feared power of the OAG to formulate its recommendations. The fact that the chair of the committee is typically not a member of the government increases the chances that the committee agenda and proceedings can escape the dictates of the government (the present Chair, Kevin Sorenson, is a Conservative member). The committee also has a clerk who organizes its proceedings and research help from the Library of Parliament (see Figure 18.2). All in all, one might conclude that the committee "appears to occupy a central position in holding government accountable for its spending."[12]

However, a closer look shows that the committee suffers the fate of legislative bodies in modern parliamentary systems. The lack of expertise, the party discipline, the excessive partisanship, and the feeling that MPs could do something better than looking at issues of financial management all work against ensuring that government finances are used efficiently. The PAC also suffers from a unique drawback: its greatest strength is

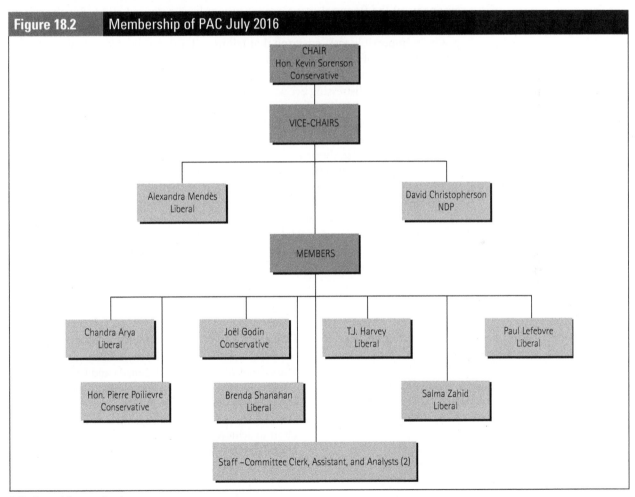

Figure 18.2   Membership of PAC July 2016

© The House of Commons, Canada

Chapter 18 / Management of Financial Resources

its greatest weakness. The OAG reports give the committee a sound basis for reviewing government spending. But the reliance on the OAG—90% of committee work relates to the OAG—makes it appear that the real power is the Auditor General. As noted earlier, the OAG strives to protect against this perception; but the fact is that the OAG is much better known to Canadians than the PAC.

The Third Aim

The attempt to achieve the aim of sound financial management shows a commitment to rigour and the rules of parliamentary government. The Treasury Board Secretariat produces a set of Estimates almost daunting in its thoroughness, and Parliament responds with a system of committees whose mandate is to turn proposals into laws. Departments and the Treasury Board together form two lines of defence against inefficiency and misuse of funds, now law, with the Comptroller General of Canada and the Chief Financial Officers acting as lead actors in this battle. The Office of the Auditor General and its leader bring their formidable analytical powers into play in order to uncover inefficiencies. And the Public Accounts Committee ends the effort by publicizing and reviewing the work of the OAG to ensure that Parliament gets a view of how funds have been used. The whole process seems so exhaustive as to be embarrassingly redundant in many places and suffocating to anyone daring to go against its precepts.

The truth is that there is a strong commitment to rigour and the rule of law. The components of the financial management system have a desired effect. But the system has its shortcomings. The expectation that the Estimates will be considered meticulously imposes an impossible task, ensuring that failure will inevitably accompany any assessment of the review of Estimates. The House of Commons and its committees show themselves to be without the capability and even the desire to consider the nation's finances. Both limitations are distressing because in a way they cannot be fixed. Politicians are not accountants or financial officials but rather creatures whose success relies on remaining in power or seeking to gain it. Few politicians are going to get re-elected because they went over the Estimates—unless of course they run into some political issue like the Sponsorship Scandal—so they have no wish to pour over ledgers. Also, most are without the skills to determine the effective use of tax dollars. The CGO and CFOs face within their environment senior appointed officials who pay relatively little heed to concerns of financial management; the payoff for those officials lies in policy proposals, not financial management. The OAG is powerful and has an impressive impact, but it is an institution operating from the outside. All in all, the third aim is pursued with great vigour and achieves some victories along the way. But it is still the case that success remains elusive. The budgetary process is incomplete because the final aim receives too little attention.

Points to Know

- The third aim or duty of budgeting is ensuring efficient use of expenditures made available through the first two aims.

- The third duty amounts to a process of financial management involving Parliament, the Treasury Board Secretariat, government agencies, and the Office of the Auditor General.

- Parliament's role in financial management is to turn budgetary expenditures into law after reviewing the budget and the Main and Supplementary Estimates.

- Parliament also reviews the employment of expenditures through the Public Accounts Committee.

- The Comptroller General of Canada and Chief Financial Officers located in agencies monitor and assess use of expenditures during the fiscal year.

- The process of financial management contributes to the effort to achieve efficient use of expenditures, but the effort falls short of its goal. Lack of both capability and commitment largely explain this outcome.

Review Questions

1. How can the Treasury Board Secretariat be shown to be one of the key players in the financial management process?

2. What is the impact of Parliament on the Main Estimates?

3. What are the weak points and the strong points in the financial management process?

4. The formal role of the Auditor General is simply to conduct audits of government spending, yet it is a powerful player in the management of government finances. How can this be?

5. The agencies and bodies responsible for managing government finances are thorough in their work, but they fall short of successfully carrying out the third aim of public budgeting. Why is this so?

Notes

1. Treasury Board of Canada Secretariat, *2015–16 Estimates: Parts I and II The Government Expenditure Plan and Main Estimates*, II:113.
2. Treasury Board of Canada Secretariat, *Financial Management*, accessed May 5, 2015, http://www.tbs-sct.gc.ca/fm-gf/index-eng.asp.
3. Treasury Board of Canada Secretariat, *About Financial Management*, p. 1, accessed July 25, 2016, http://www.tbs-sct.gc.ca/ip-pi/structure/fm-gf-eng.asp.
4. Official from Comptroller's Office, quoted in David A. Good, *The Politics of Public Money*, 2nd ed. (Toronto: University of Toronto Press, 2014), 230.
5. Ibid., 219.
6. See Liane E. Benoit and C.E.S. (Ned) Franks, "For Want of a Nail: The Role of Internal Audit in the Sponsorship Scandal," in Commission of Inquiry into the Sponsorship Program and Advertising Activities, *Restoring Accountability: Research Studies*, Volume 2 (Ottawa: Her Majesty the Queen in Right of Canada).
7. David A. Good, *The Politics of Public Money: Spenders, Guardians, Priority Setters, and Financial Watchdogs Inside the Canadian Government* (Toronto: University of Toronto Press, 2007), 121.
8. Office of the Auditor General of Canada, *What We Do*, accessed July 18, 2016, http://www.oag-bvg.gc.ca/internet/English/au_fs_e_371.html.
9. Ibid., 7.
10. Ibid., 6.
11. Ibid., 1.
12. Good, *The Politics of Public Money*, 2nd ed., 263.

Glossary

Note: The numbers in parentheses following each item refer to the page(s) on which further elaboration on that item can be found.

A

accountability The obligation to answer for fulfilling responsibilities. (p. 20)

active representation A bureaucracy is only considered representative if the policies emanating from the policy-making process actually reflect the interests of the groups in the general population that are being passively represented. (p. 276)

administrative accountability The obligation of public servants to answer for fulfilling responsibilities that flow from the authority given them. Similar in meaning to the concept of *objective responsibility*. (pp. 14, 21)

administrative law The branch of public law concerned with relations between the government and individual citizens. It deals with the legal limitations on the actions of governmental officials and on the remedies that are available to anyone affected by a transgression of these limits. (p. 203)

administrative or public service ethics Principles and standards of right conduct in public organizations. Normally used interchangeably with the term administrative morality. (p. 24)

advocating An activity similar to lobbying except that the impact of the activity addresses not only to the interests of group members but also those interests located outside the group. (p. 235)

alternative service delivery (ASD) The trend in recent years for governments to search for more innovative and efficient ways to deliver services than through traditional departments and agencies. (p. 143)

B

BOOT (build-own-operate-transfer) In this arrangement, the private partner builds and operates a particular service (e.g., bridge, sports facility, etc.) for a specified period of time, after which the facility reverts to the government. (p. 151)

bureaucracy Literally meaning "rule by desks or offices," it is a method of administratively organizing numerous people who need to work together in large or complex public or private organizations. (p. 29)

C

captive agency theory A theory that holds that regulatory agencies eventually become captive of, or controlled by, the interests they were established to regulate. (p. 139)

casual employee Individual who is appointed to the public service for no more than 90 days in a calendar year in any one government department or agency in either full- or part-time positions. (p. 269)

central agency An agency that has a substantial amount of continuing legitimate authority to intervene in and direct the activity of departments. (p. 104)

classical federalism A concept according to which the powers of government are divided so that the general and regional governments are each, within a sphere, coordinate and independent. (p. 217)

coercive power Individuals who possess this type of power are able to influence the behaviour of others either through punishment or the threat of punishment for non-compliance. (p. 68)

COGO (company-owned-government-operated) In this arrangement, a company owns a facility that it has built for government. The government then pays a fee to the private company to rent the facility. (p. 151)

collaborative federalism A term employed to characterize a period in the 1990s when both orders of government realized the importance of cooperation in achieving policy outcomes important to the federal government and the provinces. (p. 218)

collaborative partnership This is one of several different types of partnership (the others are contributory, consultative, and operational). It is considered to be the truest form of partnership in that it involves mutual dependency and the sharing of financial resources, decision making, risks, and rewards. (p. 151)

collective ministerial responsibility The responsibility of ministers as a group (i.e., as members of the cabinet) for the policies and management of the government as a whole. (p. 188)

co-location This is the practice of bringing together different government departments or offices into the same building to make it more convenient for citizens to access services. It is one aspect of *integrated service delivery*. (p. 144)

common law Law derived from custom and judicial precedent rather than statutes. (p. 205)

competitive federalism A term used to describe highly conflictual federal–provincial relations during the 1960s, 70s, and 80s, when the provinces challenged the federal government on major issues relating to energy, fiscal arrangements, and the Constitution. (p. 218)

contracting-out In this situation the government enters into a contractual arrangement with a private sector company or non-profit organization to provide a publicly-funded service. Also known as *outsourcing*. (p. 152)

cooperative federalism A term used to describe federal–provincial relations when the constitutional division of powers is preserved but federal and provincial ministers and public servants engage in consultation and coordination to reach joint decisions on matters of mutual concern. (p. 218)

core public administration The more than 75 federal departments, agencies, and commissions identified in Schedules I and IV of the *Financial Administration Act* for whom the Treasury Board is the employer and that are the main part of the federal public service. (p. 256)

court government A type of government that places a great deal of power in the hands of the prime minister and a select group of valued counsellors. Employed by some to describe the nature of the Canadian government. (p. 171)

Crown agency A term that applies to two types of public sector organizations: 1) Crown corporations; and 2) statutory and other agencies. Along with government departments, they represent a traditional organizational form. (p. 115)

Crown corporation A corporation in the ordinary sense of the term, whose mandate relates to industrial, commercial, or financial activities, but that also belongs to the state. Also known as *public enterprise*. (p. 115)

D

decentralization A system of organization that involves placing actual decision-making power in the hands of units outside the centre of power, either geographically or organizationally. (p. 45)

deconcentration The physical dispersal of operating units with only limited delegation of decision-making authority. (p. 45)

Department of Finance A central agency responsible for advising cabinet on economic matters. The Department also formulates fiscal and tax policies. (p. 112)

departmental corporation An organizational form, established through legislation, which is responsible for delivering service, conducting research, or performing regulatory functions. It has greater autonomy than a government department, but relies mostly on appropriations (although some do generate user fees too). (p. 148)

deployment The appointment of an employee to another position at the same level as his or her existing position, or to a higher or lower level, provided there is no change in the employee's personnel classification. (p. 270)

deputy minister (DM) The administrative head of a government department. Appointed by the prime minister or premier. Also referred to as the deputy head. (p. 103)

deregulation The elimination of government regulatory control over an industry so that the industry can operate through the dictates of the private enterprise system. (p. 136)

digital divide This is a situation of inequality in service delivery that arises as a result of the fact that not all citizens have equal access to technology (e.g., the Internet and social media accessed through smart phones). (p. 157)

digital era governance (DEG) One of the governance theories that emphasizes the transformative impact of information technologies and changes to information systems on the practice of public administration. (p. 84)

E

economic regulation Sometimes referred to as "old" or "direct" regulation, these are the restrictions placed by government on such things as pricing, competition, or the methods of production for particular industries or markets. (p. 120)

efficiency A measure of performance that may be expressed as a ratio between input and output. The use of administrative methods and resources that will achieve the greatest results for a specific objective at the least cost. (p. 14)

emergency federalism A term used to describe federal–provincial relations during the two world wars and the Depression; these relations were characterized by a growth in federal power vis-à-vis the provinces. (p. 217)

employee takeover This is a type of contracting out arrangement whereby former government employees establish a private company to provide a service that they had previously provided while working for government. (p. 152)

employment equity An approach or program designed to identify and systematically remove employment policies, practices, and procedures that exclude or place at a disadvantage certain groups that have been historically under-represented in the public service. (p. 279)

entrepreneurial government A prescription for administrative reform outlined by David Osborne and Ted Gaebler comprising ten key principles that would enable governments to reinvent themselves by becoming more flexible, adaptable, and innovative. Closely associated with the shift towards NPM, particularly in the North American context. (p. 76)

equity The act of treating people equally and without bias. (p. 15)

esprit de corps The morale and sense of unity of a group based on its shared interests and responsibilities. (p. 40)

Estimates Documents that lay out the allocation of proposed expenditures to departments for the forthcoming fiscal year and constitute a request of the House of Commons for authority to expend these resources. (p. 314)

executive federalism A term used to describe federal–provincial relations characterized by the concentration of authority at the top of each participating government and the formalized quality of the relations between the two orders of government. (p. 218)

Expenditure Management System (EMS) The federal government's expenditure budget process, which is designed to provide more information to Parliament and other decision makers. Its centre point is each department's business plan, an approach that ensures that the department is focusing on its main area of responsibility. (p. 308)

expert power Individuals who have specialized knowledge or expertise can exert expert power over those who do not. (p. 68)

F

fairness The quality of deciding without discriminatory intent. (p. 15)

federalism A political system in which the powers of the state are formally divided between central and regional governments by a written constitution but in which these governments are linked in a mutually interdependent political relationship. (p. 216)

Financial Administration Act The statute that governs the regime of financial accountability for federal departments and agencies. (p. 128)

Full Supply An appropriation of funds provided by Parliament that covers the difference between the total funds requested in the Estimates and funds initially made available through Interim Supply. (p. 316)

G

globalization A process of integration and interaction between peoples, private sector corporations, and governments around the world that has been propelled by international trade and investment. (p. 8)

GOCO (government-owned-company-operated) In this arrangement, the government owns a particular facility and allows a private company to operate it so as to capitalize on the private company's expertise. (p. 151)

governance A broad category of public administration theories dealing with the distribution and exercise of authority, decision making, and accountability. More specifically, it recognizes that the state is no longer solely responsible for these processes, but rather they are shared with a variety of state and non-state actors. (p. 74)

governor general The representative of the Queen in Canada; functions as the head of state when the Queen is not in Canada. (p. 94)

governor-in-council The governor general acting on the formal advice of the cabinet. (p. 94)

Government 2.0 Efforts to make government more open, transparent, and engaging by providing open data to citizens and groups and harnessing the power of collaborative technologies. (p. 154)

H

hierarchy of needs A concept developed by Abraham Maslow that suggests workers can be motivated by the satisfaction of a number of different needs ranging from basic shelter and food to self-actualization. As workers' lower-level needs are satisfied, they are motivated by desires to satisfy higher-level needs. (p. 56)

horizontal administrative coordinative department Usually considered to be the least influential departments, these entities provide other departments with the various supports (i.e., goods and services) that they require to fulfill their mandates. (p. 97)

horizontal management A type of management process that involves two or more departments and, increasingly, non-governmental bodies. (p. 173)

horizontal policy coordinative department These are the government departments (also known as *central agencies*) that have the responsibility for coordinating the overall policy agenda of the government. (p. 97)

human resources planning The process through which a government strives to ensure that it has the appropriate quantity and quality of employees to carry out its responsibilities. (p. 269)

I

"ideal-type" bureaucracy According to Max Weber, complex organizations would be more efficient when they reflected certain key characteristics, including hierarchy, specialization of labour, employment and promotion based on merit, full-time employment, the use of written files, and decisions based on impersonal rules. (p. 33)

incremental budgeting A style of budgeting characterized by small annual adjustments in spending accompanied by occasional large increases or decreases in expenditures. (p. 305)

indeterminate employee Individuals who are appointed to the public service for an unspecified period of time (i.e., these are permanent positions). (p. 269)

individual ministerial responsibility The responsibility of the minister, as the political head of the department, to answer to the legislature and through the legislature to the public both for his or her personal acts and for those of departmental subordinates. (p. 188)

informal organizational behaviour The formal structural aspects of an organization do not fully explain patterns of behaviour and interaction. Organizations contain many informal elements, such as personal interests and goals that may diverge from formally stipulated organizational goals, and informal associations or cliques, which dictate how people actually work together. (p. 49)

integrated service delivery A term that refers to the process of coordinating government service delivery within and between levels of government. It involves bringing together and integrating related services so they can be accessed in a single, seamless experience (also referred to as a single-window service delivery). (p. 146)

integrity A disposition to distinguish right from wrong and to do the right thing. (p. 15)

interdepartmental interaction Interactions between different departments. (p. 173)

interest group Organizations of private persons who join together to further their mutual interests by influencing public policy. (p. 234)

intergovernmental policy capacity (IPC) A measure of the ability of governments in a federal state to combine their efforts to create effective policy outcomes. (p. 229)

intergovernmental relations The interactions between and among the federal, provincial, and territorial governments in the Canadian federal system. (p. 216)

Interim Supply A limited appropriation of funds provided by Parliament at the beginning of the fiscal year until the full Estimates have been improved. (p. 316)

international organization A type of Crown corporation established through international agreements whereby Canada either owns shares or has the ability to appoint or elect members to its governing body. (p. 119)

intradepartmental interaction Interactions within one department. (p. 173)

J

job classification The process by which jobs are assigned to an occupational group within an occupational category and to a level within that group. (p. 269)

joint enterprise A type of Crown corporation whereby the shares are held jointly by the Government of Canada and another level of government. (p. 117)

judicial review Authority of the courts to assess the legality of an action of the legislative or executive branches of government. (p. 203)

L

legitimate power Also known as positional power, individuals with this form of power are able to influence the behaviour of others based on their formal position within the organization's hierarchy of authority. (p. 68)

lieutenant governor The representatives of the Queen in the provinces. (p. 94)

lieutenant-governor-in-council The lieutenant governor acting on the formal advice of a provincial cabinet. (p. 94)

line function Any kind of daily operation that is directly involved in provision of goods or services by an organization. In government, those involved in a line function provide services directly to citizens. (p. 43)

line-item budgeting A style of budgeting that emphasizes the object of expenditure (salaries, stationery) rather than the purpose of the expenditure. (p. 303)

lobbying A legitimate means by which groups and individuals try to influence government decisions by direct contact with politicians or public servants. Usually associated with the activities of *interest groups*. (p. 235)

M

managerialism A theoretical perspective on organization that emphasizes setting clear organizational goals and giving employees the flexibility and autonomy to pursue these goals. (p. 74)

memorandum to cabinet The key mechanism by which policy proposals are brought forward by ministers for consideration and approval by their cabinet colleagues. The formal means by which deputy ministers provide confidential policy advice to their ministers. (p. 169)

merit principle A principle according to which (1) all citizens should have a reasonable opportunity to be considered for employment in the public service and (2) selections must be based exclusively on qualification or fitness for the job. To be distinguished from the *merit system*. (p. 260)

merit system The mechanism in use at any time by which the goals of the *merit principle* are achieved. An administrative device that can and should be adapted to changing circumstances. (p. 260)

minister An elected politician who serves as the political head of a government department. (p. 102)

mixed enterprise A type of Crown corporation whereby the shares are held jointly by the Government of Canada and one or more private interests. (p. 117)

multilevel governance An intergovernmental arrangement whereby city governments enter into working relations with federal or provincial governments (or both together) to address policy challenges that are important to urban areas; arrangement may also include the participation of non-governmental actors. (p. 219)

N

new public governance (NPG) First articulated by Stephen Osborne, this is another variant of the governance theories, which is centred on the promotion of the common good and emphasizes collaboration between multiple stakeholders. (p. 84)

new public management (NPM) A style of management that borrows heavily from private sector principles and focuses on values like customer service, flexibility in delivery, entrepreneurship, and empowerment. (p. 73)

non-governmental actor Citizens and representatives of institutions located outside of government who strive to influence elected and appointed officials and participate in the making and administration of public programs and policies. (p. 233)

O

objective responsibility The responsibility of a person or an organization to someone else, outside of self, for some thing or some kind of performance. Similar in meaning to accountability or answerability. (p. 22)

occupational category A broad range of occupations of the same type, distinguished by the nature of the duties performed and the education required. Examples in the federal public service are the Executive Group and the Operational categories. (p. 269)

Office of the Auditor General (OAG) The officer of Parliament who performs an annual audit of the public accounts and prepares reports to Parliament on the government's financial stewardship. (p. 319)

open federalism A term used to describe the period of federal–provincial relations during the early 2000s, where the federal government worked to bring a return to a classical type of federalism in which each order of government tended to its own constitutional responsibilities. (p. 219)

open government A global movement across all levels of government, the aim of which is to promote greater transparency and accountability, to provide citizens with greater access to information and data, and to foster citizen engagement. (p. 88)

open systems theory An approach to the study of organizations that emphasizes that organizations are a part of, and must interact with, their environment. (p. 65)

operating department An administrative unit comprising one or more organizational components over which a minister has direct ministerial management control. (p. 94)

order-in-council An official proclamation made by the governor-in-council; usually a government regulation. (p. 101)

organization development (OD) A participative approach to management that emphasizes team development and allows members of the organization to work together to identify and correct problems. (p. 61)

organizational humanism (human relations school) An approach to management and motivation that emphasizes the dignity and needs of workers in the workplace. Usually associated with social psychologists such as Roethlisberger and Mayo. (p. 54)

other subsidiaries and associates These are corporate entities whereby less than 50 percent of their shares are owned by one or more parent Crown corporations. (p. 117)

P

parent corporation A type of Crown corporation whose shares are directly and wholly owned by the Government of Canada. (p. 117)

participatory management A style of management emphasizing the desirability of workers actually being involved in decision making. (p. 61)

passive representation A situation whereby the demographic makeup of the bureaucracy reflects that of the general population. An assumption is made that a passively representative bureaucracy will act in the interests of their counterparts in the general population when formulating public policy. (p. 276)

patronage The appointment of persons to government service or their advancement within the service on the grounds of contributions, financial or otherwise, to the governing party rather than based on merit. (p. 39)

pay equity A system that permits comparisons to be made between different jobs performed for the same employer. A shorthand term for equal pay for work of equal value. To be distinguished from equal pay for equal work, which requires that men and women be paid the same for doing the same job. (p. 291)

performance budgeting A style of budgeting that relates expenditure to specific activities to determine unit costs of providing services. (p. 304)

performance management A method for improving the performance and productivity of employees, teams, and organizations. It involves setting performance objectives and expected behaviours, then measuring the results against these measures and providing feedback. (pp. 78, 271)

policy community or **policy network** A cluster of interested groups (government organizations, interest groups, international agencies, interested companies and individuals, and journalists) organized around a particular policy. This group has a strong influence on the making of that policy. (p. 236)

political culture The values, beliefs, and attitudes we hold about political life. (p. 9)

political neutrality A constitutional doctrine or convention according to which public servants should not engage in activities that are likely to impair or appear to impair their impartiality or the impartiality of the public service. (p. 14)

politics–administration dichotomy The idea that a clear distinction can be made between the responsibilities of elected executives, who make policy decisions, and the responsibilities of public servants, who execute these decisions. (p. 16)

POSDCORB Building on the work of Henri Fayol, this acronym was developed by Luther Gulick and Lyndal Urwick as a means of highlighting the key steps in the administrative process: planning, organizing, staffing, directing, coordinating, reporting, and budgeting. (p. 43)

post-bureaucratic organization A type of organization that eschews the qualities of traditional bureaucracies and stresses flexibility, decentralization, and citizen-centred delivery of services. (p. 75)

power The capacity to secure the dominance of one's goals or interests. There are two forms of power—control and influence. (p. 162)

Prime Minister's Office (PMO) The *central agency* providing partisan policy advice to the prime minister. It is most concerned with relations between the prime minister and the media and the party. (p. 106)

privative clause Statutory provision designed to prevent judicial review of the decisions of administrative tribunals. (p. 209)

Privy Council Office (PCO) The central agency, comprising career public servants, providing policy advice and administrative support to cabinet and its committees. (p. 109)

program budgeting A style of budgeting that allocates funds by program and attempts to measure the impact of expenditures on the goals and objectives of programs. (p. 304)

Public Accounts The series of documents containing the government's year-end financial statements. (p. 319)

public bureaucracy Also called the public service, it is the system of authority, people, offices, and methods government uses to achieve its objectives; the means by which the practice of public administration is carried out. (p. 3)

public choice theory The use of economic principles to analyze political activity. It suggests that people take political action to further their self-interest. (p. 74)

public interest The common good or welfare of the general public, which guides the actions of government. (p. 4)

public involvement A broad range of direct and indirect forms of participation by members of the public in government decision making. (p. 244)

public–private partnership (P3) Arrangement whereby the government partners with one or more private sector entities to deliver a service. (p. 150)

public servant Also referred to as civil servants or bureaucrats, these are the appointed officials who are employed by government. They provide advice, manage resources, and provide services to citizens. (p. 1)

Public Service Commission An independent agency that serves Parliament as the guardian of the merit principle in human resources management. It is responsible for recruitment, staffing, and promotion in the public service. (p. 18)

public value governance One of the most recent governance theories, whereby the purpose of collaboration between various state and non-state actors is to create public value. The focus is on public sector values, particularly democratic values, in place of concerns about efficiency and effectiveness. (p. 85)

Q

quasi-federalism A term used to describe the early decades of the Canadian federation during which the federal government dominated the provincial governments, in part by making frequent use of the federal constitutional powers to disallow and reserve provincial legislation. (p. 216)

R

recruitment The process of attracting suitable candidates for employment in the public service. (p. 270)

referent power Individuals who possess referent power are able to influence the behaviour of others because those followers admire and respect the power wielder. Followers aspire to be like this person and have a need to gain his or her approval. (p. 68)

representative bureaucracy The idea that the social composition of the bureaucracy should reflect that of the population as a whole. Also that larger numbers of persons from certain under-represented groups (e.g., women, minority groups) should be brought into the public service. (p. 276)

responsiveness Service both to the public and to political authorities. (p. 15)

reward power Individuals who possess this type of power are able to provide some type of tangible or intangible reward (such as better pay, time off, or bonuses) to influence the behaviour of others. (p. 67)

S

scalar chain The formal line of authority in an organization moving in a straight line from the top to the bottom of the organizational hierarchy. (p. 40)

scientific management A management style that emphasizes tailoring the physical nature of work to the physical abilities of workers. Characterized by time-and-motion studies and precise work standards. Usually associated with Frederick W. Taylor. (p. 39)

selection The process through which candidates for public service positions are screened by such means as application forms, written examinations, and interviews. (p. 270)

separate agency Government organizations for which the Treasury Board is not the employer, although the Public Service Commission retains exclusive authority to make appointments. Some, but not all, of the employees working in the separate agencies are counted as members of the federal public service. (p. 256)

service agency A special type of departmental corporation that typically provides a service for which there is no private sector competition. As a separate employer, it has greater financial and human resources management flexibility. (p. 149)

service quality This is a variation of TQM, which was adopted in the public sector beginning in the late 1980s. While TQM emerged from a manufacturing setting and focused on improving production systems, service quality is concerned with enhancing service and customer satisfaction. (p. 62)

shared-governance corporation A type of Crown corporation in which the federal government retains no financial interest but has the ability to appoint members to its governing structures. (p. 118)

social media A term that refers to electronic communication that conveys information, ideas, videos, proposals, and other items of interest. Relevant for public administration is the use of social media to marshal or organize public sentiment about a particular event or action and to allow for quick and easy availability of government messages and policies. (p. 241)

social movement Informal networks of private citizens with shared beliefs who seek to influence government and the larger society, through protest and other non-traditional modes of influence. (p. 248)

social regulation Also known as "new" regulation, these are the restrictions placed by government to control the behaviour of individuals or organizations in order to protect the welfare of society. (p. 120)

span of control The number of subordinates reporting to a particular supervisor. (p. 40)

staff function Those employed in this capacity, such as those in the accounting, human resources or legal departments, provide advice and support to those who are engaged in a line function. (p. 43)

statutory and other agencies A particular type of Crown agency, also known as agencies, boards, and commissions (ABCs), they perform a wide range of functions (administrative, quasi-judicial, advisory, and regulatory) in government. One of the traditional organizational forms. (p. 115)

subjective responsibility The responsibility a person feels toward others. Often described as personal or psychological responsibility. Similar in meaning to identification, loyalty, and conscience. (p. 22)

Supplementary Estimates A request for funds in addition to the original estimates. Usually requested towards the end of the fiscal year. (p. 315)

T

target (designated) group Since it is not feasible to have a bureaucracy that is an exact representation of all key demographic groups in society, the Canadian government has decided to ensure that the federal bureaucracy is representative of four target groups: women, visible minorities, Aboriginals, and persons with disabilities. (p. 278)

term (determinate) employee Individuals who are appointed to the public service for a specific period of time (e.g., a contract of six months or more). (p. 269)

Theory X/Theory Y Developed by Douglas McGregor to describe different managers' views of workers. Theory X holds that workers are basically lazy and need to be closely watched. Theory Y holds that workers are highly motivated and will voluntarily work hard. (p. 57)

total quality management (TQM) A style of participative management popularized in the 1980s and early 1990s. It requires changing an organization's culture to focus on establishing and maintaining high standards of quality, especially with respect to meeting customer expectations. (p. 62)

trained incapacity A concept that refers to the fact that actions continue to be based on skills and training that worked successfully in the past but produce inappropriate responses when circumstances change. (p. 49)

Treasury Board (TB) A cabinet committee consisting of the president of the Treasury Board, the minister of finance, and four other cabinet ministers. Responsible for preparation of the expenditure budget and for administrative management in departments. (p. 111)

Treasury Board Secretariat (TBS) The central agency that assists the Treasury Board in carrying out its responsibilities. (p. 111)

U

unilateral federalism A depiction of a short period at the turn of the century where the federal government imposed its views on arrangements involving both Ottawa and the provinces and enacted programs largely in areas of provincial jurisdiction. (p. 218)

unity of command The bureaucratic principle that holds that all employees must report to one, and only one, supervisor in order to minimize confusion and misdirection. (p. 33)

unity of direction The bureaucratic principle that holds that there should be only one leader and one plan for organizing activities to accomplish an objective. (p. 40)

V

values Enduring beliefs that influence the choices made by individuals, groups, or organizations from among available means or ends. (p. 14)

vertical constituency department Also referred to as line departments, these are the organizations that have primary responsibility for delivery of programs and services to citizens. (p. 97)

visible minority A person (other than an Aboriginal person) who is non-white in colour/race, regardless of place of birth. (p. 289)

W

wholly-owned subsidiary These are corporate entities whereby 100 percent of their shares are owned by one or more parent Crown corporations. (p. 117)

Bibliography

Chapter 1

Gow, Iain. "Evolution of Disciplinary Approaches and Paradigms in the Study of Public Administration in Canada." In *The Evolving Physiology of Government: Canadian Public Administration in Transition*, edited by O.P. Dwivedi, Tim A. Mau, and Byron Sheldrick. Ottawa: University of Ottawa Press, 2009.

Harell, Allison, and Lyne Deschâtelets. "Political Culture(s) in Canada: Orientations to Politics in a Pluralist, Multicultural Federation." In *Canadian Politics*, 6th edition, edited by James Bickerton and Alain-G. Gagnon. Toronto: University of Toronto Press, 2014, 229–248.

Henry, Nicholas. *Public Administration and Public Affairs*, 11th edition. Toronto: Pearson, 2010.

Jaskyte, Kristina. "Work Values of Public, Nonprofit, and Business Employees: A Cross-Cultural Evidence." *International Journal of Public Administration*, 39(3) (2016): 184–193.

Johnson, David. *Thinking Government: Public Administration and Politics in Canada*, 3rd edition. Toronto: University of Toronto Press, 2011.

Kernaghan, Kenneth. "Public Administration." *The Canadian Encyclopedia*. http://www.thecanadianencyclopedia. ca/en/article/public-administration/ (accessed July 10, 2016).

——————. "Speaking Truth to Academics: The Wisdom of Practitioners," *Canadian Public Administration* 52(4) (December 2009): 503–523.

Kernaghan, Kenneth, Brian Marson, and Sandford Borins. *The New Public Organization*. Toronto: The Institute of Public Administration of Canada, 2000.

Kettl, Donald. *The Global Public Management Revolution*, 2nd edition. Washington, D.C.: The Brookings Institution, 2005.

Lyonds, Sean T., Linda E. Duxbury, and Christopher Higgins. "A Comparison of Values and Commitment of Private Sector, Public Sector and Parapublic Employees." *Public Administration Review* 66(4) (2006): 605–618.

MacGregor Dawson, R. *The Civil Service of Canada*. Oxford: Oxford University Press, 1929.

Malloy, Jonathan. "The Next Generation? Recruitment and Renewal in the Federal Public Service." In *How Ottawa Spends 2004–2005: Mandate Change in the Paul Martin Era*, edited by G. Bruce Doern. Montreal & Kingston: McGill-Queen's University Press, 2004, 277–295.

Moore, Mark. "Managing for Value: Organizational Strategy in For-Profit, Nonprofit, and Governmental Organizations." *Nonprofit and Voluntary Sector Quarterly* 29(1) (2000): 183–208.

Nutt, Paul. "Comparing Public and Private Sector Decision-Making Practices." *Journal of Public Administration Research and Theory* 16(1) (2005): 289–318.

Painter, Martin, and B. Guy Peters. "The Analysis of Administrative Traditions." In *Tradition and Public Administration*, edited by Martin Painter and B. Guy Peters. Basingstoke: Palgrave Macmillan, 2010, 3–16.

Pal, Leslie A. *Beyond Policy Analysis: Public Issue Management in Turbulent Times*, 5th edition. Toronto: Nelson Education, 2014.

Peters, B. Guy, and Jon Pierre. "Introduction: The Role of Public Administration in Governing." In *The Sage Handbook of Public Administration*, Concise Second Edition, edited by B. Guy Peters and Jon Pierre. London: Sage Publications, 2014, 1–11.

Pfiffner, John M., and Robert Presthus. *Public Administration*, 5th edition. New York: Ronald Press, 1967.

Prince, Michael. "New Mandate, New Money, New Politics: Federal Budgeting in the Post-Deficit Era." In *How Ottawa Spends, 1998–1999: Balancing Act—The Post-Deficit Mandate*, edited by Leslie Pal. Toronto: Oxford University Press, 1998, 31–55.

Rasmussen, Ken. "The Administrative Liberalism of R. MacGregor Dawson." *Canadian Public Administration* 33(1) (Spring 1990): 37–51.

Richardson, Ivan L., and Sidney Baldwin. *Public Administration: Government in Action*. Columbus, Ohio: Charles E. Merrill, 1976.

Savoie, Donald J. *Whatever Happened to the Music Teacher? How Government Decides and Why*. Montreal & Kingston: McGill-Queen's University Press, 2013.

Thomas, Paul. "Two Cheers for Bureaucracy: Canada's Public Service." In *Canadian Politics*, 6th edition, edited by James Bickerton and Alain-G. Gagnon. Toronto: University of Toronto Press, 2014, 177–198.

Villard, H.S., and W.W. Willoughby. *The Canadian Budgetary System*. New York: Appleton, 1918.

Wake Carroll, Barbara. "Making It Happen: An Introduction to Public Administration in Canada" In *Approaching Public Administration: Core Debates and Emerging Issues*, edited by Roberto P. Leone and Frank L.K. Ohemeng. Toronto: Emond Montgomery Publications, 2011, 1–8.

Wilson, James Q. *Bureaucracy: What Government Agencies Do and Why They Do It*. New York: Basic Books, 1989.

Woll, Peter, editor. *Public Administration and Policy*. New York: Harper & Row, 1966.

Chapter 2

Aucoin, Peter. "New Political Governance in Westminster Systems: Impartial Public Administration and Management Performance at Risk." *Governance* 25(2) (March 2012): 177–199.

_____. "New Public Management and New Public Governance: Finding the Balance." In *Professionalism and Public Service: Essays in Honour of Kenneth Kernaghan*, edited by David Siegel and Ken Rasmussen. Toronto: University of Toronto Press, 2008, 16–33.

Canadian Broadcasting Corporation. "Budget Watchdog Questions Flaherty's Deficit Accounting." November 29, 2012. http://www.cbc.ca/news/politics/budget-watchdog-questions-flaherty-s-deficit-accounting-1.1173709 (accessed July 19, 2016).

Conteh, Charles. "Rethinking Accountability in Complex and Horizontal Network Delivery Systems." *Canadian Public Administration* 59(2)(2016): 224–244.

Dimock, Susan, et al. *Ethics and the Public Service: Trust, Integrity, and Democracy.* Toronto: Nelson, 2013.

Dowdell, R.H. "Public Personnel Administration." In *Public Administration in Canada,* 4th edition, edited by Kenneth Kernaghan. Toronto: Methuen, 1982.

Finer, Herman. "Administrative Responsibility in Democratic Government." *Public Administration Review* 1(4) (1941): 335–350.

_____. "Better Government Personnel." *Political Science Quarterly* 51(4) (December 1936): 569–599.

Friedrich, Carl J. "Public Policy and the Nature of Administrative Responsibility." In *Public Policy*, edited by Carl J. Friedrich and Edward S. Mason. Cambridge: Harvard University Press, 1940.

_____. "Responsible Government Service under the American Constitution." In Carl J. Friedrich, William Carl Beyer, Sterling Denhard Spero, John Francis Miller, and George A. Graham, *Problems of the American Public Service.* New York: McGraw-Hill, 1935.

Government of Canada. *Values Alive: A Discussion Guide to the "Values and Ethics Code for the Public Sector."* http://www.tbs-sct.gc.ca/psm-fpfm/ve/code/va-vaq-eng.asp (accessed June 25, 2016).

_____. *Values and Ethics Code for the Public Sector.* Ottawa: Her Majesty the Queen in Right of Canada, 2011.

_____. *Values and Ethics Code for the Public Service: Democratic, Professional, Ethical and People Values.* https://www.tbs-sct.gc.ca/pubs_pol/hrpubs/tb_851/vec-cve-eng.pdf (accessed July 19, 2016).

Government of Ontario. Reg. 381/07: Conflict of Interest Rules for Public Servants (Ministry) and Former Public Servants (Ministry). https://www.ontario.ca/laws/regulation/070381 (accessed June 27, 2016).

Heintzman, Ralph. "Public-Service Values and Ethics: Dead End or Strong Foundation?" *Canadian Public Administration* 50(4) (2007): 573–602.

Jarvis, Mark D., and Paul G. Thomas, "The Limits of Accountability: What Can and Cannot Be Accomplished in the Dialectics of Accountability?" In *From New Public Management to New Political Governance: Essays in Honour of Peter C. Aucoin*, edited by Herman Bakvis and Mark D. Jarvis. Montreal & Kingston: McGill-Queen's University Press, 2012, 271–313.

Kernaghan, Kenneth. "Political Rights and Political Neutrality: Finding the Balance Point." *Canadian Public Administration* 29(4) (Winter 1986): 639–652.

Kernaghan, Kenneth, Brian Marson, and Sandford Borins. *The New Public Organization.* Toronto: Institute of Public Administration of Canada, 2000.

Langford, John W. "Acting on Values: An Ethical Dead End for Public Servants." *Canadian Public Administration* 47(4) (2004): 429–450.

Mosher, Frederick C. *Democracy and the Public Service.* New York: Oxford University Press, 1968.

O'Neill, Tim. *Review of Canadian Federal Forecasting: Processes and Systems.* June 2005.

Savoie, Donald J. *Thatcher, Reagan, Mulroney: In Search of a New Bureaucracy.* Toronto: University of Toronto, 1994.

_____. *Whatever Happened to the Music Teacher? How Government Decides and Why.* Montreal & Kingston: McGill-Queen's University Press, 2013.

Task Force on Public Service Values and Ethics. *A Strong Foundation: Report of the Task Force on Public Service Values and Ethics.* Ottawa: Canadian Centre for Management Development, 1996.

Thomas, Paul G. "The Changing Nature of Accountability." In *Taking Stock: Assessing Public Sector Reforms*, edited by B. Guy Peters and Donald J. Savoie. Montreal & Kingston: McGill-Queen's University Press, 1998, 348–393.

_____. "Two Cheers for Bureaucracy: Canada's Public Service." In *Canadian Politics*, 6th edition, edited by James Bickerton and Alain-G. Gagnon. Toronto: University of Toronto Press, 2014, 177–198.

Tupper, Alan, and Lori Turnbull. "The Ethics of Public Service and the Challenge of Public Service Ethics." In *From New Public Management to New Political Governance: Essays in Honour of Peter C. Aucoin*, edited by Herman Bakvis and Mark D. Jarvis. Montreal & Kingston: McGill-Queen's University Press, 2012, 46–69.

Chapter 3

Albrow, Martin. *Bureaucracy.* London: Macmillan, 1970.

Andrews, Rhys, and Marc Esteve, "Still Like Ships that Pass in the Night? The Relationship Between Public Administration and Management Studies." *International Public Management Journal* 18(1) (2015): 31–60.

Aucoin, Peter. "The Design of Public Organizations for the 21st Century: Why Bureaucracy Will Survive in Public Management." *Canadian Public Administration* 40(2) (Summer 1997): 290–306.

Barnard, Chester. *The Functions of the Executive*. Cambridge, MA: Harvard University Press, 1962.

Barzelay, Michael. *Breaking Through Bureaucracy: A New Vision for Managing Government*. Berkeley and Los Angeles, CA: University of California Press, 1992.

Bassett, Glenn. "From Job Fit to Cultural Compatibility: Evaluating Worker Skills and Temperament in the '90s." *Optimum* 25(1) (Summer 1994): 11–17.

Beetham, David. *Bureaucracy*, 2nd ed. Minneapolis: University of Minnesota Press, 1996.

Blau, Peter, and Richard W. Scott. *Formal Organizations*. San Francisco: Chandler, 1962.

Budd, Leslie. "Post-Bureaucracy and Reanimating Public Governance: A Discourse and Practice of Continuity?" *International Journal of Public Sector Management* 20(6) (2007): 531–547.

Dawson, R. MacGregor. "The Canadian Civil Service." *Canadian Journal of Economics and Political Science* 2(3) (August 1936): 288–300.

Denhardt, Robert B., and Thomas J. Catlaw. *Theories of Public Organization*, 7th ed. Stamford, CT: Cengage Learning, 2015.

Fayol, Henri. *General and Industrial Management*, translated by Constance Storrs. London: Pitman, 1971.

Gilbreth, Frank B., Jr., and Ernestine Gilbreth Carey. *Cheaper by the Dozen*. New York: Thomas Y. Crowell, 1948.

Good, David A. *The Politics of Public Management: The HRDC Audit of Grants and Contributions*. Toronto: University of Toronto Press, 2003.

Goodsell, Charles. *The Case for Bureaucracy: A Public Administration Polemic*, 3rd ed. Chatham, NJ: Chatham House Publishers, 1994.

Gulick, Luther. "Notes on the Theory of Organization." In *Papers on the Science of Administration*, edited by Luther Gulick and Lyndall Urwick. New York: Augustus M. Kelley, 1969.

Harmon, Michael M., and Richard T. Mayer. *Organization Theory for Public Administration*. Boston: Little, Brown, 1986.

Hodgetts, J.E., William McCloskey, Reginald Whitaker, and V. Seymour Wilson. *The Biography of an Institution: The Civil Service Commission of Canada, 1908–1967*. Montreal: McGill-Queen's University Press, 1972.

Kernaghan, Kenneth, Brian Marson, and Sandford Borins. *The New Public Organization*. Toronto: Institute of Public Administration of Canada, 2000.

Lindquist, Evert. "Public Administration Research and Organization Theory: Recovering Alternative Perspectives on Public Service Institutions." In *The Physiology of Government: Canadian Public Administration in Transition*, edited by O.P. Dwivedi, Tim A. Mau, and Byron Sheldrick. Ottawa: University of Ottawa Press, 2009, 40–71.

McLaren, Robert I. *Organizational Dilemmas*. Chichester, U.K.: John Wiley & Sons, 1982.

McLean, Jesse, and David Bruser. "Inside Ottawa's Fight with a Drug Giant." *Toronto Star*, June 1, 2015.

Meier, Kenneth J., and John Bohte. "Span of Control and Public Organizations: Implementing Luther Gulick's Research Design." *Public Administration Review* 63(1) (January/February 2003): 61–70.

Merton, Robert K. "Bureaucratic Structure and Personality." *Social Forces* 18(4) (1940): 560–568.

Olsen, Johan P. "Maybe It Is Time to Rediscover Bureaucracy." *Journal of Public Administration Research and Theory* 16(1) (January 2006): 1–24.

Osbaldeston, Gordon F. *Organizing to Govern*. Toronto: McGraw-Hill Ryerson, 1992.

Osborne, David, and Peter Plastrik. *Banishing Bureaucracy: The Five Strategies for Reinventing Government*. Reading, MA: Addison-Wesley Publishing Company Inc., 1997.

Osborne, David, and Ted Gaebler. *Reinventing Government: How the Entrepreneurial Spirit Is Transforming the Public Sector*. Reading, MA: Addison-Wesley Publishing Company Inc., 1992.

Pfeffer, Jeffrey. "Like Ships Passing in the Night: The Separate Literatures of Organization Theory and Public Management." *International Public Management Journal* 9(4) (2006): 457–465.

Raadschelders, Jos, and Eran Vigoda-Gadot. *Global Dimensions of Public Administration and Governance: A Comparative Voyage*. Hoboken, NJ: John Wiley & Sons, 2015.

Riggs, Fred W. "Introduction: Shifting Meanings of the Term 'Bureaucracy.'" *International Social Science Journal* XXXI(4) (1979): 563–584.

Selznick, Philip. "Foundations of the Theory of Organization." *American Sociological Review* 13(1) (1948): 25–35.

Shafritz, Jay M., J. Steven Ott, and Yong Suk Jang, editors. *Classics of Organization Theory*, 8th edition. Toronto: Harcourt College Publishers, 2015.

Simon, Herbert. *Administrative Behavior*. New York: The Free Press, 1957.

Tompkins, Jonathan R. *Organization Theory and Public Management*. Belmont, CA: Thomson Wadsworth, 2005.

Weber, Max. *Economy and Society: An Outline of Interpretative Sociology*, edited by Guenther Roth and Claus Wittich. Berkeley: University of California Press, 1978.

Winslow Taylor, Frederick. *The Principles of Scientific Management*. New York: W.W. Norton, 1967.

Wulf, Julie. "The Flattened Firm: Not as Advertised." *California Management Review* 55(1) (Fall 2012): 5–23.

Chapter 4

Argyris, Chris. *Integrating the Individual and the Organization*. New York: John Wiley & Sons, 1964.

_____. *Personality and Organization: The Conflict Between System and the Individual*. New York: Harper & Row, 1957.

Cohen, Steven, and Ronald Brand. *Total Quality Management in Government*. San Francisco: Jossey-Bass Publishers, 1993.

Deming, W. Edwards. *Quality, Productivity, and Competitive Position.* Cambridge, MA: Massachusetts Institute of Technology, Center for Advanced Engineering Study, 1982.

Denhardt, Robert B. *Public Administration: An Action Orientation.* Pacific Grove, CA: Brooks/Cole Publishing Company, 1991.

——————. *Theories of Public Organization.* Pacific Grove, CA: Brooks/Cole, 1984.

Drucker, Peter F. *The Practice of Management.* New York: Harper & Row, 1954.

Easton, David. *A Framework for Political Analysis.* Englewood Cliffs, NJ: Prentice-Hall, 1965.

Etzioni, Amitai. *Modern Organizations.* Englewood Cliffs, NJ: Prentice-Hall, 1964.

Feigenbaum, Armand V. "Linking Quality Processes to International Leadership." In *Making Total Quality Happen,* edited by Frank Caropreso. New York: The Conference Board, 1990.

Flumian, Maryantonett, Amanda Coe, and Kenneth Kernaghan. "Transforming Service to Canadians: The Service Canada Model." *International Review of Administrative Sciences* 73(4) (December 2007): 557–568.

Follett, Mary Parker. *Creative Experience.* New York: Peter Smith, 1951.

——————. *Dynamic Administration: The Collected Papers of Mary Parker Follett,* edited by Elliot M. Fox and L. Urwick. London: Pitman, 1973.

——————. *The New State.* Gloucester, MA: Peter Smith, 1965.

French, John, and Bertram Raven. "The Bases of Social Power." In *Studies in Social Power,* edited by Dorwin Cartwright. Ann Arbor, MI: The University of Michigan, 1959, 150–167.

Galbraith, Jay. *Designing Complex Organizations.* Reading, MA: Addison-Wesley, 1973.

Garvin, David A., and Artemis March. "A Note on Quality: The Views of Deming, Juran, and Crosby." In Harvard Business Review, *Unconditional Quality.* Boston, MA: Harvard Business School Press, 1991.

Golembiewski, Robert T. *Humanizing Public Organizations.* Mt. Airy, MD: Lomond Press, 1985.

Hackman, J. Richard, and Greg R. Oldham. *Work Redesign.* Reading, MA: Addison-Wesley, 1980.

Harmon, Michael M., and Richard T. Mayer. *Organization Theory for Public Administration.* Boston, MA: Little, Brown, 1986.

Heffron, Florence. *Organization Theory and Public Organizations.* Englewood Cliffs, NJ: Prentice-Hall, 1989.

Herzberg, Frederick. "One More Time: How Do You Motivate Employees?" *Harvard Business Review* 46 (January/February 1968): 59–62.

——————. *Work and the Nature of Man.* Cleveland: The World Publishing Company, 1966.

Herzberg, Frederick, Bernard Mausner, and Barbara Bloch Snyderman. *The Motivation to Work.* New York: John Wiley & Sons, 1959.

Jablonski, Joseph R. *Implementing Total Quality Management: An Overview.* San Diego: Pfeiffer & Company, 1991.

Jaques, Elliott. "In Praise of Hierarchy." *Harvard Business Review* 68(1) (January–February 1990).

Katz, Daniel, and Robert L. Kahn. *The Social Psychology of Organizations.* New York: John Wiley & Sons, 1966.

Kernaghan, Kenneth, Brian Marson, and Sandford Borins. *The New Public Organization.* Toronto: IPAC, 2000.

Lasswell, Harold. *Politics: Who Gets What, When and How.* New York: McGraw-Hill, 1936.

Lewin, Kurt. "Frontiers in Group Dynamics." *Human Relations* 1(1) (1947): 5–40.

Marson, Brian. "Building Customer-Focused Organizations in British Columbia." *Public Administration Quarterly* 17(1) (Spring 1993): 30–41.

Martin, Denis. "Culture and Client Service at the Department of Fisheries and Oceans." *Optimum* 24 (Winter 1993): 99–104.

Maslow, Abraham H. *Eupsychian Management.* Homewood, IL: Dorsey Press, 1965.

——————. *Motivation and Personality.* New York: Harper & Row, 1970.

McGregor, Douglas. *The Human Side of Enterprise.* New York: McGraw-Hill, 1960.

Moss Kanter, Rosabeth. "Power Failure in Management Circuits." *Harvard Business Review* 57(4) (July–August 1979): 65–75.

Office of the Chief Human Resources Officer. *2014 Public Service Employee Survey: Summary Report.* Ottawa: Her Majesty the Queen in Right of Canada, February 2015. www.tbs-sct.gc.ca/psm-fpfm/modernizing-modernisation/pses-saff/dr-rd-eng.pdf (accessed August 6, 2016).

Perrow, Charles. *Complex Organizations: A Critical Essay.* Glenview, IL: Scott, Foresman, 1972.

Peters, B. Guy. *The Politics of Bureaucracy: An Introduction to Comparative Public Administration,* 6th edition. New York: Routledge, 2010.

Pfeffer, Jeffrey. *Managing with Power: Politics and Influence in Organizations.* Boston, MA: Harvard Business School Press, 1994.

Rahnema, Saeed. *Organization Structure: A Systemic Approach.* Toronto: McGraw-Hill Ryerson, 1992.

Rankin, Tom, and Archie Gardner. "New Forms of Work Organization in the Federal Public Service: The Case of CFB Shearwater/UNDE Local 80409." *Optimum* 24 (Spring 1994): 25–36.

Robey, Daniel. *Designing Organizations,* 3rd ed. Homewood, IL: Richard D. Irwin, 1990.

Roethlisberger, F. J.. and William J. Dickson. *Management and the Worker.* Cambridge, MA: Harvard University Press, 1964.

Sashkin, Marshall, and Kenneth J. Kiser. *Putting Total Quality Management to Work.* San Francisco: Berrett-Koehler Publishers, 1993.

Savoie, Donald J. *Power: Where Is It?* Montreal and Kingston: McGill-Queen's University Press, 2010.

Shafritz, Jay M., and J. Steven Ott, editors. *Classics of Organization Theory*, 5th ed. Toronto: Harcourt College Publishers, 2001.

Tompkins, Jonathan R. *Organization Theory and Public Management*. Belmont, CA: Thomson Wadsworth, 2005.

Wilson, V. Seymour. "The Influence of Organization Theory in Canadian Public Administration." *Canadian Public Administration* 25(4) (Winter 1982): 545–563.

Chapter 5

Aberbach, Joel D., and Tom Christensen. "Citizens and Consumers: An NPM Dilemma." *Public Management Review* 7(2) (2005): 225–245.

Aucoin, Peter. "New Public Management and New Public Governance: Finding the Balance." In *Professionalism and Public Service: Essays in Honour of Kenneth Kernaghan*, edited by David Siegel and Ken Rasmussen. Toronto: University of Toronto Press, 2008, 16–33.

_____. *The New Public Management: Canada in Comparative Perspective*. Montreal: IRPP, 1995.

Bakvis, Herman, and Luc Juillet. *The Horizontal Challenge: Line Departments, Central Agencies and Leadership*. Ottawa: Canada School of Public Service, 2004.

Bao, Guoxian, Xuejun Wang, Gary Larsen, and Douglas Morgan. "Beyond New Public Governance: A Value-Based Global Framework for Performance Management, Governance and Leadership." *Administration & Society* 45(4) (2012): 443–467.

Barzelay, Michael, with the collaboration of Babak J. Armajani. *Breaking Through Bureaucracy: A New Vision for Managing in Government*. Berkeley: University of California Press, 1992.

Benzie, Robert. "Queen's Park to Hire Guru for Online Services." *Toronto Star*. June 15, 2016.

Boutilier, Alex. "Ottawa in Internet Dark Ages." *Toronto Star*. March 15, 2016.

Brown, David. "Information, Technology and Canadian Public Administration." In *The Handbook of Canadian Public Administration*, 2nd ed., edited by Christopher Dunn. Toronto: Oxford University Press, 2010, 521–537.

Bryson, John, Barbara Crosby, and Laura Bloomberg, editors. *Public Value and Public Administration*. Washington, DC: Georgetown University Press, 2015.

Christensen, Tom, and Per Lægreid. "Governance and Administrative Reforms." In *The Oxford Handbook of Governance*, edited by David Levi-Faur. Oxford: Oxford University Press, 2012, 255–267.

_____. "The Whole-of-Government Approach to Public Sector Reform." *Public Administration Review* 67(6) (Nov/Dec 2007): 1059–1066.

Clerk of the Privy Council. *Fifth Annual Report to the Prime Minister on the Public Service of Canada*. Ottawa: Privy Council Office, 1998. www.clerk.gc.ca/eng/feature.asp?pageId=150 (accessed June 24, 2016).

Denhardt, Janet V., and Robert B. Denhardt. *The New Public Service: Serving, Not Steering*. Armonk, NY: M.E. Sharpe, 2003.

Denhardt, Robert B. *The Pursuit of Significance: Strategies for Managerial Success in Public Organizations*. Belmont, CA: Wadsworth Publishing Company, 1993.

Doern, G. Bruce, and Christopher Stoney. "The Harper Majority, Budget Cuts and the New Opposition." In *How Ottawa Spends, 2012–2013: The Harper Majority, Budget Cuts and the New Opposition*, edited by G. Bruce Doern and Christopher Stoney. Montreal and Kingston: McGill-Queen's University Press, 2012, 3–34.

Dunleavy, Patrick, Helen Margetts, Simon Bastow, and Jane Tinkler. "New Public Management Is Dead—Long Live Digital-Era Governance." *Journal of Public Administration Research and Theory* 16(3) (July 2006): 467–494.

Dwivedi, O.P., and James Iain Gow. *From Bureaucracy to New Public Management: The Administrative Culture of the Government of Canada*. Peterborough: Broadview Press, 1999.

Eliassen, Kjell, and Nick Sitter, *Understanding Public Management*. London: Sage Publications, 2008.

Goldsmith, Stephen, and William Eggers. *Governing by Network: The New Shape of the Public Sector*. Washington, DC: The Brookings Institute, 2004.

Good, David A. *The Politics of Public Management: The HRDC Audit of Grants and Contributions*. Toronto: Institute of Public Administration of Canada and the University of Toronto Press, 2003.

Government of Canada. *Horizontal Initiatives Database*. www.tbs-sct.gc.ca/hidb-bdih/home-accueil-eng.aspx.

Gow, Iain. "Evolution of Disciplinary Approaches and Paradigms in the Study of Public Administration in Canada." In *The Evolving Physiology of Government: Canadian Public Administration in Transition*, edited by O.P. Dwivedi, Tim A. Mau, and Byron Sheldrick. Ottawa: University of Ottawa Press, 2009, 2–39.

Gruening, Gernod. "Origin and Theoretical Basis of New Public Management." *International Public Management Journal* 4 (2001): 1–25.

Halligan, John. "A Comparative Perspective on Canadian Public Administration Within an Anglophone Tradition." In *The Evolving Physiology of Government: Canadian Administration in Transition*, edited by O.P. Dwivedi, Tim A. Mau, and Byron Sheldrick. Ottawa: University of Ottawa Press, 2009, 292–311.

Hood, C. "A Public Management for All Seasons?" *Public Administration* 69(1) (March 1991): 3–19.

Kernaghan, Kenneth, Brian Marson, and Sandford Borins. *The New Public Organization*. Toronto: Institute of Public Administration of Canada, 2000.

Kettl, Donald. *The Global Public Management Revolution*. Washington, DC: Brookings Institution Press, 2005.

Lodge, Martin, and Derek Gill. "Toward a New Era of Administrative Reform? The Myth of Post-NPM in New Zealand." *Governance* 24(1) (January 2011): 141–166.

Morgan, Douglas, and Craig Shinn. "The Foundations of New Public Governance." In *New Public Governance: A Regime-Centred Perspective*, edited by Douglas Morgan and Brian Cook. New York: M.E. Sharpe Inc., 2014, 3–12.

Osborne, David, and Ted Gaebler. *Reinventing Government: How the Entrepreneurial Spirit Is Transforming the Public Sector*. Reading, MA: Addison-Wesley, 1992.

Osborne, Stephen. "The (New) Public Governance: A Suitable Case for Treatment?" In *The New Public Governance: Emerging Perspectives on the Theory and Practice of Public Governance*, edited by Stephen Osborne. New York: Routledge, 2010, 1–16.

Osborne, Stephen, Zoe Radnor, and Greta Nasi. "A New Theory for Public Service Management? Toward a (Public) Service-Dominant Approach." *American Review of Public Administration* 43(2) (2012): 135–158.

Peters, B. Guy, and John Pierre. "Governance Without Government? Rethinking Public Administration." *Journal of Public Administration Research and Theory* 8(2) (April 1998): 223–243.

Peters, Thomas J., and Robert H. Waterman, Jr. *In Search of Excellence: Lessons from America's Best-Run Companies*. New York: Harper & Row Publishers, 1982.

Pollitt, Christopher. *The Essential Public Manager*. Maidenhead: Open University Press, 2003.

—————. "How Do We Know How Good Public Services Are?" In *Governance in the Twenty-First Century: Revitalizing the Public Service*, edited by B. Guy Peters and Donald J. Savoie. Montreal & Kingston: McGill-Queen's University Press, 2000, 119–152.

Pollitt, Christopher, and Peter Hupe. "Talking About Government: The Role of Magic Concepts." *Public Management Review* 13(5) (2011): 641–658.

Rhodes, R.A.W. "The New Governance: Governing Without Government." *Political Studies* 44(4) (1996): 652–667.

—————. "Understanding Governance: Ten Years On." *Organization Studies* 28(8) (2007): 1243–1264.

Savoie, Donald J. "What Is Wrong with the New Public Management?" *Canadian Public Administration* 38(1) (Spring 1995): 112–121.

Stark, Andrew. "What Is the New Public Management?" *Journal of Public Administration Research and Theory* 12(1) (January 2002): 137–151.

Stoker, Gerry. "Public Value Management: A New Narrative for Networked Governance?" *American Review of Public Administration* 36(1) (March 2006): 41–57.

Thomas, Paul G. "Why Is Performance-Based Accountability So Popular in Theory and So Difficult in Practice?" In *Holy Grail or Achievable Quest? International Perspectives on Public Sector Performance Management*, edited by John Herhalt. Brussels: KPMG International, 2008, 169–191.

Torfing, Jacob, and Peter Triantafillou. "What's in a Name? Grasping New Public Governance as a Political-Administrative System." *International Review of Public Administration* 18(2) (2013): 9–25.

Treasury Board of Canada Secretariat. *Canada's Action Plan on Open Government, 2014–2016*. Ottawa: Her Majesty the Queen in Right of Canada, 2014. www.open.canada.ca/en/content/canadas-action-plan-open-government-2014-16 (accessed June 24, 2016).

—————. "Whole of Government Framework." www.tbs-sct.gc.ca/ppg-cpr/frame-cadre-eng.aspx (accessed June 24, 2016).

Chapter 6

Atkinson, Michael M., Daniel Béland, Gregory P. Marchildon, et al. *Governance and Public Policy in Canada: A View from the Provinces*. Toronto: University of Toronto Press, 2013.

Aucoin, Peter. "Organizational Change in the Machinery of Canadian Government: From Rational Management to Brokerage Politics." *Canadian Journal of Political Science* 19(1) (March 1986): 3–27.

Axworthy, Thomas S. "Of Secretaries to Princes." *Canadian Public Administration* 31(2) (Summer 1988): 247–264.

Beardsley, Keith. "What It's Really Like to Work in the PMO." *Power & Influence* 4(1) (Winter 2015): 3–5.

Bernier, Luc, Keith Brownsey, and Michael Howlett. *Executive Styles in Canada: Cabinet Structures and Leadership Practices in Canadian Government*. Toronto: University of Toronto Press, 2005.

Brodie, Ian. "In Defence of Political Staff." *Canadian Parliamentary Review* 35(3) (Autumn 2012): 33–39.

Campbell, Colin, and George J. Szablowski. *The Superbureaucrats*. Toronto: Macmillan, 1979.

Canada. Department of Finance. *Jobs, Growth and Long-Term Prosperity: Economic Action Plan 2013*. Ottawa: Her Majesty the Queen in Right of Canada, 2013.

Canada. Department of Transport. *2015-2016 Report on Plans and Priorities*. Ottawa: Her Majesty the Queen in Right of Canada, 2015.

Commission of Inquiry into the Sponsorship Program and Advertising Activities. *Restoring Accountability: Recommendations*. Ottawa: Her Majesty in Right of Canada, 2006.

—————. *Who Is Responsible? Summary*. Ottawa: Her Majesty the Queen in Right of Canada, 2005.

Doern, G. Bruce. "Horizontal and Vertical Portfolios in Government." In *Issues in Canadian Public Policy*, edited by G. Bruce Doern and V. Seymour Wilson. Toronto: Macmillan, 1974.

Doern, G. Bruce, and Richard W. Phidd. *Canadian Public Policy: Ideas, Structure and Process*, 2nd ed. Scarborough: Nelson Canada, 1992.

Fekete, Jason. "Harper's Office Spared Worst of Cuts as Quarter of PM's 100-Strong Staff Paid $100K or More." *The National Post*, April 12, 2002. http://news.nationalpost.com/news/canada/almost-quarter-of-pmo-staff-paid-100k-or-more (accessed September 20, 2015).

Finley, Diane. "Defence Procurement Strategy," speaking notes for the Honourable Diane Finley, Minister of

Public Works and Government Services, announcing the Defence Procurement Strategy. Economic Club of Canada, Ottawa, February 5, 2014. http://www.tpsgc-pwgsc.gc.ca/medias-media/dm-ms/2014-02-04-eng.html (accessed February 15, 2015).

Fraser, Graham. "The Man Who Really Saved the Government." *Toronto Star*, May 22, 2005.

Glor, Eleanor D. "Patterns of Canadian Departmental Survival." *Canadian Public Administration* 54(4) (December 2011): 551–566.

Hodgetts, J.E. *The Canadian Public Service: A Physiology of Government.* Toronto: University of Toronto Press, 1973.

Kelly, James B. *Governing with the Charter: Legislative and Judicial Activism and Framers' Intent.* Vancouver: UBC Press, 2005.

Leblanc, Daniel. "New Chief of Staff Ray Novak has Long Ties to Harper." *Globe and Mail*, May 19, 2013. www.theglobeandmail.com/news/politics/new-chief-of-staff-ray-novak-has-long-ties-to-harper/article12023016 (accessed September 22, 2015).

MacKinnon, Leslie. "How Stephen Harper's Inner Circle Has Changed." *CBC News*, May 24, 2014. www.cbc.ca/news/politics/how-stephen-harpers-inner-circle-has-changed-1.2652571 (accessed September 22, 2015).

Martin, Don. "PM Can't Keep Blaming Messenger." *National Post*, February 22, 2006.

Osbaldeston, Gordon. *Organizing to Govern.* Toronto: McGraw-Hill Ryerson, 1992.

Robertson, Gordon. "The Changing Role of the Privy Council Office." *Canadian Public Administration* 14(4) (Winter 1971): 487–508.

Savoie, Donald J. *Whatever Happened to the Music Teacher?* Montreal and Kingston: McGill-Queen's University Press, 2013.

Studlar, Donley T., and Gary F. Moncrief. "Women's Work? The Distribution and Prestige of Portfolios in the Canadian Provinces." *Governance* 12(4) (October 1999): 379–395.

Treasury Board of Canada Secretariat. *Report on Plans and Priorities 2015–16.* Ottawa: Her Majesty the Queen in Right of Canada, 2015.

Tremblay, Manon, and Daniel Stockemer. "Women's Ministerial Concerns in Cabinet, 1921–2010: A Look at Socio-Demographic Traits and Career Experiences." *Canadian Public Administration* 56(4) (December 2013): 523–541.

Chapter 7

Armstrong, Robert. *Broadcasting Policy in Canada*, 2nd edition. Toronto: University of Toronto Press, 2016.

Benzie, Robert. "Hydro One's New Share Offer Should Raise $1.7B." *Toronto Star*, April 5, 2016. www.thestar.com/news/queenspark/2016/04/05/next-wave-of-hydro-one-shares-for-sale-soon.html (accessed June 6, 2016).

Bergevin, Philippe, and Finn Poschmann. *Reining in the Risks: Rethinking the Role of Crown Financial Corporations in Canada.* C.D. Howe Institute Commentary No. 372. Toronto: C.D. Howe Institute, February 2013.

Bernier, Luc. "The Future of Public Enterprises: Perspectives from the Canadian Experience," *Annals of Public and Cooperative Economics* 82(4) (2011): 399–419.

Bird, Malcolm G. "Alberta's and Ontario's Liquor Boards: Why Such Divergent Outcomes?" *Canadian Public Administration* 53(4) (December 2010): 509–530.

_____. "Canadian State-Owned Enterprises: A Framework for Analyzing the Evolving Crowns." *Policy Studies* 36(2) (2015): 133–156.

Boardman, Anthony, and Aidan Vining. "A Review and Assessment of Privatization in Canada." University of Calgary School of Public Policy *SPP Research Papers* 5(4) (January 2012): 1–31.

Borins, Sandford F. "World War Two Crown Corporations: Their Wartime Role and Peacetime Privatization." *Canadian Public Administration* 25(2) (Fall 1982): 380–404.

Canadian Broadcasting Corporation. #*Creating Connections: Annual Report, 2014–2015.* Ottawa: CBC/Radio-Canada Corporate Communications, 2015.

Canadian Food Inspection Agency. *2016–2017 Report on Plans and Priorities.* Ottawa: Her Majesty the Queen in Right of Canada, 2016.

Carpenter, Daniel, and David Moss, editors. *Preventing Regulatory Capture: Special Interest Influence and How to Limit It.* New York: Cambridge University Press, 2014.

Crisan, Daria, and Kenneth J. McKenzie. "Government-Owned Enterprises in Canada." University of Calgary School of Public Policy *SPP Research Papers* 6(8) (February 2013): 1–29.

Doern, G. Bruce. *Red Tape, Red Flags: Regulation for the Innovation Age.* Ottawa: Conference Board of Canada, 2007.

_____. "Smart Regulation, Regulatory Congestion and Natural Resources Regulatory Governance." In *How Ottawa Spends 2004–2005: Mandate Change in the Paul Martin Era*, edited by G. Bruce Doern. Montreal & Kingston: McGill-Queen's University Press, 2004, 245–274.

Dyck, Rand, and Christopher Cochrane. *Canadian Politics: Critical Approaches*, 7th edition. Toronto: Nelson, 2014.

Economic Council of Canada. *Reforming Regulation.* Ottawa: Minister of Supply and Services, 1981.

External Advisory Committee on Smart Regulation. *Smart Regulation: A Regulatory Strategy for Canada.* September 2004. http://publications.gc.ca/collections/Collection/CP22-78-2004E.pdf (accessed June 8, 2016).

Financial Consumer Agency of Canada. *2016–2017 Business Plan.* Ottawa: Her Majesty the Queen in Right of Canada, 2016.

Harris, Stephen. "The Global Financial Meltdown and Financial Regulation: Shirking and Learning—Canada in an International Context." In *How Ottawa Spends, 2010–2011: Recession, Realignment and the New Deficit*

Era, edited by G. Bruce Doern and Christopher Stoney. Montreal and Kingston: McGill-Queen's University Press, 2010, 68–86.

Hodgetts, J.E. *The Canadian Public Service: A Physiology of Government, 1867–1970*. Toronto: University of Toronto Press, 1976.

Iacobucci, Edward M., and Michael J. Trebilcock. "The Role of Crown Corporations in the Canadian Economy: An Analytical Framework." University of Calgary School of Public Policy *SPP Research Papers* 5(9) (March 2012): 1–41.

Ireland, Derek, and Kernaghan Webb. "The Canadian Escape from the Subprime Crisis? Comparing the US and Canadian Approaches." In *How Ottawa Spends, 2010–2011: Recession, Realignment and the New Deficit Era*, edited by G. Bruce Doern and Christopher Stoney. Montreal and Kingston: McGill-Queen's University Press, 2010, 87–106.

Johnson, David. "Regulatory Agencies and Accountability: An Ontario Perspective." *Canadian Public Administration* 34(3) (Autumn 1991): 417–434.

Johnson, David. *Thinking Government: Public Administration and Politics in Canada*, 3rd edition. Toronto: University of Toronto Press, 2011.

Liquor Control Board of Ontario. *Let's Get Together: Annual Report 2014–2015*. Toronto: LCBO Corporate Communications, 2015.

National Energy Board. Board Member Operating Model, February 2016. www.neb-one.gc.ca/bts/whwr/gvrnnc/brdmmbrprtngmdl-eng.pdf (accessed May 19, 2016).

O'Brien, Audrey, and Marc Bosc, editors. *House of Commons Procedure and Practice*, 2nd edition. Ottawa: House of Commons, 2009.

Organisation for Economic Cooperation and Development. *Canada: Maintaining Leadership Through Innovation*. Paris: OECD, 2002.

Privy Council Office. *A Guide Book for Heads of Agencies: Operations, Structures and Responsibilities in the Federal Government*. Ottawa: Privy Council Office, August 1999. www.pco-bcp.gc.ca/index.asp?lang=eng&page=informatioon&sub=publications&doc=guide2/table-eng.htm (accessed May 15, 2016).

_____. *Guide to Making Federal Acts and Regulations*, 2nd edition. Ottawa: Her Majesty the Queen in Right of Canada, 2001.

Statistics Canada. "Mandate and Objectives." www.statcan.gc.ca/eng/about/mandate (accessed May 15, 2016).

Sossin, Lorne. "Does Independence Matter? From Elections Canada to the Nuclear Watchdog, the Harper Government Seems to Disagree." *Literary Review of Canada* (July-August 2008). www.reviewcanada.ca/magazine/2008/07/does-independence-matter/ (accessed June 1, 2016).

Stemshorn, Barry, and Robert W. Slater. "Potential for a Regulatory Breakthrough? Regulatory Governance and Human Resource Initiatives." In *How Ottawa Spends, 2008–2009: A More Orderly Federalism?* edited by

Allan M. Maslove. Montreal and Kingston: McGill-Queen's University Press, 2008, 59–81.

Strick, John. *The Economics of Government Regulation: Theory and Canadian Practice*. Toronto: Thompson Educational Publishing Inc., 1994.

_____. "Regulation and Deregulation." In *The Handbook of Canadian Public Administration*, 1st edition, edited by Christopher Dunn. Toronto: Oxford University Press, 2002, 263–278.

Treasury Board of Canada Secretariat. *Midterm Evaluation of the Implementation of the Cabinet Directive on Streamlining Regulation*. Ottawa: Treasury Board, May 2011. www.tbs-sct.gc.ca/report/orp/2011/cdsr-dcrrtb-eng.asp (accessed June 8, 2016).

_____. "Overview of Institutional Forms and Definitions." http://www.tbs-sct.gc.ca/hgw-cgf/finances/rgs-erdg/cc-se/institution/forms-formulaires-eng.asp (accessed May 12, 2016).

_____. *Review of the Governance Framework for Canada's Crown Corporations*. Ottawa: Her Majesty the Queen in Right of Canada, 2005.

Trebilcock, M.J., and J.R.S. Prichard. "Crown Corporations: The Calculus of Instrument Choice." In *Crown Corporations in Canada: The Calculus of Instrument Choice*, edited by J. Robert S. Prichard. Toronto: Butterworths, 1983.

Wolf, Charles, Jr. *Markets or Governments: Choosing Between Imperfect Alternatives*, 2nd edition. Cambridge: MIT Press, 1993.

Chapter 8

Aberbach, Joel, and Tom Christensen. "Citizens and Consumers: A NPM Dilemma." *Public Management Review* 7(2) (June 2005): 225–246.

Auditor General of Ontario. *Annual Report, 2014*. Toronto: Queen's Printer for Ontario, 2014. www.auditor.on.ca/en/content/annualreports/arreports/en14/2014AR_en_web.pdf44 (accessed July 6, 2016).

Berardi, Jennifer. "The Niagara Casinos Partnership: Game of Chance?" In *Professionalism and Public Service: Essays in Honour of Kenneth Kernaghan*, edited by David Siegel and Ken Rasmussen. Toronto: University of Toronto Press, 2008, 207–235.

Boardman, Anthony, Matti Siemiatycki, and Aidan Vining. "The Theory and Evidence Concerning Public-Private Partnerships in Canada and Elsewhere." University of Calgary School of Public Policy *SPP Research Papers* 9(12) (March 2016): 1–28.

Brown, David. "The Canada Revenue Agency as Separate Employer: Anomaly or Model for the Future?" *Canadian Public Administration* 52(4) (December 2009): 569–590.

Campion-Smith, Bruce. "Major Canadian Airports Could Be Sold Off." *The Toronto Star*, July 4, 2016.

Canada. *Voluntary Sector Task Force, An Accord Between the Government of Canada and the Voluntary Sector*. Ottawa: Privy Council Office, 2001.

Canadian Council for Public–Private Partnerships. "Canadian PPP Project Database." www.projects. pppcouncil.ca/ccppp/src/public/search-project (accessed July 6, 2016).

Dutil, Patrice, Cosmo Howard, John Langford, and Jeffrey Roy. *The Service State: Reality, Rhetoric and Promise.* Ottawa: University of Ottawa, 2010.

Evans, Bryan, and Halina Sapeha. "Are Non-Government Policy Actors Being Heard? Assessing the New Public Governance in Three Canadian Provinces." *Canadian Public Administration* 58(2) (June 2015): 249–270.

Fafard, Patrick, François Rocher, and Catherine Coté. "Clients, Citizens and Federalism: A Critical Appraisal of Integrated Service Delivery in Canada." *Canadian Public Administration* 52(4) (December 2009): 549–568.

Ford, Robin, and David Zussman. "Alternative Service Delivery: Transcending Boundaries." In *Alternative Service Delivery: Sharing Governance in Canada*, edited by Robin Ford and David Zussman. Toronto: KPMG Centre for Government Foundation and Institute of Public Administration of Canada, 1997.

Good, David A., and Barry Carin. "Alternative Service Delivery," August 2003. Draft, prepared by the Canadian Team as part of the CEPRA project on "Sector and Regional Specifics of Reformation of Budgetary Institutions".

Heintzman, Ralph, and Brian Marson. "People, Service and Trust: Is There a Public Sector Service Value Chain?" *International Review of Administrative Sciences* 71(4) (December 2005): 549–575.

Hjartarson, Josh, Alexandra Schwenger, and Liam McGuinty. *Unlocking the Public Service Economy in Ontario: A New Approach to Public–Private Partnership in Services.* Toronto: Ontario Chamber of Commerce, 2014.

Kernaghan, Kenneth. "Moving Towards Integrated Public Governance: Improving Service Delivery Through Community Engagement." *International Review of Administrative Sciences* 75(2) (2009): 239–254.

——————. "Moving Towards the Virtual State: Integrating Services and Service Channels for Citizen-Centred Delivery." *International Review of Administrative Sciences* 71(1)(March 2005): 119–131.

——————. "Putting Citizens First: Service Delivery and Integrated Public Governance." In *The Evolving Physiology of Government: Canadian Public Administration in Transition*, edited by O.P. Dwivedi, Tim A. Mau, and Byron Sheldrick. Ottawa: University of Ottawa Press, 2009, 249–269.

——————. "Serving Seniors: Innovation and Public Sector Service Delivery." *The Innovation Journal: The Public Sector Innovation Journal* 20(2) (2015): 1–18.

Kernaghan, Kenneth, Brian Marson, and Sandford Borins. *The New Public Organization.* Toronto: Institute of Public Administration of Canada, 2000.

Laforest, Rachel. "Shifting Scales of Governance and Civil Society Participation in Canada and the European Union." *Canadian Public Administration* 56(2) (June 2013): 235–251.

Levin, Mike. "Company Booms in Wake of Privatization." *Business Edge News Magazine* (May 2005), http://www.businessedge.ca/archives/article.cfm/company-blooms-in-wake-of-privatization-9579.

NavCanada. "Governance." www.navcanada.ca/EN/about-us/Pages/governance.aspx.

Osborne, David, and Ted Gaebler. *Reinventing Government: How the Entrepreneurial Spirit Is Transforming the Public Sector.* Reading, MA: Addison-Wesley, 1992.

Phillips, Susan, and Karine Levasseur. "The Snakes and Ladders of Accountability: Contradictions Between Contracting and Collaboration for Canada's Voluntary Sector." *Canadian Public Administration* 47(4) (Winter 2004): 451–474.

Reddick, Christopher, and Michael Turner. "Channel Choice and Public Service Delivery in Canada: Comparing E-Government to Traditional Service Delivery." *Government Information Quarterly* 29(1) (January 2012): 1–11.

Roy, Jeffrey. *From Machinery to Mobility: Government and Democracy in a Participative Age.* New York: Springer-Verlag, 2013.

——————. "Gov. 2.0, Mobility and Inclusion: A Critical Examination of Social Assistance Reform in Ontario, Canada." In *Information and Communication Technologies in Public Administration: Innovations from Developed Countries*, edited by Christopher Reddick and Leonidas Anthopoulos. Boca Raton: CRC Press, 2015, 235–254.

Stefanick, Lorna. "Government Outsourcing of Service Provision: Be Careful What You Wish For." In *Approaching Public Administration: Core Debates and Emerging Issues*, edited by Roberto Leone and Frank Ohemeng. Toronto: Emond Montgomery Publications, 2011, 244–254.

Travis, Leah. "National Capital Commission Employee Takeover Corporations." In Deputy Minister Task Force on Service Delivery, *Toward Citizen-Centred Service Delivery: Case Studies.* Ottawa: Canadian Centre for Management Development, 1996.

Treasury Board of Canada Secretariat. "Becoming a Special Operating Agency." https://www.tbs-sct.gc.ca/pubs_pol/opepubs/TB_B4/bsoa-doss01-eng.asp (accessed July 5, 2016).

——————. "Overview of Institutional Forms and Definitions." http://www.tbs-sct.gc.ca/hgw-cgf/finances/rgs-erdg/cc-se/institution/formsformulaires-eng.asp (accessed July 5, 2016).

——————. "Policy on Alternative Service Delivery." April 1, 2002. http://www.tbs-sct.gc.ca/pubs_pol/opepubs/TB_B4/asd-dmps01eng.asp#Toc853882 (accessed June 30, 2016).

Tsasis, Peter. "The Politics of Governance: Government–Voluntary Sector Relationships." *Canadian Public Administration* 51(2) (June 2008): 265–290.

Tumin, Zachary, and Archong Fung. *From Government 2.0 to Society 2.0: Pathways to Engagement, Collaboration and Transformation.* Cambridge: Harvard Kennedy School of Government, 2010.

Vining, Aidan, and Anthony Boardman. "Public–Private Partnerships in Canada: Theory and Evidence." *Canadian Public Administration* 51(1) (March 2008): 9–44.

Zussman, David. "Alternative Service Delivery in Canada." In *The Handbook of Canadian Public Administration*, 2nd edition, edited by Christopher Dunn. Toronto: Oxford University Press, 2010, 250–267.

Chapter 9

Brooks, Stephen. *Canadian Democracy,* 8th edition. Toronto: Oxford University Press, 2015.

Carson, Bruce. *14 Days: Making the Conservative Movement in Canada.* Montreal & Kingston: McGill-Queen's University Press, 2014.

Dahlstrom, C., et al., editors. *Steering from the Centre: Strengthening Political Control in Western Democracies.* Toronto: University of Toronto Press, 2011.

Government of Canada. *Open and Accountable Government: A Guide for Ministers and Ministers of State.* Ottawa: Her Majesty the Queen in Right of Canada, 2015.

Harris, Michael. *Party of One: Stephen Harper and Canada's Radical Makeover.* Toronto: Viking, 2014.

Hockin, Thomas A., editor. *Apex of Power: The Prime Minister and Political Leadership in Canada,* 2nd edition. Scarborough: Prentice-Hall, 1977.

Privy Council Office, *Memorandum to Cabinet,* 2013.

Savoie, Donald J. "The Federal Government: Revisiting Court Government in Canada." In *Executive Styles in Canada: Cabinet Structures and Leadership Practices in Canadian Government,* edited by Luc Bernier, Keith Brownsey, and Michael Howlett. Toronto: University of Toronto Press, 2005.

_____. "Power at the Apex: Executive Dominance." In *Canadian Politics,* 6th edition, edited by James Bickerton and Alain-G. Gagnon. Toronto: University of Toronto Press, 2014.

_____. *Whatever Happened to the Music Teacher? How Government Decides and Why.* Montreal & Kingston: McGill-Queen's University Press, 2013.

Simpson, Jeffrey. *The Friendly Dictatorship.* Toronto: McClelland & Stewart, 2001.

Chapter 10

Akin, David. "Non-Partisan to Partisan: Federal Politicians Pluck their Staff from the Civil Service." *Toronto Sun,* March 15, 2016. http://www.torontosun.com/2016/03/15/non-partisan-to-partisan-federal-politicians-pluck-their-staff-from-the-civil-service (accessed June 21, 2016).

Bakvis, Herman, and Luc Juillet. *The Horizontal Challenge: Line Departments, Central Agencies, and Leadership.* Ottawa: Canada School of Public Service, 2004. http://publications.gc.ca/Collection/SC103-1-2004E.pdf (accessed July 11, 2015).

Benoit, Liane E. "Ministerial Staff: The Life and Times of Parliament's Statutory Orphans." In Commission of Inquiry into the Sponsorship Program & Related Activities, *Restoring Accountability: Research Studies, Volume 1: Parliament, Ministers and Deputy Ministers.* Ottawa: Her Majesty in Right of Canada, 2006.

Bourgault, Jacques. "Federal Deputy Ministers: Serial Servers Looking for Influence." In *Deputy Ministers in Canada: Comparative and Jurisdictional Perspectives,* edited by J. Bourgault and C. Dunn. Toronto: University of Toronto Press, 2014.

Brodie, Ian. "In Defence of Political Staff." *Canadian Parliamentary Review* (Autumn 2012): 33–39.

Doberstein, Carey. "Metagovernance of Urban Governance Networks in Canada: In Pursuit of Legitimacy and Accountability." *Canadian Public Administration* 56(4) (December 2013): 584–609.

Doyle, Simon. "Chiefs of Staff: Meet the People Behind All of Trudeau's Ministers." *Toronto Globe and Mail.* http://www.theglobeandmail.com/news/politics/globe-politics-insider/chiefs-of-staff/article28148253/ (accessed June 21, 2016).

Government of Canada. *Open and Accountable Government: A Guide for Ministers.* Ottawa: Her Majesty the Queen in Right of Canada, 2015.

Government of Canada, Privy Council Office. *Guidance for Deputy Ministers.* http://www.pco.gc.ca/index.asp?lang=eng&page=information&sub=publications&doc=gdm-gsm/doc-eng.htm#TOC1_3 (accessed August 4, 2016).

Howard, Cosmo, and Susan Phillips. "Moving Away from Hierarchy: Do Horizontality, Partnerships, and Distributed Governance Really Signify the End of Accountability?" In *From New Public Management to New Political Governance: Essays in Honour of Peter C. Aucoin,* edited by Herman Bakvis and Mark D. Jarvis. Montreal & Kingston: McGill-Queen's University Press, 2012.

Osbaldeston, Gordon. "Dear Minister." *Policy Options* 9 (June/July 1988): 3–11.

_____. "Job Description for DMs." *Policy Options* 9 (January 1988): 33–38.

Savoie, Donald J. *Whatever Happened to the Music Teacher? How Government Decides and Why.* Montreal & Kingston: McGill-Queen's University Press, 2013.

Task Force on Horizontal Relations. *Managing Horizontal Policy Issues.* December 1996. http://publications.gc.ca/collections/Collection/SC93-8-1996-3E.pdf (accessed July 11, 2015).

Thomas, Paul. "Who Is Getting the Message: Communications at the Centre of Government." In Oliphant Commission, *Public Policy Issues and the*

Oliphant Commission: Independent Research Studies. Ottawa: Public Works and Government Services, 2010.

Treasury Board Secretariat. *Horizontal Initiatives Database.* 2015. http://www.tbs-sct.gc.ca/hidb-bdih/home-accueil-eng.aspx (accessed July 11, 2015).

Chapter 11

Aucoin, Peter, Jennifer Smith, and Geoff Dinsdale. *Responsible Government: Clarifying Essentials, Dispelling Myths and Exploring Change.* Ottawa: Canadian Centre for Management, 2004.

Aucoin, Peter, Mark D. Jarvis, and Lori Turnbull. *Democratizing the Constitution: Reforming Responsible Government.* Toronto: Emond Montgomery Publications, 2011.

Franks, Ned (Professor Emeritus of Political Science, Queen's University, as an individual) at the Public Accounts Committee. March 21, 2007. https://openparliament.ca/committees/public-accounts/39-1/44/prof-ned-franks-1/only/ (accessed August 6, 2016).

Government of Canada. *Open and Accountable Government: A Guide for Ministers, 2015.* Ottawa: Her Majesty in Right of Canada, 2015.

Jeffrey, Brooke. *Dismantling Canada: Stephen Harper's New Conservative Agenda.* Montreal & Kingston: McGill-Queen's University Press, 2015.

Lindquist, Evert, and Ken Rasmussen. "Deputy Ministers and New Political Governance: From Neutral Competence to Promiscuous Partisans to a New Balance?" In *From New Public Management to New Political Governance: Essays in Honour of Peter C. Aucoin,* edited by Herman Bakvis and Mark D. Jarvis. Montreal & Kingston: McGill-Queen's University Press, 2012.

Malloy, Jonathan, and Scott Millar. "Why Ministerial Accountability Can Still Work." In *How Ottawa Spends: The Harper Conservatives - Climate of Change, 2007–2008,* edited by G.B. Doern. Montreal and Kingston: McGill-Queen's University Press, 2007.

Parliamentary Centre. *Backgrounder.* September 2004. http://www.parlcent.org/en/wpcontent/uploads/2011/04/articles_and_papers/MPs_and_Committees_Backgrounder_EN.pdf (accessed August 19, 2015).

Privy Council Office. *Accounting Officers: Guidance on Roles, Responsibilities and Appearances Before Parliamentary Committees.* 2007. http://www.pco-bcp.gc.ca/docs/information/publications/ao-adc/2007/ao-adc-eng.pdf/ (accessed August 19, 2015).

Rathgeber, Brent. *Irresponsible Government: The Decline of Parliamentary Democracy in Canada.* Toronto: Dundurn, 2014.

Savoie, Donald J. *Breaking the Bargain: Public Servants, Ministers and Parliament.* Toronto: University of Toronto Press, 2003.

Sossin, Lorne. "Bureaucratic Independence." In *Handbook of Canadian Public Administration,* 2nd edition, edited by Christopher Dunn. Toronto: Oxford University Press, 2010.

_____. "Speaking Truth to Power? The Search for Bureaucratic Independence in Canada." *University of Toronto Law Journal* 55(1) (Winter 2005): 1–59.

Standing Committee on Public Accounts, House of Commons. *Governance in the Public Service of Canada: Ministerial and Deputy Ministerial Accountability.* May 2005. http://www.parl.gc.ca/HousePublications/Publication.aspx?DocId=1812721&Language=E&Mode=1&Parl=38&Ses=1 (accessed August 18, 2015).

Thomas, Paul G. "Parliament and the Public Service." In *The Handbook of Canadian Public Administration,* 2nd edition, edited by Christopher Dunn. Toronto: Oxford University Press, 2010.

_____. "The Past, Present and Future of Officers of Parliament." *Canadian Public Administration* 46(3) (Fall 2003): 287–314.

Chapter 12

Braverman, Lisa. *Administrative Tribunals: A Legal Handbook.* Aurora: Canada Law Book Inc., 2001.

CBC. "Unanimous Ruling Says Ottawa has Jurisdiction Over All Indigenous People." April 14, 2016. http://www.cbc.ca/news/aboriginal/metis-indians-supreme-court-ruling-1.3535236 (accessed August 7, 2016).

Clark, Campbell, and Bill Curry. "Absolving Chretien, Judge Blasts Gomery." *Globe and Mail,* June 27, 2008. http://www.theglobeandmail.com/news/national/absolving-chretien-judge-blasts-gomery/article675611/ (accessed August 7, 2016).

Fine, Sean. "Documents Reveal Government's Scramble to Enact Niqab Requirements." *Globe and Mail,* September 23, 2015. http://www.theglobeandmail.com/news/national/documents-reveal-governments-scramble-to-enact-niqab-requirements/article26486680/ (accessed August 7, 2016). Fine, Sean, and Gloria Galloway. "Ruling Makes Niqabs an Election Issue." *Globe and Mail,* September 19, 2015.

Gall, Gerald. *The Canadian Legal System,* 5th edition. Toronto: Thomson Carswell, 2004.

Hogg, Peter. *Constitutional Law of Canada,* 5th edition. Supplemented, Loose-Leaf. Toronto: Carswell, 2015.

Jones, David P., and Anne de Villars. *Principles of Administrative Law,* 6th edition. Toronto: Thomson Carswell, 2014.

Kelly, James B. *Governing with the Charter: Legislative and Judicial Activism and Framers' Intent.* Vancouver: UBC Press, 2005.

Law Reform Commission of Canada. *A Catalogue of Discretionary Powers in the Revised Statutes of Canada.* Ottawa: Information Canada, 1975.

MacIvor, Heather. *Canadian Politics and Government in the Charter Era.* Toronto: Nelson Thomson, 2006.

McLachlin, Beverly, Rt. Hon., Chief Justice of Canada. "Administrative Tribunals and the Courts: An Evolutionary Relationship." May 27, 2013.

http://www.scc-csc.ca/court-cour/judges-juges/spe-dis/bm-2013-05-27-eng.aspx (accessed June 20, 2016).

Savoie, Donald J. *Breaking the Bargain: Public Servants, Ministers, and Parliament.* Toronto: University of Toronto Press, 2003.

Chapter 13

Black, Edwin R. *Divided Loyalties: Canadian Concepts of Federalism.* Montreal: McGill-Queen's University Press, 1975.

Boismenu, Gerard, and Peter Graefe. "The New Federal Tool Belt: Attempt to Build Social Policy Leadership." *Canadian Public Policy* XXX(1) (2004): 71–89.

Boyer, J. Patrick. *Our Scandalous Senate.* Toronto: Dundurn Press, 2014.

Bradford, Neil. "Canada's Urban Agenda: A New Deal for the Cities?" In *Canadian Politics,* 4th edition, edited by James Bickerton and Alain-G. Gagnon. Peterborough: Broadview Press, 2004.

Brown, Douglas M. "Getting Things Done in the Federation: Do We Need New Rules for an Old Game?" In *Constructive and Cooperative Federalism?* Montreal: Institute for Research on Public Policy, 2003. www.policy.ca/policy-directory/Detailed/890.html (accessed August 11, 2016).

Cameron, David, and Richard Simeon. "Intergovernmental Relations in Canada: The Emergence of Collaborative Federalism." *Publius: The Journal of Federalism* 32(2) (Spring 2002): 49–72.

Curry, Bill. "Ottawa Lowers Expectations for Climate Deal with Provinces." *Globe and Mail,* February 10, 2016.

Friendly, Martha and Linda A. White. "No-laterialism: Paradoxes in Early Childhood Education and Care in the Canadian Federation." In *Canadian Federalism: Performance, Effectiveness, and Legitimacy,* 3rd edition, edited by Herman Bakvis and Grace Skogstad. Toronto: University of Toronto Press, 2012.

Inwood, Gregory J., Carolyn Johns, and Patricia L. O'Reilly. "Intergovernmental Officials in Canada." In *Canada: The State of the Federation 2002,* edited by J. Peter Meekison, Hamish Telford, and Harvey Lazar. Montreal & Kingston: McGill-Queen's University Press, 2004.

—————. *Intergovernmental Policy Capacity in Canada: Inside the Worlds of Finance, Environment, Trade, and Health Policy.* Montreal & Kingston: McGill-Queen's University Press, 2011.

Maioni, Antonia. "Health Care." In *Canadian Federalism: Performance, Effectiveness, and Legitimacy,* 3rd edition, edited by Herman Bakvis and Grace Skogstad. Toronto: University of Toronto Press, 2012.

McCarthy, Shawn. "Ottawa Seeks to Set National Minimum on Carbon Pricing." *Globe and Mail,* February 17, 2016.

McCarthy, Shawn, and Gloria Galloway. "First Ministers Agree to Forge National Climate Strategy." *Globe and Mail,* November 24, 2015.

Meekison, J. Peter, Hamish Telford, and Harvey Lazar. "The Institutions of Executive Federalism: Myths and Realities." In *Canada: The State of the Federation 2002,* edited by J. Peter Meekison, Hamish Telford, and Harvey Lazar. Montreal & Kingston: McGill-Queen's University Press, 2004.

Papillon, Martin. "Canadian Federalism and the Emerging Mosaic of Aboriginal Multilevel Governance." In *Canadian Federalism: Performance, Effectiveness, and Legitimacy,* 3rd edition, edited by Herman Bakvis and Grace Skogstad. Toronto: University of Toronto Press, 2012.

Russell, Peter. *Constitutional Odyssey: Can Canadians Become a Sovereign People?* 3rd edition. Toronto: University of Toronto Press, 2004.

SCICS, Press Release – Communique of Canada's First Ministers. March 3, 2016. http://www.scics.gc.ca/english/Conferences.asp?a=viewdocument&id=2400 (accessed June 17, 2016).

Simeon, Richard. "The Federal–Provincial Decision Making Process." In Ontario Economic Council, *Issues and Alternatives—1977: Intergovernmental Relations.* Toronto: Ontario Economic Council, 1977.

Simeon, Richard, and Ian Robinson. "The Dynamics of Canadian Federalism." In *Canadian Politics,* 4th edition, edited by James Bickerton and Alain-G. Gagnon. Peterborough: Broadview Press, 2004.

Simeon, Richard, Ian Robinson, and Jennifer Wallner. "The Dynamics of Canadian Federalism." In *Canadian Politics,* 6th edition, edited by James Bickerton and Alain-G. Gagnon. Peterborough: Broadview Press, 2014.

Skogstad, Grace. "International Trade Policy and the Evolution of Canadian Federalism." In *Canadian Federalism: Performance, Effectiveness, and Legitimacy,* 3rd edition, edited by Herman Bakvis and Grace Skogstad. Toronto: University of Toronto Press, 2012.

Smiley, Donald V. "The Rowell-Sirois Report, Provincial Autonomy, and Post-War Canadian Federalism." *Canadian Journal of Economics and Political Science* 28 (February 1962): 54.

Trudeau, Justin P.J. Letter to the Hon. Paul Davis, September 2, 2015. https://www.liberal.ca/letter-to-the-council-of-the-federation/ (accessed August 11, 2016).

—————. Speech to the Federation of Canadian Municipalities Conference. June 10, 2015. https://www.liberal.ca/justin-trudeaus-speech-to-the-federation-of-canadian-municipalities-conference/ (accessed October 11, 2015).

—————. Minister of Environment and Climate Change Mandate Letter. http://pm.gc.ca/eng/minister-environment-and-climate-change-mandate-letter (accessed August 11, 2016).

Vile, M.J.C. *The Structure of American Federalism.* London: Oxford University Press, 1961.

Wheare, K.C. *Federal Government,* 4th edition. London: Oxford University Press, 1963.

Winfield, Mark, and Douglas Macdonald. "Federalism and Canadian Climate Change Policy." In *Canadian Federalism: Performance, Effectiveness, and Legitimacy*, 3rd edition, edited by Herman Bakvis and Grace Skogstad. Toronto: University of Toronto Press, 2012.

Chapter 14

Bell, Rogers, and Telus. Letter to Prime Minister Trudeau regarding upcoming spectrum auction. July 9, 2013. https://www.northumberlandview.ca/?module=news&type=user&func=display&sid=23576 (accessed March 10, 2016).

Bruni, Frank. "How Facebook Warps Our Worlds." *New York Times*, May 22, 2016. http://www.nytimes.com/2016/05/22/opinion/sunday/how-facebook-warps-our-worlds.html?_r=0 (accessed May 22, 2016).

Clancy, Peter. "Business Interests and Civil Society in Canada." In *Group Politics and Social Movements in Canada*, 2nd edition, edited by Miriam Smith Toronto: University of Toronto Press, 2014.

Cope, George, President and CEO of Bell Canada. "An Open Letter to all Canadians." http://www.bell.ca/an-open-letter-to-all-canadians (accessed March 10, 2016).

Dobby, Christine. "Telus Takes Battle Over Ottawa's Wireless Spectrum Policy to Federal Court." *Financial Post*, July 29, 2013. http://business.financialpost.com/fp-tech-desk/telus-takes-battle-over-ottawas-wireless-spectrum-policy-to-federal-court?__lsa=d42c-e709 (accessed May 20, 2015).

Fell, Anthony. "Canada's Telecom Arrogance." *Financial Post*. August 12, 2013. http://business.financial-post.com/fp-comment/canadas-telecom-arrogance (accessed May 20, 2016).

Fierlbeck, Katherine. *Health Care in Canada: A Citizen's Guide to Policy and Politics*. Toronto: University of Toronto Press, 2011.

Good, David A. *The Politics of Public Management*. Toronto: University of Toronto Press, 2003.

Government of Canada, "Consulting with Canadians." http://www1.canada.ca/consultingcanadians/ (accessed August 10, 2016).

Health Canada. *Health Canada Policy Toolkit for Public Involvement in Decision Making*. Ottawa: Minister of Public Works and Government Services, 2000.

Health Council of Canada. *Primer on Public Involvement*. http://www.cprn.org/documents/45131_en.pdf (accessed August 10, 2016).

Laforest, Rachel. "Deep and Wide: Citizen Engagement in the Era of Social Media." In *Canadian Public Administration in the 21st Century*, edited by Charles Conteh and Ian Roberge. New York: CRC Press, 2013.

Laforest, Rachel, and Susan Phillips. "Citizen Engagement: Rewiring the Policy Process." In *Critical Policy Studies*, edited by Michael Orsini and Miriam Smith. Toronto: UBC Press, 2007.

Lynch, Michael Patrick. *The Internet of Us: Knowing More and Understanding Less in the Age of Big Data*. New York: Liveright Publishing Corporation, 2016.

Marland, Alex. "Political Communication in Canada: Strategies and Tactics." In *Canadian Politics*, 6th edition, edited by James Bickerton and Alain-G. Gagnon. Toronto: University of Toronto Press, 2014.

Montpetit, Éric. "Are Interest Groups Useful or Harmful? Take Two." In *Canadian Politics*, 6th edition, edited by James Bickerton and Alain-G. Gagnon. Toronto: University of Toronto Press, 2014.

_____. "Governance and Interest Group Activities." In *Canadian Politics*, 4th edition, edited by James Bickerton and Alain-G. Gagnon. Peterborough: Broadview Press, 2004.

_____. "Public Consultations in Policy Network Environments: The Case of Assisted Reproductive Technology Policy in Canada." *Canadian Public Policy* XXIX (2003): 97.

Moore, James, Hon., PC, MP, Minister of Industry. "A Telecom Policy for All Canadians." http://www.jamesmoore.org/august132013 (accessed September 16, 2016).

Orsini, Michael. "Of Pots and Pans and Radical Handmaids: Social Movements and Civil Society." In *Canadian Politics*, 6th edition, edited by James Bickerton and Alain-G. Gagnon. Toronto: University of Toronto Press, 2014.

Pariser, Eli. *The Filter Bubble: What the Internet Is Hiding from You*. New York: Penguin Press, 2011.

Phillips, Susan D., and Michael Orsini. *Mapping the Links: Citizen Involvement in Policy Processes*. Ottawa: Canadian Policy Research Networks, 2002.

Pross, Paul. *Group Politics and Public Policy*. Toronto: Oxford University Press, 1986.

_____. "Pressure Groups: Adaptive Instruments of Political Communication." In *Pressure Group Behaviour in Canadian Politics*, edited by Paul Pross. Toronto: McGraw-Hill Ryerson, 1975.

Roy, Jeffrey. "The Promise (and Pitfalls) of Digital Transformation." In *Approaching Public Administration: Core Debates and Emerging Issues*, edited by Roberto P. Leone and Frank L.K. Ohemeng. Toronto: Emond Montgomery Publications, 2011.

Savoie, Donald J. *What Is Government Good At? A Canadian Answer*. Montreal & Kingston: McGill-Queen's University Press, 2015.

Shields, Kristin, Gwen DuBois-Wing, and Ellis Westwood. "Share Your Story, Shape Your Care: Engaging the Diverse and Disperse Population of Northwestern Ontario in Healthcare Priority Setting." *Healthcare Quarterly*, 13(3) (May 2010): 86–90. doi:10.12927/hcq.2010.21821.

"Verizon Not Entering Canada's Wireless Market After All." *cbc.ca*. http://www.cbc.ca/news/business/verizon-not-entering-canada-s-wireless-market-after-all-1.1339361 (accessed August 10, 2016).

Young, Lisa, and Joanna Everitt. *Advocacy Groups*. Vancouver: UBC Press, 2004.

Chapter 15

Auditor General of Canada. "Streamlining the Human Resource Management Regime." *Report of the Auditor General of Canada.* Ottawa: Department of Public Works and Government Services, April 2000.

Brown, Kerry. "Human Resource Management in the Public Sector." *Public Management Review* 6(3) (2004): 303–309.

Canada. *Blueprint 2020: Getting Started—Getting Your Views. Building Tomorrow's Public Service Together,* June 2013. www.clerk.gc.ca/local_grfx/bp2020/bp2020-eng.pdf (accessed June 9, 2015).

—————. *Public Service 2000: The Renewal of the Public Service of Canada.* Ottawa: Supply and Services Canada, 1990.

—————. *Public Service 2000: The Renewal of the Public Service of Canada – Synopsis.* Ottawa: Minister of Supply and Services, 1990.

—————. *Sixteenth Annual Report to the Prime Minister on the Public Service of Canada.* Ottawa: Her Majesty the Queen in Right of Canada, 2009.

—————. *2014 Public Service Employee Survey: Summary Report.* Ottawa: Her Majesty the Queen in Right of Canada, February 2015.

Canada. House of Commons. *5,000 Bilingual Positions to Be Filled Every Year: The Role of Post-Secondary Institutions in Promoting Canada's Linguistic Duality. Report of the Standing Committee on Official Languages.* Ottawa: Communication Canada, 2009.

Clerk of the Privy Council. *Fifteenth Annual Report to the Prime Minister on the Public Service of Canada.* Ottawa: Privy Council Office, 2008.

—————. *Fifth Annual Report to the Prime Minister on the Public Service of Canada.* Ottawa: Supply and Services Canada, 1997.

—————. *Fourth Annual Report to the Prime Minister on the Public Service of Canada.* Ottawa: Supply and Services Canada, 1996.

—————. *Seventh Annual Report to the Prime Minister on the Public Service of Canada.* Ottawa: Privy Council Office, 2000.

D'Avignon Committee. *Report of the Special Committee on the Review of Personnel Management and the Merit Principle.* Hull: Supply and Services Canada, 1979.

Dawson, R. McGregor. The Canadian Civil Service." *Canadian Journal of Economics and Political Science* 2 (August 1936): 288–300.

—————. *The Civil Service of Canada.* Oxford: Oxford University Press, 1929.

—————. *The Principle of Official Independence.* London: P.S. King and Son, 1922.

Dwivedi, O.P., and James Iain Gow. *From Bureaucracy to Public Management: The Administrative Culture of the Government of Canada.* Toronto: Broadview Press, 1999.

Glenn, Ted. "The State of Talent Management in Canada's Public Sector." *Canadian Public Administration* 55(1) (March 2012): 25–51.

Governor General. *Here for All Canadians: Stability, Prosperity, Security. Speech from the Throne to Open the First Session of the Forty-First Parliament of Canada.* June 3, 2011.

Ingraham, Patricia W., B. Guy Peters, and Donald P. Moynihan. "Public Employment and the Future of the Public Service." In *Governance in the 21st Century: Revitalizing the Public Service,* edited by B. Guy Peters and Donald J. Savoie. Montreal & Kingston: McGill-Queen's University Press, 2000, 385–422.

Johnson, David, and Andrew Molloy. "The Quiet Crisis and the Emergence of La Relève: A Study of Crisis Perception and Executive Leadership within the Canadian Federal Public Service, 1997–2002." *Canadian Public Administration* 52(2) (June 2009): 203–223.

Juillet, Luc. *The Public Service Commission and the Implementation of the Public Service Employment Act (2003).* Ottawa: Public Service Commission, March 2011.

Juillet, Luc, and Ken Rasmussen. *Defending a Contested Ideal: Merit and the Public Service Commission of Canada, 1908–2008.* Ottawa: University of Ottawa Press, 2008.

Lammam, Charles, Milagros Palacios, Feixue Ren, and Jason Clemens. *Comparing Government and Private Sector Compensation in Ontario.* Vancouver: The Fraser Institute, February 2015.

Lavigna, Robert J., and Steven W. Hays. "Recruitment and Selection of Public Workers: An International Compendium of Modern Trends and Practices." *Public Personnel Management* 33(3) (Fall 2004): 237–253.

Lindquist, Evert, and Gilles Paquet. "Government Restructuring and the Federal Public Service: The Search for a New Cosmology." In *Government Restructuring and Career Public Services,* edited by Evert Lindquist. Toronto: Institute of Public Administration of Canada, 2000, 71–111.

Lindquist, Evert, Ian Clark, and James Mitchell. "Reshaping Ottawa's Centre of Government: Martin's Reforms in Historical Perspective." In *How Ottawa Spends 2004–2005,* edited by G. Bruce Doern. Montreal & Kingston: McGill-Queen's University Press, 2004, 317–347.

Lowe, Graham. *Employer of Choice? Workplace Innovation in Government: A Synthesis Report.* Ottawa: Canadian Policy Research Network, 2001.

Mallett, Ted. *A Comparison of Public-Sector and Private-Sector Salaries and Benefits.* Toronto: Canadian Federation of Independent Business, March 2015.

Malloy, Jonathan. "The Next Generation? Recruitment and Renewal in the Federal Public Service." In *How Ottawa Spends 2004–2005: Mandate Change in the Paul Martin Era,* edited by G. Bruce Doern. Montreal & Kingston: McGill-Queen's University Press, 2004, 277–295.

May, Kathryn. "The 'Golden Age' of Public Service is on the Horizon—If Canada Hires More Millennials: Scott Brison." *The National Post,* February 16, 2016. www.news.nationalpost.com/news/canada/canadian-politics/the-golden-age-of-public-service-is-on-the-horizon-if-canada-hires-more-millennials-scott-brison (accessed May 2, 2016).

_____. "Kevin Page Dismisses Privy Council's Blueprint 2020 as 'Empty Vessel'." *Ottawa Citizen*, December 25, 2013. www.ottawacitizen.com/news/national/kevin-page-dismisses-privy-councils-blueprint-2020-as-empty-vessel (accessed June 10, 2015).

Mueller, Richard. "Public- and Private-Sector Wage Differentials in Canada Revisited." *Industrial Relations* 39(3) (July 2000): 375–400.

Office of the Auditor General. *Report of the Auditor General of Canada to the House of Commons—2001.* Ottawa: Supply and Services Canada, 2001.

Palacios, Milagros, and Jason Clemens. *Comparing Public and Private Sector Compensation in Canada.* Vancouver: The Fraser Institute, 2013.

Peters, B. Guy. "The Future of Reform." In *Governance in the Twenty-First Century: Revitalizing the Public Service*, edited by B. Guy Peters and Donald J. Savoie. Montreal & Kingston: McGill-Queen's University Press, 2000, 425–436.

Prime Minister's Advisory Committee on the Public Service. *Second Report of the Prime Minister's Advisory Committee on the Public Service.*

_____. *Seventh Report to the Prime Minister: Modernizing the Employment Model.* March 2013.

Public Service Commission. *Annual Report 2004–2005.* http://www.collectionscanada.gc.ca/webarchives/20071121062637/http://www.psc-cfp.gc.ca/arp-rpa/2005/rpt-eng.pdf#page=12&zoom=auto,-73,702 (accessed July 27, 2016).

_____. *Merit and Non-Partisanship Under the Public Service Employment Act* (2003). Ottawa: Public Service Commission of Canada, 2011.

_____. "New Direction in Staffing—Message from the Public Service Commission to All Public Servants." April 1, 2016. www.psccfp.gc.ca/plcy-pitq/message-eng.htm (accessed June 29, 2016).

_____. *The Road Ahead: Recruitment and Retention Challenges for the Public Service.* Ottawa: Public Service Commission of Canada, February 2002.

Public Service Human Resources Management Agency of Canada. "Welcome to HR Council Online." *Human Resources Council.* July 12, 2006. www.hrma-agrh.gc.ca/hr-rh/hrc-crh/index_e.asp.

Public Service Labour Relations Board. http://pslreb-crtefp.gc.ca/index_e.asp (accessed June 25, 2015).

Raffel, Jeffrey A., Peter Leisink, and Anthony E. Middlebrooks, editors. *Public Sector Leadership: International Challenges and Prospects.* Cheltenham, UK: Edward Elgar, 2009.

Royal Commission on Government Organization. *Report.* 5 volumes. Ottawa: Queen's Printer, 1962–63.

Savoie, Donald J. *Breaking the Bargain: Public Servants, Ministers and Parliament.* Toronto: University of Toronto Press, 2003.

_____. *Court Government and the Collapse of Accountability in Canada and the United Kingdom.* Toronto: University of Toronto Press, 2008.

_____. *Thatcher, Reagan, Mulroney: In Search of a New Bureaucracy.* Toronto: University of Toronto Press, 1994.

Shim, Deok-Shob. "Recent Human Resource Developments in OECD Member Countries." *Public Personnel Management* 30(3) (Fall 2001): 323–347.

Task Force on Public Service Values and Ethics. *A Strong Foundation: Report of the Task Force on Public Service Values and Ethics.* Ottawa: Canadian Centre for Management Development, 1996.

Treasury Board of Canada Secretariat. *Demographic Snapshot of the Federal Public Service, 2014.* June 1, 2015. www.tbs-sct.ca/res/stats/demo14-eng.asp.

_____. *Directive on Performance Management* (April 2014), Appendix. www.tbs-sct.gc.ca/pol/doc-eng.aspx?id=27146 (accessed June 20, 2016).

_____. *Employment Equity in the Public Service of Canada, 2013–14: Annual Report to Parliament.* Ottawa: Her Majesty the Queen in Right of Canada, 2015).

_____. "The Key Leadership Competency Profile, March 2015." www.tbs-sct.gc.ca/psm-fpfm/learning-apprentissage/pdps-ppfp/klc-ccl/klcp-pccl-eng.asp (accessed July 14, 2016).

_____. *Policy Framework for People Management* (July 2010). www.tbs-sct.gc.ca/pol/doc-eng.aspx?id=19134 (accessed June 20, 2016).

_____. *Policy on Learning, Training and Development* (January 1, 2006). http://www.tbs-sct.gc.ca/pol/doc-eng.aspx?id=12405 (accessed July 14, 2016).

Whittington, Les. "Flaherty's Message: Victory Opens Way to Spending Clampdown." *The Toronto Star*, May 13, 2011. www.thestar.com/business/2011/05/13/flahertys_message_victory_opens_way_to_spending_clampdown.html (accessed June 2, 2015).

Zussman, David, and Jak Jabes. *The Vertical Solitude: Managing in the Public Sector.* Halifax: The Institute for Research on Public Policy, 1989.

Chapter 16

Andrew, Caroline. "Women and the Public Sector." In *The Handbook of Canadian Public Administration*, edited by Christopher Dunn. Toronto: Oxford University Press, 2002, 159–168.

Bourgault, Jacques. *Profile of Deputy Ministers in the Government of Canada.* Ottawa: School of Public Service, 2004.

Healy, Theresa, and Sue Genge. *Pay Inequity: Canadian Labour Congress Analysis of the "Public Sector Equitable Compensation Act,"* Research Paper #47. Ottawa: Canadian Labour Congress, February 27, 2009.

Impact Research. "Native People and Employment in the Public Service of Canada." A report prepared for the Public Service Commission, October 1976.

Kennedy, Brandy. "Unraveling Representative Bureaucracy: A Systematic Analysis of the Literature." *Administration & Society* 46(4) (2014): 395–421.

Luciani, Patrick. *Economic Myths: Making Sense of Canadian Policy Issues*. Toronto: Pearson Education Canada Inc., 2004.

Mosher, Frederick. *Democracy and the Public Service*. New York: NY: Oxford University Press, 1968.

Ng, Eddy S., and Greg J. Sears. "Toward Representative Bureaucracy: Predicting Public Service Attraction Among Underrepresented Groups in Canada." *Review of Public Personnel Administration* (2014): 1–19. DOI: 10.1177/0734371X14544546.

Pay Equity Task Force. *Pay Equity: A New Approach to a Fundamental Right – Pay Equity Task Force Final Report*. Ottawa: Her Majesty the Queen in Right of Canada, 2004.

Porter, John. "The Bureaucratic Elite: A Reply to Professor Rowat." *Canadian Journal of Economics and Political Science* 25 (May 1959): 207–209.

_____. "Higher Public Servants and the Bureaucratic Elite in Canada." *Canadian Journal of Economies and Political Science* 24 (November 1958): 483–501.

Public Service Alliance of Canada. "Economic Leadership and the Prosperity of Canadian Women." A Submission to the House of Commons Standing Committee on the Status of Women, May 14, 2014. www.psacunion.ca/economic-leadership-and-prosperity-canadian-women (accessed July 27, 2015).

Public Service Commission. *Annual Report 1971*. Ottawa: Information Canada, 1972.

_____. *Guidance Series – Integrating Employment Equity in the Appointment Process*. Ottawa: Public Service Commission of Canada, December 2005. www.psc-cfp.gc.ca/plcy-pltq/guides/equity-equite/guid-orie-eng.htm (accessed July 21, 2015).

_____. *History of Employment Equity in the Public Service and the Public Service Commission of Canada*. Ottawa: Public Service Commission of Canada, October 2011.

_____. *Members of Employment Equity Groups: Perceptions of Merit and Fairness in Staffing Activities*. Ottawa: Her Majesty the Queen in Right of Canada, March 2014.

_____. *Merit—Achieving Representativeness*. Ottawa: Public Service Commission of Canada, March 2008.

_____. *PSC Glossary*. Ottawa: Public Service Commission of Canada, February 2012. www.psc-cfp.gc.ca/abt-aps/gls/index-eng.htm#e (accessed June 30, 2105).

_____. *The Road Ahead: Recruitment and Retention Challenges for the Public Service*. Ottawa: Public Service Commission of Canada, February 2002.

Rowat, Donald C. "On John Porter's Bureaucratic Elite in Canada." *Canadian Journal of Economics and Political Science* 25 (May 1959): 204–207.

Royal Commission on Equality in Employment. *Report*. Ottawa: Minister of Supply and Services, 1984.

Royal Commission on Government Organization. *Report*. Ottawa: Queen's Printer, 1963.

Royal Commission on the Status of Women. *Report*. Ottawa: Information Canada, 1970.

Statistics Canada. *Projections of the Diversity of the Canadian Population 2006 to 2031*. Ottawa: Minister of Industry, 2010. www.statcan.gc.ca/pub/91-551-x/91-551-x2010001-eng.pdf (accessed July 21, 2015).

Tellier, Paul, Clerk of the Privy Council and Secretary to the Cabinet. *Public Service 2000: A Report on Progress*. Ottawa: Minister of Supply and Services, 1992.

Treasury Board of Canada Secretariat. "Affirmative Action in the Public Service." News release, June 27, 1983.

_____. *Annual Report on Official Languages 2013–14*.

_____. *Demographic Snapshot of the Federal Public Service, 2014*. http://www.tbs-sct.gc.ca/psm-fpfm/modernizing-modernisation/stats/demo14-eng.asp (accessed July 11, 2016).

_____. *Employment Equity in the Federal Public Service 1996–97*. Ottawa: Public Works and Government Services Canada, 1997.

_____. *Employment Equity in the Public Service of Canada 2006–07 and 2007–08*. Ottawa: Her Majesty the Queen in Right of Canada, 2009. www.tbs-sct.gc.ca/rp/0608ee01-eng.asp (accessed July 24, 2015).

_____. *Employment Equity in the Public Service of Canada 2012–13*. Ottawa: Her Majesty the Queen in Right of Canada, 2013.

_____. *Employment Equity in the Public Service of Canada 2014–2015*. Ottawa: Her Majesty the Queen in Right of Canada, 2016.

_____. *Evaluation of the Official Languages Centre of Excellence*. Ottawa: Her Majesty the Queen in Right of Canada, May 2013. www.tbs-sct.gc.ca/report/orp/2013/olce-celo/olce-celopr-eng.asp (accessed July 23, 2015).

_____. *The Public Sector Equitable Compensation Act and the Reform of Pay Equity*. Ottawa: Her Majesty the Queen in Right of Canada, November 2012.

Turgeon, Luc, and Alain-G. Gagnon. "The Representation of Ethnic and Linguistic Groups in the Federal Civil Service of Belgium and Canada." *Canadian Public Administration* 56(4) (December 2013): 565–583.

Wilson, V. Seymour, and Willard A. Mullins. "Representative Bureaucracy: Linguistic/Ethnic Aspects in Canadian Public Policy." *Canadian Public Administration* 21(4) (Winter 1978): 513–538.

Chapter 17

CBC. "New Liberal Budget Bill Raises Old Concerns about Omnibus Legislation." April 24, 2016. http://www.cbc.ca/news/politics/budget-omnibus-wherry-1.3550676 (accessed June 8, 2016).

Clark, Scott, and Peter Devries. "Restoring Integrity to the Budget Process." *Inside Policy* (February–March, 2013): 6–9.

Coyne, Andrew. "Rush to Balance Budget Is a Political Imperative, not an Economic One." *National Post*, January 19 (or January 20), 2015. http://news.nationalpost.com/2015/01/19/andrew-coyne-rush-to-balance-budget-is-a-political-imperative-not-an-economic-one/ (accessed July 18, 2016).

Department of Finance. *Advantage Canada: Building a Strong Economy for Canadians.* Ottawa: Her Majesty the Queen of Right in Canada, 2007.

Doern, G. Bruce, Allan M. Maslove, and Michael Prince. *Canadian Public Budgeting in the Age of Crises: Shifting Budgetary Domains and Temporal Budgeting.* Montreal and Kingston: McGill-Queen's University Press, 2014.

Drury, C.M. *Planning-Programming Budgeting Guide.* Ottawa: Queen's Printer, 1969.

Franks, C.E.S. "Omnibus Bills Subvert Our Legislative Process." *Globe and Mail*, July 14, 2010. www.theglobeandmail.com/globe-debate/omnibus-bills-subvert-our-legislative-pro (accessed Jan. 1, 2015).

Good, David A. *The Politics of Public Money*, 2nd edition. Toronto: University of Toronto Press, 2014.

_____. "Still Budgeting by Muddling Through: Why Disjointed Incrementalism Lasts." *Policy and Society* 30 (2011): 41–51.

Gow, David. *The Process of Budgetary Reform in the Government of Canada.* Ottawa: Information Canada.

Page, Kevin. *Unaccountable: Truth and Lies on Parliament Hill.* Toronto: Viking, 2015.

Savoie, Donald J. "The Federal Government: Revisiting Court Government in Canada." In *Executive Styles in Canada: Cabinet Structures and Leadership Practices in Canadian Government*, edited by Luc Bernier, Keith Brownsey, and Michael Howlett. Toronto: University of Toronto Press, 2005.

_____. *Whatever Happened to the Music Teacher? How Government Decides and Why.* Montreal and Kingston: McGill-Queen's University, 2013.

Schick, Allen. "The Changing Role of the Central Budget Office." *OECD Journal on Budgeting* 1 (2001/02): 9–26.

Treasury Board Secretariat. *The Expenditure Management System of Canada.* Ottawa: Minister of Supply and Services, 1995.

Chapter 18

Benoit, Liane E, and C.E.S. (Ned) Franks. "For Want of a Nail: The Role of Internal Audit in the Sponsorship Scandal." In *Commission of Inquiry into the Sponsorship Program and Advertising Activities, Restoring Accountability: Research Studies*, Volume 2. Ottawa: Her Majesty the Queen in Right of Canada.

Good, David A. *The Politics of Public Money*, 2nd edition. Toronto: University of Toronto Press, 2014.

_____. *The Politics of Public Money: Spenders, Guardians, Priority Setters, and Financial Watchdogs Inside the Canadian Government.* Toronto: University of Toronto Press, 2007.

Office of the Auditor General of Canada. *What We Do.* http://www.oag-bvg.gc.ca/internet/English/au_fs_e_371.html (accessed July 18, 2016).

Treasury Board of Canada Secretariat. *About Financial Management*, p. 1, accessed July 25, 2016, http://www.tbs-sct.gc.ca/ip-pi/structure/fm-gf-eng.asp.

_____. *Financial Management.* http://www.tbs-sct.gc.ca/fm-gf/index-eng.asp (accessed May 5, 2015).

_____. *2016–17 Estimates: Parts I and II The Government Expenditure Plan and Main Estimates*, II. https://www.tbs-sct.gc.ca/hgw-cgf/finances/pgs-pdg/gepme-pdgbpd/20162017/me-bpd-eng.pdf

Index

The following notations have been used: b (box); f (figure); n (note); and t (table).

personnel and governance systems, 133

political and judicial control of, 127–131, 134

privatization, deregulation and "smart regulation" of, 134–140, 137b

public enterprise growth and evolution, 131–132

rationale for, 123–127

trends and issues for, 131–140

Crown corporations, 115–116

accountability of, 132–133

as alternative service delivery, 158n1

appointment to, 130–131

defined, 116–117

employment equity in, 280

Financial Administration Act framework for, 128

incomplete information concerning, 125

ministerial oversight of, 117–118, 118f, 128–129

ownership method, 119t

personnel and governance systems, 133

politics and, 126–131, 134

privatization, deregulation and "smart regulation" of, 134–140, 137b

public enterprise growth and evolution, 131–132

service delivery mechanisms, 147, 147f

supply security for, 126

trends and issues for, 131–140

Curran, Jim, 152–153

customer-driven government, 76–77

D

damages, awarding of, 209

Dawson, R. MacGregor, 6

decentralization
in organization theory, 45–47, 46f

decentralized government, 76

decision-making
decentralization and deconcentration of, 45–47, 46f
rule-based, 34

declaratory judgment, 209

deconcentration
in organization theory, 45–47, 46f

de Gournay, Vincent, 31

Deming, W. Edwards, 62–63

democracy, respect for, 16b

democratic values
in public service, 14

demographic changes
human resources management and, 254–259, 256b

Denhardt, Janet, 85

Denhardt, Robert, 60, 81–82, 85

departmental corporations, 148–149, 149b

departments. *See also* interdepartmental and intradepartmental interactions

basic structure, 95–96, 95f

in Canadian government, 94–104

classification systems, 96–98, 96t

definition of, 94–95

employees in, 105t

executive branch and, 101, 169

financial administration and, 317–318

legislature and, 99–101

ministerial staff and officials of, 184

operations of, 102–104, 102f, 103f

organizational structure, 98–99, 122f

deployment of employees, 270

deputy minister
defined, 103
intradepartmental relations, 179–184, 180f
statutory responsibilities of, 197–199

Deputy Ministers Human Resource Management Advisory Committee, 266–267

deregulation
Crown agencies and corporations and, 136–140

development programs for employees, 270–271

Dickson, William J., 55–56

digital divide, 156–157

digital era governance (DEG), 84

Disability Rights Social Movement, 249b

disabled persons
employment equity for, 291

Doherty, A., 6

Duffy, Mike, 168b

duties, organization of, 42–44, 43f

E

early childhood education
federal-provincial policy on, 225

economic conditions
trends in, 11f

economic regulation, 120

education programs
federal-provincial policy relations and, 225

education in public administration, 6–7, 7b

employee learning programs, 270–271

efficiency
defined, 14–15
privatization paradigm and, 135–140
public *vs.* private administration and, 4–5

Eldridge case, 211

Elections Act, 134

Elections Canada, 134, 194

Elliassen, Kjell, 83–84

emergency federalism, 217

employability
human resources management and, 256–259, 273n24

employee classification system, 269

employee takeovers (ETs), 152–153

employment
Aboriginal right to equity in, 288–289
in bureaucracy, 34–35
case study of equity in, 282b–284b
for disabled persons, equity in, 291
distribution of public service employees, 281t
equal opportunity in, 278–291
equity in, 275–293
Francophone community equity in, 284–285, 286t
pay equity in, 291–293
in public administration, 255–259, 256b, 257t, 258t, 273n11
visible minority equity in, 289–291
women's equity in, 285, 287–288

Employment and Social Development Canada, 69–70, 289

Employment Equity Act (1986), 280

Employment Equity Act (1995), 280

Employment Equity Governance Model, 290–291

enterprising government, 76

entrepreneurial government, 76

entropy
open systems theory, 65–66

Equalization program, 221–223 222f

equal opportunity in employment, 278–291

service delivery models for, 69–70
structure in Canada of, 94–112, 95f
Government 2.0, 154, 157
government-owned-company-operated (GOCO) partnerships, 151–152
governor general, 94
governor-in-council, 94
Greenpeace movement, 236
Gulick, Luther, 30, 40–44

H

habeas corpus, 209
Hackman, Richard, 59–60
Halpern v. the Attorney General of Canada et al., 211–212
Harper, Stephen, 88, 99, 108, 134, 171, 219, 225, 231n36, 302
Harvard Business Review, 65
Hawthorne experiments, 55–56
healthcare accords
federal-provincial policy and, 226
Heintzman, Ralph, 27b, 145
Henry, Nicholas, 7
Herzberg, Frederick, 54, 58–60
hierarchical structure of bureaucracy, 33, 34f, 35
executive interaction with, 162–163
flattening of hierarchy in, 41–42
hierarchy of needs, Maslow's theory of, 56–57, 56f
horizontal accountability, 24, 24b
horizontal administrative coordinative department, 97
horizontal management, 173, 175–178, 175b, 177f
horizontal policy coordinative department, 97
House of Commons committees, 195–198, 196f, 197b
Human Resources and Social Development Canada, Department of, 31–32
Human Resources Council, 266–267
human resources management
challenges in federal government for, 253–259, 272n4
collective bargaining and, 266b
failure of reform in, 262–265
historical evolution of, 260–265
legislative and governance structure for, 265–268, 268f
merit principle and, 259–260
modernization of, 263–265
overview of, 251–252, 272n2

in public sector, 252–259
public *vs.* private administration approaches to, 5–6
reform of, 261–262
tasks in, 268–272
training, development and learning, 270–271
human resources planning, 269
employment equity and, 281–284
hygiene factors
motivation and, 58–60, 59f

I

"ideal-type" bureaucracy, 33–34, 50n19
Idle No More movement, 248
"in and out" scheme
politics of Crown agencies and, 134
incomplete information
Crown agencies and, 125
Increased Ministerial Authority and Accountability (IMAA), 86
incremental budgeting, 305–306, 306b
indeterminate employees, 269
Indigenous and Northern Affairs Canada, 289
individual ministerial responsibility, 188
inducement to cooperation, 48
informal organization behaviour, 49
Information and Privacy Commissioner (IPC) (Ontario), 207
information technology (IT)
alternative service delivery and, 153–154
digital era governance and, 84
injunctions, 209
inputs
open systems theory, 65–66
Institute of Public Administration of Canada, 8
institutionalized groups, 234–235, 235f
integrated service delivery, 146, 146b
integration
in organizational humanism, 55
integrity
administrative ethics and, 24–27
in public sector, 15, 16b
interdepartmental relations, 173–174, 174b
horizontal management and, 175–178, 175b, 177f

interest groups
activities of, 235–236
case study in politics of, 240–241
defined, 234
government access and targeting, 236–239
tactics of, 238–239
types of, 234–235, 235f
intergovernmental policy capacity (IPC), 229–230, 229f
intergovernmental relations
administrative interactions, 228
federalism and, 216–226
federal-provincial constitutional relations, 223–224
federal-provincial fiscal relations, 221–223
federal-provincial policy relations, 224–226
machinery for, 226–228, 226f
interim supply, 316
international organizations, 119
international regulation
ineffectiveness of, 139
Internet, 247–248
intradepartmental relations, 173, 178–184
intragovernmental relations, 228
Ishaq, Zuma, 212–213
issue-oriented groups, 234–235, 235f

J

Jaques, Elliott, 65
Japan
quality management in, 62–64
job classification system, 269
job design
motivation and, 59–60
job training programs, 225
John Howard Society, 236
joint enterprises, 117–118
judicial review
advice to ministers by, 212
defined, 203
errors of law and, 208
forms of relief, 208–209
grounds for, 205–206
ultra vires doctrine and, 207–208
utility of, 213
judiciary
bureaucracy and, 201–213
classification of function in, 205
Crown agency control by, 127–131
discretionary powers of, 204–205
natural justice principles and, 206–207